D1549676

A HISTORY OF INLAND TRANSPORT
AND COMMUNICATION

A HISTORY OF
INLAND TRANSPORT
AND
COMMUNICATION

by

EDWIN A. PRATT

A reprint with an introductory note

by

C. R. Clinker

DAVID & CHARLES REPRINTS

7153 4703 9

This book was first published in 1912 by
Kegan Paul Trench Trubner & Co Ltd

This edition published 1970

© 1970 Introductory Note C. R. Clinker

Printed in Great Britain by
Redwood Press Limited Trowbridge Wiltshire
for David & Charles (Publishers) Limited
South Devon House Railway Station
Newton Abbot Devon

INTRODUCTORY NOTE TO 1970 EDITION

It is impossible to study the history of transport and communication in England from original sources without becoming increasingly aware of and involved in the close and vital connections between it and the development of agriculture and industry, and many other economic and social aspects of the national life. The greatly increased attention paid to the historical side of inland transport over the past forty years has inevitably widened the canvas until, by a natural process of fragmentation, each form has found itself in a separate compartment—road, river, canal, railway, street tramway and internal combustion engine—and treated as such, in more or less complete isolation.

It is questionable whether this fragmentation, and consequent isolation, is altogether a good thing. There is such close interlinking between, for example, canals and railways that a knowledge of preceding forms of transport is essential to a proper understanding of their place in the development of the whole. Segregation has, undoubtedly, enabled historians to deal at greater length and in detail with individual subjects, turnpike roads for instance; canals and railways have been subdivided, usually into companies but sometimes into areas, so large is the volume of original material now available for their study.

This isolation and subdivision has, however, had the unfortunate effect of leaving both serious students and casual reference-seekers with only two books which can be said to cover adequately and reliably the history of transport as a whole over a long period— the present volume and C. E. R. Sherrington's *A Hundred Years of Inland Transport* (1934). Of those dealing with limited periods the most outstanding is W. T. Jackman's *The Development of*

Transport in Modern England (1916), a scholarly work of great precision and fully documented, which takes the story from Roman roads down to 1850. Even one of the most frequently-studied subjects, railway history, lacks a dependable book giving detailed coverage beyond 1852.

Albeit his account ends in 1911, it is fortunate that we have Edwin A. Pratt's *History of Inland Transport and Communication in England*, for here is a readable and authentic record of the transport panorama from the earliest roads, down through the river and canal era to the electrically-operated railways of 1911. But this is not merely dry history. Pratt devotes whole chapters to examination of roads and the Church, early trading conditions, the turnpike system, disadvantages of river navigation, railways and the State, and railway rates and charges, on which he was an authority. The sources of practically all his statements and quotations are documented in the text or expanded by footnote; there is also a useful list of books, pamphlets and reports consulted in preparation of the work.

Pratt may justly be regarded as a neglected author. He wrote more than twenty books on canals and railways, one or two probably of only ephemeral interest. His special interests were the contentious subject of nationalisation, railway rates, accidents and the part played by railways in wartime. The present work was the first of a series initiated in 1912 entitled *National Industries*, edited by Henry Higgs. Only two others appear to have materialised—H. S. Jevon's *British Coal Trade* and A. W. Kirkaldy's *British Shipping* (both also reprinted by the present publishers).

It is essential that those who wish to form a clear picture of inland transport history as a whole should begin the story at the beginning, and trace the course of events leading up to the conditions as they existed in the peak years before World War I. They cannot do better than read this book through from cover to cover.

C. R. CLINKER

NATIONAL INDUSTRIES
EDITED BY HENRY HIGGS, C.B.

A HISTORY OF INLAND TRANSPORT
AND COMMUNICATION IN ENGLAND

A HISTORY OF
INLAND TRANSPORT
AND
COMMUNICATION
IN ENGLAND

BY

EDWIN A. PRATT

AUTHOR OF "RAILWAYS AND THEIR RATES"; "GERMAN VERSUS BRITISH
RAILWAYS"; "RAILWAYS AND NATIONALISATION";
"CANALS AND TRADERS"
ETC.

LONDON
KEGAN PAUL, TRENCH, TRÜBNER & CO., Ltd.
BROADWAY HOUSE, CARTER LANE, E.C.
1912

PREFATORY NOTE

DESIGNED as the introductory volume of a series of books—
by various writers—dealing with our "National Industries,"
the present work aims at telling the story of inland transport
and communication from the earliest times to the present date,
showing, more especially, the effect which the gradual development thereof, in successive stages, and under ever-varying circumstances, has had alike on the growth and expansion of
trade and industry and on the general economic and social
conditions of the country.

The various phases of inland transport described in the
course of the work include roads, rivers, canals, turnpikes,
railways, tramways, and rail-less electric traction; and the
facilities for communication of which accounts are given
comprise packhorses, waggons, stage-coaches, "flying" and
mail-coaches, private carriages, posting, hackney coaches,
cabs, omnibuses, cycles, motors, motor-buses, commercial
motors, and aeroplanes. Reference is (*inter alia*) made to
most of the English rivers and to many inland towns; the
origin, achievements, and shortcomings of canals are traced;
a complete outline of the turnpike system is given; a short
history of tramways comprises the leading points therein; the
story of the rise, development and prospects of the motor
industry is related; while the evolution and development
of the railways and their position to-day both as a means
of transport and communication and as constituting in themselves a "National Industry" are treated in such a way as to
afford, it is hoped, a comprehensive idea of the railway system
from its very earliest origin down to the strikes and the con-

troversy following the close of the Royal Commission of Inquiry in the autumn of 1911.

Incidentally, also, allusion is made to the rise of Bristol, Lynn, Liverpool, and various other ports; the early history of the textile industries, the cutlery trades, the iron trade, the salt trade, and the coal trade is briefly sketched, while the facts narrated in relation thereto should enable the reader to realise the bearing, throughout the ages, of State policy towards the general question of transport. Finally, the present situation and the future outlook are brought under review.

Even as these pages are passing through the press new developments are occurring which confirm the suggestion I have made, on page 470, that " in the dictionary of transport there is no such word as 'finality.'"

While it is still true that the electrification of the London suburban railways has not been generally adopted by the trunk companies, yet the scheme in this connection announced, on November 18, 1911, by the London and North-Western Railway Company (see page 507) supplementing the action already taken by the London, Brighton and South Coast Railway Company in regard to some of their suburban lines, is significant of a growing determination on the part of the great railway companies to defend their own interests by competing, in turn, with the electric tramways, which have absorbed so much of the suburban traffic of late years.

Following closely on this one announcement comes another, to the effect that a new company is about to set up, in the Midlands, works covering thirty-four acres for the construction of a type of petrol-electric omnibus for which great advantages over the earlier motor-omnibuses are claimed. (This, presumably, is the vehicle which the Tramways Committee of the Edinburgh Corporation, as mentioned on page 470, propose to watch in preference to deciding at once on a system of railless electric traction.)

In commenting on the former of the announcements here in question, "The Times Engineering Supplement" of November 22, 1911, observes :—

It is of importance to realise what this decision portends. The history of the matter is that the steam railways were inadequate to fulfil the requirements of the suburbs, and that an opening was thus afforded to municipalities to provide tramways of their own. It was a crude method of dealing with the problem ; it robbed the main roads of every vestige of rural character, and it added new dangers and checks to street traffic. Nevertheless it was a necessity, and it served its purpose, first, by providing facilities that were always cheap to the travellers, even if they were occasionally dear to the taxpayers ; and, secondly, by stimulating the railway companies to adopt means to get back their lost traffic. Now that the railway companies are fully alive to the opportunities offered to them by electrification, the general aspect of the problem is changed, and additional support is given to the belief that electric railways and motor-omnibuses will carry an increasing proportion of London traffic, and that from some roads at least tramways may even disappear altogether.

In other directions there are reports of individual agriculturists who are constructing light railways of their own to secure direct communication between their farms and the nearest main line railway, sympathetic local authorities having offered them practical encouragement by making only a nominal charge for the privilege of crossing the public roads where this is necessary. A new era in agricultural transport and cultivation is further foreshadowed in the announcement that it is quite reasonable to believe that resort to rail-less electric traction will serve as a means of introducing electrical supply into rural areas for agricultural purposes ; while in the House of Lords on November 22, 1911, Lord Lucas, replying for the Government to some comments made by Lord Montagu of Beaulieu on the first report of the Road Board (dealt with on page 481), said that body considered the most important thing at present was to improve the surface of the roads ; but

" they had borne in mind the fact that it would be necessary for them before long to undertake larger operations, involving heavier expenditure."

Still further developments occurring, maturing, or under consideration when the text of the present work was already in type include—

(1) A projected alliance between the tube railways and the London General Omnibus Company, following on the conspicuous success obtained by the latter in substituting motor for horsed vehicles for the 300,000,000 passengers it carries annually.

(2) The issuing of " Minutes of Evidence taken before the Departmental Committee of the Board of Trade on Railway Agreements and Amalgamations " [Cd. 5927], containing some notable expressions of opinion by railway managers concerning the future of the railway system, together with much important information on the general subject.

(3) The publication, on December 1, of the Fourth Annual Report of the London Traffic Branch of the Board of Trade [Cd. 5972], which deals with various matters already touched upon in my last three chapters, including the effects of improved transport facilities on the migration of population from the inner to the outer suburban ring; the further widening of the motor-transport delivery radius, to the advantage of urban, but to the disadvantage of suburban traders; the steady substitution of mechanical traction for horse-drawn vehicles of every type—the Report predicting, on this point, that " if two-wheeled horse cabs continue to diminish at the rate of the last two years, they will disappear before the end of 1912 "; the improbability of further material extensions of the tramway system, and the assumption that " the competition of promoters for the privilege of constructing tube railways has come to an end "; while the Report also discusses the merits of a scheme for the provision, at an estimated cost of between £20,000,000 and £30,000,000, of about 120 miles of great

arterial roads across London for the accommodation of the increasing traffic, and of still another scheme, put forward by a Departmental Committee of the General Post Office, for relieving the streets of London of a good deal of mail-van traffic by the construction of an underground electric railway, 6½ miles in length, and costing £513,000, across the centre of London from east to west, for the conveyance of Post Office matter, the Report further suggesting that this particular system might be found equally applicable to other forms of enterprise which require the use of carts for the frequent conveyance of goods in small consignments between fixed points.

(4) The passing by the House of Commons, on November 22, of a resolution expressing the opinion that a meeting should take place between the parties on whose behalf the Railway Agreement of August 19, 1911, was signed (see p. 448), "to discuss the best mode of giving effect to the Report of the Royal Commission"; the acceptance by such parties of Board of Trade invitations to a conference, in accordance with the terms of this resolution, and the holding of a conference which began, at the offices of the Board of Trade, on December 7, under the presidency of Sir George Askwith, Chief Industrial Commissioner, and resulted, on December 11, in a settlement being effected.

(5) The prospective increase, from January 1, 1912, of certain season, excursion, week-end or other special-occasion fares (many of which now work out at a rate of a halfpenny or a farthing, or even less than a farthing, per mile) as a means of assisting the railway companies to meet advances in wages, such increases in passenger fares (distinct from any increases in merchandise rates, for a like reason, as foreshadowed by the Government undertaking of August 19, 1911, alluded to on pp. 448 and 511) being already in the option of the companies, provided the latter do not exceed the powers conferred on them by their Acts, and subject to the condition that on fares of over a penny the mile Government duty must be paid.

(6) The reading, by Mr. Philip Dawson, at the Royal Automobile Club, on December 8, of a valuable paper on "The Future of Railway Electrification," in which—after detailing what had already been done in the United States, in Germany, and, in this country, on the suburban systems of the Lancashire and Yorkshire, the North Eastern and the London, Brighton, and South Coast railways—he showed the practicability and the advantages of applying electric traction (single phase system) to main-line long-distance traffic; announced that the surveys and calculations in connection with a scheme for electrifying the whole of the L.B. and S.C. Railway Company's services between London and Brighton were already far advanced; mentioned that such a transformation would allow of a 10 to 15-minute service to Brighton and of the 52-mile journey being done by non-stop trains in about 45 minutes, or by stopping trains in about 60 minutes; and declared that "the equipment of this line if, as he hoped would be the case, it were carried out, would be epoch-making in the history of British railways."

Thus the whole subject of inland transport is now so much "in the air" that the story of its gradual and varied development, as here told—and this, too, for the first time on the lines adopted in the present work—should form a useful contribution to the available literature on one of the most important of present-day problems.

EDWIN A. PRATT.

December 12, 1911.

CONTENTS

A HISTORY

OF

INLAND TRANSPORT AND COMMUNICATION

CHAPTER I

INTRODUCTORY

THE gradual improvement, throughout the centuries, of those facilities for internal communication which reached their climax in the creation of the present system of railways has constituted a dominating factor alike in our industrial and in our social advancement as a people.

Until transport had provided a ready means alike of collecting raw materials and of distributing food supplies and manufactured articles, industries of the type familiar to us to-day were practically impossible ; and until convenient and economical means of travel were afforded, England had to be considered less as a nation than as a collection of more or less isolated communities, with all the disadvantages, social and moral as well as economic, necessarily resulting ; while the social and moral progress facilitated by improved means of communication reacted, in turn, on the industries by creating new wants for manufacturers and workers to supply.

To the right understanding of the position occupied by our National Industries, it is thus necessary that the special significance of internal communication and its development should, at the outset, be clearly realised from the point of view, not alone of present-day circumstances, but, also, of conditions that either preceded the industries themselves—so far checking their growth that industrial development in Great Britain came at a much later date than in many coun-

tries on the Continent of Europe—or else aided materially in
the expansion of industries as the disadvantages and drawbacks began to disappear.

That industries existed when internal communication was
still in a primitive stage in this country is true enough ; but
they were " domestic " rather than " national," and it was
not until the advent of better means of transport that it became
possible for them to begin to pass from the one stage to the
other, and, at the same time, to exercise so important an
influence on our advancement as a nation. It is no less true
that British commerce, conducted by ships obtaining ready
access to foreign ports by traversing ocean highways, had made
much greater progress at an early period in our history than industries dependent on inland highways that were then either
non-existent or scarcely passable ; yet, though navigation might
advance still further, and though navigators might discover
still more new countries, commerce could not hope to attain
to the expansion it subsequently underwent until the industries whose operations were to be facilitated by improvement
in land communication supplied the merchants with the home
commodities which they required for sale or exchange in the
markets of the world. Whatever, again, the natural resources
of a country—and such resources have certainly been great
in our own—they may be of little material value until they
can be readily moved from the place where they exist to the
place where they can be used ; and even then it is necessary
that the cost of transport shall not be unduly high.

Transport and communication by land and water have thus
become what Prof. J. Shield Nicholson rightly calls, in his
" Principles of Political Economy," " the bases of industrial
organisation " ; and it is to industrial organisation that a
country such as ours has been indebted in a pre-eminent degree
both for its material prosperity and for the position it occupies
to-day among the nations of the world. But just as British
engineers long regarded the subject of road construction and
road repairs as beneath their notice, and left such work to be
done by any parish " surveyor," subsidised pauper or " Blind
Jack of Knaresboro'," who thought fit to engage in it, so have
most writers of history, while zealously recording the actions
of kings, of diplomatists, of politicians, and of warriors who may
have made a great stir in their day but who took only a very

small share in the real and permanent progress of the British people, bestowed only a passing reference—and sometimes not even that—on questions of trade and transport which have played a far more important part in our social and national advancement.

The history of railways has already been told by various writers. But the history of railways is only the last chapter in the history of inland transport and communication; and, though that last chapter is of paramount importance, and will here receive full recognition, it is essential that those who would form a clear idea of the position as a whole should begin the story at the beginning, and trace the course of events leading up to the conditions as they exist to-day.

CHAPTER II

IT has been assumed in some quarters that, because the main routes of travel in this country did not have to pass over lofty mountains, as in Austria and Switzerland, therefore the construction of roads here was, or should have been, a comparatively easy matter. But this is far from having been the case, the earliest opening of regular lines of communication by road having been materially influenced by certain physical conditions of the land itself.

The original site of London was a vast marsh, extending from where Fulham stands to-day to Greenwich, a distance of nine or ten miles, with a breadth in places of two or two and a half miles. The uplands beyond the Thames marshes were covered with dense forests in which the bear, the wild boar, and the wild ox roamed at will. Essex was almost entirely forest down to the date of the conquest. Nearly the whole expanse of what to-day is Sussex, and, also, considerable portions of Kent and Hampshire, were covered by a wood—the Andred-Weald, or Andreswald—which in King Alfred's time is said by the Anglo-Saxon Chronicle to have been 120 miles long and 30 miles broad. Here it was that, until even these great supplies were approaching exhaustion, the iron industry established in Sussex in the thirteenth century obtained the wood and the charcoal which were exclusively used as fuel in iron-making until the second half of the eighteenth century, when coal and coke began to be generally substituted. Wilts, Dorset and other southern counties had extensive woodlands which were more or less depleted under like conditions. Warwickshire, Northamptonshire and Leicestershire all had extensive woods. Sherwood Forest extended over almost the whole of Nottinghamshire. In Derbyshire, as shown by the Domesday Survey, five hundreds

4

out of six were heavily wooded, and nineteen manors out of twenty-three had wood on them. " In Lancashire," says Charles Pearson, in the notes to his " Historical Maps of England During the First Thirteen Centuries," " if we distinguish forest from wood, and assume that the former was only wilderness, we still have official evidence for believing that a quarter of a million acres of the land between Mersey and Ribble was covered with a network of separate dense woods."

Altogether, it is calculated by various authorities that in the earliest days of our history about one third of the surface of the soil in the British Isles was covered with wood, thicket, or scrub. Of the remainder a very large proportion was fenland, marsh-land or heath-land. " From the sea-board of Suffolk and Norfolk," says the Rev. W. Denton, in " England in the Fifteenth Century," " and on the north coast almost to the limits of the great level, stretched a series of swamps, quagmires, small lakes and ' broads.' " A great fen, 60 miles in length and 40 miles in breadth, covered a large proportion of the counties of Cambridgeshire, Huntingdonshire, Northamptonshire, Lincolnshire, Norfolk and Suffolk. A great part of Lancashire, Mr Denton further states, was a region of marshes and quaking mosses, while " from Norwich to Liverpool, and from the mouth of the Ouse at Lynn to the Mersey, where it falls into the Irish sea, a line of fen, uncultivated moors and morasses stretched across England and separated the northern counties from the midland districts, the old territory of Mercia."

Much of the surface, again, was occupied by hills or mountains separated by valleys or plains through which some 200 rivers—many of them far more powerful streams than they are to-day—flowed towards the sea. As for the nature of much of the soil of England, the early conditions are further recalled by Daniel Defoe who, in describing the " Tour through the Whole Isle of Great Britain " which he made in the first quarter of the eighteenth century, speaks of " the soil of all the midland part of England, from sea to sea," as " a stiff clay or marly earth " for a breadth of 50 miles, at least, so that it was not possible to go north from London to any part of Britain without having to pass through " these terrible clays," which were, he says, " perfectly frightful to travellers."

It was under conditions such as these that Britain obtained her first roads ; and it was, also, conditions such as these that were to affect more or less the future history of inland communication in England, adding largely to the practical difficulties experienced in making provision for adequate transport facilities.

Inasmuch as a great number of chariots were used by the Britons in their attempt to resist the invasion of Cæsar, it may be assumed that there were even then in this country roads sufficiently broad and solid on which such chariots could run ; and though evidence both of the use of wattles in the making of roads over clayey soil and of a knowledge on the part of the early Britons of the art of paving has been found, the British chariot-roads were so inefficiently constructed that few traces of them have remained.

The earliest British roads were, however, probably of the nature of tracks rather than of durable highways ; and they may have been designed less for the purposes of defence against invasion than in the interests of that British trade which, even then, was an established institution in the land.

Writing in " Archæologia," vol. xlviii (1885), Mr Alfred Tylor expresses the view that the civilisation of the Britons was of a much higher character in some respects than has till recently been supposed. From the fact that Pytheas of Marseilles, a Greek traveller who lived B.C. 330, and visited Britain, described the British-made chariots, he thinks we may assume that the Britons had discovered the art of smelting and working tin, lead and iron, and that they used these materials in the making both of chariots and of weapons. But they produced for export, as well as for domestic use. Tin, more especially, was an absolute necessity in Europe in the bronze age for use in the making of weapons both for the chase and for war, and the metallurgical wealth of Britain afforded great opportunities for trading, just as it subsequently gave the country the special importance it possessed in the eyes of the Roman conquerors.

To the pursuit of such trading the Britons, according to Mr Tylor, were the more inspired by a desire to obtain, in return for their metals the amber which, as the favourite ornament of prehistoric times, then constituted a most important article of commerce, but was obtainable only in the north of Europe.

The early importance of amber in Europe is proved, Mr Tylor
says, by its presence in many parts of Europe throughout the
long neolithic age, and, therefore, long prior to the bronze age ;
and it was mainly to facilitate the exchange of metals for this
much-desired amber that the Britons made roads or tracks
from the high grounds which they generally chose for their
habitations (thus avoiding alike the forests, the fens and the
marshes), down to the ports from which the metals were to be
shipped to their destination. Mr Tylor says on this point :—
    " The first British tin-commerce with the Continent in
prehistoric times moved, either on packhorses or by chariots,
in hilly districts, towards Essex, Norfolk, and Suffolk, that is,
in the direction from west to east ; then by sea from the
eastern British shipping ports, of which Camulodunum on the
Stour, close to the Thames (Colchester) is a type, to the Baltic.
Thus at first the ' tin ' used to find its way partly by land
and partly by sea from Cornwall to the mouths of the Elbe
and Vistula, there to meet the land caravans of the Baltic
amber commerce from the north of Europe to the south. . . .
When the land route throughout Gaul was established the tin
had to go across the English Channel, not to Brittany, across
the rougher and wider part, but to Normandy. The Isle of
Wight was nearer Normandy, and a suitable entrepôt for the
coasters meeting the fleets of ocean trading ships.[1] . . .
    " Iron and lead were, also, valuable British productions,
and could easily reach the Isle of Wight by coasting vessels
or by the British or Roman roads via Salisbury or Winchester. . . .
    " All ancient roads to British shipping ports were, of
course, British. . . . Without roads it would be impossible
to get over the low, often clay, grounds, or to reach the seaports
in chariots, as the seaports were constantly in the clay. . . .
It was impossible to reach the shipping-ports, which are all at
low levels, without roads, as the clay and sand would be
impassable for chariots. Of course packhorses could travel
where chariots could not, but if the main roads were made for
chariots they would be equally good for packhorses."
    Mr Tylor thinks there is the greater reason for assuming
that a considerable trade had thus been developed between

[1] Mr Tylor argues that Brading, in the Isle of Wight, was the favoured
point of shipment.

Britain and the Continent because Tacitus alludes to a
British prince who had amassed great wealth by transporting
metals from the Mendips to the Channel coast ; but our main
consideration is the evidence we get of the fact that Britain's
earliest roads appear to have owed their origin to the development of Britain's earliest trade.

Two, at least, of the four great roads to which the designation
" Roman " has been applied followed, in Mr Tylor's opinion,
the line of route already established by the Britons under the
conditions here indicated.   Certain it is that, although the
Romans always aimed at building their roads in straight lines,
and troubled little about ascents and descents, they followed
the British plan of keeping the routes to high and dry ground,
whenever practicable, in order to have a better chance of
avoiding alike the woods, the bogs, the clays, the water-
courses and the rivers.

Skilled road-builders though they were, the Romans shrank,
in several instances, Pearson tells us, from " the tremendous
labour of clearing a road through a forest where the trees must
be felled seventy yards on either side to secure them from the
arrows of a lurking foe."   Thus the great military roads
marked in the Itinerary of Antonine always, if possible,
avoided passing through a forest.   The roads to Chichester
went by Southampton in order to avoid the Andred-Weald
of Sussex, and the road from London to Bath did not take
the direct route to Wallingford because, in that case, it would
have required to pass through twenty miles of forest in
Buckinghamshire and Oxfordshire.   Later on, however, as
the Roman rule became more firmly established, the making
of roads through forests became unavoidable, and much
destruction of timber followed, while the fact that the trees
thus felled were left to rot on the ground alongside the roads
helped to create the quagmires and " mosses " which were
to be so great a source of trouble to road-makers in future
generations.

As regards the routes taken by the Roman roads, Mr. Tylor
says :—

" The Romans made a complete system of permanent
inland roads to connect the Continent with the military posts,
London, York, Colchester, Chester, Uriconium, Gloucester,
Winchester, Silchester, Porchester and Brading, and chief

trading towns with each other. At commanding points along or near these roads the Romans constructed camps, and so placed their legions as to protect the centres of metallurgical industry and the roads leading to them. . . . The Romans did not originate the sites of many new seaport towns or towns on large, navigable rivers, and, when they did so, as in the case of London, Richborough, Uriconium, Rochester, Canterbury, it was for strategical reasons, or indirectly connected with the traffic in minerals, the great industry of Britain during the Roman occupation as it was before it. . . . Silchester . . . was forty-five miles from London, and was on high ground away from river or forests, and not far from the junction of a number of land-routes. It was on dry ground on which waggons could travel. It was convenient for roads giving access to Cornwall for tin ; to the Mendips for lead, copper or brass ; Gloucester and South Wales for iron ; and from these termini there were routes passable to the east and south coasts of England."

From all this it would seem that the mineral wealth and the trading interests which had inspired the line of route of the earliest British roads were, side by side with military considerations, leading factors in the particular direction given to the Roman roads that followed them.

As for the Roman roads themselves, so admirably were they built that some of those laid down in ancient Rome and in France have been in use for from 1500 to 2000 years, while remains of Roman roads found in Britain, buried deeply under the debris of centuries, have still borne striking evidence of the solid manner in which they were first constructed.

But the point that here arises for consideration is, not only the high quality of the great roads the Romans built in Britain, but the broad-minded policy by which the builders themselves were influenced. The provision of a system of scientifically constructed roads wherever they went was, primarily, part of the Roman plan of campaign in the wars of aggrandisement they carried on ; but it was further designed to aid in developing the resources of the country concerned, while it was, also, carried out in Britain by the Roman State itself, on lines embracing the transport conditions of the country as a whole, and in accordance with a unified and well-planned system of internal communication on " national " lines such as no succeeding administration attempted either to follow or to direct.

Thus the great Roman roads, connecting the rising city on the Thames and the commercial centre of Britain with every part of the island, were remarkable, not only because they represented an art which was to disappear with the conquerors themselves, but, also, because they had been directly created, and were directly controlled, by a central authority as the outcome of a State road policy itself fated in turn to disappear no less effectually. The almost invariable practice in this country since the departure of the Romans has been for the State, instead of following the Roman example, and regarding as an obligation devolving upon itself the provision of adequate means of intercommunication between different parts of the country, to leave the burden and responsibility of making such provision to individual citizens, to philanthropic effort, to private enterprise, or to local authorities. The result has been that not only, for successive generations, were both the material progress and the social advancement of the English people greatly impeded, but the actual development of such intercommunication was to show, far too often (1) a lamentable want of intelligence and skill in meeting requirements ; and (2) a deficiency of system, direction and co-ordination as regards the many different agencies or authorities concerned in the results actually secured.

CHAPTER III

ROADS AND THE CHURCH

FOLLOWING the departure of the Romans, not only road-making but even road-repairing was for several centuries wholly neglected in this country. The Roman roads continued to be used, but successive rulers in troublesome times were too busily engaged in maintaining their own position or in waging wars at home or abroad to attend to such prosaic details as the repairing of roads, and they had, apparently, still less time or opportunity for converting into roads hill-side tracks which the Romans had not touched at all.

In proportion, too, as the roads were neglected, the bridges of the earlier period got out of repair, fell in altogether, or were destroyed in the social disorders of the time. So the mediæval ages found the means of internal communication by land probably worse in Britain than in any other country in western Europe.

The State having failed to acquit itself of its obligations, the Church took up the work as a religious duty. The keeping of roads in repair came to be considered, as Jusserand says in " English Wayfaring Life in the Middle Ages," " a pious and meritorious work before God, of the same sort as visiting the sick and caring for the poor." Travellers were regarded as unfortunate people whose progress on their toilsome journeys it was Christian charity to assist. In these circumstances the religious houses of the period took over the task of making or repairing both roads and bridges, the faithful being encouraged to assist in the good work, either through gifts or with personal labour, by the concession to them of special indulgencies. Jusserand tells, for instance, how Richard de Kellawe, Bishop of Durham, 1311–1316, remitted part of the penalties on the sins of those who did good work in helping to make smooth the way of the wanderer, his episcopal register

containing frequent entries of 40-day indulgencies granted to
contributors to the road-repair funds. There were benefactors,
also, who left to the monasteries lands and houses the proceeds
of which were to be applied to the same public purpose ; while
in proportion as the monasteries thus increased the extent
of their own landed possessions they became still more
interested in the making and repairing of roads in the neigh-
bourhoods in which the lands they had acquired were situated.

In those days, in fact, people bequeathed not only land,
or money, but even live stock for the repair of roads just as
they left gifts for ecclesiastical purposes, or as people to-day
make bequests to charitable institutions. The practice continued until, at least, the middle of the sixteenth century,
since in the Sixth Report of the Historical Manuscripts Commission there will be found (page 422) the last will and testa-
ment, dated May 16, 1558, of John Davye, in which the
testator says :—

" I leve and bequeithe a cowpell of oxson that I boughte the
laste yere to the building of Moulde Church where I dwell ;
And I bequieth a bullocke that I boughte of the Royde unto
the mendynge of the hye waie betwixte my howse and the
Molld."

Bequests of money or lands were also made for the construction or the maintenance of bridges, or for the freeing of
bridges from toll so that the poor could cross without payment ;
and one of the duties of the bishops, when making their
visitations, was to enquire whether or not the funds thus left
were being applied to the purposes the donors intended.

On the Continent of Europe a religious order was founded,
in the twelfth century, for the building of bridges. It spread
over several countries and built some notable bridges—
such, for instance, as that over the Rhone at Avignon ; though
there is no trace, Jusserand tells us, of these Bridge Friars
having extended their operations to this country. It was,
however, from them that laymen learned the art of bridge-
building, and in Britain, as in Continental countries, bridges
came to be considered as pious works, to be put under the
special charge of a patron saint. To this end it was customary
to build a chapel alongside an important bridge—as in the case
of the old London Bridge that replaced the original wooden
structure by Peter Colechurch, " priest and chaplain," itself

having had a chapel dedicated to Saint Thomas of Canterbury. Sovereigns or great landowners gave generous gifts for the endowment of such bridges. Although, too, there was no special order of bridge-building friars in England, guilds and lay brotherhoods, animated by the religious spirit, were formed in the reign of Richard II. (1377–1399) for the repair of roads and bridges, just as, in turn, the ordinary trading guilds which were the forerunners of the corporate bodies set up in towns undertook to " maintain and keep in good reparacion " bridges which had become " ruinous," and, also, to attend to the " foul and dangerous highways, the charge whereof the town was not able to maintain." [1]

It became customary, also, for hermits to take up their habitation in cells along the main thoroughfares, and to occupy themselves with looking after the roads, trusting to the alms of passers-by for a little worldly recompense. In one instance, at least, a hermit was allowed to put up a toll-bar— the first on record in this country—and collect compulsory payments from persons using the roads he mended. This was in 1364, when Edward III. made a decree authorising " our well-beloved William Phelippe the hermit " to set up a toll-bar on the lower slope of Highgate Hill, on the north side of London, and levy tolls for the repair of the " Hollow Way " from " our people passing between Heghgate and Smethfelde."

Jusserand sums up the situation at this period by saying that " The roads in England would have been entirely impassable . . . if the nobility and the clergy, that is to say, the whole of the landed proprietors, had not had an immediate and daily interest in possessing passable roads."

There came, however, a period of decline in religious fervour. The laity grew less disposed to give or to bequeath money,

---

[1] In the Ninth Report of the Historical Manuscripts Commission, page 290, mention is made of a charter, granted by Edward VI., giving a new municipal constitution to the "ancient borough" of Stratford-on-Avon in lieu of the franchise and local government taken away by the suppression of the guild previously existing there ; and in this charter the guild in question is spoken of as having been, in former times, "founded and endowed with divers lands tenements and possessions," the rents, revenues and profits from which were to be devoted to the maintenance of a grammar school, an almshouse, and "a certain great stone bridge, called Stratford Bridge, placed and built over the water and river of the Avon beside the said borough."

land or cattle for road-repair purposes, however much the offer of indulgences in return therefor might be increased from days to months or even to years; and the clergy, in turn, became more remiss in acquitting themselves of the obligations they had assumed as road-repairers. They accepted the benefactions, and they granted the indulgences; but they showed increasing laxity in carrying out their responsibilities. The roadside hermits, also, gathered in so much in the way of contributions, voluntary or compulsory, from passers-by that they ate and drank more than hermits ought to do, grew fat and lazy, and too often left the roads to look after themselves.

What, therefore, with neglected roads and dilapidated bridges, the general conditions of travel went from bad to worse. Church Councils, says Denton, were summoned and adjourned because bishops feared to encounter the danger of travelling along such roads. Oratories were licensed in private houses, and chapels of ease were built, because roads were so bad, especially in winter, that the people could not get to their parish churches. The charter, 47 Edward III., 1373, by which the city of Bristol was constituted a county, states that this was done in order to save the burgesses from travelling to Gloucester and Ilchester, " distant thirty miles of road, deep, especially in winter time, and dangerous to passengers." On many different occasions, too, the members of the House of Commons, assembled for a new session, could transact no business because the Peers had been detained by the state of the roads and the difficulty of travelling, and Parliament was, therefore, adjourned.

The general conditions grew still worse with the impoverishment of the monasteries by which the main part of the work had—however negligently—been done since the end of the Roman régime. As will be shown later on, various statutes had gradually imposed more and more the care of the roads on the laity, and it was upon them that the full responsibility fell with the eventual dissolution, first of the lesser, and next of the greater, monasteries by Henry VIII.

CHAPTER IV

EARLY TRADING CONDITIONS

RIVERS constituted, in the Middle Ages, the most important means of inland transport. Most of our oldest towns or cities that were not on the route of one of the Roman roads were set up alongside or within easy reach of some tidal or navigable stream in order, among other reasons, that full advantage could be taken of the transport facilities the waterways offered. So were monasteries, castles, and baronial halls, while the locating of the universities of Oxford and Cambridge on the Thames and the Cam respectively rendered them accessible by sea and river to Scottish and other students from the north who could hardly have made their way thither by land.[1]

It was, however, only a limited number of inland places that could be reached by water, and other towns or settlements were wanted. The trading opportunities of the latter were at first restricted to the packhorse, few of the roads being then adapted for even the most primitive of agricultural waggons. Long lines of packhorses, with bales or panniers slung across their backs, made their way along roads or bridle paths often inadequate to allow of two strings of loaded horses to pass one another, so that many a quarrel arose, when two teams met, as to which should go into the mud to allow the other to pass along the path proper.

Traders sending wool or other commodities by the same route were in the habit of making up companies in order to secure mutual protection against robbers, and they armed themselves and their servants as if going to battle. Like precautions were taken by merchants from the north when they started on their annual business journeys to London—

[1] The subject of rivers and river transport will be fully dealt with in later chapters.

journeys so full of peril that they were not begun until the merchant had made his will and earnestly commended himself to the protection both of St. Botolph and of his own patron saint. The "commercial travellers" of that day carried their samples or their wares in a bag lying across their horse's back, thus qualifying for the designation of "bagmen" by which they were to become known.

In the Middle Ages everyone rode except the very poor, and they had to be content to trudge along on foot. Kings and nobles, princes and princesses, gentlemen and ladies, merchants and bagmen all travelled on horseback. Women either rode astride until the introduction of side-saddles, in the fourteenth century, or else rode in pillion fashion.

The main exception to riding on horseback, in the case of ladies or of the sick or infirm, was the use of litters attached to shafts to which two horses, one in front and one behind the litter, were harnessed. Sometimes, also, "passengers" were carried in the panniers of the packhorses, instead of goods.

Certain main routes, and especially those favoured by pilgrims—such as that between London and Canterbury—must have been full of animation in those days ; but, speaking generally, no one then travelled except on business or under the pressure of some strong obligation.

Down to the end of the fourteenth century England was purely an agricultural country, and her agricultural products were exclusively for home, if not for local or even domestic consumption, with the one exception of wool, which was exported in considerable quantities to Flanders and other lands then dependent mainly on England for the raw materials of their cloth manufactures. In our own country manufactures had made but little advance, and they mainly supplied the requirements, in each instance, of a very limited area.

England was, indeed, in those days, little more than a collection of isolated communities in which the various householders, more especially in villages at a distance from any main road or navigable river, had to provide for their own requirements to a great extent. Of retail shops, such as are now found in the most remote villages, there were none at all at a period when the replenishing of stocks would have been impossible by reason of difficulties in transport ; so that while the country as a whole was mainly agricultural, there were more craftsmen in the villages, and there was greater skill possessed by individuals in the production of domestic requirements than would to-day be found among agricultural populations accustomed to depend on the urban manufacturer or the village stores for the commodities their forefathers had to make, to raise or to supply for themselves.

Each family baked its own bread, with flour ground at the village mill from the wheat or the rye grown on the family's own land or allotment ; each brewed its own ale—then the common beverage at all meals, since tea and coffee had still to come into vogue ; and each grew its own wool or flax, made its own cloth and clothing, and tanned its own leather. What the household could not do for itself might still be done by the village blacksmith or the village carpenter. Alike for ribbons, for foreign spices, for luxuries in general, and for news of the outer world the household was mainly dependent on the pedlar, with his stock on his back, or the chapman, bringing his collection of wares with him on horseback ; though even these welcome visitors might find it impossible to travel along roads and footpaths reduced by autumn rains or winter snows to the condition of quagmires.

In these conditions many a village or hamlet became isolated until the roads were again available for traffic, and rural households prepared for the winter as they would have taken precautions against an impending siege. Most of the meat likely to be required would be killed off in the late autumn and salted down—salt being one of the few absolute necessities for which the mediæval household was dependent on the outside world ; while families which could not afford to kill for themselves would purchase an animal in common and share the meat. Stores of wheat, barley and malt were laid in ; honey was put on the shelves to take the place of the sugar then almost unknown outside the large towns ; logs were collected for fuel and rushes for the floors ; and wool and flax were brought in to provide occupation for the women of the household. In the way of necessaries the provision made by each self-dependent family, or, at least, by each self-contained community, was thus practically complete—save in the one important item of fresh vegetables, the lack of which, coupled with the consumption of so much salt meat, was a frequent source of scurvy. Millstones for the village mill might, like the salt, have to be brought in from elsewhere ; but otherwise the villagers had small concern with what went on in the great world.

Such trading relations as the average village had with English markets or with foreign traders were almost exclusively in the hands of the lord of the manor, one of whose rights—and one not without significance, from our present point of view—it was to call upon those who held land under him, whether as free men or as serfs, to do all his carting for him. This was a condition on which both villeins and cottars had their holdings ; and though, in course of time, the lord of the manor might relieve his people of most of the obligations devolving upon them, this particular responsibility still generally remained. " Instances of the commutation of the whole of the services," says W. J. Ashley, in the account of the manorial system which he gives in his " Introduction to English Economic History and Theory," " occur occasionally as early as 1240 in manors where the demesne was wholly left to tenants. The service with which the lord could least easily dispense seems to have been that of carting ; and so in one case we find the entry as to the villeins, ' Whether they pay rent or no they shall cart.' "

To the lord of the manor, at least, the difficulties of road transport, whether in getting his surplus commodities to market or otherwise, must have appeared much less serious when he was thus able to call on his tenants to do his cartage.

In the towns the isolation may not have been so great as in the villages ; but the urban trading and industrial conditions nevertheless assumed a character which could only have been possible when, owing to defective communications, there was comparatively little movement and competition in regard either to manufactures (such as they were) or to workers.

The period of internal peace and order which followed the Norman Conquest led, as Ashley has shown, to the rise in town after town of the merchant guild—an institution the purpose of which was to unite into a society all those who carried on a certain trade, in order, not only to assure for them the maintenance of their rights and privileges, but also to obtain for them an actual monopoly of the particular business in which they were interested. Such monopoly they claimed against other traders in the same town who had not entered into the combination, and still more so against traders in other towns. The latter they regarded as "foreigners" equally with the traders from Flanders and elsewhere.

The merchant guilds were found in all considerable towns in the eleventh century, and they were followed, a century later, by craft guilds which aimed, in turn, at securing a monopoly of employment for their own particular members.

Coupled with the guilds there was much local regulation of the prices and qualities of commodities through the setting-up of such institutions as the "assize" of ale, of bread and of cloth ; while the justices had, in addition, considerable powers in regard to fixing the rates of wages and the general conditions of labour.

All this system of highly-organised Protection, not so much for the country as a whole as for each and every individual town in the country, might serve in comparatively isolated communities ; but it could not prevail against increased intercourse, the growing competition of developing industries, a broader area of distribution for commodities made in greater volume, and a wider demand for foreign supplies. It was thus doomed to extinction as these new conditions developed ; but it nevertheless exercised an important influence on our national advancement, since it was the impulse of corporate unity, fostered by the merchant guilds, and strengthened by the system of manorial courts for the enforcement of the local laws and customs in vogue in each separate manor before the common law of the land was established, that led to so many English towns securing, from King or overlord—and notably in the twelfth and thirteenth centuries, when the influence of the merchant guilds was especially great—those charters which so powerfully stimulated the growth of the great towns, of English citizenship, of individual freedom, and of national prosperity. Ashley well says, in this connection :—

"Wide as were the differences between a civic republic of Italy, or an imperial city of Germany with its subject territory, and a little English market town, there was an underlying similarity of ideas and purposes. Each was a body of burghers who identified the right to carry on an independent trading or industrial occupation with the right of burgess-ship ; who imposed restrictions on the acquisition of citizenship, with the object of protecting the interests of those already enjoying it ; who acted together by market regulation and inter-municipal negotiation to secure every advantage they could over rival boroughs ; who deemed it meet that every occupation should have its own organisation and its own representation in the governing authority, and who allowed and expected their magistrates to carry out a searching system of industrial supervision. Municipal magistracy was not yet an affair of routine, bound hand and foot by the laws of the State."

The general trade of the country in the Middle Ages was conducted mainly through markets and fairs.

Every town had its market and fixed market day, and such market served the purpose of bringing in the surplus produce of the surrounding agricultural district, the area of supply depending, no doubt, on the distance for which the state of the roads and the facilities for transport on them would allow of commodities being brought.

Held, as a rule, annually or half-yearly, fairs assumed much more important proportions than the (generally) weekly local markets. It was to the fairs that traders both from distant counties and from foreign countries brought wares and products not otherwise obtainable ; and it was at the fairs that the foreign merchants, more especially, bought up the large quantities of wool which were to form their return cargoes. Whereas the business done at the local markets was mainly retail, that done at the fairs was, to a great extent, wholesale, and the latter represented the bulk of such transactions as would now be done on the public exchanges or in the private warehouses of London, Liverpool, Manchester, Birmingham, and other leading commercial centres.

Fairs were essentially the outcome of defective means of communication. Going back in their origin to the days of ancient Greece, they have been found in most countries in the earlier stages of society, or under conditions which have not allowed of (1) a ready distribution of commodities, (2) sufficiently advanced manufactures, or (3) the subdivision of trade over an adequately wide area. Fairs in England began to decay in exact proportion as communications and manufactures improved and retail trade expanded ; so that to-day the survivals are either exclusively cattle fairs, sheep fairs, horse fairs, cheese fairs, and so on, or else are little more than pleasure fairs, with gingerbread stalls, shows and roundabouts for their chief attractions—mere reminiscences of old institutions which, in bygone days, were of supreme commercial importance.

They were, also, greatly influenced by religious festivals, whether in ancient Greece or in Europe. In Britain itself the commemoration of saints' days by the monasteries, the dedication festivals of churches or cathedrals, and the visitation of shrines by pilgrims brought together crowds of people whose assembling offered good opportunities for the opening up with them of a trade in commodities which they, in turn, might otherwise have some difficulty in procuring. It was, indeed, to the advantage of the Church to offer or to encourage the offering of such facilities, not only because there would thus be a greater inducement to people to come to the festivals or to visit the shrines, but also because when the fair was held on land belonging to the Church or connected with religious buildings there might be a substantial revenue gained from the tolls and charges paid by the traders. At one time the fairs were even held in churchyards ; but this practice was prohibited in the 13th year of Edward I., and thenceforward they were held on open spaces, where stalls and tents could be erected for the accommodation of the goods on sale and of the persons who had brought them, various amusements being added, or encouraged, by way of affording further attractions. The land occupied might be that of the lord of the manor, but the fairs still continued to be held chiefly on Saints' days or on the occasion of Church festivals, the actual dates being generally so fixed as to allow of the foreign or other traders attending them to arrange a circuit. The time of year preferred for the holding of fairs was either the autumn, when people whose wants were not wholly met by pedlar or chapman would be providing against the stoppage of all traffic along the roads during the winter ; or the spring, when they would want to replenish their depleted stocks. The localities mostly favoured were towns either on navigable rivers, giving access to a good stretch of country, or at the entrance to valleys whose inhabitants would be especially isolated during the winter months by their impassable roads and mountain tracks.

In course of time the fairs became, as shown by Giles Jacob, in his " Law Dictionary " (4th edition, 1809), " a matter of

universal concern to the commonwealth," as well as a valuable
monetary consideration to those who had the right to collect
the tolls ; and they were, in consequence, subjected to close
regulation.   No person could hold a fair " unless by grant
from the King, or by prescription which supposes such grant " ;
the time during which it could be kept open was announced
by proclamation, and rigidly adhered to ; " just weight and
measure " was enforced, and a " clerk of the fair " was
appointed to mark the weights.

On the other hand every encouragement was offered to
traders to attend the fairs.   " Any citizen of London," says
Jacob, " may carry his goods or merchandise to any fair or
market at his pleasure."   Mounted guards were, in some
instances, provided on the main routes leading to the fair,
in order to protect the traders from attack by robbers.   Tolls
were to be paid to the lord of the manor or other owner of the
land on which a fair was held under a special grant ; but if
the tolls charged were " outrageous and excessive " (to quote
again from Jacob), the grant of the right to levy toll became
void, and the fair was thenceforth a " free " one.   It was
further laid down that persons going to a fair should be
" privileged from being molested or arrested in it for any other
debt or contract than what was contracted in the same,
or at least, was promised to be paid there."

An especially curious feature of these old fairs was the
so-called " Court of Pie Powder "—this being the accepted
English rendering, in those days, of " pied poudré "—or
" The Court of Dusty Feet."   The court was one of summary
jurisdiction, at which questions affecting pedlars or other
(presumably) dusty-footed traders and their patrons, or
matters relating to " the redress of disorders," could be decided
by a properly constituted authority during the period of the
holding of the fair in which such questions or matters arose.

Jacob says of this old institution :—

" It is a *court of record* incident to every *Fair ;* and to be
held only *during the time* that the *Fair* is kept.   As to the
jurisdiction, the cause of action for contract, slander, &c.,
must arise *in* the fair or market, and not before at any former
fair, nor after the fair ; it is to be for some *matter concerning*
the same *fair* or *market ;* and must be done, complained of,
heard and determined the same day.   Also the plaintiff must

make oath that the contract, &c., was *within the jurisdiction* and *time* of the *fair*. . . . The steward before whom the court is held, is the judge, and the trial is by merchants and traders in the fair."

Such courts were as ancient as the fairs themselves, and they ensured a speedy administration of justice in accordance with what was recognised as merchants' law long before any common law was established. Supposed to have been introduced by the Romans, the " court of pie powder " was, according to Jacob, known by them under the name of " curia pedis pulverisati," while the Saxons called it the " ceapung-gemot," or " the court of merchandise or handling matters of buying and selling." It was, of course, the Normans who introduced the later term of " pied poudré," which the English converted into " pie powder."

One of the most ancient, and certainly the most important, of all the English fairs was the Sturbridge fair, at Cambridge, so called from a little river known as the Stere, or the Sture, which flowed into the Cam.[1]

Early records of this particular fair, according to Cornelius Walford, in " Fairs Past and Present," are to be found in a grant by King John in or about the year 1211. The fair is believed to have been originally founded by the Romans; but it may have acquired greater importance at the date of this particular charter by reason of what Cunningham, in his " Growth of English Industry and Commerce in the Early and Middle Ages," describes as the " extraordinary increase " of commerce in every part of the Mediterranean in the twelfth and thirteenth centuries, coupled with the " improvements in navigation and in mercantile practice " which " went hand in hand with this development. Englishmen," he further tells us, " had but little direct part in all this maritime activity. Their time was not come ; but the Italian merchants who bought English wool, or visited English fairs, brought them within range of the rapid progress that was taking place in South Europe."

From the middle of the twelfth to the middle of the thir-

---

[1] The fair has, also, been widely described as the " Stourbridge " fair, a name which seems to associate it, quite wrongly, with the town of Stourbridge, in Worcestershire. I have preferred to follow here the spelling favoured by Defoe and other contemporary writers.

teenth century the export of wool, leather, lead, tin and other English commodities was in the hands almost exclusively of foreign merchants, who came here both to purchase these raw materials and to dispose of the products of their own or other countries ; and Sturbridge Fair, as it happened, formed a convenient trading centre alike for foreign and for English traders, the question of inland communication being, in fact, once more the dominating factor in the situation.

Foreign goods destined for the fair were mostly brought, first, to the port of Lynn, and there transferred to barges in which they were taken along the Ouse to the Cam, and so on to the fair ground which, on one side, was bordered by the latter stream. Heavy goods sent by water from London and the southern counties, or coming by sea from the northern ports, reached the fair by the same route. Great quantities of hops brought to the fair from the south-eastern or midland counties by land or water were, in turn, despatched via the Cam, the Ouse and the port of Lynn to Hull, Newcastle, and elsewhere for consignment to places to be reached by the Humber, the Tyne, etc. Where water transport was not available the services of packhorses were brought into requisition until the time came when the roads had been sufficiently improved to allow of the use of waggons.

In his " Tour Through the Whole Island of Great Britain " Defoe gives a graphic account of Sturbridge Fair as he saw it in 1723. By that date it had become, in his opinion, " not only the greatest in the whole Nation, but in the World." It covered an area of about half a square mile, had shops placed in rows like streets, with an open square known as the Duddery, and comprised " all Trades that can be named in London, with Coffee-houses, Taverns, and Eating-houses innumerable, and all in Tents and Booths." He speaks of £100,000 worth of woollen manufactures being sold in less than a week, and of—

" The prodigious trade carry'd on here by Wholesale-men from London, and all parts of England, who transact their Business wholly in their Pocket-Books, and meeting their Chapmen from all Parts, make up their Accounts, receive Money chiefly in Bills, and take Orders : These, they say, exceed by far the sales of Goods actually brought to the Fair, and deliver'd in kind ; it being frequent for the London

Wholesale Men to carry back orders from their Dealers for ten Thousand Pounds-worth of Goods a man, and some much more. This especially respects those People, who deal in heavy Goods, as Wholesale Grocers, Salters, Brasiers, Iron-Merchants, Wine-Merchants and the like ; but does not exclude the Dealers in Woollen Manufactures, and especially in Mercery Goods of all sorts, the Dealers in which generally manage their Business in this Manner :

" Here are Clothiers from Halifax, Leeds, Wakefield and Huddersfield in Yorkshire, and from Rochdale, Bury, &c. in Lancashire, with vast Quantities of Yorkshire Cloths, Kerseys, Pennistons, Cottons, &c., with all sorts of Manchester Ware, Fustians and Things made of Cotton Wooll ; of which the Quantity is so great, that they told me there were near a Thousand Horse-packs of such Goods from that Side of the Country. . . .

" In the Duddery I saw one Ware-house or Booth, with six Apartments in it, all belonging to a Dealer in Norwich Stuffs alone, and who, they said, had there above Twenty Thousand Pounds value in those Goods alone.

" Western Goods had their Share here, also, and several Booths were fill'd as full with Serges, Du-Roys, Druggets, Shalloons, Cataloons, Devonshire Kersies, &c., from Exeter, Taunton, Bristol, and other Parts West, and some from London also.

" But all this is still outdone, at least in Show, by two Articles, which are the Peculiars of this Fair, and do not begin till the other Part of the Fair, that is to say, for the Woollen Manufacture, begins to draw to a Close : These are the Wooll and the Hops : As for the Hops there is scarce any price fix'd for Hops in England till they know how they fell at Sturbridge Fair : the Quantity that appears in the Fair is indeed prodigious. . . . They are brought directly from Chelmsford in Essex, from Canterbury and Maidstone in Kent and from Farnham in Surrey ; besides what are brought from London, the Growth of those and other places."

In the North of England, Defoe continues, few hops had formerly been used, the favourite beverage there being a " pale smooth ale " which required no hops. But for some years hops had been used more than before in the brewing of the great quantity of beer then being produced in the

North, and traders from beyond the Trent came south to
buy their hops at Cambridge, taking them back to Yorkshire,
Northamptonshire, Derbyshire, Lancashire and even to
Scotland. Of wool, according to the same authority, the
quantity disposed of at a single fair would be of the value of
£50,000 or £60,000.

In writing on this same Sturbridge fair, Thorold Rogers says,
in his " History of Agriculture and Prices " :—

" The concourse must have been a singular medley. Besides
the people who poured forth from the great towns . . . there
were, beyond doubt, the representatives of many nations
collected together to this great mart of medieval commerce.
The Jew, expelled from England, had given place to the
Lombard exchanger. The Venetian and Genoese merchant
came with his precious stock of Eastern produce, his Italian
silks and velvets, his store of delicate glass. The Flemish
weaver was present with his linens of Liége and Ghent. The
Spaniard came with his stock of iron, the Norwegian with his
tar and pitch. The Gascon vine-grower was ready to trade
in the produce of his vine-yard ; and, more rarely, the richer
growths of Spain, and, still more rarely, the vintages of
Greece were also supplied. The Hanse towns sent furs and
amber, and probably were the channels by which the precious
stones of the East were supplied through the markets of
Moscow and Novgorod. And perhaps by some of those
unknown courses, the history of which is lost, save by the
relics which have occasionally been discovered, the porcelain
of the farthest East might have been seen in many of the
booths. Blakeney, and Colchester, and Lynn, and perhaps
Norwich, were filled with foreign vessels, and busy with the
transit of various produce ; and Eastern England grew rich
under the influence of trade. How keen must have been the
interest with which the franklin and bailiff, the one trading
on his own account, the other entrusted with his master's
produce, witnessed the scene, talked of the wonderful world
about them, and discussed the politics of Europe !

" To this great fair came, on the other hand, the woolpacks
which then formed the riches of England and were the envy
of outer nations. The Cornish tin-mine sent its produce. . . .
Thither came also salt from the springs of Worcestershire . . .
lead from the mines of Derbyshire and iron, either raw or

manufactured, from the Sussex forges. And besides these, there were great stores of those kinds of agricultural produce which, even under the imperfect cultivation of the time, were gathered in greater security, and therefore in greater plenty, than in any other part of the world, except Flanders."

Other leading fairs, besides that of Sturbridge, included Bartholomew Fair, in London, and those of Boston, Chester and Winchester ; while Holinshed says of the conditions in the second half of the sixteenth century, " There is almost no town in England but hath one or two such marts holden yearlie in the same." In the case of Bartholomew Fair, its decay was directly due to the fact that there came a time when English manufacturers could produce cloth equal in quality to that from Bruges, Ghent and Ypres which had been the chief commodity sold at this particular fair, thenceforward no longer needed. But the eventual decline alike of Sturbridge and of most of the other fairs carrying on a general trade was mainly due to the revolutionary changes in commerce, industry and transport to which improved facilities for distribution inevitably led.

CHAPTER V

It was in the year A.D. 411 that the Roman legions were withdrawn from Britain, and it was not until 1555, or 1144 years after their departure, that the first general Act was passed, not for the construction, but for the repair of roads in this country. In the meantime such further construction or repairing as was actually done had been left to the Church, to private benevolence, to landowners acting either voluntarily or in accordance with the conditions on which they held their estate, or to the inefficient operation of the common law obligation that the inhabitants of a parish must repair the highways within the same.

A writer in 1823, William Knight Dehany, of the Middle Temple, in a book on " The General Turnpike Acts," comes to the conclusion, after careful research into the records of this early period, that " With the exception of the principal roads communicating with the important sea ports and fortresses of the Kingdom (probably the four great roads formed either by the Romans or Saxons), the other highways were but tracks over unenclosed grounds, where the passenger selected his path over the space which presented the firmest footing and fewest impediments, as is the case in the present day in forests and wastes in remote situations." He considers that when packhorses only were used for the transport of burdens, the state of the roads was not a subject of much interest and importance ; but certain it is that the subject became more acute when the greater traffic that resulted from expanding trade and commerce led to the roads getting into an even worse condition than they had been in previously.

The earliest road legislation that can be traced was an Act passed in 1285, in the reign of Edward I., directing that on highways leading from one market town to another " there be neither dyke, tree nor bush whereby a man may lurk to do hurt within two hundred feet on either side of the way "; but this measure was designed for the protection of travellers against robbers, and had no concern with the repair of the roads. In 1346 tolls were imposed, by authority of Edward III., for the repair of three roads in London, namely, " the King's highway between the hospital of St. Giles and the bar of the old temple (in Holborn) "; what is now Gray's Inn Road ("being very much broken up and dangerous"), and another road, supposed to be St. Martin's Lane. These tolls, according to Macpherson's " Annals of Commerce " (1805) were to be imposed for a period of two years upon all cattle, merchandise and other goods passing along the roads in question ; they were fixed at the rate of one penny in the pound on the value of the animals or goods taxed, and they were to be paid by all persons, except, curiously enough, " lords, ladies, and persons belonging to religious establishments or to the Church." Then, in 1353, " the highway between Temple-bar and Westminster being already rendered so deep and miry by the carts and horses carrying merchandise and provision at the staple that it was dangerous to pass upon it," the King required the owners of houses alongside to repair the road in consideration of the increased value of their property owing to the establishment of the staple.[1]

Reference has already been made (page 13) to the concession by Edward III. to " Phelippe the hermit " of the right to impose tolls for the repair of the road on Highgate Hill. Macpherson further says, under date 1363 :—

" The equitable mode of repairing the roads by funds collected from those who used them was now so far established that we find, besides the renewals of the tolls for the Westminster road almost annually, tolls granted this year for the road between Highgate and Smithfield, for that from Wooxbridge (Uxbridge) to London, and for the venel called Faytor (Fetter) lane in Holburn."

In the reign of Henry VIII. the first Statutes relating to

[1] "Staple" was a term applied, in the Middle Ages (1) to a town to which traders were encouraged to send their supplies of some particular commodity—wool, for example—such town becoming the recognised headquarters of the trade concerned, while the arrangement was one that facilitated the collection of the taxes imposed by the King on the traders ; and (2) to the commodity sold under these conditions.

particular highways were passed, a lord of the manor in Kent, and another in Sussex, being empowered to construct certain new roads, at their own expense, and then enclose the old ones for which the new would be substituted ; but the Act of 2 and 3 Philip and Mary c. 8, passed in 1555, was the first Highway Act in this country which applied to roads in general.

"Commerce," says Macpherson, "beginning to increase considerably in the reign of Queen Mary, and the old roads being much more frequented by heavy carriages" (a term applied at this time to wheeled vehicles of any description), the Act was passed with a view to securing a much-needed improvement. After declaring, in a preamble, that the roads had become "both very noisome and tedious to travel in and dangerous to all passengers and carriages," the Act directed that constables and churchwardens in every parish should, during Easter week in each year, "call together a number of the parochians" and choose two honest persons to serve for twelve months as surveyors and orderers of works for amending parish highways leading to any market town. These surveyors were authorised to require occupiers of land to attend each Midsummer with wains, or carts, in proportion to their holdings, such carts being furnished, after the custom of the country, with oxen, horses or other cattle and necessaries, and to be in charge of two able men. All other householders, cottagers and labourers, able to work and not being servants hired by the year, were to furnish work in their own persons, or by deputy, bringing with them "such shovels, spades, pikes, mattocks and other tools and instruments as they do make their own fences and ditches withall." Work was to be carried on for four days, of eight hours each, unless otherwise directed by the supervisors ; and constables and churchwardens were "openly in the Church to give knowledge" of appointed days. Fines for default were to be imposed at leets or quarter-sessions.

This Act was to remain in operation for seven years. In 1562 it was continued by 5 Eliz. c. 13, which, in addition to giving compulsory powers to obtain materials for road repairs, increased the "statute" labour, as it came to be called, from four to six days each year.

This principle of compulsory labour on the roads was—subject to various modifications in regard to alternative assessments—to remain in operation until the passing of the General Highway Act of 1835, when it was wholly superseded by highway rates. The labour itself, though it brought about an improvement on the previous road conditions, was from the first far from satisfactory, judging from the references made to it by Holinshed. The roads, he says, were very deep and troublesome in winter; the obligation in regard to six days' labour on them was of little avail, since the rich evaded their duty, and the poor loitered so much that scarcely two days' work was done out of the six; while the surveyors, instead of applying the labour to the amendment of roads from market town to market town, bestowed it on particular spots the repair of which conduced to their own convenience. Nor, it seems, was the power conferred on the justices to punish surveyors and parishioners if they failed in their duty of much practical avail.

No further general legislation concerning roads was passed until the Restoration, when, says Macpherson, " The vast increase of commerce and manufactures and of the capital city of London, with the concomitant increase of luxury, brought in such numbers of heavy-wheel carriages as rendered it by degrees impracticable, in most cases, for parishes entirely to keep their own part of the roads in a tolerable condition, more especially in the counties lying near London and in the manufacturing counties."

Petitions had been received from the inhabitants of various districts throughout the country praying that steps should be taken for the betterment of their roads, with the view of facilitating intercommunication, and it became evident that some more effective system for the construction and repairing of roads must be adopted.

In 1662 Parliament passed an Act (14 Car. II., c. 6) which stated that, inasmuch as former laws and statutes for mending and repairing public highways had been found ineffectual, by reason whereof, and the extraordinary burdens carried on waggons and other carriages, divers highways had become dangerous and almost impassable, churchwardens and constables or tithing men in every parish were directed to choose surveyors yearly on the Monday or Tuesday in Easter week, giving public notice thereof in church immediately after the end of the morning prayer. These surveyors were to view the highways, estimate the cost of the necessary repairs, and, with the help of two or more substantial householders, apportion the cost among persons assessed to the poor rate and owners of all classes of property exclusive of " household stuff," the stock of goods in a shop being assessed as well as the shop itself, and the personal belongings of a householder equally with the dwelling he occupied.

There was further brought about, in 1663, the definite establishment, by law, of that system of toll-taking, by means of turnpikes, the principle of which had, as we have seen, already been adopted in a few isolated instances. Macpherson speaks of the system as " the more equitable and effectual method of tolls, paying at the toll-gates (called turnpikes) by those who use and wear the roads " ; and this was the view that generally prevailed at the time. He records as follows, under date 1663, the passing of this first English Turnpike Act :—

" The antient fund for keeping the roads of England repaired was a rate levied on the land holders in proportion to their rents, together with the actual service of the men, the carts, and horses of the neighbourhood for a limited number of days. But now, by the increase of inland trade, heavy carriages and packhorses were so exceedingly multiplied that those means of repairing the roads were found totally inadequate ; neither was it just that a neighbourhood should be burdened with the support of roads for the service of a distant quarter of the Kingdom. It was therefore necessary to devise more effective and, at the same time, more equitable means of supporting the public roads, and the present method of making and repairing the roads at the expense of those who actually wear them and reap the benefit of them was now first established by an Act of Parliament (15 Car. II., c. 1.) for repairing the highways in the shires of Hartford, Cambridge and Huntingdon, by which three toll-gates (or turn-pikes) were set up at Wadesmill, Caxton and Stilton."

The highways here in question formed part of the Great North Road to York and Scotland, and the preamble of the Act stated that this " ancient highway and post-road " was, in many places, " by reason of the great and many loads which are weekly drawn in the waggons through the said places, as well as by reason of the great trade of barley and

malt that cometh to Ware, and so is conveyed by water to
the city of London . . . very ruinous, and become almost
impassable, insomuch that it is become very dangerous to all
his Majesty's liege people that pass that way." The Act
required the justices in each of the three counties to appoint
surveyors who were to provide road materials and require of
persons chargeable under the general law that they should
send waggons and supply labour in accordance with their
obligations, any extra work done by them being paid for at the
usual rates in force in the district. The surveyors were, also,
to appoint collectors of tolls who were empowered to levy,
at the toll-gates (one of these being in each of the three
counties) " for every horse, one penny ; for every coach,
sixpence ; for every waggon, one shilling ; for every cart,
eightpence ; for every score of sheep or lambs, one half-penny,
and so on in proportion for greater numbers ; for every score
of oxen or neat cattle, five pence ; for every score of hogs,
twopence " ; but no person, having once paid toll, and
returning the same day with the same horse or vehicle, or
with cattle, was to pay a second time. The Act was to remain
in operation for eleven years ; though it was, of course, then
renewed.

How the turnpike system, thus introduced, was subsequently developed throughout the land will be shown later.

Charles II., whether he personally influenced the Act of
1663 or not, showed in a very practical way his interest in the
opening up of the country to improved communications. In
1675 a remarkable work was published by John Ogilby, Cosmo-
grapher Royal, under the title of " Britannia ; A Geographical
and Historical Description of the Roads of England and
Wales." The book consisted of 100 double-page sheets of
road maps, giving, in scroll fashion, every mile of route
for eighty-five roads or itineraries, and showing distances in
each case, together with a description of each route, written
in considerable detail. The maps, without the letterpress,
were published in the same year in a separate volume, under
the title of " Itinerarium Angliæ " ; and in 1699 the descriptive
matter, without the maps, was reprinted in the form of a
handbook, under the title of " The Traveller's Guide."

In his dedication of " Britannia " to King Charles II. the
author says : " Influenced by Your Majesty's Approbation

and Munificence, I have attempted to Improve our Commerce and Correspondency at Home by Registering and Illustrating Your Majesty's High-Ways, Directly and Transversly, as from Shore to Shore, so to the Prescribed Limits of the Circumambient Ocean, from this Great Emporium and Prime Center of the Kingdom, Your Royal Metropolis."

" The Traveller's Guide " is described as " A most exact Description of the Roads of England, being Mr Ogilby's Actual Survey and Mensuration by the Wheel of the Great Roads from London to all the considerable Cities and Towns in England and Wales, together with the Cross Roads from one City or Eminent Town to another " ; while in the preface the author throws more light on the previous reference to his Majesty's munificence, saying :—

" This Description of England was undertaken by the Express Command of King Charles II., and it was at his Expence that Mr Ogilby with great exactness performed an Actual Survey and Mensuration by the Wheel of all the Principal Roads of England."

CHAPTER VI

THE carts that succeeded the early British and Roman war chariots, and enabled the villeins and cottars to do the obligatory " cartage " for the lord of the manor, were heavy, lumbering vehicles, with wheels hewn out of solid pieces of wood, and were used for private transport rather than transport for hire. The latter came in with the " wains " or " long waggons " of England's pioneer road carriers. These long waggons, according to Stow, were brought into use about the year 1564, up to which time—save for the horse litters and the agricultural carts—the saddle-horse and the packhorse had been the only means of travelling and conveying goods. The long waggon developed into a roomy covered vehicle, capable of accommodating about 20 passengers in addition to merchandise ; it had broad wheels adapted to the roads ; and it was drawn, at a walking pace, by six, eight, or more horses which (except on such long journeys as that from London to Wigan) accompanied it for the entire journey. As the forerunner of the stage-coach it was, at first, generally used not only for the heavier classes of goods (lighter qualities, and especially so when greater speed was required, still going by packhorse), but, also, by such travellers as either could not, or preferred not to, travel on horseback.

The waggons made regular journeys between London, Canterbury, Norwich, Ipswich, Gloucester, and other towns. It was in the long waggon that many a traveller in the seventeenth century made the journey between London and Dover, either going to or returning from the Continent[1] ; and, though, because of this Continental traffic, the Dover road was probably kept in as good a condition as any in the country, the long

---

[1] The earlier Continental route was by river to Gravesend and thence by road to Dover.

waggon went at so slow a pace that in 1640 the journey to Dover often took either three or four days.

To Bristol, at the beginning of the eighteenth century, long waggons were despatched three times a week, as follows :—

Left London.	Arrived at Bristol.
Wednesday	Tuesday
Saturday	Friday
Friday	Thursday

It should, however, be remembered that both the long waggon and the stage-coach which succeeded it travelled only by day, remaining for the night at some wayside inn where, in coaching language, it " slept."

When Charles Leigh wrote " The Natural History of Lancashire, Cheshire and the Peak of Derbyshire," published in 1700, the London waggons went as far north as Wigan and Standish, where they took in cargoes of coals for sale on the return journey. North of Wigan nearly all the trade was carried on by strings of packhorses or by carts. Kendal was the principal packhorse station on this line of road, sending large trains of packhorses as far south as Wigan, and over the hills, northward, to Carlisle and the borders of Scotland.

In 1753, according to " Williamson's Liverpool Memorandum Book " for that year, the Lancashire and Cheshire stage waggons left London every Monday and Thursday, and were ten days on the journey in summer and eleven in the winter. At that time no waggon or coach from the south could get nearer to Liverpool than Warrington, owing to the state of the roads. The general mode of travelling was on horseback. Four owners of post-horses in London advertised in 1753 that they started from the " Swan-with-Two-Necks," Lad Lane, every Friday morning with a " gang of horses " for passengers and light goods, and arrived in Liverpool on the following Monday evening, this being considered very good time.

The conditions of transport between London and Edinburgh in 1776, when Adam Smith published his " Wealth of Nations," may be judged from the following references thereto which he makes in a comparison between the cost of land transport and the cost of sea transport :—

" A broad-wheeled waggon, attended by two men, and

drawn by eight horses, in about six weeks' time carries and brings back between London and Edinburgh near four ton weight of goods. In about the same time a ship navigated by six or eight men, and sailing between the ports of London and Leith, frequently carries and brings back two hundred ton weight of goods. Six or eight men, therefore, by the help of water carriage, can carry and bring back in the same time the same quantity of goods between London and Edinburgh as fifty broad-wheeled waggons, attended by a hundred men, and drawn by four hundred horses."

The long waggon, supplementing alike the packhorse and the coach, which carried the lighter and more urgent commodities, continued, right down to the railway age, the means by which the great bulk of the general merchandise of the country was transported where carriage by water was not available. It remained, also, in favour with the poorer classes of travellers until late in the eighteenth century, when the stage coaches reduced their fares to such proportions that there was no longer any saving in going by the slower conveyance.

Private carriages, as an alternative alike to the horse litter and to riding on horseback, seem to have been introduced into this country, from the Continent, about the middle of the sixteenth century. In his " History of the Origin and Progress of the Company of Watermen and Lightermen of the River Thames " Henry Humpherus says that at her coronation, in 1553, Queen Mary rode in a chariot drawn by six horses, followed by another in which were " Lady Elizabeth, her sister, and Lady Ann of Cleves." He further states that in 1565 a Dutchman, Guylliam Boonen, presented to Queen Elizabeth a " coach " which was considered a great improvement on the " chariot or waggon " used at the coronation of Queen Mary. But the pioneer carriages of this date were little better than gorgeously decorated springless carts, to be ridden in along the worst of roads, and so uncomfortable that in an audience she had with the French Ambassador in 1568, Queen Elizabeth told him of " the aching pains " she was suffering in consequence of having been " knocked about " a few days before in a coach which had been driven too fast along the streets. All the same, these private " coaches " must have come into more general use by the end of the

sixteenth century, since we find Stow saying in his " Survey
of London " (1598) :—

" Of old times coaches were not known in this island. . . .
But now of late years the use of coaches, brought out of
Germany, is taken up and made so common that there is
neither distinction of time nor difference of people observed ;
for the world runs on wheels with many whose parents were
glad to go on foot."

Fynes Moryson, Gent., in the " Itinerary " he published
(1617) in the reign of James I., recording various journeys he
had made, also alludes to this greater use of private " coaches,"
and he gives some interesting details as to the general conditions of travel at that period.   He says :—

" Sixtie or seventy yeeres agoe, Coaches were very rare in
England, but at this day pride is so far increased, as there be
few Gentlemen of any account (I mean elder Brothers) who
have not their Coaches, so as the streetes of London are almost
stopped up with them. . . . For the most part Englishmen,
especially in long journies, used to ride upon their owne
horses.   But if any will hire a horse, at London they used to
pay two shillings the first day, and twelve, or perhaps eighteene
pence a day, for as many dayes as they keepe him, till the horse
be brought back home to the owner, and the passenger must
either bring him backe, or pay for the sending of him, and
find him meate both going and comming.   In other parts of
England a man may hire a horse for twelve pence the day. . . .
Likewise Carriers let horses from Citie to Citie. . . . Lastly,
these Carryers have long covered Waggons, in which they carry
passengers from City to City : but this kind of journeying is so
tedious, by reason they must take waggon very earely, and
come very late to their Innes, as none but women and people
of inferiour condition, or strangers (as Flemmings with their
wives and servants) use to travell in this sort."

These long covered waggons began to be supplemented, in
1640 or thereabouts, by stage coaches, the advent of which is
thus recorded by a contemporary writer, Dr Chamberlayne :—

" There is of late such an admirable commodiousness, both
for men and women, to travel from London to the principal
towns of the country that the like hath not been known in the
world, and that is by stage coaches, wherein any one may be
transported to any place sheltered from foul weather and foul

ways, free from endamaging one's health and one's body by
hard jogging or over-violent motion on horse back, and this
not only at the low price of about a shilling for every five
miles but with such velocity and speed in one hour as the
foreign post can but make in one day."

The " admirable commodiousness " which thus beat the
world's record of that date was a vehicle without either
springs or windows, which carried four, six or eight passengers
inside. Over the axle there was a great basket for luggage
and a few outside passengers, who made themselves as comfortable as they could among the bags and boxes, a few hand-
fuls of straw being, in their case, the only concession to luxury.
The earliest coaches carried neither passengers nor luggage
on the roof, this arrangement coming into vogue later. In
order that people should not be deterred from travelling in
these conveyances by fear of highwaymen, it was announced, in
the case of some of them, that the guards were armed and that
the coaches themselves were " bullet proof."

As against the eulogy of Dr Chamberlayne it might be
mentioned that the introduction of stage-coaches was regarded
with great disfavour by another writer, John Cressett, who
published, in 1672, a pamphlet entitled " The Grand Concern
of England Explained in Several Proposals to Parliament "
(reprinted in Harleian Miscellany, vol. viii.). Cressett evidently
belonged to those adherents to " good old times " conditions
who are opposed to all innovations ; but his pamphlet affords
much information as to the general conditions of travel at the
time he wrote.

Cressett asked, among other things, " that a stop be put
to further buildings in and about London " ; " that brandy,
coffee, mum, tea and chocolate may be prohibited " ; and
" that the multitude of Stage-coaches and caravans may be
suppressed." It is with the last-mentioned demand, only,
that we have here any " grand concern." In amplifying it
he recommends " That the Multitude of Stage-coaches and
Caravans now travelling upon the Roads may all, or most of
them, be suppressed, especially those within forty, fifty, or
sixty Miles of London, where they are no Way necessary."

The indictment he prefers against the coaches is in the
following terms :—

" These Coaches and Caravans are one of the greatest

Mischiefs that hath happened of late Years to the Kingdom, mischievous to the Publick, destructive to Trade, and preju-judicial to Lands :

" First, By destroying the Breed of good Horses, the Strength of the Nation, and making Men careless of attaining a good Horsemanship, a Thing so useful and commendable in a Gentleman.

" Secondly, By hindering the Breed of Watermen, who are the Nursery for Seamen, and they the Bulwark of the Kingdom.

" Thirdly, By lessening his Majesty's Revenues."

Alluding to the effect of coach-riding on the individual, he says :—

" Stage-coaches . . . effeminate his Majesty's Subjects who, having used themselves to travel in them, have neither attained Skill themselves nor bred up their Children to good Horsemanship, whereby they are rendered incapable of serving their Country on Horseback, if Occasion should require and call for the same ; for hereby they become weary and listless when they ride a few Miles, and unwilling to get on Horseback ; not able to endure Frost, Snow, or Rain, or to lodge in the Fields."

These last-mentioned words, " or to lodge in the fields," are especially suggestive of what might happen in those days to travellers on horseback. The writer goes on to say :—

" There is such a lazy Habit of Body upon Men, that they, to indulge themselves, save their fine clothes, and keep them-selves clean and dry, will ride lolling in one of them, and endure all the Inconveniences of that Manner of Travelling rather than ride on Horseback."

He grieves over the fact that there were not " near so many coach-horses either bred or kept in England " as there were saddle-horses formerly, and he mentions the interesting fact that the York, Chester and Exeter stage-coaches, with 40 horses a-piece, carried eighteen passengers a week to each of those three places from London, and brought the same number back—a total of 1872 for the year. His plea that, but for the coaches, this number of travellers would have required, with their servants, " at least 500 horses," instead of the 120 which sufficed for the coaches, no longer concerns us ; but his figures as to the extent of the travel in 1673 between London and cities of such importance—even in those days—

as York, Chester and Exeter, are certainly interesting. One learns from the pamphlet that there were, in addition, stage coaches then going to " almost every town within 20 or 25 miles of London."

The writer also sought to discredit coaches on the ground that they were—bad for trade ! " These Coaches and Caravans," he said, " are destructive to the Trade and Manufactures of the Kingdom, and have impoverished many Thousands of Families, whose subsistence depended upon the manufacturing of Wool and Leather, two of the Staple Commodities of the Kingdom." It was not only that saddlers and others were being cast on the parish, but tailors and drapers were also suffering because in two or three journeys on horseback travellers spoiled their clothes and hats—" Which done, they were forced to have new very often, and that increased the consumption of the manufactures, and the employment of the Manufacturers, which travelling in Coaches doth no way do."

All this must have seemed grave enough to the good alarmist ; but there was still worse to come, for he goes on to say that—

" Passage to London being so easy, Gentlemen come to London oftener than they need, and their Ladies either with them, or, having the Conveniences of these Coaches, quickly follow them. And when they are there, they must be in the Mode, buy all their Cloaths there, and go to Plays, Balls, and Treats, where they get such a Habit of Jollity and a Love to Gayety and Pleasure, that nothing afterwards in the Country will serve them, if ever they should fix their minds to live there again ; but they must have all from London, whatever it costs."

Fearing, perhaps, that these various arguments might not suffice to discredit the coaches, the pamphleteer has much to say about the discomforts of those conveyances :—

" Travelling in these Coaches can neither prove advantageous to Men's Health or Business ; For what Advantage is it to Men's Health to be called out of their beds into these Coaches, an Hour before Day in the Morning, to be hurried in them from Place to Place till one Hour, two or three within Night ; insomuch that, after sitting all Day in the Summertime stifled with Heat and choaked with Dust; or in the

Winter-time starving and freezing with cold, or choaked with filthy Fogs, they are often brought into their Inns by Torch-light, when it is too late to sit up to get a Supper ; and next Morning they are forced into the Coach so early, that they can get no Breakfast. . . .

" Is it for a Man's Health to travel with tired Jades, and to be laid fast in the foul ways and forced to wade up to the knees in Mire ; afterwards sit in the Cold, till Teams of Horses can be sent to pull the Coach out ? Is it for their Health to travel in rotten Coaches, and to have their Tackle, or Pearch or Axle-tree broken, and then to wait three or four hours, sometimes half a day, to have them mended, and then to travel all Night to make good their Stage ? "

And so on, and so on, until we come to the moral of the story, which is that people should refuse to patronise such innovations as stage-coaches, keep to the ways of their fore-fathers, and do their travelling on horseback. If they could not do that, and needs must ride in a vehicle, let them be content with the long coaches (i.e. long waggons) which were " More convenient than running coaches . . . for they travel not such long journeys, go not out so early in the Morning, neither come they in so late at night ; but stay by the Way, and travel easily, without jolting Men's Bodies or hurrying them along, as the running Coaches do."

But the denunciations, arguments and vigorous pleadings of this " Lover of his Country," as the author of " The Grand Concern " called himself, were all of no avail. The march of progress had taken another step forward, and England found it had now entered definitely on the Coaching Era.

CHAPTER VII

BEFORE dealing more fully with the development of coaches and coaching and of vehicular traffic in general, it will be desirable to revert to the new perplexities which such development brought to those who were concerned with the care of the roads, and see in what way it was endeavoured to meet them.

In Macpherson's " Annals of Commerce " the following is given under date 1629 :—

" The great increase of the commerce of England of late years very much increased the inland carriage of goods, whereby the roads were more broken than heretofore. King Charles issued his proclamation, confirming one of his father's in the 20th year of his reign, for the preservation of the public roads of England, commanding that no carrier or other person whatsoever shall travel with any waine, cart or carriage with more than two wheels nor with above the weight of twenty hundred ; nor shall draw any waine, cart or other carriage with above five horses at once."

The King Charles here spoken of was, of course, Charles I., and the 20th year of the reign of his father, James I., takes us back to 1623. That year, therefore, gives us the date for the starting of a policy, not of adapting the roads to the steadily increasing traffic, but of adapting the traffic to the roads ; and this policy, as far as successive rulers and governments were concerned (efforts in the way of actual road betterment being left almost exclusively to individual initiative or private enterprise), was persevered in more or less consistently for a period of close on two centuries.

The State policy here in question was applied mainly in two directions : (1) the restriction to a certain weight of the loads carried ; and (2) the enforcing of regulations as to the breadth of wheels. The former alone is mentioned in the references

43

just made to the proclamations of Charles I. and James I. ; and it may be explained that the stipulation as to not more than five horses being attached to any cart or waggon was itself a precaution against the drawing of what were regarded as excessive loads. Such precautions were renewed after the Restoration, when, as we have seen, there began to be a considerable expansion of trade. By 13 & 14 Chas. II., c. 6, it was laid down that no waggon, wain, cart or carriage carrying goods " for hire " should be drawn by more than seven horses or eight oxen, or carry more than 20 cwt. between October 1 and May 1, or more than 30 cwt. between May 1 and October 1, thus modifying the earlier regulations, while it further enacted that no wheels should have rims exceeding four inches in breadth ; but by 22 Chas. II., c. 12, the maximum number of horses allowed to any vehicles was again reduced to five ; and by 30 Chas. II., c. 5, the words " for hire " were deleted, the restrictions being applied to all vehicles carrying goods.

From the time of the accession of William and Mary, every few years saw fresh Acts of Parliament becoming law, changing, deleting or adding to regulations previously laid down as to weight of loads, number of horses, the order in which they should be harnessed, the breadth of the tires, the position of the wheels, the kind of nails to be used for fastening the tires, and so on, until it becomes practically impossible to follow the complicated changes from time to time, if not actually from year to year. These changes more especially applied to the number of horses or oxen by which carts and waggons could be drawn, and efforts were made to enforce the ever-varying regulations by exceptionally severe penalties. The Act 5 Geo. I., c. 11, for example, authorises any person to seize and keep possession of such number of horses as might be attached to a carter's waggon in excess of six, or to a cart, for hire, in excess of three ; though 16 Geo. II, c. 29, states that, as the restriction of three horses to a cart, under the Act of Geo. I., had been found inconvenient for farmers, and highly detrimental to the markets of the Kingdom, the number could be increased to four.

In reference to these legislative restrictions on the number of horses a farmer might attach to a single cart, it is said in " A General View of the Agriculture of Shropshire," by Joseph Plymley, Archdeacon of Salop (1803) : " Were farmers permitted to draw any number of horses, it would be of great public utility in lowering the price of these animals, which is now enormously high. The law, as it now stands, acts as a prohibition to farmers breeding horses ; for a breeding mare, or a colt under five years old, is not fit to draw one of four in a waggon, with no more than 60 bushels of barley or wheat, which is the common load of the Shropshire or Staffordshire farmers, neither being more than two tons. . . . Another evil occasioned by the law is that such farmers are obliged to keep horses of the largest size, which consume the produce of much land by eating a large quantity of corn." Whereas good waggon-horses could formerly be bought at from £10 to £15 each, they were then, " by their scarcity," costing from £25 to £35 each. Coach-horses cost " from £40 to £60."

The various provisions in respect to number of horses or oxen per cart or waggon failed to keep down the loads to a weight suited to the deficiencies of the roads—which deficiencies had continued, notwithstanding the turnpikes— and a further step was taken under 14 Geo. II., c. 42, which authorised turnpike trustees not only to erect weighing machines but to impose an additional toll of twenty shillings per cwt. on any waggon which, together with its contents, had a total weight exceeding 60 cwt. By Geo. II., c. 43, the trustees were authorised to levy the same additional toll on any vehicle drawn by six horses.

In addition to adopting these various restrictions on the weights carried, Parliament had devoted much attention to the construction of the vehicles employed. One of the provisions of an Act passed in 1719 was a regulation in respect to the breadth of the wheel-rims, or " fellies," and the use thereon of rose-headed nails, these being regarded as injurious to the roads ; though in the following year came another Act which recited that as the extending of these regulations to waggons that did not travel for hire had been found detrimental to farmers and others, and, also, to the markets of the Kingdom, they were repealed—only, however, to be revived, by 18 Geo. II., c. 33, in 1745.

Parliament was now to devote much more attention to the subject of broad wheels ; and how this came about is explained by Daniel Bourn in a pamphlet entitled, " A Treatise upon Wheel Carriages " (1763), the main purpose of which was to expound to the world the excellences of what the writer described as " that noble and valuable machine, the broad-wheeled waggon." He gives the following account of the origin of the said machine :—

" The first set of broad wheels made use of on roads in this Kingdom were erected by Mr James Morris, of Brock-Forge, near Wiggan in Lancashire ; who having a deep bad road to pass with his team advised with me upon the subject; I mentioned the making of the fellies of his wheels of an uncommon width : He accordingly made his first set thirteen inches, and the next year another of nine inches in the sole ; and his travelling with these to Liverpool, Warrington and other places, was took notice of by some persons of distinction, particularly Lord Strange, and Mr Hardman, Member for Liverpool, &c., who after making strict enquiries of Mr Morris, concerning their nature and properties, reported their utilities to the House, which occasioned an Act of Parliament being made in their favour. . . .

" Therefore let us congratulate ourselves on making thus far so happy a progress; and as the publick roads continue to mend and improve, as they polish and smooth, and arrive nearer perfection, so let us try if the carriage that travels this road may not continue to improve too, and receive a similar degree of perfection."

The Act of Parliament referred to by Bourn was, presumably, that of 26 Geo. II., c. 30, which laid down that—with certain exceptions—no cart or waggon should be allowed on any turnpike road at all unless the " fellies " of each and every wheel had a breadth of at least nine inches, the penalty for a breach of this enactment being a fine of £5, with one month's imprisonment in default of payment, and forfeiture of one of the horses, together with its harness, to the sole use and benefit of the person making the seizure. As a further encouragement of such wheels, the trustees of turnpike roads were required to accept reduced tolls for all vehicles having wheels of a breadth of nine inches. Two years later a further Act (28 Geo. II., c. 17), set forth that, the former statutes relating to cart-wheels not having answered the good purposes intended, it was now provided that for a period of three years from June 24, 1753, waggons having 9-inch wheels were to be allowed to pass free through every turnpike in the Kingdom, the trustees being authorised to protect themselves against loss from such free passage by imposing higher tolls on all carts and waggons the wheels of which were not nine inches in width.

The idea in having these broad wheels was that they would not only be less injurious to the roads than the narrow wheels, but would even tend to keep the roads in good order by helping to smooth and consolidate them in the same way as would be done by garden rollers. Mr Bourn, who was an enthusiast on the subject, even proposed to have cart and waggon wheels made of cast iron with a breadth of sixteen inches! He says in his pamphlet :—

" I would recommend having the wheels made in the following manner :—

" Let there be run out of cast iron at the founders hollow rims or cylinders, about two feet high, sixteen inches broad or wide, and from one to near two inches in thickness, according to the design or necessity of the proprietor, and the burden he intends them to bear. Let the space, or cavity between these cylinders be filled up solid with a block of wood, through the center of which insert your arbor or gudgeon, and leave it two inches and six eighths at each end longer than the cylinder; which parts must be round, and about two inches thick, being the pivots, and when the whole is well wedged the wheel is compleat.

" Here then is a solid wheel, which answers all the intentions of the garden roller ; now can anything be conceived that would have so happy a tendency upon the roads ? to render them smooth and even to harden and encrust the surface, and make it resemble a terrass walk ? I say, can anything be equal to these kind of cast iron rollers to produce the foregoing effects ? "

Without adopting Mr Bourn's 16-inch cast-iron garden rollers, the carriers of the period did, apparently, adopt the 9-inch wheels favoured by Parliament ; but as they found that, with 9-inch wheels, they could carry much heavier weights, there had to be a further resort to legislation directed to a limitation of loads. This was done by 5 Geo. III., c. 38,[1]

[1] This Act also provided that when the wheels of a waggon were so arranged that those at the back followed in a line with those in front, the two pairs thus running in one and the same groove, only half the usual tolls should be charged.

while under 6 Geo. III., c. 43,, turnpike trustees were directed
to issue orders to their collectors not to allow any waggon
or other four-wheeled carriage having wheels of less than
9 inches in breadth to pass through a toll-gate when drawn
by more than four horses without seizing one of the horses.
By 13 Geo. III., c. 84, the reduced tolls already conceded to
9-inch wheels were extended to 6-inch wheels, and it was
further provided that waggons with 16-inch wheels should pass
toll free for a year, and then pay only one-half of the tolls
to be paid by 6-inch wheeled waggons.

In order to give still further encouragement to the use
of 16-inch wheels, an Act passed in the following year provided
that any waggon having wheels of those dimensions should
pass toll-free for five years instead of one, and pay only half
toll afterwards.

Among the many other Acts that followed, mention may
be made of 55 Geo. III., c.119, which gives an especially good
idea of the infinite pains taken by the Legislature to adapt
the construction of vehicles to the apparently hopeless
deficiencies of the roads. The Act authorised road trustees
to exempt certain vehicles from tolls for overweight " provided
such Waggon, Cart or other such Carriage shall have the Soles or
Bottoms of the Fellies of all the Wheels thereof of the Breadth
of Six inches, or of Nine Inches, or of Sixteen Inches or upwards,
and be cylindrical, that is to say, of the same Diameter on the
Inside next the Carriage as on the outside, so that when such
Wheels shall be rolling on a flat or level Surface, the whole
Breadth thereof shall bear equally on such flat or level Surface ;
and provided that the opposite Ends of the Axletrees of such
Waggon, Cart or other Carriage, so far as the same shall be
inserted in the respective Naves of the Wheels thereof, shall
be horizontal and in the continuance of one straight Line,
without forming any Angle with each other ; and so that in
each pair of Wheels belonging to such Carriage, the lower Parts,
when resting on the Ground, shall be at the same distance from
each other as the upper Parts of such Pair of Wheels : Provided always," etc.

Under 3 Geo. IV., c. 126 (1822) no waggon or cart with
wheels of less breadth than 3 in. was to be used on any turnpike
road from the 1st of January, 1826, under a penalty of not
exceeding £5 for the owner and not exceeding forty shillings

for the driver ; but this provision was repealed by 4 Geo. IV., c. 95 (1823), " in compliance," says Dehany, " with a cry raised on the part of the farmers and agriculturists, who, in petitions and complaints against the Act, put forward this clause as a principal grievance."

The broad-wheel policy of successive Governments evoked a good deal of criticism from others besides farmers and agriculturists, who themselves seem to have been reduced from time to time by the ever-changing regulations and restrictions to a condition almost of despair. In speaking of the roads in the parish of Eccles, Dr Aikin, writing in 1795, says in his " Description of the Country from Thirty to Forty Miles round Manchester " that although " much labour and a very great expense of money " had been expended on them, they still remained in a very indifferent state owing to the immoderate weights drawn in waggons and carts, and he adds : " To prevent this, vain and useless are all the regulations of weighing machines ; and the encouragement of broad and rolling wheels still increases the evil, which must soon destroy all the best roads of Great Britain."

The general effect of the legislation in question was, also, thus commented on by William Jessop in an article on " Inland Navigation and Public Roads," published in vol. vi. of the " Georgical Essays " (1804) :—

" I do not know anything in this country . . . that has been more neglected than the proper construction of wheel carriages and the formation of roads. It has been generally acknowledged that for carriages of burden broad wheels, which will roll the roads, are the most eligible ; and by the exemptions which have been granted to those who use broad wheels, the legislature has certainly looked forward to the benefits to be expected from the use of them ; but never was a proposition more misunderstood, or an indulgence more abused. Of all the barbarous and abominable machines that have been contrived by ignorance, and maintained by vulgar prejudice, none have equalled the broad-wheeled carriages that are now in use ; instead of rolling the roads, they grind them into mud and dust."

Not alone cart-wheels, but even cart-wheel nails, engaged the serious attention of Parliament, and formed the subject of special legislation. The Act 18 Geo. II., c. 33, provided, among other things, that the streaks or tires of wheels were to be fastened with flat, and not rose-headed, nails ; and an Act passed in 1822, in the reign of George IV., directed that when the nails of the tire projected more than a quarter of an inch from the surface of the tire the owner of the waggon should pay a penalty of £5 and the driver one of forty shillings for every time such vehicle was drawn on a turnpike road ; though an amending Act, passed the following year, reduced the penalties to " any sum not exceeding " forty shillings for the owner and twenty shillings for the driver.

Towards the end of the long period here in question it began to be realised that what was wanted, after all, was an adaptation of the roads to the traffic rather than an adaptation of the traffic to the roads ; but the change in policy was not definitely effected until two practical - minded men, John Loudon McAdam and Thomas Telford, had introduced, at the beginning of the nineteenth century, the first attempt at really scientific road-making which had been made in this country since the departure of the Roman legions in the early part of the fifth century.

CHAPTER VIII

W<small>HILST</small> the Legislature had been actively engaged in endeavouring to adapt wheeled vehicles to roads, the number of vehicles of various types using the roads had greatly increased as the result of expanding trade and travel, combined with the further stimulus offered by that system of turnpike roads the story of which will be told in later chapters.

The vehicle that first performed in this country the functions of a public coach in transporting a number of passengers from one place to another was, of course, the long waggon, of which an account has already been given. Stage-coaches began to come into use about the year 1659, when, as shown by the " Diary " of Sir William Dugdale, there was a Coventry coach on the road. The three coaches a week between London and York, Chester and Exeter, spoken of by John Cressett as running in 1673, carrying their six passengers apiece on each journey, went, at that time, only in summer, on account of the roads ; and even in the summer it was no unusual thing for the passengers to have to walk miles at a time because the horses could not do more than drag the coach itself through the mire. The usual speed was from four to four and a half miles an hour.

The first stage-coach between London and Edinburgh ran in 1658. It went once a fortnight, and the fare was £4. In 1734 a weekly coach from Edinburgh to London was announced. It was to do the journey in nine days, " or three days sooner than any coach that travels that road " ; but either such rapid travelling as this was a piece of bluff on the part of the advertiser or the conditions of travel went from bad to worse since in 1760 the Edinburgh coach for London left only once a month, and was from fourteen to sixteen days on the way. The fact that one coach a month sufficed to carry all the passengers is sufficiently suggestive of the very small amount of travel by land between London and Scotland that went on even in the middle of the eighteenth century. Fourteen days for the journey between London and Edinburgh was then considered a very reasonable time-allowance. In 1671 Sir Henry Herbert had said in the House of Commons, "If a man were to propose to convey us regularly to Edinburgh in coaches in seven days, and bring us back in seven more, should we not vote him to Bedlam ? " [1]

In 1712 a fortnightly coach from Edinburgh to London was advertised to " perform the whole journey in thirteen days without any stoppages (if God permits), having eighty able horses to perform the whole journey." The fare was £4 10s. with a free allowance of 20 lbs. of luggage. In 1754 the Edinburgh coach left on Monday in winter and on Tuesday in summer, arrived at Boroughbridge (Yorkshire) on Saturday night, started again on Monday morning, and was due to reach London on the following Friday.

In 1774 Glasgow had been brought within ten days of London. The arrival of the coach was then regarded as so important an event that a gun was fired off when it came in sight, to let the citizens know it was really there. A 10-day coach to London was also running from Edinburgh to London in 1779, an advertisement in the *Edinburgh Courant* of that year stating that such a coach left every Tuesday, that it rested all Sunday at Boroughbridge, and that " for the better accommodation of passengers " it would be " altered to a new genteel two-end coach machine, hung upon steel springs, exceedingly light and easy."

York was a week distant from London in 1700 ; but on April 12, 1706, there was put on the road, to run three times a week, a coach which, said the announcement made respecting it, " performs the whole journey in four days (if God permits)." The time of starting on the first day was five o'clock in the morning.

The proprietors of a coach that ran between London and Exeter in 1755 promised their patrons " a safe and expeditious journey in a fortnight " ; though this record was improved on before the end of the century, the time being reduced to

[1] Passengers are to-day regularly conveyed between London and Edinburgh by train in eight and a quarter hours.

ten days. Exeter is a little over 170 miles from London, and the journey can be done to-day, by rail, in three hours.

From London to Portsmouth took, in 1703, fourteen hours, " if the roads were good."

The Oxford coach in 1742 left London at 7 a.m., arrived at High Wycombe at 5 p.m., remained there for the night, and reached Oxford the following day.

By 1751 travelling between London and Dover had so far improved that it was accomplished in two days by stage-coach, instead of three or four days by long waggon. The coach left London every Wednesday and Friday at four in the morning; the passengers dined at Rochester, stayed for the night at Canterbury, and were due at Dover " the next morning, early." The announcements made in respect to this coach state that " there will be a conveniency "—that is, a basket—" behind, for baggage and outside passengers."

The advancement made by the stage-coach over the long waggon was, however, satisfactory for a time only. By about 1734 the stage-coach itself began to find a rival in what was called " the flying coach," otherwise a stage-coach which travelled at accelerated speed. Thus the advent of a " Newcastle Flying Coach " was announced in the following terms :—

" May 9, 1734.—A coach will set out towards the end of next week for London or any place on the road. To be performed in nine days, being three days sooner than any coach that travels the road, for which purpose eight stout horses are stationed at proper distances."

In 1754 a " flying coach " between Manchester and London was started by a group of Manchester merchants who, with the developing trade of those times, doubtless felt the need for improved facilities of travel. It was announced that " incredible as it may appear, this coach will actually arrive in London four days and a half after leaving Manchester."

If the person who wrote this advertisement could only come to life again, what would he be likely to say to the fact that London and Manchester are to-day only four hours apart, and that a London merchant, after doing a morning's work in the City, can leave Euston at noon, lunch in the train, be in Manchester by four o'clock, have two hours there, leave again at six, dine in the train, and be back in London by ten ? On the other hand, what does the London merchant who can do these things (besides having the further advantages of the telegraph and the long-distance telephone) think of the business conditions in 1754, when the quickest communications between London and Manchester were by a coach doing the journey in the then " incredible " time of four days and a half ?

The enterprise of Manchester naturally stimulated that of Liverpool, and three years later it was announced that from June 9, 1757, " a flying machine on steel springs " would make the journey between Warrington and London in three days. The roads between Liverpool and Warrington being still impassable for coaches, the Liverpool passengers had to go on horseback to Warrington the day previous to the departure of the coach from that town. Manchester got a three-day coach to London in 1760. Seven years later communication by stage-coach was opened between Liverpool and Manchester, six or even eight horses being required to drag through the ruts and sloughs a heavy, lumbering vehicle which, going three days a week, then took the whole day to make the journey. In 1782 the time between Liverpool and London was 48 hours.

Down to the middle of the eighteenth century there was no direct communication by coach between Birmingham and London. The Birmingham merchant or resident who wanted to travel to London by coach, instead of on horseback, had to go four miles by road to Castle Bromwich, and there await the coach from Chester to London. In 1747, however, Birmingham got a coach of its own, and this vehicle, it was announced, would run to London in two days " if the roads permit," [1] but the roads around Birmingham were still in a deplorable condition when William Hutton published his " History " of the town. He says that from Birmingham, as from a grand centre, there radiated twelve roads to as many towns ; but on most of them one could not travel with safety in times of floods, the water, owing to the absence of causeways and bridges, flowing over the road higher than the stirrup of one's horse. At Saltley in the year 1779 he had had to pass through what was really a dangerous river. A mile from Birmingham, on the Lichfield road, a river remained

---

[1] The journey between Birmingham and London can now be done by train in two hours.

without a bridge until 1792. The road to Walsall had been " lately made good," and that to Wolverhampton was much improved ; but he speaks of the road to Dudley, twelve miles in length, as " despicable beyond description," and says the " unwilling traveller " was obliged to go two miles about, through a bad road, to avoid a worse. The roads to Stratford and Warwick were " much used and much neglected," and the one to Coventry could " only be equalled by the Dudley Road."

" A flying machine on steel springs " from Sheffield to London was started in 1760. It " slept " at Nottingham the first night, at Northampton the second, and arrived in London on the third day. Leeds showed equal enterprise.

The Bath coach, " hung on steel springs," was in 1765 doing the journey in 29 hours, the night being spent at Andover. The improvement of the Bath road allowed of Burke reaching Bristol from London in 24 hours in the summer of 1774 ; but his biographer mentions, by way of explaining how he accomplished this feat, that he " travelled with incredible speed." By 1795, however, Bath had been brought within a single day's journey of London, the traveller who started from the Angel, at the back of St. Clements Danes, at four o'clock in the morning, being due at Bath at eleven o'clock at night. The journey between Dover and London was also reduced to one day, a " flying machine " leaving at four a.m. and reaching its destination in the evening.

By 1784, in fact, flying coaches had become quite common, and their once incredible speeds even came to be regarded as far from satisfactory for travellers to whom time was of importance.

The immediate reason, however, for the next development arose through the defective postal arrangements. Hitherto the mails had been carried either by post-boys, whose contract time was five miles an hour, or, in the case of short journeys, by veterans on foot whose rate of progress was much less, though it was then a common practice to make up urgent letters as parcels, and send them by the coaches. John Palmer, manager of a theatre at Bath, finding the mail was taking three days over a journey to London which he himself often did in one, submitted to Pitt, in 1783, a scheme for the running of mail coaches at the then equivalent to "express" speed. The permanent officials of the Post Office naturally regarded such a scheme, proposed by a rank outsider, as impracticable, if not absolutely absurd, and Palmer had a sturdy fight before he got his way. The experimental service started in 1784 was an immediate success, and when it became known that letters were being carried between Bristol and London in sixteen hours, every other important town or city in the country (Liverpool being one of the first to petition) wanted to have its own postal arrangements improved in the same way. Thus there was inaugurated a "mail-coach era," which was to continue unchecked until the first despatch of mails by railway in 1830.

The earliest of the mail-coaches travelled at a rate of about six miles an hour ; but, as the roads were improved, the speed was increased to eight, nine, ten or even twelve miles an hour. The time for the Liverpool-London journey, for example, was eventually reduced to 30 hours in good weather and 36 hours in bad.

The running of these mail-coaches had a powerful influence on the whole question of road improvement, since the attainment of the best possible speed and the avoidance of delays in the arrival of the mails came to be regarded as matters of supreme importance ; while more and more of the ordinary stage-coaches were put on for travellers to whom the lower fares [1] were of greater concern than high rates of speed.

Mail coaches had the further good effect of stimulating great improvements in coach construction. The use of springs, in particular, allowed of a more compact vehicle, carrying luggage and outside passengers on the roof instead of relegating them to a basket "conveniency" behind. The competition, or, at least, the example of the mail-coaches had the further result of increasing the speed of the "flying" coaches,

[1] The fares by the stage coaches generally worked out at 2½d. to 3d. a mile outside, and 4d. to 5d. a mile inside ; and those by mail-coach at 4d. to 5d. a mile outside, and 8d. to 10d. a mile inside. An outside place on the Edinburgh mail-coach cost about 7½ guineas, and an inside place 11½ guineas, exclusive of tips to coachmen and guards at every stage, and meals and refreshments *en route*. C. G. Harper, in "The Great North Road," estimates that the total cost of a journey from London to Edinburgh by mail-coach was, for an outside traveller, 11 guineas, and for an inside traveller 15 guineas.

which now generally aimed at doing their eight or nine miles an hour ; but here, again, much depended on the state of the roads.

Supplementary to the coaching there was the system of " posting," favoured by those who did not care to patronise public vehicles, and could afford the luxury of independent travel. In the earliest form of the posting system, that is, in the days when wheeled vehicles had not yet come into general use, and people did their journeys on horseback, travellers hired horses only at the recognised posting places ; and Fynes Moryson, in his " Itinerary," narrating the conditions in 1617, says a " passenger " having a " commission " from the chief postmaster " shall pay 2½d. each mile for his horse and the same for his guide's horse ; but one guide will serve the whole company, tho' many ride together." Travellers without a " commission " had to pay 3d. a mile. The guide, presumably, brought back the horses, and, also, really guided the traveller—a matter of no slight importance when the roads were often simply tracks over unenclosed spaces with no finger-posts to point the way.

Another form of posting was the hire from place to place of horses for use in private carriages ; but the more general form was the hiring of both horse and post-chaise—a four-wheeled vehicle, accommodating, generally, three persons, and having a roof on which luggage could be strapped. Posting was a costly mode of travelling, only possible for people of wealth and distinction. Harper calculates that to " post " from London to Edinburgh must have cost at least £30 ; but it was no unusual thing, about the middle of the eighteenth century, for the Scotch newspapers to publish advertisements by gentlemen who proposed to " post " to London, inviting others to join them with a view to sharing the expense.

The condition of the streets in the towns being often no improvement on that of the roads in the country, the development of vehicular traffic, even there, was but slow. It was the example of Queen Elizabeth in riding in a " coach " through the streets of London that led to private carriages becoming fashionable, since, following thereon, " divers great ladies " had coaches made, and went about in them— much to the admiration of the populace, but much, also, to the concern of the Thames watermen, who regarded the innovation as one that foreshadowed for them a competition which did, indeed, become formidable, and even fatal, to their own occupation.

In those days and for long afterwards the Thames was the highway by means of which people of all classes went, whenever practicable, from one part of London to another, the main incentive to this general use of the river being the deplorable condition of the streets and roads. In his book on " England in the Fifteenth Century " the Rev. W. Denton tells how the King's serjeants-at-law, who dwelt in Fleet Street, and who pleaded at Westminster Hall, gave up an attempt to ride along the Strand because the Bishop of Norwich and others would not repair the road which ran at the back of their town houses. It was safer and more pleasant for lawyers to take a boat from the Temple stairs and reach Westminster by water. The Lord Mayor, on his election, not only went by water from the City to Westminster, to be received by the judges, but down to 1711, when a " Lord Mayor's Coach " was provided for him, rode on horseback from the Guildhall to London Bridge, where he embarked on the City barge, accompanied by representatives of the Livery Companies in their barges.

Transport on the Thames constituted a vested interest of great concern to the watermen, who had hitherto regarded as their special prerogative the conveyance of Londoners along what was then London's central thoroughfare ; and the story of the way in which they met the competition of vehicular traffic in the streets is worth the telling because it illustrates the fact that each successive improvement in locomotion and transport has had to face opposition from the representatives of established but threatened conditions.

The great champion of the watermen was John Taylor (1580–1654), the " Water Poet," as he called himself. When the private carriages began to increase in number he expressed his opinion of them thus :—

" The first coach was a strange monster, it amazed both horse and man. Some said it was a great crab-shell brought out of China ; some thought it was one of the pagan temples, in which cannibals adored the devil. . . .

" Since Phaeton broke his neck, never land hath endured more trouble than ours, by the continued rumbling of these upstart four-wheeled tortoises. . . . A coach or carouch is a mere engine of pride, which no one can deny to be one of the seven deadly sins."

In 1601 sympathisers with the watermen succeeded in getting a Bill passed in the House of Commons " to restrain the excessive and superfluous use of coaches." It was thrown out by the House of Lords, though in 1614 the Commons, in turn, refused to pass a " Bill against outrageous coaches." In 1622 the Water Poet published a work, " An Errant Thief," etc., in which he dealt at length with the great injury that was being done to the watermen by the coaches, saying, among other things :—

> " Carroches, coaches, jades and Flanders mares,
> Do rob us of our shares, our wares, our fares ;
> Against the ground we stand and knock our heeles,
> Whilst all our profit runs away on wheeles.
> And whosoever but observes and notes
> The great increase of coaches and of boates,
> Shall find their number more than e'er they were
> By halfe and more, within these thirty yeare ;
> Then watermen at sea had service still,
> And those that stay'd at home had worke at will ;
> Then upstart hel-cart coaches were to seek,
> A man could scarce see twenty in a weeke ;
> But now I think a man may dayly see
> More than the wherrys on the Thames can be."

In the following year he published another work, " The World Runnes on Wheeles," in which he dealt further with the woes of the watermen. But the coaches continued to increase alike in number and in public favour, and the position of the watermen became still worse in 1625, when the already numerous private carriages were supplemented in London by hackney carriages let out for hire, though these did not, at first, exceed twenty in number, while they had to be hired direct from the stables of their owners.

In 1633 it was found that the river traffic was being pre-judiced more and more by the greater use of vehicles in the streets. Whether or not in sympathy with the watermen, the Star Chamber issued an Order which said :—

" As to a complaint of the stoppage of the streets by the carriages of persons frequenting the play-house of the Blackfriars, their lordships, remembering that there is an easy passage by water unto that play-house, without troubling the streets, and that it is much more fit and reasonable that those which go thither should go by water, or else on foot, do order all coaches to leave as soon as they have set down, and not return till the play is over, nor return further than the west end of Saint Paul's Church Yard, or Fleet conduit ; coachmen disobeying these orders to be committed to Newgate or Ludgate."

Opposition to the innovation of the coaches was, however, wholly unavailing, even when supported by Star Chamber intimations that people ought to be content to " go by water or else on foot " ; and in 1634 permission was obtained for hackney coaches to ply in the streets for hire, instead of their having to remain, as heretofore, in the stables. The first public stand, for four carriages, with drivers in livery, was set up in the Strand, near Somerset House. A month or two later the watermen presented to Charles I. a petition in which they said :—

" The hackney coaches are so many in number that they pester and incumber the streets of London and Westminster, and, which is worst of all, they stand and ply in the terme tyme at the Temple gate, and at other places in the streets, and doe carry sometymes three men for fourpence the man, or four men for twelvepence, to Westminster or back again, which doing of this doth undoe the Company of Watermen."

The same year (1634) saw still another innovation, that of the sedan chair, which was to play so important a rôle in social life until towards the end of the eighteenth century, and was, in fact, not to disappear until even later, since there was a stand for sedan chairs still to be seen in St. James's Square in 1821. How the sedan chair came to be introduced is shown by a Royal Order issued as follows :—

" That whereas the streets of our cities of London and Westminster and their suburbs, are of late so much incumbered with the unnecessary multitude of coaches that many of our subjects are thereby exposed to great danger, and the necessary use of carts and carriages for provisions thereby much hindered ; and Sir Sanders Duncombe's petition representing that in many parts beyond sea people are much carried in chairs that are covered, whereby few

coaches are used among them ; wherefore we have granted
to him the sole privilege to use, let and hire a number of the
said covered chairs, for fourteen years." [1]

On January 19, 1635, there was issued a Royal Proclamation
which said that—

" The great number of Hackney Coaches of late seen and
kept in London, Westminster, and their suburbs, and the
general and promiscuous use of coaches there, are not only
a great disturbance to his Majesty, his dearest consort the
Queen, the nobility, and others of place and degree, in their
passage through the streets, but the streets themselves are
so pestered and the pavements so broken up that the common
passage is thereby hindered and made dangerous, and the price
of hay and provender, &c., thereby made exceeding dear,
wherefore we expressly command and forbid that no Hackney
or hired coach be used or suffered in London, Westminster,
or the suburbs thereof, except they be to travel at least three
miles out of the same ; and also that no person shall go in a
coach in the said streets except the owner of the coach shall
constantly keep up four able horses for our service when
required."

Vigorous efforts were made to enforce this proclamation,
and the Water Poet was especially active in the matter, in
the interests of his protégés, but all to no purpose. Two years
later the King, " finding it very requisite for our nobility and
gentry, as well as for foreign ambassadors, strangers and
others " that the said restrictions should be withdrawn, was
graciously pleased to sanction the licensing in London of fifty
hackney coaches. Such attempts at limitation must, however,
have been equally of no avail, since in 1652 there was another
order, which set forth that not more than 200 should ply in
the streets. In the following year the watermen sent a further
petition to the House of Commons, and in 1654 the Protector
issued an order limiting to 300 the number of hackney coaches
to ply in London and Westminster and six miles round,
while the number of hackney coach horses was not to exceed
600. Two years or so after this the watermen sent still another

---

[1] By an Act of Parliament passed in 1710 the number of sedan chairs
allowed to ply for hire in London was fixed at 200, but the limit was raised
in the following year to 300. This was, of course, independent of the
private sedan chairs, of which every mansion had at least one.

petition to the House of Commons. This petition of " the Overseers and Rulers of the Company of Watermen, together with their whole society," declared that their " trade or art of rowing on the water hath been long reputed very useful to the Commonwealth "; that the Company had, " ever since their incorporation, been a nursery to breed up seamen " ; that, after serving " the Commonwealth's special service at sea," they found that " the art affordeth but a small livelihood to them, and that with hard labour " ; and—

" That of late your petitioners' art is rendered more contemptible than formerly, and their employment much lessened and impoverished, by reason of the strange increase of hackney coaches, which have multiplied from about three hundred to a thousand, in eleven years last past, whereby people are discouraged from binding their sons apprentice to the trade of a waterman, and if remedy be not speedily had, there will not be a sufficient number of watermen to supply the service of the Commonwealth at sea,[1] and also your petitioners and families utterly ruined.

" That of late some rich men about the city, keep very many hackney coaches to the great prejudice, as your petitioners humbly conceive, of the Commonwealth, in that they make leather dear, and their horses devour so much hay and corn ; and also they do so fester the streets as that by sad experience divers persons are in danger of their lives, by reason of the unskilfulness of some of them that drive them, besides many other inconveniences which are too large to be here inserted."

Therefore the petitioners humbly prayed that Parliament would limit the number of such coaches.

No immediate action seems to have been taken ; but, continuous complaints being made as to the obstructions caused by the hackney coaches, a proclamation was issued on November 7, 1660, by Charles II., to the effect that hackney coaches should no longer come into the streets to be hired. The proclamation had so little effect that on July 20, 1662, the watermen sent a petition to the House of Lords, once more recounting their grievances. The House named certain Lords who were to consider the matter and report ; but Henry

[1] So numerous were—or had been—the Thames watermen and lightermen that, according to Stow, they could at any time have furnished 20,000 men for the fleet.

Humpherus, author of the " History of the Origin and Progress of the River Thames," has been unable to find that any report was made thereon. Soon after this the number of hackney coaches was increased (14 Chas. II., c. 2) to 400. In 1666, more complaints coming from the watermen, the House of Commons appointed a committee of inquiry.

In the winter of 1683–4 the disconsolate watermen had to suffer the indignity of seeing the Thames itself—their own special province—invaded by the drivers of hackney coaches ! So severe was the frost that, as told by John Evelyn in his " Diary," the Thames was frozen over " so thick as to bear, not only streets of booths in which they roasted meat, and had divers shops of wares, quite across as in a town, but coaches, carts and horses," so that " coaches plied from Westminster to the Temple, and from several other stairs to and fro, as in the streets."

By 1685 the hackney coaches seem to have established their position as successful competitors of the watermen, an Act of Parliament which placed them on a recognised and regulated footing being passed in that year, while the number to be licensed was increased in 1694 to 700, in 1711 to 800, and in 1771 to 1000.

A still further blow was given to the interests of the watermen by the introduction from Paris, in 1820, of the " cabriolet," or " cab " as it came to be called ; and yet another was dealt to them when, on July 4, 1829, Mr Shillibeer, the coach proprietor, ran the first omnibus from the Yorkshire Stingo, Paddington, to the City, and thus began a further new era in urban locomotion, supplanting, thereby, a good many of the hackney coachmen, just as they themselves had to so considerable an extent already supplanted the Thames watermen.

CHAPTER IX

THE AGE OF BAD ROADS

In the present chapter I propose to bring together the testimony of various contemporary writers with a view to enabling the reader thoroughly to realise those bad-road conditions from which, it was hoped, the country would at last be saved by the introduction of the system of turnpike roads inaugurated by the Act of 1663.

Evidence of the general character of English roads at the time the Act was passed, and, also, probably, for a considerable period afterwards, is afforded by the maps and descriptions of routes given by Ogilby in his " Britannia " (see page 33). The maps indicate by means of lines and dots where the roads had been enclosed, by hedges or otherwise, on one side or both, and where they were still open. Taking the series of maps for the route from London to Berwick, and so on to Scotland, one finds that for a distance of about twenty-five or thirty miles from London, the road was then mostly enclosed; and from that point, through a large part of Hertfordshire, Cambridgeshire, Huntingdonshire, Northamptonshire, Rutland, Lincolnshire and Nottinghamshire, only occasional stretches, mostly in the neighbourhood of towns, and often for lengths of no more than half a mile each, were enclosed either on one side of the road or both. The enclosures began again about six miles south of York, and continued for a short distance on the north of that city; but beyond York they became still more rare, and from Morpeth (Northumberland) to Berwick, a distance of about fifty miles, the total extent of enclosed road did not exceed six miles. Taking roads in the west, it is shown that in forty miles or so between Abingdon and Gloucester there was not a single enclosure.

What all this meant was that, where there had been no enclosure, the road was simply a track across commons, fens, marshes, heaths, etc., or through woods, where drivers of carts, waggons or coaches picked and chose to the best advantage, discarding an old path when it became a deep rut or was otherwise impassable, in favour of a new one alongside, or some distance away, and leaving the new one, in turn, when it got into the same state as the old.[1]

The crossing of heaths and other open spaces was rendered the more difficult by the general absence of finger-posts.[2] In some instances land-beacons were constructed as a guide to travellers. One which had a height of seventy feet, served as a landmark by day and was provided with a lantern at night, was raised in 1751 by Squire Dashwood on a dreary, barren and wholly trackless waste in the neighbourhood of Lincoln known as Lincoln Heath. The lantern was regularly lighted until 1788. The beacon itself stood until 1808, when it fell and was not rebuilt.

One especially important factor in the situation was the nature of the soil.

I have already mentioned, on page 5, Defoe's references in his " Tour " to this particular matter ; but the description he gives of some of the roads which crossed the 50-mile belt of " deep stiff clay or marly " soil throws a good deal of light on the conditions of travel in his day. Thus, in dealing with the roads from London to the north, he says :—

" Suppose we take the great Northern Post Road from London to York, and so into Scotland ; you have tolerably good Ways and hard Ground, 'till you reach Royston about 32, and to Kneesworth, a Mile farther : But from thence you enter upon the clays which, beginning at the famous Arrington Lanes, and going on Caxton, Huntington, Stilton, Stamford, Grantham, Newark, Tuxford (called for its Deepness Tuxford in the Clays), holds on 'till we come almost to Bautree, which

---

[1] Incidentally, this fact may explain why country roads to-day, still following old tracks, often have so many twists and turns when, one might think, they could just as well have been made straight.

[2] A writer in the " Westminster Review " for October, 1825, referring to the lack of finger-posts, says : "There is scarcely a parish in the country, and not one in the remoter parts, where a stranger can possibly find his way, for want of this obvious remedy. South Wales is an inextricable labyrinth ; it is a chance if there is a finger-post in the whole principality. Cornwall and Devonshire are as bad. If by chance they are once erected they are never repaired or replaced. The justices know their own roads and care nothing for the traveller."

is the first town in Yorkshire, and there the Country is hard and sound, being Part of Sherwood Forest.

"Suppose you take the other Northern Road, by St. Albans. . . . After you are pass'd Dunstable, which, as in the other Way is about 30 Miles, you enter the deep Clays, which are so surprisingly soft, that it is perfectly frightful to Travellers, and it has been the Wonder of Foreigners, how, considering the great Numbers of Carriages which are continually passing with heavy Loads, those Ways have been made practicable ; indeed the great Number of Horses every Year kill'd by the Excess of Labour in those heavy Ways, has been such a Charge to the Country, that new Building of Causeways, as the Romans did of old, seems to me to be a much easier Expence. From Hockley to Northampton, thence to Harborough, and Leicester, and thence to the very Bank of Trent these terrible Clays continue ; at Nottingham you are pass'd them, and the Forest of Sherwood yields a hard and pleasant Road for 30 miles together."

On the road to Coventry, Birmingham and West Chester he had found the clays " for near 80 miles " ; on the road to Worcester " the Clays reach, with some intermissions, even to the Bank of the Severn," and so on with other roads besides.

Bourn, to whose " Treatise upon Wheel Carriages," published in 1763, earlier reference has also been made, said, among other things, in support of his scheme of broad-wheeled waggons :—

" So late as thirty or forty years ago the roads of England were in a most deplorable condition ; those that were narrow were narrow indeed, often to that degree that the stocks of the wheels bore hard against the banks on each side, and in many places they were worn below the level of the neighbouring surface many feet, nay, yards perpendicular, and a wide-spreading, bushy hedge, intermixed with old half-decayed trees and stubbs, hanging over the traveller's head, intercepted the benign influence of the heavens from his path, and the beauties of the circumjacent country from his view, made it look more like the retreat of wild beasts and reptiles than the footsteps of men.

" In other parts, where the road was wide, it might be and often was too much so, and exhibited a scene of a different aspect. Here the wheel carriage had worn a diversity of tracks which were either deep, or rough and stony, or high or low, as mother nature had placed the materials upon the face of the ground ; the spaces between these were frequently furzy hillocks or thorny brakes, through or among which the equestrian traveller picked out his entangled and uncouth steps. To these horrible, hilly, stony, deep, miry, uncomfortable, dreary roads the narrow wheel'd waggon seems to be best adapted, and these were frequently drawn by seven, eight, or even ten horses, that with great difficulty and hazard dragged after them twenty-five or thirty hundred, seldom more."

A writer in the " Gentleman's Magazine " for November, 1752, declares that the roads from London to Land's End, and even those as far as Exeter, Plymouth or Falmouth, were then still " what God left them after the flood " ; while in comparing England with some of the Continental countries, he says :—

" Nothing piques me more than that a trumpery despotic government like France should have enchanting roads from the capital to each remote part of use. Some roads in Holland are very fine. . . . The republic of Berne hath made lately three or four magnificent roads, some of which are near 100 miles in length, and that, too, in a country to which Cornwall, Derbyshire, Cumberland and Westmoreland are perfect carpet ground."

Sydney Smith professed to know—approximately—the number of " severe contusions " he received in going from Taunton to Bath " before stone-breaking McAdam was born." He put the figure at " between 10,000 and 12,000."

In Sussex the roads were especially bad. In 1702, the year of Queen Anne's accession to the throne, Charles III. of Spain paid a visit to London, travelling by way of Portsmouth. Prince George of Denmark went from Windsor to Petworth to meet him, and an account of this 40-mile journey by road says :—

" We set out at six in the morning . . . and did not get out of the carriages (save only when we were overturned or stuck fast in the mire) till we arrived at our journey's end. 'Twas a hard service for the Prince to sit fourteen hours in the coach that day without eating anything, and passing through the worst ways I ever saw in my life. . . . The last nine miles of the way cost us six hours to conquer them."

Defoe tells how the transport of timber from the neighbourhood of Lewes to Chatham by road sometimes took two or
three years to effect. He saw there twenty-two oxen engaged
in dragging " a carriage known as a ' tug ' " on which the
trunk of a tree had been loaded ; but the oxen would take it
only a short distance, and it would then be thrown down again
and left for other teams to take it still further short distances
in succession. He also speaks of having seen, at Lewes,
" an ancient lady, and a lady of very good quality," going to
church in a " coach " drawn by six oxen, " the way being
stiff and deep that no horses could go in it."

There would seem to have been difficulties not only in going
to church in Sussex but even in getting buried there, for in the
" Sussex Archæological Collections " mention is made of the
fact that in 1728 Judith, widow of Sir Richard Shirley, of
Preston, Sussex, directed in her will that her body should be
brought for burial to Preston, " if she should die at such time
of the year as the roads thereto were passable."

An authority quoted in the article on " Roads " in Postlethwayt's " Dictionary " (1745), in referring to "that impassable county of Sussex," bears the following testimony thereto :
" I have seen, in that horrible country, the road 60 to 100
yards broad, lie from side to side all poached with cattle, the
land of no manner of benefit, and yet no going with a horse
but at every step up to the shoulders, full of sloughs and holes,
and covered with standing water."

On the other hand the bad roads were regarded by many
of the inhabitants of Sussex as a distinct advantage. They
afforded increased facilities for the smuggling operations
practised there down to the beginning of the nineteenth
century, by rendering pursuit more difficult.

Arthur Young is an especially eloquent witness as to the
conditions of travel in England about the year 1770. In
making his tours through the country, with a view to investigating and reporting on the state of agriculture, he passed over
all sorts of roads, and, though some of them were " good,"
" pretty good," and even " very good "—these compliments
being more especially paid to roads constructed by the country
gentry at their own cost—he experiences a difficulty in finding
words sufficiently strong in which to express himself when he
attempts to describe the roads that were really bad ; and this

was the case in regard to many of the turnpike roads on which alleged improvements had been carried out.

The following examples of his experiences are taken from his " Six Months' Tour through the North of England " :—

" From Newport Pagnel I took the road to Bedford, if I may venture to call such a cursed string of hills and holes by the name of road ; a causeway is here and there thrown up, but so high, and at the same time so very narrow that it was at the peril of our necks we passed a waggon with a civil and careful driver."

" From Grinsthorpe to Coltsworth are eight miles, called by the courtesy of the neighbourhood a turnpike ; but in which we were every moment either buried in quagmires of mud or racked to dislocation over pieces of rock which they call mending."

" From Rotherham to Sheffield the road is execrably bad, very stony and excessively full of holes."

" Those who go to Methley by Pontefract must be extremely fond of seeing houses, or they will not recompense the fatigue of passing such detestable roads. They are full of ruts, whose gaping jaws threaten to swallow up any carriage less than a waggon. It would be no bad precaution to yoke half a score of oxen to your coach to be ready to encounter such quagmires as you will here meet with."

" To Coltsworth. Turnpike. Most execrably vile ; a narrow causeway, cut into rutts that threaten to swallow one up."

" To Castle Howard. Infamous. I was near to being swallowed up by a slough."

" From Newton to Stokesby, in Cleveland. Cross,[1] and extremely bad. You are obliged to cross the moors they call Black Hambledon, over which the road runs in narrow hollows that admit a south country chaise with such difficulty that I reckon this part of the journey made at the hazard of my neck. The going down into Cleveland is beyond all description terrible, for you go through such steep, rough narrow, rocky precipices that I would sincerely advise any friend to go an hundred miles about to escape it."

" From Richmond to Darlington, by Croft Bridge. To Croft Bridge, cross, and very indifferent. From thence to Darlington is the great north road and execrably broke into

[1] Cross = cross road.

holes, like an old pavement ; sufficient to dislocate ones bones."

"To Lancaster. Turnpike. Very bad, rough and cut up."

"To Preston. Turnpike. Very bad."

"To Wigan. Ditto. I know not in the whole range of language terms sufficiently expressive to describe this infernal road. To look over a map, and perceive that it is a principal one, not only to some towns, but even whole counties, one would naturally conclude it to be at least decent ; but let me most seriously caution all travellers who may accidentally propose to travel this terrible country to avoid it as they would the devil ; for a thousand to one but they break their necks or their limbs by overthrows or breakings down. They will here meet with rutts which I actually measured four feet deep, and floating with mud only from a wet-summer ; what therefore must it be after a winter ? The only mending it receives is the tumbling in some loose stones, which serve no other purpose but jolting a carriage in the most intolerable manner. These are not merely opinions but facts, for I actually passed three carts broken down in these eighteen miles of execrable memory."

"To Warrington. Turnpike. This is a paved road, and most infamously bad. . . . Tolls had better be doubled and even quadrupled than allow such a nuisance to remain."

"From Dunholm to Knotsford. Turnpike. It is impossible to describe these infernal roads in terms adequate to their defects. Part of these six miles I think are worse than any of the preceding."

"To Newcastle. Turnpike. This, in general, is a paved causeway, as narrow as can be conceived, and cut into perpetual holes, some of them two feet deep, measured on the level ; a more dreadful road cannot be imagined ; and wherever the country is in the least sandy the pavement is discontinued, and the rutts and holes most execrable. I was forced to hire two men at one place to support my chaise from overthrowing, in turning out from a cart of goods overthrown and almost buried. Let me persuade all travellers to avoid this terrible country, which must either dislocate their bones with broken pavements or bury them in muddy sand."

"I must in general advise all who travel on any business but absolute necessity to avoid any journey further north than Newcastle. All between that place and Preston is a country, one would suppose, devoid of all those improvements and embellishments which the riches and spirit of modern times have occasioned in other parts. It is a track of country which lays a most heavy tax upon all travellers and upon itself. Such roads are a much heavier tax than half a crown a horse for a toll would be. Agriculture, manufactures and commerce must suffer in such a track as well as the traveller. . . . Until better management is produced I would advise all travellers to consider this country as sea, and as soon think of driving into the ocean as venturing into such detestable roads."

That the roads in the south of England were no improvement on those in the north is shown by the same writer's " Six Weeks Tour through the Southern Counties of England and Wales," wherein he says :—

" Of all the cursed roads that ever disgraced this kingdom in the very ages of barbarism, none ever equalled that from Billericay to the King's Head at Tilbury. It is for near 12 miles so narrow that a mouse cannot pass by any carriage ; I saw a fellow creep under his waggon to assist me to lift, if possible, my chaise over a hedge. . . . I must not forget the eternally meeting with chalk waggons, themselves frequently stuck fast till a collection of them are in the same situation that twenty or thirty horses may be tacked to each to draw them out one by one."

Of the " execrably muddy road " from Bury to Sudbury, in Norfolk, he says : " For ponds of liquid dirt and a scattering of loose flints, just sufficient to lame every horse that moves near them, with the addition of cutting vile grips across the road under pretence of letting water off, but without the effect, altogether render at least 12 out of these 16 miles as infamous a turnpike as ever was travelled." As for Norfolk in general, he declares that he " does not know one mile of excellent road in the whole country."

Conditions in and around London were not much better than in the country. In 1727 George II. and his Queen were the whole night in making their way from Kew Palace to St. James's. At one particularly bad place their coach was overturned. In 1737 the time usually occupied, in wet weather, in driving from Kensington to St. James's Palace was two hours—assuming that the vehicle did not stick in the mud. Writing from Kensington in this same year, Lord Hervey said : " The road between this place and London is grown so infamously bad that we live here in the same solitude as we would do if cast on a rock in the middle of the ocean ; and all the Londoners tell us there is between them and us an impassable gulf of mud."

Middleton, again, speaking in his " Survey of Middlesex " of the Oxford Road at Uxbridge, in 1797, says that during the whole of the winter there was but one passable track on it, and that was less than six feet wide, and was eight inches deep in fluid sludge.

In 1816 the Dublin Society made a grant of £100 to defray the cost of a series of experiments to be carried out by Richard Lovell Edgeworth at the Society's premises in Kildare Street, Dublin, with a view to ascertaining " the best breadth of wheels, the proper weight of carriages and of burthen, and the best form of materials for roads." Edgeworth's report, published under the title of " An Essay on the Construction of Roads and Carriages " (second edition, 1817), includes, in its introductory matter, a short account of the history and development of roads. After pointing out that before vehicles for the conveyance of goods were in use little more was required than a path on hard ground which would bear horses ; that all marshy grounds were shunned ; that inequalities and circuitous roads were of much less consequence than was the case when carriages, instead of packhorses, began to be employed, he proceeds :—

" When heavier carriages and greater traffic made wider and stronger roads necessary, the ancient track was pursued ; ignorance and want of concert in the proprietors of the ground, and, above all, the want of some general effective superintending power, continued this wretched practice until turnpikes were established. . . .

" The system of following the ancient line of road has been so pertinaciously adhered to that roads have been sunk many feet, and in some parts many yards, below the surface of the adjacent ground; *so that the stag, the hounds and horsemen have been known to leap over a loaded waggon, in a hollow way, without any obstruction from the vehicle.*"

After this the reader will better appreciate the fact that in

the course of a report on agriculture in the county of Northampton, in 1813, it was stated that the only way of getting
along some of the main roads there in rainy weather was by
swimming !

Nor is there any lack of testimony as to the prejudicial effect
on trade and agriculture of the deplorable condition into which
so many of the roads had fallen.

Whitaker, in his "Loidis and Elmete" (1846), speaking of
the impediments to commerce and manufactures in the Leeds
district prior to the rendering of the Aire and Calder navigable,
impediments which, he declares, "it will be difficult for a
mind accustomed only to modern ideas and appearances to
conceive," says :—

"The roads were sloughs almost impassable by single carts,
surmounted at the height of several feet by narrow horse-
tracks, where travellers who encountered each other sometimes tried to wear out each other's patience rather than either
should risk a deviation. Carriage of raw wool and manufactured goods was performed on the backs of single horses,
at a disadvantage of nearly 200 to 1 compared to carriage by
water. At the same time, and long after, the situation of a
merchant was toilsome and perilous. In winter, during which
season the employment of the working manufacturer was
intermitted, the distant markets never ceased to be frequented.
On horse-back before day-break, and long after night-fall,
these hardy sons of trade pursued their object with the spirit
and intrepidity of a fox chase, and the boldest of their country
neighbours had no reason to despise their horsemanship
or their courage."

There is the evidence, also, of Henry Homer, author of "An
Enquiry into the Means of Preserving Publick Roads,"
published in 1767. He regarded the state of the roads and
the difficulties of internal communication as among the chief
reasons for the backward state of the country in the reign
of Queen Anne (1702–1714), saying on this subject :—

"The Trade of the Kingdom languished under these
Impediments. Few People cared to encounter the diffi-
culties, which attended the Conveyance of Goods from the
Places where they were manufactured, to the Markets, where
they were to be disposed of. And those, who undertook this
Business, were only enabled to carry it on in the Wintry-

Season on Horseback, or, if in Carriages, by winding Deviations from the regular tracks, which the open country afforded them an Opportunity of making. . . . The natural Produce of the Country was with Difficulty circulated to supply the Necessities of those Counties and trading Towns, which wanted, and to dispose of the superfluity of others which abounded. Except in a few Summer-Months, it was an almost impracticable Attempt to carry very considerable quantities of it to remote Places. Hence the Consumption of the Growth of Grain as well as of the inexhaustible stores of fuel, which Nature has lavished upon particular Parts of our Island, was limited to the Neighbourhood of those Places which produced them ; and made them, comparatively speaking, of little value to what they would have been, had the Participation of them been enlarged.

" To the Operation of the same Cause must also be attributed, in great Measure, the slow Progress which was formerly made in the Improvement of Agriculture. Discouraged by the Expence of procuring Manure, and the uncertain Returns, which arose from such confined Markets, the Farmer wanted both Spirit and Ability to exert himself in the Cultivation of his Lands. On this Account Undertakings in Husbandry were then generally small, calculated rather to be a Means of Subsistence to particular Families than a Source of Wealth to the Publick."

Postlethwayt's authority on the roads of Sussex declared that their condition at that time (1745) " hardly admits the country people to travel to markets in winter, and makes corn dear at the market because it cannot be bought, and cheap at the farmer's house because he cannot sometimes carry it to market." This fact is confirmed by G. R. Porter, who, in his " Progress of the Nation " (1846), gives the authority of an inhabitant of Horsham, Sussex, then lately living, for the tradition that at one time sheep or cattle could not be driven to the London market at all from Horsham, owing to the state of the roads, and had to be disposed of in the immediate neighbourhood, so that " under these circumstances a quarter of a fat ox was commonly sold for about fifteen shillings, and the price of mutton throughout the year was only five farthings the pound."

In Devonshire the Rev. James Brome, who published in

1726 a narrative of "Three Years Travels in England, Scotland, and Wales," found the farmers carrying their corn on horseback, the roads being too narrow to allow of the use of waggons.

Altogether the need for improved facilities for inland communication in the interests alike of travellers and of traders was great beyond all question, and there was unlimited scope for the operation of such improvement as was represented by the turnpike system, now coming into vogue.

It was, however, not so much the general needs of the country as the rebellion in Scotland in 1745, accompanied by such disasters for the Royalist troops as their defeat at Preston Pans, which had led the Government to pay special attention to the subject of road-making and road-improvement. Between 1726 and 1737 General Wade, employing in summer about 500 soldiers on the work, had constructed in Scotland itself some 250 miles of what were, in point of fact, military roads, being designed as a means of reducing disorder in that country. The communications between Scotland and England still remained, however, very defective, and, though English cavalry and artillery had gone forward bravely enough when the rebellion broke out, they found roads that, apart altogether from any question of fighting on them, were not fit for them even to move upon ; so that while the troops from the south were hampered and delayed by the narrow tracks, the ruts and the bogs which impeded their advance, the enemy, more at home in these conditions, had all the advantage.

No sooner, therefore, had the rebellion been overcome than the Government, recognising that, even if turnpikes were set up along the roads on the border between Scotland and England, the tolls likely to be raised there would be wholly inadequate for the purpose, themselves took in hand the work of road construction and improvement ; and this action gave impetus to a movement for improving roads in England and Wales generally.

Down to this time the turnpike system had undergone very little development. For a quarter of a century after it had been applied, by the Act of 1663, to the Great North Road, no Turnpike Acts at all were sought. A few were then obtained, but until the middle of the eighteenth century, at least, even if not still later, travellers from Edinburgh to London met with no turnpikes until they came within about 110 miles of their destination. Newcastle and Carlisle were still connected by a bridle path only, while a writer in the " Gentleman's Magazine " for November, 1752, in alluding to the journey from London to Falmouth, says that " after the first 47 miles from London you never set eyes on a turnpike for 220 miles."

The policy adopted by the Government so far stimulated the action of private enterprise that between 1760 and 1774 no fewer than 453 Turnpike Acts were passed for the making and repairing of roads, and many more were to follow.

CHAPTER X

THE TURNPIKE SYSTEM

THE fundamental principle of the turnpike system was that of transferring the cost of repairing main roads from the parish to the users.

The mediæval practice, under which the roads were maintained by religious houses, private benevolence and individual landowners, had, of course, still left the common law obligation that each and every parish should keep in repair the roads within its own particular limits, the Act of Philip and Mary, with its imposition of statute duty, being, in effect, only a means for the regulation and carrying out of such requirement. The parishioners were even indictable if they failed to keep the roads in repair.

But in proportion as trade and travel increased, the greater became alike the need for good roads and, also, the apparent injustice of requiring the residents in a particular parish to do statute labour on roads, or to pay for labour thereon, less in the interest of themselves and their neighbours than in that of strangers, or traffic, passing through on the main road from one town to another. In effect, also, whether such requirement were reasonable or not, the work itself was either not done at all or was done in a way that still left the roads in a condition commonly described as " execrable."

The principle that the users should pay for the main roads by means of tolls was thus definitely adopted ; but the obligation in regard to other than main roads still rested in full with the parish. It was not, however, until the passing of 24 Geo. II., c. 43, that turnpike roads were mentioned as distinct from " highways," this being the accepted designation for roads for which the parish was responsible. When the adoption of the turnpike system became more general, that is to say, about the year 1767, the turnpike roads were maintained—or were supposed to be maintained—by tolls, and the statute labour and contributions in lieu thereof were mainly appropriated to the cross roads constituting the parish highways, on which no turnpikes were placed ; though certain proportions of the statute labour or statute labour contributions also became available for turnpike roads which could not otherwise be properly maintained.

At first there was a pronounced disinclination on the part of the public in various parts of the country to tolerate toll-bars. It might be supposed that, the state of the roads having generally been so deplorable, everyone would have welcomed their amendment under almost any possible conditions. Defoe, at least, was enthusiastic over the prospect of better roads that turnpikes foreshadowed. Alluding to them in his " Tour," he says : " And 'tis well worth recording, for the Honour of the present Age, that this Work has been begun, and is in an extraordinary Manner carry'd on, and perhaps may, in a great Measure be compleat within our Memory, as to the worst and most dangerous Roads in the Kingdom. And this is a Work of so much general Good that certainly no publick Edifice, Alms-house, Hospital or Nobleman's Palace, can be of equal Value to the Country with this, nor at the same time more an Honour and Ornament to it."

But there was another point of view which is thus expressed by Whitaker in " Loidis and Elmete " : " To intercept an ancient highway, to distrain upon a man for the purchase of a convenience which he does not desire, and to debar him from the use of his ancient accommodation, bad as it was, because he will not pay for a better, has certainly an arbitrary aspect, at which the rude and undisciplined rabble of the north would naturally revolt."

Objections to turnpikes had been further fomented by demagogues who went about the country proclaiming that the gates which were being put up were part of a design planned by the Government to enslave the people and deprive them of their liberty.

Not only did many individuals in various parts of the country refuse to use the turnpike roads, or to pay toll if they did use them, but in some instances the gates were destroyed, by way of making the protests more emphatic. In 1728 it was thought necessary to pass a general Act against " ill-designing and disorderly persons " who had " in various parts of this Kingdom associated themselves together, both by day and by night, and cut down, pulled down, burnt and otherwise destroyed several turnpike gates and houses which have been erected by authority of Parliament for repairing divers roads by tolls, thereby preventing such tolls from being taken, and lessening the security of divers of her Majesty's good subjects for considerable sums of money which they have advanced upon credit of the said Acts, and deterring others from making like advances." Persons convicted of such offences were— without any discretion being given to the justices — to be committed for three months' imprisonment, and were, also, to be whipped at the market cross. These penalties appear to have been unavailing, since we find that four years later the punishment, even for a first offence, was increased to seven years' transportation.

But the hostility increased rather than diminished. In the " Gentleman's Magazine " for 1749 there is an account of some turnpike riots in Somerset and Gloucestershire which began on the night of the 24th of July and were not suppressed until the 5th of the following month. A start was made with the destruction of the gates near Bedminster by " great numbers of people." On the following night a crowd bored holes in the gates at Don John's Cross, a mile from Bristol, blew up the gates with gunpowder, and destroyed the toll-house. Cross-bars and posts were erected next day, in place of the gates, and the turnpike commissioners took it in turns to enforce payment of the tolls. At night " a prodigious body of Somersetshire people," armed with various instruments of destruction, and some of them disguised in women's clothes, went along the roads to an accompaniment of drum-beating and much shouting, demolished the turnpikes, and pulled down the toll-houses. Re-erected, the gates were guarded by a " body of seamen, well armed with musquets, pistols and cutlasses " ; but two nights afterwards the rioters were out again, this time with rusty swords, pitch-forks, axes, guns, pistols and clubs. They demolished and burned some turnpikes which had been put up a third time, and destroyed others besides. By August 3 " almost all the turnpikes and turnpike-houses " in the neighbourhood of Bristol had been demolished ; but a report dated Bristol, August 1^, says : " By the arrival of six troops of dragoon guards on the 5th, we are secured from all insults of the country people who immediately dispersed and posts and chains are again erected, and the tolls levied, but the turnpikes are fixed nearer the city."

The revolt in Yorkshire referred to by Whitaker occurred in 1753, four years later than the disturbances in the west. At Selby the inhabitants were summoned by the bellman to assemble at midnight, with hatchets and axes, and destroy the turnpikes. They obeyed the summons, and any gate left unprotected was soon level with the ground. In the neighbourhood of Leeds the rioting was especially serious. Whitaker says concerning it :—

" The public roads about Leeds were at that time narrow, generally consisting of a hollow way that only allowed a passage for carriages drawn by a horse in a single row, and an elevated causeway covered with flags or boulder stones.

" The attempt to improve this state of the public roads excited great discontent among the lower classes of the people, who formed the design of pulling down all the turnpike bars in the neighbourhood."

They pulled down, or burned down, as many as a dozen in one week ; and when some of the rioters had been arrested, and were on their way to York Castle, their friends attempted a rescue, following this up by assaulting the magistrates and breaking some windows. Troops were called out, and, warnings and the firing of blank cartridge being of no avail, ball cartridges were used, with the result that two or three persons were shot dead, and twenty-two were wounded, some fatally.

Whatever the justification for the turnpikes that gave rise to this popular discontent, the way in which the system itself was developed was certainly open to criticism.

The precedent set by the Act of Charles II. in the grouping together of several counties, and in conferring on the justices the powers of chief control, was wholly disregarded. Instead of even an improvement on this procedure being effected by the creation of a national system of turnpike roads, directed by some central authority, and responding in regard to internal communication to the wants of the country as a whole, there was called into being an almost endless number of purely local trusts, each taking charge of, as a rule, from ten to twenty miles of road, each concerned only in its own local, or even its own personal, interests, and each operating under conditions that involved an excessive expenditure with, too often, the most unsatisfactory of results for the general public.

The defects of the system thus brought about were well recognised by various authorities at a time when they were still being experienced to the full.

The Select Committee appointed by the House of Commons in 1819 to consider the subject of public highways said in the course of their report :—

" The importance of land-carriage to the prosperity of a country need not be dwelt upon. Next to the general influence of the seasons . . . there is, perhaps, no circumstance more interesting to men in a civilised state than the perfection of the means of interior communication. It is a matter, therefore, to be wondered at, that so great a source of national improvement has hitherto been so much neglected. Instead of the roads of the Kingdom being made a great national concern, a number of local trusts are created, under the authority of which large sums of money are collected from the public, and expended without adequate responsibility or control. Hence arises a number of abuses, for which no remedy is provided, and the resources of the country, instead of being devoted to useful purposes, are too often improvidently wasted."

Writing in 1823, Dehany said in reference to the Act of 1663, " It is to be regretted that this plan of passing one Act applicable to a considerable district, and carrying it into execution under the superintendence of the magistracy, was not pursued, instead of parcelling out the roads into smaller divisions, with independent bodies of trustees " ; while the " Westminster Review," in its issue for October, 1825, argued that the whole system of roads should be one, and continued :—

" Such a work might have been thought the duty of the Government most interested in it ; but that Government seems generally to be otherwise occupied. Leaving all to individual exertion, it perhaps often leaves too much ; since there are matters in which individual exertion has an insufficient interest, while there are others which it is unable to accomplish without unjustifiable sacrifices. We do not desire the perpetual, nor even the frequent interference of Government, that is most certain; but there is an useful medium between the inter-meddling of some of the continental states and that neglect, or, rather, discountenance, which our own throws on numerous matters where its aid would be of use, and which, without that aid, cannot be accomplished. . . . The freedom of uni-versal communication is the object, and it is to little purpose that one portion of a road be good if the other is impassable. It is a national and not a private concern."

Under the conditions actually brought about it was left for any group of landowners and others in any particular district where better roads were needed to apply to Parliament for an Act authorising them to raise a loan in order to meet the initial cost of making or repairing a road, and to set up gates or bars where they could enforce payment of tolls out of which to recoup themselves for their expenditure and meet the costs of maintenance. Theoretically, these were simply temporary expedients, and the turnpike trustees, having once provided a good road, and got their money back, would take down the toll-gates again, and leave the road for the free use of the public. Hence every Turnpike Act was granted only for a limited period, generally about twenty years, and had to be renewed at the end of that term if, as invariably happened, the debt on the road had not been cleared off, and the need for toll-collection still remained. The cost of procuring the periodical continuance of all these Acts was, in itself, a not inconsiderable burden on the finances of the trusts. In, for example, the twenty-four years from 1785 to 1809, the number of Turnpike Acts, whether new Acts or renewals of old ones, passed by the Legislature was no fewer than 1062.

One result of the excessive localisation of the turnpike system was that trusts of absurdly large proportions were created to look after absurdly small stretches of road. " The fundamental principle," says a writer in the " Edinburgh Review " for October, 1819, " is always to vest the whole management in the hands of the country gentlemen ; and, as they act gratuitously, it has been the policy of the law to appoint in each act a prodigious number of commissioners—frequently from one hundred to two hundred, for the care of ten or fifteen miles of road ; and thus a business of art and science is committed to a promiscuous mob of peers, squires, farmers and shopkeepers, who are chosen, not for their fitness to discharge the duties of commissioners, but from the sole qualification of residence within a short distance from the road to be made or repaired."

That the best interests of the community could be served under these conditions was an impossibility. The "Edinburgh Review" declares, in fact, that the whole time of the meetings of turnpike trusts was "occupied in tumultuous and unprofitable discussions, and in resolving on things at one meeting which run a good chance of being reversed at the next; that the well informed and civilized commissioners become very soon disgusted with the disorderly uproar, or the want of sense, temper or honesty of some of their companions; and that the management finally falls into the hands of a few busy, bustling, interested persons of low condition, who attend the meetings with no idea of performing a public duty, but for the purpose of turning their powers, by some device or other, to the profit of themselves or of their friends or relations."

The writer of the article on "Roads" in "Rees' Cyclopædia" is no less condemnatory of the whole system, speaking of the "violent disputations and bickerings" at the meetings of the trustees, where, he says, "a proposed new line of road or, perhaps, the repair of an old one, will sometimes be contested with as great keenness and vehemence as if the parties were contending whether Great Britain shall be a monarchy or a republic."

Each trust, again, had its own organisation, with attorney, treasurer, clerk and surveyor; and one may assume that each of these individuals, in turn, was inspired by no greater sense of public duty than were many of the trustees themselves, and was much more concerned in what he could make out of the business for himself than in helping to provide through routes of communication in the interests of the community. The surveyors were, generally speaking, hopelessly incompetent. The short length of road in charge of a trust and the consequent limitation of the amount received for tolls did not, as a rule, warrant the payment of an adequate salary to a really qualified man, and the individual upon whom the courtesy title of "surveyor" was conferred was often either the pensioned servant of a local landowner or some other person equally unfit to be entrusted with those functions of road-management which the trustees, whether as the result of their mutual differences or otherwise, generally left in his hands. The "Edinburgh Review," in the article already quoted, declares that "the state of the roads displays no symptoms of well qualified commissioners. They leave the art and science of the business to their surveyor—who is commonly just as much in the clouds as themselves as to his own proper calling. With a laudable veneration for his forefathers, he proceeds according to the antient system of things, without plan or method ; and fearing no rivalry, and subject to no intelligent control, he proceeds, like his predecessors, to waste the road money on team work and paupers, and leave nothing for the public like a road but the name and cost of it."

Nevertheless, the turnpike system, defective in itself, badly administered, and burdensome to the toll-payers, did bring about an improvement in roads which previously had too often received little or no attention ; and this improvement, as will be shown in the chapter that follows, had a material influence on trade, travel and social conditions ; though it was not to attain its maximum results until the turnpike roads had been supplemented by a further system of scientific road-making and road-repairing.

CHAPTER XI

In strong contrast to the vigorous denunciations of Arthur Young of so many, though not all, of the roads over which his extensive journeyings through England had led him, are the statements of other authorities, writing about the same time, as to the commercial and social advantages resulting from such improvements as had been brought about. The conflict of testimony appears inconsistent until one remembers that, bad as were the particular conditions which Arthur Young describes, the general conditions were, nevertheless, better than before. Just as the first bone-shaking stage-coach, without springs, seemed to Chamberlayne an "admirable commodiousness," such as the world had never before seen, so, in the view of the writers who had not the same experience of travel as Arthur Young, turnpike roads of any kind may have appeared a vast improvement on the boggy roads or the narrow bridle paths they had succeeded.

Whatever, again, the dangers and discomforts of so many even of the new turnpike roads, there is no doubt that a distinct stimulus was given to trade and travel as the result not only of the better roads but of the better vehicles that could be, and were being, used on them. Agriculture, industries, commerce and social progress all, in fact, took another step forward as these opportunities for transport and communication relatively improved.

Under the influence, possibly, of such considerations as these Henry Homer, writing in 1767, regards with great satisfaction the general outlook at that time. He says :—

" Our very Carriages travel with almost winged Expedition between every Town of Consequence in the Kingdom and the Metropolis. By this, as well as the yet more valuable Project of increasing inland Navigation, a Facility of Communication is soon likely to be established from every Part of the Island to the sea, and from the several places in it to each other. Trade is no longer fettered by the Embarrasments, which attended our former Situation. Dispatch, which is the very life and Soul of Business, becomes daily more attainable by the free Circulation opening in every Channel, which is adapted to it. Merchandise and Manufactures find a ready Conveyance to the Markets. The natural Blessings of the Island are shared by the Inhabitants with a more equal Hand. The Constitution itself acquires Firmness by the Stability and Increase both of Trade and Wealth which are the Nerves and Sinews of it.

" In Consequence of all this, the Demand for the Produce of the Lands is increased ; the Lands themselves advance proportionably both in their annual Value and in the Number of Years-purchase for which they are sold, according to such Value. . . .

" There never was a more astonishing Revolution accomplished in the internal System of any Country than has been within the Compass of a few years in that of England.

" The carriage of Grain, Coals, Merchandize, etc., is in general conducted with little more than half the Number of Horses with which it formerly was. Journies of Business are performed with much more than double Expedition. Improvements in Agriculture keep pace with those of Trade. Everything wears the Face of Dispatch ; every Article of our Produce becomes more valuable ; and the Hinge, upon which all these Movements turn, is the Reformation which has been made in our Publick Roads."

In the article on " Roads " in Postlethwayt's " Dictionary " (1745) it is declared that the country had derived great advantage from the improvements of the roads, and from the application of tolls collected at the turnpikes. Travelling had been rendered safer, easier and pleasanter. " That this end is greatly answered," we are assured, " everyone's experience will tell him who can remember the condition of the roads thirty or forty years ago." There had been, also, a benefit to trade and commerce by the reduced cost of carriage for all sorts of goods and merchandise. On this especially interesting point the writer of the article says : " Those who have made it their business to be rightly informed of this matter have, upon inquiry, found that carriage is now 30 per cent

cheaper than before the roads were amended by turnpikes."
He proceeds to give a number of examples of such reductions
in freight, among them being the following :—

"From Birmingham to London it is said there is not less
than 25 or 30 waggons sent weekly ; 7s. per hundred was
formerly paid, the price now paid is from 3 to 4s. per hundred.

"From Portsmouth to London the common price was 7s.
per hundred, the Government paid so in Queen Anne's war,
and now only 4 to 5s. per hundred is paid ; and in the late
war arms and warlike stores for his Majesty's service were
carried at the rate of 4 or 5s. per hundred.

"From Exeter to London, and from other towns in the
west of like distance the carriage of wool and other goods is
very great, especially in times of war.—12s. per hundred was
formerly paid, now only 8s. per hundred. The same can be
affirmed with respect to Bristol, Gloucester and the adjacent
counties."

While the traders and the consumers were, presumably,
both benefitting from these reduced charges, the carriers also
gained, by reason of the greater loads they were able to take
with the same number of horses. On this point the writer
says : " The roads in general were formerly so bad and deep,
so full of holes and sloughs that a team of horses could scarce
draw from any place of 60 miles distant, or upwards, above
30 hundred weight of goods ; whereas the same team can now
draw with more ease 50 or 60 hundred." On the other hand
he did not overlook the fact that the keeping up of the turnpike
roads was " a prodigious expense to the nation," so that,
in his opinion, the reduction in transport charges was only
" a seeming alleviation " of the general burden.

At the time Defoe made his tour of England the turnpike
system was still in its infancy ; but he is very eulogistic over
the improvements then already made.

Having, as already mentioned on p. 65, described the roads
from London to the North across the clay-belt of the Midlands,
Defoe tells how " turnpikes or toll-bars " had been set up on
" several great roads of England, beginning at London, and
proceeding through almost all those dirty deep roads " in
the midland counties especially, " At which Turn-pikes all
Carriages, Droves of Cattle and Travellers on Horse-back are
obliged to pay an easy Toll ; that is to say, a Horse a Penny,

a Coach three Pence, a Cart four Pence, at some six Pence to eight Pence, a Waggon six Pence, in some a Shilling, and the like ; Cattle pay by the Score, or by the Head, in some Places more, in some less." Several of these turnpikes had been set up of late years and " great Progress had been made in mending the most difficult Ways."

On these roads toll was, of course, being taken by authority of Act of Parliament ; but there was one road, at least, on which tolls were being enforced without Parliamentary sanction ; for Defoe goes on to say :—

" There is another Road, which is a Branch of the Northern Road, and is properly called the Coach Road . . . and this indeed is a most frightful Way, if we take it from Hatfield, or rather the Park Corners of Hatfield House, and from thence to Stevenage, to Baldock, to Biggleswade and Bugden. Here is that famous Lane call'd Baldock Lane, famous for being so impassable that the Coaches and Travellers were oblig'd to break out of the Way even by Force, which the People of the Country not able to prevent, at length placed Gates and laid their lands open, setting men at the Gates to take a voluntary Toll, which Travellers always chose to pay, rather than plunge into Sloughs and Holes, which no Horse could wade through.

" This terrible Road is now under Cure by the same Methods, and probably may in Time be brought to be firm and solid."

In regard to the turnpike system in general he says :—

" The Benefit of these Turnpikes appears now to be so great, and the People in all Places begin to be so sensible of it, that it is incredible what Effect it has already had upon Trade in the Counties where the Roads are completely finished ; even the Carriage of Goods is abated, in some Places, 6d. per hundred Weight, in others 12d. per hundred, which is abundantly more Advantageous to Commerce than the Charge paid amounts to. . . .

" Besides the benefits accruing from this laudable Method we may add, The Conveniency to those who bring fat Cattle, especially Sheep, to London in the Winter from the remoter counties of Leicester and Lincoln, where they are bred : For before, the Country Graziers were obliged to sell their Stocks off in September and October when the Roads began to be bad, and when they generally sell cheap ; and the Butchers and Farmers near London used to engross them, and keep them till December and January, and then sell them, though not an Ounce fatter than before, for an advanced price to the Citizens of London ; whereas now the Roads are in a Way to be made everywhere passable the City will be serv'd with Mutton almost as cheap in the Winter as in the summer, and the profit of the advance will be to the Country Graziers, who are the original Breeders and take all the Pains.

" This is evidenc'd to a Demonstration in the Counties where the Roads are already repair'd, from whence they bring their fat Cattle, and particularly their Mutton, in Droves, from Sixty, Seventy or Eighty Miles without fatiguing, harrassing or sinking the Flesh of the Creatures, even in the Depth of the Winter."

Whether or not the fat cattle and the sheep were really able to do their long walk to London without fatigue and loss of flesh, it is certain that the naturally bad condition of the roads leading to London was made worse by the " infinite droves of black cattle, hogs and sheep " which passed along them from Essex, Lincolnshire and elsewhere. When the roads were being continually trodden by the feet of large heavy bullocks, " of which," says Defoe, " the numbers that come this way "—that is, out of Lincolnshire and the fens— " are scarce to be reckon'd up," the work done by the turnpike commissioners in the summer was often completely spoiled in the winter. Among, therefore, the many advantages of the rail transport of to-day we may reckon the fact that the roads and highways are no longer worn to the same extent as before by cattle and sheep on their way to the London markets.

Defoe alludes, also, to the influence of improved communications on the development of the fish industry, with the subsidiary advantage of improving the food supplies of the people, saying, in this connection—

" I might give Examples where the Herrings which are not the best Fish to keep, used, even before these Reparations were set on foot, to be carried to those Towns, and up to Warwick, Birmingham, Tamworth and Stafford, and though they frequently stunk before they got thither, yet the people were so eager for them, that they bought them up at a dear Rate; whereas when the Roads are every where good they will come in less Time, by at least two Days in Six of what they used to do, and an hundred times the quantity will be consumed."

Until, again, the advent of better roads, food supplies and provender—peas, beans, oats, hay, straw, etc.—for London were brought in on the backs of horses. In proportion as the roads improved and were made available for carts and waggons the area of supply widened, and the counties immediately adjoining London even petitioned Parliament against the extension of turnpikes into the remoter counties. These other counties, they alleged, would, from the cheapness of their labour, be able to sell their grass and corn cheaper in the London market than the nearer counties, and would reduce the rents and ruin the cultivation in the latter. Here, of course, the producer wanted protection against competition, and wished to retain the benefit of his geographical advantage. The broader view as to the effect of improved communications on national progress in general was expressed by Adam Smith. In Book I., chapter xi., Part I., of his " Wealth of Nations," he says :—

" Good roads, canals, and navigable rivers, by diminishing the expense of carriage, put the remote parts of the country more nearly upon a level with those in the neighbourhood of the town. They are upon that account the greatest of all improvements. They encourage the cultivation of the remote, which must always be the most extensive circle of the country. They are advantageous to the town, by breaking down the monopoly of the country in its neighbourhood. They are advantageous even to that part of the country. Though they introduce some rival commodities into the old market, they open many new markets to its produce. Monopoly, besides, is a great enemy to good management, which can never be universally established but in consequence of that free and universal competition which forces everybody to have resource to it for the sake of self-defence."

The conditions under which the traders of the country in general conducted their business was, naturally, influenced, if not altogether controlled, by the conditions of locomotion.

Hutton tells us in his " History of Birmingham " that the practice of the Birmingham manufacturer for, perhaps, a hundred generations was to keep within the warmth of his own forge. The foreign customer, therefore, applied to him for the execution of orders, and regularly made his appearance twice a year.

Concerning the Manchester trade, Dr Aikin, in his " Description of the Country from Thirty to Forty Miles round Manchester " (1795), says :—

" For the first thirty years of the present century, the old established houses confined their trade to the wholesale dealers in London, Bristol, Norwich, Newcastle, and those who frequented Chester fair. . . . When the Manchester trade began to extend the chapmen used to keep gangs of pack-horses, and accompany them to the principal towns with goods in packs, which they opened and sold to shop-keepers, lodging what was unsold in small stores at the inns. The pack-horses brought back sheep's wool, which was bought on the journey, and sold to the makers of worsted yarn at Manchester, or to the clothiers of Rochdale, Saddleworth and the West Riding of Yorkshire. On the improvement of the turnpike roads waggons were set up, and the pack-horses discontinued ; and the chapmen only rode out for orders, carrying with them patterns in their bags. It was during the forty years from 1730 to 1770 that trade was greatly pushed by the practice of sending these riders all over the kingdom, to those towns which before had been supplied from the whole-sale places in the capital places before mentioned."

Thus one effect of the improvement in communications was to allow of the Manchester manufacturers establishing direct relations with retailers in the smaller towns who had hitherto been supplied by the wholesale dealers in the large towns, one set of profits being saved. Dr Aikin adds :—

" Within the last twenty or thirty years the vast increase of foreign trade has caused many of the Manchester manu-facturers to travel abroad, and agents or partners to be fixed for a considerable time on the Continent, as well as foreigners to reside at Manchester. And the town has now in every respect assumed the style and manners of one of the com-mercial capitals of Europe."

In an article headed " Change in Commerce," published in No. XI. of " The Original," (1836), Thomas Walker gives (" by tradition," as he says) some particulars as to the methods of business followed by a leading Manchester mer-chant who was born there early in the eighteenth century and realised a sufficient fortune to be able to have a carriage of his own when not half a dozen were kept in the town by persons connected with business.

" He sent the manufactures of the place into Nottinghamshire, Lincolnshire, Cambridgeshire, and the intervening counties, and principally took in exchange feathers from Lincolnshire and malt from Cambridgeshire and Nottinghamshire. All his commodities were conveyed on pack-horses, and he was from home the greater part of every year, performing his journeys entirely on horseback. His balances were received in guineas, and were carried with him in his saddle-bags. He was exposed to the vicissitudes of the weather, to great labour and fatigue, and to constant danger. . . . Business carried on in this manner required a combination of personal attention, courage, and physical strength not to be hoped for in a deputy. . . . The improvements in the way of carrying on commerce, and its increase, may be attributed in a great degree to the increased facility of communication, and the difference between the times I have alluded to and the present is nearly as great as between a pack-horse and a steam-carriage."

Walker also mentions that in the early days of the trader here referred to Manchester was provided with wine by a wine merchant who lived at Preston and carried his supplies to Manchester on horseback. The quantity then consumed, however, was but small, as " men in business confined themselves generally to punch and ale, using wine only as a medicine or on very extraordinary occasions."

A no less interesting phase of the improvements being brought about, and one to which I shall revert in the chapter on " The Canal Era," was found in the influence of better communications on the social conditions of the people.

That these conditions had been greatly prejudiced by the bad roads is beyond all question. Villages which could be reached only with difficulty in summer, and were isolated from the rest of the world for four or five months in the autumn, winter and early spring, were steeped in ignorance and superstition. True it is that in such communities as these the games, sports, customs and traditions which represented the poetry of old English life survived the longest, and have not even yet disappeared before the march of Modern Progress. But no less true is it that such communities were the longest to foster that once popular belief in witchcraft which meant, not merely the looking askance at any decrepit old creature who was believed to have turned the milk sour in the pails, or to have stopped the cows and ewes from breeding, but the putting to death of many thousands of supposed " witches " in England and Scotland in the sixteenth and seventeenth centuries. The total number of victims in the first eighty years of the seventeenth century alone is estimated by Dr Charles Mackay, in " Memoirs of Extraordinary Popular Delusions,"ᵃ at forty thousand ! This particular mania was certainly shared by Kings, Parliaments and ecclesiastics no less than by ignorant villagers ; but it decreased in proportion as general intelligence increased, and the increase in general intelligence was materially influenced by those improvements in locomotion and communication which led to wider knowledge and a greater intermingling of the classes.

The same isolation fostered the belief in ghosts, goblins, wraiths, kelpies and other inhabitants of the world of spirits, whose visitations or doings probably formed a leading topic of conversation as the isolated family sat round the fire in the long winter months, wives and daughters busy, no doubt, with their distaffs, their spinning-wheel or their needlework, but none the less able to tell or to listen to the favourite stories.

The whole conditions of existence were of the most circumscribed kind. Many a village got no news at all of what was happening in the world except such as the pedlar might bring, or, alternatively, might circulate through his London-printed " broadsides," telling of some great victory, giving the last dying speech of a noted highwayman, or recording the death of one ruler and the succession of another, of which events the villagers might not hear for two or even three months after they had occurred. " Whole generations," in the words of Samuel Smiles (" Early Roads and Modes of Travelling "), " lived a monotonous, ignorant, prejudiced and humdrum life. They had no enterprise, no energy, little industry, and were content to die where they were born."

In the Elizabethan era, and even later, inhabitants of the northern counties were regarded by dwellers in the south as people among whom it would be dangerous for them to go.

English navigators were entering on voyages of discovery and conquest in distant seas, where they would fearlessly encounter the enemies of England or the Indians of the New World, at a time when their fellow-countrymen at home would have shrunk from the perils of a journey across the wilds of Northumberland or of an encounter with the supposed savages of Lancashire.

Even when it was a matter of visiting friends, journeys to distant parts of the country were but rarely undertaken. In the " Gentleman's Magazine " for December, 1752, it was remarked that English people were readily going to France, where they spent in 1751 nearly £100,000 ; but though a rich citizen in London who had relatives or friends in the west of England might hear of their welfare half a dozen times in his life, by post, " he thinks no more of visiting them than of traversing the deserts of Nubia."

On the other hand, one result of this limitation in the facilities for home travel was to give to many a county town a far greater degree of social distinction that it can claim to-day.

Just as in mediæval times England had consisted of so many separate self-governing and self-dependent communities, each with the house of the lord of the manor as the " hub " of its own little universe, so—in the days when communications had certainly, though still only relatively, improved—did the county town become the recognised centre of social life and movement for each and every county where there was any pretence to social life at all. The country gentry, with their wives and daughters, came to regard a visit to the county town, and indulgence there in a round of balls, feasts, visits and functions, in the same light as a season in London is regarded at the present date.

London in the seventeenth century, if not even down to the middle of the eighteenth, was, for all practical purposes, as far away from the western counties of England as London to-day is from Vienna or St. Petersburg. Visits to the Metropolis were then, indeed, of extremely rare occurrence. In Macaulay's sketch of " The State of England in 1685," forming chapter iii. of his " History of England," there is a diverting account of what must have happened to the lord of a Lincolnshire or Shropshire manor when he appeared in Fleet Street, to be " as easily distinguished from the resident population as a Turk or a Lascar," and to be subjected to numerous " vexations and humiliations " until, enraged and mortified, he returned to his mansion where " he was once more a great man, and saw nothing above himself except when at the assizes he took his seat on the bench near the judge, or when at the muster of the militia he saluted the Lord Lieutenant."

Adding to such " vexations and humiliations " the cost, the inconveniences and the perils of a journey to London—perils, too, that arose from highwaymen as well as from the roads themselves—the country gentleman was generally content to seek his social distractions nearer home than London. To quote again from Macaulay :—

" The county town was his metropolis. He sometimes made it his residence during part of the year. At all events he was often attracted thither by business and pleasure, by assizes, quarter sessions, elections, musters of militia, festivals and races. There were the halls in which the judges, robed in scarlet and escorted by javelins and trumpets, opened the King's commission twice a year. There were the markets at which the corn, the cattle, the wool and the hops of the surrounding country were exposed for sale. There were the great fairs to which merchants came from London, and where the rural dealer laid in his annual stores of sugar, stationery, cutlery and muslin. There were the shops at which the best families of the neighbourhood bought grocery and millinery."

Defoe, in his " Tour," affords us some interesting glimpses of the social life of various country towns in the first quarter of the eighteenth century. Dorchester he describes as " indeed a pleasant town to live in. . . . There is," he says, " good company and a good deal of it," and he thinks " a man that coveted a retreat in this world might as agreeably spend his time, and as well, in Dorchester " as in any town he knew in England. Exeter was " full of gentry and good company." He has much to say in praise of social life in Dorsetshire. In Plymouth " a gentleman might find very agreeable society." Salisbury had " a good deal of good manners and good company." The " neighbourhood " of " Persons of Figure and Quality " caused Maidstone to be " a very agreeable place to live in," and one where a " Man of Letters and Manners " would always " find suitable Society both to Divert and Improve himself," the town being, in fact, one of " very great

Business and Trade, and yet full of Gentry, of Mirth, and of Good Company." King's Lynn, the head-quarters of so important a shipping business in those days, he found " abounding in very good company," while of York he writes : " There is abundance of good Company here, and abundance of good Families live here, for the sake of the good Company and cheap living ; a Man converses here with all the World as effectually as at London ; the Keeping up of Assemblies among the younger Gentry was first set up here, a thing other Writers recommend mightily as the Character of a good Country and of a Pleasant Place."

The general effect, from a social standpoint, of the combination of better roads and better coaches is well told in an essay " On the Country Manners of the Present Age," published in the " Annual Register " for 1761. The writer has much to say that is of interest from the point of view of the present work, but the following extracts must suffice :—

" It is scarce half a century since the inhabitants of distant counties were regarded as a species almost as different from those of the Metropolis as the natives of the Cape of Good Hope. . . . Formerly a journey into the country was considered almost as great an undertaking as a voyage to the Indies. The old family coach was sure to be stowed with all sorts of luggage and provisions ; and perhaps in the course of the journey a whole village together with their teams, were called in to dig the heavy vehicle out of the clay, and to drag it to the next place of wretched accommodation which the road afforded. Thus they travelled like the caravan over the deserts of Arabia, with every disagreeable circumstance of tediousness and inconvenience. But now the amendments of the roads with the many other improvements of travelling have in a manner opened a new communication between the several parts of our island. . . . Stage-coaches, machines, flys and post chaises are ready to transport passengers to and fro, between the metropolis and the most distant parts of the Kingdom. The lover now can almost literally annihilate time and space, and be with his mistress before she dreams of his arrival. In short the manners, fashions, amusements, vices and follies /of the metropolis now make their way to the remotest corners of the land as readily and speedily, along the turnpike road, as, of old, Milton's Sin and Death, by means of their marvellous bridges over the Chaos from the infernal regions to our world.

" The effects of this easy communication have almost daily grown more and more visible. The several great cities, and we might add, many poor country towns, seem to be universally inspired with the ambition of becoming the little Londons of the part of the country in which they are situated."

But if the easy communication rendered possible by turnpike roads and flying coaches conferred on the country towns a hope of becoming so many little Londons, the day was to come when a still easier communication by means of railway lines and express trains was to take provincial residents just as readily to the great and real London, and so deprive not a few provincial centres of much of that social life and distinction which the improved transport facilities had brought them.

In London itself, as may also be learned from Defoe, the betterment of the roads around the metropolis led to the citizens flocking out in greater numbers than ever to take lodgings and country houses in " towns near London," which many people having business in the City had not been able to do before because of the trouble involved in riding to and fro on the bad roads. We are told, further, of the consequent increase in the rent of houses, and of the greater number of dwellings being built, in places the roads to which had thus been improved, as compared with other suburban districts to which the turnpike system had not yet been extended.

We have here the beginnings of that creation of a Greater London which has since undergone such enormous developments, and has led to the almost complete disappearance of the custom, once in vogue in the City of London, of a merchant or tradesman living on the same premises as those in which he carried on his business.

Of the various circumstances that led to the eventual decline and fall of the turnpike system, which, with all its faults and short-comings, had at least helped to bring about the improvements in trade, transport and social conditions here described, I shall speak in Chapter xxiii.

CHAPTER XII

SCIENTIFIC ROAD-MAKING

ONE question which naturally arises in connection with the turnpike roads is, " Why was it, when there was so widespread an organisation of turnpike trusts, and when so much money was being spent on the repair of the roads, that the roads themselves were still so defective, and only relatively better than they had been before ? "—this being the real position, notwithstanding the praises bestowed on the turnpike system by those who were gratified with the stimulus given to trade, travel and commerce by the improvements actually made.

The answer is that although a vast amount of road-making or road-repairing was going on, at the very considerable expense of the road users, and to the advantage of a small army of attorneys, officials and labourers, it was not road-making of a scientific kind, but merely amateur work, done at excessive cost, either with unintelligent zeal or in slovenly style, and yielding results which mostly failed to give the country the type of road it required for the ever-increasing traffic to which expanding trade, greater travel, and heavier and more numerous waggons and coaches were leading.

Before the adoption of scientific road-making, the usual way of forming a new road was, first to lay along it a collection of large stones, and then to heap up thereon small stones and road dirt in such a way that the road assumed the shape of the upper half of an orange, the convexity often being so pronounced that vehicles kept along the summit of the eminence because it was dangerous for them, especially in rainy weather, to go along the slope on either side.

This form of road was adopted in order to ensure good drainage for rain-water ; and in this connection the writer on " Roads " in Postlethwayt's " Dictionary " (1745) says :—

" The chief and almost the only cause of the deepness and

98

foulness of the roads is occasioned by the standing water which, for want of due care to draw it off by scouring and opening ditches and drains and other water courses, and clearing of passages, soaks into the earth, and softens it to such a degree that it cannot bear the weight of horses and carriages."

But the result of making roads in the shape of a semi-circle was that the central ridge was speedily crushed down, and ruts were formed along the line of traffic passing over the loose materials used. These ruts, again, defeated the purpose of the original high convexity by becoming troughs for the retention of rain and mud, the latter being rendered worse with each fresh churning up it received from the wheels of waggon or stage-coach.

The road-maker thus required to be speedily followed by the road-repairer ; and *his* method of procedure has been already indicated in Arthur Young's description of the road to Wigan, where he says, " The only mending it receives is the tumbling in some loose stones, which serve no other purpose but jolting a carriage in the most intolerable manner."

The mending of hundreds of miles even of turnpike roads had never gone any further than this. There was no cohesion in collections of loose stones, mainly in their natural and more or less rounded form, and the expectation that they would be crushed and consolidated into a solid mass by extra-broad waggon wheels, in accordance with Acts of Parliament in that case made and provided, remained unfulfilled. The stones were simply displaced and thrown aside by the traffic, the inevitable ruts reappearing in due course ; while, as the rain-water passed readily through them, the roads became elongated reservoirs of water in rainy weather, and were most effectively broken up by frost in winter.

It was from conditions such as these that Thomas Telford and John Loudon McAdam came to rescue the country.

There had been one road-reformer before them, in John Metcalf, a native of Knaresboro', where he was born in 1717. Though totally blind from the age of six, he developed abundant resources, and became successively fiddler, soldier, chapman, fish-dealer, horse-dealer and waggoner. Taking at last to road-making, he constructed about 180 miles of road in Yorkshire, Lancashire, Cheshire and Derby, rendering an important service to the two first-mentioned counties, more especially by improving their means of communication at a time when they were greatly in need of better roads on account of their then rapidly increasing trade and industry. But though Metcalf did good work in these directions, and achieved some noteworthy successes in carrying solid roads across difficult bogs, he introduced no really new system, and the chief progress made did not come until after his death, in 1810.

Son of a shepherd at Eskdale, Dumfriesshire, where he was born in 1757, Telford started life as a stonemason's apprentice, but became an engineer, and undertook many important works, including canals, bridges, harbours and docks. Here, however, we are concerned with him only as a builder of roads —a department in which he showed great skill and activity.

On the appointment, in 1803, of a body of Commissioners who were to improve the system of communications in Scotland (one half of the expense being defrayed by Parliamentary grants, and one half by local contributions), Telford was selected to carry out the work, and he constructed 920 miles of road and 1,117 bridges in the Highlands, and 150 miles of road between Glasgow, Cumbernauld (Dumbarton) and Carlisle. Then, in 1815, money having been voted by Parliament for the improvement of the Holyhead road, with a view to the betterment of communications with Ireland, Telford was entrusted with the task, which involved the making or improvement of, altogether, 123 miles of road.

Telford's own opinion of the roads of England and Scotland was thus expressed in the evidence he gave before the Select Committee of the House of Commons in 1819 :—

" They are in general very defective both as to their direction and inclination ; they are frequently carried over hills, which might be avoided by passing along the adjacent valleys . . . there has been no attention paid to constructing good and solid foundations ; the materials, whether consisting of gravel or stones, have seldom been sufficiently selected and arranged ; and they lie so promiscuously upon the roads as to render it inconvenient to travel upon them. . . . The shape of the roads, or cross section of the surface, is frequently hollow in the middle ; the sides incumbered with great banks of road dirt, which have accumulated in some places to the height of six, seven, or eight feet; these prevent the water from falling into the side drains; they also throw a considerable shade upon the road, and are gross and unpardonable nuisances. The materials, instead of being cleaned of the mud and soil with which they are mixed in their native state, are laid promiscuously upon the road."

In planning new roads Telford cut right through the hills, wherever possible, in order to avoid unduly steep gradients. In making the roads he first arranged a solid foundation of pieces of durable stone, from 4 in. to 7 in. in size, these being carefully put into position by hand, with the broadest side downward, and packed with small stones in between. On the rough pavement thus formed he laid an upper course of small broken stones, with a binding of one inch of gravel. Between the two courses a drain was set across the road every hundred yards, Telford attaching great importance to the carrying off of all water that might percolate through the upper course on to the lower. He gave a uniform and only moderately convex shape to the surface of the road, abandoning, in this respect, the ideas of his more amateur predecessors. But his system was one that called for much labour and care, as well as for an abundant supply of the needful materials, and the cost of carrying it out was proportionately high, if not, in some situations, prohibitive.

McAdam preferred to be considered a road-repairer rather than a road-builder, and his methods differed materially from those of Telford. He became, also, much more of a propagandist in the work of road-improvement, enforcing his theories with such success that he brought a new word into the English language, roads made or mended according to the main principles he laid down having been known ever since his day as " macadamised."

Born in Ayrshire in 1756—one year before Telford—McAdam went to America at the age of 14 to start life in the counting-house of his uncle in New York. Subsequently he became a successful merchant, and returned in 1783 to Scotland, where he bought the estate of Sauchrie, and then, in 1785, began to devote his attention to road-making, which was to occupy his thoughts and absorb his energies for the rest of his days. Roads he came to regard as, in his own words, " perhaps the most important branch of our domestic economy." Many new roads were then being constructed in Scotland, and he himself became a commissioner of roads in that country. He also began a systematic course of travel over the roads of England and Scotland, covering, by 1814, no fewer than 30,000 miles.

In 1810 McAdam commenced a series of experiments in the construction of roads, and he published the following year some " Observations on the Highways of the Kingdom," recording the opinions he had formed as the result of his twenty-seven years' inquiries.

By this time the question had, indeed, become acute. The prosperity of the country had undergone much expansion, but the improvement of the roads, notwithstanding the extension of the turnpike system, had in no way kept pace with the general progress and the growing needs of the nation. Parliamentary Committees were still devoting close attention to that good old stock subject, the width of cart-wheels. In 1806 there was a Select Committee appointed " to take into consideration the Acts now in force regarding the use of Broad Wheels, and to examine what shape is best calculated for ease of draught and the Preservation of the roads." This Committee presented two reports, and like Committees were appointed in the Sessions of 1808 and 1809, each of these Committees making three reports. What Parliament itself was doing at this period in the way of cart-wheel legislation has already been told.

So there was abundant scope for the activities of someone who could offer new ideas, and when, in 1811, a Select Committee was appointed " to take into consideration the Acts in force regarding the Highways and Turnpike Roads in England and Wales, and the expediency of additional regulations as to the better repair and preservation thereof," [1] McAdam came forward with his proposals, as contained in the aforesaid " Observations " presented by him to the Committee in question.

---

[1] Similar Committees were, also, appointed in 1819, 1820, and 1821. In the report it eventually issued, the Committee of 1811 said : " By the improvement of our roads, every branch of our agricultural, commercial and manufacturing industry would be materially benefitted. Every article brought to market would be diminished in price ; the number of horses would be so much reduced, that by these and other retrenchments, the expense of five millions would be annually saved to the public."

McAdam began by saying that " In all three reports of Committees of the House of Commons on the subject of roads, they seem to have principally in view the construction of wheeled carriages, the weights they were to draw, and the breadth and form of their wheels ; the nature of the roads on which these carriages were to travel had not been so well attended to." Proceeding to give the results of his own investigations, he expressed the view that the bad condition of the roads of the kingdom was owing to the injudicious application of the materials with which they were repaired, and to the defective form of the roads ; and he assured the Committee that the introduction of a better system of making the *surface* of the roads, and the application of scientific principles which had hitherto never been thought of, would remedy the evil.

The basis of his system, as defined on this and subsequent occasions, was the covering of the surface of roads with an impermeable crust, cover or coating, so that the water would not penetrate to the soil beneath, which soil, whatever its nature, and provided it was kept dry, would, he argued, then bear any weight likely to be put upon it.

His method of securing the said impermeable crust was by the use of an 8 in. or 10 in. covering of *broken* stones, these being not more than about 1½ inches each in size, or more than about six ounces each in weight. Such broken stones, if properly prepared and properly laid on a road, would, he showed, consolidate by reason of their angles, and, under the pressure of the traffic, be transformed into a " firm, compact, impenetrable body," which " could not be affected by vicissitudes of weather or displaced by the action of wheels." The broken stones, with their angular edges, would, in effect, dovetail together into a solid crust under a pressure which, applied to pebbles or flints, would merely cause them to roll aside, in the same way as shingle on the seashore when passed over by a cart or a bathing van.

The difference between his broken stones and the more or less rounded stones with which the roads were then being repaired was, McAdam declared, the difference between the stones that were thrown down in a stream to form a ford and the shaped stones used to construct the bridge that went over the stream ; while inasmuch as the road-arch, or crust, he formed would rest on the ground, and be impermeable to rain-water, there would be no need to have underneath it either a stone foundation or a system of drainage ; though he held it as essential that the subsoil should be perfectly dry when the " metal," or covering of broken stone, was laid in position. Keeping the water out of the road by this means, he would prevent the road itself from being broken up by the action of frost, and he would have a more elastic surface than if there were a solid stone foundation under the metal. The thickness of his consolidated cover of broken stones would, he further argued, be immaterial to its weight-carrying capacity.

In 1816 McAdam became surveyor of roads in the Bristol district, and the object lessons in road-mending which he provided there were so convincing that his system began to be generally approved in 1818. In 1827 he was appointed Surveyor-General of Roads, and in the same year he issued a ninth edition of his " Remarks on the Present System of Road-Making."

In this publication he states, among other things, that very considerable sums were being raised annually in the kingdom, principally from tolls, on account of turnpike roads, and these funds were expended, nominally under the protection of Commissioners, but practically under the surveyors. Every Session there were numerous applications to Parliament by turnpike trusts for powers to increase their tolls in order to pay off their debts and to keep the roads in repair. In the Session of 1815 there were 34 such petitions ; in 1816 there were 32, and " all passed as a matter of course." The condition of the turnpike roads was, nevertheless, most defective, and that of the parish roads was " more deplorable than that of the turnpike roads." Legislative enactments for the maintenance and repair of the parish roads were so inadequate that these roads " might be considered as being placed almost out of the protection of the law." In the result " The defective state of the roads, independent of the unnecessary expense, is oppressive on agriculture, commerce and manufactures by the increase of the price of transport, by waste of the labour of cattle, and wear of carriages, as well as by causing much delay of time."

As for Scotland, he declared that " The roads in Scotland are worse than those in England, although materials are more abundant, of better quality, and labour at least as cheap, and the toll duties are nearly double ; this is because road-making, that is the surface, is even worse understood in Scotland than in England." He mentions that the Postmaster-General had been obliged to give up the mail-coach from Glasgow to Ayr on account partly of the bad roads and partly of the expense, there being ten turnpike gates in 34 miles of road.

The roads were, in fact, McAdam continued, " universally in want of repair." Ample funds were already provided ; but the surveyors employed by the turnpike trusts were " mostly persons ignorant of the nature of the duties they are called on to discharge," [1] and the money brought in by a continual and apparently unlimited increase of the tolls was " misapplied in almost every part of the Kingdom." In some new roads made in Scotland the thickness of the materials used exceeded three feet ; [2] but, said McAdam, " the road is as open as a sieve to receive water " ; and what this meant he was able to show by pointing to the results of weather conditions on bad roads in the month of January, 1820. A severe frost was succeeded by a sudden thaw, accompanied by the melting of much snow, and the roads of the kingdom broke up in an alarming manner, causing great loss, much delay of the mails, and endless inconvenience. The cause of the trouble was explained by McAdam thus :—

" Previous to the severe frost the roads were filled with water which had penetrated through the ill-prepared and unskilfully-laid material ; this caused immediate expansion of the whole mass during the frost, and, upon a sudden thaw, the roads became quite loose, and the wheels of the carriages penetrated to the original soil, which was also saturated with water, from the open state of the road. By this means many roads became altogether impassable."

On the 1000 miles of road to which his own system had

[1] It was shown in evidence before the Select Committee of 1819 that the "surveyors" in a certain district included a miller, an undertaker, a carpenter, a coal merchant, a publican, a baker, "an infirm old man," and "a bedridden old man who had not been out of his house for several months." Nineteen times out of twenty, it was declared, the appointment was "a perfect job."

[2] McAdam had found the roads at Bristol loaded with an accumulation two or three feet deep of stones, which had been thrown down during a series of years with the idea of "repairing" the roads. Such roads became his quarries for stones to be broken by hand.

been applied there had, he further said, been no breaking up at all by reason of frost.

The figure here given suggests the extensive adoption of McAdam's system which was then proceeding. It was not only that old roads were being repaired according to his plan, but there was much construction of " macadamised " roads, the deficiencies of the existing roads having discouraged and checked the provision of new ones. Between 1818 and 1829, as told by Porter, in his " Progress of the Nation," the length of turnpike roads in England and Wales was increased by more than 1000 miles. In proportion, also, as the turnpike roads increased alike in number and in quality, through the wider adoption of McAdam's system, there was a corresponding impetus given to coaching in respect both to number of vehicles and to increase of speed, leading up to those " palmy days " of coaching which were only to close with the spread of the railway.

It is true that McAdam's plans were not adhered to exactly as he first laid them down. Greater experience led later authorities to attach more importance to a foundation than McAdam had been disposed to do; though they did not necessarily have foundations laid by hand, after the manner of Telford's buried pavements. Later, the introduction, also, of the steam-roller was to revolutionise the art of making macadamised roads.

Nor can it be disputed that McAdam and Telford had both, to a certain extent, been anticipated. In an article on roads published in the " Quarterly Review," in 1820, the observation is made in respect to them that " Many of the practices of each of these gentlemen had been previously adopted in a variety of instances ; but it required zeal and perseverance like theirs to recommend the entire system to the attention of the public."

Other persons might have recommended the use of broken stones, and these are said to have been already employed in Switzerland before McAdam came on the scene ; but it was his lucid explanation of the scientific bearing of angular as opposed to round stones ; his untiring zeal in travelling thousands of miles over English and Scottish roads in order to see and study everything for himself ; and his advocacy of scientific road-making with such indefatigable energy, though to his own impoverishment (until Parliament voted him re-compense), that led to the conspicuous and world-wide success his system eventually attained.

Writing in 1826, " Nimrod " said : " Roads may be called the veins and arteries of a country, through which channels every improvement circulates. I really consider Mr McAdam as being, next to Dr Jenner, the greatest contributor to the welfare of mankind that this country has ever produced."

This may seem, to-day, to be exaggerated praise ; but if the reader looks at the matter from the point of view from which " Nimrod " himself must have regarded it, and tries to realise how greatly the deplorable state of the roads—before McAdam began to repair them—was hampering social life, travel, trade, commerce and national industries, he will probably conclude that such praise, at such a period, and in such circumstances, was far from being undeserved.

The turnpike system lasted well into the railway period, and the story of its gradual decline and the causes that led thereto has still to be told. Before, however, dealing further with these aspects of the general question I propose to revert to the subject of rivers and river navigation ; to show, next, how canals and canal transport were developed ; and then to give an account of the rise of that railway system which was so materially to affect alike rivers, canals and turnpike roads as well.

CHAPTER XIII

IN the earliest days of our history, and for many generations later, navigable rivers exercised a most important, if not a paramount, influence on the settlement of tribes, the location of towns, the development of trade and the social life of the people. They were natural highways, open to all who possessed the means of using them, at a time when men had otherwise still to make roads for themselves ; and in a land covered to so great an extent with forest and fen such natural highways were of exceptional value. They offered a ready means of reaching points in the interior of the country which would otherwise have been more or less inaccessible. They allowed of the transport, in craft however primitive, of commodities too heavy or too bulky for conveyance by pack-horse along the narrow paths trodden out on the hill-sides, winding through woods, or picked out across bog, plain, or morass.

Rivers further helped to develop that civilisation which is directly encouraged by facility of communication between groups of people who would otherwise assuredly remain backward in social progress. It will even be found that down to the turnpike, if not, indeed, to the railway, era in this country, communities dwelling on the banks of navigable rivers, and thus possessing a ready means of communication at all times with others having a like advantage, attained to a higher degree of culture, refinement and social standing than people in localities where, remote from any river or passable highway, they were shut off by bad roads from all intercourse with their fellow-men for, at least, the whole of the winter months.

In C. H. Pearson's " Historical Maps of England During the first Thirteen Centuries " there is abundant evidence of the way in which towns and trading centres in Britain grew up

along the course of navigable rivers, while the country. at
any distance therefrom remained unoccupied, however important the places that may be found there to-day. On the
map of Saxon England, for instance, mention is made of
Gleaweceaster (Gloucester ; spelling from " Saxon Chronicle "), Teodekesberie (Tewkesbury ; " Domesday "), Brycg-
north (Bridgnorth ; " Saxon Chronicle "), and Scrobbesbyrig
(Shrewsbury ; " Saxon Chronicle "), but no one can doubt
that these places attained to their early importance mainly
because of their situation on the river Severn. Other typical
inland cities or towns include London and Oxford on the
Thames ; Ware on the Lea ; Rochester on the Medway ; Peterborough on the Nen ; Lincoln on the Witham ; York on the
Ouse ; Doncaster on the Don ; Cambridge on the Cam ; Norwich
on the Yare ; Colchester on the Colne ; Ludlow on the Terne ;
Exeter on the Exe ; Winchester on the Ouse (Sussex) ; Hereford on the Wye ; Chester on the Dee ; Caerleon (Isca) on
the Usk ; and so on with many other places, the location of
which alongside a river must doubtless have been due, in part,
it may be, to the convenience of water supply, and in part,
also, to the greater fertility of the river valley, but more
especially to the facility offered by the water highway for
transport when other highways were either lacking or far less
convenient.

Adam Smith, in his " Wealth of Nations " (Book I.,
chapter xi., pages 20–1), compares the cost of sending goods
by road from London to Edinburgh with that of forwarding
them by sea, and adds :—

" Since such are the advantages of water carriage it is
natural that the first improvements of art and industry should
be made where that conveniency opens the whole world for a
market to the produce of every sort of labour, and that they
should always be much later in extending themselves into the
inland parts of the country. The inland parts of the country
can for a long time have no other market for the greater part
of their goods but the country which lies round about them,
and separates them from the sea coast and the great navigable
rivers. The extent of their market, therefore, must for a long
time be in proportion to the riches and populousness of that
country, and consequently their improvement must always
be posterior to the improvement of that country. In our

North American colonies the plantations have constantly
followed either the sea coast or the banks of the navigable
rivers, and have scarce anywhere extended themselves to any
considerable distance from both."

On the Continent of Europe the location of the chief inland
centres of trade, commerce, and industry was no less decided
by the convenience of transport afforded by the great navigable
rivers, as shown (to give two examples only) by Augsburg on
the Danube and Cologne on the Rhine.

In Britain there were found to be advantages in having a
port, not at the mouth of a river, but as far inland as the
vessels employed could go. One of these advantages lay in the
fact that, the further inland the river-port, the greater was the
protection against the Danish or Norwegian pirates who, at
one time, infested the seas around our shores ; but the main
reasons for the preference are somewhat quaintly expressed
by " R. S.," in a pamphlet, published in 1675, entitled
" Avona ; or a Transient View of the Benefit of making Rivers
of this Kingdom Available. Occasioned by observing the
Scituation of the City of Salisbury, upon the Avon, and the
Consequence of opening that River to that City." The writer
says :—

" There is more advantage to those places, which, being
seated far within the Land (as this [1] is), do enjoy the benefit
of Commerce by Sea, by some Navigable River, than to those
Port-Towns which are seated in some Creeke or Bay only, and
are (as I may call it) Land-lock'd, having no passage up into
the Land but by Carriages, as we see in Poole and Lynn, in
Dorset, and in a number of other Port-Towns of like Scituation
in other places quite round the Island : For such places,
though the Sea brings in commodities to them, yet they can
neither without great charge convey those commodities higher
up into the Land, nor, without the like charge, receive the Inn-
land commodities to export again : Whereas, Cities seated
upon navigable Rivers far within the Land look like some
Noble Exchange of Nature's own designing ; where the Native
and the Forreigner may immediately meet, and put off to each
other the particular commodities of the growth of their own
Countreys ; the Native (as a Merchant) receiving the Forreign
Goods at first hand, and exchanging his own for them at the

[1] Salisbury.

very place where they are made, or grow ; or, at most, going
no further to it, than to his ordinary Market."

Thus the ideal river-ports were those that were situated,
not only a good distance inland, but in close connection with
a Roman or other road along which commerce could be readily
brought or distributed, the land journey being reduced to
the smallest and most convenient proportions. The advantage
was still greater where the small sea-going vessels could be
carried by a tidal stream right up to the town to which their
cargo was consigned.

• As against these advantages, however, there was the disadvantage that, the further inland the river-port, the greater
was the risk that access to it might become impracticable
either through the formation of shallows in the river-bed or
because the larger build of vessels in later years could not
pass where the smaller and more primitive type of ship of
earlier days had gone without difficulty.

From one or other of these causes many English rivers on
which considerable traffic formerly passed have dwindled in
importance, even if they have not ceased to be navigable at all ;
and many inland places that once flourished as river, or even
as " sea "-ports, would to-day hardly be regarded in that light
at all, as shown, for example, by the fate of Lewes on the
Sussex Ouse, Deeping on the Welland, Cambridge on the Cam,
Ely on the Ouse, West Dean on the Cuckmere, and Bawtry
on the Idle. York and Doncaster, though situated so far
inland, once considered themselves seaports because of their
river connection with the coast, so that, as told by the Rev. W.
Denton, in " England in the Fifteenth Century," they claimed
and exercised the right of sharing in " wrecks at sea " as
though they stood on the seaboard instead of high up the
course of the Ouse or the Don.

The Romans not only supplemented their road transport
by river transport but they sought to improve the latter by the
construction of river embankments. In the case of the Trent
and the Witham they even cut a canal—the Fossdyke—in
order to establish direct communication between them.
Just, however, as road-making became a lost art here on their
departure from Britain, so did an interval of a thousand years
elapse before there was any material attempt to follow their
example in effecting improvements in river navigation. The

initial advantage, therefore, lay with towns located on rivers which were naturally navigable and remained navigable both for a considerable extent and for a considerable period, without need of amendment ; though river navigation, as a whole, did not attain to its highest development until, as will be shown in the chapter that follows, much had been done, especially in connection with streams not naturally navigable, to overcome the various impediments or difficulties to effective transport.

All the same, the part that English navigable rivers, great or small, have played in the social and economic progress of the country has been one of undeniable magnitude and importance, and offers many points of general interest.

These considerations more especially apply to the river Severn, which, in conjunction with such of its tributaries as the Wye and the Warwickshire Avon, was once the great highway for the trade and traffic, not only of the western counties, but of, also, a considerable area in Wales and the midland and northern counties, enabling the districts it more directly served to attain an early development long before others which were then still struggling with the disadvantages of bad roads, however much they may since have outstripped them in the race for industrial advancement.

The Severn itself was naturally navigable from Welshpool, Montgomeryshire, a distance of 155 miles by a very winding stream to where the river empties itself into the Bristol Channel. This was the greatest length of navigation, unaided by artificial means, of any river in the kingdom. The early Britons passed along it in their coracles, and, as these were supplemented by vessels of an improved type, trade was developed, towns and cities—each a storehouse or an entrepôt for a more or less considerable area—began to arise on the banks, while Bristol attained to the dignity of a great national port when Liverpool was still only an insignificant fishing village.

It was in connection with the Severn that the question arose as to the right of the community to regard a navigable river as a public highway, the same as if it were a road dedicated to general use.

The writer of the article on " Rivers " in the " Penny Cyclopædia " (1841) observes that : " In rivers which are navigable, and in which the public have a common right to passage, the King is said to have ' an interest in jurisdiction,' whether the rivers were the King's property or private property. These rivers were called ' fluvii regales,' ' haut streames le roy,' or ' royal streams,' because of their being dedicated to public use, all things of public safety and convenience being under his care and protection." Navigable rivers being thus, the writer continues, the King's highway by water, many of the incidents belonging to a highway on land attached to such rivers, and any nuisances or obstruction upon them, even though occurring on the private land of any person, might be made the subject of indictment.

In regard to the Severn and the right of access thereto, it was found necessary, in 1430–1, following on complaints which had been made to Parliament, to pass an Act (9 Hen. VI., c. 5) for the protection of boatmen in the Severn estuary against " many Welshmen and ill-disposed persons " who " were used to assemble in manner of war and stop trows, boats and floats or drags on their way with Merchandise to Bristol, Gloucester, Worcester, and other places, hewing these craft in pieces, and beating the sailors with intent to force them to hire boats from the said Welshmen, for great sums of money, an evil example and great impoverishment of a King's liege people, if remedy were not hastily provided."

Under this Act the Severn was declared a free river for all the King's subjects to carry on within the stream of the river. The Act made no mention, however, of any right on the part of the boatmen to use the land alongside the river for the purpose of towing their vessels ; and in regard to this point the writer in the " Penny Cyclopædia " says : " Though a river is a public navigable river, there is not, therefore, any right at common law for parties to use the banks of it as a towing path."

By an Act passed in 1504 riparian owners along the Severn were authorised, notwithstanding the earlier enactment of the freedom of the river itself, to take " reasonable recompense and satisfaction " from every person going upon their land to draw a boat. There is no evidence that the landowners availed themselves of this authority ; but in a later Act, passed in 1532, it was stated that although, " time out of mind," people had used, without any imposition or toll, a path

one foot and a half broad on each side of the river for drawing
their boats, " of late certain covetous persons " had " interrupted " those so using the said paths, " taking of them fines
and bottles of wine," and the Act imposed a penalty
of forty shillings on anyone attempting to enforce such
tolls, except as regards the reasonable recompense which the
riparian owners could claim.   This enactment seems to have
been due to the action of local officials in Worcester, Gloucester
and other places on the river in seeking, as told in Nash's
" History and Antiquities of Worcestershire " (1781), to
raise revenue for their cities or towns by taxing traders who
used the Severn for the transport of their commodities.

The importance of the Severn, from the point of view of trade
and commerce, in the middle of the sixteenth century, is
suggested by what William Harrison wrote of it in his
" Description of the Sauerne " (1577) : " As the said stream,
in length of course, bountie of water, and depth of chanell
commeth farre behind the Thames, so for other commodities,
as trade of merchandize, plentie of cariage . . . it is nothing
at all inferiour to or second to the same."

One reason for the early commercial prosperity of the Severn
towns was the important trade in flannels which they carried
on with Wales ; though the industry was, also, considerably
developed in the Severn counties themselves.   Made mostly
in the farm-houses and cottages of Montgomeryshire, Merion-
ethshire and Denbighshire, before the days of factories, the
flannels and webs were taken by the makers to the fortnightly
market at Welshpool.   This was a convenient centre for the
drapers from Shrewsbury, who, journeying thither along the
Severn, would, at one time, buy up the entire stock ; though
later on they had competitors in the traders from Wrexham
and other places.   Although carried on only as a domestic
industry, the making of these Welsh flannels underwent
considerable expansion, Archdeacon Joseph Plymley saying,
in his " General View of the Agriculture of Salop," published
in 1803, " The manufacture in Wales by means of jennies
introduced into farm-houses and other private houses is four
times as great, I am told, as it was twenty years ago."

At Shrewsbury the wares thus brought down the Severn
from Wales were purchased mostly by merchants from London
who either sent them to Continental markets or else consigned

them to South America or the West Indies, for conversion there into clothing for the slaves.

As the demand increased, flannels and webs were more and more produced in and around Shrewsbury itself and other parts of Shropshire. Shrewsbury also developed a large manufacture of coarse linens, linen threads, and other textiles, and eventually attained to such prosperity that Defoe says of it, in his " Tour " :—

" This is indeed a beautiful, large, pleasant, populous and rich Town ; full of Gentry, and yet full of Trade too ; for here, too, is a great Manufacture, as well of Flannel, as also of white Broadcloth, which enriches all the Country round it. . . . This is really a Town of Mirth and Gallantry, something like Bury in Suffolk, or Durham in the North, but much bigger than either of them, or indeed than both together. . . . Here is the greatest Market, the greatest Plenty of good Provisions, and the cheapest that is to be met with in all the Western Part of England ; the Severn supplies them here with excellent Salmon, but 'tis also brought in great Plenty from the River Dee, which is not far off, and which abounds with a very good Kind. . . . There is no doubt but the Cheapness of Provisions, joined with the Pleasantness and Healthiness of the Place, draws a great many Families thither, who love to live within the Compass of their Estates."

Archdeacon Plymley speaks of Shrewsbury as having been, " chiefly from the advantage of the river, for several centuries past, a sort of metropolis for North Wales."

Bewdley, which had obtained its charter from Edward IV., was another Severn town which developed an extensive trade in the exportation not only of Welsh flannels but of timber, wool, leather, combs and sailors' caps. All these were sent down the river to Bristol, whence the Bewdley dealers received, in return, imported groceries and other commodities for distribution throughout Wales and Lancashire. Bridgnorth also attained to considerable importance as a convenient point for the transport to Bristol, via the Severn, of goods brought by road from a Hinterland extending to Lancashire and Cheshire.

There was, again, much traffic to and from towns situate on the Warwickshire Avon, which enters the Severn at Tewkesbury after passing through Stratford, Evesham, Pershore and other towns. Defoe says of this affluent of the Severn : " The Navigation of this River Avon is an exceeding advantage to all this part of the Country and also to the Commerce of the City of Bristol. For by this River they derive a very great trade for sugar, oil, wine, tobacco, iron, lead, and in a word all heavy goods which are carried by water almost as far as Warwick ; and return the corn, and especially the cheese is brought back from Gloucestershire and Warwickshire to Bristol."

The Wye, which enters the estuary of the Severn below Chepstow, after passing through or along the borders of the counties of Montgomery, Radnor, Brecknock, Hereford, Monmouth and Gloucester, was, with its own tributary, the Lug, not made navigable until 1661, when an Act (14 Car. II.) was passed, the preamble of which set forth that —

" Whereas the making Navigable, or otherwise passable for Barges, Boats, Leighters, and other Vessels the Rivers Wye and Lugg and other Rivulets and Brooks falling into the said Rivers in the County of Hereford and other adjacent Counties, and so navigable into the River of Seaverne, may (with God's blessing) be of great advantage, and very convenient and necessary not onely to the said Counties, But also to the Publick, By import and export of Corn and encrease of Commerce and Trade, and improving the yearly value of lands in the parts near adjoyning thereunto, besides the great and extraordinary preservation of the High-ways, and most profitable and necessary to and for the City of Hereford for conveyance thereby of Coles, fuel and other necessaries to the said City, whereof there is now great scarcity and want, and far greater hereafter like to grow, if some Help therefore be not made and provided. Be it therefore," etc.

That the merchants of Bristol derived great advantage from river as well as from sea transport is well shown by Defoe. Not only, he tells us, did they carry on a great trade, but they did so with less dependence on London than the merchants of any other town in Britain. He says :—

" The shopkeepers in Bristol who, in general, are all Whole-sale Men, have so great an Inland trade among all the Western Counties that they maintain Carriers just as the London Tradesmen do, to all the principal Countries and Towns, from Southampton in the south to the Banks of the Trent, north, and though they have no navigable river that way yet they drive a very great trade through all those counties."

The " two great rivers," the Severn and the Wye, enabled them, also, to " have the whole trade of South Wales, as it were, to themselves," together with the greater part of that of North Wales,[1] while the sea gave them access to Ireland, where they were carrying on a trade which, says Defoe, was not only great in itself but had " prodigiously increased " in the last thirty years, notwithstanding the greater competition of the Liverpool merchants.

The transport facilities offered by the Severn were a further material factor both in the local development of great coal, iron and other industries, at a time when like industries were still in their infancy in the north, and in the increase of the general wealth of the western counties. In regard to Shropshire, Archdeacon Plymley writes that the inhabitants of the county, having such ready communication both with the interior of the country and with the sea, had opened mines of iron, stone, lead, lime, etc., and had, also, established very extensive iron manufactures. As the result of all this enterprise, much capital had been drawn into the district ; a great market had been opened for the agricultural produce of the country ; the ready conveyance of fuel and manure had enabled the cultivation of the soil to be carried on even beyond the demands of the increasing consumption ; and all had so operated together as to increase the wealth and well-being of Shropshire in general.

Some interesting facts as to the conditions under which the navigation of the Severn was conducted in 1758 are given in a communication published in the " Gentleman's Magazine " for that year (pages 277–8) from G. Perry, of Coalbrookdale, under the heading, " A Description of the Severn." The following passages may be quoted :—

" This river, being justly esteemed the second in Britain, is of great importance on account of its trade, being navigated by vessels of large burden more than 160 miles from the sea, without the assistance of any lock. Upwards of 100,000 tons of coals are annually shipped from the collieries about Madeley

---

[1] " Wines and groceries," says Archdeacon Plymley, " are brought up the Severn from Bristol and Gloucester to Shrewsbury, and so on to Montgomeryshire."

and Broseley to the towns and cities on its banks, and from
thence into the adjacent countries ; also great quantities of
grain, pig and bar iron, iron manufactures and earthen wares,
as well as wool, hops, cyder, and provisions are constantly
exported to Bristol and other places, from whence merchants'
goods, &c., are brought in return. The freight from Shrewsbury to Bristol is about 10s. per ton, and from Bristol to
Shrewsbury 15s., the rates to the intermediate towns being
in proportion.

" This traffic is carried on with vessels of two sorts ; the
lesser kind are called barges and frigates, being from 40 to
60 feet in length, have a single mast, square sail, and carry
from 20 to 40 tons ; the trows, or larger vessels, are from 40 to
80 tons burthen ; these have a main and top mast, about
80 feet high, with square sails, and some have mizen masts ;
they are generally from 16 to 20 feet wide and 60 in length,
being, when new, and completely rigged worth about 300*l*."

Their number having greatly increased, he had " an exact
list " taken of all the barges and trows on the Severn in May,
1756, and this list he gives. The total number of owners
was then 210, and the total number of vessels was 376. Among
the places mentioned are the following :—

TOWN.				OWNERS.		VESSELS.
Shrewsbury .	.	.	.	10	...	19
Madeley Wood	.	.	.	21	...	39
Broseley	.	.	.	55	...	87
Bridgnorth .	.	.	.	47	...	75
Bewdley	.	.	.	18	...	47
Worcester	.	.	.	6	...	21
Tewkesbury .	.	.	.	8	...	18
Evesham-upon-Avon.		.	.	1	...	2
Gloucester .	.	.	.	4	..	7

Of the disadvantages that attended navigation on the
Severn I shall speak in chapter xv, in connection with the
decline of river transport in general.

What the Severn group of rivers, with Bristol as the head-
quarters of their navigation, were on the west coast, the Wash
group and the port of Lynn were on the east coast.

The Wash group comprised : (1) the Bedford Ouse and its
tributaries, with a main outlet at Lynn ; (2) the Welland,

with Spalding for its inland port ; and (3) the Witham, which passes through the Fens and into the Wash by way of Boston. There is abundant testimony available as to the former great importance of these rivers.

Defoe says of Lynn : " There is the greatest extent of Inland Navigation here, of any Port in England, London excepted. The Reason whereof is this, that there are more Navigable Rivers empty themselves here into the Sea, including the Washes, which are branches of the same Port, than at any one Mouth of Waters in England, except the Thames and the Humber."

Nathaniel Kinderley, in his work on " The Ancient and Present State of the Navigation of the Towns of Lynn, Wisbeach, Spalding and Boston " (2nd edition, 1751), speaks of the Bedford Ouse as having five rivers emptying themselves into it from eight several counties; and he says that it " does therefore afford a great Advantage to Trade and Commerce, since hereby two Cities and several great Towns are therein served, as Peterborough, Ely, Stamford, Bedford, St. Ives, Huntington, St. Neots, Northampton, Cambridge, Bury St. Edmunds, Thetford, &c., with all Sorts of heavy commodities from Lyn ; as Coals and Salt (from Newcastle), Deals, Fir-Timber, Iron, Pitch and Tar (from Sweden and Norway), and Wine (from Lisbon and Oporto) thither imported, and from these Parts great Quantities of Wheat, Rye, Cole-Seed, Oats, Barley, &c., are brought down these Rivers, whereby a great foreign and inland Trade is carried on and the Breed of Seamen is increased. The Port of Lyn supplies Six Counties wholly, and three in Part."

Another writer of the same period, Thomas Badeslade, who published in 1766 a " History of the Ancient and Present State of the Navigation of the Port of King's Lyn and of Cambridge and the rest of the trading Towns in those Parts," took up the argument that the number of inhabitants, the value of land, the trade, the riches and the strength of every free State were great in proportion to their possession of navigable rivers ; and he went on to declare that " Of all the Navigable Rivers in England the River of the Great Ouse is one of the chief, and Lyn sits at the door of this river, as it were the turnkey of it."

The various large and populous towns (as already mentioned)

which stood either upon the Ouse itself or upon one of the other rivers connecting with it were, he proceeded, all dependent on its navigation, and all of them were supplied by the merchants of Lynn with what he described as "maritime commodities.". "Their Exports and Imports," he declared, "enrich and Furnish the Country; and raise a great Revenue to the Government, and in all National advantages the Port of Lyn is equalled by few Ports of this Kingdom." But, owing to neglect of the Ouse, there was the risk that the river would "in a very short time" be "lost to navigation," and all, he continued, agreed that "If something be not done this Country will be rendered uninhabitable, and the Navigation of the Port of Lynn will be lost, and the University of Cambridge, and all the great Towns situate on the Rivers for the benefit of Navigation must with it decay and become impoverished; and the Customs and Duties of the State be in Consequence thereof greatly lessened."

Happily our national well-being has not depended on navigable rivers, as Badeslade thought it did, and, though the condition of the Bedford Ouse has got far worse than it was when he wrote, the University of Cambridge and the various towns in question still, happily, survive. But even in Badeslade's time the Ouse was beginning to get, as he says, "choaked up," and he recalls the year 1649 when "keels could sail with Forty Tun freight 36 miles from Lynn towards Cambridge at ordinary Neip-Tides, and as far as Huntingdon with Fifteen Tun Freight. And Barges with Ten Chaldron of coals could sail up Brandon River to Thetford; and as far in proportion up the Rivers Mildenhall, &c., &c. By all which Rivers the Port of Lynn was capable of the most extensive Inland navigation of any Port of England."

How Lynn served as the port for the great quantities of foreign produce and, also, for the hops and other commodities sent from London and the south-western counties for the Sturbridge fair at Cambridge has already been told (see page 24). It was, also, through Lynn and Boston that a large proportion of our commerce with Normandy, Flanders and the Rhine country was conducted; and Lynn, especially, grew in wealth and importance, and further developed, as Defoe found, into a town having considerable social attractions.

Concerning the Witham, Joseph Priestley says, in his

" Historical Account of the Navigable Rivers, Canals and Railways of Great Britain " (1831), it has been thought that previous to the Norman Conquest the river was a tideway navigation for ships to Lincoln. That it was navigable at a very early period he thinks may be inferred from the fact that the Fossdike Canal, " an ancient ' Roman Work,' " was scoured out by Henry I. in the year 1121 for the purpose of opening a navigable communication between the Trent and the Witham at the city of Lincoln in order that that place, which was then in a very flourishing condition and enjoying an extensive foreign trade, might reap all the advantages of a more ready communication with the interior.

Another most important group of rivers, from the point of view of inland navigation, was the series which have their outlet in the Humber. This group includes the Yorkshire Ouse and the Trent, both naturally navigable.

The Ouse (York) is formed by the confluence of the Ure and the Swale sixty miles above the Trent Falls, where, after passing through York, Selby, and Goole, it joins the Trent and forms the Humber estuary. Under a charter granted by Edward IV., in the year 1462, the Lord Mayor and Aldermen of York were to " oversee and be conservators " of this river, as well as of the Aire, the Wharfe, the Derwent, the Don, and the Humber, all of which are connected with it. Of the city of York, as he found it in or about the year 1723, Defoe says :—

" No City in England is better furnished with Provision of every Kind, nor any so cheap, in proportion to the goodness of Things ; the River being so navigable and so near the Sea, the Merchants here trade directly to what port of the world they will ; for Ships of any Burthen come up within thirty Mile of the City, and small Craft from sixty or eighty Ton, and under, come up to the very City."

The navigable Trent was for many centuries the chief means of communication between south and north, and Nottingham, as the capital of the Trent district, became a place of great importance. It was along the Trent that the King's messengers passed on their way to York, in preference to braving the dangers of the road through Sherwood Forest. The burgesses of Nottingham were required to take charge of them as soon as they came to the river and conduct them safely to

Torksey, whose burgesses, in turn, had to take them to the Humber, and so on up the tidal Ouse to York.

To the town of Burton-on-Trent by packhorse or waggon, down the Trent by barge to Hull, and thence by sailing vessel along the east coast and up the Thames, was once a favoured route for the consignment of cheese from Cheshire to the London market. In Defoe's time the quantity of Cheshire cheese thus passing along the Trent, either for London or for east coast towns, was 4000 tons a year. Owing to the state of the roads the Trent route was the only practicable alternative the Cheshire cheese makers had to what they called the " Long sea " route to London, " a terribly long, and sometimes dangerous Voyage " (says Defoe) by way of the Mersey, Land's End, the English Channel and the Thames. In describing the conditions of navigation on the Trent he tells us that, " The Trent is Navigable by Ships of good Burthen as high as Gainsbrough, which is near forty Miles from the Humber by the River. The Barges without the Help of Locks or Stops go as high as Nottingham, and further by the Help of Art to Burton-upon-Trent in Staffordshire. The Stream is full, the Channel deep and safe, and the Tide flows up a great Way between Gainsborough and Newark. This, and the Navigation lately, reaching up to Burton and up the Derwent to Derby, is a great Support to and Encrease of the Trade of those counties which border upon it."

In speaking more fully of Nottingham Defoe says : " The Trent is Navigable here for Vessels or Barges of great Burthen, by which all their heavy and bulky Goods are brought from the Humber and even from Hull ; such as Iron, Block-tin, Salt, Hops, Grocery, Dyers Wares, Wine, Oyl, Tar, Hemp, Flax, &c., and the same vessels carry down Coal, Wood, Corn ; as also Cheese in great Quantities from Warwickshire and Staffordshire."

From an article " On Inland Navigations and Public Roads," by William Jessop, published in the Georgical Essays, Vol. IV. (1804), I gather that merchandise was carried on the Trent at a cost of eight shillings a ton for a distance of seventy miles, and that " in point of expedition " vessels frequently made the journey of seventy miles and back in a week, including the time for loading and unloading—a degree of despatch which Jessop evidently regarded as very creditable, since he adds,

" This has been done by the same vessel for ten weeks successively, and would often be done if they were not obliged to
wait for their lading."

One of the affluents of the Trent, the little river known as
the Idle, joins it at Stockwith, 21 miles from the junction of
the Trent with the Humber ; and seven miles up the Idle is
the once-famous " port " of Bawtry.

This particular place fulfilled all the conditions of what
I have already described as the ideal port of olden days. Not
only was it far inland, bringing a considerable district into
communication with the sea, but it was situated—eight miles
south-east of Doncaster—on the Great North Road, at the
point where this road enters the county of York. Until the
navigation of the Don was improved, under an Act passed in
1727, the Hull, Trent, Idle and Bawtry route was preferred
to the Hull, Ouse, Aire, Don, and Doncaster route alike for
foreign imports into Yorkshire and for Yorkshire products
consigned to London or to places abroad ; and Bawtry,
known to-day, to those who know it at all, as only a small
market town in Yorkshire, was at one time of considerable
importance.

In the reigns of Edward III. and Edward IV., as told by the
Rev. Joseph Hunter, in " The History and Topography of
the Deanery of Doncaster " (1828), the lords of the manor
of Bawtry were " of the prime of English nobility," while
the market established there dated from the beginning of the
thirteenth century. When the sovereign or any members of
the Royal Family travelled in state to the north, they were
usually met at Bawtry by the sheriff of the county and a
train of attendants.

More to our present purpose, however, is the fact that,
down to the opening of the second quarter of the eighteenth
century this inland port of Bawtry was the route by which
most of the products of Sheffield, of Hallamshire, and of the
country round about, destined for London, for the eastern
counties, or for the Continent, passed to their destination.
From Sheffield to Bawtry was a land journey of twenty miles,
and thus far, at least, packhorses or waggons had to be
utilised over such roads as there then were. The Idle is
described by Defoe as " a full and quick, though not rapid and
unsafe Stream, with a deep Channel, which carries Hoys,

Lighters, Barges or flat-bottomed Vessels out of its Channel into the Trent." In fair weather these vessels, taking on their cargo at Bawtry, could continue the journey from Stockwith, where the Trent was entered, to Hull; but otherwise the cargo was transhipped at Stockwith into vessels of up to 200-ton burthen, which were able to pass from the Humber along the Trent as far as Stockwith whether laden or empty. By means of this navigation, to quote again from Defoe :—

"The Town of Bautry becomes the Center of all the Exportation of this Part of the Country, especially for heavy Goods, which they bring down hither from all the adjacent Countries, such as Lead, from the Lead Mines and Smelting-Houses in Derbyshire, wrought Iron and Edge-Tools, of all Sorts, from the Forges at Sheffield, and from the Country call'd Hallamshire, being adjacent to the Towns of Sheffield and Rotheram, where an innumerable Number of People are employed. Also Millstones and Grindstones, in very great Quantities, are brought down and shipped off here, and so carry'd by Sea to Hull, and to London, and even to Holland also. This makes Bautry Wharf be famous all over the South Part of the West Riding of Yorkshire, for it is the Place whither all their heavy Goods are carried, to be embarked and shipped off."

One can thus well credit Hunter's statement that there appear to have been several persons residing at Bawtry in the Middle Ages who had been enriched by the commerce of " the port," as the place was, in fact, described in the Hundred Rolls; but when one thinks of the great extent of the industries of the Sheffield district as carried on at the present day, it is certainly interesting to learn of the conditions under which they were developed, and the circuitous route by which their products once reached London and the markets of the world.

The industries grew, however, in spite of all the difficulties in transport. The iron trade had existed in Hallamshire since the reign of Henry II. (1154–1189). Sheffield cutlery was well known in the Middle Ages. It was in high repute in Queen Elizabeth's time. In the early part of the eighteenth century the industries of the district were increasing at a greater rate than ever. In 1721 the weight of Hallamshire manufactures sent in the direction of the Humber was 13,000 tons; and the greater proportion of this quantity must have passed through the port of Bawtry and thence along the river Trent.

The Thames, England's greatest river, does not, so far as it serves the port of London and facilitates the immense trade there carried on, enter so much into consideration from the point of view of strictly " internal communication " as some of the lesser rivers already mentioned, the position alike of London, Liverpool, Newcastle, Southampton, etc., relating to ports, docks, harbours and commerce in general rather than to the particular forms of inland transport here under review. One must not forget, however, that, above the port of London itself the navigation of the Thames was, from very early times, of the greatest advantage to a considerable extent of country, and that the value of these services was further increased by various tributaries of the Thames.

The fact that settlement originally followed the course of rivers is abundantly shown by the number of cities, towns, monasteries, abbeys and conventual establishments set up of old in the Thames valley. The convenience, also, of water transport must have had much to do with the locating of a University at Oxford, on the Thames, just as it did with the establishment of a University at Cambridge, on the Cam, each being thus rendered accessible to scholars from Scotland and elsewhere who would have found it impracticable to make so long a journey under the early conditions of road travel. The Thames became, further, the main highway for the various counties through which it flowed, included therein being some of the most fertile districts in the land ; and, though London may owe its pre-eminence mainly to foreign trade, passing between the port of London and the sea, the facilities for communication offered above the port of London by the Thames for the full extent of its navigable length were, in the pre-railway days more especially, of incalculable advantage both to the districts served thereby and to the Metropolis itself.

This advantage becomes still more striking when we take into account the rivers that form important tributaries of the Thames.

The Lea was described in a statute of 1424 as " one of the great rivers, which extendeth from the town of Ware till the water of the Thames, in the counties of Hertford, Essex and

Middlesex " ; and along this river there was carried at one
time a very considerable quantity of produce and merchandise.
The history of Ware goes back to, at least, the ninth century,
when the Danes took their ships up to the town but were
outmanœuvred by King Alfred, who diverted the stream,
and left the vessels stranded. Not only was the founding of
Ware on the spot where it stands due to the convenience of
water communication, but Ware itself was one of the ideal
ports of the time, inasmuch as it was so far inland, and was in
convenient reach of several counties.

The navigation, as far as Godalming, of the Wey, which falls
into the Thames at Weybridge, opened up a great part of
Surrey and the adjoining counties to water communication
with London. In recording his visit to Guildford, Defoe
says of the Wey that a very great quantity of timber was
carried along it, such timber being not only brought from the
neighbourhood of that town, but conveyed by road from
" the woody parts of Sussex and Hampshire above 30 miles
from it " ; though he significantly adds that this was done
" in the Summer," the Sussex roads being, as I have already
shown, probably unequalled for badness, and especially in the
winter, by those of any other county in England. Defoe
further says in regard to the Wey that it was "a mighty
support" to the "great corn-market" at Farnham. Meal-
men (as he calls them) and other dealers obtained corn at
Farnham, and brought much of it by road to the mills on the
Wey, a distance of about seven miles. In these mills it was
ground and dressed, and it was then sent in barges to London,
" as is practiced," Defoe adds, " on the other side of the
Thames for above fifty miles distance from London."

The Medway was another means of communication between
a considerable extent of country and the Thames. It was
utilised, not alone for sending timber from the woods of
Sussex and Kent to the port of London or elsewhere, but, also,
for the distribution of general produce. Defoe says of Maidstone, the chief town on the Medway, that " from this Town
and the Neighbouring Parts London is supplied with more
particulars than from any single market Town in England."

In addition to these great groups of rivers, many single and
minor rivers led to the opening up of inland ports which
served in their day a most useful purpose.

The Exe allowed of Exeter carrying on a considerable foreign trade. Defoe tells of the " vast quantities " of woollen manufactures sent from Exeter direct to Holland, as well as to Portugal, Spain and Italy. The Dutch, especially, gave large commissions for the buying of Devonshire serges, which were made not only in Exeter but at Crediton, Honiton, Tiverton and in all the north part of the county, giving abundant employment to the people. Defoe speaks of the serge-market at Exeter as, next to that at Leeds, " the greatest in England." He had been assured, he says, that in this market from £60,000 to £100,000 worth of serges had been sold in a week.

In the neighbouring county of Somerset, Taunton was the inland port to which coal conveyed in sea-going vessels from Swansea to Bridgwater was taken in barges along the navigable Parrett. Heavy goods and merchandise from Bristol—such as iron, lead, flax, pitch, tar, dye-stuffs, oil, wine, and groceries of all kinds—were received there in the same way. From Taunton these commodities were distributed, by packhorse or waggon, throughout the county.

Whatever the original capacity of rivers naturally navigable, there came a time when, by reason either of their inherent defects or of the use of larger vessels, they required a certain amount of regulation ; and there came a time, also, when it was deemed expedient to render navigable by art many rivers that were not already adapted thereto by nature. In this way the necessity arose for much river legislation, together with much enterprise in respect to river improvement, in the days when the only alternatives to river transport were the deplorably defective roads.

CHAPTER XIV

RIVER IMPROVEMENT AND INDUSTRIAL EXPANSION

THE earliest legislation applying to navigable rivers referred only to the taking of salmon or to restrictions on weirs and other hindrances to navigation. Regulations in regard to these matters began to be enforced in 1285, and numerous statutes relating more especially to the removal alike of weirs, jetties, mills, mill-dams, etc., causing obstruction to boats, were passed; though in 1370 and subsequently there were complaints that the said statutes were not observed.

The first Act for the improvement of an English river was, according to Clifford, as told in his " History of Private Bill Legislation," a statute of 1424 (2 Hen. VI.), which appointed a commission " to survey, redress and amend all the defaults " of the river Lea. Six years later there was a further Act which set forth that, owing to the number of shoals in the river, ships and boats could not pass as they ought; and the Chancellor was authorised to appoint Commissioners to remove the shoals. The Commissioners were further empowered to take tolls from passing vessels, though the Act was to be in force for only three years, and was, in effect, not renewed.

We have here the introduction, not alone of the improvement of river navigation by Act of Parliament, but of the principle of toll-collection on rivers as a means of raising funds for defraying the cost, on the principle that those who benefitted should pay. It will, also, be seen that this first legislative attempt at river improvement related only to dredging and deepening the channel of the stream to which it applied.

Next, as we are further told by Clifford, came the straightening of rivers, or their partial deviation by new cuts; and here, again, the Lea stands first in the Statutes. The preamble of an Act (13 Eliz., c. 18), passed in 1571, " for bringing the river Lea to the north side of the city of London," stated :—

" It is perceived by many grave and wise men, as well of the city of London as of the country, that it were very commodious and profitable both for the city and the country that the river of Lea, otherwise called the Ware river, might be brought within the land to the north part of the city . . . through such a convenient and meet cut as may serve for the navigation of barges and other vessels, for the carrying and conveying as well of all merchandizes, corn and victuals, as other necessaries from the town of Ware and other places to the city . . . and also for tilt-boats and wherries for conveying of the Queen's subjects to and fro, to their great ease and commodity."

The Corporation of the City of London were authorised to construct and act as conservators of the new channel, and Commissioners in Middlesex, Essex and Hertfordshire were again entrusted with the duty of freeing the river from shoals and shallows.

A number of other Acts relating to the Lea followed, but mention need only be made here of one passed in 1779 which stated that, inasmuch as the trustees appointed under earlier enactments could not, without further advance in the rates they were already empowered to enforce, liquidate the charges falling upon them in respect to the outlay for works done on the river, they were authorised to increase those rates.

In the seventeenth century, especially in the period following the accession of Charles II. to the throne (1660), much attention was paid to river improvement. A rapid expansion of commerce, of industries and of wealth had followed alike the planting of colonies in the West Indies and on the continent of North America, the development of home manufactures, the reclamation of many waste spaces through the operation of enclosure Acts, and the improvements brought about in cultivation. The need for better means of communication in order to open up districts then more or less isolated, to provide better transport for raw materials and manufactured goods, and to facilitate the carriage of domestic and other supplies needed by the increasing population, thus became more and more apparent.

In many instances the condition of the roads and the prejudicial results upon them of heavy traffic were adduced as the main reason for a resort to improvements of river navigation. An Act (21 Jas. I., c. 32), passed in 1624, for deepening the navigation of the Thames from Bercott to Oxford, stated that it was designed " for the conveyance of Oxford freestone by water to London, and for coal and other necessaries from London to Oxford, now coming at a dear rate only by land carriage, whereby the roads are becoming exceedingly bad." It was further stated, in the preamble, that " the said passage will be very behoveful for preserving the highways leading to and from the said university and city and other parts thereabouts " which, owing to " the continual carriages by carts," had become dangerous for travellers in winter, " and hardly to be amended or continued passable without exceeding charge." In 1739 there was passed an Act (14 Geo. II., c. 26), "for the betterment and more easy and speedy portage " on, the Medway of timber from the woods of Sussex and Kent, which timber could not be " conveyed to a market but at a very large expense by reason of the badness of the roads in these parts."

Various far-seeing, patriotic and enterprising individuals took a leading part in pioneering the movement in favour of improved river navigation which, for a period of about 100 years—until, that is, the advent of the canal era—was to be developed with much zeal and energy, though not always with conspicuous success. Especially prominent among these pioneers were William Sandys, Francis Mathew and Andrew Yarranton ; and it is only fitting that some mention should here be made of these three worthies, each of whom shared the fate of so many other pioneers, in so far as he was a man in advance of his time.

Sir William Sandys, of Ombersley Court, in the county of Worcester, obtained, in 1636, an Act of Parliament which granted powers for making navigable the Warwickshire Avon from the Severn, at Tewkesbury, to the city of Coventry, and, also, the Teme, on the west side of the Severn, towards Ludlow. Some of the works thus carried out are still rendering good service. In 1661 he secured further Acts for making navigable the rivers Wye and Lugg and the brooks running into them in the counties of Hereford, Gloucester and Monmouth. Here he anticipated much of what was to be done a century later by Brindley, in connection with canal construction, inasmuch as he obtained powers not simply to deepen the beds of the rivers and to straighten their courses, but to construct new channels, to set up locks, weirs, etc., to provide towing-paths, and to dig new channels where required. This last-mentioned proposal constituted, as will be seen later on, the idea that led up to the eventual transition from navigable rivers to artificial canals, the new " cuts " on the former being the connecting link between the two.

The Wye was found to be an exceptionally difficult stream to tame and control, and Sandys' attempt to make it navigable by locks and weirs on the pound-lock system was a failure. The scheme was, however, afterwards carried through on different lines ; and in summing up the results John Lloyd, Junr., says in " Papers Relating to the History and Navigation of the Rivers Wye and Lugg " (1873) :—

" Although, through the uncertainty of its stream, the Wye was never brought to answer the purpose of a regular conveyance, its navigation has proved of great service throughout the county of Hereford. Throughout the last [1] century most of the coal consumed in Hereford and its neighbourhood was brought up in barges after a flood. Various other heavy articles, such as grocery, wines and spirits, having been first conveyed from Bristol to Brockweir in larger vessels, were carried up thence in barges at a much easier rate than by land carriage. In return the boats were freighted with the valuable oak timber, bark, cider, wheat, flour and other produce of the county. The opening of the towing-path for horses by the Act of 1809 gave a further impetus to navigation, and especially to the trade in coal from Lidbrook, and while every river-side village could boast of its quay and its barge, the quay walls at Hereford were thronged with loading and unloading barges. . . .

" Since the opening of the Hereford, Ross and Gloucester Railway, in 1855, and the consequent dissolution of the Towing-path Company, nearly all navigation on the Wye above Monmouth has ceased."

Francis Mathew addressed, in 1655, to Oliver Cromwell, " Lord Protector of the Commonwealth," a powerful argument in favour of " The Opening of Rivers for Navigation," the benefit thereof which he sought to show being, as his title-page said, " exemplified by the Two Avons of Salisbury and Bristol,

[1] Eighteenth.

with a Mediterranean Passage by Water for Billanders of Thirty Tun between Bristol and London." The writer described his little book as a plea that " England's fair valleys and rich Inlets through which so many noble Rivers insinuate themselves might with the imitation of the industrious Netherlanders be made in many places docible of Navigation, to the inestimable comfort, satisfaction, ease and profit of the publick." " Rivers," he further observed, " may be compared to States-men, sent abroad ; they are never out of their way so they pass by great Cities, Marts, Courts of Princes, Armies, Leaguers, Diets and the like Theatres of Action, which still contribute to the increase of their Observation ; So Navigable Rivers, the more places of Note they pass by, the more they take up, or bring, still gleaning one Commodity or other from the Soyl they pass through, and are supplied by every Town they touch at with imployment."

Into the details of his scheme for establishing direct water communication between Bristol and London there is now no need to enter. Suffice it to say that the two cities had to wait many years before the idea he foreshadowed was carried into effect. But I must not omit to mention one of the arguments advanced by Mathew in support of his general proposals, since it has a direct bearing on the conditions of road transport at this period, and the reasons based thereon in favour of improvements in river navigation. Thus he urged, among other things, " the facility of Commerce from one place to another, and the cheapness of transportation of Commodities without so much grinding and plowing up our high-wayes, which maketh them now in so many places impassable. You shall see," he continued, " Western Waggons, which they call Plows, carry forty hundred weight ; insomuch as between Bristol and Marlborough they have been enforced at a Hill they call Bagdown-hill, to put twenty beasts, Horse and Oxen, to draw it up : This great abuse by this means would be taken away, by keeping our high-wayes pleasant ; and withal, by this transportation of Commodities by River, the price of Commodities would fall."

Oliver Cromwell had other matters than roads and rivers to engage his attention, and Francis Mathew got from him no favourable response to his proposals. But in 1670 he dedicated to Charles II. and " the Honorable Houses of

Parliament " a new edition of his scheme under the title of " A
Mediterranean Passage by Water from London to Bristol,
and from Lynne to Yarmouth, and so consequently to the City
of York for the great Advancement of Trade and Traffique."
In the course of his Dedication he said :—

" Observing by traversing this island, that divers Rivers
within the same may be moulded into such Form as will
admit of Vessels of thirty Tun burden, or upwards, to sail in,
unto the great Relief of divers Countryes in this Island, by
means of the same, at less than half the Rates now paid for
Land carriage . . . and considering at how easy a Charge . . .
the same may be brought to pass . . . I humbly presume . . .
to become Importunate to your most Excellent and Royal
Majesty for the enterprize of and ready effecting this Work,
being an Undertaking so Heroick, that 'tis beyond the Level
of any others to attempt."

Among the reasons he now advanced in favour of removing
the obstructions and difficulties to be met with in the making
of rivers navigable were the " Wonderful Improvement to
much Trade," and especially the trade in coal ; " the great
Ease of the Subject " ; increased public revenue—

" And what is well and worthy of Observing, the High-
wayes hereby will be much preserved, and become a very
acceptable work to the Country, which now notwithstanding
their great cost, is a grievous Toil as well to Man as beast,
being now so unnecessarily plowed up by Waggons of Prodigious Burthens, which in this Island are dayly travelling."

Andrew Yarranton, who brought out in 1677 a remarkable
book, entitled " England's Improvement by Land and Sea,"
might be described as a Pioneer of Protection as well as an
early champion of improved inland communication. He
considered that the best way of fighting the Dutch, who were
then a source of trouble to the country, would be, not to go to
war with them, but to capture their trade and commerce.
To this end he elaborated a scheme under which, instead of
importing every year " vast quantities " of " linen cloth of
all sorts," of iron, and of woollen goods, England would
" settle " these industries here, fostering them by means
of import duties to be imposed on foreign manufactures for a
period of seven years, and supplementing those duties by the
setting-up of a general system of banking, itself, in turn,

made secure by a general land register. The linen industry, he advised, should be established in the counties of Warwick, Leicester, Northampton, and Oxford, where, among other considerations, navigable rivers would be available for the purposes of transport; and he goes on to say, in words which, though written more than two and a quarter centuries ago, seem only to have anticipated much that we hear from the tariff reformers of to-day, that by this means, " we should prevent at least two millions of money a year from being sent out of the Land for Linen Cloth, and keep our people at home who now go beyond the Seas for want of imployment here."

In his references to the iron trade, Yarranton speaks of the " infinite quantities of raw iron " then being made in Monmouthshire and the Forest of Dean, and he says that the greatest part of what he calls the " Slow Iron " made in the Forest of Dean " is sent up the Severne to the Forges, into Worcester-shire, Shropshire, Stafford-shire, Warwick-shire and Cheshire, and there it's made into Bar-iron : And because of its kind and gentle nature to work, it is now at Sturbridge, Dudly, Wolverhampton, Sedgley, Wasall, and Burmingham and thereabouts wrought into all small Commodities and diffused all England over, and thereby a great Trade made of it ; and when manufactured sent into most parts of the World " ; though in Worcestershire, Shropshire, Staffordshire, Warwickshire and Derbyshire there were already great and numerous ironworks in which, he adds, " Much Iron is made of Metal or Iron Stone of another nature quite different from that of the Forest of Deane."

Having sketched his ideas of such reorganisation of industry as would, in his opinion, help the country both to beat the Dutch without fighting and, also, to provide work for all the poor people in England, he proceeded : " That nothing may be wanting that may conduce to the benefit and incouragement of things manufactured, as in cheap carriage to and fro over England, and to the Sea at easie rates, I will in the next place shew you how the great Rivers in England may be made navigable, and thereby make the Commodities and Goods carried, especially in Winter time, for half the rate they now pay."

The schemes he especially recommended in this connection were for the establishing of communication between the

Thames and the Severn, and between the Dee and the Severn ; and he argued that there would be a further advantage from the point of view of the national food supply, as an improvement in river navigation would allow both of corn being more easily brought to London and of the setting up of great granaries, at Oxford for the advantage of London, and at Stratford-on-Avon for the benefit of towns on the Severn. He further says :—

" I hear some say, You projected the making Navigable the River Stoure in Worcestershire ; what is the reason it was not finished ? I say it was my projection, and I will tell you the reason it was not finished. The River Stoure and some other Rivers were granted by an Act of Parliament to certain Persons of Honour, and some progress was made in the work ; but within a small while after the Act passed it was let fall again. But it being a brat of my own I was not willing it should be Abortive ; therefore I made offers to perfect it, leaving a third part of the Inheritance to me and my heirs for ever, and we came to an agreement. Upon which I fell on, and made it compleatly navigable from Sturbridge to Kederminster ; and carried down many hundred Tuns of Coales, and laid out near one thousand pounds, and then it was obstructed for Want of Money, which by Contract was to be paid."

To describe, in detail, all the various schemes for the improvement of river navigation which were carried out, more especially in the second half of the seventeenth century and the first half of the eighteenth (irrespective of the many others that succumbed to the complaint spoken of by Yarranton—want of money), would take up far too much space ; but a few typical examples, which have a direct bearing on the development of British trade, commerce and industry, may be of interest.

Until the year 1694, when the improvement of the Mersey was taken in hand, Liverpool had no chance of emerging from a situation of almost complete isolation, and of competing with ports some of which, though now ports no longer, or far outstripped by the Liverpool of to-day, were then of vastly greater importance than Liverpool from the point of view of national commerce.

Nature, unaided by man, had not been so considerate to

Liverpool as she had been to Bristol, to Lynn, to Hull or to Boston. These, and other ports besides, stood on streams which were naturally navigable for more or less considerable distances into the interior of the country, whereas the Mersey was not naturally navigable for more than about fifteen or twenty miles above Liverpool. The navigation even of the estuary as far as Liverpool presented difficulties and dangers in stormy weather, owing to sand-banks, violent currents and rapid tides ; but beyond Runcorn the Mersey was not then navigable at all. Nor were the tributaries of the Mersey—the Irwell and the Weaver—navigable.

Liverpool was thus shut off from communication with the interior by river, and for a long time the town was not in a much better position as regards roads. No Roman road came nearer to Liverpool than Warrington, and, down to 1750 (as I have already shown), the road between Warrington and Liverpool was not passable for coaches or carriages. On the east Liverpool was practically isolated from the rest of the country by the high range of hills dividing Lancashire from Yorkshire, and there were the still more formidable hills of the Lake District on the north. The early route for a journey to the south from Liverpool was to cross the Mersey at Monk's Ferry, Birkenhead, and then pass through the forest of Wirral to Chester. Here there was found a Roman road, along which a coach to London was running in the reign of James II. (1685–1688), whereas the first coach from Warrington to London did not start until 1757.

So long as our commercial relations were mainly with Continental or other ports which could be more conveniently reached from the east or the south coast, or from Bristol, and so long as the industries of Lancashire and Yorkshire were but little developed, or found an outlet abroad in these other directions, the comparative isolation of Liverpool was a matter of no great national concern ; though how, in effect, Liverpool compared with other seaports or river-ports in the thirteenth century is shown by the fact (as told by Thomas Baines, in his " History of the Commerce and Town of Liverpool ") that whereas the aggregate value of trading property in Liverpool, Lancaster, Preston and Wigan—the only four towns in Lancashire which then acknowledged possessing such property at all—was given in an official return for the year 1343 as £233, equal to £3495 of our present money; the equivalent value to-day of the trading property of Bristol at the same period would be £30,000, and that of Nottingham, then the great inland port of the Trent, £50,000.

That was a time when, as the same authority says, " Liverpool stood nearly at the extremity of the known world." But when the known world was enlarged by the addition thereto of the New World of America, and when commerce with the lands across the Atlantic began to develop, and the industries of Lancashire and Yorkshire to grow apace, the need for improved communications with the port of Liverpool became more and more acute.

Such need was the greater, too, because of the fate that was overtaking the much earlier and hitherto far more prosperous port of Chester. Established as a fortress of the first order by the Romans, at the western end of one of their famous roads, and favoured alike by Saxons and Normans, Chester had developed into a flourishing commercial port from which, more especially, intercourse with Ireland was conducted, and it was still the port through which travellers passed to or from Ireland for a long time after Liverpool began to compete actively for the Irish goods traffic. Richard Blome, who visited Chester in 1673, describes it in his " Britannia " as " the usual place for taking shipping for Ireland, with which it has a very great intercourse, and a place of very considerable trade."

But, as against the advantage it offered as an inland port, situate twenty-two miles from its estuary, and dealing with the products of an especially productive county, Chester had the disadvantage due to the enormous masses of sand which were driven into the Dee by Atlantic storms, to the full fury and effects of which the open estuary was exposed. This evil began to grow serious soon after the Conquest, and the port of Chester steadily declined as the port of Liverpool steadily rose, the trade lost by the one helping to build up the prosperity of the other.

The benefits resulting from the improvements carried out on the Mersey when, under the Act of 1694, navigation was extended from Runcorn to Warrington, began to be immediately felt ; but they also brought out more clearly the great necessity for still further amendment. How merchandise went across country in those days is shown in a letter written in 1701 by Thomas Patten, a Liverpool citizen who had taken a leading part in the movement that led to the Mersey being made navigable as far inland as Warrington. Referring to a certain consignment of tobacco which was to be despatched from Liverpool to Hull, on behalf of a trader at Stockport, Patten says that, as the tobacco could not be carried in the hogshead all the way by road from Warrington to Hull, and as the sea route from Liverpool to Hull would have taken too long, the tobacco was first forwarded by cart, in twenty or thirty hogsheads, from the quay at Warrington to Stockport. There it was made up into canvas-covered parcels, and then sent on by packhorse—three parcels to a horse—a distance of thirty-six miles by road to Doncaster, and from Doncaster it was conveyed by river for the remainder of the distance to Hull. Baines, who gives the letter in his " History of Lancashire and Cheshire," remarks : " Such was the mode of conveying goods up to that time, and for upwards of thirty years after. It is evident that there could be no great development of trade and commerce so long as the modes of communication were so tedious and costly."

The improvement on the Mersey itself led to a further scheme for making the Mersey and Irwell navigable from Warrington to Manchester, thus establishing direct water communication between Liverpool and Manchester, as an alternative to transport by road. A survey of the two rivers was carried out in 1712, and a prospectus was issued in which it was said :—

" The inland parts of Lancashire and Yorkshire being favoured with a great variety of valuable manufactures in woollen, linen, cotton, &c., and that in very great quantities, has made that neighbourhood as populous, if not more so, than (London and Middlesex excepted) the same extent of any part of Great Britain. The trades of these counties extend considerably through the whole island, as well as abroad, and the consumption of groceries, Irish wool, dyeing stuffs, and other important goods consequently is very great ; but as yet not favoured with the conveniency of water carriage, though Providence, from the port of Liverpool up to the most considerable inland town of Lancashire, Manchester, has afforded the best, not yet employed, rivers of Mersey and Irwell for that purpose."

It was not until the passing of the Mersey and Irwell Navigation Act, in 1720, that the work of rendering these rivers navigable between Warrington and Manchester was begun, and another twenty years elapsed before it was completed. The result of this " conveniency of water carriage " when it was, at last, obtained, was to reduce the cost of transport of goods and merchandise from forty shillings a ton by road to ten shillings a ton by river. The goods traffic between Liverpool and Manchester at this time amounted to about 4000 tons a year ; but it had, prior to the provision of water transport, naturally been restricted to the quantity that could be carried by the packhorses, carts and waggons of those days. Hence the river navigation gave the advantage of a transport not only cheaper in price but greater in capacity. It will be seen later on, however, that the Mersey and Irwell navigation subsequently developed disadvantages for which a remedy was sought in the construction of the Duke of Bridgewater's canal.

An Act, passed in 1720, for making the river Weaver navigable from Winsford Bridge, beyond Northwich, to Frodsham Bridge, near the junction of the Weaver with the Mersey (a distance of about twenty miles), was not only of further material advantage to the port of Liverpool but a first step in an important development of the salt mines of Cheshire. These mines have been described as " incomparably the richest of the salt mines and brine pits of England " ; but at the date in question their working was greatly hampered by transport costs and difficulties in the matter both of fuel and of the distribution of the salt, when made.

Fuel was required for heating the furnaces and the pans in which the brine was evaporated into salt ; and in the earliest days of the industry the salt-makers used for this purpose faggots of wood brought from the forests on the borders of Cheshire and Staffordshire. As long as these supplies were available, the principal seat of the salt trade was at Nantwich, in the higher part of the Weaver, and near to the forests where the wood was obtained. But the forests got depleted in course of time, and the industry then moved to other works lower down the river which could be operated with coal brought from the Lancashire coal-field. This coal, however, had to be carried, by cart or packhorse, a distance of twelve or fourteen miles ; and inasmuch as two tons of coal were required for every three tons of fine salt made, the cost of transport of raw materials was a serious item.

As for the manufactured salt, that was distributed in the same way, even such small consignments as could then alone be sent to Liverpool having to be taken thither by road. In the circumstances the salt trade remained comparatively undeveloped in Cheshire while it was making great advance at Newcastle-on-Tyne, where the coal readily obtained, by water, from the neighbouring coal-fields was used in the production of salt from sea-water. In the time of the Stuarts the manufacture of salt was one of the most important of Newcastle's industries and articles of export.

When, under the Act of 1720, the Weaver was made navigable as far as the Northwich and Winsford Bridge salt works, the land journey for Lancashire coal was reduced from twelve or fourteen miles to five or six miles, and the salt could be sent direct to Liverpool by water. The greatest impetus to the Cheshire salt industry (to the consequent detriment, and eventual extinction, of that at Newcastle-on-Tyne, though with a further advantage to the trade of Liverpool) was, however, not given until the makers were enabled to get their coal all the way by water through the supplementing of the now navigable Weaver by the Sankey Canal—of which more hereafter.

In the same year that the Act for improving the navigation of the Weaver was passed, Parliament sanctioned a no less important work on the river Douglas, which passes through Wigan, and has its outlet in the Ribble estuary, at a point about nine miles west of Preston. Wigan is situated on a part of the Lancashire coal-fields which contains some of the richest and most valuable seams of coal to be found in Lancashire ; but down to 1720 the only means of distributing this coal was by cart or packhorse. The opening of the Douglas to navigation allowed of the coal being sent by water to the estuary of the Ribble, and thence forwarded up the Ribble to Preston, or, alternatively, along the coast either to Lancaster in the one direction or to Liverpool and Chester in the other. These were tedious routes, and the voyage from the Ribble estuary along the coast was often very dangerous on account both of storms and of sand-banks. The lines of water com-

munication were, nevertheless, so much cheaper than land
carriage that they were followed for about fifty years—until
a safer and more expeditious waterway was provided through
the opening of the Leeds and Liverpool Canal.[1] Thomas
Baines, from whose " History of the Town and Commerce of
Liverpool " I glean these details, adds :—

" With all its defects, the Douglas navigation may be
regarded as the primary cause of the manufacturing prosperity
of the town of Preston, which it was the first means of supplying with cheap fuel for its workshops and factories. It may,
also, be considered as one of the early causes of the commercial
prosperity of Liverpool, which has always been much promoted
by the possession of cheap and abundant supplies of coal and
salt."

The rendering of the Aire and Calder navigable, under an
Act of Parliament passed in 1699, was an important event for
the then rising manufacturing towns of Leeds, Wakefield,
Halifax, Bradford and Huddersfield, situate on or within a
convenient distance of one or other of these two rivers which,
joining at Castleford, ten miles below Leeds, thence flow
in a combined stream to their junction with the Yorkshire Ouse,
and so on to the Humber and the ports of Hull and Grimsby.
The event in question was no less interesting because it marked
a further development in an industrial transition which constitutes a leading factor in the economic history of England.

The textile industries originally established in the eastern
counties by refugees from the Netherlands and France afterwards spread through the southern and western counties,
attaining in each district to a very considerable growth long
before they were of any importance in those northern counties
with which they were afterwards mainly to be associated. The
migration to the north occurred at a time when the woollen
industries were paramount and the cotton industries had still
to attain their subsequent stupendous growth. It occurred,
also, long before the Aire and the Calder were made navigable,
so that, in this case, we cannot say the industrial centres
already mentioned as being situated on or near to those two
Yorkshire rivers were set up there, as the towns on the river

[1] The Douglas navigation was afterwards purchased by the proprietors
of the Leeds and Liverpool Canal, who substituted an artificial cut for part
of the natural channel of the river.

Severn had mainly been, in order to secure the convenience of river transport.

The chief reason why the bleak and barren moorlands of the north were preferred to the fair and fertile plains of the south for the further expansion of these great national industries was that, in the days when the steam-engine of James Watt was as yet far off, the heavier rainfall in the English Highlands of the north and north-west, together with the more numerous streams pouring down mountain sides both of greater height and of greater extent than in the south, gave to the cloth-makers, not only the abundant water supply they wanted, but, also, the particular kind of motive power, through the use of water-wheels, on which they then mainly relied for the working of their machinery.

It was in the interests of this power derived from falling water that the textile industries first migrated from the eastern counties—where the streams flow but slowly, and from comparatively slight elevations—to the western counties, where there are streams coming from hills of from 800 to 1000 feet in height. These, for a time, answered better the desired purpose, though only to be more or less discarded, in turn, for northern or north-western streams which, with a greater rainfall, had their rise on heights of from 1500 to 2000 feet, and were so numerous that almost every one of the "small" manufacturers who set up business for himself on the otherwise cheerless slope of a Yorkshire hill-side could have a brook, a rivulet, or a mountain torrent of his own, or, at least, make abundant use of one before it passed on to serve the purposes of his neighbour.

In alluding to the woollen trade as affected by these conditions, Dr Aikin remarks in his "Description of the Country from Thirty to Forty Miles round Manchester" (1795), "It would seem as if a hilly country was particularly adapted to it, since it almost ceases where Yorkshire descends into the plain"; though the position has, of course, been entirely changed by the general resort to steam in preference to water power.

Other industries, besides those relating to textiles, whether woollen or, at a later period, cotton, took advantage of the same favourable conditions, as shown in the case of Sheffield, where the earliest of the cutlers who were to make Hallamshire goods famous throughout the world settled down at the confluence of the Sheaf and the Don because those streams afforded them the best available means of operating their tilt-hammers.[1]

In the early stage of this transition period the streams were desired and utilised solely as an aid to manufacturing purposes. As the towns or the industrial centres developed, however, there grew up increasing need for improved means of transport—supplementary to the roads of that day—in order, more especially, to facilitate the better distribution of the commodities then being produced in ever-increasing quantities. It was this need that led to the Act of 1699, giving powers for rendering the Aire and the Calder navigable. Petitions in favour thereof were presented by the " clothiers " (as cloth-makers were then called) of various towns likely to derive advantage from the scheme, and some of these petitions afford an interesting insight into the conditions under which the cloth industry was carried on in Yorkshire and Lancashire in the closing years of the seventeenth century.

A petition from the " clothiers " of Leeds said, " That Leeds and Wakefield are the principal towns in the north for cloth ; that they are situated on the rivers Ayre and Calder, which have been viewed, and are found capable to be made highways which, if effected, will very much redound to the preservation of the highways and a great improvement of trade ; the petitioners having no conveniency of water carriage within sixteen miles of them, which not only occasions a great expense, but many times great damage to their goods, and sometimes the roads are not passable."

The clothiers of " Ratchdale " (Rochdale) stated that they were " forty miles from any water carriage " ; those of Halifax said they " have no water carriage within thirty miles, and much damage happens through the badness of the roads by the overturning of carriages " ; and those of Wakefield said of the scheme :—

" It will be a great improvement of trade to all the trading towns of the north by reason of the conveniency of water

[1] In giving an account of a visit he paid to Derbyshire in 1713, Dr. William Stukeley says in his "Itinerarium Curiosum" (2nd ed., 1776): "At the smelting works they melt down the lead ore, and run it into a mould, whence it becomes pigs, as they call it ; the bellows continually are kept in motion by running water."

carriage, for want of which the petitioners send their goods twenty-two miles by land carriage (to Rawcliffe) the expense whereof is not only very chargeable but they are forced to stay two months sometimes while the roads are impassable to market, and many times the goods receive considerable damage, through the badness of the roads by overturning."

The general conditions of life in Yorkshire towns in Defoe's day, when the Aire and Calder had been made navigable, but when bad roads still dominated the situation from a social and domestic standpoint, are shown in the account he gives of his visit to Halifax. After explaining how the people devoted themselves mainly to cloth production and imported most of their household requirements, he says :—

" Their Corn comes up in great quantities out of Lincoln, Nottingham and the East Riding ; their Black Cattle and the Horses from the North Riding, their Sheep and Mutton from the adjacent Counties every way, their Butter from the East and North Riding, their Cheese out of Cheshire and Warwickshire, more Black Cattle also from Lancashire. And here the Breeders and Feeders, the Farmers and Country People find Money flowing in plenty from the Manufactures and Commerce ; so that at Halifax, Leeds and the other great manufacturing Towns, and adjacent to these, for the two months of September and October a prodigious Quantity of Black Cattle is sold.

" This Demand for Beef is occasioned thus : the usage of the People is to buy in at that Season Beef sufficient for the whole Year which they kill and salt, and hang up in the Smoke to dry. This way of curing their Beef keeps it all the Winter, and they eat this smoak'd Beef as a very great Rarity.

" Upon this foot 'tis ordinary for a Clothier that has a large Family, to come to Halifax on a Market Day, and buy two or three large Bullocks from eight to ten Pounds a-piece. These he carries home and kills for his Store. And this is the reason that the markets at all those times of the Year are thronged with Black Cattle, as Smithfield is on a Friday, whereas all the rest of the year there is little extraordinary sold there."

We have here full confirmation of what I have already said as to the way in which people in former days provisioned their houses in the autumn for the winter months, during which the roads would be impassable and food supplies from outside unobtainable.

The trading conditions of the period are shown by the accounts of the once-famous cloth market of Leeds given, in his " Ducatus Leodiensis ; or the Topography of Leedes," by Ralph Thoresby (1715), and, also, in his " Tour," by the ever-picturesque Defoe.

Thoresby, who speaks of " the cloathing trade " as being " now the very life of these parts," tells us that the Leeds cloth-market was held on the bridge over the Aire every Tuesday and Saturday down to June 14, 1684, when, for greater convenience, it was removed to Briggate, the " spacious street " leading from the bridge into the town. Already, in Thoresby's day, Leeds was the manufacturing capital of the district, and he speaks of its cloth-market as " the life not of the town only but of these parts of England."

Defoe, in his account of the market, describes it as " indeed a Prodigy of its kind, and not to be equalled in the world." He tells how, making their way to Leeds at an early hour in the morning from the surrounding district, the " clothiers," each bringing, as a rule, only a single piece of cloth, assembled at the various inns, and there remained until the ringing of a bell, at seven o'clock in the summer, or a little later in the winter, announced that trestles, with boards across them for the display of the cloth, had been duly fixed in the roadway, and that the market had opened. Thereupon the clothiers, without rush or haste, and in the most solemn fashion, would leave their inns, and step across the footpath to the " stalls " in the roadway. Standing quite close to one another, they then put down their cloth on the boards, which would soon be completely covered with rolls of cloth arranged side by side. While the clothiers were so engaged, the merchants would have left their houses, entered the market, and begun their inspection of the goods displayed for sale, so that within fifteen minutes of the ringing of the bell the market would be in full operation. When a merchant saw a piece of cloth which suited his requirements he would lean across the boards, and whisper in the ear of the clothier the price he was prepared to give, this practice of whispering being adopted in order that the other clothiers standing immediately alongside should not hear what was said. The clothier agreed or disagreed, without any attempt at " bargaining." If satisfied with the offer, he would instantly pick up the cloth, and go off with it to the merchant's house, where the transaction would be completed. Within less than half an hour the clothiers would be seen thus leaving the market ; in an hour the business would be over, and at half-past eight the bell would be rung again, to announce that the market had closed and that there must be no more sales. Any clothier who had not sold his cloth would then take it back with him to his inn.

" Thus," says Defoe, " you see Ten or Twenty thousand Pounds value in cloth, and sometimes much more, bought and sold in little more than an hour. . . . And that which is most admirable is 'tis all managed with the most profound Silence, and you cannot hear a word spoken in the whole Market, I mean by the Persons buying and selling ; 'tis all done in whisper. . . . By nine a Clock the Boards are taken down, and the street cleared, so that you see no market or Goods any more than if there had been nothing to do ; and this is done twice a week. By this quick Return the Clothiers are constantly supplied with Money, their Workmen are duly paid, and a prodigious Sum circulates thro' the Country every week."

It is no less interesting—and, also, ﾉ o less material to the present inquiry as to the influence of transport conditions on trade—to learn how the cloth purchased in these particular circumstances was disposed of in days when travel through the country was still attended by so many difficulties.

The supplies intended for home use were distributed in this manner : Leeds was the head-quarters of a body of merchants who were in the habit of going all over England with droves of packhorses loaded up with the cloth which had been bought in the open-air market, as already described. These travelling merchants did not sell to householders, since that would have constituted them pedlars. They kept to the wholesale business, dealing only with shopkeepers in the towns or with traders at the fairs ; but they operated on such a scale that, Defoe says, " 'tis ordinary for one of these men to carry a thousand pounds value of Cloth with them at a time, and having sold it at the Fairs or Towns where they go, they send their Horses back for as much more, and this very often in the Summer, for they chuse to travel in the summer, and perhaps towards the Winter time, tho' as little in Winter as they can, because of the badness of the Roads."

Other of the buyers on the Leeds market sent their purchases to London, either carrying out commissions from London traders or forwarding on consignment to factors and warehousemen who themselves supplied wholesale and retail dealers in London, besides despatching great quantities of coarse goods abroad, especially to New England, New York, Virginia, etc. The Russian merchants in London also sent "an exceeding quantity" to St. Petersburg, Riga, Sweden, Dantzic and Pomerania.

Still another group of buyers was represented by those who had commissions direct from traders in Holland, Germany and Austria, the business done by the members of this group being "not less considerable" than that done by the others.

It was mainly on account of this London and foreign trade that the Act for making the rivers Aire and Calder navigable was obtained, there being secured a waterway communication by means of which the cloth could be sent direct from Leeds, Wakefield and other industrial centres to Hull, there to be shipped to London or to Continental ports, as desired.

The facilities for navigation thus afforded subsequently had a still greater influence on the development of the Yorkshire coal trade, coal being taken from Wakefield or Leeds to the Humber, and thence conveyed up the Ouse to York, or to the numerous towns situate on the Trent or other rivers. By the same navigation the Yorkshire towns received most of their supplies, either as imported into Hull from abroad, or as received there from London or the eastern counties, these supplies including butter, cheese, salt, sugar, tobacco, fruit, spices, oil, wine, brandy, hops, lead, and all kinds of heavy or bulky goods. For the merchants of Hull this meant a business to be compared only with that of the merchants of Lynn and Bristol.

Some of the many river improvement Acts passed in the period here under review were not secured without a certain amount of opposition, and the case of the Don, more especially, offers a striking example of that conflict of rival interests, even in the case of rivers, which later on was to give rise to many a Parliamentary battle in the days, first of canals, and then of railways.

How the cutlers of Sheffield and the steel manufacturers and others of Hallamshire in general had been accustomed to forward their goods by road to the inland port of Bawtry, thence to be sent down the Idle and on by the Trent and the Humber to Hull, has already been told. (See pp. 123–4.) There came a time, however, when this preliminary land journey of twenty miles from Sheffield to Bawtry was found of great disadvantage to the trade of the district ; and in 1697 leave was given to bring in a Bill to allow of the Don, already navigable to Doncaster, being rendered navigable to Sheffield, in order that merchandise might be sent by that stream direct from Sheffield to the Ouse, and so on to the Humber and the port of Hull. But the opposition offered by representatives of the Bawtry, Trent and other interests—who rightly foresaw in the scheme impending ruin for most of the traffic on the Idle—was so powerful that the Bill was thrown out. A further Bill, with a like object, was introduced, and strongly supported, in the following Session. It was still more vigorously opposed, there being what Hunter describes as "a war of petitions," and it was not proceeded with.

For a time nothing further was done ; but in the meanwhile Sheffield was rapidly advancing to the position of one of the leading industrial centres in the country, and the compulsory twenty-mile journey by road to the chief port of consignment for Sheffield goods sent to London or abroad when there was a river flowing through Sheffield itself, was felt to be an intolerable infliction, as well as a serious prejudice to the local industries.

In 1722, therefore—twenty-four years after the last of the earlier attempts—the Master Cutler of Sheffield and the Cutlers' Company petitioned Parliament to allow the improvement of the Don navigation to proceed. The corporation of Doncaster sent a like petition, and so did the corporations of Manchester, Stockport and several other places. But the established interests still controlled the situation, and the design once more failed.

Four years later (1726) the Sheffield cutlers made still

another effort, and this time, although the opposition was
again very powerful, it was agreed in Committee of the House
of Commons that power should be given to the Cutlers'
Company to make the Don navigable from Doncaster, not to
Sheffield itself, but to Tinsley, three miles from Sheffield ;
and, also, to maintain a turnpike road from Sheffield to
Tinsley. A Bill to this effect was passed, and in 1727 the
corporation of Doncaster obtained powers to remove certain
obstructions from the Don ; but, under an Act of 1732, the
carrying out of the whole scheme was transferred to an independent body, the Company of Proprietors of the River
Don Navigation. It proved, says Hunter, writing in 1828,
" eminently beneficial to the country " ; but the reader will
see that the Sheffield cutler or manufacturer still had to
forward his goods three miles by road before they could be
sent, first along the Don, then along the Ouse, then down
the Humber to Hull, and then (if they were consigned to
London) by sea along the east coast, and finally up the Thames
to the Metropolis. These were the conditions until the year
1821, when the three-mile journey by road was saved by the
opening of a canal between Sheffield and the Don at Tinsley,
affording, as was said, " easy accommodation with the coast
and London."

CHAPTER XV

DISADVANTAGES OF RIVER NAVIGATION

IT will have been assumed, from the two preceding chapters, that rivers, whether naturally navigable or rendered navigable by art, were of material service in supplementing defective roads, in opening up to communication parts of the country that would then otherwise have remained isolated, and in aiding the development of some of the greatest of our national industries.

While this assumption is well founded, yet, as time went on, the unsatisfactory nature of much of the inland river navigation in this country became more apparent.

Some of the greatest troubles arose from, on the one hand, excess of water in the rivers owing to floods, and, on the other, from inadequate supplies of water due either to droughts or to shallows.

The liability to floods will be at once apparent if the reader considers the extent of the areas from which rain water and the yield of countless springs, brooks, and rivulets may flow into the principal rivers. In the Report of the Select Committee of the House of Lords on Conservancy Boards, 1877, there was published a list which showed that the 210 rivers in England and Wales had catchment basins as follows :—

1000 miles and upwards	11
500 ,, to 1000 miles	14
100 ,, ,, 500 ,,	59
50 ,, ,, 100 ,,	24
10 ,, ,, 50 ,,	102
Total	210

The rivers having catchment basins of 1000 miles or upwards are given thus :—

Name.	County.	Length. Miles.	Area of Basin. sq. miles.	Tributaries. No.	United length. miles.
Humber .	York . .	37	1229	2	55
Mersey .	Lancaster. .	68	1707	6	188
Nen . .	Northampton .	99	1055	1	11
Ouse . .	York . .	59½	4207	11	629
Ouse . .	Cambridge .	156¼	2894	8	212
Severn .	Gloucester .	178	4437	17	450
Thames .	— .	201¼	5162	15	463
Trent . .	Lincoln . .	167½	3543	10	293
Tyne . .	Northumberland	35	1053	6	154
Witham .	Lincoln . .	89	1052	4	75
Wye . .	Hereford . .	148	1655	9	223

In times of heavy storms or of continuous rainy weather, rivers which drain up to 5000 square miles of country may well experience floods involving a serious impediment to navigation.

The Severn, which brings down to the Bristol Channel so much of the water that falls on Plinlimmon and other Welsh hills, and is joined by various streams, draining, altogether, as shown above, an area of 4437 square miles, is especially liable to floods. In a paper read before the Institution of Civil Engineers in 1860, Mr. E. L. Williams stated that floods had been known to raise the height of the Severn 18 ft. in five hours, and they had not infrequently caused it to attain a height of 25 ft. above the level of low water. The Thames and the Trent, also, are particularly liable to floods, and so, down to recent years, when considerable sums were spent on its improvement, was the Weaver.

It has been asserted in various quarters that less water runs in English rivers now than was probably the case centuries ago, when the abundant forests caused a greater rainfall. This may be so, but, on the other hand, a number of witnesses examined before the Select Committee of 1877 expressed the belief that the water flowing into the rivers had increased of recent years, owing to the improved land drainage, which drained off rapidly and sent down to the sea much rain water that previously would have passed into the air again by evaporation.

In the matter of high tides, " Rees' Cyclopædia " (1819) says that the tide " often " rises at the mouth of the Wye

to a height of 40 ft.; while " Chambers' Encyclopædia " gives
47 ft. above low-water mark as the height to which the tide
has been known to rise in the same river at Chepstow.

Of the floods in the Yorkshire Ouse Rodolph De Salis
says in " Bradshaw's Canals and Navigable Rivers of England " (1904): " The non-tidal portion of the river above
Naburn Locks is liable to floods, which at York often reach
a height of 12 ft., and have been known to attain a height
of 16 ft. 6 in. above summer level."

The liability of English rivers to a shortage of water would
seem to be as great as their liability to excess of it. In
Archdeacon Plymley's " General View of the Agriculture
of Shropshire " (1803) there is published a table, compiled
by Telford, giving the heights reached by the Severn between 1789 and 1800. It shows that, as against some very
serious floods and inundations, the river often, during the
dates mentioned, ran for considerable periods with a stream
of no more than sixteen inches of water ; that it frequently
had less than a foot of water ; and that in times of extreme
drought the depth of water had been reduced to nine inches.
In 1796, the period during which barges could be navigated
even down-stream with a paying load did not exceed two
months, and " this interruption," it is stated, " was severely
felt by the coal-masters, the manufacturers of iron, and the
county in general."

The navigation of the Trent is declared in " Rees' Cyclopædia " to be " of vast importance to the country " ; yet
the authority of John Smeaton, who had examined the river
in 1761, is given for the statement that in several places the
ordinary depth of water did not exceed eight inches. In the
upper part of the river there were, in 1765, more than twenty
shallows over which boats could not pass in dry weather
without flushes of water.

The inadequate depth of water may be due, not alone to
drought, but to the formation of shoals or shallows owing to
the rapid fall of the river, its excessive width, or the amount
of sediment brought down from the hill-sides or washed
from the bed over which it flows. Alternatively, much silting-
up may be caused by the sand brought into the river by in-
coming tides, and not always washed out again by out-going
tides.

In an undated pamphlet, entitled " Reflections on the General Utility of Inland Navigation to the Commercial and Landed Interests of England, with Observations on the Intended Canal from Birmingham to Worcester," by the proprietors of the Staffordshire Canal, stress is laid on the trouble caused by the shoals in the Severn, and some facts are given as to the way in which traders had to meet the uncertainties offered by river transport.   The pamphlet says :—

" A principal defect of the present conveyance arises from the shoals in the river Severn above Worcester, an evil incurable.   The fall from Stourport to Diglis, near Worcester, is nineteen feet ; and the river is, what this fact alone would prove, full of shoals.   These shoals impede the current of the stream, and retain the water longer in the bed of the river. Let these shoals be removed, the water will pass off, and the *whole* of the river become too shallow for navigation.   Locks on the river could alone correct this defect ; but these would overflow the meadows, impede the drainage of the land, and do an injury to the landowners, which parliament can never sanction.

" This defect gives rise to others—to *uncertainty as to the time of the conveyance*—for it is only at particular periods that there is water sufficient for the navigation—to delays from a want of men[1] and expence from the increased number which the strong current requires.   It gives rise, also, to a double transhipping of commodities sent from Birmingham down the Severn, first from the canal at Stourport, and secondly at or near Worcester, as the barges which this shoal water will admit are too small to navigate much below.

" The delays and damage incidental to such a navigation have induced the manufacturers of Birmingham to employ land carriage at a great expence—many waggons are constantly employed at the heavy charge of 4*l.* per ton from Birmingham to Bristol alone to convey goods or manufactures which cannot await the delay or damage to which in the present navigation they are necessarily exposed ;—large

---

[1] Barges were towed up-stream on the Severn by men.   Writing in 1803, Archdeacon Plymley said : " A horse towing-path is now established from Bewdley to Coalbrookdale, which is more and more used, and it is hoped will soon be extended, the office of towing barges by men being looked upon as very injurious to their manners."

quantities of manufactures and the materials of manufactures are likewise sent to Diglis to be conveyed by the Severn in vessels that cannot navigate higher up the river."

In the Trent frequent shallowness of water was due, partly to the excessive breadth of the stream, in places, and partly to the large quantity of " warp," or silt, brought into the river from the Humber estuary by the tides, and left there until scoured out again when the river was in flood.

The Wash group of rivers was specially liable to the silting-up process. Nathaniel Kinderly, writing of the position at Lynn in 1751, said : " The Haven is at present so choaked up with sand that at Low-water it is become almost a Wash, so as to have been frequently fordable." Of the Nen he says it " cannot possibly be preserved long, but is in danger of being absolutely lost," owing to the silting-up of its bed. As for the Witham, the welfare of the port of Boston was threatened so far back as the year 1671, judging from an Act (22 & 23 Chas. II. c. 25) passed in that year, the preamble of which stated :—

" Whereas there hath been for some hundreds of yeares a good navigacion betwixt the burrough of Boston and the river of Trent by and through the citty of Lincolne, and thereby a great trade managed to the benefit of those parts of Lincolnshire, and some parts of Nottinghamshire, and Yorkshire, which afforded an honest employment and livelyhood to great numbers of people. But at present the said navigacion is much obstructed and in great decay by reason that the rivers or auntient channells of Witham and Fossdyke, which runn betwixt Boston and Trent are much silted and landed up and thereby not passable with boats and lyters as formerly, to the great decay of the trade and intercourse of the said citty and all market and other towns neare any of the said rivers, which hath producet in them much poverty and depopulation. For remedy thereof and for improvement of the said navigacion, may it please your most excellent Majestie that it may be enacted," etc.

Among various other conditions of river navigation may be mentioned—the extremely serpentine courses of some of the rivers, two miles often having to be made for each mile of real advance ; the ever-varying channels in some of the streams ; the arduous labour of towing against strong currents, especially when, in the absence of towing-paths for horses, this work had to be done by men ; and the destruction, by floods, of the river banks or of works constructed on them.

I have here sought to catalogue, with passing illustrations, the principal troubles attendant on inland river navigation. That the physical disadvantages in question have continued, in spite of all River Improvement Acts, and notwithstanding a considerable outlay, may be seen from the report issued, in 1909, by the Royal Commission on Canals and Waterways.

In regard to the Thames the report says that the commercial traffic above Staines has become a very insignificant quantity, and " if the Thames is to be converted into an artery of commercial navigation, there is need for much improvement above Windsor, but still more so above Reading."

On the Severn there is now practically no navigation above Stourport. Much money has been spent on the river since the Severn Navigation Act of 1842 ; the channel has been deepened and dredged, and, " up to Worcester, at any rate, the river is now one of the best of English waterways." But, in spite of the considerable sums expended on improvements, the traffic fell from 323,329 tons in 1888 to 288,198 tons in 1905, a decline in seventeen years of over 35,000 tons. High water in the river renders it impossible for the larger estuary-going vessels to pass under certain of the bridges, so that, as one witness said, " A vessel may go up when the water is low, and a freshet may come, and the vessel may not be able to get back again for perhaps many days."

The Warwickshire Avon, once navigable from Stratford to the Severn, is now navigable only from Evesham, and even from that point " there is hardly any commercial traffic."

The Trent is navigable to-day to the junction with the Trent and Mersey Canal, at Derwent mouth, " when there *is* plenty of water." The report says :—

" The great difficulty on the Trent, in its present condition, is the want of sufficient depth of water in dry seasons ; in wet seasons traffic is impeded by floods. The river Trent is a fine river and a most important part of the main route connecting the Midland waterway system and the town and colliery district of Nottingham with each other and with the estuary of the Humber. It appears, for want of necessary works of improvement, to be in an inefficient state for these purposes. There is, at present, no certainty that a barge carrying seventy or eighty tons of cargo from the port of Hull to Newark or Nottingham will arrive at its destination without being lightened on its way. A witness said, ' Very often the traffic in dry seasons is left waiting for two or three weeks on the road between Hull and Newark, which, of course, is a very poor way of getting on with business.' "

On the Ouse (York), below Naburn Lock, the conservators find it difficult to keep the channel at its proper depth by reason of the great deposits of floating sand, or " warp," distributed by the tides, the scour of the river being insufficient to carry the warp out to sea. Vessels are at times unable to navigate for several days, obstructive shoals are formed, and the line of the channel is frequently altered.

On the Bedford Ouse the traffic on the upper parts of the river has come to an end, and, though there is still a small amount between Lynn and St. Ives, " the river is in many places very shallow and choked with weeds and mud, so that barges are often stopped for days, and the use of steam traction, up to St. Ives, is impossible."

The Nen from Northampton to Wisbech is " navigable with difficulty "—where the water is sufficient at all—by barges of the smallest size ; but sometimes navigation even by these barges is impracticable for weeks together in certain parts of the river. Between Northampton and Peterborough the course of the Nen is extremely tortuous. " It would," says the report, " take a barge nearly three days to travel the sixty-one miles by water, while the railway can carry goods from Northampton to Peterborough in two hours."

It is thus evident that rivers, whether navigable naturally or rendered so by art, must be regarded as water highways possessed of considerable disadvantages and drawbacks in respect to inland traffic when they are on the scale and of the type found in England. Dependent on the forces of Nature—ever active and ever changing—rivers must needs be the exact opposite of the fixed and constant railway line unless those forces can be effectually controlled under conditions physically practicable and not too costly. " Rivers," says L. F. Vernon-Harcourt, in his book on " Rivers and Canals," " are not always suitable for navigation, in their natural condition, even in the lower portions of their course ; and, owing to the continual changes taking place in their channels and at their outlets, they are liable to deteriorate if left to themselves." Left to themselves the English rivers, like the Roman and the British roads, were for a thousand years after the departure of the Romans, and the liability to deteriorate may well have shown itself during this period, before even the earliest of the River Improvement Acts was passed ; though the deterioration due to the ceaseless operations of Nature may obviously continue in spite of all Acts of Parliament, and notwithstanding a great expenditure of money.

The fate that has overtaken so many English rivers which once counted as highways of commerce may be compared with the fate that, also through the operation mainly of natural causes, has overtaken many of our once flourishing sea ports.

When, in the thirteenth century, Liverpool was raised to the rank of a free borough, there were between thirty and forty places which, whether situated on the coast or some distance inland (as in the case of York), were counted as sea-ports. Their order of importance at that time is shown by the following table (taken from Baines's " History of Liverpool "), which gives the taxation then levied on each ; though the amounts stated should be multiplied by fifteen to ascertain their equivalent in the money of to-day :—

	£	s.	d.		£	s.	d.
London	836	12	10	Seaford	12	12	2
Boston	788	15	3	Shoreham	20	4	9
Southampton	712	3	7	Chichester	23	6	0
Lincoln	656	12	2	Exmouth	14	6	6
Lynn	651	11	11	Dartmouth	3	0	6
Hull	344	14	7	Esse	7	4	8
York	175	8	10	Fowey	48	15	11
Dunwich	104	9	0	Pevensey	16	17	10
Grimsby	91	15	1	Coton		11	11
Yarmouth	54	16	6	Whitby		4	0
Ipswich	60	8	4	Scarborough	22	14	0
Colchester	16	8	0	Selby	17	11	8
Sandwich	16	0	0	Barton	33	11	2
Dover	32	6	1	Hedon	18	15	9
Rye	10	13	5	Norwich	6	19	10
Winchelsea	62	2	4	Orford	11	7	0

Of these ports the majority have ceased to be available for the purposes of foreign commerce. Dunwich, once a considerable town, the seat of a bishopric, and the metropolis of East Anglia, had its harbour and its royal and episcopal palaces swept away by encroachments of the sea. Hedon, in the East Riding of Yorkshire, returned two members of Parliament in the reign of Edward I., and was a more important centre of trade and commerce than Hull; but its harbour, getting choked up by sand, was converted into a luxuriant meadow, and the ports of Hull and Grimsby now reign in its stead. Sandwich, Romney, Hythe, all the Cinque ports except Dover, and various other ports, got choked up with sand, while others that have been able to retain a certain amount of traffic are to-day only the ghosts of their former selves.

It is certain that in the case of English navigable rivers of any type, much might require to be done, and spent, in order to keep navigation open. With most of them it was a matter of carrying on an unceasing warfare with elemental conditions. Patriotic men like Sandys, Mathew and Yarranton might bring forward their schemes, companies might raise and spend much money on river navigation, and municipal corporations might do what they could, within the range of their means and powers; but the inherent defects and limitations of the navigation itself were not always to be overcome by any practical combination of patriotism, enterprise and generous expenditure even when—and this was far from being always the case—the requisite funds were actually available.

Vernon-Harcourt is of opinion that "the regulation, improvement and control of rivers constitute one of the most important, and, at the same time, one of the most difficult, branches of civil engineering"; and this difficulty must have been found still greater in the last half of the seventeenth and the first half of the eighteenth centuries, when river improvement was engaging so much attention, but when civil engineering was far less advanced than is the case to-day.

Whatever, too, the degree of success attained in the efforts made to overcome the results of floods and droughts, of shoals and shallows, of river mouths choked by sand washed in from the estuaries, of streams unduly broad from lack of

adequate embankments, and of ever-varying channels, whatever the energy and the outlay in meeting or trying to meet
conditions such as these, there still remained the consideration that, even assuming all the difficulties in regulating,
improving and controlling could be surmounted, river transport itself was an inadequate alternative to bad roads, (1)
because of the length of the land journey that might have
to be made before the river was reached ; and (2) because
even the best of the rivers only served certain parts of the
country, and left undeveloped other districts which were
unable to derive due benefit from their great natural resources
by reason of defective communications.

Each of these points calls for some consideration, in order
that the position of the traders at the period in question
may be clearly understood.

In regard to the distance at which manufacturers might be
situated from a navigable river, I would point to the position
of the pottery trade in North Staffordshire.

The pottery industry had been introduced into Burslem in
1690, though it made comparatively little progress until the
time of Josiah Wedgwood, who began to manufacture there
in 1759. One of the reasons for the slow growth, down to his
day, was the trouble and expense the pottery-makers experienced in getting their raw materials and in sending away
their manufactured goods.

Following on the improvement of the Weaver, under the
Act of 1720, there were three rivers of which the pottery-
makers in North Staffordshire made more or less use—the
Weaver itself, the Trent and the Severn. On the Weaver
the nearest available point to the Potteries was Winsford
Bridge, a distance of twenty miles by road. On the Trent
the principal river-port for the Potteries was Willington,
about four miles east of Burton-on-Trent, and over thirty
miles by road from the Potteries. To the Severn inland ports
the distances by road from the Potteries, via Eccleshall and
Newport, were :—

From	To	Miles.
Newcastle (Staff.) .	Bridgnorth . .	. 39
Burslem . . .	,, . .	. 42½
Newcastle (Staff.) .	Bewdley . .	. 54
Burslem . . .	,, . .	. 57½

From Winsford the pottery-makers received, by pack-horse or waggon, supplies of clay which had been sent from Devonshire or other western counties by sea to Liverpool, and there transhipped in barges, in which it was sent twenty miles down the Weaver, thence to be carried twenty miles by road. From Willington they received flints which had been brought by sea, first to Hull, then forwarded by barge along the Humber to the Trent, and so on to Willington, to be carried thirty miles by road.

Manufactured pottery for London or for the Continent was sent by road to Willington, and then along the Trent and the Humber to Hull, where it was re-shipped to destination. Exports were, also, despatched either to the Severn, along which they were taken in barges to Bristol, or via the Weaver to Liverpool. Concerning the Severn route it is stated in " The Advantages of Inland Navigation " (1766), by Richard Whitworth, afterwards M.P. for Stafford : " There are three pot-waggons go from Newcastle and Burslem weekly, through Eccleshall and Newport to Bridgnorth, and carry about eight tons of pot-ware every week, at 3*l*. per ton. The same waggons load back with ten tons of close goods, consisting of white clay, grocery and iron, at the same price, delivered on their road to Newcastle. Large quantities of pot-ware are con-veyed on horses' backs from Burslem and Newcastle to Bridgnorth and Bewdley for exportation—about one hundred tons yearly, at 2*l*. 10*s*. per ton."

The cost of land transport, along roads of the worst pos-sible description, was considerable in itself. In a pamphlet published in 1765, under the title of " A View of the Ad-vantages of Inland Navigations, with a Plan of a Navigable Canal intended for a Communication between the Ports of Liverpool and Hull " (said to have been written by Josiah Wedgwood and his partner, Bentley), it is stated that be-tween Birmingham and London the cost of road transport amounted to about eight shillings per ton for every ten miles, but along the route of the proposed canal, and in many other places, the cost was nine shillings per ton for every ten miles. The pamphlet adds, on this particular point :—

" The burthen of so expensive a land carriage to Winsford and Willington, and the uncertainty of the navigations from those places to Frodsham, in Cheshire, and Wilden, in Derby-

shire, occasioned by the floods in winter and the numerous
shallows in summer, are more than these low-priced manufactures can bear ; and without some such relief as this under
consideration, must concur, with their new established competitors in France, and our American colonies, to bring these
potteries to a speedy decay and ruin."

It was, again, as we further learn from Whitworth's little
work, by the navigable Severn and Bristol that even Manchester manufacturers sent their goods to foreign countries
in the days when Liverpool had still to attain pre-eminence
over the south-western port.   Every week, we are told, 150
packhorses went from Manchester through Stafford to Bewdley
and Bridgnorth, these being in addition to two broad-wheel
waggons which carried about 312 tons of cloth and Manchester
wares in the year by the same route, at a cost of £3 10s. per
ton.   The distance, via Stafford, from Manchester to Bridgnorth is 84 miles ; that from Manchester to Bewdley is
99 miles, and what the roads at this time were like we have
already seen.

The quantity of salt sent from Cheshire to Willington, to
proceed thence along the Trent to Hull for re-shipment to
London and elsewhere, is put in Josiah Wedgwood's pamphlet
at " many hundred tons " a year.   The navigable Trent was
thus taken advantage of for the purposes of distribution ;
but to get to Willington from the Northwich or other salt
works in Cheshire involved a road journey of about forty miles.

Whitworth also gives much information as to what he calls
the " amazing " development the iron industry had undergone along the Severn valley at the time he wrote (1766) ;
and he more especially mentions that the total annual output of twenty-two furnaces and forges situate within a distance
of four miles of the route of a canal he proposed should be
constructed between Bristol, Liverpool, and Hull was £624,000
—a figure which in those days appears to have been regarded
as something prodigious.   But the iron-works in question,
though having the advantage of the navigable Severn in one
direction, suffered from transport disadvantages in another,
since their Cumberland ore (of which, says Whitworth, a
very small furnace used at least 1100 tons a year) was brought
down the Weaver to Winsford, in Cheshire, whence it had to
be transported by road to the works on the Severn " at six

shillings per ton for a very small distance." On the basis of
52,780 tons only (though, we are told, " they frequently send
iron to . . . Chester and many other places at a great distance "), Whitworth calculates that the 32 forges in question
were then paying a net sum of £32,500 a year for land transport, only, of the ore and pig-iron they received, and of the
manufactured iron they sent away. " I have dwelt thus
long," he says, in concluding his somewhat copious details,
" upon the iron trade to show that no branch of manufacture
can reap more immediate benefit from the making of these
canals for navigation, or more sensibly feel the want of them
when other ports of the Kingdom have them."

Of coal, he further shows, some 12,000 tons a year were
going from the Shropshire collieries to Nantwich, on the
Weaver, at a cost of ten shillings per ton for land carriage
only, apart from the supplementary cost of river transport.
In the opposite direction the farmers of Cheshire and Staffordshire brought about 1000 tons of cheese annually, by road,
to Bridgnorth fair—presumably for redistribution thence via
the Severn among the various centres of population in the
western counties, and also in Wales. The cheese was carried
in waggons, and, on the basis of the journey taking, altogether,
three or four days, Whitworth calculates that the cost to
the farmers in getting the cheese to Bridgnorth must have
been about thirty shillings for every two tons.

One of the subsidiary disadvantages attendant on river
transport of which mention should be made was the pilfering
of goods that went on, more especially when the barges were
stopped in the open country, perhaps for days together, by
reason of shallow water. In " A View of the Advantages of
Inland Navigations " it is said, on this point :—

" It is, also, another circumstance not unworthy of notice
in favour of canals, when compared with river navigation,
that as the conveyance upon the former is more speedy and
without interruptions and delays, to which the latter are
very liable, opportunities of pilfering earthen wares, and
other small goods, and stealing and adulterating wine and
spirituous liquors, are thereby in a great measure prevented.
The losses, disappointments and discredit of the manufacturers, arising from this cause are so great that they frequently choose to send their goods by land at three times

the expense of water carriage, and sometimes even refuse to supply their orders at all, rather than run the risque of forfeiting their credit and submitting to the deductions that are made on this account.

" We may also add, with respect to the potteries in Staffordshire, that this evil discourages merchants abroad from dealing with those manufacturers, and creates innumerable misunderstandings between them and the manufacturers."

These complaints seem to have been made not without good cause. In 1751 it had been found expedient to pass an Act " for the more effectual prevention of robberies and thefts upon any navigable river, ports of entry or discharge, wharves or quays adjacent." Any person stealing goods of the value of forty shillings from any ship, barge, boat, or any vessel on any navigable river or quay adjacent thereto, was, on conviction, to *suffer death !* The penalty seems to have been modified into one of transportation ; and in 1752 thirteen persons were convicted under the new Act, and sent across the seas.

Many traders could not derive any advantage from river transport. This was the case with the cheese-makers of Warwickshire when they sought to compete with those of Cheshire, or, alternatively, with those of Gloucester, who could take their cheese by road to Lechdale or Crickdale, on the Thames, and send it down that river to London. "The Warwickshire Men," says Defoe, "have no Water Carriage at all, or at least not 'till they have carry'd it a long way by Land to Oxford, but as their Quantity is exceedingly great, and they supply not only the City of London but also the Counties of Essex, Suffolk, Norfolk, Cambridge, Huntingdon, Hertford, Bedford, and Northampton, the Gross of their Carriage is by mere dead Draught, and they carry it either to London by Land, which is full an hundred miles, and so the London cheese-mongers supply the said counties of Essex, Suffolk and Norfolk, besides Kent and Sussex and Surrey by Sea and River Navigation ; or the Warwickshire Men carry it by Land once a Year to Sturbridge Fair, whence the Shopkeepers of all the Inland Country above named come to buy it ; in all which Cases Landcarriage being long, when the Ways were generally bad it made it very dear to the Poor, who are the chief Consumers."

While, also, Bedfordshire was producing " great quantities of the best wheat in England," the wheat itself had to be taken, from some parts of the county, a distance of twenty miles by road to the markets of Hertford or Hitchin, whence, after being bought and ground into flour, it was taken on, still by road, a further distance of twenty-five or thirty miles to London. The farmers and millers of Bedfordshire were thus unable to enjoy the same advantages of river transport as were open to those on the Wey or the Upper Thames.

In addition to all this, representations came from many different quarters of the neglect of natural advantages and other opportunities where means of transport apart from bad roads were wholly lacking. Numerous pamphlets issued in favour of one canal scheme or another pointed to the opportunities that were being lost or allowed to remain dormant. In, for example, " A Cursory View of the Advantages of an Intended Canal from Chesterfield to Gainsborough," published in 1769, it was said : " The country contiguous to Chesterfield abounds chiefly with bulky and ponderous Products, such as Lead, Corn, Timber, Coals, Ironstones and a considerable Manufacture of earthen Ware, all of which have been for Ages past conveyed by Land, at a prodigious Expense." An advocate of a navigable canal between Liverpool and Hull had much to say about the undeveloped resources of that district. Whitworth declared that there were " many large mines of valuable contents," such as stone, iron ore, and marble, together with " quarries of various sorts," that would be " opened and set to work," if only inland navigation were better developed, while the cheapening of the cost of raw materials would, he declared, lead manufacturers to embark on new enterprises. Archdeacon Plymley told how, even at the date he wrote (1803), there was, in many of the midland and southern parishes of Shropshire, " no tolerable horse-road whatever," adding, " and in some that have coal and lime these articles are nearly useless from the difficulty of bringing any carriage to them."

However substantial, therefore, the results to which the navigable rivers had led, it was found by the middle of the eighteenth century that there was real need for entirely new efforts, and these were now to be made in the direction of supplementing alike rivers and roads by artificial waterways.

CHAPTER XVI

THE initiation, in the middle of the eighteenth century, of the British Canal Era was primarily due, not to any examples in canal construction already offered by the ancients, by the Chinese and other Eastern nations, or by Continental countries, but to a natural transition from certain forms of river improvement already carried out in England.

I have shown, on page 131, that when, in 1661, Sir William Sandys obtained his Act for making the Wye and the Lugg navigable, he secured powers, not only for the usual deepening and embanking of the river itself, but for cutting new channels where these might be of advantage, in order to avoid windings of the stream or lengths thereof which offered exceptional difficulties to navigation. In proportion as river improvement increased, the adoption of these " side cuts," as they were called, with pound-locks to guarantee their water supply, was more and more resorted to, and they became one of the most important of the measures by which it was sought to overcome the difficulties that river navigation so often presented.

In 1755 the Corporation of Liverpool and a number of merchants of that port obtained Parliamentary powers to deepen three streams flowing from the St. Helens coal fields and combining to form the Sankey Brook, which drains into the Mersey at a point two miles below Warrington. The promoters sought, by making the Sankey Brook navigable, to bring Liverpool into direct communication with the twelve or fourteen rich beds of coal existing in the St. Helens district of Lancashire, and thus to gain a great advantage for their town.

For many generations the fuel consumed at Liverpool consisted mainly of peat, or turf, of which there were great quantities in Lancashire. At one time, says Baines, in his

" History of the Commerce and Town of Liverpool," the turbaries around the town were considered of great value. The Act passed in 1720 for the navigation of the Douglas had allowed of coal from the pits at Wigan being taken down that river to the Ribble estuary, and then along the coast to the Mersey estuary, and so on to Liverpool ; but the advantage which would be offered by a shorter and safer route was obvious, and the Sankey Brook scheme was taken up with much earnestness.

The original idea, that of making the brook itself capable of being navigated, was found to be impracticable. Not only did the stream wind a great deal, but after heavy rains on the surrounding hills the whole valley through which the brook ran was liable to floods, and these would have effectively stopped navigation so long as they continued. Happily the powers obtained by the promoters included one which allowed of " a side cut " ; and the first plan was abandoned in favour of a canal separate from the brook, though cut parallel with it somewhat higher on the hillsides, where the floods would be less felt. The canal was to be provided with locks, overcoming the fall of 90 feet in twelve miles to the Mersey, together with a pound, fed by the brook, on the highest level, to ensure an adequate water supply.

The immediate result of the construction of this pioneer canal was, not only to provide a convenient coal supply for Liverpool, but, also, in conjunction with the earlier rendering of the Weaver navigable, to put the salt industry of Cheshire in direct water communication with the Lancashire coalfields. These advantages led (1) to a great expansion of the Cheshire salt industry ; (2) to a substantial increase in the export of salt from Liverpool ; and (3) to the ruin of the salt trade of Newcastle-on-Tyne, since, when the makers on the Weaver could readily get an abundance of coal, they, with their great natural stores of brine noted for its superlative quality and strength had a great advantage over the makers on the Tyne, who obtained their salt from the waters of the sea.

It is thus incontestable that the Sankey Brook Canal both started the Canal Era and formed the connecting link between the river improvement schemes of the preceding 100

years and the canal schemes which, themselves a great
advance thereon, were to be substituted for them, only to be
supplanted in| turn |by the still further development in
inland communication brought about by the locomotive.

All the same, it was the canals of Francis, Duke of Bridgewater, as constructed by James Brindley, a remarkable genius
and a great engineer, which gave the main incentive to the
canal movement.

The chief purpose of the Bridgewater canals was to meet
the deficiencies of the Mersey and Irwell navigation by providing new waterways, cut through the dry land, and carried
across valleys and even over rivers without any connection
with streams already navigable or capable of being rendered
navigable,—an advance on the precedent established by the
Sankey Canal.

The Duke's first artificial waterway was from his collieries
at Worsley to the suburbs of Manchester. His coal beds at
Worsley were especially rich and valuable ; but, although
they were only about seven miles from Manchester, and
although Manchester was greatly in need of a better coal
supply for industrial and domestic purposes, it was practically
impossible to get the coal carried thither from Worsley at
reasonable cost. The seven-mile journey by bad roads was
not to be thought of. The alternative was transport by the
Mersey and Irwell navigation, which was, in fact, within
convenient reach of the collieries. But the company of proprietors would not abate their full charge of 3s. 6d. per ton
for every ton of coal taken along the navigation even in the
Duke's own boats, and in 1759 the Duke obtained powers to
construct an independent canal. Possessing no technical
skill himself (though he is said to have been greatly impressed
by what he had seen, in his travels, of the grand canal of
Languedoc, in the south of France), he called in James
Brindley to undertake the carrying out of his plans.

Born in 1716, in the High Peak of Derbyshire, and appren-
ticed to a wheelwright whose calling he adopted, Brindley
had been brought up entirely without school learning. Though
in his apprenticeship days he taught himself to write, his
spelling was so primitive that even in his advanced years he
wrote—in a scarcely decipherable hand—" novicion " for
navigation, " draing " for drawing, " scrwos " for screws,

" ochilor servey " for ocular survey, and so on. But he made up for his lack of education by being a perfect genius in all matters calling for mechanical skill, combining therewith a quickness of observation, a fertility of resource, and a power of adaptability which led to no problem being too great for him to solve, and no difficulty too great for him to overcome. Arthur Young, who had opportunities of judging of his work and character, speaks of his " bold and decisive strokes of genius," and tells of his " penetration, which sees into futurity, and prevents obstructions unthought of by the vulgar mind merely by foreseeing them."

Under Brindley's direction the canal from Worsley to Manchester was duly constructed, and, though a professional engineer had derided, as " a castle in the air," Brindley's design of carrying the canal on a viaduct over the Irwell at Barton (in order to maintain the waterway at the same level, and so avoid the use of locks down one side of the river valley and up the other), the result showed that the new plan (sanctioned by a further Act obtained in 1760) was perfectly feasible, and had been carried out with complete success. To coal consumers in Manchester the new water-way meant that they could obtain their fuel at half the price they had previously paid, while to the Duke it meant that he now had a market for all the coal his collieries could produce.

The canal from Worsley to Manchester was opened for traffic in July, 1761 ; but before the financial results of the one scheme had been established the Duke had projected another and still more ambitious scheme—that of a canal between Manchester and Liverpool, on the surveys for which Brindley started in September of the same year.

The need for a further improvement in the transport con-ditions between Manchester and Liverpool was undeniable. The opening of the Mersey and Irwell navigation, under the Act of 1720, had been of advantage when bad roads were the only means of communication ; but there were disadvantages in river transport which were now felt all the more because in forty years both Manchester and Liverpool had made much progress, and the necessity for efficient and economical transport between the two places was greater than ever.

The Mersey and Irwell navigation followed, in the first place, a very winding course, the bends and turns being such that the rivers took from thirty to forty miles to pass a distance of, as the crow flies, not more than twenty or twenty-five. Then the boats could not pass from Liverpool up to the first lock, above Warrington Bridge, without the assistance of a high tide, and they could only pass the numerous fords and shallows higher up the stream in great freshes or, in dry seasons, by the drawing of great quantities of water from the locks above. Alternatively, there might be an excess of water due to winter floods, and then navigation would be stopped altogether. Aikin, in referring to the navigation in the book he published in 1795, says : " The want of water in droughts, and its too great abundance in floods, are circumstances under which this, as well as most other river navigations, has laboured." He adds : " It has been an expensive concern, and has, at times, been more burthensome to its proprietors than useful to the public." Even in the most favourable conditions of tide or water supply, the boats had to be dragged up and down the stream by men, who did the work of beasts of burden until the construction of the rival waterway led to the navigation proprietors employing horses or mules instead.

That there were great delays in the river transport, occasioning much loss and inconvenience to Manchester traders, will be easily imagined. As it happened, too, whether the navigation were burthensome to the proprietors or not, they took the fullest advantage they could out of their monopoly, at the expense of the traders. They maintained the highest rates in their power, and when goods were damaged in transit, or when serious losses were sustained through delays, they refused all redress.

It is no wonder that, in all these circumstances, the Manchester merchants were often obliged to return even to the bad roads for their transport, and this although road carriage between Manchester and Liverpool cost forty shillings a ton, as against twelve shillings a ton by river. The traders of each town welcomed the Duke of Bridgewater's proposal to construct a competitive waterway which would be navigable at all times, independently of tides, of droughts and of floods, would be nine miles shorter than the rivers, and the tariff on which for the goods carried was not to exceed six shillings per ton.

Manchester residents were no less in need of improved communication than were the Manchester and Liverpool traders. Smiles, in his "Life of James Brindley," speaks of the difficulty experienced in supplying the increasing population with food, and says : "In winter, when the roads were closed, the place was in the condition of a beleaguered town, and even in summer, the land about Manchester itself being comparatively sterile, the place was badly supplied with fruit, vegetables and potatoes, which, being brought from considerable distances, slung across horses' backs, were so dear as to be beyond the reach of the mass of the population. The distress caused by this frequent dearth of provisions was not effectually remedied until the canal navigation became completely opened up."

Nevertheless, the opposition offered to the Duke of Bridgewater's new scheme was vigorous in the extreme. His first project for taking the Worsley coals to Manchester by canal had gone through unopposed ; but the second one, which seemed to threaten the very existence of the Mersey and Irwell navigation, put the proprietors thereof on their most active defence. Just as those having vested interests in the Idle and the Trent had opposed the improvement of the Don, so now did the river interests rise in arms against the canal interests, foreshadowing the time when these, in turn, would fight against the railways. "Not even," says Clifford, in his "History of Private Bill Legislation," "the battles of the gauges, or any of the great territorial struggles between our most powerful railway companies, were more hotly contested than the Duke of Bridgewater's attack in 1761–2 upon the monopoly of the Mersey and Irwell navigation."

When the Duke applied for powers to construct his canal from Manchester to Runcorn, where it would connect with the Mersey, the proprietors of the Mersey and Irwell navigation petitioned against it on the ground that there was no necessity for the canal as the Mersey and Irwell navigation, with which it would run parallel, could convey more goods than the existing conditions of trade required ; that the canal could confer no real advantage on the public; that the proprietors of the river navigation had spent over £18,000 thereon ; that "great part of their respective fortunes" was at stake ; that they had expended their money on the navigation on the faith of their being protected by Parliament; and that for Parliament now to allow a canal to be established to compete with them would be a gross interference with their vested rights. Active opposition was also offered by landowners whose property was to be either taken for the canal or, as they argued, would be deteriorated by it in value; and still more opposition came from traders interested in the river navigation. The controversy of the pro-canal and anti-canal parties even got mixed up with politics, Brindley writing in his notebook that " the Toores mad had agane ye Duk " (" the Tories made head against the Duke ").

But, in the result, the Duke got his Bill, and Brindley proceeded to make the canal. It proved to be a far more costly work than had been anticipated. In a total length of about twenty-four miles from Longford Bridge, Manchester (where it connected with the Worsley Canal), to Runcorn, it passed through a bog with a quicksand bottom; it crossed two rivers; it required numerous aqueducts, and it necessitated the provision of many road bridges and culverts, together with a flight of locks at Runcorn to overcome the difference between the canal level and the Mersey level, this being the first occasion on which locks of this kind had been constructed in England.

Even the Duke of Bridgewater's ample fortune did not suffice to meet the expense of the costly work he had thus taken upon himself. There came a time when his means were exhausted, and he found the greatest difficulty in replenishing them. No one either in Liverpool or in Manchester would honour for him a bill for £500 on a then doubtful enterprise. There were Saturday nights when the Duke had not sufficient money to pay the men's wages, and when he had to raise loans of £5 or £10 from among his tenants. He reduced his personal expenditure to £400 a year, while the recompense that Brindley received from him for carrying out schemes which were to be the wonder of England and introduce a new era in locomotion never exceeded three-and-sixpence a day, and was more often only half a crown a day.

The Duke eventually surmounted his financial difficulties by borrowing, altogether, £25,000 from Messrs. Child, the

London bankers, and the new canal was partly opened for traffic in 1767, although the Runcorn locks were not completed till 1773. The total amount spent by the Duke on his two canals was £220,000.

In 1772 the Duke added to the usefulness of his Manchester-to-Runcorn canal by establishing passenger boats which could accommodate sixty passengers, and on which they were carried twenty miles for a shilling. He afterwards had larger boats, holding from 80 to 120 passengers, the fares on these being 1s., 1s. 6d. and 2s. 6d. per twenty miles, according to class. Each of these boats, says Macpherson, in his "Annals of Commerce," was "provided with a coffee house kept by the master ; wherein his wife serves the company with wine and other refreshments."

The effect of the new canal on the trade and commerce of Manchester and Liverpool was considerable. It diverted to Liverpool the stream of export traffic which had previously gone from Manchester via Bridgnorth and the Severn to Bristol ; it enabled Manchester manufacturers to obtain raw materials more readily from Liverpool, to supplement the cheaper supplies of coal they were already obtaining from Worsley ; and it opened up the port of Liverpool to a wider stretch of country than could otherwise benefit from the facilities thereof, to the advantage both of Liverpool itself and of industrial Lancashire, though other canal schemes, leading to like results, were to follow.

Even before the Manchester and Runcorn Canal was opened for traffic, Brindley had started on a much bolder project. The new scheme was one for a canal connecting the Mersey with the Trent, and, also, with the Severn, thus opening up direct inland water communication between Liverpool, Hull and Bristol, and affording an alternative to road transport not only for the Potteries, but, by means of branch canals, for the industrial centres of Staffordshire and Worcestershire, then, as it were, more or less land-locked.

In the same year (1755) in which the Bill for the construction of the Sankey Canal was obtained, the Corporation of Liverpool already had under consideration a scheme for a canal from the Mersey to the Trent ; but no definite action was then taken, and it was left for private enterprise to carry out the idea. The chief promoters were Earl Gower (ancestor of the Duke of Sutherland), the Duke of Bridgewater, the Earl of Stamford, Josiah Wedgwood, and various other land-owners and manufacturers. Parliamentary powers were obtained in 1766, and the work of construction, as planned by Brindley, was begun at once. The name of " Grand Trunk " was given to the undertaking, the idea being that the waterway would form the main line of a system of canals radiating from it in various directions, and linking up the greater part of the country south of the Trent with the three ports mentioned.

We have here the first suggestion of any approach to a real system of inland communication, as applying to the country in general, which had been attempted since the Romans made the last of their great roads in Britain. Apart from the natural limitations of navigable rivers, the turn-pike roads so far constructed had been chiefly designed to serve local interests, and successive rulers or Governments had either failed to realise the importance of carrying out a well-planned scheme of inland communication, embracing a great part even if not the whole of the country, or had been lacking in the energy, or the means, to supply what had become one of the greatest of national wants.

There was thus all the more credit due to the little group of far-sighted, enterprising and patriotic individuals whose names I have mentioned that they should themselves have undertaken work which was to have an important influence on the industrial and social conditions of the country. Yet the nature of the conditions under which the Trent and the Mersey section of the Grand Trunk system was made afforded an early example of the physical difficulties attendant on canal construction in England which were to be a leading cause of the decline of canals as soon as the greater advantages of the railway and the locomotive had been established.

Canals were superior to rivers in so far as they could be taken where rivers did not go, and could be kept under control in regard to water supply without the drawbacks of floods or droughts, of high tides, or of being silted up by sand or mud. It is, indeed, reported that when, after he had made a strong pronouncement in favour of canals, James Brindley was asked by a Parliamentary Committee,

" Then what do you think rivers are for ? " he replied, " To supply canals with water."

On the other hand, water would not flow up-hill in canals any more than in rivers, and in the making and operation of canals there was, literally as well as figuratively, a great deal of up-hill work to do.

Between the Mersey and the Trent there were considerable elevations which formed very difficult country for water transport. These elevations had to be overcome by the gradual rising of the canal, by means of locks, to a certain height, by the construction, at that point, of a tunnel through the hills, and by a fresh series of locks on the other side, to allow of a lower level being reached again. The rise of the Trent and Mersey Canal from the Mersey to the summit at Harecastle, near the Staffordshire Potteries, was 395 ft., a final climb of 316 ft. being made by means of a flight of thirty-five locks. Through Harecastle Hill there was driven a tunnel a mile and two-thirds in length, with a height of 12 ft. and a breadth of 9 ft. 4 in.[1] South of this tunnel the canal descended to the level of the Trent, a fall of 288 ft., by means of forty locks. In addition to this the canal, in its course of 90 miles, had to pass through four other tunnels and be carried across the river Dove by an aqueduct of twenty-three arches and at four points over windings of the Trent, which it followed to its junction therewith at Wilden Ferry.

These engineering difficulties were successfully overcome by Brindley, and the canal was opened for traffic in 1777. The benefits it conferred on industry and commerce, having in view the unsatisfactory alternative means of transport, were beyond all question. English traders saw established across the island, from the Mersey to the Humber, a line of inland navigation which, apart from the long and tedious voyage round the coast, and, also, from the scarcely passable roads, was the first connecting link in our national history between the ports of Liverpool and Hull. But of even greater importance were the facilities for making use of either or both of these ports—the one on the west coast, and the other on the east coast—which were opened up to manu-

---

[1] Subsequently supplemented by a tunnel of larger dimensions alongside, constructed by Telford.

facturers and traders in the midland districts, and especially when the Trent and Mersey Canal was supplemented by the Wolverhampton (now the Staffordshire and Worcestershire) Canal, connecting the Trent with the Severn ; the Birmingham Canal; the Coventry Canal (which gave through navigation from the Trent via Lichfield and Oxford, to the Thames) ; and others.

Of the many districts benefitted it was, perhaps, the Potteries that received the maximum of advantage. Fourteen years before the Trent and Mersey Canal was opened for traffic—that is to say, in 1763—Josiah Wedgwood perfected a series of improvements in the pottery industry which foreshadowed the probability of the manufacture of coarse pottery—already carried on in North Staffordshire for many years—developing into the production of wares of the highest excellence, for which a great market would assuredly be found not only throughout England but throughout the world. The one drawback to an otherwise very promising outlook lay in the defective communications. The roads were hopelessly bad and the navigable rivers were far distant. It was almost impossible to get sufficient clay for the purposes of raw material, and the cost and the risk of damage involved in long land journeys before the goods could be put on the water, for carriage to London or the Continent, almost closed those markets for the Staffordshire manufacturer.

In 1760—three years before Josiah Wedgwood started his new era in pottery manufacture—the number of workers engaged in the industry did not exceed 7000 persons ; and not only were they badly paid and irregularly employed but in their position of almost complete isolation from the rest of humanity they were, as Smiles puts it in his " Life of James Brindley," " almost as rough as their roads." They were ill-clad, ill-fed and wholly uneducated ; they lived in dwellings that were little better than mud huts ; they had to dispense with coal for fuel, since the state of the roads made its transport too costly for their scanty means ; they had no shops, and for such drapery and household wares as they could afford to buy they were dependent on the packmen or the hucksters from Newcastle-under-Lyme. Their favourite amusements were bull-baiting and cock-fighting.

Any stranger who ventured to appear among such a people, devoid as they were of most of the attributes of civilisation, might consider himself fortunate if he escaped rough usage simply because he was a stranger.

Of conditions such as those to be found in the Potteries at the period in question one gets some glimpses in William Hutton's " History of Birmingham " (1781). He tells of a place called Lie Waste, otherwise Mud City, situate between Halesowen and Stourbridge. The houses consisted of mud, dried in the sun, though often destroyed by frost. Their occupants, judging from the account he gives of them, could have been little better than scarcely-clad barbarians. Of a visit he paid to Bosworth Field in 1770 the same writer says :—

" I accompanied a gentleman with no other intent than to view the field celebrated for the fall of Richard the Third. The inhabitants enjoyed the cruel satisfaction of setting their dogs at us in the street, merely because we were strangers. Human figures, not their own, are seldom seen in those in-hospitable regions. Surrounded with impassable roads, having no intercourse with man to humanize the mind, no commerce to smooth their rugged manners, they continue the boors of nature."

How industry and improved communications may tend to civilise a people, as well as ensure economic advance-ment, was now to be shown in the case of the Potteries. Wedgwood's enterprise led to the employment of far more people ; the better means of communication allowed both of the industry being greatly developed and of the intro-duction of refining influences into a district no longer isolated ; and the combination of these causes had a striking effect on the material and the moral conditions of the workers.

In giving evidence before a House of Commons Committee in 1785, eight years after the Mersey and Trent Canal was opened, Wedgwood was able to say that there were being employed in the Potteries at that time from 15,000 to 20,000 persons on earthenware manufacture alone—an increase of from 8000 to 13,000 in twenty-five years, independently of the opening of new branches of industry. Work was abundant, and the general conditions were those of a greatly enhanced comfort and prosperity.

Then, also, when John Wesley visited Burslem in 1760 he wrote that the potters assembled to laugh and jeer at him. " One of them," he says, " threw a clod of earth which struck me on the side of the head ; but it neither disturbed me nor the congregation." In 1781 he went to Burslem again. On this occasion he wrote : " I returned to Burslem ; how is the whole face of the country changed in about 20 years ! Since which, inhabitants have continually flowed in from every side. Hence the wilderness is literally become a fruitful field. Houses, villages, towns, have sprung up, and the country is not more improved than the people."

This actual experience of John Wesley's would seem to confirm the view expressed by Sir Richard Whitworth in the observations he offered to the public in 1766 on " The Advantages of Inland Navigation." It was, he argued, trade and commerce, and not the military force of the Kingdom, which could alone enrich us and enable us to maintain our independence ; but there were millions of people " buried alive " in parts of the country where there were no facilities for transport, and where they had hitherto been " bred up for no other use than to feed themselves." What advantage would not accrue to the nation when these millions were brought into the world of active and productive workers ! " Hitherto," he continued, " the world has been unequally dealt, and, though all the inhabitants of this island should have an equal right to the gifts of nature in the advantages of commerce, yet it has only happened to those who live upon the coasts to enrich themselves by it, while as many millions lie starving for want of opportunity to forward themselves into the world. Though the city, village, or country in which they live is at the lowest ebb of poverty it will, in a short time, by trade passing through it, alter its very nature and the inhabitants become, from nothing, as it were, to a very rich and substantial people ; their very natural idea of mankind, and their rude and unpolished behaviour, will be altered and soothed into the most social civility and good breeding by the alluring temptations of the beneficial advantage of trade and commerce."

The opening of the Grand Trunk and other canals connecting with it led to such reductions in the cost of carriage as are shown in the following figures, from Baines's " History

of Liverpool," where they are quoted as from " Williamson's
Liverpool Advertiser " of August 8, 1777 :—

COST OF GOODS TRANSPORT PER TON.

BETWEEN		BY ROAD.				BY WATER.		
		£	s.	d.		£	s.	d.
Liverpool and Etruria . . .		2	10	0	...	0	13	4
,, ,, Wolverhampton .		5	0	0	...	1	5	0
,, ,, Birmingham .		5	0	0	...	1	5	0
Manchester and Wolverhampton .		4	13	4	...	1	5	0
,, ,, Birmingham .		4	0	0	...	1	10	0
,, ,, Lichfield .		4	0	0	...	1	0	0
,, ,, Derby . .		3	0	0	...	1	10	0
,, ,, Nottingham .		4	0	0	...	2	0	0
,, ,, Leicester .		6	0	0	...	1	10	0
,, ,, Gainsborough .		3	10	0	...	1	10	0
,, ,, Newark .		5	6	8	...	2	0	0

Thus the cost of transport by canal was in some instances
reduced to about one-fourth of the previous cost by packhorse or road waggon.

Under the new conditions the numerous manufactures in
the Birmingham and Black Country districts obtained their
raw materials much cheaper than they had done before,
and secured much better facilities for distribution, the difference in cost in sending guns, nails, hardware, and other
heavy manufactures from Birmingham to Hull by water
instead of by road being in itself a considerable saving, and
one likely to give a great stimulus to the industries concerned.
Ores from the north were brought at less expense to mix
with those of Staffordshire, and the iron-masters there were
enabled to compete better with foreign producers. The
manufacturers of Nottingham, Leicester and Derby were
afforded a cheap conveyance to Liverpool for their wares.
The fine ale for which Burton was famous had been sent to
London by way of the Trent, the Humber and the Thames
since, at least, the early part of the seventeenth century, and,
exported from Hull, it had won fame for the Burton breweries
in all the leading Baltic ports and elsewhere. It was now
to be conveyed by water to the port of Liverpool, and find
fresh or expanded markets opened out for it from the west
coast, as well as the east. Cheshire salt obtained a better

distribution ; the merchants both of Hull and of Liverpool could now send groceries and other domestic supplies throughout the midland counties with greater ease, and with much benefit to the people ; while among still other advantages was one mentioned by Baines : " Wheat which formerly could not be conveyed a hundred miles, from corn-growing districts to the large towns and manufacturing districts, for less than 20s. a quarter, could be conveyed for about 5s. a quarter."

The towns which had least cause for satisfaction were Bridgnorth, Bewdley and Bristol, the traffic that had previously gone by the long land route from the Potteries to the Severn, and so on to Bristol, being now diverted to Liverpool by the Grand Trunk Canal, just as the salt of Cheshire had been taken there on the opening of the Weaver navigation, and the textiles of Manchester on the completion of the Duke of Bridgewater's canal.

These developments had, consequently, a further influence on the growth of the once backward port of Liverpool, and such growth was to be stimulated by the Leeds and Liverpool Canal.

Sanctioned by Parliament in 1769, six years before the Grand Trunk Canal was opened, the Leeds and Liverpool Canal was mainly designed to overcome the natural barrier, in the form of a chain of lofty hills, which separated Lancashire from Yorkshire, serving to isolate Liverpool and to keep back from her the flow of trade and commerce from industrial centres on the other side of the hills which should otherwise have regarded Liverpool as their natural port. The canal was further intended to open up more fully than had been done before the great coal-fields of Lancashire, ensuring a better distribution of their mineral wealth both to Liverpool and to the manufacturing towns of Lancashire ; while, by connecting with the Aire at Leeds, the capital of the Yorkshire woollen industry, the canal was to provide another cross-country connection, by inland navigation, between Liverpool and Hull.

The work of constructing the Leeds and Liverpool Canal included (1) the piercing of the Foulridge Hills by a tunnel, 1640 yards long, which alone took five years of constant labour ; (2) an aqueduct bridge of seven arches over the

Aire ; and (3) an aqueduct carrying the canal over the Shipley valley. The total length of navigation was 127 miles, with a fall from the central level of 525 ft. on the Lancashire side, and of 446 ft. on the Yorkshire side. The entire work of construction extended over 41 years, and the total cost was £1,200,000.

The effect of the Leeds and Liverpool Canal on the industrial districts of Lancashire and Yorkshire was no less remarkable than the effect of the Grand Trunk Canal on the industries west or south of the Trent. When the Leeds and Liverpool Canal was formed there was, as Baines observes in his " Lancashire and Cheshire," not one town containing 10,000 inhabitants along the whole of its course from Liverpool to Leeds. With the improved facilities afforded for the conveyance of raw materials and manufactured goods from or to the port of Liverpool came a new era for the textile trades all along the route of the canal—and the now busy and well-populated towns of Wigan, Blackburn, Nelson, Keighley, Bradford and Leeds are indebted in no small degree for their industrial expansion to the better means of communication which the Leeds and Liverpool Canal, in the days when railways were still far off, opened up to them.

Still another canal that was made in order to establish a line of communication west and east, and to serve important intermediate districts, was the Rochdale Canal, which starts from Manchester, rises by a succession of locks to a height 438 ft. above the Manchester level, and, fed on the hill summit by some great reservoirs, descends to the river Calder at Sowerby Bridge, the point from which that river is navigable to the Humber.

Connection with the Calder, and thus with the cross-country navigation of which it formed a part, was also obtained by means of the Huddersfield Canal, a waterway twenty miles in length which, starting from Ashton, rises 334 ft., to the Saddleworth manufacturing district (situate in the wildest part of the Yorkshire hills), passes through a tunnel three miles long, and descends 436 ft. on the Huddersfield side in reaching the level of the Calder.

The reader will have concluded from these references to other canals that, although the Duke of Bridgewater had found a difficulty in raising the means with which to complete his canal to Runcorn, public confidence in canals must have been reassured, and ample money must have been forthcoming, to allow of these further costly and important schemes being undertaken. This conclusion is abundantly warranted. The position following the construction of the Bridgewater canals was thus described, in 1796, in " A Treatise on the Improvement of Canal Navigation," by R. Fulton :—

" So unacquainted were the people with the use of canals, and so prejudiced in favour of the old custom of river navigations, that the undertaking was deemed chimerical, and ruin was predicted as the inevitable result of his Grace's labour. . . . Yet it was not long finished when the eyes of the people began to open ; the Duke could work on his canal when floods, or dry seasons, interrupted the navigation of the Mersey ; this gave a certainty and punctuality, in the carriage of merchandize, and ensured a preference to the canal ; the emoluments arising to the Duke were too evident to be mistaken ; and perseverance having vanquished prejudice, the fire of speculation was lighted, and canals became the subject of general conversation."

The farming community, more especially, had looked with suspicion upon this new-fangled idea of sending boats across fields and up and down the hill-sides. The author of " A Cursory View of the Advantages of an Intended Canal from Chesterfield to Gainsborough " (1769) finds, however, a sufficient excuse for them in the conditions of locomotion and transport with which alone they had hitherto been familiar. He says :—

" Though this useful set of Men, the Farmers, will undoubtedly reap a Proportion of Advantages from the Execution of this beneficial Scheme, they are far from being satisfied, and seem to reflect upon it with many Doubts and Fears. Custom, indeed, and Occupation in Life, cast a wonderful Influence on the Opinions of all Mankind ; it is therefore by no means surprizing that men, whose Forefathers, for Ages, have been inured to rugged and deep Roads, to wade after their Beasts of Burden up to the Knees in Mire, to see their loaded Waggons stick fast in Dirt ; Men, who from their interior, inland Situation, are almost totally unacquainted with all Objects of Navigation ; it is by no means strange, that People, so unaccustomed, should consider an Attempt, to introduce a navigable Canal up to the Town of Chesterfield, and within the Air of the Peak-Mountains, with alarming Ideas, with Suspicion and Amazement."

Another set of scruples was thus dealt with by Richard Whitworth—himself a canal enthusiast—in his " Advantages of Inland Navigation " (1766) :—

" It has been a common objection against navigable canals in this Kingdom that numbers of people are supported by land carriage, and that navigable canals will be their ruin. . . . I must advance an alternative which would free the carrier from any fear of losing his employment on selling off his stock of horses, viz.:—That no main trunk of a navigable canal ought reasonably to be carried nearer than within four miles of any great manufacturing town, . . . which distance from the canal is sufficient to maintain the same number of carriers, and employ almost the same number of horses, as usual, to convey the goods down to the canal in order to go to the seaports for exportation. . . . If a manufacturer can have a certain conveniency of sending his goods by water carriage within four miles of his own home, surely that is sufficient, and profit enough, considering that other people must thrive as well as himself, and a proportion of profit to each trade should be the biassing and leading policy of this nation."

In some instances certain towns did succeed in maintaining a distance of several miles between themselves and the canals they regarded with prejudice and disfavour. They anticipated, in this respect, the action that other towns were to take up later on in regard to railways ; and in the one case as in the other there was abundant cause for regret when the places concerned found they had been left aside, much to their detriment, by a main route of trade and transport.

Other alarmists predicted the ruin of the innkeepers ; protested against the drivers of packhorses being deprived of their sustenance ; prophesied a diminution in the breed of draught horses ; declaimed against covering with waterways land that might be better used for raising corn ; and foreshadowed a detriment to the coasting trade that, in turn, would weaken the Navy, " the natural and constitutional bulwark of Great Britain "—this being a phrase which,

no doubt, was rolled out with great effect in the discussions
that took place.

The discovery, however, that canals were likely to be not
only exceedingly useful but a profitable form of investment
was quite sufficient to overcome all scruples, and even to
give rise, in 1791–4, to a " canal mania " which was a prelude
to the still greater " railway mania " of 1845–6.   In the four
years in question no fewer than eighty-one canal and navigation Acts were passed.

So great had the eagerness of the public to invest in canal
shares become that when, in 1790, the promoters of the
Ellesmere Canal held their first meeting, the shares for which
application was made were four times greater than the number
to be issued.   In 1792, when a meeting was held at Rochdale
to consider the proposed construction of the Rochdale Canal,
£60,000 was subscribed in an hour.   In August, 1792, Leicester
Canal shares were selling at £155, Coventry Canal shares at
£350, Grand Trunks at the same figure, and Birmingham and
Fazley shares at £1170.   At a sale of canal shares in October,
1792, the prices realised included—Trent navigation, 175
guineas per share ;   Soar Canal (Leicestershire) 765 gs. ;
Erewash Canal, 642 gs. ;   Oxford Canal, 156 gs. ;   Cromford
Canal, 130 gs. ;   Leicester Canal, 175 gs., and ten shares in
the Grand Junction Canal (of which not a single sod had
then been cut) at 355 gs. premium for the ten.

The spirit of speculation thus developed led to the making
of a number of canals which had no real prospect of remunerative business, were commercial failures from the start, and
involved the ruin of many investors.   Canals of this type are
still to be found in the country to-day—picturesque derelicts
which some persons think the State should acquire and put
in order again because it is " such a pity " they are not made
use of.

Dealing with the general position as it was in 1803, Phillips
wrote in his " General History of Inland Navigation " (4th
edition) :—" Since the year 1758 no less than 165 Acts of
Parliament have received the royal assent for cutting, altering, amending, etc., canals in Great Britain, at the expense
of £13,008,199, the whole subscribed by private individuals ;
the length of ground which they employ is 2896½ miles. . . .
Of these Acts 90 are on account of collieries opened in their

vicinity, and 47 on account of mines of lead, ore, and copper which have been discovered, and for the convenience of the furnaces and forges working thereon."

Among the more typical of the canals, in addition to those already mentioned, were—the Grand Junction Canal, connecting the Thames with the Trent, and thus with both the Mersey and the Humber ; the Thames and Severn Canal ; the Ellesmere, connecting the Severn with the Dee and the Mersey ; the Barnsley Canal (of which Phillips says : " The beneficial effects of this canal, in a rich mineral country, hitherto landlocked, cannot fail to be immediately felt by miners, farmers, manufacturers and the country at large ") ; the Kennet and Avon (opening, according to the same authority, " a line of navigation, sixteen miles in length, over a country before very remote from any navigable river ") ; the Glamorganshire Canal (" has opened a ready conveyance to the vast manufactory of iron established in the mountains of that country ") ; the extensive network of the Birmingham Canal system ; the Shropshire Union, which connects the Birmingham Canal with Ellesmere port, on the Mersey, and has branches to Shrewsbury, Llangollen, Welshpool and Newtown ; and the Manchester, Bolton and Bury Canal. To the last-mentioned, constructed under an Act of Parliament passed in 1791, Baines alludes as follows in his " Lancashire and Cheshire " :—

" The River Irwell flows directly down from Bury to Manchester, and the river Croal, which flows through Bolton, joins the Irwell between Bury and Manchester ; but neither of these streams was considered available, by any amount of improvement that could be given to it, for the purposes of navigation. They are both of them very impetuous streams, occasionally sending down immense torrents of water, but at other times so shallow as not to furnish sufficient depth of water for the smallest vessels. Instead, therefore, of wasting time and money upon them, a canal was cut at a considerably higher level, but following the general direction of the river Irwell."

The Manchester, Bolton and Bury Canal was thus a further example of the resort to artificial canals, with water channels capable of regulation, in preference to further schemes for rendering rivers navigable.

How the situation brought about by the creation of the network of navigable waterways thus spread, or being spread, throughout the country was regarded by an impartial observer in the " Canal Mania " period is shown by the following comments thereon by Dr Aikin :—

" The prodigious additions made within a few years to the system of inland navigation, now extended to almost every corner of the Kingdom, cannot but impress the mind with magnificent ideas of the opulence, the spirit and the enlarged views which characterise the commercial interest of this country. Nothing seems too bold for it to undertake, too difficult for it to achieve ; and should no external changes produce a durable check to the national prosperity, its future progress is beyond the reach of calculation. Yet experience may teach us, that the spirit of project and speculation is not always the source of solid advantage, and possibly the unbounded extension of canal navigation may in part have its source in the passion for bold and precarious adventure, which scorns to be limited by reasonable calculations of profit. Nothing but highly flourishing manufactures can repay the vast expense of these designs. The town of Manchester, when the plans now under execution are finished, will probably enjoy more various water-communication than the most commercial town of the Low Countries has ever done. At the beginning of this century it was thought a most arduous task to make a *high road* practicable for carriages over the hills and moors which separate Yorkshire from Lancashire ; and now they are pierced through by *three navigable canals !* Long may it remain the centre of a trade capable of maintaining these mighty works ! "

The day was to come, however, when it would be a question, not of the additions made to inland navigation justifying the expense incurred, but of the inherent defects of the said " mighty works," the increasing manufactures, and the introduction of still better methods of transport and communication giving to canals a set-back akin to that which they themselves had already given to navigable rivers.

CHAPTER XVII

THE INDUSTRIAL REVOLUTION

CONTEMPORANEOUSLY with the canal period in England came an industrial revolution which was to place this country—hitherto distinctly backward in the development of its industries—at the head of manufacturing nations, but was, also, to show that, however great the advantages conferred by canals, as compared both with rivers and with roads, even canals were inadequate to meet the full and ever-expanding requirements of trade and transport.

The main causes of this industrial revolution were—the application of a number of inventions and improved processes to leading industries; the incalculable advantages derived from steam power; the immense increase in the supplies of cotton, coal, minerals and other raw materials; the greater wealth of the nation, allowing of much more capital being available for industrial enterprises; and the improvement, not alone in inland communication, but in ship-building and the art of navigation, foreign markets being thus reached more readily at a time when the general political and economic conditions were especially favourable to the commercial expansion abroad which followed on our industrial expansion at home.

Woollen manufactures, originally established here with the help of workers introduced from Flanders in the time of Edward III., had had a long pre-eminence, obtaining a vested interest which led to the advent of a new rival, in the form of cotton manufacturers, receiving, at first, very scanty encouragement. Woollens had made such progress that, even before the Restoration, a market was (as Dowell tells us) opened for our goods, not only in Spain, France, Italy and Germany, but also in Russia and Baltic and other ports, while they were carried by way of Archangel into Persia, and also made a market for themselves in Turkey.

A great part of England was turned into sheep farms for the production of wool, and by 1700 the value of woollen goods exported had risen to £3,000,000.

At this time the import of raw cotton was only about 1¼ million lbs.[1] To such an extent had the woollen, and, also, the linen, industries been placed under the " protection " of the governing powers that until 1721 it was a penal offence in England to weave or sell calico—that is, a fabric consisting entirely of cotton ; and down to 1774 anyone who made or sold a fabric having more than half its threads of cotton was liable to prosecution. Not until 1783 was the prohibition of British-made calicoes removed and the production in this country of all-cotton goods allowed by legislators who had been unduly solicitous of the welfare of British industry. When, in 1776, Adam Smith published his great work on " The Wealth of Nations," he certainly did state that Christopher Columbus had brought back from the New World some bales of cotton, and had shown them at the court of Spain ; but he did not think it necessary to mention that a cotton industry had been started here, and was likely to contribute to the wealth of the United Kingdom.

The imports of raw cotton slowly increased to 2,000,000 in 1720, and to 3,000,000 lbs. in 1751. In 1764, the year in which Hargreaves introduced the spinning jenny, they were still not higher than 4,000,000 lbs. But the successive inventions, during the course of about three decades, alike of Hargreaves, Arkwright, Crompton, Cartwright and others gave such an impetus to the industry that by 1800 the importation of raw cotton (greatly facilitated by the further invention, in 1793, of Eli Whitney's appliance for separating cotton from the cotton seed) had risen to 52,000,000 lbs., while the value of all kinds of cotton products exported increased between 1765 and 1800 from £800,000 to £5,800,000.

This rapid progress would not, however, have been possible but for the facilities for obtaining cheap power afforded by the condensing steam-engine of James Watt, who had taken out a patent for his invention in 1769, though it was not till 1776 that he built and sold his first engine, on which he further improved in 1781. Steam-power, of far greater force

---

[1] The imports of raw cotton into the United Kingdom in 1910 were 17,614,860 cwts., or nearly 1973 million lbs., valued at £71,716,808.

and utility, and capable of being produced anywhere, thus took the place of the water-power, only available alongside streams, on which, as we have seen, the earlier success of the woollen industry, especially as carried on among the hills of Yorkshire, had been established. It was by water-power that the spinning machine so recently introduced by Sir Richard Arkwright was operated until James Watt had shown that steam could be used to better advantage. Then the setting up at Papplewick, Nottinghamshire, in 1785, of a steam-engine for the operation of cotton machinery marked, also, the decline of domestic manufactures and the advent of that factory system which was to bring about a complete transformation in the industrial conditions of the United Kingdom.

Yet just as the improvements in cotton production would have been incomplete without the steam-engine, so, also, would the invention even of the steam-engine have been of little service but for an abundant supply of coal, and but, also, for the possession of a ready and economical means of moving the coal from the localities where it was to be found to those where it was wanted for the purposes of the " steam age " that was about to open.

The greater demand for fuel and the increased facilities for supplying it led to the greater development of various inland coal-fields, in addition to those already long in operation in the Newcastle district, and having there the advantages of river and sea as an aid to distribution. The need, also, of coal for the operation of the steam-engine in the countless number of new industries or new works that followed on James Watt's improvements had an important influence on fixing the location of fresh industrial centres.

Coal-mining, again, was powerfully accelerated in the same period by the iron industry, which itself was undergoing developments no less remarkable than those attending the expansion of the cotton industries, and having no less a bearing on the problem of efficient inland transport.

Down to the year 1740 the smelting of iron-ores—an industry carried on here from very early days in our history—was done entirely with wood charcoal. For this reason the early seat of the iron industry was in the forests that, as already told, once covered so large an area in Sussex, Kent and Surrey, and afforded what may, at one time, have appeared to be a practically limitless supply of fuel.

The three counties in question thus attained to a high degree of industrial importance and prosperity at a time when Lancashire and Yorkshire were still regarded by dwellers in the south as inhabited by a scarcely civilised people. Lord Seymour, who was made by Henry VIII. Lord High Admiral of England, and ended his life on the scaffold in 1549, was the owner of iron-works in Sussex. The cannon and shot which Drake, Hawkins and Frobisher took with them on their ships were supplied by these southern foundries. Of the position of the industry in 1653, when there were 42 forges and 27 furnaces in the Weald of Sussex, the author of " Glimpses of our Ancestors in Sussex " says : " Sussex was then the Wales and the Warwickshire of England. Foreign countries sought eagerly for its cannon, its culverines and falconets. . . . Its richly decorated fire-backs and fantastic andirons were the pride of lordly mansions. London sent here for the railings that went round its great cathedral ; Sussex ploughshares, speeds and other agricultural implements and hardware were sent all over the kingdom."

Fears, however, had already been excited in Henry VIII.'s day that the continued destruction of forests, in order to supply the iron-works with fuel, would lead to a timber famine ; and in Queen Elizabeth's reign such a prospect, foreshadowing a shortage of timber for shipbuilding purposes at the very time when a conflict with Spain was regarded as inevitable, was looked upon as involving a possible national disaster. A subsidiary complaint against the industry was that the traffic to and from the iron-works injured the roads. Legislation was therefore passed prohibiting, under severe penalties, any increase in the number of iron-works in the three counties mentioned, except on land already occupied or able to furnish of itself a sufficient supply of timber. Exportation of iron was also prohibited, and it was even considered good policy to import iron, rather than to make it, and so preserve the still available timber for other purposes.

By the early part of the eighteenth century the iron industry, after exhausting the timber supplies of Sussex, had disappeared from that county ; but it flourished in Shropshire, where it found both fuel and iron-stone in the Forest of Dean, while the Severn provided water-power and inland navigation. The industry was also carried on in Staffordshire ; and here, in the reign of James I., some important experiments were made in the direction of using coal instead of wood in the manufacture of iron ; but this idea was not fully developed until Abraham Darby had shown, in 1735, how coke, in combination with a powerful blast, could be substituted for wood. What is regarded as the real turning-point in the iron industry followed in 1760, when Dr Roebuck built, at the Carron works, his new type of blast furnace, in which coke was to be used.

An impetus was thus given to the industry, and an impetus it certainly needed, inasmuch as the production of iron in the United Kingdom had sunk in 1740 to 17,350 tons. Then, in 1783, Henry Cort, of Gosport, patented his process for converting pig-iron into malleable iron through the operation of " puddling " in a common air-furnace consuming coal, and in 1784 he patented a further process for turning malleable iron into bars by means of rollers instead of forge hammers.

These further inventions were of much service ; but the greatest advance of all followed on the application of steam to iron-making, as one of the many results of James Watt's achievements. Steam enabled the manufacturers to get a far more powerful blast in the new furnaces, at a consumption of about one-third less of coal, than had been possible in the process of smelting carried on with the help of water-power. The use, also, of coal instead of timber for fuel, and of steam-power in place of water-power, made the iron-masters independent both of the forests and of the rivers of southern England, and led to the further expansion of the iron industry being transferred to such districts as Staffordshire, the north-east coast, Scotland and South Wales, where the now all-important coal could be obtained no less readily than the iron-ore.

So the migration of some of the greatest of our national industries from south to north, begun by the streams on Yorkshire hills, was completed by the steam-engine of James Watt.

The effect on the iron industry itself of the improvements in manufacture was prodigious. The 17,350 tons of iron which were alone produced in 1740 came from 59 furnaces, using charcoal only. In 1788 the number of furnaces had increased to 85, and the output to 68,300 tons, of which 55,200 tons had been produced by coke, and only 13,100 tons by charcoal. In 1796, when the charcoal process had been almost entirely given up, the number of furnaces was 121 (in England and Wales 104 ; in Scotland 17), and the production was 124,879 tons. In this same year Pitt proposed to put a tax on coal, and the following year he sought to impose one on pig-iron ; but a taxing of raw material was not to be tolerated, and he had to abandon each project.

Adding to these details corresponding figures for other years in the Canal Era, we get the following table :—

IRON FURNACES AND PRODUCTION IN ENGLAND, WALES AND SCOTLAND.

Year.	Number of furnaces.	Production (tons).
1740	59	17,350
1788	85	68,300
1796	121	124,879
1802	168	170,000
1806	227	250,000
1820	260	400,000
1825	374	581,367

This great increase in the output of iron meant, also, a considerable expansion in the engineering trades of the country in general, in the hardware trades of Birmingham, in the cutlery trade of Sheffield, and in many other trades besides. It led to the opening up of new centres of activity and industry in addition to a greater aggregation of workers in centres already established ; while the combined effect on the coal industry itself of all these developments is well shown by the following figures, giving the output of coal in the United Kingdom, for the years mentioned, as estimated by the Commissioners of 1871 :—

YEAR.	TONS.
1700	2,612,000
1750	4,773,828
1770	6,205,400
1790	7,618,728
1795	10,080,300

The rapid expansion in the last half of the eighteenth century of the various industries here mentioned, and of many others besides, led to a corresponding growth in the industrial towns ; and this, in turn, meant an increase in the wants of the community, and the opening up of new and even huge markets for agricultural produce. Such produce, also, was now obtainable in greater quantity owing to the fact that more land was being brought under cultivation. In 1685 it had been estimated that there were in England about 18,000,000 acres of fen, forest and moorland. Of this total 3,000,000 acres had been brought under cultivation before 1727. But from that time many enclosure Acts were passed, no fewer than 138 becoming law between 1789 and 1792 ; and, though it by no means follows that all the land so enclosed was actually cultivated, the greater opportunities opening out to agriculture when more and more workers were being collected into factories and manufacturing districts, and becoming more and more dependent on others for food supplies which, under the old conditions of life and industry, people grew for themselves, were beyond all question, while agricultural production was itself advanced by the supply of those better and cheaper aids to husbandry which followed on the improvements in iron manufacture.

To meet the enormously increased demands for the transport alike of raw materials, of manufactured articles and of domestic supplies in the period of industrial revolution which thus began to develop about the middle of the eighteenth century, something more was wanted than rivers, offering uncertain navigation, and only available in particular districts, and highways deplorably bad in spite of Turnpike Acts and much wasteful expenditure, another half-century having still to elapse before Telford showed the country how roads should be made, and McAdam told how they should be mended.

In these circumstances, and during the period here in question, it was canals that were mainly looked to as a means of supplying the transport requirements then growing at so prodigious a rate. Invention and production had already far surpassed the means of efficient distribution. England was on the eve of the greatest industrial expansion of any country in Europe ; but she was starting thereon with probably the worst means of inland transport of any country in

Europe. Canals appeared to be the one thing needed ; and every fresh canal constructed was heralded with joy because it foreshadowed, among other things, better trade, more employment, higher wages, cheaper fuel and provisions, and less of the isolation from which many a land-locked community was suffering.

Some of the accounts given by Phillips, in his " General History of Inland Navigation," of the opening of various canals afford interesting evidence of the satisfaction with which the populace greeted the new waterways. I give a few examples :—

" 1798.—The Herefordshire and Gloucestershire canal from Gloucester to Ledbury is completed ; the opening of this navigation took place on the 30th of March, when several of the proprietors and gentlemen of the committee embarked . . . in the first vessel freighted with merchandise consigned to Ledbury, which was followed by three others laden with coal. They passed through the tunnel at Oxenhall, which is 2192 yards in length, in the space of 52 minutes. . . . Both ends of the tunnel, as well as the banks of the canal, were lined with spectators, who hailed the boats with reiterated acclamations. It is supposed that upwards of 2000 persons were present on their arrival at Ledbury. . . . The advantages which must result from this inland navigation to Ledbury and the adjoining country are incalculable. In the article of coal the inhabitants of this district will reap an important benefit by the immediate reduction in price of at least 10s. per ton. Coals of the first quality are now delivered at the wharf, close to Ledbury, at 13s. 6d., whereas the former price was 24s. per ton."

" 1799.—The new canal from Sowerby-bridge to Rochdale was lately opened for business. The Travis yacht first crossed the head level, decorated with the Union flag, emblematical of the junction of the ports of Hull and Liverpool, with colours flying, music playing, attended by the Saville yacht, and thousands of spectators ; a display of flags on the warehouses, and sound of cannon, announced to the rejoicing neighbourhood the joyful tidings, which in the evening were realised by the arrival of several vessels, laden with corn and timber."

" 1800.—The Peak Forest canal . . . was opened on the

1st of May. The completion of this bold and difficult undertaking, through numerous hills and valleys, precipices and
declivities, is an object of general admiration."

Yet in these same records—published in 1803—and among
his accounts of the crowds, the flags, the music and the
cannon that had then so recently welcomed the opening of still
more canals, Phillips tells of an innovation destined eventually
to supplant the canal system by reason of advantages which
he himself seems to have recognised, though he naturally
did not then anticipate all that was to follow. The said
innovation is thus recorded by him under date " 1802 " :—

" The locks, canal and basin, from which the Surrey iron
rail-way now in agitation, is to commence at Wandsworth,
have been lately opened and the water admitted from the
Thames. The first barge entered the lock amidst a vast
number of spectators, who rejoiced at the completion of this
part of the important and useful work. The ground is laid
out for the rail-way, with some few intervals, all the way to
Croydon ; and the undertakers are ready to lay down the
iron ; it is expected to be ready by midsummer.

" N.B. The iron rail-ways are of great advantage to the
country in general, and are made at an expense of about
300l. per mile. The advantage they give for the conveyance
of goods by carts and waggons, seems even to surpass, in
some instances, those of boat carriage by canals."

So we come to the story of the railway, which had, however,
been undergoing development, from very primitive conditions,
for a considerable period even prior to this notable event on
the banks of the Thames in 1802.

CHAPTER XVIII

EVOLUTION OF THE RAILWAY

THE early history of the railway is the early history of the English coal trade.

Down to the sixteenth century the fuel supply of the country alike for manufacturing and for domestic purposes was derived almost exclusively from those forests and peat-beds that once covered so large a portion of the area of the British Isles. Coal was not unknown, though it was then called " sea-coal," a name distinguishing coal from charcoal, and given to it because the fact of the earliest known specimens being found on the shores of Northumberland and of the Firth of Forth—where there are outcrops of the coal measures —led to the belief that the black stone which burned like charcoal was a product of the sea. The name was retained, as an appropriate one, when coal was brought to London by sea from the north.

Coal is known to have been received at various dates during the thirteenth century in London (which then already had a Sacoles, or Sea-coal, Lane), in Colchester, in Dover and in Suffolk ; but it was used mainly by smiths and lime-burners ; and it was used by them still more when the con-struction of feudal castles and ecclesiastical buildings in and following the Norman period called for work not to be done efficiently with fires of wood or charcoal. The use of coal as fuel for domestic purposes remained, however, extremely limited. Unlike wood and charcoal, coal was not suitable for burning in the centre of rooms then unprovided with chimneys, while coal smoke was regarded as an intolerable nuisance, and as seriously detrimental to health. It was on these grounds that when, in the fourteenth century, brewers, dyers and others in London were found to be using coal, a Royal Proclamation was issued interdicting its use by any person not a smith or a lime-burner, and appointing a commission of Oyer and Terminer to see to the punishment of all offenders.

For a further considerable period the use of coal continued very partial ; but in the sixteenth century great uneasiness began to be felt at the prospective exhaustion of the timber supplies of the country, and various enactments were passed with a view to checking the destruction of the forests. Great attention began to be paid to the use of sea-coal as a substitute for wood, and an improvement in domestic architecture led to a more general provision of fire-places with chimneys, thus allowing of a resort to coal fires for domestic purposes. Chimneys began to appear, in fact, in numbers never seen before. Harrison, writing in 1577, grieves over the innovation of coal fires, and recalls the good old times of wood and peat when, as he touchingly says, " our heads did never ake."

Queen Elizabeth retained the prejudice against sea-coal, and would have none of it. Ladies of fashion, sharing, as loyal subjects, her Majesty's objections, would, in turn neither enter a room where coal was burning nor eat of food cooked at a coal fire. But James I., whose ancestors had long favoured coal fires in Scotland—and, it may be, thus made themselves responsible for the name of " Auld Reekie " conferred on Edinburgh—had coal brought for fires in his own rooms in Westminster Palace. When this fact became known Society changed its views, and decided that the hitherto obnoxious sea-coal might be tolerated, after all. Howes, writing in 1612, was then able to speak of coal as " the generall fuell of this Britaine Island."

In the result, and especially following on the development in trade and industry which came with the Restoration, there was a great increase in the demand for coal. In 1615 the coal fleet engaged in the transport of sea-coal to London, and other ports on the east and south-east coasts—where fuel was scarcest—comprised (as stated in " A History of Coal Mining in Great Britain," by Robert L. Galloway) 400 vessels. In 1635, or only twenty years later, the number had increased to between 600 and 700, and by 1650, or thereabouts, the total had further risen to 900 vessels, these figures being exclusive of the foreign fleets carrying coal to France, Holland and Germany.

The collieries that were more especially required to meet this increased demand were those in the immediate neighbourhood of the Tyne, since they offered the advantages of thick seams of coal of excellent quality and close alike to the surface and to a navigable river. The proportions to which the industry had already attained in the year 1649 are shown by Grey, in his " Chorographia, or a Survey of Newcastle-upon-Tine," where he says : " Many thousand people are imployed in this trade of coales : many live by working of them in pits : many live by conveying them in waggons and waines to the river Tine. . . . One coal merchant imployeth five hundred or a thousand in his works of coal."

The one great difficulty in the way of development lay in the trouble experienced in getting the coal from the pit-banks to the river for loading into the keels, or barges, by which it would be conveyed to the sea-going colliers lying below the bridge at Newcastle.

The established custom was to send the coal to the river by carts, or wains, or even in panniers slung across the backs of horses ; and in Robert Edington's " Treatise on the Coal Trade " (1813) mention is made of various collieries which had up to 600 or 700 carts engaged in this service. Inasmuch, however, as the art of road-making in general was then still in its elementary stage, one can well imagine that, with all this traffic along them, the roads between the collieries and the Tyne must have been in a condition that added greatly both to the difficulties and to the cost of transport. Nicholas Wood, in his " Practical Treatise on Rail-roads " (1825), gives an extract, dated 1602, from the book of a Newcastle coal company, showing that " from tyme out of mynd " the coal carts had brought eight bolls—equal to about 17 cwt.—of coal to the river ; but added that " of late several hath brought only, or scarce, seven," a fact sufficiently suggestive of the deplorable state to which the colliery roads had been reduced even at the opening of a century that was to bring about so great an increase in the demand for coal.

Bad as the position was for the collieries located near to the Tyne, it was worse for those situate at any distance from the river, since, under the road conditions then prevailing, it was practically impossible for the owners of the latter collieries to get their coal to the river at all, or to secure any share in a trade offering such great opportunities and undergoing such rapid expansion. The coal had but a nominal value so long as it could not be got away from the pit-banks.

The first attempt to overcome the difficulties of the situation was in the direction of laying parallel courses of stone or wood for the waggon wheels to run upon; but here we have the equivalent of a partially-paved roadway rather than of actual rails. The latter came when the parallel wheel-courses of wood were reduced to what William Hutchinson, in his " View of Northumberland " (1778), calls " strings of wood," for the accommodation of " large unwieldy carriages or waggons."

Nicholas Wood says that these wooden rails had a length of about six feet, and were five or six inches in thickness, with a breadth of about the same proportions. They were pegged down to sleepers placed across the track at a distance of about two feet apart, so that one rail reached across three sleepers. The spaces between the sleepers were filled in with ashes or small stones, to protect the feet of the horses. The waggons were in the form of a hopper, being much broader and longer at the top than at the bottom. At first all four wheels of the waggon were made either of one entire piece of wood or of two or three pieces of wood fastened together, the rim, in either case, being so shaped as to have on one side a projection, or flange, which would keep the wheel on the rails.

This, then, was the earliest example of a *rail*way—the fundamental principle of which is, of course, the use of *rails* to facilitate the drawing or the propulsion of a moving body, and not the particular form of motive power (however great the importance, in actual practice, of this matter of detail) by which the traction is secured.

The date of the first " rail-way " (so called) in the form described, and in accordance with the principle mentioned, is uncertain; but Galloway, in his " History of Coal Mining," mentions a document dated 1660 which refers to a sale of timber used in the construction of waggon-ways; while Roger North, writing in 1676, describes the then existing railways in terms which suggest that they were, at that date, a well-established institution. Speaking generally, therefore, one may assume that the pioneer rail-ways were brought into operation somewhere about the middle of the seventeenth century—if not still earlier. Taking 1650 as an approximate date, this would mean that the first rail-way must have been made about one hundred and eighty years before the opening of that Liverpool and Manchester line with which the history of railways is often assumed to have begun.

Hutchinson speaks of the collieries on the Tyne as being, at the time he wrote (1778), " about twenty-four in number," and he further says of them that they " lie at considerable distances from the river." On account of these considerable distances the colliery managers had to secure way-leaves for their rail-ways from the owners of intervening land, so as to obtain access to the Tyne. Thus Roger North, in the account he gives of the railways in the Newcastle district, says : " When men have pieces of land between the collieries and the rivers, they sell leave to lead coals over their ground, and so dear that the owner of a rood of ground will expect 20l. per annum for this leave." In some instances the total payment for a way-leave seems to have amounted to £500 a year. Statutory powers were not required for the rail-ways so long as they were used only for private purposes, though when they crossed a public road the assent of the local authorities was necessary.

The rails, sleepers and wheels, all of wood, came mostly from Sussex or Hampshire, and the writer of an article on the Tyne railways, published in the " Commercial and Agricultural Magazine " for October, 1800, speaks of the use on them of so much timber as " the more extraordinary " because the necessities of the coal mines had previously " used up every stick of timber in the neighbourhood," so that " the import from returning colliers (coal-ships) was the sole resource." Such import, also, would appear to have been considerable, the making of wooden rail-ways on the north-east coast being the means of developing an important industry in rails and wheels in the southern counties.

One of the importers on the Tyne was William Scott, father of Lords Stowell and Eldon, and his " Letters," included in M. A. Richardson's " Reprints of Rare Tracts " (Newcastle-upon-Tyne, 1849), give some interesting details on the subject. Scott, in addition to being himself engaged in mining, acted as agent for southern producers of wooden rails and wheels for colliery rail-ways; and his letters show that in and about the year 1745 the consignments were coming to hand in " immense quantities." Scott seems to have had great trouble in restraining the zeal of the southerners. He tells one correspondent that " Wheels are at present a great drug from so many yt. came last year. Rails will be wanted, but the people pays so badly for them that wo^d weary eny body to serve them." To another he says : " I find the best oak rails will scarcely give 6d. p yd this year." To correspondents at Lyndhurst, New Forest, he writes : " I fancy the dealers in wn. wheels will expect to have wheels soon 'em given, if such great numbers continue coming." Mr West, of Slyndon, near Arundel, Sussex, is told that not more than five shillings can be got for the best wooden wheels, and that " dealers are so full that they have not room for any wheels." On March 27, 1747, Scott writes concerning wheels : " No less than about 2000 com'd within these 14 days from Lyndhurst consign'd to different people " ; and two months later he announces that he has resolved to receive " no more such goods as wooden wheels, rails and such like from anybody."

Most of the Tyne collieries were at a higher level than the river, and in the construction of the rail-ways it was sought to obtain a regular and easy descent, regardless of route or distance, to the " staith," or shipping-stage, from which the coal would be loaded either into the keels (barges) employed to take it along the river to the colliers, or, in the case of longer distance rail-ways, direct into the collier itself, the bottom of the waggons being made after the fashion of a trap-door to facilitate discharge. Gradual descent was further aimed at because it allowed of the loaded waggons moving along the rail-way by reason of their own weight.

How this prototype both of the railway and of express trains as known to us to-day was operated is well shown in a " Description of a Coal-Waggon," with an accompanying illustration, contributed to the " General Magazine of Arts and Sciences " for June, 1764, by John Buddle, of Chester-le-street, Durham, who subsequently became manager of the Wallsend Colliery. In the illustration a horse is depicted drawing, by means of two ropes fastened to its collar, a loaded four-wheeled coal waggon along a rail-way preceded by a man who, having a bundle of hay underneath one arm,

holds some of the hay a few inches in front of the horse so
that the animal, stretching forward to get the hay, draws
along the waggon more readily. Buddle explains that the
waggon is " conducted or drove by a single man, called the
Waggon-man, whose most common action on the road is,
inticing the horse forward with a bit of hay in his hand,
which he supplies from under his arm, a quantity of hay
sufficient for a day being kept in the Hay-poke," that is,
in a receptacle at the back of the waggon. Suspended over
one of the hind wheels is a " convoy," or brake, formed of
a curved and strong-looking piece of wood (described in the
text as alder-wood), which is attached at one end to the
waggon, and held in a loop at the other. " Its use," says
Buddle, " is to regulate the motion of the waggon down the
sides of the hills (called by the waggon men runs) making
it uniform. . . . The waggon-man, taking the end out of the
loop, lets it down upon the wheel, and, placing himself astride
upon the end, with one foot on the waggon-soal he presses
more or less, according to the declivity of the run ; the Convoy
acting at that time as a leaver."

Buddle further says : " Waggon men, in going down very
steep Runs, commonly take their horses from before, and
fasten them behind their waggons,[1] as they would inevitably
be killed was the convoy to break (which frequently happens)
or any other accident occasion these waggons to run *amain*.
Nor is this fatal consequence attendant only on the horses,
but the drivers often receive broken bones, bruises, and
frequently the most excruciating deaths. Indeed, in some
places, a most humane custom is established, which is, when
any waggon-man loses his horse, the other Waggon-men go
a Gait for the poor sufferer, which is little out of their profits,
and purchase him another horse."

About 1750, according to Nicholas Wood, cast-iron wheels
were introduced ; but in 1765 wooden wheels were still
mostly used at the back of the waggon, to allow of the convoy
getting a better grip when the waggon was going, by its own

[1] Not only was it a case of the cart going before the horse, on a
descending road, but in some instances there was attached to the waggon
a sort of horse-trolley on which the animal itself could ride down-hill, and
thus reserve its strength for taking back the empty waggon on a second
pair of rails alongside.

weight, down an incline ; though even then the danger of accident was, as Buddle's observations suggest, sufficiently grave. On this same point it is said by T. S. Polyhistor, in a " Description of a Coal Waggon," given in the " London Magazine " for March, 1764 :—

" They commonly unloose the horse when they come to the runs, and then put him too again when down ; the reason of their taking him off at such places is because, were the convoy to break, it would be impossible to save the horse from being killed, or if the waggon-way rails be wet sometimes a man cannot stop the waggon with the convoy and where the convoy presses upon the wheel it will fire and flame surprisingly ; many are the accidents that have happened as aforesaid ; many hundred poor people and horses have lost their lives ; for was there ever so many waggons before the waggon that breaks its convoy and has not got quite clear of the run, they are all in great danger, both men and horses, of being killed."

Polyhistor also states that the quantity of coal one of these waggons would draw on the rails was 19 " bolls," or " bowls," as he calls them. This gave a load of about 42 cwt. of coal, as compared with the load of 17 cwt., or less, to which the waggons on the ordinary roads at the collieries had been reduced. The advantage from the point of view of transport was obvious ; but no less certain, also, was the risk to life and limb when a waggon with over two tons of coal was allowed to run down an incline checked only by a primitive wooden brake, with a man seated on one end of it to press it against a wheel. In wet weather boys or old men were employed to sprinkle ashes on the rails ; but there were times when the rail-ways having a steep descent could not be used at all.

Introduced on the Tyne, the rail-way was adopted in 1693 by collieries on the Wear, and it also came into vogue in Shropshire and other districts. In 1698 a rail-way was set up on Sir Humphry Mackworth's colliery at Neath, Glamorganshire ; but after it had been in use about eight years it was condemned by a grand jury at Cardiff as a " nuisance," and the portion crossing the highway between Cardiff and Neath was torn up. In a statement presented, rebutting the allegation of the grand jury, it was said : " These waggon ways are very common and frequently made use of about Newcastle and also at Broseley, Benthal and other places in Shropshire, and are so far from being nuisances that they have ever been esteemed very useful to preserve the roads, which would be otherwise made very bad and deep by the carriage of coal in common waggons and carts."

The Tyneside colliery rail-way was, in fact, widely adopted; though it underwent many improvements long before there was any suggestion of operating the new form of traction by means of locomotives.

The first improvement on the original wooden rail pegged on to the sleepers was the fastening on it of another rail, in order that this could be removed, when worn down, without interfering with the sleepers. This arrangement was known as the "double way"; and Nicholas Wood says of it: "The double rail, by increasing the height of the surface whereon the carriage travelled, allowed the inside of the road to be filled up with ashes or stone to the under side of the upper rail, and consequently above the level of the sleepers, which thus secured them from the action of the feet of the horses." He adds that on the first introduction of the double way the under rail was of oak, and afterwards of fir, mostly six feet long, and reaching across three sleepers, and was about five inches broad on the surface by four or five inches in depth. The upper rail was of the same dimensions and almost always made of beech or plane tree.

The next improvement was the nailing of thin strips, or "plates," of wrought iron on to the double rail wherever there was a steep descent or a considerable curve, thus diminishing the friction. These "plates" were about two inches wide and half an inch thick, and they were fastened on to the wooden rails with ordinary nails. They constituted the first step towards the conversion of wooden rail-ways into an iron road, and Nicholas Wood thinks it very likely that the diminution of friction resulting from their use may have suggested the substitution of iron rails for wooden ones.

Cast-iron rails began to come into use about 1767. Their brittleness was, at first, found to be a great disadvantage; but this defect was subsequently overcome, to a certain extent, by the use of smaller waggons, which allowed of a better distribution of weight over the rail. Then in or about

1776 " plates " or " rails " (the two expressions seem to have been used somewhat indiscriminately) were cast with an inner flange, from two to three inches high, so that waggons with ordinary wheels could be taken upon them and be kept on the plate, or rail, by means of this flange.

John Curr, manager of the Duke of Norfolk's collieries, near Sheffield, who claimed to have invented these flanged " plates," describes them in his " Coal Viewer and Engine Builder's Practical Companion " (1797), as being six feet long, three inches broad, half an inch thick, from 47 lbs. to 50 lbs. in weight, and provided with nail holes for fastening them direct on to oak sleepers. Lines so constructed became known as " plate-ways," " tram-ways," or, alternatively, " dram-ways."

The derivation of the words tram and tramway has given rise to a certain amount of discussion from time to time, and the fallacy that they come from the name of Benjamin Outram, of the Ripley iron-works, Derbyshire, who, in the last quarter of the eighteenth century, advocated the flanged-plate system of rail-way, has been especially favoured. It was, however, merely a coincidence that "tram" formed part of his name, and this popular theory here in question is quite unfounded.

The real origin of " tram " is indicated, rather, by the following list of possible derivations, which I take from Skeat's " Etymological Dictionary " :—

Swedish : Tromm, trumm, a log, or the stock of a tree ; also a summer sledge.

Middle Swedish : Tråm, trum, a piece of a large tree cut up into logs.

Norwegian : Tram, a door-step (of wood). Traam, a frame.

Low German : Traam, a balk or beam ; especially one of the handles of a wheel-barrow.

Old High German : Drām, trām, a beam.

Thus in its original signification the word tram, or its equivalent, was applied either to a log of wood or to certain specified objects made of wood.

The word itself was in use in this country as far back as the middle of the sixteenth century, since on August 4, 1555, a certain Ambrose Middleton, of Skirwith, Cumberland (as recorded in the Surtees Society " Publications," vol. xxxviii., page 37, note), made a will in which he left " to the amendinge of the highwaye *or tram*, from the weste ende of Bridgegait, in Barnard Castle, 20s." There is no reason to doubt that the " highwaye or tram " here referred to was a road across which logs of wood had been laid, the name " tram " being applied thereto by reason of its aforesaid original significa- tion. It is, further, easy to understand how, when the pioneer rail-ways were made entirely of wood, the word tram-way should, for that reason, still be applied to them. Just, also, as " tram " had already passed from a log of wood to a wooden sledge or.to a wheelbarrow handle, so it was given by pit- men in the north of England to the small waggon in which coal was pushed or drawn along in the workings.

When " plates " were nailed on to the wooden rails of the early rail-ways the use of the word tram-way may still have been regarded as appropriate ; it was retained for the plates or rails provided with a flange, and lines constructed with flanged plates or rails were, in turn, called plate-ways, tram- ways, or dram-ways to distinguish them from other ways or roads made with rails having no flange.

In course of time the wooden rails which had been the original justification for the use of the word or prefix " tram " disappeared, and even the flanged rails were to be met with only on canal or colliery lines ; but " tramway "—now a complete misnomer—is the name still given in this country to what in the United States are more accurately known as street railways.

Of the vast number of people in the United Kingdom who daily use the word tramway, or speak of " going by tram," few, probably, realise how they are thus recalling the days alike of log-roads and of those rail-ways of wood which were the pioneers of the iron roads of to-day.

The designation, also, of " platelayer " was originally applied to the men employed to lay the " plates " of which I have spoken ; but although workers on the permanent way are now, surely, *rail*-layers rather than *plate*-layers, they are still known by the original name.

The system of flanged plates, or rails, was widely adopted ; but when, in 1785, it was proposed to build a 3-mile plate- way, or tram-way, of this type between Loughborough and the Nanpantan collieries, the commissioners of a turnpike road it was necessary to cross objected, on the ground that the raised flange would be dangerous to traffic passing along the road. Following on these objections, William Jessop, the engineer of the proposed line, decided, in 1788, to abandon flanged plates and flat wheels, and to substitute for them flat rails and flanged wheels.[1] He proceeded to cast some " edge-rails " which overcame the scruples of the road commissioners, and the Loughborough and Nanpantan rail-way was opened in 1789, being the first having iron rails with a flat surface, on the " edge " of which wheels with a flange on their inner side were run. The plate, or tram, system of flanged rails still had many advocates, and for a time there was much controversy as to the respective merits of the two systems; but the principle introduced by Jessop was eventually adopted for railways in general, and became one of the most important of the developments that rendered possible the attainment of high speeds in rail transport. " The substitution of the flanged wheel for the flanged plate was," said Mr. James Brunlees, C.E., in his presidential address in the Mechanical Science Section at the 1883 meeting of the British Association, " an organic change which has been the forerunner of the great results accomplished in modern travelling by railway."

For some thirty years after Jessop's improvement, the rails, of whichever kind, were still made of cast-iron, wrought-iron rails, tried at Newcastle-upon-Tyne in 1805, not coming into general use until about 1820, when John Birkenshaw, of the Bedlington iron-works, invented an efficient and economical method of rolling iron bars suitable for use as railway lines.[2] By 1785 iron rails, even though only cast-iron rails, had widely taken the place of the wooden rails which had then been in use for over a hundred years.

---

[1] In the first instance projections were cast on the rails to allow of their being attached to the wooden sleepers; but, as these projections were found to break easily, they were cast separately in the form of " pedestals," or " chairs," into which, after they had been fastened to the sleepers, the rails could be fixed with pieces of wood.

[2] Mr Brunlees is of opinion that the plating of rails with a steel surface was probably begun about 1854, and that it was not until eight or ten years later they were made entirely of steel. " Now," he said in his address, " owing to the improvements in the manufacture of steel rails, they can be produced as easily and as cheaply as iron rails."

The substitution, from about 1767, of iron rails—even though they were only cast-iron rails—for wooden ones became the great event in the development of railways at this period, and gave the newer lines their distinguishing feature as compared with their predecessors. Each fresh line made took the credit of being an " *iron* rail-way " ; and not only did that designation remain in vogue in this country for several decades but it fixed, also, the names of the railway systems in various Continental countries, as shown by the term " Chemin de Fer " in France and Belgium, " Eisenbahn " in Germany, Austria and Switzerland ; " Strada ferrata " in Italy, and " Ferrocarril " in Spain (the English equivalent in each instance being " Iron Road "), and by the name of Holland Iron Railway Company (" Hollandsche Yzeren Spoorvegs-maatschappy ") by which one of the oldest of the railway companies in Holland—where it was founded in 1837—is still known.[1]

One factor in the preference shown for iron rails over wooden ones was the consideration of cost. Alluding to the wooden railways of Durham, in his " General View " of the agriculture of that county, drawn up for the Board of Agriculture in 1810, John Bailey, of Chillingham, says : " Of late years, on account of the high price of wood, iron railways have been substituted." With an increase in the price of timber, owing to the greater scarcity thereof, as the available supplies in the southern counties became more depleted, the time may well have come when, apart from other considerations, it was found cheaper in the north to make cast-iron rails than to import wooden ones. The need for importing so much timber was further diminished, from about 1739, by the substitution, in many instances, of blocks of stone for

[1] The adoption of the designation "Iron," as applied to the railway systems abroad, was probably influenced to some extent by Thomas Gray's " Observations on a General Iron Rail-way." First published in 1820, the work had gone through five editions by 1825, and in a letter addressed, in 1845, to Sir Robert Peel, urging the claims of Gray to generous treatment by the State, on the ground of his being the " author " (*sic*) of the railway system, Thomas Wilson wrote : " His name and his fame were spreading in other lands ; his work was translated into all the European languages, and to the impression produced by it may be attributes the popular feeling throughout Germany and France in favour of rail-road which has terminated in the adoption of his railway system in Germany and Belgium especially."

the wooden sleepers previously used, the iron being either spiked to wooden plugs inserted in holes made in the stones or else fastened by wooden pins into cast-iron " pedestals," as John Bailey calls them, fixed in the stones.

Wooden rails did not, however, entirely and immediately give way to iron rails. On the contrary, the old system was so far maintained that, according to " The Industrial Resources of the Tyne," wooden railways could still be found on the collieries in that district as late as 1860.

Among the advantages derived from the substitution of iron rails for wooden rails was the fact that a horse could draw, on the level, heavier loads than before. On the other hand, the heavier the load the greater was the danger in taking the waggons down hill-sides with only a wooden brake to check their speed ; and this danger was increased to an even greater degree when the use of iron rails involved the abandonment of the wooden wheels which had hitherto been retained at the back of the waggons in order that the brake should act more effectively. Still further improvements thus became necessary, and these first took the form of inclined planes on which the law of gravity was employed, loaded waggons raising empty ones, or having their own descent regulated, by means of a rope passing round a wheel at the top of the incline. Later on stationary engines and chains were substituted for the wheel and the rope, horses then being employed on the level only.

Bailey says on this point : " Waggon ways have generally been so contrived that the ascents were not greater than a single horse could draw a waggon up them ; but some cases have happened lately where it required more than one horse, and steam engines have been substituted for horses for drawing waggons up these ascents. At Urpeth waggon way five or six waggons are drawn up at one ascent, by a steam engine placed at the top."

Here, then, we have another stage in the process of evolution that was going on. The stationary engine at the top of an incline drawing up, or regulating the descent of, heavier loads, on iron rails, was the first employment on railways of that steam power which was afterwards to develop into the locomotive capable to-day of taking heavy trains at a speed of a mile a minute. In those early days, however, speed was not regarded as a matter of any importance. Colliery managers were quite satisfied with a steady three miles an hour.

Although the general conditions of the pioneer railways were, apparently, so primitive, some of the lines were more ambitious and more costly than might, at first, be supposed. Among them were lines from five to ten miles in extent which served the double purpose of (1) enabling collieries in, for example, the Hinterland of the Tyne to benefit from the ever-expanding trade in coal; and (2) providing them with the means of discharging direct into the colliers below Newcastle bridge, thus saving the preliminary transport in, and trans-shipment from, the coal barges on the river. In these five- or ten-mile distances there were often considerable declivities to overcome, in order that the ideal of a gradual descent should be secured, and the cuttings, embankments, bridges and other works thus carried out were often closely akin to much of the railway construction with which we are familiar to-day. Thus Dr. Stukeley, in his " Itinerarium Curiosum," says in describing the visit he paid to the Tanfield Collieries, Durham, in 1725 :—

" We saw Col. Lyddal's coal-works at Tanfield, where he carries the road over valleys filled with earth, 100 foot high, 300 foot broad at bottom : other valleys as large have a stone bridge laid across : [1] in other places hills are cut through for half a mile together ; and in this manner a road is made, and frames of timber laid, for five miles to the river-side."

Arthur Young, also, who visited the Newcastle-on-Tyne district in 1768, says in his " Six Months Tour through the North of England " : " The coal waggon roads from the pits to the water are great works carried over all sorts of inequalities of ground so far as the distance of nine or ten miles."

The staiths at the river end of the Tyne railways are de-scribed in the " Commercial and Agricultural Magazine " as " solid buildings, two stories high ;. into the upper story the

[1] The stone bridge here referred to allowed of an easy transport across the valley from the collieries to the Tyne. Constructed by a local mason, the bridge soon fell down, and was rebuilt in 1727, the architect thereupon committing suicide to spare himself the anxiety of any possible further collapse of his work. In Brand's " History and Antiquities of Newcastle " (1789) it is stated that the span of the bridge was 103 feet, that the height was 63 feet, and that the cost of the structure was £1200.

waggon-way enters, and a spout projecting over the river shoots the coals into the keels, or a trap-door drops the coals into the lower story, whence they must be shovelled into the keels afterwards."

John Francis expresses the opinion, in his " History of the English Railway " (1851), that probably by 1750 there was scarcely an important colliery that had not its own railway. Such lines as these, however, were of a private character, serving the interests only of the companies or the individuals making them, without offering transport facilities to other traders in return for tolls, and requiring no Act of Parliament so long as they retained this character, did not require to cross public roads, and could be constructed by agreement among the landowners concerned. The more important development came when the canal companies themselves desired to supplement their canals by railways which anyone paying the stipulated tolls could use in connection with canal transport. Under these conditions the companies had to seek for further powers from Parliament, and this they began to do about the middle of the eighteenth century.

The Trent and Mersey Canal Act of 1776, for example, authorised the construction of a " rail-way " from the canal to the Froghall quarries, a distance of three and a half miles.[1] In 1802 the same company obtained authority to construct three " railways " extending from their canal in various directions. The preamble of the Act (42 Geo. III. c. 25) recited that the lines would be of " great advantage to the extensive manufactories of earthenware . . . and of public utility," and the Act accordingly sanctioned the lines " for the passage of waggons and carriages of forms and constructions, and with burthens suitable to such railways, to be approved by the company," at rates duly specified. These various railways, together with the Trent and Mersey Canal itself, were, in 1846, taken over by the North Staffordshire Railway Company, whose general manager, Mr W. D. Phillipps, informs me that portions of two of them are still in daily use. They are laid with cast-iron tram plates, with flanges to keep the wheels in place, and ordinary waggons

---

[1] In the Company's further Acts of 1783 and 1785 this line was still spoken of as a "rail-way," with the hyphen; but in their Act of 1797 it had become a railway—without the hyphen.

and carts use them to get from the canal basin to the high road, a few hundred yards away, the same rate of toll being charged as on the canal. Mr Phillipps further says: "Our Froghall tramway rises 400 feet from the level of the canal to the quarry, passing by means of a tunnel through an intermediate hill, and it is worked entirely by gravitation, there being four inclined planes of various lengths and inclinations. The gauge is 3 feet 6 inches. It is practically the same as when laid down over 100 years ago. We convey over it nearly 500,000 tons of limestone annually, and I find it a cheap and expeditious mode of conveyance."

I would call special attention to these details because it was, no doubt, the fact that ordinary road carts, with flat-edged wheels, could be taken along the flanged plates of the early railways, and were so taken under authority of the Acts of Parliament here in question, that originally established the idea both of a common user of the railways by traders employing their own vehicles upon them and of competition being thus ensured between different carriers. The pioneer public railways, provided as accessories to canal transport, were, indeed, looked upon as simply a variation, in principle, of the ordinary turnpike road. They were roads furnished with rails, and available for use, on payment of the authorised tolls, by anyone whose cart-wheels were the right distance apart.

The position in this respect was entirely changed when the system of railway operation came to be definitely fixed on the principle of edge-rails and flanged wheels, with locomotives in place of horses; yet the legislation immediately following the spread of railways on this vastly different basis was still determined, as regarded their use by the public, by the precedent originally established under the conditions here narrated.

While thus operated on the toll principle of a turnpike road—the pioneer "railway stations" being themselves simply the equivalent of toll-houses—the early railways were all associated with canal or river transport. Robert Fulton says in his "Treatise on the Improvement of Canal Navigation" (1796) that "Rail-roads have hitherto been considered as a medium between lock-canals and cartage, in consequence of the expence of extending the canal to the particular works in its neighbourhood "; and, in the course of a detailed argument in favour of small boats, of from two to five tons burden, in preference to the unduly large ones—as he considered them—then in vogue, he adds : " Rail-ways of one mile or thereabouts will, no doubt, be frequently necessary, where it may be difficult to find water at the extremity, or when the trade from the works is not sufficient to pay the expence of machinery,[1] and, its extent being one mile, can be of little importance to the country."

That Parliament itself, at this time, looked upon railways only as accessories to canals is shown by a reference to the " House of Commons Journals," where, under date June 19, 1799, it is reported that a Committee appointed, on the 10th of the same month, " to consider the expediency of requiring notices to be given of an intended application to Parliament for leave to bring in a Bill for the making of Ways or Roads usually called Railways or Dram Roads, or for the renewal or alteration of an Act passed for that purpose," had adopted the following resolution : " That it is the opinion of this Committee, That the Standing Orders of the House of the 7th of May, 1794, relating to Bills for making Navigable Canals, Aqueducts and the Navigation of Rivers, or for altering any Act of Parliament for any or either of those purposes, be extended to Bills for making any Ways or Roads, commonly called Railways or Dram Roads, except so much of the said Standing Orders as requires," etc. The resolution was agreed to by the House on the 25th of the same month.

Towards the close of the century it became customary for canal companies applying to Parliament for powers, or extensions of existing powers, to seek for authority to make railways, waggon ways or stone roads in connection with their canals ; and these they were generally authorised to lay down to any existing or future mines, quarries, furnaces, forges or other works within a distance of, at first four, subsequently eight, miles of such canal. They were, also, authorised to construct any bridges necessary for giving access to the canal. If, after being asked to make a railway, waggon road or bridge, under these conditions, the canal company refused so to do, the person or persons concerned

Stationary engines.

could carry out the work at his or their own cost and charges, without the consent of the owner of the lands, rivers, brooks or water-courses it might be necessary to cross, though subject to the payment to them of compensation under conditions analogous to those in force in regard to the construction of canals. One Act of this type, the Aberdare Canal Act, 1793, goes on to say : " Every such rail way or waggon road and bridge . . . shall . . . be publick and open to all persons for the conveyance of any minerals, goods, wares, merchandizes and things, in waggons and other carriages," of a specified construction, " and for the passage of horses, cows and other meat cattle, on payment to the person or persons at whose charge and expense such rail way or waggon road shall have been made or erected " of the same rates as would be payable to the canal company under like conditions.

It was in South Wales, even more than on the Tyne, that the early railways eventually underwent their greatest development. In " Illustrations of the Origin and Progress of Rail and Tram Roads and Steam Carriages or Loco-motive Engines" (1824), by T. G. Cumming, Surveyor, Denbigh, we read :—

" As late as the year 1790 there was scarcely a single railway in all South Wales, whilst in the year 1812 the rail-ways, in a finished state, connected with canals, collieries, iron and copper works, &c., in the counties of Monmouth, Glamorgan and Carmarthen alone extended to upwards of one hundred and fifty miles in length, exclusive of a very considerable extent within the mines themselves, of which one company at Merthyr Tydvil possessed upwards of thirty miles underground connected with the stupendous iron works at that place ; and so rapid has been the increase of rail-ways in South Wales of late years that at the present period they exceed four hundred miles, exclusive of about one hundred miles underground."

The whole of these lines were on the tram-plate, or flanged-rail, principle, while solid blocks of stone were, in Wales, generally substituted for wooden sleepers. Cumming further says :—

" In the extensive mining districts south of the Severn, including South Wales, the rail and tram roads are very numerous, and here, perhaps, more than in any part of the

United Kingdom, owing to the steepness, great irregularity and impracticable nature of the ground, they have been of the most essential utility in supplying the place of canals. . . .

" There are numerous tram roads connected with the canal between Cardiff and Merthyr Tydvil, in Glamorganshire. The extent of rail road about Merthyr Tydvil alone is very considerable ; besides which, in the same neighbourhood are the Hirwaen, Aberdare, and Abernant tram roads, and a great variety of others communicating with the vast works on the hills in the vicinity."

One of the South Wales tramroad schemes—though not specifically mentioned by Cumming—is of exceptional interest inasmuch as it represented, probably, the first attempt ever made to introduce a railway as a direct rival of and competitor with a canal, instead of being simply a feeder thereof. The attempt was a failure, but it nevertheless constitutes a landmark in early railway history.

The story begins with the granting, in 1790, of an Act for the cutting of a canal between Merthyr and Cardiff by the Company of Proprietors of the Glamorganshire Canal Navigation, improved means of transport being then much needed in the interests of the iron-works and other industrial undertakings in the district. The Act of 1790 authorised the company to spend £90,000 on the canal ; but this amount was found to be inadequate, and in 1796 a second Act sanctioned the raising of a further £10,000, and, also, the cutting of a short extension at the Cardiff end.

The opening of the canal for traffic is thus recorded by J. Phillips in the fourth edition (1803) of his " General History of Inland Navigation " :—

" Feb. 1794. The canal from Cardiff to Merthir-Tidvil is completed, and a fleet of canal boats have arrived at Cardiff laden with the produce of the iron works there, to the great joy of the whole town. The rude tracks, through which the canal passes in some places are constantly improving, from the happy and healthful toil of the husbandman, and in a few years will be forgotten in a garden of verdure and fertility. This canal is 25 miles long ; it passes along the sides of stupendous mountains. Nothing appears more extraordinary than, from a boat navigating this canal, to look down on the river Taaf, dashing among the rocks 100 yards below. The fall from Merthir-Tidvil to Cardiff is nearly 600 feet."

In a later reference, dated 1802, Phillips says that the completion of the Glamorganshire Canal " has opened a ready conveyance to the vast manufacture of iron established in the mountains of that country, and many thousands of tons are now annually shipped from thence."

The canal, however, failed to meet all requirements, a scheme for a railway, or dram-road, between Cardiff and Merthyr being projected in the same year that the waterway was first opened.

In " Rees' Cyclopædia " (1819) it is stated : " The railways hitherto constructed were private property, or for the accommodation of particular mines or works, and it was not, we believe, until about the year 1794 that Mr Samuel Homfray and others obtained an act of Parliament for constructing an iron dram-road, tram-road or rail-way between Cardiff and Merthyr Tidvill in South Wales, that should be free for any persons to use, with drams or trams of the specified construction on paying certain tonnage or rates per mile to the proprietors." Tredgold, in his " Practical Treatise on Railroads " (1825), makes a similar statement as regards the granting of an Act in 1794, saying that " in consequence of the upper part of the Cardiff or Glamorganshire canal being frequently in want of water, the Cardiff and Merthyr railway or tram-road was formed parallel to it, for a distance of about nine miles, chiefly for the iron works of Plymouth, Pendarran and Dowlais," with a continuation, however, making a total distance of about 26¾ miles. The tramway, he further says, " appears to have been constructed under the first Act ever obtained for this species of road."

These statements have been accepted and repeated by various writers ; but a search of the " House of Commons Journals " for 1794 fails to show that any such Act was passed. The scheme in question seems to have been projected, in 1794, by certain ironmasters, who found that their own traffic on the canal was being prejudiced by a preference given to the traffic of their rivals ; but the project for a tramway or railway from Merthyr to Cardiff was abandoned —for a time—in favour of one from Merthyr to a place then called Navigation, and now known as Abercynon, where the canal would be joined, and traffic could be tran-shipped.

The tramway in question is thus referred to in " The Scenery, Antiquities and Biography of South Wales, from Material Collected during two Excursions in the year 1803," by B. H. Malkin (second edition, 1807) :—

" At the Aqueduct, where the Canal is carried over the River, an iron rail-road for the present ends ; and from the Wharf at this place [Navigation] the Canal is the only conveyance for heavy goods to Cardiff ; the length of it—as far as it has already been completed—is 10 miles, but it was designed to have extended from Merthyr Tydfil to Cardiff, and it is said that one horse would have been able to draw 40 tons of iron the whole distance of 26 miles in one day ; I understand, however, that it is not likely to be finished, and, indeed, it is much more necessary where it is now made from the occasional want of water lower down where the confluence of many and copious streams affords a more certain supply to the Canal."

The line had evidently been constructed, not under any special Act, but by the authority of powers already granted by clause 57 of the Glamorganshire Canal Company's own Act, which, framed on the general lines already mentioned, conferred upon all persons owning, renting, leasing, or occupying property containing any mines of coal, iron-stone, limestone or other minerals, or the proprietors of any furnaces or other works lying within the distance of four miles from some part of the canal the right to make any railways or roads over the lands or grounds of any person or persons, or to make any bridges over any river, brook or watercourse, for the purpose of conveying the coal, iron, etc., to the said canal.

It will be noticed that this clause appears to limit to four miles the length of any tramway constructed in virtue of its provisions, whereas the length of the line actually made was, in effect, nine miles from Merthyr and ten from Dowlais. It is understood, however, that the constructors of the tramway successfully contended that, so long as their mines or works were within four miles of the canal, they were at liberty to lay down the tramway to such point on the canal as they thought proper to select, and they chose Navigation because it suited them best.

There is reason to believe, although actual proof is lacking, that the original design of continuing this tramway to Cardiff was not carried out because of the opposition of the canal company. Certain it is that the project for such a tramway was revived in 1799. Under date February 18, in that year, the " House of Commons Journals " record that William Lewis (Alderley), William Taitt, Thomas Guest, Joseph Cowles, and John Guest, being a firm of ironmasters in the parish of Merthyr Tydvil, known as the Dowlais Iron Company ; Jeremiah Homfray, Samuel Homfray, Thomas Homfray and William Forman, ironmasters, of Merthyr Tydvil, known by the name of Jeremiah Homfray and Co. ; Richard Hill and William Lewis (Pentyrch Works) petitioned the House for leave to bring in a Bill for the construction of a " dram road " from or near Carno Mill, in the parish of Bedwelty and the county of Monmouth to Cardiff, with branches to Merthyr and Aberdare.[1]

The petitioners declared that such dram-road would " open an easy Communication with several considerable Ironworks, Collieries, Limestone Quarries and extensive Tracks of Land, abounding with Coal, Limestone and other Minerals, whereby the Carriage and Conveyance of Iron, Coal, Lime, Timber and all kinds of Merchandize to or from the different Places bordering on the said intended Road will be greatly facilitated and rendered less expensive than at present, and will tend greatly to improve the Lands and Estates near the said Road, and the said Undertaking will, in other Respects, be of great Public Utility."

The petition was referred to a Committee, who reported favourably on March 8, and the Bill was presented and read a

---

[1] The length of the main line from Carno Mill to Cardiff was to be 26 miles, the branches increasing the total to 44 miles. The estimates of expenditure put the cost of land and construction at £31,105, exclusive of £894 10s., for "obtaining the Act, etc." The items in respect to the main line were as follows :—

	£	s.	d.
Forming the road and laying the dram rails, making the fences, etc., £220 per mile	5720	0	0
Iron dram rails, 44 tons per mile, at £6 per ton	6864	0	0
Sleepers, £40 per mile	1040	0	0
Purchase of land, 26 miles at £75 per mile	1950	0	0
Extra allowance, £100 per mile	2600	0	0
	£18,174	0	0

first time on March 15. Then, however, came the opposition
from the canal company. On April 8, as the " Journals "
further record, the Commons received a petition from the
Company of Proprietors of the Glamorganshire Canal Navigation setting forth that they had been authorised under two
Acts to make and maintain a navigable canal from Merthyr
to Cardiff; that they had expended on this undertaking
a sum of £100,000; that they had seen the Bill above-
mentioned, and, they proceed :—

" That the Dram Road or Way, proposed to be made by
the said Bill, will pass from one End thereof to the other,
nearly parallel, and in almost every Part near to the said
Canal; and in some places will cross the same; and that
the Petitioners were induced to undertake the making of the
said Canal, in hopes of being repaid the Expence thereof,
with proper remuneration for the Risk of the said Undertaking,
by the Carriage of Coal, Lime, Iron, Timber, and other goods
and Merchandizes thereon, but if the said Dram Road or
Way should be made as proposed they would be deprived
of a great Part of those Advantages which they apprehend
they have had granted and secured to them, and are therefore now fully entitled to, by the said Two Acts, without the
Country adjacent or the Public in General, receiving any
particular Benefit or Advantage."

The company further pleaded that under their Acts they
were " restrained from ever receiving more than a moderate
Dividend on their Shares, and whenever the Profits of the
Canal shall be more than sufficient to pay the same, their
Rates of Tonnage are to be lowered ;[1] and for that reason, as
well as many others, of equal Justice, they conceive they
should be secured in the possession of all the advantages
proposed to be granted to them by the said Acts."

The House ordered that the petition do lie upon the table
until the said Bill be read a second time, and that counsel be
then heard on both sides. On May 3 a day was appointed
for the second reading, and on May 4 the House received a
further petition from landowners, tradesmen and others in
support of the Bill. The " Journals," however, contain no
record of the second reading having been reached, and their

[1] In regard to this particular plea, see further references to the
Glamorganshire Canal Company on pages 238-9.

only further reference at all to the Bill is in the " General
Index " to the volumes for 1790–1801, where, under the
heading " Navigations : Petitions to make Dram Roads to
Canals, &c.," it is said of the Bill in question " Not proceeded in."

There is no reason to doubt that this first scheme for the
construction of a railway—even though under the name of a
" dram road "—which would have been not only independent
of canal transport but in direct competition therewith, was
killed through the opposition of the then powerful canal
interests. The tradition in Cardiff is that the Glamorganshire
Canal Company " got hold " of the leading promoters, and
persuaded them to abandon their scheme by electing them
members of the managing committee of the canal. Whether
or not some additional inducement was offered to them is
not known. In any case, there was no further attempt to
set up a railway in direct and avowed competition with a
canal until the great fight over the Liverpool and Manchester
Railway Bill, a quarter of a century later.

The significance of all these facts will be found still greater
in the light of what I shall have to say subsequently in regard
to the influence of canal interests and canal precedents alike
on railway development and on railway legislation.

In some instances the railways belonging to the period
here under review were constructed by the canal companies
not merely as feeders to the canals but as substitutes for
lengths of canal where the making of an artificial waterway
presented special difficulties. The Lancashire Canal Company, incorporated in 1792, laid a line of railway for five
miles, passing through the town of Preston, to connect two
sections of canal. The Ashby Canal Company, under an Act
of 1794, avoided a considerable expense in the construction
of locks by supplementing thirty miles of canal on the level
with intermediate lengths of railway to the extent of another
twenty miles. Writing in 1884, Clement E. Stretton says,
in his " Notes on Early Railway History," concerning these
old tram-roads of the Ashby Canal Company : " One part
has since been altered and absorbed into the Ashby and
Worthington Railway ;[1] but the branch from Ticknall tram-

---

[1] Amalgamated by the Midland Railway Company.

way wharf to Tucknall has never been relaid or altered in any way, and, therefore, is a most interesting relic of ancient times. To see waggons with flat wheels drawn over cast-iron rails one yard long by a horse, cannot fail to interest those who watch the workings of railways, and it most clearly shows the great improvements made and the perseverance which has been required to develop the present gigantic railway system out of such small beginnings."

The Charnwood Forest Canal, again, concerning which I shall have more to say later, was a connecting link between two lines of edge-railway, the purpose of the combined land and water route being to enable Leicestershire coal to reach the Leicester market.

It will thus be seen that, whilst the coalowners introduced railways in the first instance, it was the canal companies themselves who, in the days before locomotives, mainly developed and established the utility of a new mode of traction which was eventually to supersede to so material an extent the inland navigation they favoured. It was open to those companies to adapt their undertakings much more com-pletely to the new conditions, if they had had sufficient fore-sight and enterprise so to do.

The signs of the times were obvious enough to those who were able and willing to read them, and there were many indications that canals would assuredly be not only supple-mented, but supplanted, by railways. An impartial authority like Thomas Telford, in adding a postscript to an article on "Canals" which he had contributed to Archdeacon Plymley's "General View of the Agriculture of Shropshire," wrote under date November 13, 1800 :—

"Since the year 1797, when the above account of the inland navigation of the county of Salop was made out, another mode of conveyance has frequently been adopted in this country to a considerable extent ; I mean that of form-ing roads with iron rails laid along them, upon which the articles are conveyed on waggons, containing from six to thirty cwt. ; experience has now convinced us that in countries whose surfaces are rugged, or where it is difficult to obtain water for lockage, where the weight of the articles of pro-duce is great in comparison with their bulk, and where they are mostly to be conveyed from a higher to a lower level,—

that in those cases, iron rail-ways are in general preferable to a canal navigation.

" On a rail-way well constructed, and laid with a declivity of 55 feet in a mile, one horse will readily take down waggons containing from 12 to 15 tons, and bring back the same waggons with four tons in them. . . .

" This useful contrivance may be varied so as to suit the surface of many different countries at a comparatively moderate expense. It may be constructed in a manner much more expeditious than navigable canals ; it may be introduced into many districts where canals are wholly inapplicable ; and in case of any change in the working of the mines or manufactures, the rails may be taken up and put down again, in a new situation, at a moderate expense."

Thomas Gray, writing in 1821, warned investors in canal shares that the time was " fast approaching when rail-ways must, from their manifest superiority in every respect, supersede the necessity both of canals and turnpike roads, so far as the general commerce of the country was concerned." He further expressed the conviction that " were canal proprietors sensible how much their respective shares would be improved in value by converting all the canals into railways, there would not, perhaps, in the space of ten or twenty years remain a single canal in the country."

Blinded by their prosperity, however, the canal companies failed to adopt the necessary measures for ensuring its continuance, though the Duke of Bridgewater himself saw sufficient of the new rival to get an uneasy suspicion of what might happen. " We may do very well," he is reported to have said to Lord Kenyon, when asked about the prospects of his canals, " if we can keep clear of those —— tram-roads." Unfortunately for the canal interests, though fortunately for the country, the qualified tram-roads were not to be kept clear of, but, with the encouragement they got from those they afterwards impoverished, were to bring the Canal Era to a close, and to inaugurate the Railway Era in its place.

CHAPTER XIX

THE RAILWAY ERA

BETWEEN 1801 and 1825 no fewer than twenty-nine " iron railways " were either opened or begun in various parts of Great Britain. The full list is given by John Francis in his " History of the English Railway." It shows, as Francis points out, that from Plymouth to Glasgow, and from Carnarvon to Surrey, " there was scarcely a county where some form of the railway was not used." Most of these new railways were, however, still operated in conjunction with collieries or ironworks and canals or rivers, as the following typical examples show :—

1802 : Sirhowey Tramroad, built by the Monmouthshire Canal Company in conjunction with the Tredegar Iron-works; length, eleven miles ; cost £45,000.

1809 : Forest of Dean Railway, for conveying coals, timber, ore, etc., to the Severn for shipment ; length, seven and a half miles ; cost £125,000.

1809 : Severn and Wye Railway, connecting those rivers ; length, 26 miles ; cost £110,000.

1812 : Penrhynmaur Railway, Anglesey ; a colliery line, seven miles long, consisting of a series of inclined planes.

1815 : Gloucester and Cheltenham Railway, connecting with the Berkeley Canal at Gloucester.

1817 : Mansfield and Pinxton Railway, connecting the town of Mansfield, Nottinghamshire, with the Cromford Canal at Pinxton basin, near Alfreton, Derbyshire ; cost £32,800.

1819 : Plymouth and Dartmoor Railway ; length 30 miles ; cost £35,000.

1825 : Cromford and High Peak Railway, connecting the Cromford and Peak Forest Canals, and rising, by a series of elevations, 990 feet ; length 34 miles ; cost £164,000.

The first Act for a really *public* railway, in the sense in which that term is understood to-day, and as distinct from railways serving mainly or exclusively the interests of collieries, iron-works and canal navigations, was granted by Parliament in 1801 for the Surrey Iron Rail-way, which established a rail connection between the Thames at Wandsworth and the town of Croydon, with a branch to some mills on the river Wandle whose owners were the leaders in the enterprise. The total length was about nine and a half miles. According to the Act, the line was designed for " the advantage of carrying coals, corn and all goods and merchandise to and from the Metropolis." Constructed with flanged rails, or " plates," fixed on stone blocks, the line was available for any ordinary cart or waggon of the requisite gauge. The conveyances mostly used on it were four-wheeled trucks, about the size of railway contractors' waggons. They belonged either to local traders or to carriers who let them out on hire, it being doubtful whether the company had any rolling stock of their own. The motive power was supplied by horses, mules or donkeys. Chalk, flint, fire-stone, fuller's earth and agricultural produce were sent from Croydon— then a town of 5700 inhabitants—to the Thames for conveyance to London. The return loading from the Thames was mainly coal and manure. Two sets of rails were provided, and there was a path on each side for the men in charge of the horses.

Referring to the Surrey Iron Rail-way in his " History of Private Bill Legislation," Clifford says :—

" The Act of 1801, upon which the rest of this early railway legislation was framed, follows the canal precedents in their provision for managing the company's affairs, for raising share and loan capital, and for compensating landowners. Only the use of horse power was contemplated. The tracks, when laid down, were meant, like canals, for general use by carriers and freighters. The companies did not provide rolling stock ; any person might construct carriages adapted to run upon the rails, and if these carriages were approved certain maximum tolls applied to the freight they might carry. . . . Passenger traffic was not expected or provided for. . . . Such was the first Railway Act, passed at the beginning of the century with little notice by Parliament or people, but now a social landmark, prominent in that stormy period of history."

This was, however, in point of fact, only a further development of the still earlier railway legislation (see page 210), which required the proprietors of lines laid down for general traffic to allow anyone who pleased to run his own vehicles thereon, subject to certain regulations and to the payment of specified tolls.

The Surrey Iron Rail-way was also a landmark in railway history because, although in itself of very small extent, it was originally designed to serve as the first section of a railway which, made by different companies, as capital could be raised, would eventually have extended from the Thames to Portsmouth.[1] The second section was the Croydon, Merstham and Godstone Iron Railway, which Parliament sanctioned in 1803. From Croydon this further railway was to carry the lines on to Reigate, with a branch from Merstham to Godstone Green, a total distance of sixteen miles in addition, that is, to the nine and a half miles of the Surrey Iron Rail-way. Both companies, however, drifted into financial difficulties, and had to apply to Parliament again, in 1806, for fresh powers, while the lines of the second company never got beyond the chalk quarries at Merstham.

In the absence of the through traffic it had been hoped eventually to secure, the local business alone available was evidently inadequate to meet the charges on a capital outlay which, at that time, may have been regarded as not inconsiderable, inasmuch as the Surrey Iron Rail-way attained to a good elevation at its southern end, while the Croydon, Merstham and Godstone line went through a cutting thirty feet deep, and crossed a valley by an embankment twenty feet high. After a chequered career, the Merstham line was acquired by the Brighton Railway Company in 1838 and closed, being then no longer required. The Surrey line lingered on till 1846, when, with the sanction of Parliament, its operation was discontinued, the rails being taken up and sold by auction.

---

[1] My authority for this statement is a newspaper article, headed "Centenary of the First Railway Act," written in 1901 by W. P. Paley, and to be found in a collection of railway pamphlets in the British Museum (08235 i 36). The name of the journal is not stated ; but the writer of the article gives such precise details concerning the line in question that his information is evidently authentic.

It was unfortunate that these two pioneer public railways were a failure because, had they succeeded, and had they really formed the first sections of a through line of communication between the Thames and Portsmouth, there would have been established a further precedent—and one of much greater value than that of a common user—the precedent, namely, of a trunk line made by companies co-operating with one another to give continuous communication on a well-organised system, in place of collections of disconnected lines designed, at the outset, to serve the interests only of particular localities, with little or no attempt at co-ordination.

Yet the principle of a general public railway had, at least, been established by the Surrey and Merstham lines, and this principle underwent further important development by the Stockton and Darlington Railway, the first Act for which was obtained in 1821.

The only purpose originally intended to be served by the Stockton and Darlington Railway was the finding of a better outlet for coal from the South Durham coalfield. A company, with Edward Pease as the moving spirit, was formed in 1816, but two years later the projectors were still undecided whether to make a canal or " a rail or tramway." George Overton, who preceded George Stephenson as a distinguished railway engineer, wrote to them, however, advising the latter course. " Railways," he said, " are now generally adopted, and the cutting of canals nearly discontinued " ; and he told them, further, that within the last fifteen years the great improvements made in the construction of tram-roads had led to the application of the principle to a number of new roads. His advice was adopted, and the first Act, obtained after several unsuccessful efforts, authorised the making and maintaining of " a railway or tramroad " from the river Tees, at Stockton, to Witton Park Colliery, with various branches therefrom. The line would, the Act said, be " of great public utility by facilitating the conveyance of coal, iron, lime, corn and other commodities from the interior of the county of Durham to the town of Darlington and the town and port of Stockton," etc.

It was first intended to use wooden rails, and to rely on horse-power, no authority for the employment of locomotives being obtained under the Act of 1821 ; but George Stephenson, on being appointed engineer to the line, persuaded the company to adopt iron rails in preferenee to wooden ones, and to provide a locomotive such as he had already constructed and successfully employed at Killingworth Colliery. Two-thirds of the rails laid were of malleable iron and one-third of cast iron. It was not, however, until September, 1824, that the order was actually given for a locomotive, some of the promoters having still shown a strong preference for the use of stationary engines and ropes.

The line was opened for traffic on September 27, 1825, and the locomotive which had been ordered—the " Locomotion " as it was called—was ready for the occasion. It weighed seven tons, and had perpendicular cylinders and a boiler provided with only a single flue, or tube, 10 inches in diameter and 10 feet in length, the heat being abstracted therefrom so imperfectly that when the locomotive was working the chimney soon became red-hot.[1] The usual speed was from four to six miles an hour, with a highest possible of eight miles an hour on the level.

The company made provision for the anticipated goods traffic by having 150 waggons built ; but they started with no idea of themselves undertaking passenger traffic. Their first Act had laid down that " Any person is at liberty to use and run a carriage on the railway, provided he complies with the bye-laws of the company " ; and J. S. Jeans, in his history of the Stockton and Darlington Railway published (1875) under the title of " Jubilee Memorial of the Railway System," says : " It was originally intended to allow the proprietors of stage-coaches or other conveyances plying on the route of the proposed new railway to make use of the line on certain specified conditions." This, too, is what actually happened ; for although, a fortnight after the opening of the line, the railway company themselves put on the line a springless " coach," known as the " Experiment," and drawn by a horse, several coach proprietors in the district availed themselves of their statutory right to run their own coaches on the railway, first, of course, providing them with wheels adapted to the rails. They paid the railway company

[1] In succeeding engines a double tube, bent in the form of the letter U, was fixed. Stephenson provided his " Rocket " with 25 tubes, thus giving a further substantial increase in the heating surface.

the stipulated tolls, and had the advantage of requiring to
use no more than a single horse for each coach. These horse
coaches for passengers seem to have run in the intervals
when the lines were not occupied by the locomotive engaged
in drawing the coal waggons.

In a letter published in the " Railway Herald " of April 27,
1889, John Wesley Hackworth, whose father, Timothy
Hackworth, was for some time engineer on the Stockton
and Darlington Railway, says that twenty miles of the line
were at first worked by horses and locomotive in competition,
and at the end of eighteen months it was found that horse
traction was costing only a little over one-third of the traction by locomotive. Meanwhile, also, the value of the £100
shares had fallen to £50. In view of these results the directors
had decided to abandon locomotive power, and depend
entirely on horses; but Timothy Hackworth said to them,
" If you will allow me to construct an engine in my own
way I will engage it shall work cheaper than animal power."
He received the desired authority, and the " Royal George,"
built by him, was put into operation in September, 1827. It
confirmed the assurance which had been given, and, says
Timothy Hackworth's son, " finally and for ever " settled
the question of the respective merits of horse and steam
traction on railways.

Horse coaches still continued to run on the lines, however,
in addition to the mineral and goods trains, and in January,
1830, the company had to draw up a time-table fixing the
hours of departure for the coaches, thus ensuring a better
service for the public, and, also, protecting travellers against
any possible encounter with the locomotive as the horse
ambled along with them on the railway.

By October, 1832, seven coaches, belonging to various
proprietors, were doing fifty journeys a week between different
places on the line; so that thus far the original idea of Parliament, in enforcing against railways the principle of a common
user of their lines by the public, had appeared to be warranted.
A year later, however, the railway company, finding, as
Jeans tells us, that it would be more convenient and more
advantageous for them to take the whole carrying trade in
their own hands and supersede the horses by steam locomotives, bought out, on what were considered generous terms,

the interests of the four coach proprietors then carrying passengers on their own account on the lines.

Actual experience had thus nullified the expectation that a railway would be simply a rail-road upon which anyone would be able to run his own conveyances as on an ordinary turnpike road.

From October, 1833, the whole of the passenger traffic (then undergoing rapid expansion) was conducted by the company. In April, 1834, the directors, who had by this time acquired some other and better engines, announced that they had commenced to run, six times a day, both "coaches" (for passengers) and "carriages" (for goods) by locomotives; and this date, probably, marks the final disappearance of the horse as a means of traction for passenger traffic on public railways in England, though the word "coaches," introduced into the railway vocabulary under the circumstances here narrated, has remained in use ever since among railway men as applied to rolling stock for passenger traffic.

Unlike its predecessors in Surrey, and though facing various difficulties at the outset, the Stockton and Darlington line attained to a considerable degree of prosperity. After undergoing various extensions from time to time, and playing a leading part in the industrial expansion of the district it served, it was incorporated into what is now the North-Eastern Railway system.

Summing up the respects in which the Stockton and Darlington line had carried forward the story of railway development, we find that it (1) established the practicability of substituting locomotive for horse traction on railways; (2) introduced the provision of waggons by the railway company, instead of leaving these to be found by carriers and traders; (3) proved that railways were as well adapted to the transport of passengers as they were to the carriage of goods; (4) showed by actual experience that the idea of a common user of railways was impracticable; and (5) prepared the way for the eventual recognition, even by Parliament itself, of the principle that transport on a line of railway operated by locomotives must, in the nature of things, be the monopoly of the owning and responsible railway company.

While the Surrey Iron Rail-way and the Stockton and

Darlington Railway had been thus seeking to establish themselves as public railways, there was no lack of advocates of
what were then called "general rail-ways," to be laid either
on the ordinary roads or on roads made for the purpose ;
and such general railways were especially advocated for
districts where canals could not be made available.

Dr James Anderson, writing on "Cast Iron Rail-ways"
in the issue of his "Recreations in Agriculture, Natural
History," etc., for November, 1800, had already strongly
recommended them as "an eligible mode of conveyance where
canals cannot be conveniently adopted " ; and he especially
advised the construction of one railway in London, from
the new docks on the Isle of Dogs to Bishopsgate Street,
and another between London and Bath, "for the purpose of
conveying unsightly loads, leaving the roads, as at present,
open for coaches and light carriages." Such railways, he
argued, would render great service in relieving the ordinary
road of heavy traffic, and help to solve the road problem
of that day—all the more acute because McAdam had not
yet shown the country how roads could and should be made
or repaired.

On February 11, 1800, Mr Thomas, of Denton, read a
paper before the Newcastle Literary Society recommending
the introduction of railways, on the colliery principle, for
the general carriage of goods ; and R. L. Edgeworth urged,
in "Nicholson's Journal," in 1802, that for a distance of
ten miles or more one of the great roads out of London should
be provided with four tracks of railway operated by stationary
engines and circulating chains for fast and slow traffic in
each direction.

But the most strenuous advocate of all was Thomas Gray.
Both before and subsequent to the publication, in 1820, of
the first edition of his "Observations on a General Rail-way,"
he had been pressing his views, in the form of petitions, letters
or articles, on members of the Government, peers of the
realm, M.P.'s, corporations, capitalists, reviews and newspapers. His idea was that there should be six trunk lines
of railway radiating from London, with branch lines linking
up towns and villages off these main routes ; but he was
looked upon as a visionary, if not as a crank and a bore whose
impracticable proposals were not deserving of serious con-

sideration. It was evidently Thomas Gray whom the " Quarterly Review " had in mind when it said, in March, 1825 : " As to those persons who speculate on making railways general throughout the Kingdom, and superseding all the canals, all the waggons, mail and stage-coaches, post-chaises, and, in short, every other mode of conveyance by land and water, we deem them and their visionary schemes unworthy of notice."

In the result Gray was left to spend the last years of his life in obscurity and poverty, and the further development of the railway system of the country was proceeded with on lines altogether different from, and far less efficient, than those he had recommended.

The greatest impetus to the movement was now to come, not from any individual pioneer, but from the Liverpool and Manchester Railway ; and this line, in turn, was due far more to purely local conditions and circumstances than to any idea of encouraging the creation of a network of railways on some approach, however remote, to a national or " general " system. The original cause of the Liverpool and Manchester line being undertaken was, in fact, nothing less than extreme dissatisfaction among the traders both of Liverpool and of Manchester with the then existing transport arrangements between these two places.

Just as the Duke of Bridgewater had drawn his strongest arguments in favour of a canal from the shortcomings of the Irwell and Mersey navigation, so now did the traders base their case for a railway mainly on the deficiencies and shortcomings alike of the river navigation and of the canal by which the rivers had been supplemented.

There were, in the first place, physical difficulties. By whichever of the two water routes goods were sent from Liverpool to Manchester, the barges had first to go about eighteen miles along the Mersey to Runcorn, being thus exposed for that distance to the possibly adverse winds and strong tides of an open estuary. The boats often got aground, and many wrecks occurred during stormy weather. On the canal itself the boats could often go with only half loads in the summer, and they were liable to be stopped by frost in winter, while the canal was closed altogether for ten days every year for repairs.

Supplementing these physical disadvantages of the navigation was the attitude of the waterway interests towards the traders whom they held at their mercy. Theoretically there was competition between the rivers and the canal; but the agents of both extorted from the traders the highest possible charges for a most inefficient service.

Joseph Sandars, who was to take a leading part in the movement for a railway between Liverpool and Manchester, has some strong things to say about the " exorbitant and unjust charges of the water carriers " in a " Letter " on the subject of the proposed railway which he published in 1824. He alleged that, whereas the Duke of Bridgewater had been authorised by his Acts to charge not more than two shillings and sixpence per ton for canal dues, his agents had, by various devices, which Sandars details, exacted five shillings and two-pence per ton. The trustees had, also, obtained possession of all the warehouses alongside the canal at Manchester, and they were thus able to exact whatever terms they pleased from the bye-carriers and traders. If the canal trustees carried the goods in their own vessels they were entitled to charge six shillings per ton; and their aim seems to have been to render it impossible for the independent carriers to do their business at a lower rate than this. When the carriers, using boats of their own, would not pay the same rate as if the trustees had themselves done the carrying, they were not allowed to land the goods.

Then, by acquiring all the warehouses and all the available land at Preston Brook and Runcorn, the trustees had likewise got control over navigation on the Trent and Mersey Canal, which joins the Bridgewater Canal at Preston Brook. Sandars speaks of Mr Bradshaw, to whom the Duke of Bridgewater had, by his will, given absolute control of his undertakings, as a dictator of canal transport. " No man," he says, in giving examples of the wide extent of the interests that Bradshaw controlled or sought to influence, " can bring a Bill forward for a canal in any part of the Kingdom but Mr Bradshaw interferes as a sort of canal Neptune, directing where, how, and at what price it shall run. He has tortured the trade of the country to become tributary to him in all directions. Every man, every corporate body, seems spell-bound the moment Mr Bradshaw interposes his authority."

As for the profits of the undertaking, Sandars says : " There is good reason to believe that the nett income of the Duke's canal has, for the last twenty years, averaged nearly £100,000 per annum."

The Old Quay Company had refrained from exceeding the amounts they were authorised to charge for tolls on the Irwell and the Mersey ; but there was no restriction on them in regard to traffic they themselves carried, and Sandars alleges that they, also, had secured all the warehouse accommodation on their own line of route, and had almost monopolised the carrying trade, since a bye-carrier's business could hardly be conducted without warehouses. They were thus making far more money than they could have got from the statutory tolls alone. So profitable had the undertaking become that the thirty-nine original proprietors had, Sandars continues, " been paid every other year, for nearly half a century, the total amount of their investment." An immense revenue was being raised at the expense of the merchants and manufacturers, " and for no other purpose than to enrich a few individuals who were daily violating Acts of Parliament, Acts which, by a long course of cunning policy," they had contrived to convert into " the most oppressive and unjust monopoly known to the trade of this Kingdom— a monopoly which," Sandars goes on to declare, " there is every reason to believe compels the public to pay, in one shape or another, £100,000 more per annum than they ought to pay."

The agents of the two companies not only agreed between themselves what charges they would impose but, autocrats as they were, they established a despotic sway over the traders. They set up, says Francis, " a rotation by which they sent as much or as little as suited them, and shipped it how or when they pleased. They held levees, attended by crowds who, admitted one by one, almost implored them to forward their goods. One firm was thus limited by the supreme wisdom of the canal managers to sixty or seventy bags a day. The effects were really disastrous ; mills stood still for want of material ; machines were stopped for lack of food. Of 5000 feet of pine timber required in Manchester by one house, 2000 remained unshipped from November, 1824, to March, 1825."

Merchants whose timber was thus delayed in transit were fined for allowing it to obstruct the quays; and Sandars tells of one who paid £69 in fines on this account during the course of two months. It was less costly and more convenient to leave the delayed timber where it was, and pay the fines, than to keep moving it to and fro between quay and timber yard; though the effect—especially as the imports of timber increased—was to block up, not only the quays, but the neighbouring streets, which thus became almost impassable for carts and carriages.

Corn and other commodities had often to be kept back eight or ten days on account of a lack of vessels. It sometimes happened that commodities brought across the Atlantic in three weeks were detained in Liverpool for six weeks before they could be sent on to Manchester. The agents would not carry certain kinds of merchandise or particular descriptions of cotton at all. Alternatively they would tell a trader: " We took so much for you yesterday, and we can take only so much for you to-day." " They limited the quantity," says Francis, " they appointed the time, until the difficulties of transit became a public talk and the abuse of power a public trouble. The Exchange of Liverpool resounded with merchants' complaints; the counting-houses of Manchester re-echoed the murmurs of manufacturers."

To avoid serious delays either to raw materials or to manufactured articles the traders were often forced to resort to road transport " because," says Sandars, " speed and certainty as to delivery are of the first importance "; and he adds on this point, " Packages of goods sent from Manchester, for immediate shipment at Liverpool, often pay two or three pounds per ton; and yet there are those who assert that the difference of a few hours in speed can be no object. The merchants know better."

The example already set in so many different parts of the country in the provision of rail-ways, or railways, as they were now being generally called, may well have suggested that in a resort to this expedient would be found the most practical solution of the problem which had caused so much trouble to the traders. Sandars himself says that inasmuch as the two companies were " deaf to all remonstrances, to all entreaties," and were " actuated solely by a spirit of mono-

poly˜and extortion," the only remedy the public had left
was to go to Parliament and ask for permission to establish
a new line of conveyance—and one, also, that possessed
decided advantages over canal or river transport.

But here there arose a consideration which had a material
bearing on the problem immediately concerned, and was to
affect the further development of the railway system in
general.

Numerous as were the lines already existing at this time,
none of them directly competed with the waterways. They
were feeders rather than rivals of the canals. Even the
Surrey Iron Rail-way and the Stockton and Darlington line,
though operating independently of the canal companies,
had not come into conflict with them. In the one instance—
that of the Merthyr and Cardiff dram-road—in which a railway had hitherto been projected in direct competition with a
canal the scheme had been either killed or bought off by the
canal interests. But the proposed Liverpool and Manchester
Railway was avowedly and expressly designed to compete
with the existing water services. It was not simply to supplement the waterways. It threatened to supplant them.

So the waterway companies, representing very powerful
interests—inasmuch as by 1824 the amount invested in canal
and navigation schemes was about £14,000,000—might well
think it necessary to take action in defence of their own position. Down to this time they had regarded the railway as
either a friend or a non-competitor, and they had either extended to it a sympathetic support or had, at least, regarded
it with a feeling of equanimity. Henceforward they had to
look upon it as an opponent.

The project for a Liverpool and Manchester Railway would
seem to have first begun to assume definite shape in or about
1822, when William James, a London engineer, who had
already proposed a " Central Junction Rail-way or Tram-
road " from Stratford-on-Avon to London, made surveys
between Liverpool and Manchester, and prepared a set of
plans. The certain prospect, however, of vigorous opposition
from the waterway interests led some of the traders to think
they had better make terms with the men in possession, if
they could ; and in that same year the corn merchants of
Liverpool memorialised the Bridgewater trustees, asking both

for a reduction in the rate of freight and for better accommodation. Bradshaw replied with an unqualified refusal, and he treated as idle talk the then much-discussed project of a line of railway.

There is no doubt that if, at this period, reasonable concessions had been made to the traders the building of the Liverpool and Manchester Railway, although, of course, inevitable, would have been delayed to a later period. The traders shrank, at first, from an open fight, and the project of 1822 was allowed to drop for a time. The situation was found to be so hopeless, however, that in 1824 they decided that mere concessions from the waterway interests would no longer suffice, and that the provision of an alternative means of transport had become imperative. A Liverpool and Manchester Railway Company was now formed, and on October 29, 1824, there was issued a prospectus which was, in effect, a declaration of war against the waterway parties who had so mercilessly abused the situation they thought they controlled. This document, after mentioning that the total quantity of merchandise then passing between Liverpool and Manchester was estimated at 1000 tons a day, proceeded :—

" The committee are aware that it will not immediately be understood by the public how the proprietors of a railroad, requiring an invested capital of £400,000 can afford to carry goods at so great a reduction upon the charge of the present water companies. But the problem is easily solved. It is not that the water companies have not been able to carry goods on reasonable terms, but that, strong in the enjoyment of their monopoly, they have not thought proper to do so. Against the most arbitrary exactions the public have hitherto had no protection, and against the indefinite continuance or recurrence of the evil they have but one security. *It is competition that is wanted*, and the proof of this assertion may be adduced from the fact that shares in the Old Quay Navigation, of which the original cost was £70, have been sold as high as £1250 each ! "

The canal interests in general had, however, anticipated the definite challenge thus given, and there had already been a call to arms in defence of common interests. In a postscript to the prospectus just referred to it was mentioned that the Leeds and Liverpool, the Birmingham, the Grand Trunk and other canal companies had issued circulars calling upon " every canal and navigation company in the Kingdom to oppose *in limine*, and by a united effort, the establishment of railroads wherever contemplated."[1]

By this time, therefore, the projectors of the Liverpool and Manchester Railway were threatened with the opposition, not alone of the Bridgewater trustees and of the Old Quay Navigation trustees, but of the canal and river navigation interests throughout the country. As Thomas Baines well describes the position in his " History of Liverpool," " The canal proprietors, with an instinctive sense of danger, justly appreciated what they affected to despise, and, with one accord, and with one heart and mind, resolved to crush the rival project which threatened to interrupt, if not to destroy the hopes of prescription and the dreams of a sanguine avarice."

The real strength of the opposition thus being worked up against not only the Liverpool and Manchester Railway but public railways in general will be better understood if I supplement the references I have already made to the shares of canal and navigation companies by a few further figures, showing the financial position to which the waterways had attained, and the extent of the vested interests they represented at the particular period now in question.

In a pamphlet published in 1824, under the title of " A Statement of the Claim of the Subscribers to the Birmingham and Liverpool Rail-road to an Act of Parliament ; in reply to the Opposition of the Canal Companies " (quoted in the fifth, or 1825, edition of Thomas Gray's " Observations on a General Iron Rail-way "), it is stated that the amount of capital originally subscribed for the old Birmingham Canal Company was about £55,000, in shares of £100, subject to a stipulation that no one person should hold more than ten shares. The pamphlet proceeds :—

---

[1] That this attitude of organised hostility on the part of the canal companies was well maintained is shown by the following extract from the " Manchester Advertiser " of January 30, 1836 : " The proprietors of the Ayre and Calder navigation and of the Canals, have resolved to organise an opposition to all railways whatever in Parliament. The canal proprietors are thus openly setting themselves in opposition to one of the greatest improvements of the age."

" By various subsequent Acts and collateral cuts, this canal, which has now changed its name to the style of the ' Birmingham Canal Navigation Company,' is extended to a distance of about 60 miles of water, containing 99 locks or thereabouts, 10 fire engines to raise water, number of bridges not known to the present writer.

" The original shares are computed to have cost the proprietors £140 each. In 1782 they were marketably worth £370, and in 1792, £1110. In 1811 an Act increased the shares 500 to 1000, or, in other words, for marketable convenience divided them. In 1813 the half share was sold as high as £585. In 1818 power was given to the company of proprietors further to subdivide the shares as they should deem advisable, on due public notice, etc. The shares are now in eighths. Thus at the present time, and at the last quoted prices in Wetenhall's list, there are 4000 shares of eighths, marketably worth £360 per eighth, each receiving an annual dividend of £12–10–0. Thus the original cost, compared with the present value of the 500 shares, is as £70,000 to £1,444,000, the original share having risen from £140 sterling (or thereabouts) to the sum of £2840."

Shares in the Loughborough Navigation cost the first holders £142–17–0 each. In the " European Magazine " for June, 1821, they are quoted at £2600 a share, and the dividend then being paid is given as 170 per cent. In the issue of the same magazine for November, 1824, the price per share is £4700, and the dividend is shown to have risen to 200 per cent.

Among other canal shares quoted in the " European Magazine " for the dates mentioned are the following :—

COMPANY.	SHARE.	1821		1824	
		PRICE.	DIVIDEND.	PRICE.	DIVIDEND.
	£	£	£	£	£
Coventry. . .	100	970	44	1350	44 and 61
Erewash . . .	100	1000	56	—	58
Leeds and Liverpool	100	280	10	570	15
Oxford . . .	100	630	32	900	32*
Staffordshire and					
Worcestershire .	100	700	40	950	40
Trent and Mersey .	200	1750	75	2250	75*

* And bonus.

The following further quotations are from "Wetenhall's Commercial List" for December 10, 1824 :—

COMPANY.	SHARE.			PRICE.			DIVIDEND.		
	£	s.	d.	£	s.	d.	£	s.	d.
Ashton and Oldham . .	97	18	0	310	0	0	5	0	0
Barnsley . . .	160	0	0	340	0	0	12	0	0
Grand Junction . .	100	0	0	296	0	0	10	0	0
Glamorganshire . .	172	13	4	280	0	0	13	12	8
Grantham . . .	150	0	0	190	0	0	10	0	0
Leicester . . .	140	0	0	390	0	0	14	0	0
Monmouthshire . .	100	0	0	245	0	0	10	0	0
Melton Mowbray . .	100	0	0	255	0	0	11	0	0
Mersey and Irwell . .	—			1000	0	0	35	0	0
Neath . . .	100	0	0	400	0	0	15	0	0
Shrewsbury . .	125	0	0	206	0	0	10	0	0
Stourbridge . .	145	0	0	220	0	0	10	10	0
Stroudwater . .	150	0	0	450	0	0	31	10	0
Trent and Mersey (half share) .	100	0	0	2300	0	0	75	0	0*
Warwick and Birmingham .	100	0	0	320	0	0	11	0	0
Warwick and Knapton .	100	0	0	280	0	0	11	0	0

* And bonus.

These figures, it will be seen, are given for years when the "canal mania"—at its height between 1791 and 1794—had long been over, and they suggest, therefore, *bona fide* market values based on business done and dividends paid. High as they are, it is doubtful if they tell the whole story. I have mentioned on page 218 that in their petition to the House of Commons against the proposed railway, or tramway, between Merthyr and Cardiff, the Glamorganshire Canal Company represented that they were restrained by their Act from paying more than a "moderate" dividend. The dividend they were authorised to pay was one of eight per cent; but there is a tradition in South Wales that the company, after checking effectively the threatened railway competition, attained to phenomenal prosperity, and resorted to an ingenious expedient as a means of deriving further pecuniary advantage from the waterway without exceeding the statutory limitation in regard to the dividend to be paid. This expedient took the form of a suspension of all tolls for a large part of every year, the use of the canal being free to the public for the period so arranged. In some years, it is said, no tolls were paid for six months at a time. This practice was found preferable, for certain members of the managing committee— ironmasters or large traders in the district—to a reduction of tolls to be in force throughout the year, their practice being to keep back their own consignments, whenever possible, till the free period, which they could fix to suit their convenience. When the principal shareholders were traders using the canal, it did not matter to them whether their profits came wholly in dividends or partly in dividends and partly in free carriage. Traders, however, who could not wait for their supplies or store their manufactured goods until the free period came round had to pay the full rates of tolls for, at least, the period during which these were enforced.

I shall refer later to the effect on railway legislation of the power and influence to which the waterways had attained. The consideration for the moment is that, even allowing for a certain number of minor or of purely speculative canals which were admittedly failures, the waterway interests, consolidating their forces, were able, by virtue of their position at the time in question, to organise a powerful and widespread opposition to a rival form of transport then still in its infancy, though obviously capable of eventually becoming a formidable competitor.

The canal interests also made every effort to work up an opposition on the part of representatives of the landed interests, who, however, developed such strong hostility of their own towards the iron road that the arguments of the canal proprietors were hardly needed to arouse them to violent antagonism to the scheme. Popular prejudices, too, were well exploited, and the most direful predictions were indulged in as to what would result from the running of locomotives, so that, for a time, the promoters even abandoned the idea of using locomotives at all.

The combined canal and land interests scored the first victory on the Liverpool and Manchester Bill, which was thrown out in 1825 ; but it was reintroduced and passed in 1826, the opposition of the Bridgewater trustees having, in the meantime, been overcome by a judicious presentation to them of a thousand shares in the railway.

The promoters thus established the new principle of direct

competition between railways and waterways ; but otherwise the Liverpool and Manchester differed from the Stockton and Darlington, at the outset, and as a line of railway, only in the fact that the former was to be provided throughout with malleable iron rails, whereas the latter had two-thirds malleable iron and one-third cast iron. On the one line as on the other, the use of locomotives had not been decided upon from the start ; and, unless the Liverpool and Manchester had not only adopted locomotives but, as was, of course, the case, improved on those of the Stockton and Darlington, it would have shown little real advance in actual railway operation.

The motive power to be used on the Liverpool and Manchester remained uncertain when George Stephenson and his "navvies" were attacking the engineering proposition of Chat Moss. It was still uncertain in October, 1828—or two years after the passing of the Act—when three of the directors went to Killingworth colliery, to see the early locomotive which Stephenson had made there, and to Darlington to see the locomotives then operating on the Stockton and Darlington line. They decided that "horses were out of the question" ; but even then the point remained doubtful whether the Liverpool and Manchester should be provided with locomotives or have stationary engines at intervals of a mile or two along the line to draw the trains from station to station by means of ropes. How the directors sought to solve the problem by offering a premium of £500 for a locomotive which would fulfil certain conditions ; how George Stephenson won the prize with his "Rocket" ; and how the "Rocket," with a gross load of seventeen tons, attained a speed of twenty-nine miles an hour, with an average of fourteen—whereas counsel for the promoters had only promised a speed of six or seven miles an hour—are facts known to all the world.

If the Stockton and Darlington Railway had had the honour of introducing the locomotive, it was the Rainhill trials, organised by the Liverpool and Manchester Company, which gave the world its first idea of the great possibilities to which alike the locomotive and the railway might attain. In this respect the Liverpool and Manchester line carried railway development far beyond the point already attained by the Stockton and Darlington, although no fundamentally new principle in railway working was set up. The Liverpool and Manchester line did, however, establish a new departure in proclaiming direct rivalry with the then powerful canal interests, and the warfare thus entered on, and persevered in until the railway system had gained the ascendancy, was to affect the whole further history of railway expansion and control.

CHAPTER XX

THE monopolist tendencies of the waterway interests, the magnitude of the profits secured, and the resort by traders to the building of railways as an alternative thereto and as a means of meeting the transport requirements of expanding industries, were factors in the development of the railway system that operated as direct causes in the construction of other lines besides the Liverpool and Manchester. From these particular points of view the story of the Leicester and Swannington Railway is of special significance.

In the closing years of the eighteenth century, when the Canal Era was in full operation, the various new projects put forward included one for constructing a canal, eleven miles in length, down the Erewash valley to connect with the Trent, thus facilitating the transport of coal and other products from Nottinghamshire and Derbyshire to places served by that river; and another for rendering the Soar navigable from its junction with the Trent to Leicester, this being known as the Loughborough Navigation. These two schemes were to form part of a network of important waterways, the Soar Navigation joining the Leicester Navigation, and this, in turn, communicating with the Leicestershire branch of the Grand Junction Canal, thus eventually giving a direct route from Derbyshire, Nottinghamshire and Leicestershire to London.

The Leicestershire coalowners regarded these proposals with great uneasiness. They were then supplying Leicester with coal conveyed there by waggon or packhorse from the collieries on the other side of Charnwood Forest, and they foresaw that the proposed navigations would give the Derbyshire and Nottinghamshire coalowners a great advantage over them in the Leicester market. They accordingly offered a strong opposition to the schemes, and persisted until the projectors

of the Loughborough Navigation undertook to make that
Charnwood Forest Canal which, with its edge-railway at
each end (see page 220), would connect the Leicestershire coal-
fields at Coleorton and Moira with Leicester, and so allow
of the threatened competition from the north of the Trent
being duly met.

The Loughborough Navigation and its Charnwood Forest
extension were completed in 1798; but in the succeeding
winter the Charnwood Forest Canal burst its banks, and the
damage done was never repaired, the Loughborough Navigation trustees (who, though forced to construct the canal, did
not consider themselves obliged to maintain it) finding it to
their advantage, from a traffic point of view, to enable the
Derbyshire and Nottinghamshire coalowners to have a virtual
monopoly on the Leicester market. It was under these conditions that the Loughborough Navigation shares advanced,
by 1824, from their original value of £142 17s. each to no less
a sum than £4700.

The local waterway interests maintained their supremacy
and were, indeed, complete masters of the situation for over
thirty years; but the days of their 200 per cent dividends
were then numbered. Influenced by what the traders of
Liverpool and Manchester were doing to fight the canal and
river monopolists there, the Leicestershire coalowners got,
in 1830, an Act of Parliament authorising them to build a
railway from Swannington to Leicester. This line would give
them the facilities they wanted for their coal; but it was
to be a " public," and not merely a private, railway. By one
of the clauses of the Act it was provided that " all persons
shall have free liberty to use with horses, cattle and carriages
the said railway upon payment of tolls." These tolls were
arranged alike for passengers and for goods and minerals,
and they varied according to whether the travellers and
traders provided their own conveyances or used those of
the railway company. In the former case passengers were
to pay twopence halfpenny each per mile, and in the latter
case threepence per mile, the tolls for goods and minerals
being in like proportion. In a later Act, however, passed
in 1833, it was declared that " whereas the main line hath
been constructed with a view to locomotive steam engines
being used, it might be very injurious to the said railway and

inconvenient and dangerous if horses or cattle were used," and the rights thus granted to the public under the first Act were now withdrawn.

Opened in 1832, the Leicester and Swannington Railway restored to the Leicestershire colliery-owners the advantage in the Leicester market of which the canal companies had enabled their north-of-the-Trent competitors to deprive them for so many years ; and it was now the turn of the Nottinghamshire and Derbyshire coalmasters to consider what they should do to meet the new situation which had arisen. They first had conferences with the directors of the Loughborough, Erewash and Leicester Navigations, and sought to induce them to grant such reductions in tolls as would enable them to compete with the Leicestershire coal, now that this was no longer shut out from Leicester by the dry ditch in Charnwood Forest. But the only concessions the canal companies would make were regarded as wholly inadequate by the Nottinghamshire coalmasters, who, meeting at a little inn at Eastwood, on August 16, 1832, resolved that " there remained no other plan for their adoption " than to lay a railway from their collieries to the town of Leicester. They formed a Midland Counties Railway Company, obtained an Act, built their line, and so laid the foundations of the great system now known to us as the Midland Railway. Into that system the Leicester and Swannington was absorbed in 1846.

The position to-day of the waterways which for thirty years controlled more or less the transport conditions of the three counties in question, brought great wealth to their owners, and, by their sole regard for their own interests, forced the traders to resort to railways, is shown by the Fourth or Final Report of the Royal Commission on Canals and Waterways. From this one may learn that the Loughborough and Leicester Navigations, which follow the course of the Soar, are liable to floods and are, also, sometimes short of water, in consequence of the want of control over the supply of water to mills ; and although, with the Grand Junction Canal, they offer " the most direct inland water route " to London for the traffic of Derby, Nottingham and Leicester and of the large coal districts, they serve at present, adds the Report, but an insignificant part of the traffic which travels by this route.

In effect, the very efforts made by the canal companies to preserve the monopoly they had so long and so profitably enjoyed were only a direct means of encouraging railway expansion ; though few great institutions, destined to lead to a great social and economic revolution, have established their position in the face of more prejudice, greater difficulties, and less sympathetic support from " the powers that be " than was the case with the railways.

The traders of the country were naturally favourable to them, since the need for improved means of communication, following on the ever-expanding trade and industry of the land, was becoming almost daily more and more acute. But the vested interests, as represented alike by holders of canal shares, by turnpike road trustees and investors, and by the coaching interests, were against the railways ; the Press of the country was to a great extent against them ; leaders in the literary and the social worlds either ignored or condemned them ; landowners first opposed and then blackmailed them ; Governments sought to control and to tax rather than to assist them ; and then, when the railways had proved that they were less objectionable than prejudiced critics had assumed, and were likely even to be a source of profitable investment, they were boomed by speculators into a popularity that led both to successive " railway manias " and to the whole railway system being still further burdened with an excessive capital expenditure which has been more or less to its prejudice ever since.

Some of the early denunciations by those who would have considered themselves, in their day, to be leaders of public opinion, if not of light and learning, afford interesting examples of the hostility which railways, in common with every innovation that seeks to alter established habits and customs, had to encounter.

In the article published in the " Quarterly Review " for March, 1825, in which proposals for making railways general throughout the country are condemned as " visionary schemes unworthy of notice," it is further said in reference to the Woolwich Railway :—

" It is certainly some consolation to those who are to be whirled at the rate of eighteen or twenty miles an hour, by means of a high pressure engine, to be told that they are in no danger of being sea-sick while on shore, that they are not to be scalded to death, nor drowned by the bursting of the boiler ; and that they need not fear being shot by the scattered fragments, or dashed in pieces by the flying off or the breaking of a wheel. But, with all these assurances we should as soon expect the people of Woolwich to suffer themselves to be fired off upon one of Congreve's ricochet rockets as trust themselves to the mercy of such a machine, going at such a rate. Their property they may, perhaps, trust ; but while one of the finest navigable rivers in the world runs parallel to the proposed railroad, we consider the other twenty per cent which the subscribers are to receive for the conveyance of heavy goods almost as problematical as that to be derived from the passengers. We will back old Father Thames against the Woolwich Railway for any sum."

In " John Bull " for November 15, 1835, railways are spoken of as " new-fangled absurdities," and it is declared that " those people who judge by the success of the Manchester and Liverpool Railroad, and take it as a criterion for similar speculations, are dunces and blockheads." In the case of that particular railway, the writer argues, the distance was short, the passengers were numerous, the " thing " was new and the traffic was great—above all the distance was short ; but it did not follow that railways were going to succeed elsewhere. He continues :—

" Does anybody mean to say that decent people, passengers who would use their own carriages, and are accustomed to their own comforts, would consent to be hurried along through the air upon a railroad, from which, had a lazy schoolboy left a marble, or a wicked one a stone, they would be pitched off their perilous track, into the valley beneath ; or is it to be imagined that women, who may like the fun of being whirled away on a party of pleasure for an hour to see a sight, would endure the fatigue, and misery, and danger, not only to themselves, but their children and families, of being dragged through the air at the rate of twenty miles an hour, all their lives being at the mercy of a tin pipe, or a copper boiler, or the accidental dropping of a pebble on the line of way ?

" We denounce the *mania* as destructive of the country in a thousand particulars—the whole face of the Kingdom is to be tattooed with these odious deformities ; huge mounds are to intersect our beautiful valleys ; the noise and stench of locomotive steam-engines are to disturb the quietude of the peasant, the farmer and the gentleman ; and the roaring of bullocks, the bleating of sheep and the grunting of pigs to keep up one continual uproar through the night along the lines of these most dangerous and disfiguring abominations. . . .

" Railroads . . . will in their efforts to gain ground do incalculable mischief. If they succeed they will give an un-natural impetus to society, destroy all the relations which exist between man and man, overthrow all mercantile regulations, overturn the metropolitan markets, drain the provinces of all their resources, and create, at the peril of life, all sorts of confusion and distress. If they fail nothing will be left but the hideous memorials of public folly."

In " Gore's Liverpool Advertiser " for December 20, 1824, mention is made of some of the objections then being raised against railways, these being described as " exceedingly trifling and puerile." " Elderly gentlemen," it is said, " are of opinion that they shall not be able to cross the rail-roads without the certainty of being run over ; young gentlemen are naturally fearful that the pleasant comforts and conveniencies of their foxes and pheasants may not have been sufficiently consulted. Ladies think that cows will not graze within view of locomotive engines, and that the sudden and formidable appearance of them may be attended with *premature* consequences to bipeds as well as quadrupeds. Farmers are quite agreed that the race of horses must at once be extinguished, and that oats and hay will no longer be marketable produce."

Other alarmist stories were that a great and a scandalous attack was being made on private property ; that there was not a field which would not be split up and divided ; that springs would dry up, meadows become sterile and vegetation cease ; that cows would give no milk, horses become extinct, agricultural operations be suspended, and houses be crushed by the railway embankments ; that ruin would fall alike on landowners, farmers, market gardeners and innkeepers ; that manufacturers' stocks would be destroyed by sparks from the locomotives ; that hundreds of thousands of people, including those who had invested in canals, would be beggared in the interests of a few ; and that (as an anti-climax to all these predictions of national disaster) the locomotive, after all, would never be got to work because, although its wheels might turn, it would remain on the lines by reason of its own weight—a theory which, long pondered over by men of science, led to early projects of " general " railways being based on the rack-and-pinion principle of operation, and was only abandoned when someone had the happy idea of making experiments which proved that the surmise in question was a complete delusion.

I reproduce these puerilities of the early part of the nine-teenth century, not simply for the entertainment of the reader, but because it is a matter of serious consideration how far they affected the cost of providing the country with rail-ways, and whether, indeed, the traders who smile at them to-day may not still be paying, in one way or another, for the consequences they involved.

The keener the prejudice, the greater the hostility and the more bitter the denunciations when railways were struggling into existence, the more vigorous became the antagonism of landowners, the higher were the prices demanded for land, the more costly, by reason of the opposition, were the pro-ceedings before Parliamentary Committees, and the heavier grew that capital expenditure the interest on which would have to be met out of such rates and charges as the railways, when made, would impose.

To a certain extent one may sympathise with landowners who feared that the amenities of their estates might be pre-judiced by an innovation of which so much evil was being said ; but, as a rule (to which there were some very honour-able exceptions) it was found that their scruples in regard alike to their own interests and to the national welfare even-tually resolved themselves into a question of how much money could be got out of the companies. Thus the extortionate prices paid for land often had no relation to the actual value of the land itself. They were simply the highest amount the railway company were prepared to pay the landowner for the withdrawal of his threatened opposition. If the company resisted the exorbitant demands made upon them, and would not give a sufficiently high bribe, they were so strongly opposed that they generally lost their Bill when they first applied for it to Parliament. Thereupon they would yield, or effect a compromise on, the terms asked for, announce that they had made amicable arrangements with the opposition, re-introduce their Bill in the following Session, and then succeed in getting it passed.

It might happen, even then, that the companies obtained their powers subject only to a variety of hampering or vexatious restrictions which the landed gentry or others were able to enforce in order that due respect should be shown to their fears or their prejudices. In some of the earlier railway Acts the companies were forbidden to use any " locomotives or moveable engines " without the written consent of the owners or occupiers of the land through which their lines passed. One of the clauses of the Liverpool and Manchester Act provided that " no steam engine shall be set up in the township of Burtonwood or Winwick, and no locomotive shall be allowed to pass along the line within those townships which shall be considered by Thomas Lord Lilford or by the Rector of Winwick to be a nuisance or annoyance to them from the noise or smoke thereof." The same two individuals secured insertion of a clause in the Warrington and Newton Railway Act to the effect that every locomotive used within the parishes mentioned should be " constructed on best principles for enabling it to consume its own smoke and preventing noise in the machinery or motion thereof," and should use " no coal, but only coke or other such fuel " as his lordship and the rector might approve.

The story of the London and Birmingham Railway is especially significant of the general conditions under which the English railway system came into being.

Industrial expansion had brought about great developments in the Birmingham and Black Country districts, the population in Birmingham alone having increased from about 50,000 in 1751 to 110,000 in 1830. Wide possibilities of increasing trade and commerce were being opened up, but these were seriously hampered by the disadvantages experienced in the matter of transport. Small parcels of manufactured goods could be sent by coach, and a good deal of wrought iron —in small quantities per coach—was also distributed in the same way during the course of the year. For bulky goods or raw materials the only means of transport between Birmingham and London was by canal, and this meant a three-days' journey. Over 1000 tons a week were then going from Birmingham to London by water ; but there was great need for a means of communication at once more speedy and more trustworthy. Goods were delayed in transit even beyond the three days ; they were rejected by the shippers because they did not arrive in proper time ; they were sometimes held up by frost on the canal between Birmingham and London and lost their chance of getting to the Baltic before the spring ; while, alternatively, they might be pilfered or lost on the canal journey, and so not get even as far as London. There was often much difficulty, also, in obtaining raw materials.

In the result manufacturers had to refuse orders because they could not execute them in time, and the local industries were not making anything like the advance of which, with better transport facilities, they would have been capable. The business that Birmingham manufacturers should have been doing with Italy, with Spain, or with Portugal was found to be drifting more and more into the hands of Continental competitors who had greater advantages both in obtaining raw materials on the spot and in distributing their manufactured goods. It was further argued that in view of the struggle then proceeding between this country and Continental countries for commercial supremacy, the improvement of the means of transport, even as regarded Birmingham and London, was a matter of national, and not simply of local, concern.

It might well be assumed that such considerations as these would have appealed to the patriotic instincts of the English people, and especially to those of the landed gentry. Yet the issue, in January, 1832, of the first prospectus of the London and Birmingham Railway Company, and the introduction of their Bill in February of the same year, led to opposition, to extortion and to actual blackmail of the most determined and most merciless description.

The Bill passed in the Commons, but it was thrown out in the Lords. Its rejection there was attributed to the landowners, who, it was declared, had " tried to smother the company by the high price they demanded for their property." The inevitable negotiations followed. Six months after the defeat of the Bill the directors announced that the " measures " they had taken with a view to removing " that opposition of dissentient landowners and proprietors which was the sole cause of their failure . . . had been successful to a greater extent than they had ventured to anticipate. The most active and formidable had been conciliated," and the Bill would be introduced afresh in the following Session. This was done, and the Bill became an Act, receiving the Royal assent on May 6, 1833.

The nature of the " measures " which had succeeded in overcoming the opposition may be judged from some facts mentioned by John Francis, who says that land estimated in value at £250,000 cost the company three times that amount. One landowner, in addition to getting £3000 for a certain plot, extorted £10,000 for what he called " consequential damages " ; though, instead of injuring the remainder of his property, the line increased its value by twenty per cent. For land used only as agricultural holdings the company is said to have had to pay at the rate of £350 an acre.

But this was not all. There was the opposition of towns as well as the greed of individuals to be taken into account. According to Robert Stephenson's original survey, the London and Birmingham Railway was to pass through Northampton, where, also, it was proposed to establish the company's locomotive and carriage works. The opposition in Northampton, however, was so great that in order to meet it the company altered their plans and arranged for the line to pass at a distance from that town. They further undertook to start their locomotive works at Wolverton, and thus not interfere with the amenities of Northampton.

How much the town and trade of Northampton lost as the result of its scruples could hardly be told ; but the consequences to the railway company of this enforced alteration of route were as serious as any of the extortions practised by the landowners. The line had now to pass through a tunnel at Kilsby, five miles distant from Northampton, and a contractor undertook to cut this tunnel for £90,000. But, while engaged on the task, he came upon a quicksand which reduced him to despair and led to his throwing up the contract. Robert Stephenson thereupon took the work in hand and he had to have 1250 men, 200 horses and thirteen steam-engines at work raising 1800 gallons of water per minute night and day

for the greater part of eight months before the difficulty
was overcome. By the time the tunnel was completed the
cost of construction had risen from the original estimate of
£90,000 to over £300,000, this enormous expenditure having
been incurred, not because it was necessary for the line, as
first designed, but to meet the opposition and spare the feelings
of the then short-sighted dwellers in the town of Northampton.

The London and Birmingham Railway, with its terminus
at Euston, was eventually opened for traffic throughout in
September, 1838. It was, of course, one of the lines subsequently amalgamated to form the London and North-Western
Railway.

The first Bill of the Great Western Railway, applied for in
1834, was strenuously opposed and defeated. The second
Bill, brought forward in the following session, was less
strenuously opposed, and was duly passed. In the interval
the opposition of the dissentient landowners had been " conciliated " ; and, commenting thereon (in 1851), John Francis
says :—

" The mode by which the opposition of landholders was
met bears the same sad character as with other railways.
Every passenger who goes by the Great Western pays an
additional fare to meet the interest on this most unjust
charge ; and every shareholder in this, as in other lines,
receives a less dividend than he is entitled to from the same
cause. Nor does the blame rest with the conductors of the
railway. They were the agents of the shareholders and were
bound to forward their interests. The principle of the case
to them was nothing. They were bound to get the Act at
the cheapest possible rate, and if the law gave their rich
opponents the power of practically stopping the progress of
the line, and those opponents chose to avail themselves of
the law, the shame rests with the proprietor of the soil, and
not with the promoter of the railway. Fancy prices were
given for fancy prospects, in proportion to the power of the
landowner. Noblemen were persuaded to allow their castles
to be desecrated for a consideration. There can be no doubt—
it was, indeed, all but demonstrated—that offers were made
to and accepted by influential parties to withdraw their
opposition to a Bill which they had declared would ruin them,
while the smaller and more numerous complainants were

paid such prices as should actually buy off a series of long and tedious litigants."

The promoters of that most unfortunate of lines, the Eastern Counties—predecessor of the Great Eastern Railway of to-day—found themselves faced with serious opposition in the Lords after they had got their Bill through the Commons ; " but," says the first report, " the directors, by meeting the parties with the same promptness and in the same fair spirit which had carried them successfully through their previous negotiations, effected amicable arrangements with them," and the company was incorporated in 1836. The negotiations must, however, have been carried through with greater promptness than discretion, for, to save the fate of their Bill, the directors undertook to pay one influential landowner £120,000 for some purely agricultural land which was said to be then worth not more than £5000. After they had secured their Bill they made persistent attempts to get out of paying the £120,000 ; and, altogether, they so shocked John Herapath that in successive monthly issues of his " Railway Magazine " all references to the Eastern Counties Railway Company were encircled by a black border.

In another instance a company proposed to meet the opposition of certain landowners by carrying the line through a tunnel, which would enable them to avoid the property in question. The tunnel would have cost £50,000, and the land-owners said, " Give us the price of that tunnel and we will withdraw our opposition." The company offered £30,000, and the landowners agreed to be " conciliated " on this basis. They still came off better than the objector who began by demanding £8000 and finally accepted £80. John Francis, too, relates the following story : " The estate of a nobleman was near a proposed line. He was proud of his park and great was his resentment. In vain was it proved that the new road would not come within six miles of his house, that the highway lay between, that a tunnel would hide the inelegance. He resisted all overture on the plea of his feelings, until £30,000 was offered. The route was, however, afterwards changed. A new line was marked out which would not even approach his domain ; and, enraged at the prospect of losing the £30,000, he resisted it as strenuously as the other."

There were some honourable exceptions to the general

tendency to extort as much as possible from the railway companies. Among these may be mentioned the voluntary return by the Duke of Bedford of a sum of £150,000 paid to him as compensation, his Grace explaining that the railway had benefitted instead of injuring his property; and by Lord Taunton of £15,000 out of £35,000 because his property had not suffered so much as had been anticipated. Exceptions such as these do not, however, alter the fact that, as stated by Francis in 1851, the London and Birmingham Company had had to pay for land and compensation an average of £6300 per mile, the Great Western £6696, the London and South Western £4000 and the Brighton Company £8000 per mile.

One argument, at least, which can be advanced in favour of State railways—as applying, however, to a country beginning the creation of a railway system, or building new railways, rather than to one taking over an existing system—is that extortions in respect to land could not be practised on the State in the same way as they have been practised on English railway companies left by their Government to make the best terms they could with those who were in a position to drive the hardest of bargains with them. In Prussia, for example, the securing of land for any new lines wanted for the State railway system is a comparatively simple matter. If the landowner and the responsible officials cannot agree to terms, the matter is referred to arbitration, though with every probability that the landowner will get no more than a fair sum, and will not be able to extort fancy figures under the head of consequential damages or as the " price " of his withdrawing any opposition he might otherwise offer.

Apart from other considerations, and taking only the one item of land, the State lines of Continental countries may well have cost less to construct than the English lines, while both in the United States and in Canada the pioneer railway companies had great stretches of land given to them, by State or Federal Government, not alone for their lines, but as a further means of assisting them financially.

When one finds how the cost of creating the railway system in our own country was swollen, under the conditions here stated, to far greater proportions than should have been the case, and when one remembers that the excessive capital

expenditure involved in meeting extortionate demands had
either to remain unremunerative or be made good out of the
payments of travellers and traders, it is evident that comparisons between English and foreign railway rates and fares
may be carried to unreasonable lengths if they ignore conditions of origin by which the operation of the lines concerned
must necessarily have been more or less influenced.   Francis
himself says on this point, while confessing that " every line
in England has cost more than it ought " :—

" The reader may learn to moderate his intense indignation
when, anathematising railways, he remembers with what
unjust demands and impure claims they had to deal, and
with what sad and selfish treatment it was their lot to meet.
They owe nothing to the country ; they owe nothing to the
aristocracy.   They were wronged by the former ; they were
contumaciously treated by the latter."

Another factor, apart from cost of land, in swelling the construction capital of British railways to abnormal proportions
has been the cost of Parliamentary proceedings ; and here,
again, State railways have had the advantage.   In Prussia
the obtaining of sanction for the building of an additional
line by the State railways administration is little more than
a matter of official routine ; whereas in England the expenses
incurred by railway companies in obtaining their Acts have
often amounted to a prodigious sum—to be added, of course,
to the capital outlay which the users of the railway will be
expected to recoup, or, at least, to pay interest on.

An especially striking example was that of the Blackwall
Railway, now leased to the Great Eastern Railway Company.
The cost of obtaining the Act for this line, which is only five
miles and a quarter in length, worked out at no less a sum
than £14,414 per mile, the total cost being thus £75,673.   The
amounts paid by certain other companies in securing their
Parliamentary powers are given as follows by G. R. Porter in
his " Progress of the Nation " (1846) :—

Birmingham and Gloucester . .	£22,618
Bristol and Gloucester . .	£25,589
Bristol and Exeter . . .	£18,592
Eastern Counties . . .	£39,171
Great Western. . . .	£89,197

Great North of England . . .	£20,526
Grand Junction	£22,757
Glasgow, Paisley and Greenock .	£23,481
London and Birmingham . . .	£72,868
London and South Western . .	£41,467
Manchester and Leeds . . .	£49,166
Midland Counties	£28,776
North Midland	£41,349
Northern and Eastern . . .	£74,166
Sheffield, Ashton-under-Lyne and Man-chester	£31,473
South-Eastern	£82,292

In some cases, Porter explains, the sums here given contain the expenses of surveying and other disbursements which necessarily precede the obtaining of an Act of incorporation. On the other hand, they include only the costs defrayed by the proprietors of the railway, and not the expenses incurred by parties opposing the Bills. Nor do they include the expenses incurred in connection either with rival schemes or with schemes that failed altogether; though, in these instances, of course, there would be no chance of recouping the outlay out of rates and fares. No fewer than five different companies, for instance, sought for powers to construct a line from London to Brighton, and the amounts they expended are given by John Francis as follows :—

Rennie's line	£72,000
Stephenson's	£53,750
Cundy's	£16,500
Gibb's	£26,325
South-Eastern	£25,000
Total . . .	£193,575

Another company, the name of which is not given by Francis, had so vigorous a fight that they spent nearly £500,000 before they got their Act ; but still worse than this was the fate of the Stone and Rugby Railway, whose promoters spent £146,000 on attempts made in two successive sessions to get an Act (the Committee on the first Bill sitting on 66 days) and then failed. In another instance the promoters expended £100,000 with a like result.

After the early companies had got their Acts and obtained their land they still, as railway pioneers, had to bear the expense of some very costly experiments, of which railways constructed at a later date had the advantage. The idea that the locomotive would be able to haul trains only on the level involved much unnecessary expenditure on engineering works, while the battle of the gauges led to a prodigious waste of money alike in Parliamentary proceedings and in the provision of lines, embankments, cuttings, bridges and viaducts adapted to a broad gauge eventually abandoned in favour of the narrower gauges now in general use.

The facts here mentioned will have given the reader some idea of the conditions under which the railways so greatly needed in the interests of our national industries were handicapped from the very outset by an unduly heavy expenditure ; but there were still other influences and considerations which materially affected the general position, more especially as regards questions and consequences of State policy towards the railway system in general.

CHAPTER XXI

RAILWAYS AND THE STATE

FROM the earliest moment of there being any prospect of railways, operated by locomotives in place of animal power, coming into general use, the attitude of the State towards their promoters was one less of sympathy than of distrust; and this distrust was directly due to the experience the country had already had of the waterway interests, whose merciless exactions and huge dividends had led to the fear that if the railway companies, in turn, were to get a monopoly of the transport facilities of the country, they might follow in the footsteps of the inland navigation companies unless they were restrained either by law or by the enforcement of the principle of competition.

Public sentiment, which Parliament is assumed to represent, and of which our legislation is supposed to be the outcome, was divided between, on the one hand, the landed gentry, the canal proprietors (each alike hostile to the railways until they found they had more to hope for from exploiting them), and the inevitable opponents of innovations of any kind; and, on the other hand, the traders, by whom the railways were being cordially welcomed, not only because of the greater and better transport facilities they offered, but also because they presented an alternative to the canals, the earlier enthusiasm for which had been greatly moderated by the prospect of an improved means of transport.

Without adopting wholeheartedly the views of either of these two opposing parties, Parliament regarded the position with much concern lest there might be a renewal, in another form, of what we have seen to be the grasping tendencies of monopolistic canal companies; and the distrust inspired, under these particular circumstances, and from the very outset, towards railway companies which were preparing to create a revolution in the transport conditions of the

258

country—a revolution the State was not itself disposed to effect or to finance—was powerfully to influence much of the subsequent railway legislation, if, indeed, it has even to-day entirely disappeared.

At first it was assumed that competition in rail transport would be assured, and the dangers in question proportionately reduced, by different carriers using their own locomotives, coaches and carriages on the railway lines, which alone, it was thought, would be owned by the railway companies constructing them. In some of the earlier railway Acts there was even a provision that the railway companies could lease their tolls, as turnpike trustees were doing. But the apparent safeguard in the form of competition between rival carriers disappeared when it was found (1) that, although a railway company was required to allow a trader's own horse or locomotive to use the line, it was under no obligation to afford him access to stations and watering-places, or to provide him with any other facilities, however indispensable these might be to the carrier's business ; (2) that the tolls charged by the railway companies were heavier than the carriers could afford to pay ; (3) that the entire operation of a line of railway worked by locomotives must necessarily be under the control of the owning and responsible company ; and (4) that railway companies would have to become carriers of goods as well as owners of rails.

A Parliamentary Committee which sat in 1840, and of which Sir Robert Peel was a member, had reported in the strongest terms that the form of competition originally designed was both impracticable and undesirable, and that monopoly upon the same line, at all events as regarded passengers, must be looked upon as inevitable. " Your Committee," said the report, " deems it indispensable both for the safety and convenience of the public, that as far as locomotive powers are concerned, the rivalry of competing parties on the same line should be prohibited " ; though, as some check to the consequent monopoly of the railway companies, they suggested that the Board of Trade should act as a supervising authority, with power to hear complaints, consider bye-laws, etc.

A witness for the Grand Junction Railway Company, who gave evidence before this Committee, said that any person might run his own engine on the Grand Junction, and in one instance this was done by a trader who had a locomotive on the company's line for drawing his own coal ; but the witness apprehended the greatest possible inconvenience from any general resort to such powers. On the Liverpool and Manchester, also, anyone might run his own engines on the line ; but, the witness added, " no one does."

The Royal Commission of 1865 summed up the position thus :—" No sooner were railways worked on a large scale with locomotive power than it was found impracticable for the general public to use the line with carriages and engines, and railway companies were compelled to embark in the business of common carriers on their own line, and conduct the whole operations."

When, in these circumstances, it was made certain that any idea of competition between carriers using a railway company's lines in the same manner as an ordinary highway would have to be abandoned, it became the established policy of the State to promote competition between the railway companies themselves by encouraging the construction of competitive lines or otherwise, thus still protecting, as was thought, the interests of railway users, and checking any monopolistic tendencies on the part of the railway companies. The futility, however, of seeking to compel railway companies to compete with one another had already been pointed out by Mr James Morrison, whose speech on the subject in the House of Commons on May 17, 1836, confirms, also, the theory I have suggested as to the attitude adopted towards the railway companies being traceable to fears engendered by the undue prosperity of the canal and navigation companies.

If, argued Morrison, after one company had spent a large sum on a line to Liverpool, another company were encouraged to spend as much again, with a view to providing a competition which would keep down the charges, the two would inevitably arrive at some understanding by which the original charges would be confirmed ; and the Legislature, he contended— though the Legislature never acted on his contention—was " bound to prevent, as far as it could, the unnecessary waste of capital " on the building of unnecessary lines to promote a competition he held to be futile. The safeguarding of the public interests could, he thought, be effected in another way.

"The history of the existing canals, waterworks, etc., afforded," he went on, " abundant evidence of the evils " of allowing too much freedom in the matter of rates ; and he quoted the high prices at which the shares of the Loughborough Canal and the Trent and Mersey Canal were then still being sold,[1] adding : " The possession of the best, or, it may be, the only practicable line, and the vast capital required for the formation of new canals, have enabled the associations in question, unchecked by competition, to maintain rates of charges which have realised enormous profits for a long series of years."

The remedy he recommended in preference to competition was that when Parliament established companies for the formation of canals or railroads it should invariably reserve to itself the power to make such periodical revisions of the rates and charges as it might deem expedient, examining into the whole management and affairs of each company, and fixing the rates and charges for another term ; the period he favoured being one of twenty years.[2]

There was no suggestion, at this time, that the railway companies *had* abused their powers. The only suggestion—and expectation—was that *because* the canal companies had abused theirs, the railway companies might, and doubtless would, do the same, unless they were prevented ; and it will

---

[1] See page 237.

[2] In the Taff Vale Railway Act of 1836 (the same year as that in which Morrison made his proposals) the company were prohibited from paying a dividend of more than seven per cent when the full tolls were charged, or of more than nine per cent after the tolls had been reduced by twenty-five per cent ; and the shareholders were required, at any meeting at which these maximum dividends were declared, to make such reasonable reductions in the amount of the rates to be paid during the following year as would, in their opinion, reduce the profits to the seven or nine per cent level. It was further provided that, for the purpose of " better ascertaining the amount of the clear profits upon the said railway," the company should submit their accounts to the Justices in Quarter Sessions, who were to make such reductions in the rates to be collected during the year next ensuing as would, in their judgment, reduce the profits to the prescribed minima. Mr A. Beasley, general manager of the Taff Vale Railway, who gives this information in an article on " How Parliament Harassed Early Railways," published in " The Railway Magazine" for November, 1908, adds : " The gentlemen of Quarter Sessions were never called upon to undertake this formidable task as the clauses were repealed by the Company's Act of 1840."

be found that this was mainly the position throughout the whole of the subsequent controversies.

Morrison's proposal was approved in the House of Commons, and on May 17 he brought in a Bill for giving effect to it in regard to all new railways, to be sanctioned in that or any subsequent Session. But the prospect of a Parliamentary limitation of the profits a railway might earn had a most depressing effect on the railway interests, and on July 11 Sir Robert Peel urged that the question should be decided without further delay inasmuch as " this branch of commercial enterprise was injured and almost paralysed." On the following day the Bill was brought up again, and it was then defeated.

In the same Session (1836) the Duke of Wellington moved, and carried, in the House of Lords a general clause, to be inserted in all railway Acts, the effect of which would have been to give to Parliament the power of dealing as it might think fit with any railway company during the next year. John Herapath thereupon inserted in the current issue of his " Railway Magazine " a letter addressed to the Duke of Wellington, in the course of which he said :—

" No person can doubt your Grace's intentions are honourable to all parties. Fearful of the consequences of overgrown monopolies, you are anxious to put some salutary restrictions to those bodies riding, as you apprehend, roughshod over the public ; and you are anxious to do this before they become too powerful to be ruled. Every honest and right-minded man must be satisfied that such are needful ; nor is there a company got up on honourable principles that would object to any reasonable measure, in which a due regard is paid to their own interests, and a proper consideration is had to all the circumstances of their situation and risk. But in common fairness these must be taken into account."

Defending the railways, and keenly criticising the attitude of the State towards them, Herapath further said :—

" No man knows better than yourself that these works, if they are at all likely to be beneficial to the nation—which everyone in his sober senses admits—will form a great and brilliant era in its prosperity. Nay, my Lord Duke, permit me to ask you if they have not been a Godsend towards the preservation of this country, by giving a new impetus to industry and trade, and saving us from that anarchy and confusion to which distress was fast hurrying a large proportion of our population ? With all these advantages staring us in the face, what have the Government done to promote railways ? Have they done a single thing ? I am not conscious of one. Have they removed a single impediment ? Not to my knowledge ; but they have raised several. Have they contributed a single farthing ? Rather, I believe, by the intolerable and vexatious oppositions permitted in passing the bills, have been the cause of spending many hundred thousands, which, like another national debt, will prey to the end of time on the vitals of public industry."

The Duke's proposed clause was dropped, and was heard of no more ; but Herapath's prediction as to the equivalent of " another national debt " being imposed on public industry was to be verified by the course of subsequent events still more than by any avoidable expenditure then already incurred.

If, again, as Herapath said, the Government had done nothing to promote railways, they had not been backward in seeking advantage from them in the interests both of the Exchequer and of the Post Office.

Within two years of the opening of the Liverpool and Manchester line, a tax of one-eighth of a penny per mile for every passenger conveyed on the railway was imposed, and the directors of the Liverpool and Manchester, then struggling into existence, announced that, in consequence of the tax, they would be obliged to charge the public higher fares. By 1840 the Exchequer receipts from the tax amounted to £112,000. Two years later, following on a great public agitation, Peel substituted for the mileage tax a tax of five per cent on receipts from passenger traffic, and in 1844 the tax (which had been especially oppressive on the poorer class of travellers) was abolished in the case of third-class passengers carried at fares not exceeding a penny a mile in " Parliamentary trains," stopping at every station.[1]

The local authorities, with Parliamentary sanction, also subjected the railways to a degree of taxation against which

[1] Under the Cheap Trains Act of 1883 the duty was remitted in the case of all fares not exceeding the rate of one penny a mile, and was reduced to two per cent on fares exceeding that rate for conveyance between urban stations within one urban district.

Mr G. C. Glynn, chairman of the London and Birmingham Railway, in a speech (at a meeting of his company) quoted by Francis, protested in the following terms : " Then comes the last item of local taxes and parochial rates ; these, gentlemen, we do take exception to. . . . The county assessors and the parties to whom appeal from them is made seem actuated by one principle, namely, to extract every farthing they can from the railway property. We ask no boon, we ask for no favour from Government on this subject ; but we do ask for justice."

The railways had to submit to the taxation, but they won the day as against certain excessive and, as they considered, intolerable demands made upon them by or on behalf of the Post Office.

In 1838, based on the recommendations of a Select Committee of the House of Commons on the transmission of mails by railway, the Government introduced a Bill which, in effect, placed the entire railway system of the country, then and for all future time, at the command and under the supreme control of the Postmaster-General. That functionary was empowered by the Bill to call upon the railway companies to provide him with—at their own cost—special or ordinary trains for carrying the mails at any hour of the day or night, proceeding at such speed, and calling or not calling at such places, as he might direct, the companies giving security to the Queen by bond for duly complying with all Post Office orders, and being made liable to a penalty of £20 in respect to every railway officer, servant or agent, who might disobey any Post Office order. If the Post Office wished to use its own engines and conveyances it was to be at liberty to do so without paying any rates or tolls whatever ; and it was, also, to be free to clear away any obstructions to its engines, and use any of the railway company's appliances it wanted. The railway companies were, in return, to be assured a " fair remuneration " for (in effect) the wear and tear of the rails ; but, lest this payment might be too much for the Post Office, the Postmaster-General was further authorised to recoup himself by carrying, not simply the mails, but *passengers*, in the trains he might think fit to command or to run, thus competing on the railway lines with the companies whose property he was virtually to annex.

The companies declared they were willing to render every reasonable facility to the Post Office ; but they protested most vigorously against what they called " the absurd and tyrannical clauses " of the Bill.

These were, nevertheless, defended in the Commons on behalf of the Government, the Attorney-General saying " he had no doubt if the prerogative of the Crown were put in force, the Post Office and the troops and stores might be transmitted along the railroads without the payment of any tolls whatever ; though he thought the companies should have a fair remuneration for the accommodation given."

Sir James Graham, on the other hand, wanted to know what were the Queen's rights on the Paddington Canal. He understood that troops were frequently moved from Paddington to Liverpool by canal, but were always paid for as passengers. Lord Sandon, too, declared that the question was whether the public interest conferred a right upon the Post Office to take possession of railroads, and make use of them without the slightest remuneration whatever. That the railways should be subject to control he readily admitted ; but there was a wide difference between justifiable control and absolute sway, between fair remuneration and robbery, for such it would be to use the property of these companies without paying for it.

The companies, according to a statement in the " Railway Magazine " for August, 1838, where a summary of the debate will be found, had been " prepared not merely to petition but to act "—whatever this may mean. The Government, however, adopted a more conciliatory attitude towards them by either withdrawing or amending the clauses which had evoked these protests, and an amicable settlement of the future relations between the railways and the Post Office was then effected.

The rejection of Morrison's Bill and the withdrawal of the Duke of Wellington's motion, following on their adverse criticism by the railway interests, had committed the Government still more to their policy of stimulating competition between the railway companies themselves, thus, they considered, diminishing the risk of seeing any of them become too prosperous a monopoly. It was in full accord with this policy that encouragement was given to the creation of many small, independent, and more or less competing lines, and that no attempt was made to encourage the provision, either by individual companies or by groups of companies, of " trunk lines " of the type which Thomas Gray and others had been urging on the country with so much though with such futile persistence.

The advent of the new means of transport was, in fact, marked by the complete absence of any centralised effort with a view to securing the network of a railway *system*, so planned or so co-ordinated as to make the best possible provision for the country as a whole, and especially for the rapidly increasing necessities of trade, commerce and industry. The failure to act on these lines was, however, only in accordance with the previous policy, or no-policy, which had successively left the improvement of rivers, the making of roads, the construction of canals and the provision of turnpikes either to private benevolence or to private enterprise, influenced mainly by considerations of local or personal interests.

Much had certainly been done in these various directions by those to whom the State had thus relegated the carrying out of public works which in most other countries—as regards main routes, at least—are regarded as a matter of national obligation. But, apart from any question of providing State funds, the lack even of intelligent direction and efficient supervision by a central power, qualified to advise or to organise private effort, had led both to a prodigious waste of money and to results either unsatisfactory in themselves or in no way commensurate with the expenditure incurred. The same conditions now were to lead, in regard to the railways, to a further waste of money, to disastrous speculation, to infinite confusion, to the piling up of a huge railway debt, and to the provision of innumerable small lines which were to remain more or less independent and disconnected *fragments* of a railway system until the more enterprising companies began, on their own initiative, to amalgamate them into through routes of traffic.[1]

The general position at the period here in question was well stated by G. R. Porter in his " Progress of the Nation "

[1] Professor Hadley states, in " Railroad Transportation," that in 1844 the average length of English railroads was fifteen miles.

(1846), where he wrote, on the subject of railway development :—

" The *laissez faire* system which is pursued in this country to such an extent that it has become an axiom with the Government to undertake nothing and to interfere with nothing which can be accomplished by individual enterprise, or by the associated means of private parties has been pregnant with great loss and inconvenience to the country in carrying forward the railway system. Perhaps there never was an occasion in which the Government could with equal propriety have interfered to reconcile the conflicting interests involved, and to prevent public injury arising from the false steps so likely to be made at first in bringing about a total revolution in the internal communication of the country. It is not meant by these remarks to infer that Government should have taken into its own hands the construction of all or any of the railroads called for by the wants of the community ; but only to suggest the propriety and advantage that must have resulted from a preliminary inquiry, made by competent and uninterested professional men with a view to ascertain the comparative advantages and facilities offered by different lines for the accomplishment of the object in view. If this course had been adopted before any of the numerous projects were brought forward for the construction of lines of railway between all imaginable places, and if it had been laid down as a rule by the legislature that no such projected line could be sanctioned or even entertained by Parliament which was not in accordance with the reports and recommendations of the Government engineers, the saving of money would have been immense. The expensive contests between rival companies in which large capitals had been so needlessly sunk would then have been wholly avoided ; and it might further have followed from this cause that, a kind of public sanction having been given to particular lines and localities, much of that personal opposition which has thrown difficulties in the way of works of great and acknowledged utility would never have been brought forward."

In making these remarks, Porter was only giving expression to views entertained in various influential quarters, and to a certain extent he did but anticipate, or re-echo, according to the precise date at which his observations had been

written, certain views and proposals put forward by the
Select Committee of 1844, of which Mr Gladstone (then
President of the Board of Trade) was chairman. In the Fifth
Report of this Committee it is said :—

" The Committee entertain very strongly the opinion that
in the future proceedings of Parliament railway schemes
ought not to be regarded as merely projects of local improvement, but that each new line should be viewed as a member
of a great system of communication, binding together the
various districts of the country with a closeness and intimacy
of relation in many respects heretofore unknown."

So long, the Report continued, as railways were considered
to be of problematical benefit, and were in general subject
to extensive opposition on the part of the owners and occupiers
of land, and of the inhabitants of the districts they traversed,
there might have been reasons for ensuring a very full, and,
in some points of view, a disproportionately full, representation
to local interests ; but " The considerations which tend to
attach to railways a national rather than a local character gain
weight from year to year as those undertakings are progressively consolidated among themselves, as the points of
contact between them are multiplied, and as those that
were first isolated in comparison are thus brought into relation with gradually extending ranges of space, traffic and
population."

The Select Committee went on to give their reasons for
considering that the ordinary machinery of Private Bill
Committees, with their separate and unconnected proceedings, and an individual existence commencing and ending
with each particular Bill, was inadequate and unsatisfactory;
and they especially pointed to the fact that hitherto it had
not been customary to examine railway Bills "systematically
and at large with reference to public interests." There were
various questions which could not be thoroughly sifted under
the mode of procedure then in vogue, and the Committee
recommended that, with a view to assisting the judgment of
the Houses of the Legislature, all future railway Bills should,
previously to coming before Parliament, be submitted to
the Board of Trade for their report thereon. They further
said—and these observations have a special significance in
view of events that were to follow :—

" The Committee entertain the opinion that the announcement of an intention on the part of Parliament to sift with
care the particulars of railway schemes, to associate them
with the public interest (in the cases of all future schemes and
of all subsisting companies which may voluntarily accede to
such an arrangement). . . will produce very beneficial effects
in deterring parties from the attempt to entrap the public
by dishonest projects, in securing railway projects against
the shocks to which in periods of great commercial excitement
it must otherwise be liable from such causes," etc.

Praiseworthy as was the design thus put forward by Mr
Gladstone's Committee, it failed to bring about the results
anticipated.

In accordance with the recommendations made, a special
department of the Board of Trade, under the direction of
Lord Dalhousie, was created, in August, 1844, to inquire
into and report to Parliament on all new railway schemes and
Bills, with a view to guiding the Private Bill Committees of
both Houses. The special department was more especially
to report as to the positive and comparative advantages to
the public of any Bills proposed for the construction of competing lines.

A great deal was hoped for from this new arrangement, and
the decisions of the department as to which of the schemes
then being promoted they would recommend for first consideration by Parliament were keenly awaited.

The expansion of the railway system had, by this time,
proceeded so far that by the end of 1843 Parliament had
authorised the construction of 2390 miles of railway, of which
2036 miles were then open for traffic. The capital of these
lines was £82,800,000, and of this amount about £66,000,000
had been raised. A good deal of wild speculation in 1836–7
had been followed by a reaction, and the railway market was
still depressed in 1843 ; but in 1844 interest in railway enterprise was greatly stimulated by the announcement that the
Liverpool and Manchester, the Grand Junction, the London
and Birmingham and the York and Midland were paying
dividends of from ten to twelve per cent each, and that the
Stockton and Darlington was paying fifteen per cent. The
shares in existing companies rose in value, a number of new
companies were formed, and companies already operating

projected branches in defence of their own interests against threatened competition. It was at this juncture that Mr Gladstone's Committee presented its Report and that, following thereon, the special department of the Board of Trade was called upon to undertake its responsible duties.

On November 28, 1844, the department intimated that the points it would particularly inquire into in regard to railway Bills then before it were (1) ability and *bona fide* intentions of the promoters to prosecute their application to Parliament in the following Session ; (2) national advantages to be gained ; (3) local advantages ; (4) engineering conditions ; and (5) cost of construction, prospective traffic and working expenses. On the last day of the year the department announced which Bills they proposed to recommend, and subsequently they issued reports giving their reasons. Strong protests were raised by the disappointed projectors, and on the opening of the Session of 1845 Sir Robert Peel announced that the Government intended to leave railway Bills, as before, to the judgment of the Private Bill Committees.

This meant the virtual setting aside of the newly-formed department, though its actual existence was not terminated until the following August. It meant—since each Private Bill Committee would deal only with the merits of a particular scheme—the definite abandonment of any opportunity for securing, through an authority dealing with railway projects as a whole, the realisation of the ideal of Mr Gladstone's Committee that " each new line should be viewed as a member of a great system of communication, binding together the various districts of the country with a closeness and intimacy of relation " previously unknown. It meant, also, the adoption of a policy of free trade in railways, without protection for established interests, and to any and every honest promoter or dishonest speculator who had a scheme to propose it gave, in effect, *carte blanche* to bring it forward.

Much disappointment was felt at this collapse of Mr Gladstone's apparently well-devised scheme, and the policy adopted in regard to it was keenly criticised. Francis quotes, for instance, the following passages from " Railway Legislation," the authorship of which, however, I have been unable to trace :—

" Swayed by motives which it is difficult to fathom, the

two Houses, with singular unanimity, agreed . . . to give unrestricted scope to competition. . . . Little regard was paid to the claims and interests of existing railway companies, still less to the interests of the unfortunate persons who were induced to embark in the new projects for no better reason than that they had been sanctioned by Parliament. . . . The opportunity of confining the exceptional gauge within its original territory was also for ever thrown away. By an inconceivable want . of statesmanlike views and foresight, no effort was made to connect the isolated railways which then existed by new links into one great and combined system in the form in which they would be most subservient to the wants of the community and to the great ends of domestic government and national defence. Further, the sudden change from the one extreme of determined rejection or dilatory acquiescence to the opposite extreme of unlimited concession gave a powerful stimulus to the spirit of specula-tion, and turned nearly the whole nation into gamblers."

Francis himself says of the position thus brought about :—

" All hope of applying great general principles passed away. Every chance of directing the course of railways to form a national system of communication was lost. . . . The legisla-tive body—to appropriate the idea of Mr Morrison—com-mitted the mistake of converting the Kingdom into a great stock exchange, and of stimulating the various members of the railway system to a deep and deadly struggle, destructive of order and fruitful of vice."

This may seem to be unduly strong language; but what actually and immediately followed on the course of events here in question was—the Railway Mania of 1845–6.

By the summer of 1845 the country had gone railway mad. In the Session of 1843 the number of railway Acts passed had been twenty-four, showing no more than a normal development of the railway system in meeting the legitimate needs of the country. In the Session of 1844 the number increased to thirty-seven. In the Session of 1845 there were no fewer than 248 railway Bills. In the next Session Bills were deposited with the Board of Trade for the construction of 815 new lines of railway, with a length of 20,687 miles, and capital powers to the extent of £350,000,000. Of these 815 Bills many were abortive for technical reasons, or because the necessary deposit was not paid ; but over 700 of them reached the Private Bill Office.

How every class of society joined in the scramble for shares ; how extravagant prices were given for the scrip of lines which, when completed, could not for years have covered their working expenses ; how half-pay officers, ticket-porters and men, even, in receipt of parish relief put down their names on the " subscription " lists for thousands of pounds' worth of shares, on their being paid a fee—sometimes as low as five shillings—for so doing ; how " frenzy seized the whole nation " ; how " there was scarcely a family in England which was not directly or indirectly interested in the fortunes of the rail " ; and how the inevitable collapse reached every hearth and saddened every heart in the Metropolis, bringing many families both there and elsewhere to ruin, will be found recorded in detail by John Francis, in his " History of the English Railway," and need not be enlarged upon here.

In referring to the events of this period, the Report of the Joint Committee on the Amalgamation of Railway Companies, 1872, admits that " One effect of the favour shown by Parliament to competing schemes was to encourage a large number of speculative enterprises." Leaving aside the enterprises, of whatever type, that did not survive the passage through Parliament, I compile, from figures given in Clifford's " History of Private Bill Legislation," the following table showing new lines of railway actually sanctioned by Parliament during the Sessions 1845–7 :—

YEAR.	NUMBER.	MILES.	CAPITAL.
1845	118	2700	£56,000,000
1846	270	4538	£132,000,000
1847	190	1354	£39,460,000
Totals	578	8592	£227,460,000

These figures indicate sufficiently the magnitude of the schemes in respect to which, during so short a period as three years, Parliament assumed the responsibility of giving its express sanction and approval.

The period of speculation was followed by the inevitable reaction, and in 1850 it was found necessary to pass an Act

" to facilitate the abandonment of railways and the dissolution of railway companies." Of the 8592 miles of railway sanctioned in the three Sessions, 1845–7, no fewer than 1560 miles were (as shown by the Report of the Royal Commission on Railways, 1867), abandoned by the promoters under the authority of the Act ; while a further 2000 miles of railway, requiring 40 millions of capital, are said by the Report of the 1853 Committee to have been abandoned without the consent of Parliament.

To the extent indicated by these abandonments the railway situation was certainly relieved. But the mania and the resultant panic had serious consequences in regard not alone to investors in the schemes that failed but also to the companies that survived.

Apart from projects designed to open up entirely new districts—many of them of a perfectly genuine and desirable character—there were others directly devised to compete with existing lines and capture some of the remunerative traffic these were then handling ; and it was, as I have shown, quite in accordance with the accepted principle of State railway-policy that such competition should be encouraged, in preference to any " districting " of the country among particular companies or to the creation or co-ordination of an organised system of railways on the lines proposed by Mr Gladstone's Committee.

The existing companies, finding that the territory already " allotted " to them (as they considered) was being invaded, or was in danger of being invaded, felt themselves forced, for the purposes of self-defence, to enter on a number of protective schemes which might not, at the time, otherwise have been warranted. Clifford says on this point in his " History of Private Bill Legislation " : " As the Government took no steps to prevent the promotion of competitive railways, tending to diminish the profits of existing companies, the latter sought to protect themselves as they best could, and justified their many unprofitable extensions and amalgamations as measures forced upon them by the leave-alone policy of the Government."

Confirmation of this statement will be found in a speech delivered on February 23, 1848, by Mr C. Russell, M.P., chairman of the Great Western Railway Company, at the sixth half-yearly meeting, at Paddington, of the South Wales Railway Company (of which he was also chairman), and reported in " The Times " of the following day. Referring to a pamphlet which had been issued attacking the policy of the Great Western Railway Company, Mr Russell said :—

" If their engagements were extensive, and he did not deny that they were so, they had been entered in only as a matter of necessity. They all arose out of the mania of 1845–46, and even in the pamphlet in question it had been admitted that the Great Western was not one of those companies which at that time had promoted any of the many schemes which were afloat. He, as far as he was concerned, had not only not promoted these projects, but had taken every means in his power to check them. In January, 1846, in his place in Parliament he had predicted the results if some steps were not at once adopted to put a curb upon reckless speculation ; but most unfortunately for all parties that was not the view which was taken by the House of Commons. Mr Hudson and other gentlemen maintained that the course he recommended would be an unfair interference with private enterprise, and the consequence was that schemes involving altogether the sum of £125,000,000 passed through the Legislature in that year. The Great Western had remonstrated with the President and the Vice-President of the Board of Trade, and, left to their own resources, they had been compelled, in self-defence, to look after their own interests by getting hold of all the rival or contemplated rival schemes."

In some instances the existing companies guaranteed interest to the shareholders of branches and extensions which were feared as rivals. F. S. Williams, in " Our Iron Roads," says of such lines as these that while many of them were accepted as feeders they " proved for a time to be only suckers."

The effects of the mania on the finances of existing railway companies was further shown by the fact that, in order to pay their contractors, some of the companies were obliged during the crisis to raise money at from ten to thirty, and, in some instances it is said, even at fifty per cent discount. Then, also, the shares in ten leading companies suffered between 1845 and 1847 a depreciation in value estimated at

£18,000,000. The following are typical examples of the falls experienced :—

COMPANY.	SHARES.	JULY, 1845.	APRIL 4, 1848.	DECLINE.
	£	£	£	£
London and Birmingham	100	243	126	117
Great Western . .	80 (paid)	205	88	117
Midland	100	187	95	92
London and Brighton .	50	76	28½	47½

While the general situation in the railway world had been thus developing, there was a revival, in 1846, of the idea that the work of Private Bill Committees in respect to railway schemes should be supplemented by some other form of inquiry into their merits.

Writing on this subject in the issue of his " Railway Magazine " for July, 1837, John Herapath had said :—

" It has long been anxiously expected that Parliament would take some steps to relieve itself from the onerous duties of investigating and deciding on railway matters. Probably no tribunals can be less fitted for inquiries of this kind than Parliamentary Committees, of which the House of Commons has lately given a demonstrative proof in the case of the Brighton line. After Committees of the two Houses had sat nearly the whole of last session, and a Committee of the Commons for thirty-five days of the present ; after the Committee's reports had been made on each of the lines and near 300,000l. of the subscribers' money had been wasted, the House of Commons stamped its own opinion of all those labours by giving them the ' go-by,' and referring the whole four lines to the judgment of a military engineer."

As for the element of uncertainty in the decisions of Parliamentary Committees, F. S. Williams is responsible for the statement that six railway Bills rejected by Commons Committees in 1844 were passed on precisely the same evidence in 1845 ; that of eighteen Bills rejected in 1845 seven were passed unaltered in 1846 ; and that of six Bills thrown out by Committees of the House of Lords in 1845 four were adopted by other Committees in 1846.

The failure, however, of the special department of the Board of Trade, created on the recommendation of Mr Gladstone's Committee to meet the requirements of the situation, was complete. In giving evidence before the Select Committee of 1881, the secretary of the Board of Trade, Mr T. Farrer (afterwards Lord Farrer), referring to the work of Lord Dalhousie's department, said the reports made " were very able, but they were thrown over immediately they got to the House." When, he declared, the Board of Trade had taken all the means in their power to make a full report, " it was treated as waste paper. The Board might just as well have made no report at all." On the other hand, he admitted that the reports had not been of much actual value, the Board of Trade having no power to call the parties before them and take evidence.

Apart from a feeling of jealousy entertained by members in general and Private Bill Committees in particular towards any curtailment of their powers, privileges and functions by departmental officials, experience had shown that the Private Bill Committees, after examining witnesses, getting expert testimony and hearing counsel, were better able to ascertain the facts of particular schemes than the special department, while the latter had lost credit, also, on account of its recommendations in regard to amalgamations.

The first scheme of this kind on which it was asked to report was one for an amalgamation between the Liverpool and Manchester Railway, the Grand Junction Railway (from Liverpool to Birmingham) and the North Union (from Warrington to Preston). The Bill was opposed by public bodies and traders in the leading towns of Lancashire, and Lord Dalhousie's report favoured the opposition ; but the Select Committee on the Bill nevertheless assented to an amalgamation which was, in effect, to lead to the creation of the London and North-Western system of to-day. The department also reported unsuccessfully in 1845 against the amalgamation of the Chester and Birkenhead with the Chester and Holyhead Railway—two other lines which were first united to each other and then to the London and North-Western. It further reported against various proposed amalgamations and arrangements in the Midland Counties ; so that, as the Report of the Select Committee of 1872 points out, the department would have objected strongly to such combinations as the present London and North-Western Railway, the

Great Western, the North-Eastern, the Midland, the Great Northern and the Great Eastern.

These considerations should be borne in mind by those who might otherwise be disposed to criticise the attitude adopted by the Government of 1845 towards the special department here in question.

The one experiment had been a failure—with, as we have seen, deplorable consequences for the country and serious prejudice to *bona fide* railways ; but Committees of both Houses, appointed in 1846, were now to recommend another. They advised the creation of a Board of Commissioners of Railways who were to discharge the dual functions of (1) seeing that the railway companies did not contravene the provisions of their special Acts or of any general Statutes ; and (2) report to Parliament, if so directed, upon any pending railway Bills.

An Act to this effect was passed in 1846 ; but in the following Session there was introduced a Bill which proposed greatly to increase the powers of the Board of Commissioners. Clifford says, concerning this Bill, that it made the Commissioners, in effect, arbiters of all railway legislation. Promoters were not even to survey an intended line until the Commissioners gave permission. When the survey was made one of their officers was to report upon the project. With them plans and sections were to be deposited ; they were to examine into compliance with Standing Orders and report to Parliament upon engineering merits and proposed rates. Considerable authority was also vested in them over existing railways. They were to report annually to Parliament upon tolls, fares and charges, and upon the regularity or irregularity of trains ; and they might call for returns as to traffic and many other details of management, inspect the books and documents of railway companies, and settle disputes between companies having termini or portions of line in common.

" Parliament," Clifford further tells us, " was again jealous of this proposed interference with legislation." The railway companies also protested, and the measure was received with such general disfavour that it was withdrawn before it reached a second reading. As for the Board of Commissioners, instead of getting more authority it got less. Part of its functions were re-united to those of the Board of Trade in 1848, and the remainder followed in 1851, whereupon the new authority ceased to exist.[1]

Once more, therefore, railway Bills were left to be dealt with on their individual merits by Private Bill Committees operating on lines to which, not simply John Herapath, but Mr Gladstone's own Committee, had taken exception ; and once more was a set-back given to the aspiration for the establishment of some central authority which could organise, co-ordinate or otherwise consolidate the still rapidly increasing railways on the basis of a national system of rail communication. The difficulty might, perhaps, have been met by the creation of a Minister of Communications, who would have held a position somewhat similar to that of the Minister of Public Works in Prussia or in France, and have discharged a useful function as director-in-chief, or, at least, as adviser-in-chief, in regard alike to railways, roads, rivers and canals. Such a Minister, being a member of the Government, might have acted or recommended without wounding the susceptibilities of Private Bill Committees or of individual members ; he might have organised or been the means of organising an efficient system of railways at an earlier date and at far less cost ; and he might have saved both the country from its enormous losses on the wild-cat projects of unscrupulous schemers during the mania period and *bona fide* companies from much of the excessive capitalization into which they were driven.

Whether or not the problems of the situation could have been solved in this manner, the fact remains that it was the railway companies themselves who—in spite of the established policy of the State, directed to the maintenance of railway competition, and in spite of the disapproval of amalgamations by one Parliament Committee after another — brought about the conveniences of through travel or through transit. It was they themselves who, by amalgamation or otherwise, instigated the creation of the " great " companies which both ensured these conveniences and effected a complete transformation in the general railway position, to the great advantage of everyone concerned.

[1] The present Railway and Canal Commission, which, however, has no functions in regard to advising on railway Bills, was created in 1873 for a period of years, and was made permanent in 1888.

Before, however, reaching this stage in their development, the railways had had some other struggles with the Government on questions of State policy arising out of those aforesaid feelings of suspicion and distrust, and due to the same fear as before that the companies would be sure to abuse their position unless they were restrained from so doing.

Following on the recommendations of the Committee of 1840, and with a view to safeguarding the public interests in regard alike to safety and to reasonable treatment, some important statutory powers had already been conferred on the Board of Trade. Under the Regulation of Railways Act, 1840, notice was to be given to the Board of Trade of the opening of all new lines of railway ; such lines were to be inspected by Board of Trade inspectors ; various returns in respect of traffic, tolls, rates and accidents were to be made to that body, to which, also, all existing bye-laws affecting the public were to be submitted for confirmation. In 1842 a further Act gave the Board power to delay the opening of any new line until they were satisfied that all the necessary works had been effectively constructed. Mr Glyn, chairman of the London and Birmingham Railway, said of this measure : " It is a Bill which I do not hesitate to say is, on the whole, calculated to do the interests of railways very considerable service."

But the attitude of the companies was no longer favourable when Mr Gladstone's Committee of 1844 proposed to confer on the Board of Trade some drastic powers for the periodical revision of railway rates, and likewise sought to lay down the terms on which the State might acquire all future lines of railway. The proposals in question were incorporated in a Bill which was brought in by Mr Gladstone ; but the measure met with strenuous opposition from the railway interests, and the modifications introduced before it became law were of such a nature that the Act has never been put into operation.

In regard to the revision of rates, the Act laid down that if, after the lapse of twenty-one years (not fifteen, as proposed in Mr Gladstone's first Bill), any railway sanctioned after the passing of the Act had paid ten per cent for three years, the Treasury (not the Board of Trade) might reduce the rates, guaranteeing, however, a ten per cent dividend to the company, while the revised rates and the guarantee were to continue for another twenty-one years. Needless to say, railway companies in general do not pay ten per cent dividends, though in 1844 ten per cent was regarded as quite a reasonable dividend for a railway, in view of what the canal companies had been paying; while no such guarantee as that suggested is ever likely to be made by the Treasury. Provisions authorising the Board of Trade to make deductions from the guaranteed income as penalties for what they might regard as mismanagement, and prohibiting a company from increasing its capital pending a revision of rates, without the sanction of the Board of Trade, were so vigorously opposed that they were abandoned.

The clauses of the Act relating to State purchase were to apply only to new lines of railway, the 2320 miles of railway sanctioned prior to the Session of 1844—and including many of the chief links in the great trunk lines of to-day—being expressly excluded. As regarded railways sanctioned in the Session of 1844, or subsequently thereto, it was enacted that after the lapse of fifteen years the Treasury might acquire them for twenty-five years' purchase of the average annual profits for the preceding three years; but if those profits were less than ten per cent, the amount was to be settled by arbitration. It was further enacted that no railway less than five miles in length should be bought; that no branch should be acquired without purchase of the entire railway; that the policy of revision or purchase was not to be prejudiced by the Act; that "public resources" were not to be employed to sustain undue competition with independent companies; and, finally, that no revision of rates or State purchase of lines should take place at all without an Act of Parliament authorising the guarantee or the purchase, and determining how either was to be done.

To argue, as many advocates of the nationalisation of railways habitually do, that the basis for State purchase has already been established by the Act of 1844 is to set up a theory which is obviously inconsistent with the real facts of the situation.

Commenting on this Act of 1844 the Joint Committee on the Amalgamation of Railway Companies (1872) say in their report :—

" It would be impossible to deal with railways made since 1844 without dealing with railways made before that time, since both form part of the same systems.

" As regards the revision of rates, no Government would undertake to try experiments in reducing rates on an independent company whose income they must guarantee ; and efficient or economical administration could scarcely be expected from a railway company whose rates were cut down and whose dividend at ten per cent was guaranteed by Government.

" Whatever value there may be in the notice given to the companies by this Act of their liability to compulsory purchase by the State, over and above the general right of expropriation possessed by the latter in such cases, its terms do not appear suited to the present condition of railway property or likely to be adopted by Parliament in case of any intention at any future time on the part of Parliament to purchase the railways."

The proposals contained in the Bill, and modified into the Act of 1844, were, of course, simply a further development of the then established policy of the State in taking precautions against the evils that might result from railway monopoly.

A greater degree of apparent success was, at first, to attend those further precautionary measures which took the form of encouraging the construction of competing lines, leading both to new and to existing companies invading the so-called " territory " of other companies, as distinct from the provision of lines in districts which had no railways at all.

There was at this time much discussion as to the rights of established companies.

When the proposal for the appointment of the Committee of 1840 was under discussion in the House of Commons, Sir Robert Peel had contended that a material distinction was to be drawn between new companies approaching Parliament for the first time and companies which, relying on the faith of Parliament, had invested their capital in the construction of railways. " Parliament, it was true, might repent of the indiscretion and levity with which it had granted those powers . . . but he would advise Parliament to be very cautious how it interfered with the profits or management of companies which had been called into existence by the authority, and had invested their money on the faith, of Parliament." Mr Gladstone's Committee of 1844 also declared that they had been " governed throughout their consideration of the subject by the strongest conviction that no step should be taken by Parliament which would either induce so much as a reasonable suspicion of its good faith with regard to the integrity of privileges already granted, and not shown to have been abused, or which would prospectively discourage the disposition now so actively in operation to extend the railway system by the formation of new lines."

On the other hand, there was that ever-present and ever-active dread of what *might* happen if the railway companies *did* become grasping and merciless monopolists.   There was, also, the fact that while there would be direct competition between two railways having the same terminal points, each line might further serve a more or less considerable and important intermediate stretch of country which otherwise would be left without railway accommodation at all.

For one or other of these reasons competing lines continued to be sanctioned, notwithstanding Special Committees' recommendations and railway companies' protests.   One such protest, giving a specific example of the tendencies of the day, was made in a memorial to the Board of Trade, dated June 26, 1857, and headed, " Proposed Remedies for Railway Grievances."   The memorial, signed by Sir John Hall, Bart., and six others, and addressed to Lord Stanley of Alderley, president, and Mr Robert Lowe, vice-president, of the Board of Trade, had been drawn up at the request of those two gentlemen as a more detailed statement of facts to which their attention had already been called.   Five specific grievances were dealt with, and the first of these was " The Tendency of Parliament to concede competing or otherwise unnecessary lines."   Under this head the memorialists state :—

" It is not our desire that the railway system should be legislatively restricted within its present limits, or that existing shareholders should by any process whatever be nominally or practically gifted with a monopoly of the means of railway transit.   We should submit to the introduction of new lines of railway wherever called for by absolute public necessity. . . . In such cases, however, we consider that the Legislature would only be doing justice to its previous enactments in

giving former applicants time to complete their engagements
so that they might be able, at the proper time, to exhibit
their ability and their willingness to consider the wants of
the public as well as their proper remuneration."

The memorialists mention the fact that in 1853 several
new lines were sanctioned, the period fixed for their completion being 1858, and they proceed :—

"Already, however, before these lines are opened, others
are promoted in competition with them—promoted, not by a
complaining locality, but in some cases by existing companies,
in others by persons whose only apparent object is to sell the
schemes to advantage when Parliament has sanctioned their
construction. In such instances as these we humbly submit
that the Legislature should not permit the introduction of
new lines until it has seen whether or not the company in
possession can fulfil its engagements, and whether, also, such
company should not be permitted an opportunity of electing
to extend its undertaking, or to leave further effort to the
discretion of the Legislature."

Whilst the State was thus maintaining its own policy of
competition, the railway companies were equally persistent in
keeping to their policy of amalgamation ; so that, as the Joint
Committee of 1872 remarked, " A new line was sure sooner
or later to join the combination of existing railways, and to
make common cause with them."

Practical railway experience was showing that the ordinary
ideas of competition, as regarded commercial undertakings
in general, did not and could not be made to apply to railways
beyond a certain point. The capital sunk alike in obtaining
a railway Act, in acquiring and adapting land, with provision
of embankments, cuttings, viaducts, bridges, tunnels, etc.,
for the railway lines, and in supplying the various necessary
appurtenances, railway stations, and so on, was irredeemable,
since, in the case of failure of the line, due to competition or
otherwise, the capital invested could not be realised again,
the land, rails, buildings, etc., on which it had been spent being
of little or no value for other than railway purposes. There
could thus be no transfer of capital from one undertaking to
another, as in ordinary commercial affairs.

In addition to this it might be that interest would have to be
paid on two lots of railway capital in a district where the

traffic was sufficient to allow of the financial obligations of only a single company being efficiently met, any success achieved by the new company depending (until the available traffic increased) on its power to divert business and profits from the other company.

Hence it might well occur that " the best laid schemes " of Parliament and Parliamentary Committees, in approving competitive lines, resulted only in the companies concerned coming to, at least, a friendly understanding ; and it might even be that the public did not eventually benefit at all, because, as the Joint Committee of 1872 say, " The necessity of carrying interest on the additional capital required for the new line tends sometimes, in the end, to raise rather than to reduce the rates."

Economic considerations, again, apart altogether from those monopolistic tendencies on the fear of which the policy of the State had been founded, were quite sufficient to account for the absorption of one company by another, and especially of small companies by larger ones, not so much to avoid competition as to ensure the provision of through routes operated under one and the same management, involving less outlay on working expenses, and providing greater advantages to the public than if the same length of line belonged to a number of different companies.

The lines between London and Liverpool, for example, were originally divided between three companies, and the same was the case with the lines between Bristol and Leeds. In some instances the companies were not on good terms with one another, and they ran their trains to suit their own convenience. Even when they were on good terms, they might not have any interests in common, apart from (at one time) offering as few comforts and conveniences as possible to the third-class traveller, and compelling him at least to complete his journey by going first class, if he wished to get to his destination the same night.

As early as 1847 attempts had been made by some of the companies to overcome the glaring defects of the original system of railway construction by establishing the Railway Clearing House, with a view to facilitating through traffic and allowing of a better adjustment of accounts when passengers or goods were carried over various lines in return for a single payment. The companies persevered, however, in their further policy of amalgamation and consolidation, and in 1853 the number and magnitude of schemes with these objects in view created such alarm on the part both of politicians and of traders that a further Select Committee—known as Mr. Cardwell's Committee—was appointed.

The members of this Committee pointed out in their report that the whole tendency of the companies was towards union and extension, that competition ended in combination, and that the companies were able in great measure to attain these ends by agreements with one another without the authority of Parliament. The economy and the convenience resulting from amalgamation were admitted by the report; but, though still no proof was offered, or suggestion made, that the companies were actually abusing the greater powers they had thus secured, there was an obvious under-current of alarm in the minds of the Committee as to the many undesirable things which large concerns *might* do.

The Committee were opposed to any " districting " of the country between different companies, and they recommended that, while working agreements might be allowed, amalgamations between large companies should not. As an example of the combinations they deprecated, I might mention that they pointed with evident feelings of much concern to the fact that if the amalgamation schemes then being proposed by the London and North-Western Railway Company were conceded, they would involve the union under one control of a capital of £60,000,000, a revenue of £4,000,000, and 1200 miles of railway, with the further result of " rendering impossible the existence of independent rival trunk lines." One wonders what the members of this Committee would have said had they been told that by the end of 1910 (as shown by the Board of Trade " Railway Returns ") the London and North-Western would control a total authorised capital of (in round figures) £134,000,000, have gross receipts in a single year amounting to £15,962,000, and be operating 1966 route miles of line, equivalent to 5490 miles of single track (including sidings), besides being only one of half a dozen great trunk lines.

A much more practical result of the deliberations of this Committee was seen in certain provisions of the Railway and Canal Traffic Act, 1854, which laid down that every railway company should afford proper facilities for receiving and forwarding traffic ; that no undue or unreasonable preferences should be given ; and that where the systems were continuous the companies should afford due and reasonable facilities for the interchange of traffic, without undue preference or obstruction. In this way it was sought to bring about greater co-ordination between the numerous small lines, and secure a better provision for through traffic. The Act is well described by the Select Committee of 1872 as " a measure valuable in fact and most important in its scope and intention." It may have been further anticipated that companies which, as the result of the Act, secured running powers or free interchange of traffic over the lines of other companies—and especially as regards lines having access to London—would be less ready to agree to absorption by them ; but if this expectation were, indeed, entertained, it was not realised.

The companies, in fact, continued to develop their commercial undertakings in accordance with what they regarded as commercial principles, and the Joint Committee on the Amalgamation of Railway Companies, 1872, taking a much broader view of the situation than previous Committees had done, pointed out how small had been the effect of the policy sought to be enforced against the railways, since the combinations which had enabled the great trunk lines to attain to the position they occupied at that date had been effected " contemporaneously with reports against large combinations," those reports having had " little influence upon the action of Private Bill Committees," and not staying " the progress of the companies in their course of union and amalgamation." The Committee further said, on the subject of " districting " :—

" Among the various suggestions which naturally occur when dealing with the question of amalgamation, one of the most obvious and most important is to the effect that for the future some endeavour should be made to compel railways in amalgamating to follow certain fixed lines or principles. . . . If at an earlier period in railway history such an attempt had been successfully made, there is no doubt that it might have provided us with a railway system, if not more efficient, at any rate far less costly than that which we now possess. But considering *the policy, or want of policy*, which has hitherto been pursued, and the interests which have grown up under it, the difficulties of laying down any fixed policy for the future are very formidable."

The words in this extract which I have put in italics, representing, as they do, the views of a Joint Committee of the House of Lords and of the House of Commons, justify, I would suggest, much of the criticism in which I have here ventured to indulge.

Among the conclusions at which the Committee arrived were the following :—

" Past amalgamations have not brought with them the evils which were anticipated."

" Competition between railways exists only to a limited extent, and cannot be maintained by legislation."

" Combination between railway companies is increasing and is likely to increase, whether by amalgamation or otherwise."

" It is impossible to lay down any general rules determining the limits or the character of future amalgamations."

In support of their views in regard to the first of these conclusions, the Committee pointed especially to the North-Eastern and the Great Eastern Railway Companies, each of which had so far pursued a policy of amalgamation that the report speaks of the former as " pervading and possessing one of the wealthiest and most important districts of the Kingdom," and of the latter as having " almost exclusive possession of the principal centres to which it extends."

The Committee did not suggest that either of these companies had abused its powers, or taken undue advantage of such " monopoly " as it had secured in the districts concerned. In fact, of the North-Eastern Railway they said :—
" That railway, or system of railways, is composed of thirty-seven lines, several of which formerly competed with each other. Before their amalgamation they had, generally speaking, high rates and fares and low dividends. The system is now the most complete monopoly in the United Kingdom . . . and it has the lowest fares and the highest dividends of any English railway." As for the Great Eastern, instead of abusing their " almost exclusive possession " of the Eastern Counties, everyone knows that the Company have won for themselves the credit of pioneering the movement for offering exception-

ally low rates and other special facilities for the transport of agricultural produce, and, also, of having done more, perhaps, than any other single railway company to enable working men to live in healthy suburbs around London.

The whole position in regard to the prospective abuse of a so-called monopoly due to railway amalgamations is, in fact, much misunderstood.

A railway company which controls, or practically controls, the traffic in a certain section of the country is especially interested in developing that traffic because it will enjoy all the advantages thereof, without having to share them with a rival. For this reason, instead of restricting facilities, such a company seeks to increase them ; instead of imposing extortionate fares and rates it aims, not merely at immediate profits on the transport of particular commodities, but at encouraging such a development of the district in general as will ensure its prosperity, increase its population, expand its trade, *and* create more traffic of all kinds in a not far distant future.

It was precisely this idea that led the Great Eastern Railway Company to set the example it did in seeking to develop the interests of its agricultural districts. The more these interests expanded, and the more profitable the agricultural industry became to the people living in those districts, the greater would be the demand for household supplies, for furniture, for pianos, for building materials, and for countless other commodities, most of which would bring additional traffic to the line apart from the greater amount of agricultural produce carried, and apart, also, from the further inevitable increase in passenger traffic.

Cornwall, again, might be regarded as the " monopoly " of the Great Western Railway ; but what person would suggest that the Great Western have not sufficiently boomed " the Cornish Riviera " ?

Nor is there necessarily a " monopoly " simply because a particular district is served by a single railway. If the Great Eastern did not take people to East-coast resorts at reasonable rates, or if the Great Western charged excessive fares for the journey to Cornwall, holiday-makers would, in each case, go elsewhere. If either company, or any other company, sought to get too much for carrying milk to London, milk would be obtained by the metropolitan dealers from other districts, instead ; and so on with most other commodities.

Indirect competition, on sound economic lines, may, therefore, still exist even when a railway company is, after many amalgamations, in the possession of an apparent monopoly. The law of supply and demand will still regulate both prices and charges. When, on the other hand, an attempt is made to enforce an artificial and non-economic competition by Act of Parliament, the inevitable result is that the companies concerned find it to their advantage to combine, or to agree, rather than to compete in rates and fares under conditions that would not only be mutually disadvantageous, but confer no lasting benefit on the public they seek to serve.

How the ultimate result of railway policy, as here described, has been to bring about the creation of great systems out of small ones may be seen from the following typical examples, showing in each case the number of lesser companies absorbed, leased or worked as the result of amalgamations, of leases in perpetuity, or otherwise ; though the figures do not include railways which have been vested in two or more companies jointly :—

NAME OF COMPANY.	LENGTH OF LINE.[1] Miles.	COMPANIES AMALGAMATED OR LINES LEASED.
Great Central	753	15
Great Eastern	1133	26
Great Northern	856	22
Great Western	2993	115
Lancashire and Yorkshire	589	14
London and North-Western	1966	59
London and South-Western	964	40
London, Brighton and South Coast.	454	19
Midland	1531	35
North-Eastern	1728	41
South-Eastern and Chatham	629	29
Caledonian	1074	41
North British	1363	45
Great Northern of Ireland	560	14
Great Southern and Western (Ireland)	1121	19

[1] The figures in this column are taken from the Board of Trade Railway Returns for 1910.

The process of amalgamation has been carried even further than these figures suggest, some of the companies absorbed into the great systems having themselves previously amalgamated a number of still smaller companies. The North-Eastern, for example, came into existence in 1854, through a combination of three companies—the York, Newcastle and Berwick, the Leeds Northern, and the York and North Midland—which three companies then represented between them what had originally been fifteen separate undertakings. Since 1854 the North-Eastern Company have purchased or amalgamated thirty-eight other companies, one of which, the Stockton and Darlington (absorbed in 1863), was already an amalgamation of eleven companies.[1]

That the conveniences of travel and the advantages to traders have been greatly enhanced by the substitution of these few great companies for a large number of small ones is beyond question, and actual experience has shown that the fears of grave evils resulting from prospective abuses of the railway " monopoly " brought about by amalgamations such as these have been mainly imaginary, notwithstanding the fact that they have formed the basis of so much of the policy of the State in its dealings with the railways.

There are still various small and even diminutive companies which have escaped the fate of being swallowed up by their big neighbours. One of the smallest engaged in a general traffic—as distinct from dock or mineral lines—is the Easingwold railway, Yorkshire, which connects with the North-Eas-

---

[1] When giving evidence before the Departmental Committee on Railway Agreements and Amalgamations, on June 21, 1910, Mr A. Beasley, general manager of the Taff Vale Railway Company, called attention to the fact that in "Bradshaw's Railway Manual" for 1909 there was published a special index of all the railways of which notices had appeared in that publication during sixty years (practically covering the whole position), the total of such railways, including light railways, being 1129. Of this number 86 were recorded as having been abandoned, closed or wound up, leaving a balance of 1043. In "Bradshaw's Railway Guide" for March, 1910, only 110 railways—including light railways, railways operated by joint committees, as well as railways in the Isle of Man, the Isle of Wight, and Jersey—were given as being in actual operation. "That shows," continued Mr Beasley, "that there must have been 933 railways, all separately authorised, most of them separately constructed, and many of them, for a time, separately worked, which have been purchased, amalgamated, leased or otherwise absorbed or taken over by other undertakings."

tern at Alne, but still maintains an independent existence.
According to the Board of Trade Returns for 1910 the Easingwold Railway consists of two miles of line, or three miles if we
include sidings, and it owns one locomotive, two carriages for
the conveyance of passengers and one goods waggon. It
carried in 1910 a total of 33,888 passengers, 5547 tons of
minerals and 11,214 tons of general merchandise. Its total
gross receipts from all sources of traffic for the year amounted
to £2358, and the net receipts, after allowing for working
expenses, were £936. The authorised capital of the company
is £18,000, of which £16,000 has been paid up.

Small as this line is, it serves a useful purpose; but the
policy of amalgamation, followed up by leading companies
with such pertinacity, and in spite of so much distrust and
opposition, has, happily, saved the railway system of the
country from remaining split up among an endless number of
companies of the Easingwold type—even though they might
have had more than three miles of railway and a single
locomotive each.

Other developments of State policy towards the railways
have applied to ensuring both perfection of construction and
safety in operation.

In the former respect the English lines have been built with
a solidity and a completeness not to be surpassed by the
railways of any other country in the world. Even in sparsely
populated districts where, under similar circumstances, the
American or the Prussian railway engineer would lay down
only such a line as would be adequate to the actual or prospective traffic, would give the passengers no platform, would
provide little more than a shed for a railway station, and would
expect the public to be content with a level crossing and look
out for the trains, a British railway company is obliged to
respect State requirements by laying down a line equal to the
traffic of a busy urban centre, give the passengers such platforms as will enable them to enter or leave the trains without
the slightest inconvenience, erect well-built and more or less
commodious station buildings, and, it may be, arrange for
bridges, viaducts or underground passages such as in other
countries would be found only in centres having a substantial
amount of traffic.

Apart, in fact, from any question as to expenditure on

Parliamentary proceedings and on the acquiring of land, the cost simply of building the railway itself has, generally speaking, been far greater in this country than, under corresponding geographical and traffic conditions, has been the case elsewhere.   Judging from the example of the Prussian State Railway administration it is extremely doubtful if, had the British railway system been constructed, owned and operated by the State, instead of being left to private enterprise, any responsible Chancellor of the Exchequer would have authorised so great a degree of expenditure, in the interests of an absolute perfection of construction under all possible conditions, as that which has been forced upon commercial companies dependent for their capital on the money they could raise from investors.

Less scope for criticism is offered by the provision of the most complete of safety appliances in regard to signalling and other phases of railway operation.   The desirability of reducing the risk of railway accidents to an absolute minimum is beyond the range of all possible dispute.   Yet, as a matter of detail, the substantial cost of ensuring this all-important element of safety, no less than the exceptionally heavy outlay on the lines themselves, has helped still further to increase that capital expenditure a return on which is only to be secured by the investors from the revenue the companies can get from the railway users.

When we look for the ultimate and combined results of the various conditions touched upon in this and the preceding chapter—excessive cost of land, abnormal expenditure on Parliamentary proceedings and various aspects of State policy and control—we find them in the fact that, whether or not the British railways are really the best in the world, they have certainly been the most costly.

Comparisons with other countries may be misleading unless we remember that published statistics as to the cost of construction of the world's railways apply to route mileage—or, otherwise, " length of line "—and that the English lines have a large proportion of double, treble and other multiple track, while in more sparsely populated countries the railways, except in and around the large towns, consist to a far larger extent of single track.   The actual position is not, therefore, quite so bad as the comparative figures appear to show. But, even allowing for these considerations, the following table

—which I compile from data published in the " Bulletin of the International Railway Congress Association " for February, 1911—may be regarded as conveying the moral of the story I have here been seeking to tell :—

CONSTRUCTION COST OF THE RAILWAYS OF DIFFERENT COUNTRIES.

COUNTRY.	SYSTEM.	YEAR.	MILES.	CONSTRUCTION TOTAL. £	CAPITAL PER MILE. £
Great Britain and Ireland	Entire	1905	22,843	1,272,600,000	55,712
Germany .	,,	1908	35,639	813,300,000	22,821
France . .	Main lines	1906	24,701	706,700,000	28,611
Belgium .	State lines	1907	2,523	93,600,000	37,088
Netherlands .	Entire	1897	1,653	28,700,000	17,350
Denmark .	State	1909	1,218	13,250,000	10,884
United States of America	—	1908	233,632	3,521,200,000	15,071
Canada .	—	1907	22,447	269,850,000	12,022

CHAPTER XXII

DECLINE OF CANALS

CONSIDERING that, in spite of the unreasonableness, the exactions and the large profits of many of the canal companies in the later days of their prosperous monopoly, the canals themselves had rendered such invaluable service to the trade, commerce and industry of the country, the question may well have arisen why they were not allowed, or enabled to a greater extent than was actually the case, to continue their career of usefulness.

There has, indeed, for some years been in the United Kingdom a canal-revival party which favours the idea that either the State or the local authorities should acquire and improve the canals with a view to enabling them better to compete with the railways—which, as the story of the Liverpool and Manchester line shows, were at one time expressly designed as competitors of and alternatives to the canals.

So far has this resuscitation idea been carried that in December, 1909, the Royal Commission on Canals and Waterways reported in favour of the State acquiring, widening and otherwise bringing up to date a series of canals radiating from the Birmingham district, and establishing cross-country connections between the Thames, the Mersey, the Severn and the Humber. The reasons for the decline of the canals and the practicability, or otherwise, of reviving them may thus be regarded as questions of more than merely historical or academic interest for (1) the traders who might benefit from the said revival ; (2) the traders who certainly would not benefit, but who, in conjunction with (3) the general taxpayer, might have to contribute to the cost if the State did acquire the canals and failed to make them pay.

The " real commercial prosperity of England " has well been dated from the period of early canal development, when artificial waterways began to supplement the deficiencies of navigable streams limited to certain districts and liable to floods, droughts and other disadvantages, and of ill-made roads which even the turnpike system had failed to adapt to the requirements of heavy traffic. In these conditions the movement either of raw materials or of manufactured articles other than those which could be carried on packhorses had, as we have seen, been rendered all but impossible in many parts of the country on account either of the difficulties or of the excessive cost of transport. Canals, constituting a great improvement on any other existing conditions, came to the rescue, and supplied the first impetus to that industrial revolution which the railways were to complete.

This was a great work for the canals to have accomplished, and it was a work that was essentially done by private enterprise. Clifford says that " Parliament, by its legislation in furtherance of canals and of agriculture, probably contributed more largely to the national prosperity than by any group of public measures passed towards the close of the last [eighteenth] century." There is here not a word of recognition for Brindley, the Duke of Bridgewater and the other pioneers of the canal movement, or for the private investors who provided the £14,000,000 spent on the actual " furtherance " of canals. Parliament did not inspire, originate or in any way improve the canals ; it found none of the money which they cost, nor did it even seek to direct their construction on any such well-organised system of through and uniform lines of communication as would have made them far more useful, and assured them, probably, a longer lease of life. Yet Mr Clifford has no hesitation in giving all the praise to Parliament because it *allowed* the canal promoters and proprietors to carry out the work on their own initiative, and at their own risk, as the improvers of rivers and the providers of turnpike roads had done before them.

" Canals in this country," says the Final Report of the Royal Commission on Canals and Waterways, " were constructed upon no general scheme or system. As soon as it was seen that they were a profitable investment, independent companies were formed in every district, and, according to their influence or their means, obtained from Parliament Acts conceding powers to make canals of the most varying length and character." If, in conceding these powers, Parliament had established some central authority with a view to securing such uniformity in construction and such connected routes as were practicable, it would have rendered a greater service than by simply approving schemes put forward in what the Final Report itself describes as a " piecemeal " fashion. This, however, was not done ; nor, in fact, was action taken to prevent the canal companies, after they had shown their enterprise and risked their millions, from becoming in the pre-railway days grasping monopolists whose one idea was to exploit the trader to their own advantage, leading him to welcome the railways, as an alternative to the canals, still more cordially than he had previously welcomed the canals as an alternative to the roads and rivers.

So long as the locomotive remained in a comparatively undeveloped stage, the canal companies refrained from regarding railways as serious rivals, and continued to look upon them in the light, rather, of contributors of traffic to the waterways ; but in proportion as the locomotive was improved and the rivalry of the railways became more and more pronounced the canal companies grew alarmed for the prospects of their own concerns. They entered on no new undertakings—the last inland canal, as distinct from ship canals, was completed about 1834—and they got anxious as to the future of those they had on their hands. They had first scoffed at the railways as " nothing but insane schemes," or as costly " bubbles," and they had then worked up a powerful opposition against them. Having failed in each of these directions, they next took steps which they would have done well to take earlier—they reduced their tolls, and they also began to consider how they could improve their canals.

In 1835 there was a general reduction of rates on the Old Quay Navigation between Liverpool and Manchester, but this belated policy of seeking to make terms with the traders did not prejudice the fortunes of the new railway between those places. As regards the improvements sought to be introduced on the canals, Nicholas Wood, in the third edition (1838) of his " Practical Treatise on Rail-Roads," says :—

" Canals, ever since their adoption, have undergone little or no change ; some trivial improvements may have been effected in the manner of passing boats from one level to another, and light boats have been applied for the conveyance of passengers ; but in their general economy they may be said to have remained stationary. Their nature almost prohibits the application of mechanical power to advantage in the conveyance of goods and passengers upon them ; and they have not, therefore, partaken of the benefits which other arts have derived from mechanical science.

" The reverse of this is the case with railroads ; their nature admits of almost unrestricted application of mechanical power upon them, and their utility has been correspondingly increased. . . .

" At the time of the publication of the first[1] and second[2] editions of this work scarcely any experiments had been made on a large scale to elucidate the capabilities of canal navigation —none, certainly, satisfactory ; since then the competition of railways has aroused the dormant spirit of the canal proprietors, and various experiments have been made to ascertain the amount of resistance of boats dragged at different velocities ; attempts have been likewise made to adapt the power of steam to propel the boats upon them, and other experiments have been adopted to increase their activity as a mode of traffic, and especially for the conveyance of passengers."

These various experiments had little practical result, and the navigation companies found it more to their advantage, in many instances, to make good use of their position and influence, while they were still a power in the land, and force the railway companies either to buy them out entirely or to guarantee them against loss. Such results were generally secured either by first threatening opposition to the railway Bills, and then stating the price for withdrawing therefrom, or, alternatively, by projecting schemes for the competitive lines of railway specially favoured by the State policy of the day, and likely, therefore, to be readily conceded.

When, in 1845, the Oxford, Worcester and Wolverhampton Railway Company—afterwards amalgamated with the Great Western Railway Company—were seeking powers of incorporation, they were opposed by the Severn Commissioners, who represented that they had spent £180,000 in improving the waterway, in anticipation of securing a revenue of £14,000 a year. In order to overcome this opposition and get their Bill, the railway company agreed to make up to the Severn

[1] 1825.   [2] 1832.

Commissioners any deficit between the amount of their tolls and £14,000 a year. Under this obligation the railway company paid £6000 a year for many years; but in 1890 the obligation was commuted by a payment by the Great Western Railway Company of £100,000, and by the giving up to them of certain mortgages to which they had become entitled in consideration of the Commissioners discharging them from the liability under their guarantee. In stating these facts in evidence before the Royal Commission on Canals and Waterways, Mr T. H. Rendell, chief goods manager of the Great Western Railway Company, added (Question 23,834) : " It is desirable to mention that, because it is rather suggested that State aid should be given to enable this very waterway to come into fresh competition with the railway. Of course, if that were so, it would be only fair that the Severn Commissioners should re-imburse the railway company the compensation they have received."

The acquiring of the Stratford-on-Avon Canal by the Oxford, Worcester and Wolverhampton Railway was another of many instances of purchase by a railway company being the price of withdrawal of canal opposition to railway Bills.

By threatening to apply to Parliament for powers to build an opposition railway, the Kennet and Avon Canal Company, in 1851, also induced the Great Western to buy them out, the railway company agreeing to pay £7773 a year for the canal, which has been a loss to them ever since.

In the same way the London and Birmingham Railway Company, now the London and North-Western, originally acquired control over the Birmingham Canal Navigations as the result of a declared intention on the part of the canal company, in 1845, to seek for powers to build a competing line of railway through the Stour valley. The railway company only overcame the threatened opposition by guaranteeing the canal company £4 per share on their capital, obtaining, in return, certain rights and privileges, in regard to control and operation, in the event of their having to make good any deficiency in the revenue. This they have had to do every year since 1874, with the single exception of 1875 ; and down to 1910 the total amount paid by the London and North-Western Railway Company to the proprietors of the Birmingham Canal Navigations, under this guarantee, had been no less than £874,652. The payments for the years 1906–10 were as follows : 1906, £37,017 14s. 9d. ; 1907, £22,262 2s. 7d. ; 1908, £44,690 3s. 11d. ; 1909, £45,697 10s. 3d. ; 1910, £39,720 3s. 9d.

There has been much talk in the past of railway companies having obtained possession of canals in order to " strangle " the traffic on them. It is difficult to see why, except under pressure, railway directors, who count among the shrewdest of business men, should have incurred such substantial obligations towards canals which, at the time, everyone regarded as doomed to extinction before a superior means of transport. It is equally difficult to believe that, having incurred these costly obligations, the companies deliberately " strangled " the traffic on the canals, instead of allowing them to earn—if they could—at least sufficient to cover the cost of their upkeep.

Whatever the precise conditions under which they acquired control, the railway companies were compelled by Parliament to incur obligations in regard to maintenance which have had the effect of continuing the existence of many a little-used waterway that would long ago have become hopelessly derelict if it had remained under the control of an independent canal company, instead of being kept going out of the purse of a powerful railway company in accordance with the statutory obligations imposed by Parliament.

These obligations were, of course, based on the principle of ensuring competition even though canals and railways passed under the same control, the former being supported and kept more or less efficient out of the revenues of the latter. This policy, however, was regarded as only an alternative to another, to which Parliament gave the preference—that, namely, of maintaining, if possible, a still more effective competition by strengthening the position of the canals, now the weaker of the combatants in the economic struggle, and enabling them to continue their independent existence, in preference to seeking absorption by the railways.

In 1845 an Act (8 & 9 Vic. c. 28) was passed, the preamble of which, after alluding to the provision in the Railway Clauses Consolidation Act, 1845, giving power to railway companies to vary their rates, declared that " greater competition, for the public advantage, would be obtained " if canal companies, etc., were to have like powers granted to them in respect of their canals, etc. ; and the Act therefore conferred upon them the necessary powers for varying their tolls.

The preamble of another Act passed in the same Session (8 & 9 Vict. c. 42) recited the powers given to railway companies as carriers of goods on their own lines, and stated that " greater competition, for the public advantage, would be obtained if similar powers were granted to canal and navigation companies." The Act accordingly extended to them the same powers. With a like object, and again adopting the principle sanctioned in the case of railway companies, the Act further authorised canal companies to make working arrangements between themselves, and, also, to lease their canals to other canal companies, with a view to a better provision of through water routes, and, consequently, a more active competition with the railways. Two years later another Act (10 & 11 Vict. c. 94) was passed, giving the canal companies power to borrow money for the purposes here specified.

In his presidential address to the Institution of Civil Engineers in 1885, Sir Frederick Bramwell, dealing with various matters relating to the transport conditions of the country, said : " This addition to the legal powers of the canal companies made by the Acts of 1845 and 1847 has had a very beneficial effect upon the value of their property, and has assisted to preserve a mode of transport competing with that afforded by the railways."

It is true that the powers to act as carriers were taken advantage of by leading canal companies, who worked up a good business as carriers, although, to a certain extent, with a result directly at variance with the widely accepted view that canals should carry heavy and bulky commodities, and railways the lighter and more compact goods. What actually happened was that the canal companies, as carriers, competed with the railways in the transport of domestic supplies, while the railways still carried most of the coal, iron-stone, etc., for which many people supposed that canal transport is specially adapted.

While, however, as the result of these particular powers, some of the canal companies improved their financial position, and were enabled to maintain a better competition with the railways, very little use was made of the authority given to them to combine among themselves and establish through routes, converting series of small canals into connected waterways under one and the same control, if not actually owned by one and the same company, as was being so actively done with the railways.

Some action had certainly been taken in this direction. The Birmingham Canal system of to-day is composed of three canal companies which had amalgamated prior to 1846, supplemented by a fourth which joined them in that year. The Shropshire Union, also, is formed of four canal companies originally independent. But these are only exceptions to the rule, for though the Joint Select Committee of 1872, following up what had already been done at an earlier period, recommended that the utmost facilities should be given for amalgamations between canal companies, few of such amalgamations have, as the Final Report of the Royal Commission on Canals and Waterways points out, taken place since the full establishment of railways. Goods sent to-day by canal from Birmingham, for instance, to London, to Liverpool or to Hull will pass over waterways controlled by from six to eight different authorities, according to the route followed.

One must, however, recognise the fact that the securing of uniformity of gauge and the establishment of through routes presented far greater difficulties in the case of artificial waterways than in that of railways. The physical geography of England is wholly unfavourable to efficient cross-country water transport, and this fact, in itself, is sufficient to render impracticable any such scheme of canal resuscitation as that which has been put forward by the recent Royal Commission.

The physical condition of England in relation to the building of canals is well shown in the article on " Canals " published in " Rees' Cyclopædia " (1819) where it is said, in this connection :—

" Great Britain . . . has a range of high land passing nearly its whole length, which divides the springs and rain waters that fall to the opposite coasts : we shall call this range dividing the eastern and western rivers of Britain the *grand ridge*. . . . No less than 22 of our canals now do or are intended to pass this grand ridge, forming as many navigable connections between the rivers of the east and west seas ! . . . The Dudley canal crosses this grand ridge twice, the two ends being on the eastern side, and the middle part on the western side thereof ; the Kennet and Avon crosses the eastern and western branches, into which it divides on the Chalk Hills, west of Marlborough, by which parts of this canal are in the drainage of the west, the south and the east seas ! The Coventry Canal, also, by means of its Bedworth branch, crosses the grand ridge twice. The populous and remarkable town of Birmingham is situate on high ground, near to the grand ridge, and has six canals branching off in different directions, either immediately therefrom or at no great distance, and, what is singular, owing to a loop, or sudden bend of the ridge at this place, no less than five of them traverse the grand ridge, either by means of tunnels or deep-cutting."

While the grand ridge here in question presents no difficulty to powerful locomotives, the position is altogether different with canals fed by streams of water that will not flow up-hill. In the case of the Birmingham Canal, specially referred to in the extract just given, there are three separate " levels." The lowest is 209 feet, and the highest 511 feet above sea level. Boats doing the cross-country journey, or passing between Birmingham and the coast, would have to overcome such heights as these by means of locks, lifts or inclined planes.

Here we have a very different proposition from that which is presented by canals on the flat surfaces of Holland, Belgium and North Germany—with, also, their abundant water supplies, from great rivers or otherwise—whereas the upper levels of the Birmingham Canal are kept filled with water only by means of costly and powerful pumping machinery, supplemented by reservoirs.

When the original builders of canals had to cross the grand ridge, or any other elevation over which they required to pass, they sought to economise water consumption and to keep down both cost of construction and working expenses by making the locks on the top levels only just large enough to pass boats of a small size. The dimensions of any boat making a through journey are thus controlled by those of the smallest lock through which it would require to pass. On lower levels where the water problem did not arise—or not to the same degree—the locks could well be made larger, to accommodate larger boats engaged only in local traffic.

The material differences in cost of construction and operation between waterways on a low and uniform level and those crossing considerable eminences, by means of locks, were well recognised by Parliament when approving the lists of tolls to be paid on different waterways. On the Aire and Calder the minimum toll, if a boat passed through a lock, was fixed at five shillings. On the Rochdale Canal the minimum toll for a boat crossing the summit level was ten shillings.[1] The reason for this difference is that whereas the Aire and Calder navigation is but little above sea level throughout, the summit of the Rochdale Canal is at a height of 600 feet above sea level, and is crossed by means of ninety-two locks in thirty-two miles.

The reader will see, therefore, that the want of a common gauge in the construction of artificial waterways, mainly designed, at the outset, to supply the needs of particular districts, may often have been due to more practical reasons than simply a lack of combination or a difference of view on the part of canal constructors, the problem of gauge on canals built at varying elevations, and all depending on water supply, being entirely different from any question as to the gauge or the running of railways on the same or similar routes.

" The necessity of a uniform gauge on canals as on railways," says Clifford, " is now clear enough. We need not wonder that, in the eighteenth century, Parliament was no wiser than the engineers, and had not learned this lesson." It was, however, not entirely a matter of wisdom. There were, also, these inherent defects of the canal system itself to be considered. It is very doubtful if even Parliament, had it possessed the greatest foresight, could have forced, or have persuaded, the canal companies to construct locks of precisely the same dimensions at elevations of 400, 500 or 600 feet, where water was difficult to get or costly to pump, as on canals more or less on the sea level, and deriving an abundant water supply from mountain streams or navigable rivers.

Forbes and Ashford, in " Our Waterways," also think it is much to be regretted that in this country no standard dimension was ever fixed for canals, " as has been done in France." But the superficial area of the United Kingdom,

[1] "The Law Relating to Railway and Canal Traffic"; Boyle and Waghorn. Vol. I, page 296.

304 History of Inland Transport

with its mountains and valleys, and hills and dales, presents a wholly different problem, in the matter of canal construction, from that offered by the flat surfaces of France, of Holland, of Belgium or of North Germany. In 230 miles of waterway between Hamburg and Berlin there are three locks. In this country there is an average of one lock for every mile and a quarter of canal navigation. The total number of locks is 2,377, and for each of these there must be allowed a capitalised cost of, on an average, £1360.

The fate that overtook the once prosperous canals of South Wales when the railways could no longer be suppressed by the canal companies, and were allowed to compete fairly with them, has been materially due to their own physical disadvantages in respect of the large number of locks they require to overcome the steep inclines of the mountainous district in which they were made. These facts are brought out in the Fourth (Final) Report of the Royal Commission on Canals and Waterways, where it is said :—

" The Glamorganshire and Aberdare Canals were bought by the Marquis of Bute in 1885. They form a continuous narrow waterway with a total length of about 32 miles. In this distance there are 53 locks. . . . The waterway is used at the Cardiff end by small coasting vessels, but above this point the traffic has fallen off considerably. The total tonnage carried on the canals amounted in 1888 to 660,364 tons ; in 1905 to 249,760 tons. Two railways run parallel to the canals and carry almost all the coal brought down from the collieries near the canals. The gradients from these collieries to the port are considerable. This makes the haulage of full railway trucks easy, and, on the other hand, in the case of the canal makes necessary a great number of locks relatively to the mileage, with consequent slowness of transport.

" The Swansea Canal belongs to the Great Western Railway Company. It is a narrow canal, 16½ miles in length, and has 36 locks. The traffic has diminished . . . for reasons similar to those given with respect to the Glamorganshire Canal."

Much more, however, than the provision of locks was necessitated by the physical conditions of a country naturally unsuited for artificial waterways. In some instances the canals were taken across broad valleys by means of viaducts designed to allow of the waterway being maintained at the same level ; and certain of the works thus carried out were, in their day, deservedly regarded as of considerable engineering importance. The Chirk aqueduct, which carries the Ellesmere Canal across a 700-feet stretch in the Ceriog valley, and at a height of 70 feet above the level of the river, and the Pont-cysyllte aqueduct, 1007 feet long, which takes the same canal over the river Dee, are spoken of by Phillips, in his " General History of Inland Navigation " (1803), as " among the boldest efforts of human invention in modern times." Elsewhere the canals had to pass along high embankments or through deep cuttings. Canal tunnels of up to three miles in length were not infrequent, though some of these were made so narrow—in the interests of economy—that they had no towing-path, the boats being taken through by men who lay on their backs on the cargo, and pushed against the sides of the tunnel with their feet. Alternatively, it was sometimes possible to avoid rising ground or deep valleys, necessitating locks, by making wide detours in preference to taking the shortest route, as a railway would do. Thus the distance by canal between Liver-pool and Wigan is thirty-four miles, as compared with a distance of only nineteen by rail. From Liverpool to Leeds is 128 miles by canal and eighty by rail. These windings made the canal compare still more unfavourably with the railway when it was considered that the speed of transport on the former was only about two and a half miles an hour, without counting delays at the locks ; and of these there are, between Liverpool and Leeds, no fewer than ninety-three.

But just because these engineering works had been so bold and so costly, or left so much to be desired in regard to length of route, and just because so many physical difficulties had had to be overcome, it may well have happened that when what was universally considered a better means of transport was presented, general doubts arose as to the wisdom and prac-ticability of reconstructing, in effect, the whole canal system to enable it to compete better with the railways in catering for that through traffic for which the canals themselves were so ill adapted.

Supplementing these considerations as to the physical configuration of the country is the further fact that in the colliery districts the keeping of the canals in working order involves great trouble, incessant watchfulness and very considerable expenditure on account of subsidences due to coal-mining. In my book on "Canals and Traders" (P. S. King & Son) I have told how "throughout practically the whole of the Black Country, the Birmingham Canal, for a total distance of about eighty miles, has been undermined by colliery workings, and is mainly on the top of embankments which have been raised from time to time, in varying stages, to maintain the waterway above the level of the ground that has sunk because of the coal mines underneath." Many of these embankments, as I have had the opportunity of seeing for myself, are now at a height of from twenty to thirty feet above the present surface of the land, and in one instance, at least, the subsidences have been so serious that an embankment twenty feet high and half a mile long has taken the place of what was formerly a cutting. If the Birmingham Canal had not been controlled by the London and North-Western Railway Company, who are under a statutory obligation to keep it in good and effective working condition, it would inevitably have collapsed long ago. No independent canal company, deriving its revenue from canal tolls and charges alone, could have stood the heavy and continuous drain upon its resources which, in these circumstances, the canal would have involved ; and like conditions apply to various other railway-owned canals in the north, in Wales, and elsewhere.

Concerning the Glamorganshire Canal, it is said in "Transport Facilities in South Wales and Monmouthshire," by Clarence S. Howells :[1] "The present owners have spent £25,000 on the canal since 1885 in an ineffectual attempt to revive its waning fortunes. One of its many difficulties is the subsidence caused by colliery workings."

Dealing with the general position in regard to canal transport in the United Kingdom, J. S. Jeans remarks in "Waterways and Water Transport" (1890) :—

"The railway companies have been accused of acquiring canal property in order that they might destroy it, and thereby get rid of a dangerous rival. This is probably not the case. The railway companies are fully aware of the fact that water transport under suitable conditions is more economical than rail transport. It would therefore have suited them, at the

---

[1] "Publications of the Department of Economics and Political Science of the University of South Wales and Monmouthshire," No. 2 (1911).

same rates, to carry by water heavy traffic, in the delivery of which time was not of so much importance. But the canals as they came into their possession were naturally unadapted for such traffic without being more or less remodelled, and this the railway companies have not attempted.

" When we consider the enormous disadvantages under which the majority of the canals of this country now labour, the great matter for wonder is, not that they do not secure the lion's share of the traffic, but that they get any traffic at all."

If, for the sake of argument, we leave out of account all the " enormous disadvantages " here alluded to, and assume that the physical difficulties already detailed could be overcome without much trouble or great expense (though this would, indeed, be a prodigious assumption), we should still have the fact that the number of traders in the country who could hope to benefit from any possible system of internal navigation would necessarily be limited to those in certain districts, whereas the railway can be taken anywhere, and be made to serve the interests of each and every district or community in the country.

It is true that when commodities can be sent direct from an ocean-going vessel to a works situated immediately alongside a canal, the waterway may have the advantage over the railway ; and the same may be the case as regards manufactured goods forwarded in the opposite direction. Of the 235,000 tons of flints, clay and other potters' materials brought into the Potteries district of North Staffordshire during 1910, no fewer than 200,000 tons, imported at Runcorn, Ellesmere Port or Weston Port, were taken by canal to pottery works located on or near to the canal banks. In these circumstances the North Staffordshire Railway Company, who also control the Trent and Mersey Navigation, cannot, as railway owners, compete with themselves as canal owners. In the case of the Aire and Calder, the physical conditions of which are exceptionally favourable, coal can readily be sent from the collieries immediately alongside the waterway to the steamers or the coal ships in the port of Goole. On the Birmingham Canal, also, the traffic between collieries and works, or between works and railway transhipping basins, on the same level, is already so considerable that no great increase could be accommodated without carrying out on the canal a widening which would be fabulously costly, and, also, wholly impracticable, on account of the great iron-works and other industrial establishments which line almost the entire twelve-mile route between Birmingham and Wolverhampton, forming, with their hundreds of private basins, the actual boundary of the canal on one side or the other. To " adapt " the Birmingham Canal to through traffic would produce chaos for the local traffic.

Mr Jeans thus goes a little too far when he makes the sweeping statement that " Canals as they were built a century ago have no longer any function to fulfil that is worthy of serious consideration. Their mission is ended, their use is an anachronism." Even the title given to the present chapter, " Decline of Canals," is to be read subject to the exceptions represented by those of the waterways that still answer these useful local purposes and should have every encouragement therein. Mr Jeans is, however, fully warranted in declaring that " it would be the idlest of idle dreams to expect that the canal system of this or any other country as originally constructed can be resuscitated, or even temporarily galvanised into activity, in competition with the railways."

There is a still further consideration.

Whatever the prospective advantages of resuscitation when the point of despatch and the point of delivery are both on the same canal—and especially when both are on the same level of the canal, so that passage through locks is unnecessary—it must be obvious that when commodities are despatched from, or consigned to, places situate at such a distance from a canal that supplementary transport is necessary, the cost thereof must be added to the amount of the canal charges. The sum of the two may then be so little below the cost of rail transport that the latter—coupled with the greater speed and the greater convenience in the way, perhaps, of sidings or of lines of rails coming right into the works—will be preferred. Academic theories, on paper, as to the comparative costs of hauling given weights of commodities on water and rail respectively may, in fact, be rendered futile by (1) the supplementary cost of transport to or from the waterway and of various services or conveniences included in the railway rate but not included in the canal charges ; and (2) the consideration that if a large sum of money be spent on improving the canals the interest thereon must either be met by means of increased canal charges—in which event the canal-users would have no advantage over the railway-users— or remain as a permanent burden on the community.

How the cost of the supplementary charges and services operates in practice may be shown by a reference to the London coal trade, coal being a commodity which is regarded by those who favour State ownership of the canals as one specially adapted for waterway transport.

Except as regards the consignments of sea-borne coal, the domestic coal supply of London is carried almost exclusively by rail. The trucks can generally go right up to the collieries ; they convey the coal to special and extensive railway sidings, there to await orders ; and they proceed thence, as required, to the suburban railway station or depôt nearest to the premises of the actual consumer, in any part of the country ; whereas coal sent by canal would first have to be taken from the colliery to the canal, and there be discharged into the boat, then be conveyed, say, to the Thames, next be transferred from boat to cart, and finally be taken by road across London to destination, with the subsidiary considerations (1) that with each fresh handling the coal would deteriorate in value ; (2) that the traders would lose the advantage of railway coal sidings and station depots ; and (3) that the railway truck is a better unit than the canal boat for the various descriptions or qualities of coal dealt in by the average coal merchant, whose prejudices in favour of rail transport over canal transport, when the consumers are not actually located on or quite close to the waterway, can thus be accounted for by strictly business considerations.

The conclusion is forced upon one that, notwithstanding the useful purposes which a certain number of canals are still serving, any resuscitation of canals in general, or even any provision of improved cross-country canal routes passing over the " grand ridge," at the cost of an indefinite number of millions to the country, can hardly be regarded as coming within the range of sound economics. It certainly is favoured by a larger number of traders than the comparatively small proportion who would be able, or willing, to use the canals when they had been improved ; but this support is directly due to a belief that nationalisation—though what is proposed is only a partial nationalisation—of the canals would tend towards keeping down railway rates.

In other words, the scheme is but a further development˜of that policy which aims at enforcing the principle of competition irrespective of cost, and without regard for the capital expenditure on which a fair return ought to be assured. One of the witnesses examined before the Royal Commission on Canals and Waterways said there was a local feeling against the Wilts and Berks Canal being taken in hand by the county council "because," he said, "we are all afraid of the rates ; but," he added, "from what I have heard from traders and others, they would like to see it back again, mainly as a means of cutting down railway rates." Mr Remnant, one of the Commissioners, says in his separate report, in alluding to import and export traffic, that most of the evidence given on this question " seemed to point to a desire on the traders' part, not so much for the waterways as for lower railway rates, in order to enable them to face foreign competition " ; while Mr Davison, another of the Commissioners, who also dissents from the recommendations of the Majority Report, speaks of many of the canals as being " of little economic value to the trade of the country, apart from whatever influence they may have in keeping down railway rates," though he adds : " If this latter result were otherwise secured their continued existence could not be justified on economic grounds."

Any effect which the carrying out of the Majority Report scheme of canal improvement *might* have on railway rates would, all the same, be felt only in the towns or localities directly concerned. Benefit would result to (1) those traders who could use the canals, and (2) those who, though not using the canals, obtained the lower railway rates, if reductions really were secured through the canal competition ; while traders at a distance from the waterways would not only have to help to pay the cost, though themselves deriving no benefit therefrom, but might even see two classes of their own competitors in the favoured districts gain an advantage over them—one set from State-owned and State-aided canals, and another from the local reductions in railway rates to which those canals might be expected to lead.

The proposals of the Royal Commission may well be approved by certain localities or individual traders on the line of route of the canals proposed to be taken in hand. They are hardly likely, however, to commend themselves to the traders and taxpayers of the country in general.

My own view is that if the State is prepared to find money for the purpose of cheapening the cost of transport, it could do so to better advantage if, instead of spending millions on an impracticable and partial scheme of canal resuscitation, it lightened the burden of taxation now falling on the railway companies, and thus improved their position in regard, not merely to traders in particular districts, but to the trade and industries of the United Kingdom as a whole.

CHAPTER XXIII

DECLINE OF TURNPIKES

THE inherent defects of the turnpike system must in them-selves have been fatal to its permanent continuance, irre-spective of the influence of the railways, which did not kill the turnpikes so much as merely give them the *coup de grace*.

No one can deny the adequacy of the time that Par-liament had devoted to the kindred subjects of roads and waggons. By 1838—and only a few years, therefore, later than the opening of the Liverpool and Manchester Railway—Parliament had passed no fewer than 3800 private and local turnpike Acts, and had authorised the creation in England and Wales of 1116 turnpike trusts, controlling 22,000 miles of road. But the whole system was hopelessly inefficient, wasteful and burdensome, besides being as unsatisfactory in its administration as it was in its results.

Managed or directed by trustees and surveyors under the conditions detailed in Chapter X, the actual work on the turnpike roads was mainly carried out by statute labour, pauper labour or labour paid for out of the tolls, out of the receipts from the composition for statute duty, or, as a last resource, at the direct cost of the ratepayers, who were thus made responsible for the turnpike as well as for the parish roads.

Statute labour was a positive burlesque of English local government. Archdeacon Plymley says in his " General View of the Agriculture of Shropshire " (1803) : " There is no trick, evasion or idleness that shall be deemed too mean to avoid working on the road : sometimes the worst horses are sent ; at others a broken cart, or a boy, or an old man past labour, to fill : they are sometimes sent an hour or two too late in the morning, or they leave off much sooner than the proper time, unless the surveyor watch the whole day."

In the article already quoted from the " Westminster

Review " for October, 1825, it is said : " Statute labour on the parish roads is limited to six days work and on the turnpikes to three. But it is now found generally expedient to demand or take money in lieu of labour, according to a rate to be fixed by the justices in different places. . . . In practice the statute labour was frequently a farce, half of the time being spent in going and returning and in conversation and idleness."

An authority referred to in Postlethwayt's " Dictionary " (1745) had suggested that criminals condemned to death for minor offences should, instead of being transported, be ordered to do a year's work on the highway. He further recommended, in all seriousness, that arrangements should be made with the African Company for the importation of 200 negroes as road-repairers, they being, as he said, " generally persons to do a great deal of work." Failing criminals and negroes, some of the parishes did employ paupers, gangs of whom were to be seen pretending to work at road-mending, and getting far more degeneration for themselves than they did good for the roads.

In 1835 Parliament abolished both statute labour and statute labour composition, thenceforward wholly superseded by highway rates as applying to the whole of the minor roads for which the parish was responsible.

Bad as the statute labour system had been, its abolition involved a loss to the turnpike trusts estimated at about £200,000 a year ; and this was a serious matter to trustees whose financial position was becoming hopeless in view of their liabilities and the discouraging nature of their outlook. Such discouragement was due in great part to the advent of the railways, but not entirely so, the Select Committee of 1839 on Turnpike Trusts saying in their report that " the gradual decline in the transit on turnpike roads in some parts of the country arises not only from the railways formed but from steam vessels plying on rivers and as coasting traders " ; and they added : " Whenever mechanical power has been substituted for animal power, the result has hitherto been that the labour is performed at a cheaper rate."

The cost of making and repairing turnpike roads, especially under the primitive conditions still widely retained, notwithstanding the improved methods introduced by Telford and McAdam, was in itself a most serious item, apart from the excessive expenditure on administration. Dr James Anderson says on this subject in the issue of his " Recreations " for November, 1800 :—

" I have been assured, and believe it to be true, though I cannot pledge myself for the certainty of the fact, that there is annually laid out on repairs upon the road from Hyde Park to Hounslow considerably above £1000 a mile. A turnpike road cannot be made in almost any situation for less, as I am told, than £1000 per mile ; but where it is of considerable width, as near great towns, it will run from £1500 to £2000 per mile ; and in annual repairs, including the purchase price of materials, carting them to the road, spreading, raking off, and carting away again, from £100 to £1000 a mile."

The trustees generally raised loans to meet their first expenses, payment of interest being guaranteed out of the tolls levied ; but though, at one time, and especially before the competition of railways became active, the security was regarded as adequate, an unduly costly management, combined with decreasing receipts from tolls, resulted in the piling up of huge financial liabilities which the trusts found it impossible to clear off in addition to meeting current expenditure. The Select Committee on Turnpike Trusts in 1839 reported on this subject : " The present debt of the turnpike trusts in England and Wales exceeds £9,000,000, and it is annually increasing, in consequence of the practice prevailing in several of the trusts of converting the unpaid interest into principal, the trustees giving bonds bearing interest for the amount of interest due." At this time there were no fewer than eighty-four trusts which had paid no interest on loans for several years, and there were said to be some trusts which had paid no interest for sixty years. Sir James McAdam, son of John Loudon McAdam, informed the Select Committee of 1839 that the amount of unpaid interest on the trusts at that time was £1,031,096.

In order to improve their financial position, the trustees generally adopted the expedient either of seeking Parliamentary authority to increase their tolls or of setting up the largest possible number of toll-gates along their own particular bit of road. In either case it was the road-user who paid.

The Select Committee of 1819 reported that in the three

preceding Sessions ninety turnpike trusts, seeking renewal of their Acts, had asked for authority to increase their tolls on the ground that they could not pay their debts without the assistance of Parliament. The alternative to an increase of tolls was carried so far that it became customary for the trusts to set up a toll-gate wherever there was the slightest excuse for so doing.

" In some places," says J. Kearsley Fowler, in " Records of Old Times," " as, for instance, my native town of Aylesbury, the place was literally hemmed in like a fortified city,—not even an outlet to exercise a horse without paying a toll." There were, he tells us, seven different trusts to maintain at Aylesbury alone.

Mr George Masefield, a solicitor residing at Ledbury, Herefordshire, said when giving evidence before the Select Committee on Turnpike Trusts in 1864 that in the twenty-one miles between Ledbury and Kingston, a journey he frequently made, he had to go through eight turnpike gates. In the eight miles' journey to Newent he passed through four gates and paid three times ; and in the thirteen miles to Worcester he went through six gates and paid at five.

In Gloucestershire, said the " Morning Star " of September 30, 1856, " it sometimes happens you have to pay five turnpikes in twelve miles " ; though such were the inequalities of the burden that in some other counties, said the same paper, one could go for miles without paying anything.

These inequalities had been previously pointed out in the " Westminster Review " article. In speaking of the practice followed in the location of turnpikes, the writer declared that " gates are sometimes placed so as to tax one portion and exempt another, so as to make strangers and travellers pay, while those who chiefly profit by the roads, and who destroy them most, are exempted." He further said that " the Welsh, with their characteristic cunning, have contrived to exempt their own heavy carts and to levy their tolls on the light barouches of unlucky visitors " ; that one might see, in Scotland, three toll-gates, and all to be paid, in the space of a hundred yards ; that one might, as against this, ride thirty miles without paying one toll ; and that " the inhabitants of Greenwich pay the tolls for the half of Kent."

London in 1818 had twelve turnpike trusts for 210 miles of

road. The tolls they collected in that year amounted to
£97,482 ; the expenses were £98,856, and the accumulated
debt of the dozen trusts was £62,658.

On the Middlesex side of London there were 87 turnpike
gates and bars within four miles of Charing Cross, or, including
the Surrey side, a total of 100 within a four-mile radius. " Let
the traveller drive through the Walworth gate southward,"
says J. E. Bradfield, in his " Notes on Toll Reform " (1856),
" and note how every road, every alley, every passage has its
' bar.' The inhabitants cannot move north, east, south, or
west without paying one toll ; and some of them cannot get
out of the parish without two tolls. The cry at every corner
of Camberwell is ' Toll.' " The position of Walworth and
Camberwell does not, however, appear to have been at all
exceptional. In Besant's " Survey of London " it is stated that
a map of London and its environs, published in 1835, shows
that it was then impossible to get away from town without
going through turnpikes. On every side they barred the way.

In the case of a stage-coach with four horses running every
day between London and Birmingham, the tolls paid amounted
to £1428 in the year. At one gate on the Brighton road the
tolls collected came to £2400 in the year, and of this amount
£1600 was from coaches. The payment of these tolls was a
serious tax on the coaches, though an important source of
revenue for the turnpike trustees ; and in proportion as the
coaches were taken off the roads, owing to the competition
of the railways, the financial position of the trusts became
still worse. Mail-coaches were exempted from tolls in England,
though they had to pay them in Scotland.

The amount of the tolls varied according to the trusts or the
locality. Kearsley Fowler says that in Aylesbury for a horse
ridden or led, passing through the gates, the toll was 1½d. ; for
a vehicle drawn by one horse, 4½d. ; for a carriage and pair,
9d., and so on. The tolls, he adds, fell with particular hardship on farmers, and became a tax on their trade. When
sending away their corn or other produce with a waggon and
four horses they paid, in some instances, 1s. 6d. or 2s. 3d.
If, as often occurred, the waggon passed through two gates
in eight or nine miles, the payments came to 3s. or 4s. 6d.
If the waggon returned with coal or feeding stuffs it had to
pay the same tolls over again.

Nor did the toll-payers get anything like value for their money. About fifty per cent of the amount received by the trustees, either direct from the tolls or from the persons farming them, went in interest and management expenses ; and although the remainder might be spent on road repairs, a good proportion of this was wasted because of the inefficient way in which the work was too often done. Mr Wrightson, a member of the Special Committee of 1864, declared that every toll-gate cost on an average £25 a year, and that every turnpike trust had, on an average, five toll-gates. The total number of trusts in 1864 was stated in the Fifteenth Annual Report of the Local Government Board (1886) to be 1048. An average of five toll-gates for each would give them a total of 5240 ; and an average cost of maintenance of £25 a year for this number of toll-gates gives a total of £131,000 a year as the cost simply of toll-gate maintenance, apart from salaries of official staff and other items. Mr R. M. Brereton, surveyor for the county of Norfolk, said in the course of his evidence before the Select Committee of the House of Lords on the Highway Acts (1881) : " In Norfolk we collected £15,000 a year for tolls, but we only spent £7000 a year of that actually on the roads."

It might even happen that, after costs of management and payment of interest had been met, there was no balance left for road maintenance. In the Report of the Select Committee of 1839 on Turnpike Trusts it is stated that in several instances the creditors of the trusts had exercised the power given to them under the General Turnpike Act (3 Geo. IV., c. 126) of taking possession of the tolls to secure payment of their mortgage or bonded securities and the interest due to them. " The result," says the report, " must be to throw the burden of repairs and of the maintenance of such roads on the several parishes through which they pass. Should such measures now taken by some creditors become general throughout the kingdom, the proprietors and holders of land will not only have to pay the tolls as usual, but must also be called on to defray the expense of keeping the road in a proper state for the public use, by an additional highway rate to be levied on the parishes where the tolls paid by the public are seized by the creditor."

In addition to management expenses, expenditure on the roads and payment of interest, allowance had to be made for the profits expected by those to whom the trustees farmed the tolls, offering them by auction to the highest bidder. The contractors generally had a private understanding among themselves as to the terms they were prepared to give. One of them, Lewis Levy by name, farmed from £400,000 to £500,000 of turnpike tolls within a radius of from sixty to eighty miles of London ; and we may assume that he would not have gone into the business on so large a scale as this unless it had brought him an adequate return.

The ultimate result of these various conditions was that the sum total of the indirect taxation thus collected from the public was not only great in itself, and out of all proportion to the benefits received, but was inadequate to cover an expenditure already swollen to abnormal proportions. In his evidence before the Select Committee of 1839 Sir James McAdam stated that in 1836 the gross income of the different roads was £1,776,586, and the expenditure for the year was £1,780,349, exceeding by £3,763 the whole of the income. In Lancashire alone the turnpike tolls came to £123,000 a year.

Collection of this considerable revenue from the community had, of course, been duly authorised by Parliament ; yet the trustees were under no obligation to account for the moneys they received. Not only was there free scope given for jobbery, embezzlement and malpractices in general, but the turnpike commissioners could, as the " Edinburgh Review " pointed out in 1819, abuse their trust and yet go on levying tolls, keeping possession of the road and defying complaints. The writer on " Roads " in " Rees' Cyclopædia " (1819) further declares that " either from bad management, from party influence or from chicanery and ignorance of surveyors and contractors, the roads in many places are not only laid out in the most absurd direction but are so badly constructed and kept in so wretched a state of repair that they are almost impassable."

On the other hand, the great advancement in coaching, and the higher speeds attained by the coaches during the first three decades of the nineteenth century suggest that the improvements introduced by Telford and McAdam could not have been without good effect on the chief of the main roads, at least, however inefficient the making and repairing of the turnpike and parish roads in general may still have remained.

All the same, and in spite of the greater road traffic, the financial difficulties into which the trusts drifted and the burdensome nature of the tax imposed by the toll-system on traders, agriculturists and the public were beyond all doubt.

Various attempts were made to improve the position of the trusts.

A Committee of the House of Commons recommended in 1821 that Continuance Bills for the periodical renewal of Turnpike Acts should be exempted from fees. Another Committee made a like recommendation in 1827, and subsequently a measure was passed scheduling in an annual public statute the continuation of any trusts on the point of expiring.

Then, as there was so obviously an excessive number of trusts, with a consequent undue expenditure on management, a Committee which sat in 1820 strongly recommended the consolidation of turnpike trusts around London. An Act consolidating those on the north of the Thames was passed, the preamble thereof reciting no fewer than 120 other Acts of Parliament which the new measure superseded.

In 1833, 1836 and 1839 other Committees recommended a general consolidation of trusts ; but little, apparently, was done in this direction in England, though in several counties of Scotland, as mentioned in the Report of the Select Committee of 1864, the system was greatly improved by the appointment of Road Boards which, by a consolidation of various trusts and the association of several counties for the repair and maintenance of roads, effected a material diminution in the expenses. In Ireland, also, the abolition of the system of statute labour in 1763, the placing of the business of road-making under the control of the grand juries, and the meeting both of the cost of road repairs and the payment of interest on the existing debts out of the rates of the counties and baronies led to better roads being provided at a less burdensome cost.

By a General Turnpike Act passed in 1841, justices were authorised, on proof being given to them of a deficiency in the revenue of a turnpike trust, to order the parish surveyor to pay to the trust a portion of the highway rates, to be laid out in actual repairs on parts of the turnpike road within the parish.

Bondholders petitioned Parliament that any deficiency

in their profits owing to railway competition should be made
good by the railway companies ; but although this principle
was already being enforced, in effect, in the case of many
of the canal companies, it was not adopted in that of the turnpike trusts.

The various measures resorted to did no more than afford
temporary relief to the trusts, and, in the meantime, the
obligation cast upon the community of having to support so
inefficient and so wasteful a system was found to be intolerably
vexatious and burdensome.

While some persons were praising turnpikes because of
such improvement as they had effected on the roads, the
" Gentleman's Magazine " of May, 1749, had spoken of them
as " a great disadvantage in our competition for trade with
France, where they have excellent roads without turnpikes,
which are no small tax on travellers and carriers." Not only
were the tolls a tax on all commodities carried by road, but
they constituted, to a large extent, an unprofitable tax,
because so considerable a proportion of the total amount
collected went to the support of officials, contractors, lessees,
toll-gate keepers and others, who lived on the system, and so
small a proportion—after allowing for money wasted—was
usefully spent to the direct advantage of the traders in
facilitating actual transport. The Committee of 1864 condemned the whole system of turnpike tolls as " unequal in
pressure, costly in collection, inconvenient to the public, and
injurious as causing a serious impediment to intercourse and
traffic."

In Wales popular dissatisfaction with the great increase
of toll-gates had led in 1843-4 to the " Rebecca riots," bands
of men 500 strong, their leaders disguised in women's clothes,
promenading the roads of Pembrokeshire, Cardiganshire
and Breconshire at night and throwing down the offending
gates. It was only with considerable difficulty and much
bloodshed that the disturbances were eventually suppressed by
a strong force of soldiers. A commission appointed to inquire
into the matter found there was a genuine grievance, and an
Act of Parliament was passed which consolidated the trusts
in South Wales, regulated the number of toll-gates there, and
provided for the extinction of the debt on the roads by the
advance of about £200,000, at three per cent interest, by the

Public Works Loan Commissioners, to be repaid by terminable annuities within thirty years. The loan was duly paid off by 1876.

Inasmuch as English traders and travellers simply grumbled and paid, and refrained from demonstrating as the more emotional Welshmen had done, they had to wait longer for any material relief from the grievances from which they, also, were suffering.

Down to 1864 the duty of deciding in what order turnpike Acts should be permitted to expire, instead of being renewed, was, as Mr George Sclater-Booth (Lord Basing), formerly President of the Local Government Board, informed the Select Committee of the House of Lords on the Highway Acts, when giving evidence before them in 1880, one of the functions of the Home Office, and the Home Office, he said, " was timid at that time in allowing these turnpike trusts to lapse." Pressure was brought to bear on the department with a view to effecting a more rapid extinction of the trusts ; though the ratepayers had not then realised the results to themselves of the cost of maintenance of disturnpiked roads being thrown on the parish.

Following on the report of a Special Committee of the House of Commons, recommending that the Turnpike Acts should be allowed to expire as rapidly as possible, a House of Commons Turnpike Committee was appointed in 1864 to take over the whole business from the Home Office. Thenceforward this Committee prepared every year a schedule of turnpike trusts which they thought should expire, the schedule being embodied in an annual Turnpike Acts Continuance Bill which was duly passed by Parliament. So great was the zeal shown by the Committee that from 1864 roads were disturnpiked at the rate of from 1000 to 1700 or 1800 miles a year. " This," said Mr Sclater-Booth, " has been most distinctly the policy of representative members of the House of Commons, and not the policy of the Government of the day, except in so far as the Government of the day has foreborne to exercise any interference with the Turnpike Continuance Act in Parliament."

While the reduction in the number of turnpike trusts had been an undoubted boon to users of the roads, it had thrown heavy burdens on the local ratepayers. For a period of a

century, at least, most of them had, in effect, and except in
certain circumstances, been relieved by the turnpike system
of their common law obligation to keep main roads in repair ;
but in proportion as the trusts expired the obligations in
respect to maintenance fell back again on the parishes. Under,
also, old enactments which still remained in force, not only
land and houses but many other kinds of property—stock-in-
trade, timber and " personal estate " generally—were assessed
for highways and other purposes. These conditions remained
until 1840, when an Exemption Act suspended the power
of levying rates on stock-in-trade, and other changes in the law
of assessment were made subsequently.

With the greater activity, from the year 1864, of the House
of Commons Turnpike Committee the burdens on the unfortunate parishioners became heavier than before ; and in
the Turnpike Continuance Act of 1870 there was inserted a
clause to the effect that the cost of repairing any roads disturnpiked after the passing of that Act should be borne by the
highway district, where there was one, and not by the parish.
In 1874 and 1875 the House of Commons Turnpike Committee
" made very strong complaints," Mr Sclater-Booth stated in
his evidence, that they would not have proceeded so fast
as they had done, and would not have recommended Parliament to allow so many miles of road to be disturnpiked
year by year, if they had not felt satisfied that the Government
would have provided some remedy for the injustice they
occasioned. " They seemed to me," the witness continued,
" to have had no compunction in causing the injustice to be
occasioned before any remedy was provided for it ; but,
having permitted that injustice to take place, they complained
year after year of the action, or, rather, of the non-action, of the
Government in not applying a remedy for these grievances."

No effective remedy was, in fact, provided until 1882. Early
in the Session of that year notice was given in the House of
Commons of a resolution which declared that " in the opinion
of this House immediate relief should in some form be afforded
to ratepayers from the present unjust incidence of rates
appropriated for the maintenance of main roads in England."
Mr Gladstone undertook that something should be done in
conformity with the spirit of this resolution, and thereupon a
grant designed to cover one-fourth of the cost of maintaining

disturnpiked roads was made annually by Parliament down to the year 1888, when the relief granted was increased to one-half of the total cost by a further sum of £256,000 allocated by Mr Goschen to the same purpose from his Budget for that year.

The actual expenditure under these successive grants is shown in a Report on Local Taxation made, in 1893, by Mr H. H. Fowler (afterwards Lord Wolverhampton). The amounts there given are as follows :—

YEAR.			AMOUNT EXPENDED.
			£
1883	..	..	167,165
1884	..	..	195,649
1885	..	..	205,965
1886	..	..	229,490
1887	..	..	237,123
1888	..	..	498,797
		Total	£1,534,189

After the passing of the Local Government Act of 1888 the grants were discontinued, the said Act providing that from the 1st of April, 1889, all main and disturnpiked roads should, with certain exceptions (and as distinct from parish highways), be maintained by the county councils.

Parliament had thus at least broadened out the ratepayers' burden in respect to road maintenance by spreading the charges over a larger area ; and it was, also, affording a very considerable measure of relief to the road-users in freeing them from the obligations to pay tolls for the keeping up, not simply of the roads, but of a machinery as costly as it was inefficient. There was still a third set of interests to be considered, as represented by those who had lent money to the turnpike trusts for road construction or repairs, in the expectation of getting a fair return. The proportions of the turnpike debt, the falling-off in tolls, and the mismanagement of the system generally made the outlook for the bondholders very unfavourable ; but the best that was possible, in the circumstances, was done for them.

Under an Act passed in 1872 it was laid down that, for the purpose of facilitating the abolition of tolls on any turnpike

road, the highway board and the trustees might mutually agree
that the former should take upon itself the maintenance
and repair of such road, and, also, pay off and discharge either
the entire debt in respect thereto or such sum by way of compensation as the Local Government Board, after an inquiry, might
determine. By a further Act, passed in 1873, highway boards
were authorised to raise loans for the more effective carrying
out of this arrangement, while Clifford states in his " History
of Private Bill Legislation " that " there have, also, been
Acts confirming more than 200 Provisional Orders passed
to arrange the debts of these unlucky trusts, extinguish arrears
of interest, allow compositions, and generally make the best of
some very disastrous investments."[1]

How rapid the actual decline in the number of trusts was
from the year 1864, when the House of Commons Turnpike
Committee came into existence, is shown by the following
figures, taken from the annual reports of the Local Government
Board for 1886 and 1890 :—

DATE.	NUMBER OF TRUSTS.	MILES.
December 3, 1864	1048	20,589
January 1, 1886	20	700
,, 1890	5	77

Of the five survivals on January 1, 1890, three were to
expire in that same year and one in 1896, leaving only one
the fate of which was then undecided. It may be assumed
that by the end of 1896 the system of turnpikes on public
(as distinct from private) roads, which had for so long a period
played so prominent, so vexatious, and, in many respects,
so unsatisfactory a rôle in inland communication, had wholly
disappeared.

Turnpike roads, no less than canals, undoubtedly conferred
great advantages on the growing trade and industries of the
country. Each, however, had its serious drawbacks and
disadvantages, and, in the result, the shortcomings of the
turnpikes, added to the shortcomings of the canals, gave
still greater emphasis to the welcome offered by traders to the
railways which were to become, to so large an extent, substitutes for both.

[1] The turnpike trust loans still outstanding on the 25th of March,
1887, amounted to £92,000.

CHAPTER XXIV

END OF THE COACHING ERA

WHAT are known as the " palmy days " of the coaching era began about the year 1820, and lasted until 1836. By 1820 the improvements in road-making of Telford and McAdam had led to quicker travelling and the running of far more coaches, at greater speeds, than had previously been the case. By 1836 it was evident that coaching had reached the climax of its popularity, and could not hope to maintain its position against the competition of the railways which were spreading so rapidly throughout the land.

Over 3000 coaches were then on the road, and half of these began or ended their journeys in London. Some 150,000 horses were employed in running them, and there were about 30,000 coachmen, guards, horse-keepers and hostlers, while many hundreds of taverns, in town or country, prospered on the patronage the coaches brought them. From one London tavern alone there went every day over eighty coaches to destinations in the north. From another there went fifty-three coaches and fifty-one waggons, chiefly to the west of England. Altogether coaches or waggons were going from over one hundred taverns in the City or in the Borough.

Big interests grew up in connection with the coaching enterprise. William Chaplin, who owned five yards in London, had, at one time, nearly 2000 horses, besides many coaches. Out of twenty-seven mail-coaches leaving London every night he " horsed " fourteen. He is said to have made a fortune of half a million of money out of the business ; but when he began to realise what the locomotive would do he took his coaches off the road, disposed of his stock before the railways had depreciated it, joined with Benjamin Horne, of the " Golden Cross," Charing Cross, who had himself had a large stock of horses, and founded the carrying firm of

Chaplin and Horne, which became exclusive agents for the London and Birmingham Railway. When the London and South-Western Railway Company found themselves faced with serious difficulties he devoted alike his means, his experience and his energies to helping them out of their trouble, rendering services so invaluable to the company that he soon became deputy chairman of the line, and was raised to the chairmanship in 1842. Another coach proprietor, Sherman, who had had a large number of coaches running between London and Birmingham, threw in his lot with the Great Western Railway as soon as it was opened, and did much of the London carrying business in connection with that line.

Other coach proprietors there were who, less far-sighted, or less fortunate, held on to their old enterprises, influenced, it may be, by the views of such authorities as Sir Henry Parnell, who, in the second edition of his " Treatise on Roads " (1838), declared in reference to railways :—

" The experience which has been gained from those already completed, and from the enormous expense incurred on those which are in progress, has led to a general opinion that there is little probability of more than a few of these works affording any ultimate return for the money expended upon them.

" The heavy expense which is proved by experience to be unavailable in keeping the railways and engines in repair, where great speed is the object, will in numerous cases soon make it evident that no dividends can be paid to the shareholders, and the cheaper method of using horse-power will be adopted. . . .

" The attaining of the speed of 25 or 30 miles an hour, at such an enormous expense, cannot be justified on any principle of national utility. The usefulness of communication, in a national point of view, consists principally in rendering the conveyance of all the productions of the soil and of industry as cheap as possible. . . . But a speed of 10 miles an hour would have accomplished all these purposes, and have been of great benefit to travellers, while it could have been attained at from one half to one third of the expense which has been incurred by the system that has been acted upon. It is no doubt true that travelling at the rate of 25 or 30 miles an hour is very convenient, but how it can be made to act so as to contribute very much to the benefit of the country at large it is not easy to discover. Economy of time in an industrious country is unquestionably of immense importance, but after the means of moving at the rate of ten miles an hour is universally established there seems to be no very great advantage to be derived from going faster."

It is true that an acceleration had been effected in the rates of speed attainable on improved roads, under the stimulus of mail and " flying " coaches. But these results had only been secured with consequences for the unfortunate horses which no one possessed of a spark of humanity could fail to deplore. Several coach proprietors, each owning between 300 and 400 horses, informed a House of Commons Select Committee in 1819 that those of their horses which worked within fifty miles of London lasted only three or four years, in which period the entire stock had to be renewed. Mr Horne, of Charing Cross, who kept 400 horses, said he bought 150 every year. On some roads, it was affirmed, the mortality of the horses, due in part to the bad state of the roads and in part to the accelerated speed, was so great that the average coach-horse lasted only two years. On certain roads around London it was necessary to have six horses attached to a coach in order to drag it through the two feet or so of mud which, in wet weather, was to be found on such roads as the one across Hounslow Heath.

In accounting for an increased demand for coach-horses in 1821, a paragraph from the " Yorkshire Gazette," quoted by the " Morning Chronicle " of December 27 in that year, declared that it arose out of the new regulations of the Post Office, which caused the death of two horses, on an average, in every three journeys of 200 miles. " The Highflyer of this city," the paragraph continued, " lately lost two horses, and it has cost the Manchester and Liverpool coaches seventeen horses since they commenced to cope with the mail and run ten miles an hour in place of seven or eight. . . . Several horses, in endeavouring to keep time, according to the new Post Office regulations, have had their legs snapped in two on the road, while others have dropped dead from the effort of a ruptured blood-vessel or a heart broken in efforts to obey the whip."

On one of the southern roads a coach was put on which

was run at the rate of twelve miles an hour ; but seven
horses died in three weeks, and the pace was then reduced
to ten miles an hour. An average speed even of six and a
half miles an hour was declared to be scarcely possible on
some of the roads. " It tore the horses' hearts out."

One cannot wonder that, when the fact of trains on the
Liverpool and Manchester Railway doing an average of
fifteen miles an hour with the greatest ease, and attaining to
double that speed when necessary, became known, humanitarian considerations were, in themselves, sufficient to win
preference for rail over road transport.

There was also a practical as well as a humanitarian side
to this appalling death-rate among the coach-horses. Thomas
Gray, in the course of his " Observations on a General Iron
Rail-way," showed that, reckoning the number of coach
and postchaise horses at no more than 100,000, and allowing
for renewal of stock every four years, keep and interest on
capital expenditure, the outlay would amount in twelve
years to £34,700,000 ; while a like calculation, for the same
period, in regard to the 500,000 waggon, coach, and post-
chaise horses employed on the main turnpike roads of the
country, gave a total of no less than £173,500,000.

While, again, fair-weather travellers may have enjoyed
the scenery and the poetry of motion when seated on the
top of a coach going across country in the summer-time,
there were possibilities of great discomforts and dangers
having to be faced, as well. Accidents were so frequent that
it was usual for the coaches to carry a box of carpenters' tools,
supplemented in the winter by a snow shovel. Sometimes
the coaches stuck in the mire ; sometimes they upset. They
passed through flooded roads, they were detained by fog,
they got snowed up, or their passengers might run terrible
risks from frost. On the arrival of the Bath coach at Chippen-
ham one morning in the month of March, 1812, it was found
that two passengers had been frozen to death on their seats,
and that a third was dying. In the winter of 1814 there was a
prolonged fog, followed by a severe snow-storm which lasted
forty-eight hours. In one day thirty-three mail-coaches due
at the General Post Office failed to arrive. At Christmas,
1836, there was a snow-storm which lasted nearly a week.
On December 26 the Exeter mail had to be dug out of the

snow five times. The following day fourteen mail-coaches were abandoned on different roads.

So, in proportion as the railways spread, the coaching traffic declined. In 1839 a London coach proprietor, Mr E. Sherman, of the " Bull and Mouth," told the Select Committee on Turnpike Trusts that the persons then being carried by coach were mostly timid people who did not like to go by railway, though every day it was found that the timidity was lessening, and that many individuals who formerly would not have travelled by train for any consideration were doing so in preference to going by coach.

The severity of the railway competition with the coaches was, indeed, beyond all question ; but the coach proprietors considered that their difficulty in facing it was rendered much worse by the heavy taxation on their enterprise.

The earliest stage-coaches, patronised mostly by the poorer class of travellers, were not taxed at all ; but when the " flying coaches " and the " handsome machines with steel springs for the ease of passengers and the conveniency of the country " were put on the road and attracted passengers of a better class, the owners of private conveyances began to complain of the unfairness of their being taxed while the owners of public coaches were not. Wanting more money to meet the heavy expenditure on the American war, North met the complaints of the private-carriage owners by putting a tax on the stage-coaches ; and the precedent thus established, in or about the year 1780, was followed by later Chancellors of the Exchequer, the taxation being subsequently extended alike to every class of vehicles used for coach traffic and, in 1832, to all classes of railway passengers.

In 1837 a Select Committee appointed to inquire into the taxation of internal communication reported that the taxes then in force in respect to land travelling by animal power were as follows :—

1. Assessed taxes on carriages and horses kept for private use.

2. A post-horse duty.

3. A duty on carriages kept to let for hire, being £5 5s. on each carriage with four wheels, and £3 5s. for each carriage with two wheels.

4. A license duty paid by each postmaster, being 7s. 6d. per annum.

5. Mileage duty on stage-coaches.

6. A license duty on stage-coaches, being £5 on each coach kept to run, and 1s. on each supplementary license.

. An assessed tax on coachmen and guards.

8. An assessed tax on draught horses.

There were many variations in the mileage duty on stage-coaches. In 1780 it was one halfpenny for every mile travelled ; in 1783 it was raised to a penny ; in 1797 it was twopence, while subsequent increases led up to the highest rate of all—one of fivepence halfpenny per mile for coaches licensed to carry more than ten passengers inside. It was, in part, to moderate the pressure of this tax that Shillibeer introduced the omnibus into London,[1] his first conveyance being a huge, unwieldy conveyance which, drawn by three horses, spread the fivepence-halfpenny mileage duty over twenty-two inside passengers.

The yield from the mileage duty was £194,559 in 1814, £223,608 in 1815 (when there was an increase of one halfpenny per mile for every coach) and £480,000 in 1835.

So long as the stage-coaches were well patronised, little or nothing was heard about all this taxation, which was, in effect, passed on to the traveller, who either paid without grumbling or else grumbled and paid. But when the railways began to divert more and more traffic from the roads, the duties in question fell with special severity on the coach proprietors, who then divided their maledictions pretty equally between the railway companies and the tax-gatherers.

The mileage duty was especially burdensome under the new conditions. Being assessed on the number of persons each coach was licensed to carry, and not on the number of passengers actually carried, it remained at the same amount whether the coaches ran full, half full or empty. The fact that the railways, which were depriving the coaches of their patrons, then paid their halfpenny per mile only on every four passengers actually conveyed became a grievance with the coach proprietors, who thought that the railways should be taxed on the same basis as themselves.

[1] See p. 63.

That the taxation pressed heavily on a declining business was beyond all possibility of doubt.

A petition drawn up in 1830 by proprietors of stage-coaches employed on the turnpike roads between Liverpool and various Lancashire towns showed that the taxes they paid to the Government worked out for the year as follows :—

	£	s.	d.
Duty on 33 coaches. . . .	8,455	16	8
Assessed taxes for coach servants .	261	0	0
Mileage duty	5,779	3	4
Total	14,496	0	0

In addition to this they had to pay £8005 13s. 4d. a year for turnpike tolls, while their general expenses, including horses (renewed every three years), harness, hostlers, rent of stables, hay, corn and straw, etc., but allowing for value of manure, came to £64,602 13s. 4d., their total annual expenditure thus being as follows :—

	£	s.	d.
Government duty and taxes . .	14,496	0	0
Turnpike tolls	8,005	13	4
Expenses	64,602	13	4
Total	£87,104	6	8

W. C. Wimberley, a coach proprietor of Doncaster, who gave evidence before the Select Committee of 1837, said that the Government taxation on a single coach, the " Wellington," running between London and Newcastle, for a period of 364 days, was as follows :—

	£	s.	d.
Duty for four passengers inside and eleven out, sixpence per double mile, that is up and down 278 miles . .	2529	16	0
Stamps for receipts on payment of ditto	1	12	6
Four licenses (four coaches being used successively up and down) . .	20	0	0
Assessed taxes on coachmen and guards	17	10	0
	£2568	18	6

The coach also paid, in the same period, £2537 7s. 8d. for tolls.

Another coach proprietor, W. B. Thorne, told the same Committee that on five coaches to Dover he paid for mileage duty alone in the previous year a total of £2273. On his coaches to Liverpool, Manchester and Birmingham he paid £7017 in the twelve months, and the total amount of duty he paid for all his coaches in the year was £26,717. He did not think, however, that relief from taxation would save them from being annihilated by the railways, except as regarded certain roads where the railways did not directly operate against them.

Still another coach proprietor, Robert Gray, admitted to the Committee that he did not think it would be possible for the coaches to compete on the Bath road with the Great Western Railway even if all the duty were taken off.

There was no doubt that the coaches could not have held their own permanently against the railways even if they had been relieved of taxation as soon as the success of their rivals became assured. On the other hand, if the coaches could have been afforded such relief that, while not attempting to compete with the railways on main routes where competition was hopeless, they would have been encouraged to cater for business on routes not then served by the railways, an advantage would have been gained, not only by the coach proprietors themselves, but by the public. The early days of the railway undoubtedly brought serious inconvenience to people who found themselves set down at a station ten, fifteen or twenty miles distant from their home, with no chance of their getting a coach because rail competition and Government taxation combined had made it no longer possible to run a coach on that road. If the taxation had not, as was often the case, made all the difference between profit and loss, many of the coaches would probably have held on a few years longer, by which time the railways would have been more generally developed. As it was they were withdrawn in larger numbers, at an earlier period, than would otherwise have been the case, and there were many instances of great hardship to travellers whose means did not allow of their supplementing an incomplete railway journey by hiring a vehicle specially for themselves.

The report presented by the Select Committee of 1837 admitted the inequalities of the taxation on land travelling as between the coaches and the railways; but, instead of recommending, as the coach proprietors had wanted, that the demands on the railways should be increased, the Committee expressed strong disapproval of any tax at all being imposed on internal communication. They said, among other things :—

" Very valuable evidence was submitted to your Committee by Sir Edward Lees, secretary to the Post Office at Edinburgh, as to the increased speed, security and cheapness with which the post might be conveyed over the cross-roads of Scotland by the establishment of mail cars similar to those now in use in Ireland, thereby increasing the Revenue and opening up districts now altogether destitute of any mode of public conveyance; the same remarks would necessarily apply to many cross-roads in England. The grand obstacle, however, to the establishment of these cars is the heavy taxation on travelling, which utterly deters individuals from engaging in such speculations; while in Ireland, where the roads are decidedly inferior, but where none of these taxes exist, cheap and expeditious public conveyances are everywhere to be found."

The ultimate findings and recommendations of the Committee were summed up in the following emphatic declaration:

" Your Committee earnestly recommend the abolition of all taxes on public conveyances and on carriages generally at the earliest period consistent with a due regard to the financial arrangements of the country."

Unfortunately, the financial arrangements of the country never have allowed of this recommendation being carried out, and a further period of thirty-two years was to elapse before even the moribund stage-coach business was relieved altogether of the obligation to pay mileage duty.

The burdensome nature of these duties on internal communication led to the formation of a " Committee for the Abolition of the Present System of Taxation on Stage Carriages in Great Britain "; and in some " Observations on the Injustice, Inequalities and Anomalies of the Present System of Taxation on Stage Carriages," by J. E. Bradfield, issued by this Committee in 1854, a strong case was made out in favour of such abolition. Bradfield based his main arguments on the contention that by removing restrictions placed upon the freedom of communication the general welfare of nations was promoted. The taxation of the stage-coaches conferred, he said, no advantage on the coaching enterprise, since none of the money raised in this way was expended on road improvement, while the amount of the taxation often formed an abnormally large proportion of the receipts. He mentions the case of one coach-owner in the Lake District, thirty per cent of whose receipts in the winter had to go to the Government for the duties imposed, not on the amount of business he did, but on the seating capacity of his coaches. In another instance the duties paid were forty-five per cent of the takings. Bradfield thought a fair average for the country in general would be fifteen per cent. The existing system of mileage duties enforced, he declared, an average tax of £80 per annum upon every stud of eight horses employed in stage-coaches, as against £30 for the same number used for postchaises, and £11 8s. in the case of those for private carriages.

Bradfield further quotes a Windermere coach-owner as being of opinion that there was " still great scope for coaches as feeders to the railways if only they were given greater relief in the matter of duties." He expresses his own opinion that " coaches are legitimately the streams by which the traffic should be conducted to the railways," and asks, " Why tax the stream more than the river ? "

The steady decrease in the yield from the stage-coach duties was in itself sufficiently significant of the changes in travel that were then proceeding. In 1837 the revenue from the duties was £523,856 ; but it began to decline steadily as the " palmy days " of coaching came to an end, and in 1841 it had fallen to £314,000. In 1853, when, after various modifications, the mileage duty was three-halfpence a mile, the yield was only £212,659. In 1866, after further modifications, the duty was reduced to a farthing ; and in 1869 it was repealed altogether ; though by that time the locomotive had supplanted the stage-coach except in a comparatively few localities where it still lingered, mainly, however, as a feeder to the railway.

The recent revival of coaching comes under the category of sport or recreation rather than under that of internal transport and communication.

CHAPTER XXV

RAILWAY RATES AND CHARGES

THE combined result of (1) a vast increase in industrial production ; (2) the decline in river, canal and road transport ;
and (3) the various conditions which checked competition on
and between the railways was to increase greatly the need for
transportation facilities, and to make traders and the public
in general more and more dependent on the one means of
consignment and locomotion thus so rapidly becoming
paramount. Coupled with the many technical details which,
as pioneers of the railway system, the English companies
had to work out for themselves, and, also, with the questions
arising as to the future relations between the railways and the
State, there were the further problems as to (a) the means
to be adopted to ensure that the rates and charges were
reasonable, and not likely to become unjust or oppressive,
and (b) the bases on which the rates and charges should themselves be fixed in order to secure due regard for the public
interests, to guarantee the operation of the railways on commercial lines, and to ensure for the railway investors a reasonable return on their investments.

The earliest railway rates of all were simply a toll (as on a
turnpike road) at the rate of so much per mile, or so much
per ton per mile, for the use of the rails, with an extra charge
if the railway owners supplied the waggons. This was the
practice in vogue down to the Surrey Rail-way period, the
tolls for such use of road being fixed by Parliament because
of the railway lines being a monopoly.

The next development came when the Stockton and
Darlington Railway Company obtained powers to supply
haulage by steam power or steam-engine, and were authorised
by Parliament to charge a " locomotive toll," in addition to
the road toll, when the trader made use of the company's
engines.

There was a further development when the railway companies undertook the functions of carriers, provided waggons, carriages and staff, and were authorised to make a charge for the " conveyance " of goods.

Parliament did not, at first, specify the amounts of the locomotive and conveyance tolls, but simply required that they should be " reasonable," the expectation at that time being that these tolls would be kept to reasonable limits by the competition of the outside carriers. When it was found that the outside carriers would not run their own locomotives on the railway, and that the railways would do their own carrying, the amounts which could be levied as locomotive and conveyance tolls were specified in the special Acts of the companies concerned.

At one time, therefore, the railway companies were authorised by their Acts to impose three separate charges, (1) road tolls, (2) locomotive tolls, and (3) conveyance tolls ; but in 1845 a " maximum rates clause " was introduced which grouped these different tolls into a total charge something less than the aggregate of the three.

In proportion as the railway companies themselves performed the duties of carriers, instead of leaving this branch of the transport business to the outside carrying firms, it became necessary for them to provide goods depôts and warehouses, and to have a staff available for a variety of services— loading and unloading, covering and uncovering, etc.—which were necessary in the handling of the traffic. The companies then claimed that for these " station terminals " and " terminal services " they were entitled to make charges in addition to the maximum rates, whereas it was contended on the part of the traders that these services were included in the maximum rates, and that the companies had no right to charge for them separately. After prolonged controversy and much litigation, the dispute was eventually decided in favour of the companies ; but Parliament required them to distinguish the charges for conveyance, terminals, and collection and delivery, and, finally, by the Charges Acts of 1891 and 1892, fixed the amounts of the maximum station and service terminals that each company might demand.

In the meantime much trouble had also arisen as the result of the haphazard fashion in which the railways of the country had been called into being.

The original classification of goods for transport was of the most primitive kind. In the canal companies Acts the authorised tolls and charges were generally specified in respect to only about a dozen different articles. The early railway Acts followed the canal precedent in so far that each of them contained a classification of the goods expected to go by rail, the main difference being that the list given in the railway Acts generally comprised from forty to sixty articles, divided into five or six groups.

As the railways extended, and began to deal with the great bulk of the commerce of the country, these original lists were found to be hopelessly crude and inadequate, and one of the duties undertaken by the Railway Clearing House, first set up in 1847 and incorporated by an Act of 1850, was the preparation of what became known as the Clearing House classification—a work required in the interests equally of the railways and of the traders. At the outset the Clearing House classification comprised about 300 articles. By 1852 the number had increased to 700, and in 1864 it had further expanded to 1300.

The Royal Commission of 1865 recommended that the new and improved classification thus compiled and put into operation by the companies themselves should be the basis of the classification imposed by the special railway Acts. The Committee pointed out that the rates authorised by Parliament were no longer necessarily an indication of the charges actually made in practice since these charges depended, not on the classifications in the companies' Acts, but on the Clearing House classification, by reason of which they were often lower than the statutory maxima. The Committee regarded the classification of the private Acts as defective and inharmonious, and they advised that the Clearing House classification should be enacted by some general Act which might be adopted in the private Acts by reference. The Joint Select Committee of 1872 also advised the adoption of a uniform classification ; but it was not until the passing of the Railway and Canal Traffic Act of 1888 that the recommendation was carried out.

This Act of 1888 was, in part, the outcome of reasonable dissatisfaction among the traders.

In the absence, from the outset, of any real and effective system for the organisation of railways in accordance with well-defined general principles, based on the needs of the country as a whole, great uncertainty existed as to the rates and charges to be paid. There were then no fewer than 900 Acts of Parliament which dealt with the charging powers of 976 past or present railway companies, while the only uniform classification was that of the Railway Clearing House, which had almost entirely superseded the primitive classification in the railway companies' Acts but had not yet received legal sanction.

A recommendation to the effect " that one uniform classification be adopted over the whole railway system " had been made by a House of Commons Select Committee in 1882. They considered that the adoption of this course was necessary in view of the imperfection and want of uniformity in the special Act classifications and charges, in which they had failed to discover any general principle. " In some cases," they said, " reference must be had to more than fifty Acts to determine the various rates the company is authorised to charge."

The position in regard to a new and uniform classification thus so persistently recommended was, however, complicated by the fact that the adoption thereof would involve new maximum rates, since the rates charged for the commodities carried naturally depended on the particular " class " to which those commodities had been allotted. Hence when, by the Railway and Canal Traffic Act of 1888, provision was at last made for a revised and uniform classification, each railway company was further required to submit to the Board of Trade, within a period of six months, revised schedules of maximum rates, with a view to these ultimately—after approval by Parliament—taking the place of the schedules in the existing special Acts. The new scales were, also, to include fixed maxima for " station terminals " and " service terminals," the controversy in regard to which, as already spoken of, was thus to be definitely settled.

The railway companies complied with these requirements, the revised classification and schedules of maximum rates being sent in by March, 1889, to the Board of Trade, which appointed two special Commissioners, Lord Balfour of Burleigh and Mr (afterwards Sir) Courtenay Boyle, to hold an inquiry into them on its behalf. The traders were invited to send in any criticisms they might wish to offer to the companies' proposals, and by June 3rd no fewer than 4000 objections had been received from over 1500 individuals or trading associations.

By this time the formidable nature of the work that had been undertaken began to be more fully appreciated. Not only were there the 900 Railway Acts dealing with rates and charges, but there were about 18,000 railway stations and some 40,000 pairs of stations between which business was actually transacted in regard to one or more of the 2500 articles that, by this time, were included in the Clearing House classification. As for the rates in force, we have the statement of Sir Henry Oakley that on the Great Northern Railway alone they numbered 13,000,000, while Sir Richard Moon estimated that on the London and North-Western Railway the total at this period was no fewer than 20,000,000.

The task thus imposed by Parliament on the Board of Trade in the revision of rates whose total number seemed almost as countless as the stars themselves was, indeed, of stupendous magnitude, apart altogether from the very heavy labours devolving upon each individual company in the preparation of schedules for its own particular lines. The task itself was, however, rendered still more difficult by the fact that, as pointed out by Mr Temple Franks— [1]

" No principles of revision had been laid down for guidance. The Commissioners were not told to regard either the existing statutory maxima or the actual rates then charged. Amendments to this effect had been rejected in Parliament. The Commissioners, therefore, held that the Legislature contemplated a departure from existing maxima, and that it is equitable ' to make a reduction in their present powers and fix rates based to a great extent on existing rates, but with a reasonable margin of profit for possible changes of circumstances injuriously affecting the cost of or return from the carriage of merchandise by railway.' In determining, however, the principles upon which the future maxima were to be governed, they refused to accept the proposition that they shall cover *all* existing rates and non-competitive charges."

[1] Lectures on the " History of Traffic Legislation and Parliamentary Action in Connection with Railways," delivered at the London School of Economics. See " The Railway News," November 30, 1907.

With regard to a uniform classification, the Commissioners recommended the adoption, with certain slight changes, of the existing Clearing House classification.

There is no need to record here, in detail, the exhaustive nature of the inquiries, protests, rejoinders, discussions and controversies to which the preparation of the new schedules led. Suffice it to say that these and the revised classification were eventually embodied in a series of Railway Rates and Charges Orders Confirmation Acts which, as applying to the different companies, either individually or in groups, were passed in the Sessions of 1891 and 1892, and came into operation on January 1, 1893. Under these Acts the scales of charges are divided into six parts, viz. : (1) goods and minerals, (2) animals, (3) carriages, (4) exceptional, (5) perishable commodities by passenger train, and (6) small parcels by merchandise train. Each rate is made up of two parts—conveyance and terminals. The conveyance scales for all companies are as near alike as circumstances will allow, and the maximum terminals (station terminal at each end and service terminals in respect to loading, unloading, covering and uncovering) are common to all the Confirmation Acts.

Sir Henry Oakley, who was at this time acting as secretary of the Railway Companies' Association, declared concerning the new conditions thus brought about in regard to the bases of railway rates and charges that " practically they amounted to a revolution." The maximum powers were reduced almost universally ; the classifications of the companies' own Acts were abolished, and a new and uniform one substituted ; various new scales were introduced ; the obligation was now for the first time thrown upon the companies of carrying perishables by passenger train ; and a new system of calculating rates was established. " It was not," said Sir Henry, " so much per mile for any distance beyond six miles, as it was in the original Acts, but for the first twenty miles a certain rate, for the next thirty miles a certain less rate, and for the next fifty miles a still further reduction, the effect being that, by that mode of calculating, the longer the distance the goods were carried the less the average rate per mile that was to be charged."

Within a very short time, however, of the new rates coming into force, there were louder and more vehement protests than ever on the part of the traders. The advantages of a uniform classification were fully realised, and the traders naturally did not object to the fact that (as stated in evidence by Sir Henry Oakley, in 1893), from thirty to forty per cent of the existing rates had been lowered. But they did object most strongly when they found that certain of the rates had been increased.

It was explained by some of the railway companies that, owing to the vast number of the rates involved, and to the short time between the passing of their Rates and Charges Orders Confirmation Act and the 1st of January, 1893, when such Act came in force (the period in question being in some instances not more than about four months), it had been impossible for them to complete the revision of their rate-books by the date mentioned. The class rates were ready, and what had happened was that these had been temporarily substituted for the special rates when time had not allowed of the latter being duly revised.

On the other hand it was alleged against the companies that, apart from any question of shortness of time for their revisions, they had sought to adopt a policy of recoupment, specially low non-competitive rates having been raised to the new maxima with a view to counterbalancing the decreases.

While the plea of the companies in respect to shortness of time was abundantly warranted, the counter-allegation of the traders would appear to have been not without foundation, in view of the fact that the setting of increases against the decreases was defended by the companies on the ground that, being corporations based and operated on commercial principles, they were bound to see that their revenue did not suffer, while, it was further pleaded, they were still charging no more than the rates which, having been expressly sanctioned by Parliament, were, presumably, reasonable. They gave the assurance, however, that the rates were still undergoing revision, and that the increases made were not necessarily final. They further undertook that no increases should be made which would interfere with trade or agriculture, or diminish traffic, and that, unless under exceptional circumstances, there should be no increases at all which exceeded by five per cent the rates in force in 1892.

The undertaking thus given failed to satisfy the Select Committee appointed in 1893 to inquire into these further grievances. The Committee, in their report, expressed the opinion that the course taken by the companies had been "mainly actuated by their determination to recoup themselves to the fullest extent by raising the rates of articles where the maximum rates were above the actual rates." They were of opinion that the rates not reduced by the new maxima should have been left untouched ; and they affirmed that "the margin between the old actual rates and the present Parliamentary maxima was not given by Parliament in order that immediate advantage should be taken of it, or that the policy of recoupment should be carried on, but only to meet certain contingencies, such as rises in prices and wages," etc. They also recommended that further steps should be taken to protect traders from any unreasonable raising of rates within the maxima, the Railway and Canal Commission being empowered to deal with such questions as they arose.

The outcome of all this controversy was the passing by Parliament, in the following Session, of the Railway and Canal Traffic Act, 1894, which introduced an entirely new principle in railway operation.

Turnpike trustees had always had full power to reduce and subsequently to advance their tolls, at their own discretion, provided they never sought to exceed the maxima imposed under their special Acts ; and down to this time it had been assumed that railway companies had similar powers in regard to maxima which Parliament had already expressly sanctioned in the Act or Acts of each individual company. There was—and still is—no question (except in cases of "undue preference" or "through rates") as to the right of a company to *reduce* a rate, or to transfer a commodity to a lower class, thus effecting the same object ; and there was, down to 1894, equally thought to be no question as to their right to increase a rate within the same limitations as those applying to turnpike trustees.

What the Act of 1894 did was to restrict the powers of railway companies to increase their rates even within the range of their statutory maxima. It enacted that in the event of complaints being made of any increase of rates, direct or indirect, since December, 1892 (and under the Act of 1888 a railway company had already been required to give public notice of any increase in tolls, rates or charges it proposed to make), " it shall lie on the railway company to prove that the increase is reasonable " ; and for this purpose it is not to be " sufficient to show that the charge is within any limit fixed by an Act of Parliament or by any Provisional Order confirmed by Act of Parliament." Complaint is first to be made to the Board of Trade, and, if agreement between the trader and the railway company should not follow thereon, the trader has the right of appeal to the Railway Commissioners, to whom jurisdiction to hear and determine such complaint is given. " So that," as Butterworth remarks in his " Maximum Railway Rates," " the legislation of 1888–1894 presents this remarkable result—that Parliament in 1892, after probably the most protracted inquiry ever held in connection with proposed legislation, decided that certain amounts were to be the charges which railway companies should for the future be entitled to make, and in 1894 apparently accepted the suggestion that many of the charges, sanctioned after so much deliberation, were unreasonable, and enacted that to entitle a company to demand them it should not be sufficient to show " that the charge was within the limit which Parliament itself had previously fixed.

Whether traders have really gained any balance of advantage from this further outcome of legislative policy in the assumed protection of their interests, as against the railway companies, is open to question. On the one hand they have a guarantee against increases that offer even the slightest suggestion of unreasonableness. On the other hand the Act has destroyed the element of elasticity in rate-making, inasmuch as railway managers must needs show extreme caution in granting reduced or " experimental " rates—in the interests of growing industries—when, if the experiment should fail, and the expected traffic not be forthcoming, the company must go through the formality of advertising the " increase " involved in putting the rate back to its former level, and must, also, run the risk of having to "justify" such increase before the Board of Trade or the Railway and Canal Commission. " I know of my own knowledge and my own experience," Sir George Gibb once told a Departmental Committee of the Board of Trade, "that the effect of these sections has been to prevent many reductions of rates that would have been tried experimentally."

When we pass on to consider the principles on which railway rates and charges are based we are met with so many complexities in the solution of transport problems, and with such direct conflict of interests on the part of different groups of traders, that we can in no way be surprised at the controversies and the grievances, real or imaginary, to which the subject has given rise from time to time.

The original idea that railway rates and charges should be fixed on a mileage basis, on the same principle as tolls on turnpike roads and canals, was soon found to be impracticable, and successive Parliamentary Committees have demonstrated its futility ; though its advocacy, in one form or another, has not even yet been discarded by those who think that railway rates for any given commodity should be so much per ton per mile for all traders alike, irrespective of distance and all other considerations.

One effect of such a principle of rate-fixing as this would have been to exclude the long-distance trader from any particular market, and to confer an undue advantage on the trader in the immediate neighbourhood, or at a short distance therefrom, who would thus have gained a monopoly of the market, to the disadvantage of other traders and of the local community. Nor would such a system of rate-making have answered for the railway companies themselves, since the discouragement of long-distance traffic would have restricted the area of business, and limited their sources of revenue.

Another once much-favoured theory is that the railways should charge so much for cost of service, plus a reasonable profit for themselves.

Here, in the first place, there is the impossibility of deciding what is the cost of the service rendered in regard to each commodity and each consignment thereof that is carried. No basis exists on which the most expert of railway men could decide the respective costs of transport for each and every article in a train-load of miscellaneous goods, nor could any one apportion the exact amount that each should bear in regard to interest on capital outlay and other standing charges which must needs be covered as well as the proportionate cost of actual operation.

Then we have the fact that, even if these figures could be arrived at, many of the commodities carried would be unable to pay the rates fixed thereon. This would especially apply to coal, iron-stone, manure and other things either of low value or of considerable weight or bulk. Whatever may be the real cost of carrying them, commodities of this kind cannot pay more than a certain rate. If that rate is exceeded either they will be sent in proportionately smaller quantities or they will not be sent by rail at all.

We arrive, in this way, by the logic of actual facts, at the fundamental principle, adopted by railway companies, of charging " what the traffic will bear " ; and by this is meant " charging no more than," rather than " charging as much as," the traffic will bear. Findlay, in his book on " The Working and Management of an English Railway "(fourth edition, 1891) says of the practice based on this principle :—

" The rates are governed by the nature and extent of the traffic, the pressure of competition, either by water, by a rival route, or by other land carriage ; but, above all, the companies have regard to the commercial value of the commodity, and the rate it will bear, so as to admit of its being produced and sold in a competing market with a fair margin of profit. The companies each do their best to meet the circumstances of the trade, to develop the resources of their own particular district, and to encourage the competition of markets, primarily, no doubt, in their own interest, but nevertheless greatly to the advantage of the community."

The application of the principle is worked out by the division into various classes of all minerals and merchandise carried on the railway. The classes are known respectively as A, B, C, 1, 2, 3, 4, 5, the rates charged being lowest for commodities in Class A and highest for those in Class 5. The type of article included in each class may be indicated by the following examples :—

Class A (applicable to consignments of four tons and upwards).—Coal, coke, gravel, iron-stone, limestone, stable manure, sand.

Class B (applicable to consignments of four tons and upwards).—Bricks, concrete, various articles of iron and steel, granite (in blocks), lime (in bulk), salt (in bulk), common slates.

Class C.—Parsnips, pitwood (for mining purposes), potatoes (in bulk or in sacks), salt (packed), soda, straw (hydraulic or steam-packed), waste paper (for paper-making).

Class 1.—Cardboard, cotton (unmanufactured), onions, printing paper, finished wrought iron in shafts (for driving mill wheels), soap, sugar (in bags, cases or sacks), tallow, vinegar (in casks).

Class 2.—Bacons and hams (cured and packed), celery, coffee, copper, earthenware (in casks or crates), crucibles (plumbago or clay), oranges, ropes, raw wool or yarn.

Class 3.—Baths, calicoes, carpeting, china (in hampers), combs, cotton and linen goods (in bales, boxes, etc.), cutlery, groceries, hardware, lead pencils, tea, wheelbarrows.

Class 4.—Light drapery (various), footballs, garden arches, grates, ovens or stoves, haberdashery, hats (soft felt), lamps, umbrellas.

Class 5.—Amber, engravings, feathers, cut flowers, hothouse fruit, furs, dead horses, lace, looking-glasses and mirrors, musical instruments, picture frames, silk.

These examples indicate the gradual rise in value in the articles included in the several classes, though, assuming that the traffic will bear the rate, other considerations as well as value will apply, among these being liability to damage during transit, weight in proportion to bulk, and nature of packing or cost of handling.

It is further to be remembered that although a good deal of raw material is carried in the lowest classes at rates which might work out at less than " cost " price, when every item in respect to " cost of service " and interest on capital expenditure had been allowed for, the commodities in question may reappear in various successive forms as part-manufactured or, eventually, as manufactured, articles, paying a successively higher rate, in accordance with their progressively greater value, on the occasion of each further transportation. Even when these results do not follow, the commodities carried at these low rates may help to develop the resources, or to expand the population, of a particular district, and thus serve to create traffic in other directions.

While, also, the rates for the low-value articles may not cover every item in the so-called cost of service, they do contribute to the revenue an amount which might otherwise have to be made good by the fixing of higher rates on goods in other classes. Traders dealing in commodities of the latter type do not themselves lose by the fact that minerals, raw materials, or other things are carried at rates which, although exceptionally low, are the most they can be expected to pay. No injustice is done to them because the other classes of traders concerned get lower rates than they do themselves. They may even gain—directly, because they are saved from having to cover a larger proportion of the total railway expenditure; and indirectly, because the help given to those other lines of business may either bring trade to them or else keep down the cost of production in regard to manufactured articles they deal in or which they themselves require.

The principle of charging " what the traffic will bear " does more than govern the rates as applying to visible traffic. It embraces the further principle of what Hadley, in his " Railroad Transportation," calls " the system of making rates to develop business."

An immediate result of its application, not alone in England but in various Continental countries, was to bring about a substantial reduction in rates, so that, as Hadley further says, between 1850 and 1880 railway rates were reduced, on an average, to about one-half of their former figures. It may be assumed, also, that these former figures were themselves a substantial reduction on the rates once charged under the toll system in force among the " get-rich-quick " canal companies.

There was thus a gain to the traders as regards both an increase in facilities and a reduction in the cost at which those facilities could be obtained, as compared with previous conditions. The principle in question necessarily involved discrimination between trades; but it became one of the objects of the Legislature to prevent discrimination between individual traders in the same line of business as carried on in the same town or centre.

The general position has been further influenced by the existence of an ever-active sea competition, which is said to affect probably three-fifths of the railway stations in the United Kingdom. The rates for traffic between Newcastle and London, or any other two ports, will necessarily be influenced, if not controlled, by the possibility of the commodities going by a coasting vessel if the railway company should try to get more than, in these particular circumstances, such traffic will bear. The amount of the railway rate in such a case as this will, in fact, be determined far more by the element of sea competition than by any question as to either presumptive cost of service or actual mileage.

It may well happen that between two other points, in regard to which there is no sea competition, the rates are higher than between two where there is sea competition, although the distance is the same. Here we have the elements of one of those " anomalies " which have often been urged as a reason for equal mileage rates. The inequality in the rates is, however, directly due to the inequality in the conditions. It is not a case of making the no-sea-competition places pay a rate in itself unreasonable ; it is simply a case of charging the sea-competition places no more than they would be likely to pay. There may be an apparent inconsistency ; but an increase in the rates where the sea competition exists would not necessarily be of advantage to the trader in the district where there is no such competition, though it might lead to the traffic going by sea, and involve the railway company in a loss of revenue which would not improve their position in giving the best possible terms to the inland trader. Nor could any claim by the latter to be put on the same footing as the trader on the coast, who has the alternative of sea-transport open to him, necessarily be made good. Discrimination of places, in addition to the discrimination of trades, there certainly may be ; but it is a discrimination due essentially to geography and economic laws.

Other apparent anomalies arise from the fact that where two or more railway companies have lines running to the same destination, the rates charged by each and all of them are, by arrangement between the companies concerned, generally governed by the shortest distance. Here, again, the idea of equal mileage rates is found impracticable. If the rates charged by each of the companies were arbitrarily fixed at so much per ton per mile, the line with the shortest route would naturally get all the traffic. When all charge the same between the same points all of them benefit, and the traders have the advantage of several routes instead of only one ; though there is still the " anomaly " that the trader whose consignment is carried twenty miles, and the trader whose goods are conveyed thirty miles or more to the same destination both pay the same rate.

How the general principle of a sliding scale, under which the charge per ton per mile decreases with distance over twenty miles, works out in practice may be shown by taking the case of merchandise in Class 5, the rate for which would be 4·30d. per ton per mile for a distance of up to twenty miles. For the next thirty miles the rate would be 3·70d. per ton per mile, for the next fifty miles 3·25d., and for the remainder of the distance 2·50d. If, however, the consignment travels over the lines of two or more companies on a through rate, the application of the scale begins over again in respect to the territory of each company concerned. The greatest degree of relative advantage is thus gained by the trader whose consignments travel throughout on the lines of one and the same company.

In any case, however, the effect of the principle is that traders in, say, Cornwall or Scotland are enabled to compete far more effectively on the London market with other traders who are located much nearer to London and thus pay less for rail transport, yet, it may be, do not have the same advantages in respect to economical production as the trader at the greater distance. The " tapering " railway rate—in addition to giving the companies a greater volume of long-distance traffic, and bringing greater prosperity to the long-distance places—thus helps to establish equality in the general conditions in regard to a particular market, whereas the equal mileage rate would keep the distant trader to markets within a circumscribed area, and shut him out from others at which he might otherwise hope to get a far better sale.

In the United States the effect of this " tapering " rate, when applied to large volumes of traffic carried for distances of 1000 or 2000 miles or even more, is to give a very low average rate per ton per mile, and especially so when such average is worked out for the whole of the goods and mineral traffic in the country. The United States average is, in fact, for these reasons, much lower than the corresponding average for this country, where both the average haul and the average weight per consignment are considerably less. Then, also, as the charges for terminals remain the same, whatever the length of haul, they make a material difference in the rate per ton per mile for a haul of five, ten or twenty miles while assuming infinitesimal proportions per ton per mile when spread over a haul of a thousand miles.

There is thus no real basis for the comparison formerly so often made between average cost of transport per ton per mile in the United States and the United Kingdom respectively. The only fair method of comparison is to discard averages altogether, and contrast charges for actual consignments of equal weight carried equal distances in the two countries ; and comparisons made on this basis will be found to favour the British lines rather than the American.

In some instances group rates are in operation for a series of producing centres or for a series of ports, the rates being common to all the places or ports included in the group. This arrangement is of advantage to the general body of the traders concerned, since it puts them all on a footing of equality, without reference to differences in distance ; and it is, also, of benefit to the railway companies since it simplifies the clerical work and helps further to avoid unremunerative competition.

Another important feature in connection with railway rates is the distinction between " class " rates, which represent the authorised maxima given in the railway companies' scales for the various classes already mentioned, and " special " or " exceptional " rates, in which the companies concerned have made reductions below their maximum powers, whether for the encouragement of traffic or because of such reductions being warranted by the volume or other conditions of the traffic already carried. In " The Fixing of Rates and Fares," by H. Marriott (1910), it is stated that " probably about seventy per cent of the traffic between stations in the North of England is conveyed at ' exceptional rates,' much below the statutory authority."

In my book on " Railways and their Rates " I have already given, as follows, the general principles on which these special or exceptional rates are fixed :—

(a) Volume and regularity of traffic between the points concerned.

(b) Weight per truck or by train which can be maintained by such regular traffic.

(c) General earning power of the traffic.

(d) Liability or non-liability to damage.

(e) Competition, direct or indirect, by water, by road or by other means.

(f) Special requirements of shipping traffic to or from ports.

(g) The creation of traffic by enabling new or increased business to be done.

(h) A general consideration of what the traffic will bear.

The following examples illustrate the actual difference between the class rates and the special rates at which the traffic is actually carried :—

MILES.	COMMODITY.	CLASS RATE. per ton.	SPECIAL RATE. per ton.
		s. d.	s. d.
17	Soap	8 9 (a)	7 11 (a)
107	,, ...	21 9 (a)	17 6 (a)
154	,, ...	28 2 (a)	22 9 (a)
46	Undressed leather .	17 6 (a)	15 0 (a)
179	Cotton and linen goods .	45 7 (a)	40 0 (a)
54	Common window glass .	21 9 (a)	15 10 (a)
207	,, ,, ,,	43 4 (a)	30 5 (a)
20	Iron in Class C .	5 3 (b) (c)	3 8 (b) (d)
51	Grain . . .	9 5 (b) (c)	7 6 (b) (d)
150	Common bricks .	11 0 (b) (d)	10 5 (b) (d)

Notes : (a) Collection and delivery. (b) Station to station.
(c) 2-ton lots. (d) 4-ton lots.

Yet another characteristic of English railway rates is their division into " company's risk " rates and " owner's risk " rates, the latter being a lower scale on which consignments are carried provided the trader signs either a general indemnity for the whole of his traffic or a separate owner's risk consignment note on the occasion of each despatch relieving the railway from " all liability for loss, damage, misdelivery, delay or detention, except upon proof that such loss, damage, misdelivery, delay or detention arose from wilful misconduct on the part of the company's servants."

The difficulty of proving such " wilful misconduct " in case of damage or loss has long been a grievance with traders consigning under " owner's risk " rates, and vigorous efforts have been made by them, or on their behalf, from time to time to obtain a modification of these conditions.

The railway point of view in regard to this vexed question was thus expressed by Mr F. Potter, in an address on " The

Government in Relation to the Railways of the Country,"
given to the Great Western Railway (London) Lecture and
Debating Society on February 11, 1909 :—

" Traders are apt to conveniently overlook the fact that
owner's risk rates did not precede the ordinary rates, but that
they have depended from the latter, and proposals have
actually been made that the order of things should be reversed,
and the owner's risk rates made the base rates, the company's
risk rates being arrived at by the addition of some percentage.
Traders well know the value of the insurance which the difference between the two classes of rates represents to them,
and, indeed, base their practice in making use of either rate
upon this knowledge. If the trader is prepared to be his own
insurer, that is, when there is a sufficiently wide margin between the two rates, he takes the owner's risk rate ; but if he
considers his goods are too valuable for him to accept the risk
himself, he makes the company do so by sending his freight
at the ordinary rates."

In the controversies which have arisen on this question of
owner's risk frequent reference has been made to the fact
that in Germany there is only one kind of rate, and that under
it the State railways do, nominally, assume the risk. I have,
however, already shown in my pamphlets on " German *versus*
British Railways " and " German Railways and Traders "
that unless the consignments forwarded on the German State
railways are packed so securely that it is practically impossible for them to come to any harm, they are accepted by
the railway officials only after the trader has signed a form of
indemnity declaring that the goods are either " unpacked "
or " insufficiently packed," thus absolving the State railways
of the responsibility they are supposed to accept.

Complaints respecting " preferential rates " have been an
especially fertile source of controversy and litigation. The
phrase as here used is somewhat misleading. The real ground
of complaint is against, not simply " preference," but " *undue*
preference."

If a lower rate is given for a 2-ton or a 5-ton than for a
2-cwt. or a 5-cwt. consignment, the trader in the former case
gets a distinct advantage over the trader in the latter case,
just in the same way as the wholesale man buys a large
quantity of goods at a lower price than that asked for from

the purchaser of only a very small quantity. Here, in each instance, we have "preference" strictly in accord with commercial principles.

The question really at issue turns upon the consideration whether there is undue or unfair preference. It is thus dealt with in a proviso to sub-section 2, section 27 of the Railway and Canal Traffic Act of 1888 :—

"Provided that no railway company shall make, nor shall the Court, or the Commissioners, sanction any difference in the tolls, rates or charges made for, or any difference in the treatment of home and foreign merchandise, in respect of the same or similar circumstances."

The position is thus controlled by the words "same or similar circumstances." In what is known as the "Southampton case," decided by the Railway and Canal Commission in 1895, the fact that foreign produce was being carried at lower rates by the London and South-Western Railway Company from Southampton to London than were being charged for English produce was not disputed ; but it was successfully argued (1) that lower rates might reasonably be granted for train-loads of produce capable of being loaded into the waggons at the docks and carried through, under the best transport conditions, direct to London than for small consignments, picked up at wayside stations, and loaded and carried under far less favourable traffic conditions ; (2) that there was no real detriment to local producers, since the towns concerned were importing more than they were sending away ; and (3) that in no respect were the circumstances "the same or similar." There was, said Sir Frederick Peel, one of the Commissioners, "no concurrence between the two classes of traffic, and the greater economy of transport in the dock traffic justified the lower rate."

The principle here involved disposes of, probably, most of the complaints which have been made from time to time on the subject of undue preference ; but as these complaints were especially rife in 1904, a Departmental Committee, presided over by Lord Jersey, was appointed by the Board of Trade to inquire whether or not the railway companies were according preferential treatment to foreign and colonial farm, dairy and market-garden produce from ports to urban centres as compared with home produce. The Committee declared in their report " that the evidence tendered has failed to show that the railway companies are giving undue preferential treatment to foreign and colonial produce as compared with home produce contrary to the intention and effect of existing legislation." They found that some of the traders who complained had compared rates which did not include terminal services with rates that did ; had quite wrongly divided what were, in effect, " through " rates, first subtracting the full charge of the shipping company and then assuming that the remainder could be compared with the rate from the first ; or had omitted to take into account differences in regard to bulk of consignments, packing, etc.

In effect, no British railway rate may give a preference to foreign as distinct from British produce so far as quantities, conditions and circumstances are the same. The rates are to be available for like consignments whatever the source of their origin. Where the home producer has been unable to provide the same quantities, under the same conditions and circumstances as the foreigner, he has equally been unable to avail himself of a rate open to all the world. He has had the disadvantage of the retail trader as compared with the wholesale trader. The principle involved is practically the same as that in operation on Continental State railways, where the traders who can provide the biggest loads get the advantage of the most favourable rates. On the Belgian State railways, for instance, there are special rates for 50, for 100 and even for 300-ton consignments which can obviously be taken advantage of by only a limited number of traders. But while the retail man cannot expect to get the same terms as the wholesale man, there is no adequate reason why the wholesale man should be kept to the same level as the retail man, and be refused the lower rates for his consignments to which he is entitled on account of their greater bulk or better loading. The question is certainly complicated by the fact that the wholesale man here in question is generally a foreigner ; but the railway companies could not be required to discriminate against him, and to penalise him on account of his nationality. The matters at issue must needs be looked at from the point of view of a business proposition rather than from that of expecting the railway companies to usurp the functions of the State in carrying out a policy of Protection.

Of late years far less has been heard, in the agricultural world, at least, of these allegations of undue preference. The whole position has been changed through the praiseworthy efforts of the Agricultural Organisation Society in spreading among the agricultural community a practical appreciation of the advantages of combination, as adopted by their foreign competitors, included in such advantages being the lower rates which the railways already offer for grouped or other large consignments. The excellent work carried on by the society is calculated to confer, in many different directions, much more benefit on market gardeners, dairy farmers and agriculturists in general than would be gained by them simply from seeking to persuade, or even to force, the railway companies to carry at wholly unremunerative rates the small consignments of non-associated producers, forwarded under the least favourable conditions in respect to economical transport.

As regards the machinery provided by Parliament for dealing with traders' grievances, there is, in the first place, the Railway and Canal Commission, which, taking the place of the earlier Railway Commissioners, was made a permanent body under the Act of 1888. The Court consists of two Commissioners appointed by the Board of Trade, and three *ex-officio* members, chosen from the judges of the High Court, and nominated by the Lord Chancellor, the Lord President of the Court of Session and the Lord Chancellor of Ireland for England, Scotland and Ireland respectively ; though in practice only one of the three takes part in the proceedings in connection with any case brought before the Court. The jurisdiction of the Commissioners includes powers to enforce obligations under special Acts, and to deal with questions of traffic facilities, private sidings, undue preference, through rates, etc.

Whether or not procedure before this body is too costly for other than wealthy litigants to take advantage of is a question which need not be discussed here ; but traders have the further advantage of what is known as the Conciliation Clause of the Act of 1888, which provides that " (1) Whenever any person receiving, or sending, or desiring to send goods by any railway is of opinion that the railway company is charging him an unfair or an unreasonable rate of charge, or is in any other respect treating him in an oppressive or unreasonable manner, such person may complain to the Board of Trade. (2) The Board of Trade, if they think that there is reasonable ground for complaint, may thereupon call upon the railway company for an explanation, and endeavour to settle amicably the differences between the complainant and the railway company." A resort to this expedient by aggrieved parties involves the payment of no fees or costs.

The eleventh report by the Board of Trade of their proceedings under the Conciliation Clause shows that during 1908 and 1909 the number of complaints made to them was 280—a total insignificant in comparison with the many millions of separate transactions in which the traders and the railway companies must have been concerned during the two years in question. The 280 complaints are classified as follows : Rates unreasonable or excessive in themselves, 39 ; undue preference, 65 ; rates unreasonably increased, 22 ; classification, 30 ; delay in transit, 27 ; owner's risk, 17 ; rebates, 23, through rates, 15 ; miscellaneous, 42. Settlement or partial settlement was effected in 91 cases ; in 62 the complaints were not proceeded with ; in 122 an amicable settlement could not be arrived at ; and in five the proceedings had not been completed. " In certain of the cases," the report further states, " in which an amicable settlement was not reached, it seemed clear to the Board of Trade that the complainants had no real ground for complaint."

Boyle and Waghorn are of opinion that in matters more or less personal to the applicant, or of comparatively minor importance, the procedure under this Conciliation Clause has saved much litigation ; though when questions of general principles are at issue the Board of Trade, as a rule, prefer to remit the determination of them to the Railway Commission. They further say : " The principal cause of the comparative absence of litigation lies in the fact that a law of railway traffic is being gradually evolved, reasonably considerate of the rights of both parties, and adapted to the actual circumstances of the traffic. In the early days of railways this was very far from being the case." (" The Law Relating to Railway and Canal Traffic.")

Much of the adverse criticism of railway rates and charges which has been indulged in of late years, without even any resort to an inexpensive complaint to the Board of Trade, has been due to comparisons with railway conditions in other countries.

At one time the comparison specially favoured was between English and American railway rates ; and this was persisted in until it was conclusively shown that there was, and could be, no basis of comparison between huge consignments, carried long distances, on comparatively inexpensive lines, and small average consignments, carried short distances, on the most costly railway system in the world. The element of " the same or similar circumstances " was obviously lacking.

Comparisons were then made with railway conditions in Continental countries, and various tables of comparative rates were published from time to time, in support of railway nationalisation theories or otherwise. But many of these comparisons have been wholly untrustworthy because, once more, they have not compared traffic carried under the same or similar circumstances. Exceptional rates granted, say, by the Prussian Government in the special interests of their commercial policy, but (1) applying to large consignments sent to a port for shipment, the rates being substantially higher when the commodities do not go further than the port, (2) granted in competition with routes passing through adjoining countries, and (3) being simply haulage rates, which include no additional services whatever, have been compared with English " domestic " rates for smaller quantities of traffic, or, it may be, with " paper " rates for traffic that is practically non-existent, and, therefore, has not called for special rates, while the English rates may also include a variety of supplementary services by the railway company (loading, unloading, collection, delivery, warehousing, etc.), which the Continental trader would either have to perform himself or pay for as extras.

The comparisons may thus be wholly misleading ; but, assuming that complete equality of conditions could be assured, or allowed for, and assuming that the Continental rates were then found to be lower than the really corresponding English ones, it would still be necessary to remember that in this country there have been, from the earliest period of railway development, many circumstances and conditions, due to State policy or to other causes, which have tended to swell to abnormal proportions the capital expenditure that the revenue based on rates and charges must needs cover if any reasonable return at all is to be made to the investors. There would, in fact, be no cause for surprise if rates and charges on British railways could be proved to be higher than those in force on the Continent, where the conditions attendant on railway construction and operation have differed so materially from our own. The wonder is, rather, in view of all that I have said as to the past history of our railway system, that British railway rates and charges should, generally speaking, be as low as they are.

CHAPTER XXVI

THE RAILWAY SYSTEM TO-DAY

WHATEVER the difficulties which have attended the development of British railways, the lines themselves have been spread throughout the three kingdoms to such an extent that there are now very few districts not within easy reach of a railway ; while though the different lines are still owned by, altogether, a considerable number of companies, the physical connections between them and the arrangements of the leading companies, not only for through bookings but for through trains, supplemented by the operations of the Railway Clearing House, have brought about as close an approach to a really national network of railways, connecting all the different sections of the country one with another, as could well be expected in view of the lack of co-ordination when the lines were first called into being.

At the end of 1910, according to the Railway Returns issued by the Board of Trade, the " length of line " of the railways in the United Kingdom was 23,387 miles. By itself, however, this figure does not give an adequate idea of the extent of the railway system. This is better realised by taking the figures for track mileage and sidings. A far greater proportion of the railways in England and Wales than in any other country consists of double, treble or other multiple track, so that for one mile in length of line there may be two, three or more miles of separate pairs of rails, increasing the transport facilities in proportion. The percentage of single track to total length of line in various countries is shown by the following figures :—

COUNTRY.	PER CENTAGE OF SINGLE TRACK.
England and Wales	33·0
Scotland	59·0
Ireland	80·2
United Kingdom	44·2
Prussian State railways . . .	57·3
Germany (the entire system) . . .	61·7
France (main line system) . . .	57·0

" Track mileage " in the United Kingdom is shown in the Board of Trade Returns for 1910 as under :—

TRACK.	MILES.	TRACK.	MILES.
First . . .	23,389	Ninth . . .	24
Second . .	13,189	Tenth . . .	14
Third . .	1,517	Eleventh . .	10
Fourth . .	1,192	Twelfth . . .	7
Fifth . .	236	Thirteenth . .	5
Sixth . .	143	Fourteenth . .	4
Seventh . .	70	Fifteenth . .	3
Eighth . .	44	Sixteenth–nineteenth	1 each

Corresponding figures for the United States of America, taken from an abstract issued in July, 1911, by the Interstate Commerce Commission, give the following classification of track mileage, excluding yard track and sidings :—

TRACK.	MILES.	TRACK.	MILES.
First . .	240,831	Third . . .	2,206
Second . .	21,659	Fourth . .	1,489

It will be seen from the figures relating to track mileage in the United Kingdom that there is at least one mile of railway in the United Kingdom which really consists of nineteen pairs of rails alongside one another, though counting, in length of line, as only a single mile. In the United States there seems to be no suggestion of any railroad having more than four tracks.

The length of track in the United Kingdom is 39,851 miles. To this must be added a further 14,460 miles, the length of sidings reduced to single track, giving a total, including sidings, of 54,311 miles.

Rolling stock was owned in 1910 by the different railway companies throughout the United Kingdom as follows : Locomotives, 22,840 ; carriages used for conveyance of passengers only, but including rail motor carriages, 52,725 ; other vehicles attached to passenger trains, 20,090 ; waggons of all kinds used for the conveyance of live stock, minerals or general merchandise, 745,369 ; any other carriages or waggons used on the railway, 21,360 ; total number of vehicles, excluding locomotives, 839,544. These figures are exclusive of about 600,000 waggons owned by private traders.[1]

[1] The existence of this large number of privately owned railway waggons—the greater proportion of which are in use in the coal trade—

The total weight of goods and minerals conveyed in 1910 was 514,428,806 tons, and the total number of passengers carried (exclusive of 752,663 season-ticket holders) was 1,306,728,583. The miles travelled were—by passenger trains, 266,851,217 ; by goods trains, 154,555,559 ; by mixed trains, 1,814,762, giving a total of 423,221,538 miles. It is difficult to grasp the real significance of these figures ; but, taking the train mileage alone the total distance run by trains in the United Kingdom in 1910 was equal to nearly 17,000 journeys round the world, and to four and a half journeys to the sun.

The total amount of railway capital returned as paid-up at the end of 1910 was £1,318,500,000, of which about £197,000,000, or approximately fifteen per cent, was due to nominal additions on the consolidation, conversion and division of stocks, showing a net investment of £1,120,500,000. The gross receipts of the companies during 1909 were as follows :—

SOURCE.	£	PROPORTION TO TOTAL RECEIPTS.
Passenger traffic	52,758,489	42·57
Goods	61,478,643	49·61
Miscellaneous [1]	9,688,433	7·82
Totals	123,925,565	100·00

The working expenditure in the same period amounted to £76,569,676, a proportion to total receipts of 62 per cent. The net receipts, therefore, were £47,355,889, the proportion of which to paid-up capital was 3·59 per cent.

The average rates of dividend or interest alike on ordinary

recalls the days when it was assumed that traders would provide their own rolling stock on the railways. It shows that they still do so to a considerable extent, although, of course, relying on the railway companies to supply the locomotives. It will also be seen how the questions which have arisen from time to time as to the use of a larger type of railway waggon and, also, of automatic couplers on waggons, may be complicated by the variety of ownership. There is an Association of Private Owners of Railway Rolling Stock, the objects of which are "to maintain and defend the rights and promote the interests of private owners and hirers of railway rolling stock."

[1] The receipts under this head were as follows :—
	£
Steamboats, canals, harbours and docks	5,145,640
Rents, tolls, hotels, etc.	4,542,793
	9,688,433

and on all classes of capital paid in the years from 1900 to
1909, were as follows :—

YEAR.		ORDINARY.		ALL CLASSES.
1900	..	3·34	..	3·45
1901	..	3·05	..	3·33
1902	..	3·32	..	3·45
1903	..	3·30	..	3·44
1904	..	3·26	..	3·42
1905	..	3·29	..	3·43
1906	..	3·35	..	3·46
1907	..	3·31	..	3·45
1908	..	2·99	..	3·32
1909	..	3·15	..	3·39
1910	..	3·48	..	3·53

It is pointed out in the Returns, however, that on account
of the nominal additions made to the capital of the companies
the rates of dividend or interest given in the tables are lower
than they would otherwise be.   Thus the average rates of
dividend or interest for the United Kingdom in 1910 calculated on capital exclusive of nominal additions would show :
Ordinary, 4·28 per cent (instead of 3·48 as above), and " all
classes " 4·15 (instead of 3·53) per cent.

These averages, nevertheless, allow for a large amount of
capital on which the dividend or interest paid is either *nil*
or substantially below the averages stated.

The rates of dividend on ordinary capital in 1910 were as
follows :—

	ORDINARY.	
RATES OF DIVIDEND OR INTEREST.	Amount of Capital.	Per cent of Total.
Nil	£67,358,262	13·7
Not above 1 per cent . .	29,427,057	6·0
Above 1 and not above 2 per cent .	18,072,847	3·7
,, 3 ,, 3 ,, .	87,676,759	17·8
,, 3 ,, 4 ,, .	109,788,247	22·3
,, 4 ,, 5 ,, .	38,193,955	7·7
,, 5 ,, 6 ,, .	85,503,721	17·4
,, 6 ,, 7 ,, .	54,962,066	11·2
,, 7 ,, 8 ,, .	362,000	0·1
,, 8 ,, 9 ,, .	40,000	0·0
,, 9 per cent . . .	694,907	0·1
Total	492,079,821	100 0

The various classes of capital on which the rates of dividend or interest paid in 1910 were either *nil* or not above three per cent may be shown thus :—

		RATES OF DIVIDEND OR INTEREST.		
DESCRIPTION OF CAPITAL.	Nil.	Not above 1 per cent.	Above 1 per cent and not above 2 per cent.	Above 2 per cent and not above 3 per cent.
	£	£	£	£
Ordinary . .	67,358,262	29,427,057	18,072,847	87,676,759
Preferential . .	16,607,907	631,967	2,296,250	103,019,553
Guaranteed . .	—	—	101,180	23,318,760
Loans and Debenture Stock .	558,782	676,789	4,666	189,122,426
Totals	84,524,951	30,735,813	20,474,943	403,137,498

£538,873,205

There are those who regard railway shareholders as " capitalists," and consider that the keeping of railway dividends at a low level, together with any depreciation in the value of railway stock that may result therefrom, are matters only likely to affect a comparatively few wealthy men, and not, therefore, of material concern to the country so long as the railways give the best possible service at the lowest possible rates. In the United Kingdom, however, the ownership of the railways is distributed among a far greater number of persons than is the case in the United States, where the control and the dividends of a great railway system may alike be in the hands mainly of a few financiers. That by far the larger number of shareholders in British railways have comparatively small holdings was well shown by a table published a few years ago giving the percentage of holdings of £500 or under by shareholders, exclusive of debenture-holders, in thirty-nine leading railways of the United Kingdom. An analysis of this table gives the following results :—

Number of Companies.				Percentage of Holdings of £500 or under.
2	.	.	.	. 32 to 40 per cent.
10	.	.	.	. 41 ,, 50 ,,
8	.	.	.	. 51 ,, 60 ,,
9	.	.	.	. 61 ,, 70 ,,
7	.	.	.	. 71 ,, 80 ,.
3	.	.	.	. 81 ,, 90 ,,

Total 39

It is true that many of the shareholders here in question might have invested in several companies, so that their £500 or less would not represent the full extent of their railway holdings. On the other hand, there is the fact that many of the single investments are those of friendly societies, trade unions, or other organisations representing the interests and dealing with the savings of a large number of members of the artisan class.

In any case, whether the railway shareholder be a capitalist large or small or only an ordinary thrifty middle-class person who has saved a little money which he seeks to put into something both safe and remunerative, the fact remains that since the advent of the railway era he is the person who, though supplying the means by which this huge system of inland communication has been brought into existence, has had the least consideration of all. The trader, the passenger and the railway servant have all been the subject of much legislative effort for the protection or the furtherance of their own interests, whereas the railway shareholder has been too often regarded with an absolute lack of sympathy, and treated as a person who must be severely restrained from becoming unduly wealthy at the expense of these other interests, and should be thankful that he is not deprived of his property altogether.

It has really seemed as though the aim alike of the State and of local governing authorities has been less to ensure to the railway shareholders, who have undertaken a great public work at their own risk and expense, a fair return on their enterprise than to extract from the railway system huge sums in the way of taxation.

What the railway companies have paid in the way of " rates and taxes " since 1894 is shown by the following table, which I compile from the Board of Trade Returns for 1903 and 1910 :

YEAR.		AMOUNTS PAID FOR RATES AND TAXES.		INCREASE (+) or DECREASE (−) as compared with previous year.
		£		£
1894	...	2,816,000	..	—
1895	..	3,011,000	...	(+) 195,000
1896	..	3,149,000	..	(+) 138,000
1897	..	3,249,000	..	(+) 145,000

YEAR.	AMOUNTS PAID FOR RATES AND TAXES. £	INCREASE (+) or DECREASE (−) as compared with previous year. £
1898	3,425,000	(+) 131,000
1899	3,582,000	(+) 157,000
1900	3,757,000	(+) 175,000
1901	3,980,000	(+) 223,000
1902	4,228,000	(+) 248,000
1903	4,493,000	(+) 265,000
1904	4,736,000	(+) 243,000
1905	4,933,000	(+) 197,000
1906	4,965,000	(+) 32,000
1907	4,863,000	(−) 102,000
1908	4,884,000	(+) 21,000
1909	5,010,000	(+) 126,000
1910	5,102,000	(+) 92,000

Total payments in
17 years   70,228,000

These figures show a continuous increase since 1894, with the exception only of the year 1907, when there was a decrease of £102,000 as compared with 1906, due to the activity of the railway companies in appealing against excessive assessments. The advance in the total paid in 1910 over the total for 1894 was no less than £2,286,000, or 77·9 per cent.

It should be remembered, also, that the figures given relate to sums paid for rates and taxes, and do not include the expenses incurred by the railway companies in respect both to their rates and taxes departments (conducted by highly skilled officers) and to litigation arising on their appeals against assessments they consider unfair. The total expenditure under these two heads has been estimated at over £80,000 per annum.

Since comparisons are frequently made between English and German railway rates, with a view to showing that the former are higher than the latter, it may be of interest to compare, also, the amount paid for taxation by the railways of the United Kingdom with the corresponding payments of the Prussian State railways. The length of line of the two systems is approximately the same ; yet while the taxation of the British system comes to £5,000,000 a year, that of the

Prussian State railways is only £750,000 a year. Naturally, when a Government owns the railways, it is much more interested in checking excessive taxation of the lines by the local authorities than when the railways are owned by commercial companies ; and one of the questions to which proposals in regard to the nationalisation of the British railways gives rise is whether, when the Government owned the railways, they would be willing to continue the payment from the railway revenues of all the taxation which local authorities are now able to exact from the railway companies. Presumably not ; and in that case the trader, whether or not he got lower railway rates from the State, would probably have to pay higher local rates in order to make up for the tolls no longer levied, or levied only to a much less extent, on the railway traffic.

The growth in the payments made by individual companies for rates and taxes between 1902 and 1910 may be illustrated by giving the figures for the London and North-Western, the Great Western and the Midland Companies respectively :—

YEAR.	LONDON AND NORTH-WESTERN. £	GREAT WESTERN. £	MIDLAND. £
1903	520,000	524,000	418,000
1904	572,000	558,000	435,000
1905	599,000	592,000	453,000
1906	603,000	621,000	475,000
1907	603,000	608,000	458,000
1908	610,000	638,000	436,000
1909	631,000	663,000	438,000
1910	638,000	669,000	456,000

In addition to the items coming under the head of " rates and taxes " the railway companies still have to pay to the Government the passenger duty of which I have spoken on page 263, their function here, presumably, being that of honorary tax-gatherers who are required to get the money from the British public in the interests of the national exchequer, and save the Government the cost and the trouble of collection. The passenger duty thus collected by them in 1910 came to £319,404, the total contributions of the railways to the public finances for that year being thus increased to £5,421,715.

The amounts paid in 1910 by some of the leading companies under the two heads in question may be shown thus :—

COMPANY.	RATES AND TAXES. £	GOVT. PASSEN- GER DUTY. £	TOTAL. £
Great Central . . .	149,899	4,156	154,055
Great Eastern . . .	322,894	14,296	337,190
Great Northern . . .	223,254	13,099	236,353
Great Western . . .	669,330	29,640	698,970
Lancashire and Yorkshire .	261,734	18,141	279,875
London and North-Western	638,443	50,359	688,802
London and South-Western .	268,130	34,356	302,486
London, Brighton and South Coast	209,491	31,617	241,108
Midland	455,759	16,423	472,182
North-Eastern . . .	467,404	12,982	480,386
South-Eastern and Chatham	278,505	53,015	331,520
Caledonian . . .	150,609	8,905	159,514
North British . . .	129,486	8,721	138,207

The following table shows how the sum total of the payments both for rates and taxes and for Government duty in the years from 1900 to 1910 work out (a) per train mile and (b) per mile of open railway :—

YEAR.	PER TRAIN MILE. Rates and Taxes. d.	Govt. Duty. d.	PER MILE OF RAILWAY. Rates and Taxes. £	Govt. Duty. £
1900 ..	2·24 ..	·21 ..	172 ..	18
1901 ..	2·39 ..	·22 ..	180 ..	19
1902 ..	2·53 ..	·23 ..	190 ..	19
1903 ..	2·73 ..	·23 ..	200 ..	19
1904 ..	2·86 ..	·22 ..	209 ..	18
1905 ..	2·95 ..	·22 ..	216 ..	18
1906 ..	2·87 ..	·21 ..	215 ..	18
1907 ..	2·72 ..	·20 ·..	210 ..	18
1908 ..	2·77 ..	·20 ..	210 ..	17
1909 ..	2·86 ..	·20 ..	215 ..	17
1910 ..	2·89 ..	·19 ..	218 ..	16

This question of the taxation of railways is a matter of material concern as regards (1) the direct results thereof on (*a*) rates and charges and (*b*) dividends paid—or not paid ; and (2) the general policy of the State towards the whole problem of internal communication.

As in the case of cost of land, of expenditure on Parliamentary procedure, of capital outlay on construction, and of any undue increase in cost of operation, the payments in respect to rates, taxes and Government duty can be met by the railway companies only by one or other of two expedients : either by getting the money back through the rates, charges and fares levied on the railway users (an expedient necessarily curtailed both by legislative restriction and by the economic necessity of not charging more than the traffic will bear), or, alternatively, by leaving the railway investors with only an inadequate return—if not, in respect to a large proportion of the capital, with no return at all—on their investments.

The system of assessing railways for the purpose of local rating is one of extreme complexity. It grew out of the earlier system of the taxation of canals, and, had the railway companies fulfilled the original expectation of being simply owners of their lines and not themselves carriers, the principles on which the system was based might have applied equally well to rail as to canal transport. But, while rail transport underwent a complete change, there was no corresponding adaptation of local rating to the new conditions, and the system actually in force is the outcome far less of statutory authority than of custom, as sanctioned by the judges—who have themselves had to assume the rôle of legislators—while the machinery of railway valuation differs materially in England and Wales, in Scotland, and in Ireland.[1]

In England and Wales there is a separate assessment of a railway for each and every parish through which it passes. Such assessment is divided into two parts : (1) station and buildings, and (2) railway line. The former, arrived at by a per centage on the estimated capital value of buildings and site, is a comparatively simple matter. It is in regard to the latter that the complications arise. The main consideration in each case is the amount of rent which a tenant might reasonably be expected to pay for the property assessed ; and such

[1] An excellent summary of the general position to-day will be found in "The Rating of Railways," a booklet issued by the Editor of the "Great Western Railway Magazine."

presumptive amount is arrived at in regard to the lines by calculating the amount of net earnings the railway is able to make through its *occupation* of the particular length of line that passes through the parish in question, and according to the actual value of such length of line as an integral part of one concern.

The extent of these net earnings is ascertained, in effect, by first taking the gross receipts on all the traffic that passes through the parish, and then making a variety of deductions therefrom. The cost of construction of the railway does not enter into consideration at all. The calculations are on what is called the " parochial earnings principle "—that is to say, the amount earned *in* the parish, and not the amount received from traffic arising in the parish. The railway company may have no station in the place, and the amount of traffic derived from the parish may be practically *nil ;* but the assessment of the line, on the basis mentioned, is followed out, all the same.

The main principle is the same in Scotland and Ireland, but with this important difference in detail : that in each of those countries a railway is first valued as a whole, the total value being then apportioned among the several rating areas.

It will be seen that the taxation of a railway line—as distinct from that of railway buildings—is, to all intents and purposes, the enforcement of a toll, on all traffic carried, for the privilege of passing through the parish concerned ; while there is no suggestion, as there was in the case of turnpike roads, that those who collect the toll confer an advantage on those by whom the toll is paid. The turnpike trustees did provide a road, and they were, also, under an obligation to keep it in order. The toll-payers thus got some return for their money, and, though the trade of the district, or of the country, was taxed, it was, also, directly facilitated by the toll-receivers. The railway company, on the other hand, provide and maintain their own road, without putting the parish to the slightest expense, yet the parish is authorised tó levy upon them what is, not only a toll, but a supplementary Income Tax for local purposes, based on the principle of the profits the company are supposed to make in the parish, often only because, for geographical reasons, it is necessary their lines should pass through it in going from one part of the country to another.

On page 114 I have told how, in the early part of the sixteenth century, the local authorities of Worcester, Gloucester
and other towns on the Severn sought to raise funds for their
local exchequers by taxing the traders who used the river
for the transport of their commodities ; and I have further
told how, in 1532, it was enacted that any person attempting
to enforce such toll or tax should be fined forty shillings.
But a practice held in the sixteenth century to be unjust in itself as well as prejudicial to the interests of trade, and penalised
by the Legislature accordingly, is considered quite right and
proper, and receives express legislative sanction, in the
twentieth century, though the local authorities upon whom
the toll-privilege is conferred to-day may do no more to help
the railways than Worcester and Gloucester and the other
Severn towns did to help the river traffic—and that was
nothing at all.

One result of the power thus given to local authorities
to bleed the railway companies as an easy and convenient
method of providing themselves with funds is that in a large
number of parishes throughout the country a railway company
pays the bulk of the rates, even though it may not even have
a railway station in the place.

In Chapter IV of my book on " Railways and their Rates "
I have given a table showing that in a total of 82 parishes,
divided into four groups, the proportion of local rates paid by
the London and North-Western Railway Company ranges
from 50 per cent to 86·9 per cent, although in 53 of the
parishes the company have no station. In a further table I
specify sixteen parishes in which the area of the same company's property ranges from four to fifty-eight acres, or from
1·3 per cent to 5·1 per cent of the whole of the land in the
parish, while the proportion which the railway assessment
bears to that of the entire parish ranges from 66·9 per cent to
86·1 per cent.

Being thus enabled to depend for the greater part of their
revenue on railway companies, who are given the privilege
of paying but are denied the privilege of representation or of
having any voice in the way the money they contribute shall
be spent, there are local communities which show the greater
readiness to carry out comparatively costly lighting, drainage,
education, road improvement or other such schemes because

it is a railway company that will pay most of the cost, the proportion thereof falling on the great bulk of the individual ratepayers in the parish being thus inconsiderable. Social reformers tell us of the improvements they find proceeding to-day in village life in England. What is happening to a large extent is that rural centres are providing themselves with urban luxuries at the cost of the railway companies—that is to say, at the cost either of the railway shareholders or of the railway users or both together.

The same tendency may, however, be carried further still.

On the occasion of the coronation of King George and Queen Mary, various local authorities had the less hesitation in voting supplies to defray the cost of festivities out of the rates because they knew that most of the money so voted would have to be paid by a railway company. In a letter to " The Times " of June 3, 1911, on this subject, Mr James E. Freeman, of Darlington, says :—

" The village of Carlton Miniott, near Thirsk, lately held a parish meeting to consider whether the £30 or so that will be spent in local festivities in connexion with the Coronation should be raised by means of private subscriptions or from the rates. It was decided to levy a penny rate, with the result that the North-Eastern Railway Company, which had and could have no voice in the decision, will pay £21 13s. 4d., and the loyal residents, who receive the whole of the benefit, will pay £9 11s. 8d. towards the £31 5s. that is to be expended. At the neighbouring village of South Otterington the keen-witted Yorkshiremen have profited even more from the law's absurdities. They have voted a precept of £30 on the overseers for their merry-making, and of this amount the North-Eastern Railway Company will have the satisfaction of paying a little over £25."

The " Great Western Railway Magazine " for July, 1911, in referring to the same subject, tells of " a parish having the good fortune to have a railway running through one end of it, in which a rate of threepence in the £ has been imposed. This has produced £200, all of which has been spent on eating and drinking in a population of less than 2000, while the governing idea in raising the rate appears to have been that the railway company would have to pay some £70."

Without stopping to discuss the question as to the exact

proportion in which the results of this taxation system should ultimately fall on, or be made good by (*a*) shareholders, or (*b*) traders and travellers, the policy, if not the justice, of allowing the internal transport of the country, and, therefore, the trade and industry of the country, to be subjected to this abnormal taxation, if not to this actual plundering, by constituted authorities, may well be open to question, and especially so when one bears in mind the already heavy expenditure which has fallen on the companies, and the dissatisfaction expressed, from time to time, by traders with the railway rates, by railway servants with their pay, and by shareholders with their dividends. Certain it is that in the Board of Trade " Railway Returns " all these payments on account of rates and taxes and Government duty are included among the items of " working expenditure," and are deducted from the gross receipts before arriving at the amount of the net income available for dividends or to be taken in account in regard either to reductions in rates and charges or to increases in wages.

There is no suggestion that railways should be exempted altogether from the payment of local rates ; but the complicated, anomalous and exorbitant system of taxing the traffic on their lines has long called for amendment.

So far back as 1844 Mr Gladstone's Committee declared they were " satisfied that peculiar difficulties attach to the application of the ordinary laws of rating to the case of railways which give rise to great uncertainty and inequality, as well as to expense and litigation, and they therefore consider that the subject is one which will properly call for the attention of the Legislature when any general measure for the amendment of the law and practice of rating is before it."

In 1850 the unsatisfactory nature of the law and practice in regard to railway assessments was pointed to by a Select Committee of the House of Lords on " Parochial Assessments."

In 1851 Lord Campbell adjourned the case of R. *v.* Great Western Railway Company, and expressed the hope that " before the next term Parliament might interfere " and relieve the court from the difficult position in which they were placed when called upon to administer the existing law

with regard to the rating of railways.   He added, in reference
to the matters arising in the case then before the court : " If
we settle those questions we may be considered as legislators
rather than as judges, making rather than expounding law."

In 1859 Mr Justice Wightman, in R. *v.* The West Middlesex
Water Company, said : " The whole subject matter appears to
me to be involved in so much difficulty and uncertainty that
I cannot but hope that the Legislature may interfere or make
some provision adapted to the rating of such companies as
that in question."

Among still other judges who have expressed similar views
and indulged in similar hopes may be mentioned Lord Justice
Farwell, who, in January, 1907, in the case of the Great
Central Railway *v.* the Banbury Union, said : " Fifty-six
years ago Lord Campbell protested and implored the Legislature to intervene.   His voice was the voice of one crying in the
wilderness, and I suppose ours will be equally ineffectual if
we make the same appeal."

Then, also, the Royal Commission on Local Taxation,
in the report they presented in 1901, made various recommendations in regard to the assessment of railway companies ;
but the advice of Committees and Commissioners has been
no less unavailing than the protests of judges.

Meanwhile, and pending the long-delayed action by the
Legislature, the railway companies have themselves done
what they could to protect the interests of those they represent, or of those for whose wants they cater, by appealing
against excessive and unjust assessments, and in many of
these appeals they have been successful.   Such appeals
have been warranted, not alone by unfair increases of assessments but by the fact that taxation based on earning powers
ought to be reduced as those earning powers decline ; and on
this last-mentioned point the Assessor of Railways and
Canals in Scotland is quoted in " The Rating of Railways "
as having said :—

" There is the undeniable fact, which the Board of Trade
returns amply prove, that the companies are now carrying
on their business at less remunerative rates than formerly.
The average fare per passenger carried, and the rates per ton
for goods and minerals handled, have fallen enormously ;
while, at the same time, working expenses have been con-

tinually going up, mainly owing to the demands for higher wages and shorter hours of employment, and the more stringent regulations of the Board of Trade as to block-telegraph working, brake-power, etc. Further, the increased gross or net revenues could not have been earned without a large capital expenditure for additional and more costly plant. It is well known that what would have satisfied the public twenty years ago would be deemed wholly inadequate to-day. Competition has compelled the companies to advance with the times; engines are now more powerful, carriages more comfortable, in many cases even luxurious; trains are better heated and lighted; continuous brakes and also the newest type of telegraphic instruments for signalling and working have been provided; stations are better furnished and equipped—all of which would mean a greatly increased outlay on the part of a tenant, which outlay he would undoubtedly take into account before deciding what rent he could afford to pay."

The considerations here presented in regard to the general question of railway taxation are strengthened by the fact that, although a railway company is a commercial enterprise, it has not the facilities possessed by commercial enterprises in general in meeting any increase in cost of production or working expenses by an increase in its charges to the consumer, or the person equivalent thereto. In this respect an ordinary industrial concern, producing goods for sale, is a free agent to the extent that it is restrained in its charges only by market and economic conditions; whereas the railway company, producing for sale the service known as transport, may not raise a single rate or charge in regard to the transport of goods without incurring the liability of having to " justify " such increase before either the Board of Trade or the Railway and Canal Commission. It has even been recommended recently by a Departmental Committee of the Board of Trade that like restrictions should be made to apply in the case of increases of passenger fares.

The alternative for a railway company lies in the possibility of reducing expenses; but there are limitations in this direction if perfect efficiency in all branches of the service is to be maintained, and no one would be likely to suggest that these exactions of local authorities should be made good by reductions in, for example, that especially large item of working expenses represented by the wages of railway servants.

What I have said in regard to rates and taxes in general applies no less to the increased financial burdens that would fall on railway companies in respect to the National Insurance Bill. With the main issues presented by that measure I have here no concern ; but the difference between railway companies which cannot " pass on " the heavier taxation that all measures of this type involve and the ordinary industrial companies which can should be sufficiently obvious.[1]

Clear, at least, it is that if both the Government and the local authorities continue to pile up these burdens of taxation on transport companies, themselves subject to the restrictions mentioned, the traders of the country cannot expect much relief in the railway rates of which many of them complain. It may be that the primary effect of the financial conditions thus brought about falls on the railway shareholders. It is, also, the case that the traders are well assured against any increase in rates. But the traders suffer a disadvantage as well as the shareholders because, though the railway companies may be prevented from raising their rates, they may, also, find it practically impossible to reduce rates which they would otherwise be willing to put on a lower scale. On the one hand the traders are protected from being charged more. On the other hand they are prevented from being charged less. They may not lose, but they may not gain ; and inability to secure a benefit that might otherwise be secured amounts, after all, to the equivalent of a loss. In regard, also, to the wages of the staff, these may not be reduced yet the power of companies to advance them may be curtailed by any undue swelling of working expenses in other directions.

[1] In "Insurance Legislation in Germany ; Copy of Memorandum containing the Opinions of various Authorities in Germany" [Cd. 5679], Herr E. Schmidt, Member of the Imperial Diet, and President of the German Tobacco Manufacturers' Association, is quoted as saying : " I am convinced that when the social legislation was introduced, and for the first time the large contributions for sickness insurance and later for old age and infirmity insurance had to be paid, many of us groaned. To-day, however, these contributions, which occur every year, are booked either to the general expenses account or the wages account—for they are, in fact, a part of wages—and they are naturally calculated as part of the cost of production, and eventually appear in the price of the goods, though perhaps not to the full extent in times of bad trade."

A good idea of the magnitude of the capital, the scope and extent of the operations, and the greatness and variety of the interests concerned in the working even of a single great railway company is given by the following table of what are deservedly called " interesting statistics," drawn up in regard to the Midland Railway for the year ending December 31, 1910 :—

Capital expended	£121,304,555	Waggon Stock	117,571
Authorised Capital	£193,900,517	Horses	5,158
Working Expenses	£7,716,665	Road Vehicles	7,009
Salaries and Wages	£5,015,017	Signal Cabins & Stages	1,942
Revenues :—		Miles of Teleg. Wire	31,446
Coaching	£4,058,129	Railway Telegrams	14,542,689
Goods, Mineral &		Steam Fire Engines,	
Cattle	£8,375,673	Pumps, &c.	511
Miscellaneous	£607,581	Fire Hydrants	1,619
Rates and Taxes	£450,379	Men qualified to render	
Lines owned (miles)	1,680	first aid to the	
Constructing or Au-		injured	10,037
thorised	10¾	Contributions to	
Partly owned	329	Friendly Society	£21,916
Worked over by		Sick Allowance paid by	
Engines	2,378	Friendly Society	£36,367
Train Mileage	48,472,172	Contributed to Super-	
Passengers carried	46,481,756	annuation Fund	£34,858
Season Tickets	221,862	Total number of Em-	
Coal and Coke con-		ployés	69,356
sumed (tons)	1,773,179	Uniform Staff	29,500
Minerals & General		Clerical Staff at Derby	2,519
Merchandise pass-		Workmen in all Shops	13,443
ing over line (tons)	47,533,420	Area of Carriage Works	
Engines	2,800	(Acres)	126
Carriage Stock	5,489	Acreage of Loco. Works	80

The organisation and working of the English railway system as it exists to-day are matters as to which a good deal of interest has been shown from time to time, and a certain degree of knowledge thereof is essential to an appreciation of the position that has developed from the primitive conditions already detailed. The subject is treated very fully in " The Working and Management of an English Railway," by the late Sir George Findlay, formerly general manager of the London and North-Western Railway Company, whose line he naturally dealt with in his book. Much, however, has happened since the first edition of that book was published, in 1889, and some of the details given are not applicable to present conditions. I do not propose to bring them all up to date, but it may be of advantage if I attempt to convey to the reader a general idea of the basis on which the London and North-Western, as a typical English railway, is organised and managed, leaving aside the technical data concerning construction and operation with which, although they occupy a considerable space in Sir George Findlay's book, I have here no direct concern.

The London and North-Western Railway had, on December 31, 1910, a total length of line of 1966 miles, of which 380 miles were single track and 1586 double or more. The total length of track, including sidings, in equivalent of single track, was 5490 miles. The authorised capital was £133,989,000 and the paid-up capital £125,038,000. The magnitude of the company's operations is indicated by the following figures in regard to traffic, etc., in 1910 : Number of passengers carried (exclusive of season - ticket holders), 83,589,000 ; minerals, 43,384,000 tons ; general merchandise, 10,511,000 tons ; number of miles travelled by trains, 47,463,000 ; receipts (gross) from passenger traffic, £6,699,000 ; receipts (gross) from goods traffic, £8,900,000 ; total working expenditure, £9,937,000.

The supreme control is exercised by a board of twenty directors, including a chairman and a deputy chairman. Four retire annually, and are eligible for re-election. The directors are appointed by the shareholders, all of whom have the right to express their views thereon at the half-yearly meetings of the company ; and when it is stated that the number of shareholders—debenture, preferred and ordinary—in the North-Western is 100,000, representing 90,000 holdings, and that in 45,000 cases the holding is £500 or under, it will be seen that an English railway company is a far more democratic institution than one of those great railroad systems in the United States which may be completely dominated by a single individual. Any shareholder in the London and North-Western who possesses the necessary qualification, by being the owner of ordinary stock to the value of £1,000, is eligible for appointment on the board.

The main functions of an English railway board are—to decide questions of principle and policy ; to keep close watch over the interests of the shareholders in regard to all questions of finance ; and to exercise a general control and supervision in order to ensure the thorough efficiency of the line. Subject to such general control and supervision, the working details are entrusted to railway officers possessed of the skill, judgment, experience and technical knowledge requisite thereto. It is thus no more necessary that railway directors should be railway experts than it is that the proprietor, the manager and the editor of a great daily newspaper should themselves be able to write shorthand, set up type, cast a stereo and run the machines. They can dictate policy, attend to business details and direct heads of departments without these, in their case, superfluous accomplishments. Railway directors who, going beyond their legitimate functions as aforesaid, sought to interfere with or dictate to skilled railwaymen on matters of ordinary detail or office routine would, in fact, cause friction without necessarily promoting efficiency in operation.

In practice it is not unusual for a retiring general manager to be invited to take a seat on the board either of his own or of another company ; but, generally speaking, the main qualification for a railway director, apart from the extent of his holding, is found in his possession, or assumed possession, of good business qualities, coupled with an interest in some particular part of the district the railway serves.

The full board of the London and North-Western Railway meets twice a month ; but much work is also done by committees which, as in the case of a county council or other important public body, exercise supervision over certain departments, or groups of departments, presenting minutes of their proceedings to the board for confirmation. The principal committees are the Finance Committee, the Permanent Way Committee, the Locomotive Committee, the Passenger Traffic Committee, the Goods Traffic Committee and the Debts and Goods Claim Committee. There are, in addition, various smaller committees which deal with questions arising in connection with legal business, stores, hotels, refreshment rooms, etc.

The heads of the different departments concerned attend, either regularly or as desired, the meetings of these various committees, whose members are thus kept thoroughly in touch with everything going on in regard to matters under their special cognisance.

On the subject of finance, Sir George Findlay says (and the position is still as here stated, except that certain members of the Finance Committee now meet weekly to pass current accounts for payment) :—

" The system of control over the expenditure of the Company's money is a very complete one. The general theory is that no expenditure is incurred without the direct sanction of the directors, expressed by a minute of some committee approved by the board. The district officers are, indeed, allowed to make small necessary payments, but for these vouchers are submitted monthly and, after being carefully examined, are passed by the Finance Committee. No work is done by any of the engineering departments, except ordinary maintenance and repairs, without a minute of the directors to sanction it, and, in like manner, no claim is paid, except those of trifling amount, without the authority of the ' Goods Claims Committee.' "

The executive management is carried out by the general manager, the chief goods manager, and the superintendent of the line, the heads of the various other departments—and, also, the district officers—reporting to, and being under the direction of, one or other of these three officers, or, in the case of the chief goods manager and the superintendent of the line, of their assistants.

The general manager naturally exercises general control. He is accountable to the chairman and directors for the good working of all departments, and when one takes into account the magnitude of the financial interests at stake ; the extreme complexity of the movements and details involved in the operation of so many miles of railway transporting so huge a volume of traffic ; the responsibilities of the company towards the multitudes of travellers who depend for life or limb on the perfection of the arrangements made for their safety ; the enormous value of the goods of which temporary charge is undertaken ; the questions of principle or precedent that arise in connection with a whole army of workers, no less than the matters of policy as regards development of the line or the relations with other companies, involving, it may be, introduction of or opposition to Railway Bills ; the preparation of evidence to be given before one or other of those oft-recurring Parliamentary or Departmental Committees ; together with the ever-present need of reconciling, as far as possible, the conflicting interests of public, of staff and of shareholders—when one tries to realise the full extent of all these duties, obligations and responsibilities devolving upon the general manager of a great English railway company, the holder of such a post would seem to occupy a position more onerous than that, probably, of any other British subject, even if he should not deserve to rank as a ruler of what, in the variety and extent of the interests concerned—interests greater far than those of many a Continental State—is itself the equivalent of a small kingdom.

In the chief goods manager's department there are, besides himself, an assistant goods manager, two outdoor goods managers, a mineral traffic manager and a large staff of clerks. The chief goods manager and his assistants take charge of all matters connected with merchandise and mineral traffic, apart from the actual running of the trains. They arrange the rates and conditions of carriage ; control the handling, the warehousing, and the collection and delivery of the goods ; deal with all questions of goods accommodation and goods rolling stock ; negotiate the arrangements in regard to private sidings for traders, and discharge a great number of other duties besides.

The main function of the superintendent of the line, in whose department there is, also, an assistant superintendent of the line and several assistants, is to deal with all passenger, horse, carriage and parcels traffic, and, also, the running of all trains, whether passenger, merchandise, live-stock or mineral. All questions relating to the actual working of the line, passenger stations, signals, etc., are referred to him, and the issue of all time-tables is also under his control.

The other heads of departments include : Secretary ; solicitor (with assistant solicitor) ; chief accountant ; locomotive accountant ; cashier ; chief of expenditure department ; chief of audit department ; registrar ; estate agent ; rating agent ; chief engineer (with a chief clerk and two assistant engineers, one for new works and one for permanent way) ; chief mechanical engineer (with a chief indoor assistant in locomotive department, general assistant and two outdoor assistants) ; signal superintendent ; electrical engineer ; rolling - stock superintendent ; carriage superintendent ; waggon superintendent ; stores superintendent ; horse superintendent ; police superintendent ; marine superintendent ; hotel manager ; and chief medical officer. The total number of persons engaged in these various departments, as carried on in the general offices at Euston station, without reckoning those employed elsewhere, is about 1500.

For administrative purposes the entire system, with its close on 2000 miles of railway, is divided into a number of districts, each of which is in charge of a district superintendent who is responsible for the working of the trains and the control of the staff in his district. Each district superintendent has an assistant and several travelling inspectors working under his direction, their duty being to visit regularly every station and signal box, and deal with any matters requiring attention.

In some districts the superintendents are responsible both for passenger traffic and for goods traffic. In this case they are called district traffic superintendents. They report in regard to the passenger business to the superintendent of the line and in regard to the goods business to the chief goods manager. In the most important districts the district superintendent is relieved of the management of the goods business (except as regards the working of the trains) by other district officers known as district goods managers, or goods superintendents, who are responsible to the chief goods manager at Euston.

In Dublin there is an Irish traffic manager who takes charge of all the interests of the company in Ireland, and there are agents in Paris and New York who look after the Continental and American business.

The same general principle, as applied to the various districts, operates, also, in regard to individual towns and the management of the stations therein. At the majority of the company's stations there is an agent, popularly known as the station master, who is in charge of both the passenger and the goods traffic ; and at the larger stations the work is divided between a station master—who attends to passenger traffic, and is accountable to the district superintendent—and a goods agent, who is responsible for the goods work, and is under the control of the district goods manager. The station master, in turn, has authority over the signalmen, porters and lamp-men at his station, just as the goods agent has authority over the local goods department. The chain of responsibility thus works out as follows :—

Station staff.	Goods staff.
Station master.	Goods agent.
District superintendent.	District goods manager.
Superintendent of the line.	Chief goods manager.

General manager.
Committees of the board.
Chairman and full board.

While the control through the board of directors and the general manager is complete yet, at the same time, it would be impossible to keep pace with the rapidity with which business is done at the present day unless the district officers were able to act on their own responsibility in those cases where time did not permit of matters going through the usual routine, and for that reason the district officers of a company like the London and North-Western are capable men who are able, and are encouraged, to take full responsibility when it is necessary for them to do so.

Just as the committees of the board of directors keep in touch with the chief officers and heads of departments, so do the chief officers keep in touch alike with one another and with the country officers, doing this by means of periodical con-ferences.

There is, in the first place, what is known as the " Officers' Conference." Held once a month at Euston or elsewhere, as convenient, it is presided over by the general manager, and is attended alike by the chief officers and by the district officers for both the passenger and the goods departments. At this conference the matters discussed include proposed altera-tions in the train service, mishaps or irregularities and their avoidance, suggested changes in the rules, and everything appertaining to the working, loading and equipment of the trains.

Another conference, known as the " Goods Conference," is also held monthly—generally on the day preceding the Officers' Conference—and is presided over by the chief goods manager, who meets the district officers responsible for the goods working, and discusses with them the various subjects that arise from time to time in connection with the goods traffic.

The minutes of both conferences are submitted to the directors, who are thus kept still better informed of all that is happening. Nor do the officers themselves, whether chief officers or district officers, fail to benefit from the opportunities for the exchange of views and experiences which the conferences afford.

Periodical inspections of the line, or of the stations, in various districts by the directors and the chief officers—whether both together or by the chief officers alone—afford further opportunities for checking any possible irregularities, for ensuring the provision of adequate station accommodation, for seeing that rules and regulations are properly observed, and for maintaining the thorough efficiency of the system in general.

The locomotive works of the London and North-Western Railway Company at Crewe extend over 140 acres, including 48 acres of covered-in shops, mills, etc. These works give employment to about 10,000 men and boys. In addition to the making of locomotives, the various processes carried on include the production of steel rails, girders for bridges, underframes for carriages, hydraulic machinery, cranes, bricks, gaspipes, water-pipes, drain-pipes, and a great number of other objects and appliances necessary to the construction and operation of the railway. Created by the London and North-Western Railway Company, Crewe has developed from an agricultural village into a flourishing industrial town of 42,000 inhabitants.

At Wolverton, half-way between London and Birmingham, the company build and repair their own railway carriages and road vehicles, and do much work besides in the making of station furniture, office fittings, and other requirements. The works cover 90 acres, and give employment to about 4000 hands.

The Earlstown waggon works extend over 24 acres and employ 1800 persons, Earlstown, like Crewe and Wolverton, being essentially a railway colony. In each instance—as will be shown more fully in Chapter XXVIII—liberal provision is made for the educational, social and recreative needs of the workers and their dependents.

No fewer than 82,000 persons are included in the industrial army which to-day constitutes the staff of the London and North-Western Railway. Of this total 11,000 are salaried officers and clerks and 71,000 are employed at weekly wages. A company which employs such a multitude as this, and, indirectly, ensures sustenance to a much greater number of persons, incurs obligations that are not met entirely by a stated salary or wage. Hence the company, in addition to their encouragement of schools and educational institutes, support a Superannuation Fund Association and a Widows and Orphans' Fund for the salaried staff, and various funds, on a contributory basis, for the wages staff. Other organisations supported by the company include a savings bank, a literary society, chess, rifle and athletic clubs, a temperance society and numerous coffee taverns for the staff.

CHAPTER XXVII

WHAT THE RAILWAYS HAVE DONE

To say that the railways have revolutionised trade and industries would be simply to repeat one of the commonplaces of modern economic history. Taking the general statement for granted, I would invite the reader to look a little more closely at some of the actual results that railways have, or have not, brought about.

In the first place it would be going too far to say that the Railway Age inaugurated the Industrial Era. The invention of, or the improvements in, machinery which gave so immense an impetus to our national industries preceded the opening of the particular lines of railway—the Stockton and Darlington and the Liverpool and Manchester—that were more especially to lead to the great development of the railway system on present-day lines. All the same, it was the railways that, by offering a far more effective means of transport than was already afforded by canals, rivers or roads, made it possible for the industries then already started, or for those following thereon, to attain to their present proportions.

For the creation of what is known as the factory system, with its teeming industrial populations aggregated into busy urban centres, the railways are certainly far more responsible than the earlier modes of transport. The merits or the drawbacks of that system, from the point of view of general interests, are matters that need not be discussed here. Suffice it to say that as soon as the railways had allowed of great quantities of raw material being conveyed, at especially low rates, to particular localities ; of machinery being set up there, also at lower cost than before ; of labour from the rural districts being brought in and concentrated in the same localities, and of an efficient distribution, again at lower rates, of commodities produced on a large scale under the most economical conditions ;—it was inevitable that factories should supplant home

385

industries, that manufacturers should succeed small masters, and that great towns should grow up in proportion as rural centres declined.

In helping to bring about these results—results that so materially accelerated the " economic revolution " already proceeding—railway transport also supplied a ready means for providing these urban communities with the necessaries of life.

It is only with the help of the railways that the provisioning of such vast collections of humanity as are to be found in London, Manchester, Liverpool, Birmingham, Glasgow and other centres is rendered possible. As compared with the earlier conditions of life, when households were mainly self-supporting, each providing for its own needs from its own fields, pasture or garden, the average urban family to-day is dependent on the trader for practically all domestic necessaries, and the same is mostly the case in suburban or even in country districts except, it may be, in regard to vegetables, eggs and table poultry. It is doubtful if London or any other of these great centres ever has more than, at the outside, a fortnight's supplies on hand. The complete stoppage of the railway system for any such period would thus be a national disaster. Food might still come to the ports in the same quantities as before ; but without the railways there would be no adequate means for its distribution, and the large inland towns would more especially be at a disadvantage. The mere possibility of such an eventuality may help one to realise the extent of our dependence to-day on rail transport from the point of view, not alone of trade, industry and commerce, but of our daily life and sustenance.

While it is true that many rural centres suffered a decline in population when the railways led indirectly to so many agricultural workers leaving the fields for the attractions and the supposed advantages of urban life, it is no less true that the expansion of the towns gave to those who remained in the rural centres greater markets for the sale there of such produce —and especially for such market-garden produce, eggs and poultry—as they could supply to advantage. The railways may not have annihilated distance, but they were engaged in curtailing distances ; and such curtailment became still more effective when the achievements of the locomotive were followed by the adoption of the sliding-scale principle under which the rates per ton per mile decreased in proportion as consignments were sent for a greater distance than twenty miles.

The towns and the industrial centres expanded further as rail transport afforded increased facilities for the conveyance of raw materials to works which, thanks to the steam-engine, could be set up in any part of the country, regardless of the once indispensable water power ; and the procuring of these raw materials not only gave a further great expansion to national wealth, but led to the opening up to industrial activity of many a district previously isolated and undeveloped.

Increased congestion in the towns was thus none the less supplemented by a widespread development of the interior resources of the country ; and in this respect the railways accomplished results that could not have been attained by the most complete system either of canals or of turnpike roads. There certainly were losses, besides those in the rural districts, and this was notably the case in some of the county, market, or smaller towns which no longer command the same distinction in the social and economic world as before ; but the balance as between gains and losses was in favour of an industrial expansion, a commercial development, and an unexampled increase in general prosperity.

On the general trade of the country the railway was to produce results no less striking than those that related to individual industries.

When the facilities for distributing domestic and other necessaries throughout the inland districts, and even in the most remote parts of the country, were so greatly increased, the reason for the fairs which had for many centuries played so all-important a part in English trade and commerce no longer existed, and the country hastened to deserve Napoleon's sarcasm by becoming " a nation of shopkeepers."

To the country trader the railway gave new opportunities. There was no longer any need either for his going to one of the periodical fairs or for his awaiting a call from a travelling middleman with his troop of packhorses in order to obtain supplies. Nor was it now necessary for him to purchase comparatively substantial quantities of wares at a time. Thanks to the railway, he could generally have goods sent to him direct from the manufacturer or the warehouseman in London, Manchester, Sheffield, Glasgow or elsewhere, and those goods, sent for one day and delivered the next, could be ordered by him in exactly such quantities as would suit his immediate requirements. In this way he was enabled to keep smaller stocks of a greater variety of articles, trade with less, or with better distributed, capital and anticipate a much larger turn-over. The advantage of these facilities became greater still in proportion as the post, the telegraph and the telephone gave the retailer greater opportunities for communicating his wants to the wholesale trader who supplied them.

In these circumstances village stores are to be found to-day in rural districts where shops had been non-existent down to the Railway Age, while the conditions of retail trade in probably every country town have no less changed, and have altered to a proportionate extent the conditions, also, of wholesale trade.

On the other hand, the same transport facilities which gave these opportunities to the small trader are now, to a certain extent, operating to his disadvantage, since there is an increasing tendency for retail trade to be done by the large houses which are to-day more and more dealing direct with the public, consigning to retail customers either by rail or by parcel post. In this way many of the small traders are sharing the fate of the small masters who had already been suppressed by the factory system.

The movement here in question is, of course, only a development of the dual tendency now prevalent throughout the commercial world for (1) the substitution of large or associated undertakings for numerous small and independent ones ; and (2) the abolition of middlemen ; yet such a movement could hardly have been carried out to its present actual extent but for the opportunities offered by the railway for the regular, speedy and economical transport of commodities under just such conditions as will alone allow of this further transition in trade being brought about.

So far as the railways themselves are concerned, these various developments have not been an unmixed blessing, since they have increased the tendency for the general merchandise traffic to travel in small or comparatively small consignments or parcels, involving a greater amount of

handling and of clerical work, and, therefore, an increase in
working expenses, without a proportionate gain in revenue.

The vast majority of traders in the country seem content
to live " from hand to mouth," ordering only just what they
want from day to day or from week to week, and depending
implicitly on prompt delivery by the railway whenever they
need fresh supplies. Thus we get such conditions of trade in
respect to general merchandise (distinct from minerals and
raw materials) as are suggested by the following table, showing
the total tonnage of traffic dealt with, and the average weight
per package handled, at the goods depôts mentioned :—

DEPOTS.	TOTAL OF TONS HANDLED.	NO. OF PACKAGES.	AVERAGE WEIGHT PER PACKAGE. Qrs.	lbs.
Broad Street, London . .	906	23,067	3	4
Curzon Street, Birmingham .	1615	51,114	2	14
Liverpool Stations . .	3895	79,513	3	26
London Road, Manchester .	1341	28,277	3	22

How this small-parcel-at-frequent-intervals arrangement,
so convenient for a large number of traders, increases the
work of the companies in a greater ratio than it increases their
receipts is shown by the following typical figures, worked out
by a leading railway company in respect to the comparative
increases in traffic receipts and number of invoice entries
respectively at four large stations on their system :—

STATION.	YEARS COMPARED.	INCREASE IN TRAFFIC RECEIPTS.	INCREASE IN NO. OF INVOICE ENTRIES.
A. ..	1899 and 1906 ..	2·93 ..	40·0
B. ..	1903 ,, 1907 ..	5·74 ..	28·46
C. ..	1902 ,, 1905 ..	10·36 ..	22·0
D. ..	1902 ,, 1905 ..	14·33 ..	24·3

The tendencies in the direction of repeat orders for small
consignments are no less prevalent in the case of raw materials
and bulky commodities than in that of general merchandise.
The cotton-spinner has frequent consignments of cotton, in
quantities sufficient to meet immediate needs, rather than less
frequent consignments in greater bulk. The average builder
saves yard expenses and cartage by ordering from time to time

the exact quantities of timber or the precise number of bricks
he wants for the particular work, or for a certain stage of
the work, on which he is engaged. The coal merchant orders
forward from day to day, or at intervals according to the state
of business, only the particular quantities of coal he requires
for present or prospective early needs, since the railway
arrangements generally render it unnecessary for him to
provide for more than a few days' supply at a time. So it goes
on through almost every department of present-day trade.

The advantages for the trader himself are enormous, and the
railways have encouraged him in the tendency here in question
by giving, for 2-ton or 4-ton lots, minimum special or exceptional rates which on the State railways of the Continent
would be available only for 5-ton, 10-ton or still higher
quantities. Yet when a trader has delivery made to him in
several consignments rather than one, it is evident that,
whatever the convenience to himself, the company must do
more work for their money and incur the risk, also, of having
to run two or more partly-filled waggons on separate days
in place, it may be, of one full one. Hence a further problem
in the railway world of recent years has been how to adjust
traffic arrangements to commercial conditions based on the
now established requirements of the British trader for small
consignments at frequent intervals, and yet secure for the
railways themselves the advantage of economical loading.
Much has been done in this direction by the leading companies
in the setting up of transhipping depôts and otherwise, and
substantial economies have been effected thereby.

Another respect in which railway facilities have influenced
the course of trade lies in the fact that the large warehouses,
provided by the railway companies at certain of their goods
depôts enable a large number of merchants, agents or other
traders to dispense with warehouses of their own and carry on
their business from a city office, whence they send their
instructions to the railway companies as to the destination
of particular consignments when these are to be despatched to
the purchaser. The railway companies are thus relied on to
(1) collect the goods, (2) load them into the railway waggons,
(3) transport them from one town to another, (4) unload them,
(5) remove them to the railway warehouse, (6) store them
there until they are wanted, (7) pick out, as and when required,

a particular bale or parcel from a possible pyramid of bales or parcels warehoused for the same trader ; and (8) deliver it to a given address.

In some instances all these services are included in the railway rate, a certain period of free warehousing being then allowed. In other instances, or when the free period is exceeded, a charge is made for rent ; but the trader still saves considerably as compared with what he would have to pay for a separate warehouse for himself, with rates, taxes and cost of cartage in addition.

At the autumnal meeting, on October 3, 1906, of the Executive Council of the National Chamber of Trade, held at Bradford, it was declared, in reference to the inequality in assessments for local rates, that there were in Bradford certain large concerns whose business turnover amounted to more than £40,000 a year, while the rental of the premises they occupied was not more than £100. Some exceptionally large and commodious railway warehouses in Bradford are certainly made use of by local traders under precisely such conditions as those here in question ; and it is, probably, because of these railway warehouses that the concerns alluded to are able to carry on a £40,000 business in £100 premises.

Even when the traders own extensive mills or factories they often find it convenient to allow the railway company to warehouse most of their raw material for them, sending on supplies to them as needed, a saving thus being effected in respect alike to capital outlay on land and buildings for store rooms and to rates and taxes thereon. In other instances goods are sent, as ready, to the railway warehouses at the port to await shipment, the manufacturers once more saving in not having to provide extra accommodation on their own premises for the storing of goods until a large order has been completed or until a vessel is due to leave.

The extent of this railway warehouse accommodation will be better understood if I mention that two sets of premises which constitute the Broad Street goods depôt of the London and North-Western Railway Company, in the heart of the City of London, have a total floor space of 29,500 square yards ; that the same company have at Liverpool a series of warehouses with a total of about 30,500 square yards of floor space ; that the Great Northern Railway Company have at Bradford one wool-warehouse which can accommodate from 50,000 to 60,000 bales, and another that has a storage capacity of 150,000 bales ; and that an exceptionally large goods depôt and warehouse in Manchester, with floor space equal to one and a quarter acres, cost the Great Northern Railway Company no less a sum than £1,000,000.

To illustrate the nature of the accommodation offered by, and the work carried on, in these great goods stations and warehouses, I offer a few details respecting the Bishopsgate Goods Station of the Great Eastern Railway Company.

Situate in the midst of one of the busiest of London's commercial centres and in the immediate proximity of docks, wharves, markets and warehouses carrying on, in the aggregate, an enormous business, the Bishopsgate Goods Station is a hive of activity of so extensive and varied a type that the working bees employed form a staff of no fewer than 2000 persons.

The premises, which have nine exits and entrances, are divided into three levels, known as the basement level, the rail level and the warehouse level. The total area covered by the goods station, including railway lines, yard and buildings, is twenty-one acres.

The basement level consists of a series of arches on which the lines leading into the goods station have been built. Originally the arches were designed by the railway company to serve the purposes of a general fruit, vegetable and fish market, and this market was opened in 1882 ; but the lessee of the Spitalfields market claimed certain monopoly rights under an ancient charter, and the Bishopsgate market had to be closed ; though the railway company continued to carry on a market they had previously opened at Stratford, E., subject to the payment of certain tolls to the aforesaid lessee in respect to his rights. The Stratford market, located immediately alongside lines of railway bringing produce from the most important agricultural districts of the Eastern Counties, has conferred great advantages alike on traders and on residents in the East of London. The basement arches at Bishopsgate are to-day let mainly to potato salesmen and others, who find them of the greatest convenience because loaded trucks arriving on the rail level can be lowered into the basement, there to be moved by hydraulic power to the particular arch for which the consignment is destined.

The rail level is the goods station proper. It has eleven sets of rails and five loading or unloading platforms, or " banks," while two shunting engines are constantly employed in taking loaded or empty trucks in or out. In 1910 the business done gave a daily average of 725 trucks inwards traffic, and 632 outwards traffic, a total daily average of 1,357 trucks. About eighty goods trains leave or arrive at the station during the twenty-four hours. These include two which are fitted with the vacuum brake, and give the traders and inhabitants of Lincoln and towns beyond all the advantages of an express goods service at ordinary rates—a service, that is, equivalent to what, in Germany, traders would have to pay double or treble their own ordinary rates for if they wished to ensure a corresponding speed.

Of potatoes from the fenland districts of the Eastern Counties the total quantity received at Bishopsgate during 1910 was 100,000 tons. Of green peas from Essex as many as 1000 tons have been received in a single day. Fish from Lowestoft and Yarmouth runs into an annual total of many thousands of tons.

Passengers' luggage in advance is also dealt with at Bishopsgate. This system, saving the traveller much trouble, and greatly facilitating the working of passenger traffic at the stations, is evidently advancing in favour, the packages handled at Bishopsgate having increased from 18,617 in 1900 to 87,129 in 1910.

In the matter of general merchandise, the experiences of the other railway depôts already mentioned are confirmed by those at Bishopsgate, the taking there of the number and weight of all consignments of merchandise forwarded on a particular day having shown the following results :—

Number of consignments . .	7,932
Average weight per consignment .	3 cwt. 2 qrs. 25 lbs.
Number weighing less than 3 cwts.	6,056

The total " carriage paid " entries on outwards goods traffic in 1910 numbered over 970,000. For the month of November alone the total was 87,659.

A large proportion of the commodious and well-lighted warehouse level on the top storey is let off to individual traders in what are known as " fixed spaces," the demand for which is always in excess of the supply.   Goods of great variety and of great value are stored here.   The warehouse is found especially useful in connection with the extensive goods traffic carried by the Great Eastern Railway Company between England and the Continent.

Mention might also be made of the fact that the cartage work done at Bishopsgate requires a stud of about 1100 horses and 850 road vehicles, and gives employment to nearly 800 carmen and van-guards; that nine weighbridges have been provided ; that a large staff of railway police is always on duty to regulate the traffic in or out of the station and to protect property ; that the station has its own steam fire-engine and fire brigade (the company likewise undertaking the fire insurance of goods warehoused) ; and that the general arrangements include a complete ambulance equipment for the rendering of first aid in the event of accidents to the workers.[1]

Apart from the provision of depôts and warehouses, the railway companies facilitate the operations of traders by giving them certain free periods in respect to the unloading of coal, potatoes, hay, straw and various other commodities from the railway trucks, which serve the purposes of warehouses on wheels and involve the trader in no further cost, in addition to the railway rate, provided he can find a customer and arrange for the unloading to be done within the free period allowed to him, thus escaping the alternative charge for demurrage.   Other conveniences afforded by the English railway companies to traders include the provision—for hire at cheap rates—of grain sacks, meat hampers and meat cloths. The Great Eastern Railway, for instance, who serve a district mainly agricultural, keep on hand, for the convenience of traders, from 700,000 to 750,000 sacks, 1200 meat hampers, and between 4000 and 5000 meat cloths.

Railways, as developed in England, have thus done more than increase the facilities and decrease the cost of actual transport.   They have, in various ways, increased the facilities for, and decreased the cost of the exchange of, commodities, since there is many a trader in the country who conducts his business much more with the help of a railway company's

[1] See an article on " Bishopsgate Goods Station," by Frank B. Day, in the " Great Eastern Railway Magazine " for July, 1911.

capital than he does with his own. It is not alone that trade and industry have vastly increased in volume as the result of railway operation. Trade and industry have, also, completely changed in method, while thousands of men can carry on a business of their own to-day who, in the pre-railway epoch, must have been content to be little more than hewers of wood and drawers of water.

The economy in time, also, due to the speed at which the general merchandise traffic of the country is carried, has been of no less importance than the economy in cost of transport. Of these two elements speed in delivery may often be by far the more important. Slowness in transport, as is the case on canals, may cause no inconvenience where time is immaterial and large, or comparatively large, stocks can be kept on hand ; but these considerations do not apply to the great bulk of English trading and industrial enterprises as carried on under present-day conditions. Hence to the direct saving in the cost of transport, and to the greater advantages in the exchange and distribution of commodities brought about by railways, must be added a fair allowance for gains secured indirectly through this further saving of time. So far back as 1838, and long, therefore, before goods trains were run at an equivalent to express speed, Nicholas Wood wrote in the third edition of his " Practical Treatise on Rail-roads," in comparing rail and canal transport :—

" In our comparison of the two systems of transit, we must not lose sight of the very important consequences, resulting to the commerce of the country, by the rapidity of communication effected by the railways, which far outweighs any trifling balance of economy in favour of canals, even if such do exist ; and, therefore, we presume, whenever the balance between the two modes in any degree approach each other, a preference will be given to railway communication."

Against the various advantages that improved means of transport have thus brought to the British trader must, nevertheless, in his case, be set certain disadvantages. If he can forward his commodities with greater ease, at lower rates, and in less time, to the leading markets of the country than his grandfather before him could do, he finds that, in practice, the foreigner can do the same. Where the foreigner produces at lower cost, gets the lowest available rates by reason of size of consignment, style of packing, etc., has the benefit of an earlier season and so on, he may well be able, under a system of free imports, to compete with the home producer on his own markets ; though the cost of transport to the foreigner has naturally to be reckoned from the place of origin, and not simply from the English port through which his consignments pass.

The general effect of rail transport on the trade and industry of the country was thus described by Sir John Hawkshaw in his presidential address at the Bristol meeting of the British Association in 1875 :—

" Railways add enormously to the national wealth. More than twenty-five years ago it was proved to the satisfaction of the House of Commons, from facts and figures which I then adduced, that the Lancashire and Yorkshire railway, of which I was the engineer, and which then formed the principal railway connection between the populous towns of Lancashire and Yorkshire, effected a saving to the public using the railway of more than the whole amount of the dividend which was received by the proprietors. These calculations were based solely on the amount of traffic carried by the railways and on the difference between the railway rate of charge and the charges by the modes of conveyance anterior to the railways. No credit whatever was taken for the saving of time, though in England pre-eminently time is money. Considering that railway charges on many items have been considerably reduced since that day, it may be safely assumed that the railways in the British Isles now produce, or, rather, save to the nation, a much larger sum annually than the gross amount of all the dividends payable to the proprietors, without at all taking into account the benefit arising from the saving of time. The benefits under that head defy calculation, and cannot with any accuracy be put into money ; but it would not be at all over-estimating this question to say that in time and money the nation gains at least what is equivalent to 10 per cent on all the capital expended on railways."

Sir John Hawkshaw, it will be seen, arrived at this result on the basis of the saving in rates and charges and in speed ; but one must further allow for those various supplementary services on which the railways enable the traders to effect savings in the carrying on of their business.

Nor have the political and social results of the railway system been in any degree less remarkable than the economic.

Politically, the railway has been a factor in the rise of Democracy.

The construction of railways, by giving employment to large numbers of navvies in various parts of the country, to which they moved freely as occasion required, did much to break down the restrictions to which the labouring classes had so long been subjected under laws of settlement now found to be no longer operative ; and this greater freedom of movement, combined with the wider opportunities opened out to them, had effects on the workers far beyond the results accruing to them from an industrial standpoint alone.

Under, again, the influences following on the spread of railways throughout the country, England ceased to be simply a collection of isolated communities, and attained to a greater degree of national life. Better communication helped to make men better acquainted with one another, to broaden their sympathies, to spread a better knowledge of public events at home and abroad and to establish closer links between town life and country life.

Then the railways which rendered this closer communication possible proved to be among the greatest of social levellers. The claims of the third-class passenger were recognised in course of time, in spite of the unwillingness of the pioneer companies to make them due acknowledgment ; and the day was to come when the artisan would go by the same express train as the noble lord, arrive at his destination just as soon, and, though not having quite so luxurious a seat, be afforded facilities of travel greater far than those that could once be commanded even by kings and princes. Cheap excursion trains gave to artisan and agriculturist the opportunity of visiting great towns or pleasure resorts to which, in the old coaching days, the well-to-do would alone have thought of travelling. In the same way the advantages of a concentration of life, of thought and of movement in the capital were spread by the easier means of communication to country districts, and brought the population in general into closer touch with the leaders of public opinion. The railways were the greatest disseminators of intelligence through the newspapers or books carried by train or by the post, itself no less dependent, in turn, on the railway for the facilities it conferred on the country. Without the railway a cheap and widely distributed newspaper press, such as exists to-day, would have been impossible.

So the tendency of the railway was not only to advance trade, travel and transport, but to open men's minds, to broaden the intellectual outlook of the artisan and the labourer, to place them more on a level with their social superiors, and to make them better fitted for the exercise of greater political powers.

Socially, too, the railway system constitutes a paramount factor in the national life.

Thanks to the greater facilities the railways afforded for the distribution of commodities, and thanks, also, to the greater division of labour following on the changed economic conditions, there was no need in the Railway Age for householders to practise the same domestic arts that had been more or less obligatory in the case of their forefathers. There was no longer the same necessity for each family to brew its own ale, to bake its own bread and make its own cloth, or to provide stores of salt beef and other supplies in the autumn as if for a winter siege. When the railway enabled the village shopkeeper to satisfy promptly all local requirements, in winter as readily as in summer, the whole conditions of rural life were changed.

In towns, as in villages, the railways allowed not alone of a better distribution of domestic necessaries but of distribution at lower prices. The distance at which a commodity was produced or from which it came had, as a rule, comparatively little effect on the actual selling price. The large towns, especially, had the entire country open to them as their sources of supply, and were no longer limited to the produce—and the prices—of, say, a fifteen or a twenty-mile radius.

Following closely on the necessaries came the luxuries, the cheapening of which, mainly owing to the lower cost of transport, gave even to artisans' families alternative food supplies of a kind beyond the reach even of the wealthiest in the land a century ago.

The greater consumption of fruit and vegetables, sold at the lowest possible prices, must have been of incalculable advantage to the health of the community; though this advantage would not have been possible but for the facilities afforded by the railway in the bringing of huge quantities at a low rate from even the most distant corners of the three kingdoms.[1]

If, again, the railways had to share with invention and industrial expansion the responsibility for the great increase in town life, and for the overcrowding of many an urban centre, they have, on the other hand, helped the towns to spread out into healthy suburbs, or have otherwise relieved them of much of their overcrowding by providing workmen's trains for the conveyance of artisans and labourers between their place of labour and entirely new centres of population in what once were country districts.

As for the town workers who can afford to live at greater distances, the issue of cheap season tickets and the running of business trains morning and evening have greatly extended the suburbs of London, so that City men now have their homes as far away as Brighton, Folkestone and Southend.

The encouragement thus offered by the railways to the setting up of country or even seaside homes for town workers has further tended to the improvement of the public health, in addition to effecting a complete revolution in social conditions as compared with the days when the merchant or the tradesman lived over his place of business in the very heart of the City of London.

What shall be said, also, of the effect on the national life of that " travel habit " which received its greatest development from the railways, though further encouraged in recent years by the bicycle and the motor-car ? Under the combined influences of fast trains, corridor carriages, dining, luncheon and sleeping cars and cheap fares, whether for day excursions, short-date or long-date periods, tours at home or abroad, or any other of the various combinations for which facilities are offered, the making of pleasure trips has entered so thoroughly into the habits and customs of all grades of society that the social and domestic conditions of to-day offer a complete contrast from those that prevailed in the pre-railway period. It is now only the poorest of families that fail to have an annual holiday at a seaside resort or in the country, and even in their

---

[1] In the week ending April 17, 1909, the broccoli sent from the Penzance district to various destinations throughout the country filled 1012 railway waggons, and necessitated the running of 34 special trains.

case the children may be provided for by one of the philanthropic organisations established for this purpose.

Nor does the annual summer or autumn holiday now
suffice in a vast number of British households. There are
supplementary holidays at Easter and Whitsuntide ; there
are the trips taken on the other bank holidays besides ; and,
lest all these opportunities may not suffice, the railway
companies now enable their patrons to take a little holiday,
at reduced fares, every week-end. Thanks, in fact, to the
ever-expanding facilities for travel, holiday-making—a former
innovation now developed into an established national
institution—is no longer confined to a regular holiday season.
Winter holidays, also, are coming rapidly into vogue.

The question might well be asked if indulgence in the holiday
habit is not often carried too far, especially when trips unduly
long for the time at the tripper's disposal leave it doubtful
whether the holiday-maker should not have a second holiday
in which to rest after the fatigues of the first ; though if English
people are indeed giving themselves up far too much to
pleasure, sport and recreation, the railways must certainly
share the responsibility for what is happening.

Leaving medical authorities and social reformers to decide
on the questions just raised, one may, at least, safely affirm
that the railway has been a great promoter of friendship and
family life, since visits can now readily be exchanged between
those resident in distant parts of the country, and ties can
thus be maintained that, at one time, would have been in
danger of complete severance by the difficulties or the undue
cost of journeys by road.

In addition to doing so much to re-establish our industries,
our trade and our social life and manners on the new bases
here indicated, the railway companies have also sought to
play their part in the great and responsible question of national
defence. The gravity of the issues that, in case of invasion,
would depend on the railways being able to arrange for the
rapid and safe movement of troops, of war material and of
supplies from one part of the country to another is self-evident.
It is equally clear that the necessary plans should be carefully
prepared long in advance by those most competent to make
them.

Happily the requisite provisions to this end exist in an

organisation known as the "Engineer and Railway Staff Corps," concerning which Mr C. H. Jeune says in the "Great Eastern Railway Magazine" for June, 1911, in an article accompanying a portrait (in uniform) of the general manager of the Great Eastern, Mr W. H. Hyde, who is a Lieutenant-Colonel of the corps in question :—

"In the case of the great Continental powers, with their system of compulsory military service and the State ownership of railways, immediately war is declared practically the whole of the efficient male population, including the railway staff, is ready to place itself under military discipline ; the effect being that the transport or railway department, like the infantry or artillery, becomes an integral part of the armed forces of the country. But in England the transport arrangements must of necessity be largely carried out by the railway companies with the aid of their civilian employés. As a link between the army and the companies there is an organisation, the existence of which is not widely known, designated the Engineer and Railway Staff Corps. One of the peculiar features of this body is that it consists of officers only, many of whom we dare to say have no practical knowledge of the goose step. It never drills, no band of music heralds its approach, yet its members are men of high technical ability, and the duties it performs are of great value in the schemes of national defence.

"The corps was formed in 1864 by the patriotic exertions of Charles Manby, F.R.S., an eminent civil engineer, who held the post of adjutant with the rank of Lieutenant-Colonel in the corps. It is composed of civil engineers and contractors, also general managers and other officers of railway and dock companies. At present there are, in addition to the Commandant, one honorary Colonel, thirty Lieutenant-Colonels, and twenty-four majors. Their function is to advise on the transport of troops by rail and the construction of defensive works ; to direct the application of skilled labour and of railway transport to the purposes of national defence, and to prepare in time of peace a system on which such duties should be conducted."

Selected members of the Engineer and Railway Staff Corps join with representatives of the Admiralty and the War Office in forming the War Railway Council, which deals with transport and other arrangements for mobilisation.

Before leaving this branch of the subject I may, perhaps, be excused if I look still further afield, and turn, for a moment, from what railways have done for the nation to a few examples of what they are doing for the Empire.

In Australia the railways allowed of settlements established on the coast-line of a continent (covering three million square miles) gradually stretching far inland, utilising for agricultural purposes great areas of land that must otherwise have remained little better than barren wastes.

Canada, as we know it to-day, owes her existence to the railways. "Without them," said Mr E. T. Powell, in a paper read before the Royal Colonial Institute on February 14, 1911, "the vast dominion which we are proud to call the Canadian Empire would have remained a loose aggregate of scattered agricultural communities. Quebec and Alberta must have known as much of each other as do Donegal and Kamschatka. . . . A few thousand miles of steel rail . . . have saved Canada for the Empire. . . . Every year they draw the Dominion into closer cohesion as a self-governing unit, while at the same time they cement it more firmly into the Imperial fabric."

In South Africa the railways have rendered invaluable service from the point of view alike of trade, of commerce, of colonial expansion, and of Imperial policy. Rhodesia, especially, will have been indebted to her railways for much of the future greatness to which she hopes to attain ; and no one would yet venture to limit the possible results of the Cape-to-Cairo line, when that bold undertaking shall at last have been completed.

Less generally known, perhaps, is the story of what the railway is doing both for the Empire and for civilisation on the West Coast of Africa.

Little more than a dozen years ago no railways at all had been constructed there, and most of the colonies were in a more or less disturbed condition, even if they had not been the scene of successive massacres, of sanguinary wars, of much expenditure thereon, and of human sacrifices in districts steeped in slavery, barbarism and superstition.

This was especially the case on the Gold Coast, where the

Ashantis waged wars against us in 1875, 1896 and 1901. Two years after the last of these wars the Gold Coast main line of railway was taken up to Coomassie, the capital of Ashanti. To-day the Ashantis carry on strife with us no longer. They work in the gold mines instead ; and the railway that brings the gold down to the coast has paid a five-per-cent dividend from the day it was opened.[1]

Of " Sierra Leone and Its Commercial Expansion " Mr T. J. Alldridge said, in a paper he read before the Royal Colonial Institute on March 21, 1911 (reported in " United Empire," May, 1911) :—

" The extraordinary increase in the revenue of Sierra Leone during the last few years fills one who knows the circumstances of the Colony with amazement. It could never have been achieved had communication by railway into oil-palm belts, formerly quite unworked, not been introduced by the Government. The results have been extraordinary, although as yet hardly more than the fringe of these rich forests has been reached. . . . Only since the putting down of railways into our Protectorate has the Colony of Sierra Leone made such noticeable or commercial progress. The extension in the volume of imported merchandise, the expansion in its export products, and the greatly increased revenue, stand out to-day as an extraordinary revelation of what railway communication is capable of effecting in places that were not long since un-get-at-able, but which Nature has lavishly filled with a never-failing store of indigenous wealth."

Southern Nigeria and Northern Nigeria—the former having an area of 77,000 square miles and a population of 6,500,000 Africans, and the latter an area of 256,400 square miles and an estimated population of 8,000,000—are both of them countries of enormous natural resources which are being steadily developed by railways already built or in course of construction. A writer in " United Empire " for July, 1911, says of South Nigeria : " The trade returns of 1910 have surpassed even the most optimistic expectations, but there is good reason to look forward to further considerable increases in view of railway developments, harbour improvements, road

[1] See speech by Mr Frederick Shelford at a meeting of the Royal Colonial Institute, May 24, 1910, reported in " United Empire ; the Royal Colonial Institute Journal," for August, 1910.

construction, river clearing," etc., while of Northern Nigeria he says : " When we remember that a densely-populated area, twice as large as the United Kingdom, and little more than a decade removed from the horrors of slavery, savage warfare and wholesale human sacrifices, is run by about 300 Europeans on £500,000 a year, and is rapidly arriving at conditions favourable to a great development of commerce "—such conditions including the fact that a trader can now travel from Lagos to Zaria in three days by rail, instead of taking three weeks, as before—" it is, perhaps, a record in the annals of British expansion."

As for the civilising effects of railways in West Africa, Mr P. A. Renner, an educated native, said at a Royal Colonial Institute meeting on May 24, 1910 : " In the few years I have lived on the coast I have seen an improvement which has so astonished us as to make us almost worship the white man. Previously to the introduction of railways the clan feeling and tribal strifes and feuds were very rife, and the people of one village would scarcely visit those of another. Now all this is changed."

When one looks back from the work the railway is doing to-day, in all these different directions, to those very primitive beginnings of which I have told in earlier chapters, the whole story appears to be far more suggestive of romance than of sober fact and reality. From the colliery rail-way along which John Buddle's " waggon-man " led his horse, encouraging it to greater exertion with a handful of hay, to the railway that conveys, not only passengers, but goods, at express speed, that has revolutionised our industrial, our commercial and our social conditions, and is now consolidating our Imperial interests and effecting the civilisation of once barbarian lands, it is, indeed, a far cry ; yet the sequence of events can readily be traced, while all has been done within a century and a half of the world's history.

CHAPTER XXVIII

RAILWAYS A NATIONAL INDUSTRY

HAVING seen the part that railways have played in helping to develop the industrial interests of the country in general, we may now consider (1) to what extent the railways themselves constitute a national industry, and (2) various conditions relating thereto.

The latest available statistics as to the number of all classes of railway servants connected with the working of railways, and including, as I understand, both salaried and wages staffs with the exception of heads of departments, are to be found in " Returns of Accidents and Casualties " as reported to the Board of Trade by the railway companies of the United Kingdom for the year ending December 31, 1910 [Cd. 5628]. These figures give a total of 608,750 persons, classified as follows :—

NATURE OF EMPLOYMENT.	No. of Persons employed on 31st Dec., 1910.	NATURE OF EMPLOYMENT.	No. of Persons employed on 31st Dec., 1910.
1. Brakesmen. (*See Goods Guards*.)		7. Chockers, Chain-boys and Slippers :	
2. Capstan-men and Capstan-lads :		(1) Men	288
(1) Men	1,421	(2) Boys	271
(2) Boys	140	8. Clerks :	
3. Carmen and Van-guards :		(1) Men	61,361
		(2) Boys	9,044
(1) Men	18,382	9. Engine-cleaners :	
(2) Boys	6,604	(1) Men	13,912
4. Carriage-cleaners :		(2) Boys	4,267
(1) Men	6,572	10. Engine-drivers &	
(2) Boys	286	Motormen	27,330
5. Carriage and waggon examiners . . .	3,811	11. Firemen . .	25,419
		12. Gatekeepers .	3,543
6. Checkers :		13. Greasers :	
(1) Men	9,112	(1) Men	943
(2) Boys	77	(2) Boys	753
		14. Guards (Goods) and Brakesmen	15,339

NATURE OF EMPLOYMENT.	No. of Persons employed on 31st Dec., 1910.	NATURE OF EMPLOYMENT.	No. of Persons employed on 31st Dec., 1910.
15. Guards (Passenger)	8,239	24. Permanent-way-	
16. Horse drivers .	1,159	Men . .	66,305
17. Inspectors :		25. Pointsmen .	708
(1) Permanent-way	1,029	26. Policemen . .	2,130
(2) Others . .	8,603	27. Porters :	
18. Labourers :		(1) Men .	53,388
(1) Men .	54,981	(2) Boys .	4,501
(2) Boys .	1,333	28. Shunters . .	13,281
19. Lamp-men and lamp-lads :		29. Signal Fitters and Telegraph	
(1) Men .	1,655	Wiremen . .	3,905
(2) Boys .	418	30. Signalmen . .	28,653
20. Loaders & Sheeters	4,274	31. Signal-box lads .	1,894
21. Mechanics & Artisans :		32. Station-masters .	8,684
		33. Ticket - Collectors	
(1) Men .	78,389	and Examiners .	3,904
(2) Boys .	8,294	34. Watchmen .	1,151
22. Messengers :		35. Yardsmen . .	1,299
(1) Men .	1,124	36. Miscellaneous :	
(2) Boys .	2,468	(1) Adults .	33,620
23. Number-takers :		(2) Boys .	2,563
(1) Men .	1,252		
(2) Boys .	671	Total . .	608,750

The foregoing table serves to show the great extent of the railway industry from the point of view of the number of persons directly employed therein, and it also suggests a great variety in the occupations or grades of those employed. In the latter respect, however, the information given fails to offer a complete idea of the actual situation, since over 36,000 men and boys (that is, persons under eighteen years of age) are, as will be seen, classed as " miscellaneous."

Whatever the further variety in the particular occupations included under this head, it is certain that the railway service affords employment for a greater range and diversity of talent, skill, ability or effort than probably any other single industry or enterprise on the face of the earth. From the general manager to the railway navvy, and from the chief engineer, working out intricate problems calling for a high degree of skill and scientific knowledge, to the boy who helps in the unpretending but necessary work of cleaning the engines, there is opportunity for almost every possible class or type of labour, whether skilled or unskilled.

Over and above the employees, of all grades, concerned in

" the working of railways," as here shown, there is a very considerable body of men employed by the railway companies in the building of rolling stock, the making of rails, in the provision of many other requirements, or in the doing of much other work, necessary in the construction, equipment and operation of their lines. The smaller companies are content to buy their rolling stock, and they mostly have repairing shops only ; but the larger companies have their own locomotive, carriage and waggon works in which a very considerable volume of employment is afforded to mechanics and labourers who would hardly come under the ordinary designation of " railwaymen " proper ; while in this respect the companies concerned may be regarded as not only providers of transport but as, also, in effect, engineers and manufacturers.

In order to give the reader some idea of the extent of the employment afforded by these subsidiary branches of what is still actual railway work, I give on the next page a table—for the data of which I am indebted to the companies mentioned—showing the actual or the approximate number of men employed in the leading railway works of the type in question ; though it should be added that the figures relate only to the particular works mentioned, and do not include men who may be engaged in engineering or productive work elsewhere on the same company's system.

Information as to the extent to which the railway companies of the United Kingdom in general afford employment in the directions here in question will be found in the " Census of Production (1907) " [Cd. 5254], issued in 1910, included in these returns being three tables which are given under the heading " Railways (Construction, Repair and Maintenance of Permanent Way, Plant, Rolling Stock, etc.)," and relate to (1) output ; (2) cost of materials used ; and (3) number of persons employed.

It is shown that the total value of all goods manufactured or of the work done by railway companies' employees in construction, maintenance and repair of permanent way, works, buildings, plant, rolling stock, etc. (such values being sums representing only the actual cost of manufacture or work done, and made up of wages, materials and a portion of the establishment charges), amounted for the year 1907 to

COMPANY.	WORKS.	WHERE SITUATED.	NO. OF PERSONS EMPLOYED.
Great Central	Locomotive	Gorton	2512
,,	Carriage and waggon	Dukinfield	1741
Great Eastern	Loco. and carriage	Stratford, E.	4578
,,	Waggon	Temple Mills, E.	618
Great Northern	Loco., carriage and waggon	Doncaster	6000
Great Western	Loco., carriage and waggon	Swindon	11,700
Lancashire and Yorkshire	Locomotive	Horwich	3850
,,	Carriage and waggon	Newton Heath	1960
London and North-Western	Locomotive	Crewe	9000
,,	Carriage	Wolverton	4000
,,	Waggon	Earlstown	1800
London and South-Western	Loco., carriage and waggon	Eastleigh	3600
London, Brighton and South Coast	Loco., carriage and waggon	Brighton	2035
,,	,,	Lancing	129
Midland	Locomotive	Derby	3988
,,	Carriage and waggon		4300
North-Eastern	Locomotive	Gateshead and Darlington	3953
,,	Carriage and waggon	York and Heaton	2932
,,	Waggon	Shildon	1161
South-Eastern and Chatham	Locomotive	Ashford, Kent	733
,,	Carriage and Waggon		1211
Caledonian	Loco., carriage and waggon	St. Rollax, Glasgow	2695
Glasgow and South-Western	Locomotive	Kilmarnock	986
,,	Carriage and waggon	Barassie	269
North British	Loco., carriage and waggon	Cowlairs, Glasgow	2297
Great Northern (Ireland)	Loco., carriage and waggon	Dundalk	576
Midland Great Western (Ireland)	Loco., carriage and waggon	Broadstone Station, Dublin	549

£34,703,000. The details are grouped under seven different heads, as follows :—

	Value. £
I. Engineering Department (New Works, Repairs, and Maintenance) :—	
Permanent Way	9,346,000
Roads, Bridges, Signals, and Other Works	2,686,000
Station and Buildings	1,749,000
Docks, Harbours, Wharves, and Canals	745,000
Total—Engineering Department	14,526,000
II. Locomotive Department :—	
Engines, Tools, &c. (Construction and Repairs)	7,917,000
Buildings (New Works, Repairs, and Maintenance) —not included under Head I.	175,000
Total—Locomotive Department	8,092,000
III. Carriages, Waggons, &c. :—	
Carriages (Construction and Repairs)	4,454,000
Waggons (Construction and Repairs)	3,701,000
Road Vehicles for Passengers and Goods (Construction and Repairs)	272,000
Buildings (New Works, Repairs, and Maintenance) —not included under Head I.	33,000
Total—Carriages, Waggons, &c.	8,460,000
IV. Waterworks (Repairs and Maintenance)	155,000
V. Electric Works :—	
Buildings and Lines (New Works, Repairs, and Maintenance)	148,000
VI. Steamboats (Repairs)	323,000
VII. Other Productive Departments :—	
Lamps and Fittings for Lighting Purposes	150,000
Saddlery and Harness	32,000
Tarpaulins, Waggon Covers, &c.	345,000
Clothing	19,000
Printing	69,000
Hoists and Cranes (if not previously returned under Head I.) : Construction and Repairs	303,000
Gas manufactured for Companies' use (not included under other Heads)	286,000
Electricity for Stations, &c.	128,000
Telegraphs and Telephones	481,000

	Value. £
Buildings (not returned under other Heads): New Works, Repairs, and Maintenance	92,000
Provender	308,000
Iron and Steel Manufactures	178,000
Grease	115,000
Trucks, Barrows, &c.	39,000
Other Manufactures and Work Done	454,000
Total—Other Productive Departments	2,999,000
Grand Total—Goods Made and Work Done	34,703,000

The cost of the materials used was £17,600,000. Deducting this amount from the total of the foregoing table, there is left a net sum of £17,103,000 to represent wages and establishment charges ; though it may fairly be assumed that a good deal even of the £17,600,000 which stands for cost of materials was on account of wages previously paid for the procuring or the preparation of those materials by other than non-railway servants.

The total number of persons employed by the railway companies in the manufacture of the goods or in the execution of the work comprised in the statement was 241,526, in the proportion of 232,736 wage-earners and 8790 salaried persons. This figure of 241,526, however, is not necessarily to be added to the 608,750 previously given as the number of railway servants connected with the working of railways. There is nothing to show to what extent the two tables overlap, though overlapping there obviously is, since the first table includes 66,305 permanent-way men, while the second table evidently includes the persons employed on permanent-way work, since the value of that work is put down at £9,346,000. On the other hand, some classes of servants included in the Census of Production returns are excluded from the Railway Accidents return, so that although the exact number of persons directly employed by the railway companies of the United Kingdom cannot be stated, it must be somewhere between 608,750, the total of the one return, and 850,276, the sum of the totals for both returns.

All the figures thus far given relate to work done by persons directly employed by the railway companies themselves ; but there is, in addition, a vast amount of work done for the railways by independent companies or manufacturers. Taking, for instance, railway - carriage and waggon-building factories in the United Kingdom, providing for the wants of the smaller companies at home or for railway companies in the colonies or abroad, I find from the Census of Production that this particular phase of " the railway industry " (for it must needs be regarded as included therein, notwithstanding the fact that a few of the items relate to tramcars, horse vehicles, etc.), led in 1907 to an output of goods made or of work done valued at £9,609,000. The items are :—

	£
Railway carriages for passengers, and parts thereof .	1,676,000
Railway waggons, trucks, etc.	5,340,000
Parts and accessories of railway carriages and waggons, not distinguished	129,000
Railway wheels and axles complete	771,000
Tramcars and parts thereof	572,000
Vehicles for goods, horse-drawn	75,000
Machinery and accessories	135,000
Iron and steel manufactures and structural work .	174,000
Other products	93,000
Total value of goods made . . .	8,965,000
Repair work (including repairing contracts) . .	644,000
Total value of goods made and work done .	9,609,000

The number of persons engaged in these railway-carriage and waggon-building factories when the census in question was taken was 28,193, namely, 26,492 wage-earners, and 1701 salaried staff.

When one tries to form some idea of the further volume of employment that results from the supply of the thousand and one necessaries which even the most enterprising and independent of railway companies must still procure from outside manufacturers, makers, growers or providers, it is obvious that the railways, both as an industry in themselves and in their dependence, in endless ramifications, on other industries concerned wholly or in part in supplying railway wants, must provide more or less employment for an army of workers vastly in excess even of the aforesaid 600,000 or 800,000.

In many respects the railway service proper—that is to say, the particular branches thereof which deal with actual

transport, as distinct from construction and manufacture—
offers features that are unique in their way, even if they do not,
also, bring about types of workers of a class distinct from those
to be found in the majority of other industries.

In the latter dependence is being placed more and more on
the efficiency of the machinery employed, and the person of
greatest importance to them is the machinery-inventor or
the machinery-improver. The one who works the machine
may require to have a certain degree of skill or dexterity
in carrying on the necessary process, but the more nearly
he can approach the perfection of his machine and become,
as it were, part and parcel of it, the greater will often be his
degree of success as a worker. In his case the personal equation
hardly counts. He is merely the penny put into the slot in
order that the figures may work, and any other man, or any
other penny, that fulfilled the requisite conditions might be
expected to produce the same results.

In railway operation great importance must certainly be
attached to the efficiency of the machinery, or of the system ;
but final success may depend to a very material extent on the
efficiency of the unit. Everything that human foresight and
railway experience can suggest may be done—both in the
provision of complex machinery and in the drawing-up of the
most perfect rules and regulations—to ensure safe working;
yet the ultimate factor in grave issues on which safety or
disaster will depend may be a worker who has either risen to,
or has failed to meet, a sudden emergency. In this way,
not only does the individual unit count, but the individual
unit in railway operation may be the Atlas upon whose
shoulders the railway world does, in a sense, rest. A blunder
in an ordinary factory or workshop may involve no more
than the spoiling of a machine or the waste of so much material.
A blunder on the railway may involve a terrible loss of human
life.

Railway operation is thus calculated to give to the workers
engaged in transport a keener sense of responsibility, and to
develop therewith a greater individuality, than any other
of our national industries. The railway man concerned in
operation requires to be capable both of foresight and of
initiative. It is said of a certain railway in India that a telegraphic message was one day received at head-quarters from

a station down the line to the following effect : " Tiger on platform. Send instructions." In England there is no probability of railway-station platforms being taken possession of by wandering tigers ; but if anything equivalent thereto, in the form of a sudden and dangerous emergency not provided for by rules and regulations did arise, the officials on duty would be expected to show alike resource and energy in meeting the circumstances promptly and efficiently, so far as they could, instead of waiting to ask the district superintendent or the superintendent of the line for instructions.

Independently of the ever-present dangers of actual operation, to which I shall revert later on, the fact of having to deal with such varied types of humanity as are met with on the platforms of a busy railway station, under conditions ranging between the extremes of amiability and irritability, must also tend to sharpen the wits of the average railway worker, and make a different man of him than he would be if he were to spend his working days in feeding a machine in a factory with bits of tin or leather to be shaped into a particular form. Nor, whether the railway man be concerned in passenger traffic, in goods transport, or in checking claims and accounts in the general offices, must he fail to be ever on the look-out for those who, though they may be the most honest of men in the ordinary affairs of life, never scruple to defraud a railway company when they can.

Another factor tending to differentiate the railwayman from the ordinary industrial worker is the sense of discipline—and the consequent subordination of each unit to an official superior—which must needs prevail if a great organisation is to be conducted, not simply with success for the shareholders, but with safety for the public. The maintenance of effective discipline is obviously essential to the safety of railway operation, just as it does, undoubtedly, further help to form the special type of the railway servant.

The development of the same type is being fostered to an ever-increasing degree by the special training which junior workers undergo with a view to making them, not only better fitted for the particular post they already occupy, but qualified to succeed to higher positions as opportunities for their advancement may arise.

A railway manager is not alone concerned in the working

of his line, and in the doings of his staff, day by day. He looks forward to the requirements of the line and to the constitution of the staff at least five or ten years hence, and he wants to make sure that, as the experienced men around him are lost to the service, others will be at hand equally, or even still better, qualified to take their place. He further realises that in an undertaking in which, notwithstanding its magnitude, so much depends on the unit, that unit should be encouraged, and enabled, to attain to the highest practicable stage of efficiency.

This tendency is leading to results that are likely to be both far-reaching and wide-spreading. It is a matter not only of giving to railway workers, and especially to those in the clerical and operative departments, a higher degree of technical knowledge, but, also, of rendering them equal to responsibility, of fostering their efficiency still further through their social, physical and material well-being, and of retaining them for the railway service notwithstanding (in the case of the clerical staff) the allurements of traders who look upon well-trained goods clerks, especially, as desirable assistants in the counting-house, and seek to attract them with the offer of a somewhat better wage.

The training and the higher education of railway workers have undergone important developments alike in the United Kingdom, in the United States, in Germany, in France, and elsewhere.

In the early days of the railway the most eligible person for the position of general manager was thought to be some retired naval or military officer, accustomed to controlling large bodies of men ; and the first appointments were based on this principle. But experience soon showed that in under-takings where technical, commercial and economic con-siderations were all-important, the real recommendations for leading positions were to be found, rather, in proved capacity and in thorough knowledge of railway operation and manage-ment.

Under the company system, as it prevails in the United Kingdom and the United States, railwaymen, of whatever class, are now generally taken on as boys, are trained for the position to which they are found to be adapted, and rise to higher posts according to capacity *and* opportunity—for these must needs go together. In this way it is not unusual for the general

manager on an English railway to have started as an office
boy. Many a head of department to-day entered the service
as junior clerk, and worked his way up to his present position ; there are station-masters who began as ticket clerks ;
there are guards who gained their first knowledge of railway
work as station porters, while engine-drivers are recruited
from firemen, and firemen from engine-cleaners.

For details as to what the American railway companies are
doing in the matter of " Education for Efficiency in Railroad
Service " I must refer the reader to a bulletin written by
J. Shirley Eaton and published, under this title, by the
United States Bureau of Education. Here I can do no more
than reproduce the following extract, giving in brief Mr
Eaton's view on the general situation as he finds it on the
other side of the Atlantic :—

" Railroads, as a whole, through a representative body
such as the American Railway Association, should in a comprehensive way take up the matter of the education of railway employees. As they now have committees devoted to
standards of construction, maintenance, and operating practice, they should also have a standing committee, of a character
to command confidence, who should sedulously foster a closer
relation between the railroad and educational agencies. This
could be done by roughly grouping railroad service into
classes according to the requirements of service, indicating
the efficiency required in a broad way, and studying the
curricula and course of experience leading up to such efficiency.
Such a body should officially gather all railroad literature and
accumulate the nucleus of a railroad museum. In various
ways the teaching force of educational agencies, training to-
ward railroad employ, could be drawn into study and discussion of the practical everyday problems of railroad work.
The large public policies involved in railroad operation are
to-day left to the doctrinaire or accidental publicist, when
they should be a subject of study and effective presentation
by the highest grade of trained experts which the associate
railroads could draw into their service. On the other hand,
such a standing committee could stimulate and guide the
practice of railroads in their methods of handling and in-
structing apprentices. Between the instruction and practice
in the service on the one side, and the instruction outside

the service on the other side, they could foster a closer relation, making them mutually supplementary. In developing approved plans for recruiting the service they would necessarily indicate the lines of a more direct access than now exists from the various schools to apprenticeships in the service, and suggest the best methods by which such apprenticeships would be gradually merged into the full status of regular employ at the point of special fitness."

On this side of the Atlantic the railway servants' education movement has assumed two phases—(1) secondary or technical education of junior members of railway staffs in mechanics' institutions or kindred organisations, created or materially supported by the railway companies, and already carried on during a period of, in some instances, over sixty years ; and (2) a " higher education " movement, of a much more advanced type, developed since about 1903, and conducted either in special classes held at the railway offices or in connection with a University, a mechanics' institution, a local educational body, or otherwise.

It is impossible in the space at my command to give a detailed account of what every railway company in the United Kingdom is doing in these directions. Some typical examples must suffice.

To begin with mechanics' institutions and other kindred bodies, these are by no means purely educational in their scheme of operations. They include many social and recreative features which, in effect, should play a no less important part than educational efforts in promoting the general efficiency of the railway worker by helping to give him a sound body, a contented mind, and a cheerful disposition as well as more skilful fingers or a better-cultivated brain. In the United States, judging from what Mr Eaton says on the subject, all such " welfare " work as this, though carefully fostered, is regarded by the railroad companies as a purely business proposition ; and he does not attempt to credit them with any higher motive than regard for the almighty dollar. Here, however, while there has been full recognition of the financial value of increased efficiency, the companies have, also, not failed to realise their moral obligations towards their staffs. Hence in seeking to promote the welfare of their employees they have been inspired by motives of humanity, goodwill and honourable feeling in addition to, or even as distinct from, any pecuniary advantage the shareholders themselves might eventually gain therefrom.

Crewe Mechanics' Institution dates back to 1844, when the Grand Junction Railway Company provided a library and reading-room, and, also, gave a donation for the purchase of books for the men employed in the railway works then being set up in what was, at that time, a purely agricultural district. In the following year this library and reading-room developed into a Mechanics' Institution, the primary object of the railway company being to afford to the younger members of their staff at Crewe greater facilities for acquiring theory in classes at the Institution to supplement the practical knowledge they were acquiring in the works, though the benefits of the Institution were also to be open to residents of Crewe who were not in the company's employ. The management was vested in a council elected annually by the directors and the members conjointly ; and this arrangement has continued ever since.

Larger premises were provided in 1846, in which year the Grand Junction combined with the London and Birmingham and Manchester and Birmingham Companies to form the London and North-Western Railway Company. The classes were added to from time to time until they covered the whole range of subjects likely to be of service to the students. Beginning, however, with the 1910–11 session, the art, literary and commercial classes which had been held at the Institute for sixty-four years were transferred to the local education authority, the Institute retaining the scientific and technological subjects. In addition to the ordinary work of the classes, the more recent developments of the " higher education " movement have led to systematic courses of instruction— extending over four - year periods—in (1) pure science, (2) mechanical engineering, (3) electrical engineering and (4) building construction. An Institution diploma is given to each student who completes a course satisfactorily. Visits are, also, paid to engineering works, electrical generating stations, etc. Most of the teachers are engaged at the Crewe works, and the instruction given is thus of the most practical kind.

One feature of the Institution is the electrical engineering laboratory, provided by the directors of the London and

North-Western Railway, who have further arranged for a number of apprentices to attend at the laboratory one afternoon every week to receive instruction, their wages being paid to them as though they were still on duty in the works. There is, also, a mechanics' shop, with lathes, drilling machines, etc., electrically driven.

Since 1855 the directors of the London and North-Western have given an annual donation of £20 for books to be awarded as prizes to successful students employed in their locomotive department and various other prizes and scholarships, including Whitworth scholarships, are also awarded. The Institution is affiliated with the Union of Lancashire and Cheshire Institutes, the City and Guilds of London Institute and the Board of Education, each of which bodies holds examinations and awards prizes and certificates. The library has now over 12,000 volumes.

In addition to the reading-room the Institution has coffee, smoking and recreation-rooms. Special attention is being paid to the social side of the Institution's work through the appointment of a " Teachers' Committee for Social and Recreative Development," the particular purpose of this committee being to organise sports and entertainments and to secure the formation of a literary society.

At Wolverton there is a Science and Art Institute at which many classes are held, and, although none of these are directly under the management of the London and North-Western Company, as at Crewe, the very successful and numerous courses in engineering subjects and railway-carriage building conducted by the committee of management, working in connection with the Bucks County Council, receive the active support and encouragement of the company's directors.

Science, commercial, art and domestic economy classes are also held at the L. & N.-W. Institute at Earlstown, where definite courses of instruction, in groups of subjects, and extending over at least two years, are given.

The Great Eastern Railway Mechanics' Institution, established in 1851 at Stratford New Town, has made generous provision for the education, recreation and social life of employees of that company resident in London, East. The Institution comprises a library of 9000 volumes ; reading-room ; baths (patronised by 10,000 bathers in the course of the year) ; a large hall for lectures, entertainments, balls or concerts; and a billiard-room, three quoit pitches and a rifle range, the last-mentioned being the gift of the Great Eastern directors. Science, art, technological, commercial and other evening classes to the number of over forty were held in the Institution during the Session of 1910–11. Among the subjects taught were : machine construction, applied mechanics, mathematics, electrical engineering, heat-engines, motor-car engineering, rail-carriage building, drawing, book-keeping, shorthand, physical culture, the mandoline and the violin ; while still other classes included an orchestral class and ladies' classes in " first aid " and " home nursing."

A series of practical classes, in connection with the same Institution, is also held during working hours in the Great Eastern Railway Company's works at Stratford. Arrangements are further made to extend the usefulness of these classes by visits to engineering works and electrical generating stations. Examinations are conducted in connection with the Board of Education, the City and Guilds of London Institute and the Society of Arts, and prizes, certificates and scholarships are awarded to successful students. The total number of students attending the various classes in 1910–11 was 958. The Institution at the end of 1910 had 1471 members, of whom all but 79 were in the employ of the railway company.

In 1903 the directors of the Great Eastern Railway Company gave a further proof of their appreciation of the educational work thus being carried on by granting to employee-students in the locomotive, carriage and waggon department who could fulfil certain conditions leave of absence with full pay for one or more winter sessions of about six months each, in order to afford them increased facilities for taking up the higher branches of technical study. Opportunities are also given to such students for visits to manufactories, works in progress, etc. Of the twenty-one students who had taken advantage of the arrangements in question down to the end of 1910, four had obtained the University degree of B.Sc. (Faculty of Engineering) ; four had passed the intermediate examination for the same degree ; two had obtained Whitworth scholarships, and five had been awarded Whitworth exhibitions.

Clubs formed in connection with the Institution include an athletic club, a rifle club, a quoit club, a cricket club and a football club. Concerts, illustrated lectures and various entertainments are given in the Institution during the course of each session.

The Midland Railway Institute at Derby, also going back to 1851, had a membership in 1910 of 2621. Classes in French and shorthand are held, but technical subjects are not taught, special facilities in this respect for the company's staff being provided by a large municipal technical college in the town. The Institute has a library of over 17,000 volumes, a well-stocked reading-room, a dining hall, a restaurant (for the salaried staff), a café (for the wages staff), committee rooms and a billiard-room ; while the various associations include an engineering club (which holds fortnightly meetings during the winter months for the reading and the discussion of papers, and, also, pays visits to engineering works), a natural history society (which holds indoor meetings and organises Saturday rambles), a dramatic society, a fishing club, a photographic society and a whist and billiard club.

A Mechanics' Institute and Technical School opened at Horwich in 1888 was mainly due to a grant of £5000 by the directors of the Lancashire and Yorkshire Railway Company and to the gift of the " Samuel Fielden " wing by the widow of that gentleman, for many years a director of the company. In October, 1910, there were 2224 members, of whom all but 53 were in the employ of the Lancashire and Yorkshire Railway Company. The leading features of the Institute include a dining hall, reading, magazine and smoke-rooms, a library of about 13,000 volumes, a lecture hall with seating accommodation for 900 persons, the Fielden gymnasium, a miniature rifle - range, class - rooms, and chemical and mechanical laboratories.

Science, art, technical, commercial and preparatory classes are conducted at the Institute in connection with the Board of Education, London, and the instruction given includes a continuous course of study designed to enable engineering students to make the best use of classes of direct service to them. The special arrangements thus made comprise a preliminary technical course (extended over two years), a mechanical engineering course (five years) and an electrical engineering course (four years). The classes of the Institute (exclusive of those for ambulance work) were attended in 1910–11 by over 500 students. Examinations are conducted by the Union of Lancashire and Cheshire Institutes, the Royal Society of Arts, the City and Guilds of London Institute, and the Board of Education, and numerous prizes and exhibitions are awarded.

Useful service from an educational standpoint is also rendered by the Institution's engineering and scientific club, at whose meetings the papers read and discussed have been on such subjects as " Prevention of Waste in Engineering," " Evaporation and Latent Heat," " Electric Motor-cars and their Repairs," etc. Other affiliated societies or clubs include a photographic society, an ambulance corps and a miniature rifle club (also affiliated to the National Rifle Association and the Society of Miniature Rifle Clubs). Popular lectures are given on six Saturday evenings during the winter session.

Other railway institutes are to be found at Swindon (Great Western Railway), at Vauxhall and Eastleigh (London and South-Western Railway), at York and various other centres on the North-Eastern Railway, and elsewhere.

I pass on to deal with recent developments of the higher education movement in the railway service as operated (1) by the companies themselves, or (2) by the companies in combination with outside educational authorities.

The Great Western Railway Company, on the recommendation of their general manager, Sir James C. Inglis, inaugurated at Paddington station in 1903 a school of railway signalling, designed to offer to the employees of the company a definite means by which they could acquire technical knowledge of railway working and management. The classes are conducted by the company's signalling expert, and the instruction given is based on the object lessons afforded by a model railway junction, furnished with a complete set of signalling appliances on the standard lines as laid down by the Board of Trade requirements. The experiment was so complete a success that similar schools, provided with similar models, have since been set up at various centres throughout the company's system.

In the " Great Western Railway Magazine " for November, 1911, it was announced that a revised circular dealing with these classes was then in course of preparation, and that it would include the following clause, setting out an important amendment of the scheme :—

" In order to maintain the value of the certificates awarded and the standard of efficiency of certificate holders, each holder will in future be invited to sit for re-examination before the expiry of five years from the date of his certificate. Endorsement certificates will be awarded to candidates who successfully pass the second and subsequent examinations. This step is felt to be desirable having regard to changing conditions and developments in connection with modern railway working. The date of the last certificate will be taken into account in connection with appointments, promotions, etc."

Other classes at Paddington, controlled by the chief goods manager, afford instruction in railway accounts, and enable the clerical staff to gain a better insight into matters connected with the receipt, transport and delivery of goods, and, also, the preparation of accounts and statistics both for the Railway Clearing House and for the company's audit office. Shorthand classes are also held.

Annual examinations take place in connection with all these various classes, and the students passing them receive certificates which are naturally taken into account when questions as to advancement arise. On the occasion of the distribution of certificates on January 14, 1910, the chief goods manager, Mr T. H. Rendell, said that facilities for gaining information on railway subjects were far more numerous to-day than they were forty years ago, when he joined the service. " Continuation classes of any kind," he proceeded, " were then conspicuous by their absence, and practically the only classes of this kind were those held at the Birkbeck Institute, which he attended, though he had to pay a substantial fee in respect to each subject taken. Formerly there was no organised method of acquiring knowledge of railway working, and they learnt to do right chiefly by being blamed for doing wrong."

The London and North-Western Railway Company established block telegraph signalling classes in 1910, the instruction given being facilitated by a complete working model of a double-line junction, fitted with signals and interlocking ; a set of standard block instruments and bells ; an electric train staff apparatus for single line working, and various diagrams. The lectures, given in the shareholders' meeting-room at Euston by the company's expert in signalling, were attended by students representing nearly all the different departments on the station, and the results of the examinations subsequently held were so satisfactory that the company have since established similar classes at various other centres, in addition.

To ensure the general efficiency of their clerical staff the London and North-Western Company hold (1) an educational examination which a boy must pass before he enters the service ; (2) a further examination, at the end of two years, to test the clerk's knowledge of shorthand, railway geography and the railway work on which he has been engaged ; and (3) an examination before the clerk's salary is advanced beyond £50 per annum, it being necessary for him to show a thorough knowledge of shorthand, and to write a paper on such subjects as block working, train working or development of traffic.

The Lancashire and Yorkshire Railway Company have also established, at their head offices in Manchester, a School for Signalling, the complete equipment with which it is furnished including a full-sized lever frame. Instruction is given free both to the head office staff and to the staff at the stations within a radius of twelve miles. Special lectures, also, have occasionally been given to the staff in the chief engineer's department by that officer's assistants. Another feature of the educational work of the Lancashire and Yorkshire is the sending round to the various locomotive sheds of what is known as an instruction van. A full description of this van will be found in the " Railway Gazette " for January 22, 1909.

The Great Central Railway Company, to meet their requirements more particularly at the head offices and in connection with their Continental business, adopted in 1908 a scheme designed to enable them to secure the services of a certain number of young men with higher educational qualifications than were usually possessed by those who previously presented themselves for junior clerkships. The company accordingly offer six positions annually to members of the existing staff, under twenty-five years of age, who display the highest standard of knowledge and ability in a competitive examination, the successful candidates in each year being promoted to an advanced scale of pay, and taking a " higher grade course of training," which, it is thought, should fit them to hold positions of responsibility in the future.

This higher grade course consists of periods of work, varying from three to twelve months, in eight of the principal departments, viz. the engineering, locomotive-running, goods, traffic, rolling stock, stores, marine and general manager's departments. The entire course covers a period of four years. During his stay in each of these departments the student is required to pursue a course of reading in the theory of the work in which he is engaged in that particular section ; he is given an opportunity to acquire practical knowledge of the work; he must report at the end of every month to the head of the department on the progress he has made, and, on leaving any one section, he is to send an essay to the general manager, showing the knowledge he has gained. Heads of departments or sections are also required to submit confidential reports to the general manager on the ability displayed by the student while under their supervision.

The North-Eastern Railway Company have an elaborate educational system which resolves itself into (1) preliminary tests ; (2) Part I., and (3) Part II., of a secondary examination. The subjects for examination in Part I. of the secondary examination are — (i) Regulations for train signalling by block telegraph and general rules and regulations ; (ii) goods station accounts ; (iii) passenger station accounts ; (iv) shorthand and typewriting or practical telegraphy. Those in Part II. are—Railway subjects : (i) Railway operating ; (ii) railway economics (general) ; (iii) railway and commercial geography of the United Kingdom ; (iv) law relating to the conveyance of goods and passengers by railway. Other subjects : (v) Mathematics ; (vi) commercial arithmetic and book-keeping ; (vii) methods employed in import and export trade of Great Britain ; (viii) French ; (ix) German. Instead of examining candidates in Nos. v, vi, vii, viii and ix the company will, as a general rule, accept certificates of proficiency in these subjects of recent date obtained at various specified examinations elsewhere. Each candidate is required to pass in railway operating and three other subjects, one of which must be (ii), (iii) or (iv) of the railway subjects.

It will be seen that while the subjects for Part I. cover the practical work at a station, those for Part II. deal more with the principles of railway operation. To assist clerks in preparing for these tests the company have issued several brief textbooks ; they have arranged for the delivery of series of lectures ; they are utilising railway institutes for the purpose of instruction, and they offer facilities for the circulation of standard works on railway subjects. The company also conduct at various centres railway block-telegraph signalling instruction classes fully provided with the necessary apparatus, examinations being held and certificates awarded.

Coming next to what is being done by educational bodies working in connection with railway companies, reference should first be made to the London School of Economics and Political Science.

Railway transport is a subject in which the authorities of the school have always taken great interest, and in the session of 1896–7 a course of lectures on railway economics was given at the school by Mr W. M. Acworth. On this occasion the Great Western Railway Company paid the fees for members of their staff to attend the course. When Mr Acworth gave a further series of lectures in 1897–8, the Great Eastern Railway Company also paid the fees for members of their staff who desired to attend. In 1904 seven of the leading railway companies gave a definite guarantee which allowed of a more elaborate system of railway instruction being organised at the school (now one of the schools of the University of London, as reconstructed in 1900). Under the scheme in question a complete course of instruction is given in the " History, Theory and Present Organisation of Transport," leading up, if desired, to the degree of B.Sc. (Econ.), with honours in transport. The course is under the general supervision of a " Committee of Governors on Railway Subjects," consisting of five prominent members of the railway world. The lectures are as follows :—

(A) Courses on railway subjects :—
1. Railway economics : operating (20 lectures).
2. Railway economics : commercial (20).
3. Economics of railway construction and locomotive operation (20).
4. The law of carriage by railways (20).

5. The consolidation of English railways (4).

(B) Courses on subjects useful to railway students :—

    1. Accounting and business methods. Part I. (30).

    2. Accounting and business methods. Part II. (30).

    3. Methods and applications of statistics (15).

    4. Mathematical methods of statistics : elementary (15).

Examinations are held, and certificates and medals are awarded to successful students.

The School of Economics has, also, in its library, a collection of works on transport questions which it believes to be the best of the kind in existence. It comprises no fewer than 12,000 books, pamphlets, plans, reports, etc., and, as over 5000 of these were presented by Mr Acworth, the name of the " Acworth Collection on Transport " has been given to this unique and invaluable mine of information on everything appertaining to railways and transport at home or abroad.

With the University of Manchester the Lancashire and Yorkshire Railway Company (in addition to what they have done in other directions, as already mentioned) made arrangements in 1903 for evening classes on railway economics in the interests of their staff, and these classes have been continued ever since. They are in three-year cycles, and students who go through a complete course have the advantage of receiving, from thoroughly qualified teachers, instruction in the following subjects : Railway geography and railway history of the United Kingdom and of other leading countries ; economic analysis of the railway business in relation to other businesses ; motor power and rolling stock ; goods traffic ; passenger traffic ; theory of freight rates ; accounts ; Government in relation to railways ; and railway law.

The directors of the Lancashire and Yorkshire pay the fees for any members of their clerical staff within a radius of twelve miles of Manchester who desire to attend these classes, and at the close of each session they grant to three of the most promising of the railway students scholarships which are tenable at the University for a further three years, and allow of attendance during the daytime at the classes in political economy, organisation of industry and commerce and accounting.

It was in connection with the scheme here in question that

Mr H. Marriott, now chief goods manager of the Lancashire and Yorkshire Railway, delivered the excellent course of lectures which, republished by " The Railway Gazette," under the title of " The Fixing of Rates and Fares," has become a recognised textbook on that subject.

In 1907 the directors of the same company arranged with the Victoria University, Manchester, for the delivery of a series of University Extension Lectures on railway economics at the Burnley Grammar School, paying the fees of any member of their clerical staff within a radius of twelve miles of Burnley who wished to attend. The subjects chosen were " Organisation of a Railway," " Goods Traffic," " Passenger Traffic " and " Economics," and each subject extended over three lectures.

In the autumn of 1911 arrangements were concluded between the North-Eastern Railway Company, the University of Leeds and the Armstrong (Newcastle) University for the giving at those Universities of courses of evening lectures on a variety of railway subjects, the company undertaking to pay half the fee for all members of their staff who might wish to attend.

Finally I would mention, in this connection, that, by arrangement between the Midland Railway Company and the University of Sheffield, a course of 40 lectures on economics, to extend over two years, was begun at the Midland Railway Institute, Derby, on October 11, 1911, by Mr Douglas Knopp, the special purpose of the course being to afford to members of the Midland Railway staff an opportunity of studying, free of expense to themselves, the economic features of modern industrial and commercial problems, including transportation.

Literary societies and lecture and debating societies, formed by various railway staffs, are another outcome of the aspirations of railwaymen for wider knowledge and increased efficiency. The Great Western Railway Literary Society, established in 1852, is one of the oldest institutions at Paddington. It has a library of 10,000 volumes and various social off-shoots. Another typical institution, the Great Western Railway (London) Lecture and Debating Society, founded in 1904, serves a useful function in affording opportunities for the reading of papers by heads of departments or other qualified persons on subjects likely to be of practical service to members of the staff. It was before this society that the paper on " The Government in Relation to the Railways of the Country," referred to on page 352, was read by Mr F. Potter, chief assistant to the general manager of the Great Western Railway.

Apart from the educational, literary or social organisations directly associated with particular railway companies, there are other bodies formed mainly by experts or workers in particular departments of railway construction, maintenance or operation who, whatever their position or attainments, find they are not yet too old to learn, that in the railway world there is always something new, and that advantages are to be gained by themselves from an exchange of views, opinions and experiences, apart from the benefits they may confer on juniors in helping them to advance their knowledge on technical questions. These associations are certainly to be classed among those which promote the " higher education " of the railwayman, though they may also serve various other purposes, social, provident, etc.

Among organisations of this type the Permanent Way Institution, established in 1884, and incorporated in 1908, occupies a leading position. It seeks to promote among inspectors of way and works a more thorough knowledge of all technical details connected with the discharge of their duties, and it publishes for the use of members, and persons qualified to be members, " information which may be likely to encourage and exert interchange of thought, especially with a view to create a friendly and sympathetic feeling between members and such other persons in their duties and labours, and for mutual help of members in the discharge of the same." Sections are formed in important centres throughout the United Kingdom, and the reading and discussion at the meetings of the sections of short practical papers by members, dealing mainly with matters appertaining to their employment, is regarded by the Institution as an important phase of its system of technical education. The sections are kept well supplied with literature, reports, and communications affording good material for discussion at their meetings, " and much benefit," says a prospectus issued by the Institution, " has been derived for the members from this interchange of ideas with men in similar capacities in other parts of the world, whereas the former isolation and rare opportunities for intercourse frequently caused narrow-mindedness, prejudice, reservation of manner, and the natural loss of much useful information and experience to both employer and employed."

Summer meetings, held in a centre where there are features of special interest to railwaymen, are another valuable means for the exchange of ideas between members of the Institution, for enabling them to gain fresh experiences, and for promoting social intercourse. These summer meetings have developed into " conventions " lasting a week each, and they are spoken of as having been " of untold benefit to those participating in them." The Institution has, also, various beneficent funds.

The Association of Railway Locomotive Engineers of Great Britain and Ireland is a body whose members have, for a number of years, held two meetings annually—in London in winter, and in the country in summer—for the discussion of matters of interest to railway engineers and to railway companies generally.

The Institution of Signal Engineers (Incorporated) includes in its objects " the advancement of the science and practice of signalling by discussion, enquiry, research, experiment and other means ; the diffusion of knowledge regarding signalling by means of lectures, publications, the exchange of information and otherwise ; and the improvement of the status of the signalling profession." Only railway signal or telegraph engineers, superintendents in charge of railway signalling, telegraph or kindred work, and qualified engineers in Government service are eligible for full membership ; but other officers engaged in technical work in engineering departments are eligible for associate membership, while in the autumn of 1911 the Institution was considering a scheme for student membership and the offering of annual prizes to members of the student class for papers and essays on technical subjects.

The Association of Railway Companies' Signal Superintendents and Signal Engineers was formed in 1891 with the object of affording facilities for the discussion of signalling questions by the chiefs of signalling departments on the railways of the United Kingdom. Two meetings are held each year at the Railway Clearing House.

A very useful purpose in developing the higher education,

not alone of railway workers but of the ever-widening circle of those who are interested in railway work, is being served by the Railway Club, which is established at 92, Victoria Street, London, S.W., and has, also, various provincial centres, with district representatives in Birmingham, Huddersfield, Lancaster, Glasgow and Newhaven. Founded in 1899, the club is designed to afford opportunities for bringing together all who are concerned in railway questions in general ; though some of the members specialise in locomotive problems, others in traffic problems, and so on. At the London head-quarters there is a club room well stocked with railway papers, and here, also, the members can find a comprehensive library. In the same building monthly meetings are held for the reading and discussion of papers. Some of these are of a technical character, appealing only to experts ; but subjects of more general interest are also dealt with, the programme for the 1910–11 session including papers by the Rev. W. J. Scott (president) on " Railway History: 1860–80," and by Mr E. J. Miller (hon. secretary) on " Belgian State Railways." Meetings are also held in the provincial centres, and visits are paid both there and in London to railway works, running sheds and other places of interest. The utility of the Club is greatly enhanced by the publication of its excellent little organ, " The Railway Club Journal."

From the details here given it will be seen, not only that the movement for increasing the efficiency of the railway worker, by furthering his training in railway and cognate subjects, has undergone great and varied expansion, but that railway operation and management are coming more and more to be regarded as a science, and one that, with its many problems and complexities, calls for prolonged study, effort and experience on the part of those who would attain to perfection, or even to exceptional knowledge and skill, therein.

Nor should the said details fail to excite a more sympathetic feeling on the part of the trading and travelling public towards railway workers who find they can attain to greater proficiency, and acquit themselves better of their responsibilities to the public, as well as to their company, by undergoing as much of this training, or by securing as much of this advancement in the technicalities of railway work, as their powers may warrant or their opportunities allow.

One may further anticipate that, as the various tendencies here in question are developed, there will, not only inside but outside the service, be a greater disposition to adopt the view of the American authority already quoted in his suggestion that " the large public policies involved in railroad operation are to-day left to the doctrinaire or accidental publicist when they should be the subject of study and effective presentation by the highest grade of trained experts which the associate railroads could draw into their service." When this latter result is brought about, whether through the higher education movement or otherwise, not only will the railway service be rendered still more efficient, and not only will even greater advantages be conferred on the country, but the position of the railway interests themselves should be strengthened on questions of State control in regard either to the principles of railway policy or to the details of railway operation.

Recreation and physical culture, as part of the general scheme which aims at promoting the efficiency and the personal well-being of railwaymen, are fostered in the railway world by the athletic clubs formed by the staffs of the various companies, with more or less official countenance and support, and whether in connection with mechanics' institutes or otherwise. These clubs favour, not only athletics proper but cricket, football, tennis, hockey, bowls, harriers, swimming, angling, etc. They are supplemented by a London Railways Athletic Association, which brings together the members of the different clubs in friendly rivalry, while the various gatherings and competitions have an excellent result—apart from the other advantages they confer—in fostering that social life of the railway service which tends so much to its widespread popularity.

Mention should, also, be made of the musical societies, the horticultural societies, the rifle clubs, the chess clubs and other organisations. The staff or society dinners, the outings, the smoking concerts and the presentations to retiring colleagues help still further to promote feelings of comradeship, mutual sympathy and goodwill not always to be found to anything like the same extent in commercial undertakings of other types. Such sentiments as these continue to be fostered, indeed, after the service has been left, the Retired Railway Officers' Society having been formed, in 1901, " for the purpose of bringing together those who in past years have held executive positions in the railway service of Great Britain, the Colonies or India, and for the renewal and keeping up of former friendships on the part of gentlemen once associated, in official relations, either on the same or on different railways." The objects of the society are exclusively social and friendly.

Sobriety being a virtue especially desirable on the part of those to whom so vast a number of the British public daily entrust their lives or limbs, temperance is encouraged in the railway service by the formation of Railway Temperance Unions for all the leading lines. Each union has numerous branches, and the various unions constitute, in turn, a federation known as the United Kingdom Railway Temperance Union. This movement receives much practical encouragement from railway directors and chief officers, and an active propaganda is carried on. In some places the local Temperance Union provides a Temperance Institute where the men employed at a station or in a goods yard can take their meals in comfort or spend their leisure time.

The present membership (1911) of the Temperance Union in connection with the London and North-Western Railway Company is 22,172, spread over 19 districts. The members of the same union in 1905 numbered only 4777.

Thrift in the railway service is facilitated by means of savings banks. One of these, the Great Western Railway Savings Bank, states in its nineteenth annual report that in 1910 it had 6385 depositors, who paid in a total of £109,166, drew out £69,828 and had £495,504 to their credit at the end of the year. The bank pays 3½ per cent on deposits up to £1000.

Nor are still higher things overlooked. For over forty years it has been customary for workers in the Midland Railway locomotive department at Derby to meet in one of their mess-rooms at breakfast-time, and, while having their meal, take part in a short religious service conducted by one of their number, a harmonium being provided as an accompaniment to the singing. On the day preceding the Christmas holidays the service is devoted entirely to Christmas carols or appropriate anthems.

A distinct advantage offered by the railway service is that, subject to the ability and good conduct of the individual, employment once obtained with a railway company offers a tolerable assurance of permanent and regular work. Railway companies do not run the same risk of becoming bankrupt, and of having to wind up their business, that ordinary commercial companies do, and though slackness of work may, indeed, lead to unavoidable reductions of staff, or to reduced time, in the locomotive and carriage works, the full staff will be required on the railway itself to keep it going, whatever the amount of traffic. Should the traffic fall off, and become non-remunerative, it is the shareholders who will suffer rather than the railway servants engaged in the running of trains.

This fact is of the greater importance because there may be in the railway service certain actual disadvantages, thus referred to in the " Report of the Departmental Committee on Railway Agreements and Amalgamations," issued in May, 1911 :—

" The contention of the railway servants as to the specialisation of their industry and the peculiar difficulty they find in changing their employment has a substantial foundation as regards many classes of railway servants. Men leaving one railway can seldom rely upon obtaining employment on another, except in the lower grades, as the companies usually have their own men waiting promotion. The value of a railway servant often consists largely in a special skill which is of no worth in other employments."

On the other hand, the Departmental Committee recognise that " one of the main inducements to compete for admission to the railway services is the strong presumption of the permanence of employment during good behaviour " ; and they further say that " while it would seem that the rates of pay to all ranks in the railway service do not compare unfavourably with those given in other commercial and industrial occupations, the railway companies undoubtedly profit in the quality of their services by the large range of selection they enjoy owing to the competition for situations under them."

On the subject of railwaymen's wages, various considerations arise which tend to make any general assertions, or even carefully prepared " averages " in respect thereto, of little real value.

The range of employment, from unskilled to highly skilled, is so great in the railway world that to lump together all the different grades, and then strike a so-called " average," which gives too high a figure for one large body of men and too low a figure for another, must needs be far from satisfactory.

General averages are further reduced by the inclusion therein of a large number of boys. The table given on pages 405–6 shows that the total number of railway servants employed on December 31, 1910, was 608,750 ; but in this total there are no fewer than 43,584 boys (including signal-box lads), and their wages, as boys, must needs reduce the average of the wages paid to the adults. If, for example, we add together the six shillings a week paid to a boy of fourteen or fifteen employed as engine-cleaner and the thirty shillings a week paid to a certain grade of signalmen, we get an " average " of eighteen shillings a week for the two ; but no one could argue that this result would give a real idea of actual conditions.

Then the average for the United Kingdom is below the average for England and Wales because of the inclusion in the former of the wages paid in Ireland, where the scale is distinctly lower than is the case of England and Wales ; whilst the inclusion in the figures for England and Wales of the wages for numerous small and none too prosperous lines gives a general average below what would be the actual average on the lines of the leading English companies.

Subject to these considerations, I reproduce from the Board of Trade " Report on Changes in Rates and Wages and Hours of Labour in the United Kingdom, in 1910," two tables which give the average weekly earnings of railwaymen in (1) the United Kingdom, and (2) various parts of the United Kingdom separately. The figures are based on information supplied by twenty-seven railway companies, employing over 90 per cent of the total number of railway servants in the United Kingdom ; they relate to workpeople employed in the coaching, goods, locomotive and engineers' departments, exclusive of clerical staff and salaried officers ; and they refer to actual earnings (including overtime), and not simply to rates of wages. The tables are as follows :—

I. UNITED KINGDOM

Period to which the figures relate. First week in December:—	Number employed in selected week.	Amount paid in wages in the selected week. £	Average weekly earnings per head. s. d.
1901 . . .	440,557	551,114	25 0¼
1902 . . .	448,429	559,179	24 11¼
1903 . . .	448,321	557,819	24 10½
1904 . . .	445,577	557,820	25 0½
1905 . . .	449,251	568,338	25 3½
1906 . . .	457,942	582,207	25 5¼
1907 . . .	478,690	618,304	25 10
1908 . . .	459,120	574,059	25 0
1909 . . .	459,444	582,782	25 4½
1910 . . .	463,019	596,342	25 9

II. ENGLAND AND WALES, SCOTLAND AND IRELAND

Year.	ENGLAND AND WALES.		SCOTLAND.		IRELAND.	
	Number Employed.	Average weekly earnings per Head. s. d.	Number Employed.	Average weekly earnings per Head. s. d.	Number Employed.	Average weekly earnings per Head. s. d.
1901 .	378,121	25 6¼	43,710	23 1½	18,726	19 5
1902 .	383,883	25 5¼	45,240	23 1¼	19,306	19 3¼
1903 .	384,465	25 4½	44,922	22 11½	18,934	19 5
1904 .	380,610	25 7	45,216	23 1¼	19,751	19 1½
1905 .	384,321	25 10¼	45,399	23 3¾	19,531	19 2¾
1906 .	391,661	25 11½	46,407	23 4¼	19,874	19 9½
1907 .	412,804	26 4¾	46,416	23 5½	19,470	19 8¼
1908 .	395,271	25 6¼	44,809	22 8½	19,040	19 8¼
1909 .	394,928	25 10½	45,147	23 3¾	19,369	19 11
1910 .	397,715	26 3½	46,105	23 3	19,199	20 7

Whatever the precise amount of the remuneration received, allowance must be made for various subsidiary advantages of the railway service.

Free uniforms or clothes are given to various grades, the recipients thereof on one of the leading lines including station-masters, district police and traffic inspectors, platform inspectors, yard inspectors, passenger guards, ticket collectors, foremen porters and foremen parcel porters, foremen shunters, brakesmen, shunters, signalmen, parcel porters, vanmen and boys, porters, sergeants and policemen, telegraph messengers, sleeping-car attendants and corridor attendants. Passenger guards, for example, get a summer coat and vest every two years, winter coat and vest every two years, summer trousers every year, winter trousers every year, topcoat every three years, mackintosh every four years (main line) or every three years (local line), belt (main line) when required, cap every year, and two neckties every year. The amount which a man saves by the supply of this free clothing naturally adds proportionately to the actual value of his position.

On many of the lines the companies have provided for their workers a considerable amount of cottage accommodation, with gardens and allotments, charging rentals which yield little more than a nominal return on the capital expenditure.

The Glasgow and South-Western Railway Company have organised, at Cockerhill, a model village for the accommodation of the principal section of the locomotive staff employed in the engine-sheds there. Purchase of land and construction of buildings involved the company in an expenditure of £70,000. To-day the village has a total population of 700 persons. Each tenant gets three large rooms and a kitchen for a rental of £13 a year, *plus* local rates, which amount to about 17s. a year. Attached to every house is a plot of ground where the tenant can grow his own vegetables, or cultivate his favourite flowers. The centre of social life in the village is the Railway Institute, a commodious building erected by the company, and still maintained to a certain extent at their cost. Administration of the affairs of this Institute is entrusted to a General Committee of thirty-two of the tenants, elected annually, and having different sub-committees, each of which takes charge of a particular phase of the work. The Institute has a hall (reserved on Sundays for religious meetings of a strictly non-sectarian character), reading and recreation-rooms, library and baths. The village also has a fire brigade, a children's savings bank, and a committee for the organisation of ambulance work.

A rent club, the subscription to which is one penny a week, ensures for its members the continued payment of their rent in the event of their being absent from work on account of sickness. Still another advantage offered to the tenants is

that of a season ticket between Cockerhill and Glasgow for
themselves or for members of their household at the nominal
charge of five shillings a year.

One of the latest developments in connection with the
housing of railway companies' workers has been on the Great
Eastern Railway, the chairman of the company, Lord Claud
Hamilton, saying at the half-yearly meeting on July 28,
1911 :—

" We have been asked by a portion of our staff to do something for them in respect of cottages, for although in some
districts they can obtain adequate lodging, in other districts
it is exceedingly difficult to obtain, at a reasonable rent, the
decent accommodation which they require. Now that our
prospects are improving, we have settled as from the 1st of
July to spend £10,000 a year on cottages for our workmen.
It is not a large sum, but it is as much as we can afford, and
I must tell you we can only expect to get, at the most, 2½
per cent interest on that money. But although that is a low
rate of interest, and not remunerative, the extra comfort,
satisfaction and happiness which these men and their families
will derive from healthy and adequate accommodation repays
us, I am sure, indirectly, over and over again in their more
willing service to their employers."

Railwaymen have, again, exceptional opportunities for
getting cheap holidays. In addition to the regular holidays
given to members of the salaried staff, most of the grades
of the wages staff who have a certain period of service to
their credit get from three to six days' holiday a year, with
pay. In some cases the railway company provide special
trains enabling their employees in some railway colony—
Swindon, for example—to take a holiday *en masse*, the said
colony becoming, temporarily, a deserted village. The free
passes given to members of the staff are sometimes available
for travel over the lines of other companies as well.

The concession, also, to railway servants of what are
known as " privilege tickets " enables them and their
families to travel at exceptionally low rates. These tickets
are granted so freely that the number issued by one company alone during the course of a single year has been nearly
800,000.

Provision for the railwayman's old age is assured by superannuation funds in the case of the salaried staff and by pension funds in the case of the wages staff.

The whole question in regard to the standing of these funds was investigated by a Departmental Committee which was appointed by the Board of Trade in 1908, and presented its report [Cd. 5349] in 1910. It was the position, more especially, of the superannuation funds that gave rise to the uneasiness leading up to the appointment of this Committee. The earliest of the said funds was started by the London and North-Western Railway Company in 1853, and other companies followed the example thus set, the Committee reporting on, altogether, fifteen superannuation funds brought to their notice. At first no doubt was felt as to the stability of the funds ; but when the railway companies, with a view to maintaining the efficiency of the service, enforced the retirement of officers at the age of sixty-five, or in some cases at the otherwise optional age of sixty, heavier demands were made on the funds at the same time that the benefits were being increased. Actuarial investigations disclosed substantial deficiencies, and some of the companies sought to cover these by abandoning actuarial valuations altogether and guaranteeing payment of claims out of their revenue, this being in addition to the ordinary contributions which, in one form or another, all the companies were making to the funds. A certain want of uniformity followed, and the Committee now made various recommendations in regard to the future working both of the fifteen superannuation funds and of seventeen pension funds applying to the wages staff.

There is no need here to enter into the details of the actual or proposed arrangements. Suffice it, therefore, to point to the existence of these funds, with their accumulated reserves of close on £11,000,000, as designed to assure the future of nearly 300,000 railwaymen, over and above whatever salary or wage they may receive while in active employment.

The Railway Guards' Universal Friendly Society was established in 1849 to encourage thrift and to provide, among other benefits, permanent pay for life to disabled members and annuities for the widows and orphans of deceased members. The total amount expended in relief down to the end of 1910 was over £358,000, and there were then 250 members and widows in receipt of life allowances amounting to £4758 per annum.

Further provision either for railwaymen themselves in times of distress or for their widows and orphans is made through various organisations which are supported by the contributions alike of railway servants, of the railway companies and of the general public.

At the head of these excellent bodies stands the Railway Benevolent Institution, which attained its jubilee in 1908. The objects in view, as summarised by Lord Claud Hamilton at the fifty-third annual dinner on May 4, 1911, are : (1) To grant permanent annuities to railway officers and servants in distressed circumstances ; (2) to grant permanent pensions to widows in similar circumstances ; (3) to educate and maintain orphan children between six and fifteen years of age, and then give them a start in life ; (4) to give by gratuities and by contingent annuities temporary assistance until permanent relief can be secured from the funds of the Institution ; (5) to grant gratuities from the casualty fund to injured servants and to widows of deceased servants ; (6) to enable officers and servants to insure their lives in the best approved companies on special terms ; and (7) to relieve distress whether arising among subscribers or non-subscribers.

No fewer than 157,000 railwaymen of all classes are subscribers in one form or another to the funds of the Institution, which, apart from amounts given as gratuities, conferred its benefits in 1910 on 2,672 annuitants and children, the total outgoings for the year under all heads being £55,396. To particularise only one phase of this varied activity, the number of children — mainly orphans of railwaymen killed in the service—who have been educated in the great Railway Orphanage at Derby (a branch of the Institution) has been over 2000.

Another leading railway charity, the United Kingdom Railway Officers and Servants' Association, founded in 1861 to grant assistance in time of distress and necessity to railway officers and servants, their widows and orphans, held its jubilee festival on April 28, 1911, when Viscount Castlereagh, M.P., who presided, announced that since the establishment of the Association the relief afforded had been as follows :—

	£	s.	d.
Annuitants	51,233	13	0
Sickness	100,411	7	6
Widows and members, at death .	58,956	0	0
Orphans	4,595	3	0
Special grants	9,390	11	0
Total . .	224,586	14	6

Of great advantage, also, to railway workers is the Railway-men's Convalescent Home, opened at Herne Bay, Kent, in 1901, with its recent extension in the form of a similar home at Leasome Castle, Wallasey, Cheshire, to which, by permission of King George, has been given the title of " The King Edward VII Memorial Convalescent Home for Railwaymen."

The London and South-Western Railway Servants' Orphanage was originally opened at Clapham, in 1886, for children whose fathers, at the time of their death, were in the employ of the railway company. Since July, 1909, it has been located in a commodious range of buildings erected at Woking, Surrey, for the purpose. From the time the orphanage was first opened over 400 children have been admitted to its benefits.

Thanks to a generous benefaction left by the late Mr F. W. Webb, locomotive superintendent of the London and North-Western Railway Company, the railway colony at Crewe is acquiring an orphanage which will accommodate twenty girls and twenty boys, the construction cost being estimated at about £16,000, while a further sum of £35,000 will be available for the purposes of the endowment of what has, appropriately, been named " the Webb Orphanage." In appreciation of the value of the services rendered by Mr Webb to the company, and as an indication of their sympathy with the institution, the directors of the London and North-Western Railway Company have subscribed £1000 towards the funds of the orphanage.

In addition to such support as they may render, directly or indirectly, to the recognised railway beneficent organisations, the railway companies of the United Kingdom contribute to various other institutions and associations, of various character, not directly controlled by them, and not for the exclusive benefit of their servants. Such contributions are reported to the Board of Trade, which issues an annual

return on the subject. Among those for 1910 were the
following :—

	£	s.	d
Hospitals, infirmaries and dispensaries . . .	7,832	10	6
Convalescent homes and nursing associations . .	440	17	0
Ambulance, medical, surgical aid and truss societies .	308	1	0
Benevolent and friendly societies, orphan asylums, etc.	790	19	0
Mechanics', seamen's and fishermen's institutes .	1,278	14	0
Church funds	1,365	17	8
Missions	340	6	6
Schools and technical institutes	1,137	18	0

These contributions are made by the railway companies
not so much, presumably, from motives of ordinary philan-
thropy, but in return, more or less, for benefits derived, or
that might be derived, from the institutions in question by
members of their staffs.

Adding these further subsidiary advantages to the educational, social and recreative facilities offered by the institutes,
societies and clubs already spoken of, it will be seen that there
is more to be taken into account in regard to the railway
service in general than the question of wages alone, and
especially so when the statements concerning wages are based
on " averages."

Having seen what are the advantages of the railway service,
we may pass on to consider some of its possible disadvantages.

A return issued by the Board of Trade in August, 1911,
gives the latest available information as to the once much-
discussed question of railway servants' hours of labour.
The special interest in this subject lies, of course, in the fact
that if men engaged in the movement of trains work excessive
hours the risk of accident is increased ; and the Board of
Trade are authorised, under the Act of 1889, to call for
particulars of the hours of labour of railway servants.

At one time the returns published were presented in such
a way as to make the position appear much worse than really
was the case, even after allowing for unavoidable delays from
fog, snowstorms, floods, fluctuations in traffic, and breakdowns
or other unforeseen mishaps which have been, and must needs
be, contributory causes of prolonged hours of duty. Thus,
if an engine-driver, having taken a train to some distant
station, returned home comfortably seated in a third-class
carriage, he counted in the official returns as being on duty,

as though he were still undergoing the strain of driving the engine instead of being occupied, perhaps, in smoking his pipe, or having a doze.

Following on protests by the railway companies, the returns are now published in a form less open to criticism, while the agitation raised has also led the companies to make further efforts to prevent the occurrence of excessive hours of labour as far as possible. The return for May, 1911, dealing with 109,041 servants in certain grades (guards, brakesmen, enginemen, signalmen, examiners), who worked during that month a total of 2,740,693 days, shows that the number of days on which the men were on duty for periods exceeding twelve hours by one hour and upwards amounted to 14,813, or only ·54 per cent of the total days worked.

One of the greatest drawbacks in the railway service lies in the risks of accident. The extent of these risks is shown by the General Report of the Board of Trade on Accidents on Railways of the United Kingdom during 1910.

From this I find that the number of railway servants killed in " train accidents " in 1910 was nine, and the number injured was 113. Of these, eight were killed and 109 were injured in the work of running trains ; and the proportions of these last-mentioned figures to the total number (76,327) of engine-drivers, firemen and guards employed on December 31, 1910, were : killed, one in 9541 ; injured, one in 700. Considering that the number of miles run by trains on the railways of the United Kingdom in 1910 was 423,221,000, the figures given as to injuries or fatalities to railway servants through actual train accidents do not constitute a bad record. They suggest, rather, both the extreme care with which the railway servants concerned discharge their duty and the effectiveness of the precautions taken in the interests of themselves as well as of the travelling public.

Excluding train accidents, the numbers of accidents to railway servants due to the " movement of trains and railway vehicles " in the same year were : killed, 368 ; injured 4587. The number of railway servants exposed to danger from the movement of railway vehicles being 331,296, the proportion of accidents to number employed was : killed, one in 900 ; injured, one in 72.

When these last-mentioned figures in regard to injured are

compared with the averages for earlier years, there appears to be a substantial increase ; but a " Note " thereon is given in the official returns to the following effect : " An order of the Board of Trade on the 21st December, 1906, required non-fatal accidents to be reported whenever they caused absence from ordinary work for a whole day (instead of absence preventing five hours' work on any of the next three days). This alteration caused a large apparent increase in the number of non-fatal accidents in 1907 and later years." The details in regard to the killed afford, therefore, safer guidance if one wishes to see whether the various appliances, precautions and regulations adopted by the railway companies to ensure the greater safety of those of their servants who are exposed to danger from the movement of railway vehicles are having the desired effect. Turning to Table X in the official returns, I extract therefrom the following figures :—

YEAR.					PROPORTION OF KILLED TO NUMBERS EMPLOYED.
1885–1894 (average)	.	.	.	.	I in 501
1895–1904 ,,	.	.	.	.	I ,, 665
1905–1909 ,,	.	.	.	.	I ,, 879
1910	.	.	.	.	I ,, 900

Here, therefore, we have distinct evidence of improvement in the element of risk in railway operation.

A third group of accidents to which railway servants are liable relates to those that arise in the handling of goods, in attending to engines at rest, or in other ways not connected with the movement of trains or of railway vehicles. Here the figures for 1910 are : Killed, 36 ; injured, 20,305. " The number of injured is large," says the return, " but the proportion of serious injuries is smaller than it is in the case of railway accidents proper, and it will be seen that the proportion of killed to injured is relatively low." The proportion of killed, in this third group, to the average number of railway servants exposed to risk was one in 12,546, and the proportion of injured was one in 22. A considerable number of accidents in railway goods sheds and warehouses which at one time were included in the returns of accidents in factories are now included in the returns of railway accidents.

Liability to accident, whether grave or slight, lends additional importance to the encouragement given to railwaymen by their companies to acquire a knowledge of " first aid " and general ambulance work. Ambulance corps or classes are now not only general but highly popular throughout the railway system. Instruction is given by qualified teachers ; certificates, vouchers, medallions or labels are presented to those who pass the examinations held, and not only do competitions for money or other prizes take place between teams representing the various districts of a single company's system, but an Inter-Railway Challenge Shield is annually competed for by the picked experts of the various companies, the winning of this shield being regarded as conferring a great honour on those who achieve the victory for their company.

I have here sought to give a comprehensive survey of the railway service, as a national industry, alike from its economic and from its human side, conveying some idea— even if wholly inadequate—of its extent and widespread ramifications, and showing the various influences, educational, social and otherwise, that are eminently calculated both to create a " railway type " and to give to the service characteristics that distinguish it in many respects from any other of our national industries.

While not being, perhaps, actually an ideal industry—and there are very few workers, of any rank, who would be prepared to admit that their occupation in life was absolutely free from drawbacks—the railway service offers, as we have seen, many advantages. It is, in fact, really a " service," and not simply a means of employment. One might regard it as the equivalent of a civil service operated on commercial lines. Workers in all of the many classes or grades " enter the service," as they are accustomed to say, when they are young, and they generally do so with the idea of spending their lives in it, and retiring on superannuation allowance or a pension in their old age.

Railway managers, too, want workers who come to stay. In the United States women typists are being gradually got rid of on the railway because they so often retire at the end of two or three years and get married, the experience of office work they have gained in that time being thus lost to the company. Consequently American railway managers are now showing a preference for male workers who will regard the service in the light of a future career rather than in that of a temporary employment.

That the railway service is a popular one is shown by two facts : (1) the invariably large surplus of candidates over available vacancies ; and (2) the long-service records of many of the railway workers.

In regard to the former of these points, it will suffice to say that the chairman of one of the leading English railway companies has stated that in 1906 the number of applicants for appointments on the staff of his company alone in excess of the number for whom places could be found was over 19,000.

As regards long service, instances of from forty to fifty years' work for one and the same railway company are so common that they hardly call even for passing mention. More exceptional was the case of the worker on the Great Western whose father had served the company for forty-one years, and who himself retired at the end of forty-two years, leaving a son who had then been with the company twenty-three years—a total of 106 years for one family, during three generations.

In another instance four generations employed successively on the Great Western showed a total of 147 years ; but even this record is surpassed by that of a Cardiff family. The founder of the dynasty joined the Great Western in 1840. He remained with the company forty-two years, and left with them two sons, of whom one served forty-five years, and the other forty-two years. Each of these two sons had five boys, and all ten followed the example of fathers and grandfather in becoming servants of the same company, keeping their positions for periods ranging from six to thirty years. The fourth generation is represented by four members, one of whom has already been with the company for over ten years. The total service of those members of the family who were still working on the Great Western a year or two ago was 147 years, and the aggregate for the four generations was then over 800 years. Each of the workers concerned has been employed in the locomotive department.

Notwithstanding the general popularity of the railway service, agitations and strikes have occurred from time to time ; though down to 1907 most of these arose in connection with questions of conditions of labour in regard to particular lines of railway.

In 1907 an agitation was promoted by the Amalgamated Society of Railway Servants in favour of what was called a " National All-Grades Programme " of demands for higher wages, reduced hours, etc. ; and there was a further demand that the negotiations in respect thereto should be carried on through the officers of the Amalgamated Society of Railway Servants. The companies declined to grant the concessions asked for in the " Programme," alleging that to do so would involve them in a wholly impracticable increase in their working expenses. It was subsequently stated that acceptance of the " Programme " would have increased the expenditure of the companies by between £6,000,000 and £7,000,000 per annum ; that the cost to the London and North-Western Railway Company alone would have exceeded £500,000 per annum, equal to $1\frac{1}{4}$ per cent of the company's dividend ; that on the London and South-Western it would have been equal to a two per cent dividend on the ordinary stock ; and so on with other companies in like proportion.

In the result the demand for the concession of the " Programme " became subordinate to the demand of the A.S.R.S. for " recognition " ; but this, again, was refused by the railway companies on the ground, not alone that the membership of the society included only a minority of the men qualified to join but, also, and more especially, because " recognition," involving the carrying on of negotiations through the union leaders, would, it was argued, lower the standard of discipline in a service where considerations of the public interests, and especially of the public safety, made it a matter of paramount importance that a high standard of discipline should be maintained.

Threats of a general railway strike caused much alarm, and led the Government to intervene. The negotiations carried on at the Board of Trade were based mainly on the possibility of arranging some system of conciliation by means of which further disputes would be avoided ; and eventually a fourfold scheme was arranged, comprising, in the case of each company accepting it, (1) consideration of applications by officers of the department concerned ; (2) sectional conciliation boards; (3) a central conciliation board, and (4) the eventual calling in of an arbitrator if the matters in dispute should still be undecided.

Forty-six companies adopted the scheme. The conciliation boards were elected; agreements were in many instances arranged as the result of their proceedings; and, where no settlement could be arrived at by the boards, arbitration was resorted to. Dissatisfaction with the course of procedure and its results was, however, expressed from time to time more especially by members and officers of the Amalgamated Society of Railway Servants; and such dissatisfaction became acute during the prevalence of the " labour unrest " which spread throughout the country in the summer and early autumn of 1911, affecting, more especially, the various transport services. Joint action was now taken by the Amalgamated Society of Railway Servants, the Associated Society of Locomotive Engineers and Firemen, the General Railway Workers' Union and the United Pointsmen and Signalmen's Society.

At the outset attempts had been made to show that the railwaymen had some genuine grievances against the conciliation boards on account of their " slowness," etc. ; but it soon became apparent that the trouble was mainly based on fresh demands for " recognition." On Tuesday, August 15, representatives of the four societies issued from Liverpool an ultimatum in which they offered the railway companies " twenty-four hours to decide whether they were prepared to meet immediately members of those societies to negotiate the basis of settlement of the matters in dispute " ; and they added : " In the event of this offer being refused, there will be no alternative than to respond to the demands now being made for a national railway stoppage."

The railway companies expressed their firm resolve to adhere to the principle of conciliation, and on the following Thursday the " signal " was given for a general railway strike. Only about one-third of the railway workers responded, and, though great and very grave inconvenience and loss were caused in some parts of the country, there was (owing, in part, to the calling out by the Government of a large body of troops to protect the railway operations) no such " paralysis " of the railway traffic in general as had been threatened, while public opinion was distinctly unsympathetic towards the strikers.

Meanwhile active steps had been taken by the Government to effect a settlement, and late on the Saturday night (August 19) an agreement was drawn up and signed by the parties to the negotiations.

Under this agreement the men were to return to work forthwith ; pending questions were to be referred to the conciliation boards, while the Government undertook to appoint, at once, a Royal Commission to investigate the working of the conciliation and arbitration scheme, and report what changes, if any, were desirable with a view to the prompt and satisfactory settlement of differences. It was further announced that the Government had given an assurance to the railway companies that they would propose to Parliament in the Session of 1912 legislation providing that an increase in the cost of labour due to the improvement of conditions of the staff would be a valid justification for a reasonable general increase of charges within the legal *maxima*, if challenged, under the Act of 1894.

Two statements, giving the result of the negotiations, were issued by the Board of Trade on the night of August 19. In one of these it was announced that Mr Claughton (chairman of the London and North-Western Railway Company) and Sir Guy Granet (general manager of the Midland Railway Company), who represented the railway interests at the Conference, had " stated that the recommendations of the Commission would be loyally accepted by the railway companies, even though they be averse to the contention of the companies on any question of representation, and, should a settlement be effected, any trace of ill-will which might have arisen during the strike would certainly be effaced." In the other of these official announcements it was said : " Assurances have been given by both parties that they will accept the findings of the Commission." The statements were repeated in " The Board of Trade Labour Gazette " for September, 1911.

The Royal Commission, which consisted of five members, viz. Sir David Harrel (chairman), Sir Thomas R. Ratcliffe Ellis, Mr Arthur Henderson, M.P., Mr C. G. Beale and Mr John Burnett, held twenty-five sittings, between August 28 and October 3, for the purpose of taking evidence, the witnesses examined by them during this period including thirty-four on behalf of the various railway workers' unions, ten non-unionist workers and twenty - three representatives of the railway companies.

The case presented on behalf of the railwaymen's unions was, in effect : (1) that the working of the conciliation and arbitration scheme had in various respects been very un-satisfactory, and changes therein or alternatives thereto were recommended, though in regard to the details of these changes and alternatives the witnesses did not all agree among themselves ; (2) that " recognition " of the unions, allowing of the labour unions officials—with, as was said, their " trained and experienced minds "—taking part in the negotiations with the railway companies, was essential to full justice being done to the men, who were either not competent to state their own claims or might have their position in the service prejudiced ; (3) that such recogni-tion would be in the interests of industrial peace because of the increased powers of the unions in enforcing the mainten-ance of any bargains that were made ; (4) that discipline on the railways would be strengthened if the men were confident that there would be an impartial investigation of their com-plaints ; and (5) that, as the principle of recognition was accepted in other great industries, the railway companies were not justified in refusing it to their own men.

On the other side it was contended (1) that much of the disappointment felt at the results of the awards—which had, nevertheless, led to substantial concessions being made—was due to the unreasonable hopes raised by the " National Programme," and that, although certain modifications might be made in the conciliation scheme, the principle there-of was sound, while the companies had made a " tremen-dous departure " by themselves proposing, in 1907, in the interests of peace, to concede the principle of arbitration, which involved the " revolutionary " step of taking from the directors the power of deciding what the rates of payment and the hours of labour of their workmen were to be; (2) that the four unions concerned still included only about one-fourth of the men, and that " recognition " of them would inevitably lead to interference with questions of management and discipline, without—as shown by the experiences of the North-Eastern Railway, where " recognition " had not prevented the occurrence of repeated disputes—offering any guarantee for peace, while a partial strike on certain of the Irish lines during the sittings of the Royal Commission was pointed to as showing that the union officials were unable to control their members ; (3) that the allegations as to railwaymen being unable or afraid to present their case to their own companies were unfounded, and that the real object aimed at in demanding " recognition " of the union officials was to coerce non-unionists into joining the unions which, with their increased membership, would then be in a better position to force the railways to agree to all demands ; (4) that if the companies were compelled to accept " recognition," with all the risks it would involve, they should, at the same time, be relieved of their present responsibilities in respect to the public safety and public interests ; and (5) that no analogy, in regard to " recognition," could be drawn between the railways, the continuous operation of which was essential to the wellbeing of the community, and ordinary commercial undertakings, which could suspend their working with only a limited degree of inconvenience to the public, or none at all.

The Commissioners, in their report, issued October 20, 1911, declared that in their opinion it was of the utmost importance that the initial stage of conference between the men and the companies—apt to be regarded as simply a preliminary to the later stages under the settlement scheme—should not only be maintained but facilitated. They recommended the abolition, as " redundant," of the central boards and the reference to the sectional boards of " any matter dealing with hours, wages, or conditions of service, except questions of, or bearing upon, discipline and management." Each sectional board should have a chairman selected from a panel to be constituted by the Board of Trade, but such chairman should be called on to act (virtually as arbitrator) only in the event of the sectional board being unable to agree. The men should be free to combine in the same person the duties of men's secretary and advocate at all meetings of the Board, and be at liberty to appoint to such post " any suitable person, whether an employee of the company or a person from outside " ; though this arrangement was " not intended to prevent the men from obtaining the services of a special advocate before the chairman."

Much dissatisfaction with the report—and mainly so on account of what was regarded as a wholly inadequate extension of the principle of recognition—was expressed by the men's leaders and endorsed at meetings of the men's societies, where demands were made for a general strike on a greater scale than before, while the leaders repudiated any suggestion that they had given a pledge to accept the findings of the Royal Commission of Inquiry. A new National Programme of improved conditions was put forward, but simultaneously therewith various of the leading railway companies announced revisions of their rates of wages as applying to the lower grades among their workers.

In the case of the Great Western Railway Company it was reported that between 20,000 and 30,000 men would benefit from the concessions, the immediate cost of which to the company would be £56,000 per annum, with an eventual cost, at the end of three or four years, of £78,000 per annum. The London and North-Western Company announced increases amounting in the aggregate to £80,000 a year, these being an addition to increases already made, under the arbitrator's award, at a cost to the company of £70,000 a year. The Midland Railway Company gave notice that from November 3 the minimum rate of pay for all adult members of their staff would be 22s. per week if employed in London, 20s. per week in certain large towns, and 19s. per week at all other places, the actual advances thus made to individual workers ranging from 1s. to 4s. the week.

Material concessions were also announced by the Great Central and the Caledonian, and intimation was given by other companies that they had the matter under consideration. All these concessions were, however, apparently disregarded by leaders of the extremest section among the men, who declared, in effect, that they would be satisfied with nothing short of recognition.

In the week ending November 4 representatives of the men's unions held a four-days' conference in London to consider what action should be taken, and there would seem to have been some hope on their part that, influenced by the threat of a further general strike, the Government would exercise its influence with a view to inducing representatives of the railway companies to meet the other signatories of the August agreement and discuss with them the terms of the report. On November 3 the Prime Minister, Mr Buxton and Sir George Askwith did confer with selected representatives of the companies at 10 Downing Street. No official announcement was made as to the result, but this was evidently well indicated by the following statement in " The Times " of November 4 :—

" We understand that the attitude of the directors of the railways of the country collectively is that, while they are prepared to carry out to the full the whole of the recommendations of the Inquiry Commission, they are not prepared to go any further."

Later in the same day the joint executive committee of the railway unions informed the Press that they had decided to take a ballot of their members—the papers to be returnable by December 5—on the question as to whether or not they were prepared to accept the findings of the Royal Commission and, also, " to withdraw their labour in favour of the recognition of trade unions and of a programme of all railwaymen," to be agreed upon by members of the joint executive committee.

Whatever may be the final outcome of all these controversies, the position in regard to the troubles both of 1907 and 1911 has obviously been most materially, if not, indeed, mainly, influenced by questions of trade union recognition which do not necessarily cast any reflection on the railway service itself, or detract from it as being one of the most important, most popular and most sought after of our national industries.

CHAPTER XXIX

TRAMWAYS, MOTOR-BUSES AND RAILLESS ELECTRIC TRACTION

In previous chapters I have shown that the first great highway for the citizens of London passing from one part of the capital to another was the River Thames ; that the livelihood of the watermen became imperilled by the competition successively of private carriages, hackney coaches, and cabriolets, or " cabs " ; and that these, in turn, had afterwards to face the competition of omnibuses. A still further development, leading to competition with the omnibuses, was brought about by the re-introduction of the tramway, for the purposes of street transport.

It was in the United States that street tramways first came into vogue, and it was by an American, George Francis Train, that the pioneer tramway of this type in England was laid at Birkenhead at the end of the '50's. A few other short lines followed, and some were put down—without authority—in certain parts of London, only, however, to be condemned as a nuisance on account of the hindrance to other traffic. It was not until 1868 that lines laid in Liverpool secured public favour for the innovation. Fresh tramways were laid in London between 1869 and 1871, and others followed in Glasgow, Edinburgh, Dublin and elsewhere.

All the early lines were operated by horses ; but various expedients were resorted to with the idea both of obtaining greater speed and of carrying more persons at comparatively less cost. Among these expedients were steam locomotives and underground cables, the latter for cars furnished with a grip attachment conveying to them the movement of the cables, as operated by machinery at a central depôt. The greatest impetus to the street tramway system came, however, with the application of electricity as the motive power.

The first line opened on the " trolley " system of overhead

453

wires, conveying electric current to the cars, was in Kansas City in 1884. Electric tramways were tried in Leeds in 1891, and the system was afterwards adopted in many other towns. Underground conduit and surface-contact systems were also employed, with a view to avoiding overhead wires, to which widespread objection was, especially at first, entertained ; but the latter system has been the one generally adopted.

Development of the tramway system in England was slow on account, not of any lack of enterprise on the part of business men, but of the discouraging nature of tramway legislation.

Just about the time when the original horse tramways began to come into vogue certain local authorities were cherishing strong grievances against the gas and water companies in their districts. They complained that the charges of these companies were extortionate and that the terms they asked, when invited to dispose of their undertakings to the said local authorities, were excessive. The companies, nevertheless, controlled the situation because their Parliamentary powers represented a permanent concession, and because, also, they were able to fix their own price in any negotiations upon which they might be invited to enter.

When the introduction of another public service, in the form of street tramways, seemed likely to create still another " monopoly," it was thought desirable to prevent the tramway companies from attaining to the same position as that of the gas and water companies. Powers were accordingly granted to enable the local authorities, if they so desired, to acquire the undertakings, at the end of a certain period, on terms which would be satisfactory to themselves, at least.

It was motives such as these that inspired some of the main provisions of the Tramways Act of 1870, the full title of which is " An Act to Facilitate the Construction and to Regulate the Working of Tramways " ; though in a statement presented to a Committee on Electrical Legislation of the Institution of Electrical Engineers, in 1902, the late Sir Clifton Robinson, manager of the London United Tramways Company, declared that " if it had been described as an Act to discourage the construction of tramways it would have better described the action of some of its clauses."

The Act did, undoubtedly, confer certain advantages on

tramway promoters, as well as on local authorities, since it abolished the obligation previously devolving upon them to obtain—as in the case of a railway company—a Private Bill in respect to each fresh line they desired to construct. It authorised them to apply, instead, to the Board of Trade for a Provisional Order which, on its formal confirmation by Parliament, would have all the force of a Private Act. In this way the procedure was both simplified and rendered less costly.

On the other hand, the Act of 1870 laid down (1) that the assent of the local and road authorities to a new line of tramway should be obtained ; though where the assent of authorities in respect to two-thirds of the mileage was secured the Board of Trade might dispense with that of any other objecting authority ; (2) that the frontagers were also to have a power of veto ; (3) that the original concession should be granted for a period of twenty-one years only ; and (4) that at the end of such period, or at the end of any subsequent period of seven years, the local authorities should have the option of acquiring the tramway at the " then value " of the plant, without any allowance for compulsory purchase, goodwill, prospective profits or other similar consideration.

So long as these provisions applied to horse tramways only, the companies may not have found them specially oppressive, inasmuch as there was still a prospect of their being able to make a profit within the twenty-one-year period before they were compulsorily bought out at " scrap-iron " rates, while they could expect to realise the value of their stock of horses ; though, in effect, the statutory obligations meant, even then, that towards the end of their tenure the tramway company did not spend a single shilling on the line more than was absolutely necessary to keep it in working order until the day of their eviction arrived, generally grudging even a coat of paint for the cars and refraining from any avoidable labour on the roadway. Individuals, and especially foreign visitors, unacquainted with the facts of the case, might well have considered some of the old tramway systems a discredit to the country.

When electric traction for tramway operation was introduced, there was a natural expectation on the part of the British public that the tramway companies would adopt it in place of horse traction. The companies were hampered, however, by the Act of 1870, which remained in force though a complete revolution in the conditions of street rail-transport was being brought about.

The substitution of electricity for horse-power meant (1) the provision of power stations, sub-stations and new car depôts ; (2) the fixing of overhead wires, together with fresh track-work, in the streets ; (3) the use of a heavier type of car ; and (4) the running of a much more frequent service, since only under these conditions can an electric tramway possibly be made to pay. All these things involved a very substantial increase in the capital outlay, and companies may well have hesitated to incur so great an expense with the prospect of only a twenty-one years' tenure before them ; while the position was even more hopeless in the case of companies whose tenure had already half expired.

The dissatisfaction of the public when they found that the tramway system of the country was not being brought up to date, and compared most unfavourably with tramway systems abroad, gave to the local authorities an apparent justification both for providing and for operating tramways as a special phase of municipal enterprise. At the time the Act of 1870 was passed it was assumed that, although local authorities might construct or acquire tramways, they would certainly lease them to private companies to operate.[1] In proportion, however, as the movement for municipal enterprise developed, local authorities were the more inclined to operate tramways in addition to owning them. There was no general Act giving them authority so to do, but the difficulty was overcome by the insertion in Local Bills of clauses giving to the local bodies promoting the Bills power to operate their own tramways, the reason advanced being that there were difficulties in the way of leasing the lines to companies on satisfactory conditions.

Matters were not left entirely in the hands of the municipalities, various tramway companies having sought, as their twenty-one years' tenure came to a close, to make such arrangements as would warrant an adaptation of their existing

---

[1] When the Tramways Bill of 1870 was introduced, Mr Shaw Lefevre stated that its underlying principle was to empower local authorities "to construct tramways, but not, of course, work them."

system to electric traction ; while other companies applied for powers to construct new lines or extensions of lines on the same system.   Parliament had certainly sanctioned a longer period of tenure than twenty-one years when the promoters could make an arrangement to this effect with the local authorities concerned ; and it was hardly likely that a company would incur the great expense of constructing an entirely new tramway, with electrical installation and other requirements all complete, unless they had some guarantee of a longer tenure than the statutory period.   But these very factors enabled the local authorities concerned to control the situation ; and their power to exercise this control was made still more complete by the operation of Standing Order No. 22, which applied to Private Bills for tramway schemes requirements similar to those of the Tramways Act as regards the obligation on promoters to obtain the assents of local and road authorities.

These authorities had thus an absolute veto over any new tramway schemes, and such veto might finally rest in the hands of a single local authority, controlling a sparsely populated section of the proposed mileage, yet having, perhaps, the controlling voice in being the one authority whose approval was needed to make up the requisite two-thirds.

There had been some expectation on the part of tramway promoters that the general position would be improved by the Light Railways Act, 1896, many light railways being indistinguishable from tramways.   Under this Act the assent of the local and road authorities is not required, and the frontagers' veto was done away with by it in the case of light railways ; but authority to oppose was given to railway companies, and in practice the Light Railway Commissioners held that they ought not to authorise a tramway as a light railway unless it connected the area of one local authority with another.   For these and other reasons the Act was not so beneficial in regard to tramways as had been anticipated.

In the case of tramway companies it became a matter either of paying to the local authorities the " price " they asked for their assent, or else seeing the schemes fail at the start, without any chance of having them even considered on their merits. How local authorities have used—or abused—the power of control thus possessed by them is suggested by some remarks

made by Mr Emile Garcke in an article published in " The
Times Engineering Supplement " of July 25, 1906, where he
says :—

" The right of veto is exercised not so much with the desire
to destroy a projected enterprise, but rather to exact the
utmost conditions which a promoter will accept sooner than
abandon the project. When a scheme is proceeded with in spite
of these exactions it is taken as evidence that the conditions
imposed have not been exacting enough ; and whenever the
operating company has occasion subsequently to ask the local
authority to approve anything, the company is expected to
offer more than commensurate consideration, although the
object for which the approval is desired may be primarily for
the benefit of the public. All these obstacles imply increased
capital outlay or increased working costs, and perhaps both.
If, notwithstanding these conditions, the company earns a
moderate profit, it is accused of striving only after dividends
to the prejudice of the public. If non-success of the enterprise
follows, then the company is accused of being over-capitalised
and mismanaged, and it has come to be considered an im-
pertinence for a company to offer ever so mild a protest."

On the same subject it is stated in "The Dangers of
Municipal Trading," by Robert P. Porter (1907) :—

" The use of the veto has had disastrous effects on private
enterprise. In many districts it has led to utter stagnation
of personal initiative. Good schemes have been barred by
local authorities out of pure caprice or prejudice. Other
schemes have been allowed to proceed under barely tolerable
conditions ; the undertaking has been crippled from the start
by the high price municipalities have exacted for their consent.
Others, again, have been withdrawn by the promoter because
he found it impossible to agree to the extortionate demands
of the governing bodies."

Mr Porter quotes various authorities who have expressed
strong views on the subject of the veto.

The chairman of the Parliamentary Committee which
considered a scheme of tramways promoted in Scotland said :
" The Committee desire to put on record that in their opinion
the original scheme was a good one, and calculated to be of
much use to the district ; but it has been so mutilated and
loaded with conditions by conflicting interests and the ex-

cessive demands of several local bodies that it now appears to the Committee to be wholly unworkable."

In 1902 Mr Chaplin, at one time President of the Local Government Board, stated that "what local authorities would describe as conditions are regarded by promoters—and very often, no doubt, with good reason—as neither more nor less than blackmail. This has been the subject of great complaint for years, and I do not think I should be going too far if I said that on several occasions it has led to considerable scandals."

Lest these expressions of opinion may be considered unduly severe by any reader unacquainted with the facts, I turn for some definite data to the "Exhibit to Proof of Evidence," handed in by Sir Clifton Robinson to the Royal Commission on London Traffic when he was examined before that body in 1904.[1]

In the early days of his company (the London United), the local authorities, Sir Clifton said, "had not, perhaps, fully recognised their opportunity," and the company got their assents comparatively cheaply under their first Act in 1898.

Two years later the price they had to pay for the assents of local authorities to a group of tramways in the Twickenham, Teddington and Hampton district was £202,000, or £16,000 a mile. The requirements imposed on the company took the form of "wayleaves" and of street improvements, the greater part of the latter being entirely apart from the actual needs of the tramway. The improvements in Heath Road, Twickenham, giving a 45-ft. roadway, cost for properties and works alone some £30,000. A like sum had to be spent in Hampton and Hampton Wick, where the work done included the setting back of the entire frontage of the Royal Deer Park of Bushey.

In 1901 the company sought for powers to construct twelve miles of tramway in Kingston-upon-Thames and neighbourhood. On this occasion the "concessions" wrung from

---

[1] Another of the witnesses was the Right Hon. J. W. Lowther, M.P., at that time Chairman of Committees, and now Speaker of the House of Commons. He assured the Commission that the power of "vetoing" tramways had worked a great deal of mischief. He further declared that the Standing Order had been most improperly used for the purpose of extorting all sorts of terms and conditions from tramway companies, and had subjected them to liabilities and disabilities which were never contemplated by Parliament.

them by the local authorities amounted to £66,000 for street improvements, £20,000 for bridges, and a further £68,000, capitalised value of annual payments for so-called " way-leaves." This made a total of £154,000, or £12,800 per mile, merely for assents to the construction of their lines. The details of the account included a sum of £1500 extorted by an urban district council as " a contribution towards some town improvement, not necessarily on the company's proposed line of route, but anywhere in their district the council might desire."

One item to which the company had to agree in 1902, before they could obtain an Act authorising them to build another thirteen miles of tramway, was the construction at Barnes of an embankment and terrace along the river side. It made a very pleasant promenade, and was certainly an addition to the amenities of the neighbourhood ; but it cost the tramway company £40,000. The " price " of local authorities' assents for these thirteen miles of line worked out thus : Street improvements (properties and works), £72,000 ; Barnes Boulevard, £40,000 ; " wayleaves " (capitalised), £100,000 ; a total of £412,000, or £31,600 per mile.

Altogether, in the four years, 1898–1902, the total expendi-ture of the company on street and bridge improvements in respect to less than fifty miles of tramway amounted to £745,000 ; and although, to a certain extent, the widenings, etc., were necessary for electric tramway purposes, " the bulk of the expenditure under this head," Sir Clifton declared, " was undertaken with a view to conciliate the local authorities, or was forced upon us by them as the ' price of their assents.' " To this £745,000 was to be added £241,000, the capitalised value, at five per cent, of the " wayleaves " the company had also agreed to pay, making a total of £986,500, irrespective altogether of the cost of construction and equipment of the lines.

When, in 1904, the company proposed to construct still another twenty-one miles of tramway in the western suburbs of London, " they recognised their obligations to the local and county authorities," Sir Clifton said, by proposing to undertake street, road and bridge widenings which would have cost them £217,932. They thought this a sufficiently generous " price " to pay for permission to provide the district with improved transport facilities. Instead of being satisfied, the local authorities made demands which would have involved the company in a further expenditure of £642,630, making a total of £860,562. One urban district council included in its demands the construction by the tramway company of public lavatories and a subway. In a district where the company were prepared to spend £30,000 on road improvements the county council demanded a carriageway of forty feet and wood paving throughout six and a half miles of country roads, involving the expenditure of a further £30,000.

Rather than submit to all these exactions the company abandoned their Bill. They had already abandoned sixty miles of proposed tramway extensions " owing," said Sir Clifton, " to the demands or the uncompromising attitude of the local authorities," although many of these lines would have been valuable connections with the existing tramway system, and would have served in no small degree the traffic needs of the districts concerned.

" It is not too much to say," added Sir Clifton Robinson, in concluding his statement, " that instead of giving such proposals sympathetic consideration, if not practical encouragement, the attitude assumed by the average local authority of to-day is one of hostility, inspired by a desire to extort the uttermost farthing from promoters."

In the face of experiences, or the prospect of experiences, such as these, many would-be promoters of tramway enterprise developed a natural reluctance to put their own money, or to try to induce other people to put theirs, into the business ; and even some American financiers, who thought we were much too slow in tramway matters in this country, and came over here with the combined idea of showing us how to do things and of exploiting us to their own advantage, abandoned their plans and went home again when they got to understand the bearing of our legislative enactments on the situation.

So, as time went on, the local authorities had greater excuse than ever for constructing the tramways themselves ; and most of the principal urban centres built lines of their own, sooner or later.

That there have been certain resemblances between State policy towards the railways and State policy towards the tramways may have been already noticed by the reader. Just as the one was primarily based on suspicion and distrust due to the earlier action of the canal companies, so was the other inspired by what were regarded as the shortcomings of gas and water companies. Just, also, as the local authorities, while not aiding the railways at all, were given authority to levy an abnormal taxation on them, so have they been given a free hand to exploit the tramway companies in making them pay a heavy price for assents to their enterprises. The story of tramways, again, like that not only of railways but of canals and of turnpike roads, shows the same early lack of centralised effort with a view to securing a national system ; and this piecemeal growth of tramways, rather than of a tramway system, was, undoubtedly, fostered in proportion as (1) discouragement was given to private companies, which could have operated without respect to borough boundaries and county areas, and (2) tramway construction drifted more into the hands of local authorities, whose powers did not go beyond the borders of their own particular districts.

While recognising these resemblances, one must admit that the handicapping of the tramway companies has been far more severe than that of the railway companies, by reason of the power of absolute veto possessed by local authorities in regard to tramway schemes, and the use they have made of it. Parliament certainly never foresaw the extent of such use, or abuse, when it granted the said power of veto ; and the practices in question, like the operation of tramways by the local authorities themselves, were due to a policy of drift and " leave alone " rather than to deliberate intention or expressed approval on the part of the Legislature. The misfortune is that when the new developments in tramways occurred, or that when the abuses arose and the innovations were introduced, Parliament did not revise its legislation to meet the new conditions. The Royal Commission on London Traffic reported in 1905 in favour of the abolition of the power of veto, saying : " We consider it unreasonable that any one portion of a district should be in a position to put a stop to the construction of a general system of tramways required for the public benefit, without even allowing the case to be presented for the consideration of Parliament. . . . It appears to us that instead of a ' veto ' it would be sufficient that local and

road authorities should have a *locus standi* to appear before
the proposed Traffic Board and Parliament, in opposition
to any tramway scheme within their districts, by whomsoever
such tramway scheme might be promoted." But nothing has
yet been done in the way of carrying this recommendation
into effect.

The proportions in which street and road tramways and
light railways in the United Kingdom were owned by
(a) local authorities and (b) companies and private individuals
respectively in 1909–10 are shown by the following table,
taken from official returns :—

BELONGING TO	NUMBER OF UNDERTAKINGS.	LENGTH OPEN FOR TRAFFIC. M. Ch.	CAPITAL EXPENDITURE ON LINES AND WORKS OPEN FOR TRAFFIC. £	TOTAL EXPENDITURE ON CAPITAL ACCOUNT. £
Local authorities .	176	1710 17	36,807,264	49,568,775
Companies, &c. .	124	851 34	19,294,077	24,372,884
Totals .	300	2561 51	56,101,341	73,941,659

To this table I might append the following statistics as
to the operation of street and road tramways and light railways in the United Kingdom in 1909–10 :—

Capital authorised	£93,124,187
Capital paid up	£73,260,225
Number of horses	2,365
Number of locomotive engines . . .	31
Number of cars :	
Electric	11,749
Non-electric	601
Total number of passengers carried . .	2,743,189,439
Quantity of electrical energy used (Board of Trade unit)	483,671,806
Gross receipts	£13,077,901
Working expenditure	£8,132,114
Net receipts	£4,945,787
Appropriations :—	
Interest or dividends	£1,913,872
Repayment of debt or sinking fund . .	£1,133,134
Relief of rates	£346,274
Added to Common Good funds . . .	£54,028
Aid from rates	£64,215

It will have been seen from the table given above that the
total length of tramways and light railways owned by local
authorities is double the length of those owned by companies ;

but, in the circumstances already narrated, the cause for surprise is, rather, that private companies should have been sufficiently bold or enterprising to do as much in the way of tramway construction as they have.

To the tramway patron it may seem to be a matter of no great concern whether the tramways are owned and operated by local authorities or by companies, provided they are satisfactory ; and there may even appear to be various advantages on the side of public ownership of what, since the public streets and roads are used, may be regarded as essentially a public service.

There have, however, been many suggestions that municipal tramways are too often managed on lines involving a disregard of commercial principles, and that much of the financial success claimed for them is due less to real " profits " than to the omission from the expenditure side of their accounts of inconvenient items which, if included therein, would show much less favourable results than those desired. Thus it has been represented from time to time by opponents of " municipal trading "—who have advanced many facts and figures in proof of their assertions—that large sums of money spent on street widenings for tramway purposes—that is to say, sums which a tramway company would pay from its capital account, and put down as costs of construction—are omitted from the municipal tramway accounts and classed under the head of " public improvements," to be covered out of the local rates. The general practice is to debit a third of such expenditure to the tramway, the other two-thirds coming out of the rates ; but the critics allege that, in some instances, a far greater proportion even than the two-thirds has been left to be defrayed by the general ratepayer.[1] It is further alleged that inadequate amounts are set aside for depreciation, and that the sums allowed for the use of the central office and the services of the central staff may be considerably less than the figures which ought to be allocated thereto, if the municipal tramway business were really conducted on business lines.

[1] See R. P. Porter's "Dangers of Municipal Trading," pp. 174–5, where it is stated that of over £4,000,000 spent by the London County Council on street widenings for tramway extensions only £377,000 was debited to the tramway undertaking.

Whatever the actual position may be in regard to these matters of account, which the financial experts may be left to decide, it has long been a question (1) whether it would not have been better either from the early days of street tramways or, at least, from the time when electric tramways were introduced, to have given a greater degree of encouragement to private enterprise ; and (2) whether, assuming it was necessary, or desirable, that local authorities should own the tramways, it would not have been more prudent to arrange with private companies for their operation, as is done, for example, in the case of the light railway system in Belgium. On this latter point the Royal Commission on London Traffic say in their report (1905) :—

" We think it reasonable that some profit should be derived from the tramways for the benefit of the municipality, but it does not follow that the best way of securing the largest profit will be that the municipality, even if it finds the money for construction, should undertake the task of operating. In other countries it is not unusual for municipalities to construct, purchase or otherwise acquire the tramways, but in such cases the actual working is generally left to operating companies, with provision for proper rates and general control. It is claimed that such methods yield a better financial result to municipalities, and avoid difficulties which might arise from municipal authorities carrying on a business of this kind on a large scale."

To-day we have the further question whether electric tramways, which have always constituted a more or less speculative business, have not attained the height of their possible development, and whether they are not already on their decline in face of other systems more efficient or, at least, less costly and less cumbersome.

The whole history of transport shows constant change and progress, the achievements of one generation or the " records " of one pioneer being only the starting-point of fresh advance or of still greater triumphs later on. Electric tramways themselves were, undoubtedly, as great an improvement on horse tramways as the drawing of vehicles by horses along a pair of rails had already been an advance on locomotion over the rough and rugged surfaces of badly made streets or roads. But electric tramways did not necessarily constitute finality and local authorities who built them as though for eternity are now faced by the rivalry of the motor-omnibus.

Motor-omnibuses are still to a certain extent in the experimental stage, since no one would suggest that they have yet attained to the greatest possible perfection, while further improvements in them are constantly being announced. Yet already their number has enormously increased, and they are not only competing severely with the tramway but threatening eventually to supersede it. The motor-omnibus requires no special track, no overhead wires, no power station and sub-stations, and no costly widenings of streets and roads or rebuilding of bridges. Consequently, the capital expenditure involved in the provision of a large stock of motor-omnibuses is far less, in proportion, than that entailed by electric tramways providing an equivalent service. The motor-omnibus, too, has greater freedom in a busy thoroughfare—and is thus quicker in its movements—than the tramway car, limited to a fixed track and much more liable to be detained by blocks of traffic. The motor-bus, again, can readily be transferred from one route to another where greater traffic is likely to be found, whereas the tramway, once laid, must remain where it is, whether the takings are satisfactory or not; while another material factor in the case of an electric tramway, namely, that owing to the cost of the standing equipment (power house, etc.), a fifteen-minute service is, generally speaking, the lowest economic limit,[1] does not arise in the case of the motor-omnibus, which can be run according to the actual requirements of traffic.

Still greater attention is now being paid to the subject of motor-omnibuses, inasmuch as the discouragement given to the provision of electric tramways by commercial companies—by reason of the exactions levied as the price of assents or because of the preference shown for municipal ownership—has driven private enterprise to seek alternative methods in supplying facilities for street and road traffic with the prospect of a reasonable return on the capital invested ; and one ideal in these alternative methods naturally is, in the circumstances, that they should involve a minimum of possible control by the local authorities. If, in the result, private enterprise, thus driven to adopt new expedients in locomotion, should so far

---

[1] "Electricity in Locomotion," by A. G. Whyte, 1911.

perfect a motor-omnibus, or any other alternative service, that the electric tramway will not only have a powerful competitor but be largely superseded, the position of the municipalities which first sought to exclude or to exploit private enterprise and then invested large sums in speculative tramway undertakings of their own will be sufficiently serious.

While, on the one hand, certain local authorities which have no municipal tramways are now establishing municipal motor-omnibuses—showing in this practical manner their own view of the respective claims of the two systems—others, with the intention of safeguarding the interests of their tramway undertakings rather than of securing greater transport facilities for the public, are renewing towards the motor-omnibus, as a direct competitor with municipal tramways, the hostility shown by the canal companies towards the railways when the probability of the former being supplanted by the latter began to be realised ; though it is, of course, now no longer a matter simply of one set of commercial companies competing with another.

A further rival to the electric tramway is arising in the system of railless electric traction, the fundamental principle of which is the application of electric power, derived from overhead wires, to electric cars, resembling motor-omnibuses (or alternatively, to goods lorries and vans), driven on ordinary roads without rails, and capable of being steered in and out of the traffic over the whole width of the roadway.

The advantages claimed for the system are (1) that the cost of installation is only from one-fourth to one-third of the average cost of British tramways per mile of route, the permanent way of the latter being responsible for from two-thirds to three-quarters of the capital expenditure, while maintenance of tramway lines is also very expensive ; (2) that costly street widenings are avoided ; (3) that Bills for railless electric traction projects can be laid before Parliament without first obtaining the assent of the local authorities ; (4) that such traction can be profitably installed in towns having populations insufficient to support a tramway, or having streets unsuitable for tramway rails ; (5) that it is especially useful for linking up outlying districts with tramways and railways ; for developing country and seaside places ; for the conveyance of agricultural produce from rural districts to neighbouring towns or the nearest railway; and for the transport of goods or minerals to or from railway stations or harbours over the same routes as passengers; (6) that the cars are more reliable and cheaper to operate than petrol, petrol-electric, steam or battery-driven vehicles; and (7) that inasmuch as the running of railless electric traction is practically noiseless, house property is not likely to be depreciated in value as in the case of the tramway.

The disadvantages of the system as compared with the motor-bus are (1) that the railless electric traction bus can only run along streets which have been provided with over-head wires; (2) that, even allowing for the absence of rails, the expense involved in overhead wires and power stations will still be necessary, as in the case of a tramway; (3) that by reason of the standing expenses, and in order to utilise the electric current to the best advantage, a frequent service will have to be maintained, whether the traffic really warrants it or not, whereas the motor-omnibus can be brought out and run only at such hours of the day as remunerative traffic is likely to be obtained; and (4) that railless electric traction goods vans or lorries—being able to go only along certain streets, and being unable even there to load or unload, inasmuch as these operations would prevent other railless cars from passing—would be less better adapted for urban trading purposes than commercial motors.

Railless electric traction seems to have been first adopted at Grevenbruck, Westphalia, in 1903, and since that date it has been resorted to in various other places on the Continent. In this country, apart from a short experimental line constructed at the Hendon depôt of the Metropolitan Electric Tramways, the first applications of railless traction have been at Leeds and Bradford, where, following on the obtaining of Parliamentary powers in 1910, municipal railless electric traction systems were formally opened in June, 1911, the system adopted being that of the Railless Electric Traction Construction Company, Ltd. In each case the railless traction supplements the existing municipal tramway.

At Leeds the tramway route from the City Square is followed for about a mile, and then, with the help of a special set of wires, the new system diverges, and continues to a point three miles further on; though the Parliamentary powers allow of a still further extension to the city boundary. At Bradford the railless system establishes a link a little over a mile in length between two tramway routes.

In the Session of 1911 there were about sixteen Bills before Parliament applying for powers in respect to railless traction. Some of these were promoted by local authorities, one or two were by tramway companies, one was by an omnibus company, and the remainder were schemes by various private promoters.

Municipal corporations already owning and operating tram- ways would seem to favour the railless electric traction system because it enables them (1) to utilise to greater advantage the electric power they are already generating for tramway purposes ; and (2) to provide transport facilities for parts of their district where, as is said, the traffic prospects would not warrant the laying of a tramway. It is open to consideration, however, whether the recognition by municipalities of the advantages of railless electric traction over the tramway does not itself foreshadow the eventual doom of the latter, apart altogether from any considerations that arise in respect to the motor-omnibus. It is certainly significant that in his presidential address to the ninth annual conference of the Municipal Tramways Association, in September, 1910, the general manager of the Bradford Corporation Tramways, Mr C. J. Spencer, is reported to have said :—

" In considering future developments the trackless trolley system naturally comes first into view. The introduction of this new method of transit into this country . . . will un- doubtedly extend the sphere of usefulness of the trolley system. The tramway construction boom stopped, not because every district that required better facilities was supplied, but because financial reasons made it impossible to proceed any further into districts unable to support a capital expenditure of £14,000 to £15,000 per mile of tramway laid. . . . The railless system, however, comes along with a vehicle as reliable as a tramcar, and at least as cheap to operate, but with a capital expenditure on street work so low that the bugbear of heavy interest and sinking fund charges is practically non- existent."

It remains to be seen to what extent companies or corpora- tions will be likely to start entirely new and independent schemes of railless electric traction, setting up power-houses, etc., for the purpose, in preference to running motor-buses or commercial motor vehicles. This will be the real test of the respective merits of the two systems, apart from any further utilisation of existing tramway power stations; and it is always to be remembered that still greater improvements in self-propelled buses, vans, etc., will certainly be brought about. There is certainly significance, in this connection, in the following report, published in the " Engineering Supplement " of " The Times " of November 8, 1911 :—

" The Tramways Committee of the Edinburgh Corporation have decided that nothing further is to be done for the present in connection with the proposal to adopt rail-less tramways for the city and district, in view of information which they have obtained regarding an improved type of petrol-electric omnibus which has been introduced in London. In the latter class of vehicle, they are informed, many of the disadvantages of the motor-omnibus as hitherto known have been overcome, and they consider that it would be prudent to await further developments before taking any action with regard to rail-less tramways."

Whatever the eventual issue of the rivalry between the two new systems themselves, the fact that they have been introduced at all would seem to confirm the assumption that in the dictionary of transport there is no such word as " finality." We are also left to conclude—

(1) That in the struggle between governing authorities and private enterprise the last word is not always with the former ;

(2) That the resort by local authorities both to motor-omnibuses and to railless electric traction suggests that, even in their opinion, electric tramways are being improved upon, even if they have not already had their day ;

(3) That the municipalities which checked the development of tramways by private companies—from whom an assured return might have been gained—and themselves spent, in the aggregate, many millions of public money on a form of municipal enterprise yielding doubtful results, involving great liabilities, and now, apparently, being superseded by superior systems, may eventually find abundant reason for regretting their past policy ; and

(4) That when local governing authorities do enter upon speculative commercial enterprises, they cannot, any more than

commercial companies, set up the plea of " vested interests " as against new-comers in the march of progress, but must themselves also submit to economic laws, and run the risks which commercial undertakings, even under municipal direction, necessarily involve.

CHAPTER XXX

CYCLES, MOTOR-VEHICLES AND TUBES

In addition to the developments in locomotion spoken of in the previous chapter, there have been various others to which reference should be made.

The principle of a manu-motive machine, furnished with wheels, by means of which an individual could propel himself along a road with greater speed and less exertion than in walking, goes back to the very earliest days of human history, evidences of an attempt to adapt such principle having come down to us from the times both of the Egyptians and the Babylonians.

In the last quarter of the eighteenth century and the first half of the nineteenth, various contrivances were introduced in our own country under such names as " the velocipede," " the dandy horse," " the hobby horse," " the wooden horse," and the particular form of bicycle known as " the bone-shaker." The last-mentioned became, in spite of its drawbacks, a craze in the late '60's; but it was the substitution of indiarubber for iron tires, and the production, in 1885, by J. K. Starley, of the modern rear-driven " safety," that established the practical utility of the bicycle. A succession of improvements followed, including pneumatic tires, free wheels, two-speed and three-speed gears, the adaptation of the bicycle to the use of ladies, and the supplementing of the bicycle by tricycles, sociables, tandems and the motor-cycle.

Cycles have been well defined as " the poor man's carriage "; but they are to-day favoured by every class of the community. Thanks, more especially, to the numerous local cycling clubs and the great touring clubs, of which the latter count their members by tens of thousands, cycles have materially developed the taste for travel; they have led to indulgence in outings or pleasure trips at home and abroad to an extent previously unknown; they have vastly increased the means of communication ; they have exercised a powerful influence on our general social conditions, and they have become, in a variety of ways, and with different modifications of the bicycle or the tricycle principle, an important auxiliary to the despatch of business.

Cycling has thus attained to a place of recognised usefulness in the professions, in trade, in country life, in the Post Office and even in the Army. It is no longer a hobby, a craze or exclusively a source of recreation. The cycle has definitely and permanently established its position as one of the most popular of " carriages," and, in doing so, it has itself led to the creation of a very considerable industry.

By 1895 the demand for cycles had become so great that it was then impossible for the manufacturers to meet all requirements. Over-speculation and over-production, accompanied by severe foreign competition, followed, and for a time the position of the home industry was very unsatisfactory. It has since re-established itself on sounder lines and now constitutes an enterprise of considerable local importance in various parts of the country, including Coventry, Birmingham, Nottingham and Wolverhampton.

Public prejudice and State policy were factors in the arrested development, in this country, of the application of mechanical power to road vehicles, so that while such application has its ancient history equally with the bicycle, the actual expansion thereof—on such lines that it has now become the dominating feature in road transport generally—has been brought about in quite recent times.

When, in the early years of the nineteenth century, general attention was attracted to the possibilities and prospects of using locomotives on the railway in place either of horses or of stationary engines, further projects were mooted for employing steam-propelled vehicles on ordinary roads. Trade expansion and the inefficiency of existing road-transport conditions combined to strengthen these proposals, and from about 1827 to 1835 or 1840 much enterprise was shown in the construction of steam-carriages, and more especially steam-coaches and steam-omnibuses of which various regular services, in London or in the country, were run with, at first, considerable success. The vehicles in question were designed mainly for the conveyance of passengers, and some of them attained a speed of over twenty miles an hour. There were even those who anticipated that steam-carriages on roads would be successful rivals of the locomotive on rails. Alexander Gordon, civil engineer, and an ardent supporter of steam-driven road vehicles as against railways, wrote in " An Historical and Practical Treatise upon Elemental Locomotion by means of Steam Carriages on Common Roads " (1832) :—

" It will be found that, with the exception of the Liverpool and Manchester line, and of those lines formed solely for the purpose of conveying heavy materials on a descending road, railways are, at least, of very questionable advantage where there is the possibility of having a good turnpike road and steam carriages. . . . Rail-roads have a very formidable rival in steam communication upon the common road, and the latter is of vastly greater advantage than the former."

Opposition, however, to steam-driven road coaches was hardly less vigorous than the opposition offered to the rail locomotive itself. Not only were obstructions constantly placed on the roads to prevent the steam-coaches from passing, but country squires, horse-coach proprietors, post-horse owners and representatives of the turnpike road interests combined to show the most active hostility to the new form of locomotion. The turnpike road trustees sought to make the running of the steam-coaches impossible by imposing prohibitive tolls on them. It was shown in evidence before a Parliamentary Committee that where on the road between Liverpool and Prescot horse-coaches would pay a 4s. toll, the steam-coach was charged £2 8s., while on other roads the tolls in the case of the latter were equally extortionate.

There were pioneers in those days who devoted time, toil and fortune to attempts to establish steam locomotion on the roads, only, one after the other, to retire from the contest discomfited and impoverished.

Among them was Sir Goldsworthy Gurney, who laboured for five years and expended £30,000 on his attempts to bring steam-carriages into practical and permanent use. Finding, at last, that the turnpike trustees controlled the situation, Gurney and other steam-carriage builders petitioned Parliament to investigate the subject of the opposition shown to them, and a Select Committee of the House of Commons was appointed for this purpose in 1831. It reported in favour of steam road-carriages, and recommended a repeal of the old turnpike Acts. A Bill to this effect was passed in the Commons but thrown out in the Lords. Disheartened by his losses, Gurney ceased to build and to run coaches on his own account and tried to form a company. He failed in the attempt, and he then appealed to Parliament to make him some recompense for all he had done in the interests of the public. A proposed grant of £10,000 was objected to, however, by the Chancellor of the Exchequer, and Gurney got nothing. Concluding that it was useless to continue his attempts in the face of so much discouragement, he sold off his stock-in-trade and retired from the business.

By 1835 nearly all the steam-carriages had been taken off the road, and by 1840 the considerable industry which had been developed was engaged almost exclusively—so far as it survived at all—in the production of traction engines, only spasmodic attempts being made between 1840 and 1860 to produce improved types of steam-carriages for private use.

In 1861 traction engines had so far increased in numbers that a Locomotive Act was passed mainly to fix a scale of tolls applicable to them on all turnpike roads ; though this Act further stipulated that each " locomotive " should be in charge of at least two persons, and that the speed should not exceed ten miles an hour when the vehicle was passing along any turnpike road or two miles an hour when passing through a city, town or village. An amending Act, which became law in 1865, laid down that each locomotive should be in charge of three persons ; that one of these must walk in front carrying a red flag, and that the maximum speed should not exceed four miles an hour on the highway or two miles an hour in passing through a town or village. Various other restrictions were also imposed.

It was this " red flag Act " that virtually killed off the self-propelled road-vehicle business here for the time being, except as regarded traction engines proper. A few enthusiasts made steam-carriages as a hobby, and certain manufacturers made them for export to the colonies or to India, where there were no such restrictions on their use as in this country. In India, especially, these carriages were found very serviceable in localities then unprovided with railways, though any manufacturer who even tested their capacity on a public road in England was liable to prosecution.

British inventors, thus effectively prevented by hostile legislation from improving self-propelled road-vehicles, turned their attention, instead, to tricycles and bicycles, while continental inventors, not being hampered by legislative restrictions in their own country, first converted the tricycle into a motor-vehicle, then applied the motor principle to four-wheeled waggonettes, and finally evolved some useful types of motor-vehicles which, by 1895, were being widely adopted on the Continent and more especially in Paris.

A few bold pioneers who introduced them here were repeatedly prosecuted and fined. The general position had, in fact, become even worse since 1865, because not only was a motor-car still regarded in the eye of the law as the equivalent of a traction engine or " locomotive," but, under the Highways and Locomotives (Amendment) Act, 1878, every county council was authorised to exact up to £10 for a licence which would allow of the use of such traction engine or " locomotive " only within the boundary of the authority in question, a fresh licence being thus required for each county council district through which a vehicle might pass. The only exceptions were locomotives used solely for agricultural purposes. Notwithstanding all these restrictions, there were—exclusive of vehicles of the agricultural type—about 8000 traction engines in use on our roads in 1895.

Much vigorous and practical protest led to the passing of the Locomotives on Highways Act of 1896, which became the Magna Charta of automobilism in this country. Making at last a distinction between motor-cars and traction engines, it relieved from the said restrictions any vehicle, propelled by mechanical power, the weight of which (unloaded) did not exceed three tons, or, together with that of a trailer (also unloaded), four tons. It further sanctioned the driving of such vehicle at a speed of up to fourteen miles an hour, but gave authority to the Local Government Board to reduce the speed if it thought fit—an authorisation of which the Board availed itself by fixing the speed limit at twelve miles an hour.

A great impetus was given to the use of light vehicles, and November 14, 1896, when, under the Act, the motor-car became a legal vehicle in this country, is known in automobile circles as Emancipation Day. But the Act afforded no relief in the case of motor-vehicles suitable for trade or public service purposes. Within the weights specified vehicles of these types would have been commercially unprofitable because they could not have carried a paying load. Above the said weights they were still regarded by the law, and were subject to the same regulations, as road locomotives or traction engines.

Strong representations on the subject were made by the Royal Automobile Club (then the Automobile Club of Great Britain and Ireland), the Society of Motor Manufacturers and Traders and the Commercial Motor Users' Association, which bodies claimed the right of the trading interests of the country to a greater degree of reasonable consideration. These further protests again led to good results. In 1903 a Motor-car Act was passed which, among other things, raised the speed limit to 20 miles an hour (subject to authority given to the Local Government Board to reduce the limit to 10 miles an hour in dangerous areas), and provided for the licensing of drivers and the registration and identification of cars, with a view to checking reckless driving ; while power was, also, given to the Local Government Board to increase the maximum weights allowed by the earlier Act. In January, 1904, the Board appointed a Departmental Committee to inquire into the question of increasing the maximum tare, and, after taking counsel with technical experts, trading bodies and commercial authorities, it finally issued the Heavy Motor-car Order, 1904, effecting changes in the maximum weights (unladen) as follows :—

	MOTOR CAR	MOTOR CAR AND TRAILER
Act of 1896 .	. 3 tons	4 tons.
Order of 1904	. 5 tons	6½ tons.

This Order, which came into force on the 1st of March, 1905, made possible the provision of commercial motor-services, and the full development of the motor industry, on present-day lines. It led, especially, to the creation of new types of vehicles previously unknown here, and, by allowing " heavy motor-cars "—the designation now applying to motor-vehicles over two tons in weight—to take their place in ordinary road traffic, foreshadowed changes in inland transport to which one could hardly attempt, at present, to fix any limit.

In respect to pleasure cars, detailed figures published in the issue of " The Car " for December 14, 1910, show that the number of these (as distinct from heavy motor-vehicles), registered in the United Kingdom at that date, and allowing as far as possible for those which had lapsed, was 124,860. Of motor-cycles there were 86,414. These figures convey some idea of the extent to which the automobile has been not only substituted for private horsed-carriages, as used for ordinary urban and social purposes, but adopted, also, for those longer journeys or tours which the improved means of locomotion have brought so much into vogue.

How the country is being opened up more and more to motor traffic may be shown by some references to the work in this direction by the Royal Automobile Club and the Automobile Association and Motor Union.

Founded in 1897, the Royal Automobile Club is an influential body with many-sided activities, including the provision of a club house in Pall Mall well deserving the designation of " palatial," and typical of the high standing to which automobilism has attained. More, however, to my present purpose than the social advantages offered by the club is the fact that the R.A.C. not only advises its members or associates as to the best route in regard to any tour they propose to make by motor, at home or abroad, but provides them with a complete typewritten itinerary and specially-designed maps for such tour, the information given being kept up to date by means of reports made by the members themselves. The inquirer is given, also, a guide-book for the district in question written from the point of view of the traveller by road ; he receives some confidential notes concerning the hotels *en route*, and he may arrange to retain the services, for periods of an hour, a half-day, a day, or a week, of local guides— clergymen, writers, secretaries of local societies and others— who are qualified authorities on art, archæology, architecture, natural history, topography, etc., besides having an intimate knowledge of the localities visited. In the Club itself there is a well-stocked " Travel Library," from which books can be borrowed. Should the member or the associate on tour come into conflict with the law in regard to alleged offences under

the Motor Acts, the R.A.C. will defend him in any police
court in the United Kingdom free of charge, though it reserves
to itself the right to refuse such assistance in the case of those
who may have been guilty of inconsiderate driving.

Much has been done by the R.A.C. in the provision of road
direction posts. It has, for example, put up posts or direction
boards along the whole of the Great North Road from London
to Berwick. It erects danger signs at especially dangerous
places, though at these only, as it considers undesirable any
undue multiplication of such signs by private agencies. The
R.A.C. is, further, most vigilant in defending the common
interests of motorists when these are endangered by Parliamentary Bills or in other ways.

The Automobile Association and Motor Union also has its
Touring Department, for home or foreign travel. It offers,
like the R.A.C., free defence of members prosecuted for offences
against the Motor Acts ; it has an " hotel system " of its own,
and it has shown much activity in the placing of direction
posts and danger signs on important roads throughout the
United Kingdom.

A special feature of the A.A. and M.U.'s operations is the
patrolling, by men in uniform—and provided with bicycles
or motor cycles—of 14,000 miles of roads throughout England, Wales and Scotland. It is the duty of these patrols to
give to members information of interest concerning the road,
to warn them of any dangers on the highway, and to render
them all possible assistance in case of need. They are able
to undertake minor roadside repairs ; they procure, in case
of need, fresh petrol supplies from the nearest store ; while
each is qualified to give first aid in case of accident, much
excellent service being rendered by them on the roadside
not only to members but to the public. Agents and repairers
have also been appointed by the A.A. and M.U. in all important cities and towns and in numerous hamlets at intervals
of a few miles along every main road. The agents receive or
deliver letters or telegrams, and are helpful in many ways to
the members.

In addition to these central organisations in London there
are now Associated Automobile Clubs throughout the United
Kingdom which show a great deal of local activity and offer
many advantages to their own members.

It is, again, the now general use of the automobile that has given to the improvement of the roads the greatest degree of stimulus it has received since the days of McAdam and Telford.

Speaking generally, excellent results have followed from the policy adopted by the State in transferring the charge of main roads from turnpike trustees to the county councils, and, also, in encouraging rural district councils to pay more attention to local highways other than main roads. In 1908–9, for example, the county councils spent on 27,749 miles of main roads a total of £2,739,591, and the rural district councils spent on the 95,144 miles of road under their own control a total of £2,160,492 on maintenance and repairs and £52,067 on improvements. Nor is there any reason for supposing that, under the conditions operating to-day, this expenditure is wasted or ill-spent, as was the case with so much of the outlay on roads in the pre-McAdam days of non-scientific road-making.

While the roads were being adapted to the requirements of ordinary traffic, their shortcomings from the point of view of the traffic of motor-cars and traction engines were made apparent, and called for special attention. It was not only that the suction of the india-rubber tyres raised clouds of dust and, also, injured the macadamised roads by depriving the top layer of stones of their proper binding, but the greater speed at which the motor-cars were driven made it especially necessary that the roads should be alike wide and straight, with as few awkward, if not dangerous, turns, twists or corners as possible.

The increasing use of traction engines is indicated by a report on the county roads issued by the Kent County Council. The number of traction engines licensed by that body during the year ending March 31, 1911, for use in the county, was 101, as compared with only 37 in the previous year.

Action was called for all the more because cycling and automobilism have increased the use of the roads of the United Kingdom in general to an extent that probably surpasses their use even in the palmy days of the Coaching Era. At that time it was almost exclusively along the main roads between leading cities that the coaches went in such numbers ; whereas cyclists and motorists in search of the picturesque may discard main roads and proceed, instead, along highways and by-ways where the stage-coach was never seen. The sum total of the road traffic to-day may thus be in excess of that of the Coaching Age, though, perhaps, appearing to be less because it is better distributed.

For like reasons it became necessary that not only the main roads, but the highways and by-ways, also, should receive adequate attention.

Under the Development and Road Improvement Funds Act, 1909, there was constituted, in 1910, a body known as the Road Board, having for its special function the administration of a " Road Improvement Grant." The Board was to have power, with the approval of the Treasury, (a) to make advances to county councils and other highway authorities in respect to the construction of new roads or the improvement of existing roads, and (b) itself to construct and maintain any new roads, which appear to the Board to be required for facilitating road traffic.

The funds available for the Road Improvement Grant arise from the motor spirit duties and the motor-car license duties, the last-mentioned being £1 for motor-bicycles and motor-tricycles, of whatever horse-power, and from £2 2s. to £42 for motor-cars, according to their horse-power. Motorists thus directly contribute towards the improvement of the roads, and the principle involved is the same as that under which road-users formerly paid tolls on turnpike roads ; but the present application of this principle is obviously a great improvement on the system of turnpikes, with its excessive cost of toll-collection and other disadvantages.

The amount likely to be available for grants by the Board is estimated at about £600,000 a year ; but, owing to an accumulation of funds before operations were begun, the Board started with resources amounting to £1,600,000. The grants actually made to September 30, 1911, were :—

	£
Improvement of road crusts . . .	321,445
Road widenings and improvement of curves and corners	44,856
Road diversions	16,906
Construction and improvement of bridges	23,947
Total . .	407,154

Inasmuch as applications were made to the Board up to June 30, 1911, for advances amounting in the aggregate to close on £8,000,000, there would seem still to be a great deal that requires to be done to the roads of the country to adapt them to the traffic conditions of to-day. It will be seen, however, that the combined operations of the Royal Automobile Club, the Automobile Association and Motor Union, and the Road Board constitute, in effect—and more especially from the point of view of provision of facilities for through traffic under satisfactory conditions—a national road policy far in advance of anything this country has ever seen before.

These road improvements appeal to the motorist, delighting in cross-country journeys, still more than they do to the urban trader, whose road transport does not, generally speaking, extend beyond a certain radius. But within the limits of such radius the substitution of commercial motors for horse-drawn vehicles is undergoing an expansion which seems to be restricted only by the extent of the motor-car manufacturers' powers of production, while already the use of so many commercial motors is accentuating certain changes in commercial conditions which—as it is one of the objects of the present work to show—have ever been powerfully influenced by the transport facilities of the day.

With the large wholesale and retail houses the use of the road motor is a matter not simply of economy in transport but, to a still greater degree, of doing a larger business, in less time, and over a wider area, than if horsed vehicles were used.

When urban traders send motor-vehicles a distance of over twenty or even thirty miles into the outer suburbs, and when those vehicles can cover from fifty to sixty miles in a day, distributing fresh supplies to suburban or country shopkeepers, delivering purchases to local residents, or calling on them to leave groceries, meat and other household necessaries, the possibilities of an expansion of business by the said traders are greatly increased, more especially when the local residents within the radius in question find that if they give an order to the van-man, or send it by post one day, the motor-vehicle will generally supply their wants the next day or the day following. Under this arrangement the big traders, or the big stores, in town are enabled to make their already big businesses bigger still—to their own advantage, but with a corresponding disadvantage to the local shopkeepers.

In another direction the commercial motor is assisting the operations of trading companies, caterers, grocers, tea-dealers, tobacconists, etc., who, instead of having a single huge block of departmental shops or stores, have numerous branches in all parts of London, furnishing them with viands, provisions or stock from a head depôt. In all such instances as these,—more especially when cooked food is distributed from a central kitchen,—the superiority of the motor-vehicle over the horsed van is self-evident ; while the further advantage is gained that the branch establishments can be devoted wholly, or almost exclusively, to the serving of customers, without any need for extensive kitchen arrangements or store-rooms of their own. Alternatively, the premises used for these branches need be no larger than is necessary to meet day-by-day requirements, whereas an independent trader, having only a single establishment, would want much more accommodation, involving higher rent, rates, taxes and expenses generally.

Once more the gain is on the part of the big trader as against the small one ; and once more we have evidence of the increasing tendency for the former to supersede the latter. In fact, the real competition to-day is no longer between large traders and small traders. It is a competition between the commercial giants themselves. It is a contest in which the small shopkeeper is little better than an interested spectator, with nothing more to hope for than that the particular giant who wipes out his business will, at least, be so far considerate as to offer him a situation.

In the recesses of Wild Wales there has been seen a commercial motor-vehicle which was virtually a shop or a general stores on wheels—something after the style of the familiar gypsies' van, though of a far superior type. There are evidently endless possibilities in this direction. The time may come when it will not be necessary for the rural resident to go to the shops in even the nearest town. The shops themselves— or equivalents thereto—will be brought to the very door. To a certain extent there will thus be a reversal to the habits of former days ; but between the packhorse, or the pedlar, and the motor-shop-on-wheels there will be a distinct and a very wide difference, representing generations of both scientific and economic progress. Do not such possibilities still further suggest, also, the eventual supersession of the small trader by the large one ?

In almost every class of trade or business the commercial motor is being steadily substituted for horsed vehicles. There are large retail houses in London which have each their " fleets " of up to fifty or sixty motor-vans or lorries.[1] The carrying companies would hardly be able to provide their extensive suburban services of to-day without road motors. Fishmongers, ice merchants and fruit salesmen, who especially require to have a speedy means of distributing their wares, favour the commercial motor no less than do the managers of evening newspapers. Laundry companies—to whose business a great impetus has been given of late years by the increasing resort to residential flats—find commercial motors of great service in the collections that have to be made on Mondays and Tuesdays and the deliveries effected on Fridays and Saturdays. Furniture-removers, by resorting either, for small removals, to motors carrying pantechnicons, or, for large removals, to traction-engines and regular road trains, can now cover distances of up to 100 or 150 miles a day, the " record " down to the autumn of 1911 being 166 miles in a day. Brewers, mineral-water manufacturers, oil companies, coal merchants, pianoforte-makers, brick-makers and scores of other traders, besides, are all taking to the new form of street or road transport.

Motor-vehicles are likewise succeeding horsed vehicles for fire-engines, municipal water-carts and dust-carts, street ambulances, Post Office mail-vans,[2] char-a-bancs and estate cars, the last-mentioned being constructed so that they can be used either for passengers or for goods. Theatrical companies on tour use motor-vehicles for the conveyance of themselves, *plus* belongings and scenery. Political propagandists, also on tour, move in their motor-van from one village to another with an ease that no other road vehicle could surpass. Religious missions are being sent out in motor-vans fitted up as

---

[1] The total number of commercial motor-vehicles working in the London district in August, 1911, was, according to statistics compiled by "Commercial Motor," 3500.

[2] Mails are now being sent out from London every night by motor-vans for distances of up to 100 miles.

chapels, and duly dedicated to their special purpose. Finally, after having had, through life, the advantage of all the numerous and varied motor services here mentioned, one may now be conveyed to one's last resting-place in what a writer in " Motor Traction " for June 24, 1911, describes as " a properly-equipped motor hearse."

So considerable is the expansion which the use of commercial motors has undergone, and so great and varied are the interests represented, that there is now a Commercial Motor Users' Association which, among other purposes, seeks to resist the placing of undue restrictions on users, and to extend their rights and privileges. The administration of the Association is vested in an executive committee (on which the principal industries using self-propelled vehicles for industrial purposes are represented) and various sub-committees.

Of the motor-omnibus as a competitor with the electric tramway I have spoken in the previous chapter. It is a no less serious competitor with the horse omnibus which in London, at least, if not in other cities as well, it is rapidly driving off the streets altogether. The position in London is suggested by the following figures, which give the numbers of horse-omnibuses and motor-omnibuses licensed in the years stated :—

YEAR.	HORSE.	MOTOR.	YEAR.	HORSE.	MOTOR.
1902	3736	10	1907	2964	783
1903	3667	29	1908	2557	1205
1904	3623	13	1909	2155	1133
1905	3551	31	1910	1771	1180
1906	3484	241	1911[1]	863	1665

On October 25, 1911, the London General Omnibus Company, who at one time had 17,800 horses, ran their last horse-omnibuses, these being then definitely withdrawn by them in favour of motor-omnibuses.

A like story is to be told of the rapid substitution of motor-cabs, popularly known as " taxis," for the horse-cabs which, succeeding the earlier hackney coaches, had helped to render so disconsolate the formerly important and influential, though now utterly vanished, body known as " Thames watermen." [2] Once more, in fact, the supplanters are being

[1] July 31, 1911.   [2] See pp. 58–63.

supplanted. " Growlers " and " crawlers " have had their day, and the smarter-looking and quicker-moving taxis are leaving them to share the fate of the stage-coach when it came into competition with the better form of transport represented by the railway.

How far the substitution of motor-cabs for horsed cabs has already gone in London will be gathered from the following table, taken from the report (issued in July, 1911) of the Home Office Departmental Committee on Taxicab Fares in the London Cab Trade :—

| YEAR. | MOTOR-CABS LICENSED. | HORSE-CABS LICENSED. | | |
		Hansom.	Four-wheel.	Total.
1906	96	6648	3844	10,492
1907	723	5952	3866	9818
1908	2805	4826	3649	8475
1909	3956	3299	3263	3562
1910	6397	2003	3721	4724
1911[1]	7165	1803	2583	4386

How the horse is steadily disappearing from the streets and roads is indicated by the records of a traffic census carried out by Mr. H. Hewitt Griffin on Putney Bridge, in Fleet Street, E.C., and in the Edgware Road, and published in the issues of " Motor Traction " for July 15, May 6, and October 7, 1911, respectively.

Mr Griffin has taken his Putney Bridge census for seven years in succession, and, comparing 1905 with 1911, he gives net results which may be summarised as follows :—

| TYPE OF VEHICLE. | A TWELVE HOURS' CENSUS ON | |
	Sunday, June 25, 1905.	Sunday, July 2, 1911.
Horse-drawn buses	1613 ..	33
Motor-buses	nil ..	1529
Horse cabs, carriages, etc.	715 ..	225
Motor-cars, cabs, etc.	361 ..	1943

The Fleet Street traffic census, taken for five successive years, yielded the following results for 1907 and 1911 :—

[1] Figures for March 31. On September 30, 1911, the number of taxi-cabs in London was 7360.

TYPE OF VEHICLE.	A TWELVE HOURS' CENSUS ON	
	April 23, 1907.	April 19, 1911.
Horse-drawn buses .	2241 ..	95
Motor-buses . .	995 ..	2684
Horse-cabs . .	1902 ..	391
Motor-cabs (taxis) .	48 ..	1616

In the Edgware Road the results for 1906 and 1911 were :—

TYPE OF VEHICLE.	A NINE HOURS' CENSUS ON	
	Sept. 20, 1906.	Sept. 18, 1911.
Horse-drawn buses .	1776 ..	21
Motor-buses . .	441 ..	1599
Horse-cabs . .	1051[1] ..	260
Motor-cabs (taxis) .	10 ..	1131

Statistics taken on the Portsmouth Road for the Surrey County Council on seven successive days in corresponding weeks of July, 1909, 1910 and 1911 show that the numbers of motor-vehicles passing between 8 a.m. and 8 p.m. were :—

YEAR.	NO. OF MOTORS.
1909	5,863
1910	7,823
1911	10,635

These figures give an increase in two years of 81 per cent. During twelve hours on a Saturday in July, 1911, the number of motor-vehicles counted was 3279, or an average of 273 per hour. The greatest number passing in a single hour was 524, while during the period of the heaviest traffic 90 passed in ten minutes.

All these varied and ever-extending uses to which motor-vehicles are being put would seem almost to foreshadow the time when the horse is likely to be found only at the Zoological Gardens, as a curious survival of a bygone age in traction.

Definite statistics as to the extent to which automobilism, in its manifold phases, constitutes an industry in itself are not available ; but the activities now employed on or in connection with motors, motoring, and motor transport are manifold and widespread.

[1] Figure for Sept. 24, 1907.

For many years the crippling effect of legislative restrictions greatly checked the development of motor-car construction in this country. The Act of 1896 gave a stimulus to the building of pleasure cars, but French and German makers had the advantage until British manufacturers showed they could produce cars which would bear comparison with the foreign importations.

Real expansion of the home industry came with the Heavy Motor-car Order of 1904, although even then no great degree of progress followed immediately thereon. Traders generally were reluctant to acquire commercial motors for themselves until the success of the new vehicles had been assured, and some early failures, due to faulty construction, gave commercial motors a bad name at the start. With the adoption of improved methods, their utility was fully established, and the expansion of the industry during the last four or five years has been remarkable in the extreme.

British manufacturers had already gained a world-wide reputation for their steam road-vehicles (traction engines), and they readily adapted their plant, etc., to the building of the best type of commercial motors when the initial difficulties had been overcome. While, therefore, French and German makers were still sending their pleasure motors to this country, British producers of commercial motors kept this branch of the industry in their own hands, the position to-day being that practically all the public service and commercial motors used in this country are British-made. The main if not the only chance here for foreign vehicles of these types is when the British makers cannot execute orders promptly enough to meet requirements.

In point of fact the orders coming to hand far exceed the present productive capacity of some of our manufacturers, who, in addition to seeking to supply the home market, are now sending British-made commercial motors to almost every country in the world. I am assured, by an authority in a position to know, that certain of the English and Scotch manufacturers specialising in commercial motors had so many orders on hand in October, 1911, that unless they increased their premises, and laid down fresh machinery, they would be unable to execute any more until the end of 1912.

Much enlargement or rebuilding of works is already proceeding, while manufacturers who have hitherto devoted their attention mainly or exclusively to pleasure motors are now adapting their plant, etc., to the making of commercial motors either instead or in addition. The demand for pleasure motors is limited ; that for public service motors and motor-vehicles for traders is illimitable. From the great stores which keep their " fleet " of delivery cars, and from the furniture-remover who wants the equivalent almost of a traction-engine down to the draper, the grocer or the butcher who is content with a modest three-wheel auto-carrier for loads up to five or ten cwt., every class of trader is to-day finding that, to keep pace with the times, and to deliver goods as promptly and at the same distances as his competitors, he must needs have a quicker means of road transport than a horsed-vehicle.

Then, while large traders having their fleets of motor-vehicles set up their own repairing shops, the needs of smaller traders with only two or three delivery vans are provided for by motor manufacturers or others who undertake " maintenance " on contract terms, thus saving such traders from all trouble in the matter of repairs and upkeep.

When one adds to these considerations the fact that traders not only in the United Kingdom but in the colonies, in every European country, and even as far away as Japan, are looking to English and Scotch manufacturers to supply them with motor-traction vehicles, the impression is conveyed that the further great development of the motor industry in the United Kingdom will be far less in pleasure motors, or even in the motors used by doctors and others for professional purposes, than in commercial motors ; and this impression is confirmed by a remark made by Sir Samuel Samuel at the Motor-Aviation dinner given by him at the Savoy Hotel on October 30, 1911. " The future of the motor-car industry," he said, " lay in the commercial motor traffic, the solution of the street traffic problem lay in motor-omnibuses, and in ten years time most of the tramway stock would be scrapped."

Apart from figures as to the number of public service or commercial motors—chiefly, as I have shown, of home manufacture—already in use, the only available statistics indicating the growth of the British motor industry are those given in the Board of Trade Returns concerning " cars, chassis and

parts " exported, the total value thereof being £1,502,000 in
1909 and £2,511,000 in 1910. The imports in the same years
rose from £4,218,000 to £5,065,000. It may be assumed that
the latter figures relate more particularly to pleasure cars ;
though it should be remembered that even on these, as imported from France or Germany, additional work may often
be done here—in the way of body-building or otherwise—to
the extent of £200 or so per car. Many allied trades are
likewise doing a good business in the supply of accessories.

Allowing, next, for the employment given to drivers, repairers and others, and for the sum total (if it could only be
estimated) of the amount distributed annually by motorists
among hotel proprietors and town and country tradespeople,
the circulation of money that is directly due to motoring and
motor-traction must be prodigious. As far back as 1906 it
was estimated that motor drivers alone in this country were
receiving over £5,000,000 a year in wages, that the wages
paid to men employed in the manufacture of cars and accessories amounted to nearly £10,000,000 a year, and that the
total number of drivers and others concerned in motoring was
about 230,000. But much has happened since 1906, and if
these figures accurately represent the position then, they
would have to be greatly increased to represent the position
to-day.

Thus we see that automobilism—using the word in its
widest application—has not only brought about some remarkable changes in our conditions of inland transport and communication but is itself rapidly developing into still another
of our national industries, even if it should not have done so
already.

Tube railways are an outcome of various attempts to solve
a problem in urban transport that more especially applies to
London.

When railways were first brought to the Metropolis the
prejudice against them was so strong, and the lack of foresight
as to the purpose they would eventually serve was so pronounced, that in 1846 limits were set up, on what were then
the outskirts of London, within which the lines were not to
come. The whole of the central area was to be left free from
railways, the view of a Royal Commission which considered
the subject in the year stated being that, as the proportion

of short-distance passengers by the main lines was only small, the probable demand for the accommodation of short-distance traffic would not justify the sacrifice of property or the expenditure of money that would be involved in placing the termini in crowded centres. The same Commission recommended that if, at any future time, it should be thought necessary to admit railways within the prescribed area, this should be done in conformity with some uniform plan. Under no circumstances, they urged, should separate schemes having no reference to each other be tolerated.

It was not long before the growth of London and the transport needs of its population made clear the fact that the exclusion of railways from the central area could not be maintained, though the recommendation of the 1846 Commission as regards a uniform plan was wholly disregarded.

Supplementing the omnibuses originally established between Paddington and the City in 1829 by Shillibeer came, in 1863, the first line of underground railway, connecting Paddington station with Farringdon Street, and constructed in an open cutting, where possible. An earlier idea of having one central station in London for all the different main lines of railway was discarded in favour of underground railways of the type here in question ; and the " inner circle," linking up most of the main-line termini, was eventually completed. The original restrictions in regard to the central area were also modified, such stations as those at Charing Cross, Cannon-Street, Holborn and Liverpool Street being allowed to be set up within the once sacred precincts. Branches were made from the inner circle of the underground system ; the main-line railways began to develop their now enormous suburban business ; the omnibuses were crowded in the busy hours of the day, while the tramways, though excluded from the central area still more rigidly than the railways had been, gained no lack of patronage to or from the " outer fringe."

All these facilities served a most useful purpose ; but they obviously required to be supplemented by lines of railway which would directly serve the central area of London, and both allow of easier movement from one part of London to another and enable City workers to travel more readily between their suburban homes and the immediate locality of their places of work or business. Neither surface nor over-

head railways across the centre of London were even to be
thought of, while the cost of still more underground railways
of the " shallow " type already constructed was looked upon
as almost prohibitive, though underground any further London
lines would assuredly have to be.

A way was found out of the difficulty by the construction
of deep-level iron tubes passing through the stratum of
clay underlying London, such tubes providing for lines of
railway along which trains to be worked by electricity could
pass between various stations—in still larger tubes—in
different parts of London and the suburbs.

The first of these tube railways was projected by the City
and South London Railway Company, and received the
sanction of Parliament in 1884. The line was opened in 1890,
and with it London acquired the pioneer of those tube railways
which were to effect so revolutionary a change in her general
transport conditions. The Central London Railway followed,
in 1900, and since then London has been provided with a
network of tube railways, offering facilities for a more or less
complete interchange of traffic, north and south, and east and
west, both between themselves and in conjunction with the
termini of the main line steam railways. In this way movement about and across London has been greatly facilitated.
Three of the new tubes, the Bakerloo, the Piccadilly and the
Hampstead have been united into one system by the London
Electric Railway Company, and, together with the earlier
District Railway and the London United Tramways, are under
the same control, with great advantage to everyone concerned,
while the original underground lines—the Metropolitan and
the Metropolitan District—have been electrified and vastly
improved. The disadvantages of " isolated projects " on
which successive Commissions—the London Traffic Commission among the number—have insisted so strongly have
thus, to a certain extent, been met by the principle of combination through private enterprise. No action has yet been
taken to carry out the recommendation made in June, 1905,
in the Report of the Royal Commission on London Traffic, in
regard to the formation of a London Traffic Board, though a
useful work is being done by the London Traffic Branch
appointed by the Board of Trade in August, 1907, " to
continue and supplement the work of the Royal Commission

by keeping the statistics up to date, collecting information, and studying the problem of London traffic in all its changing aspects." In the reports issued by this Branch will be found a mine of interesting data on London traffic conditions, supplementing the abundant information in the reports of the Royal Commission itself.

It is to be hoped that the sequel to these continued investigations will be the eventual creation of some such central authority as the London Traffic Board recommended. Whether this should be done by calling into existence for London an entirely new body, such as the Public Service Commission which controls all transportation questions and facilities in New York City, or whether the simpler method of enlarging the powers of the present Railway and Canal Commission should be adopted, by preference, are matters of detail which the future must be left to decide ; but the advantages that would result from a greater degree of co-ordination in the organising and regulating of London transport conditions are incontestable.

As showing the extent of the patronage which the electric railways of London, whether tube railways or otherwise, are now receiving, I might quote from the Board of Trade " Railway Returns " the following figures, giving the number of passengers (exclusive of holders of season and periodical tickets) carried in 1910 :—

COMPANY OR LINE.	NUMBER OF PASSENGERS.
Central London	40,660,856
City and South London	23,501,947
Great Northern and City	9,380,378
Waterloo and City	3,724,277
London Electric	95,647,197
Metropolitan	82,728,776
Metropolitan District	64,627,829
Whitechapel and Bow	19,886,273

CHAPTER XXXI

THE OUTLOOK

HAVING now traced the important part that improvements in the conditions of inland transport and communication have played in the economic and social development of this country, and having seen, also, the action taken therein, on the one hand by so-called " private enterprise " (defined by Samuel Smiles as " the liberality, public spirit and commercial enterprise of merchants, traders and manufacturers "), and on the other hand by State and local authorities, we have now to consider, in this final chapter, what are the prospects of further changes and developments in those transport conditions to which, judging from past experience, it would not be wise to fix finality in the matter of progress.

Thus far the railway certainly represents the survival of the fittest ; and, curiously enough, although great improvements have been made in locomotive construction, in rails, in signalling, in carriage-building and in the various departments of railway working, no absolutely new principle has been developed since the Liverpool and Manchester Railway definitely established the last of the three fundamental principles on which railway construction and operation are really based : (1) that a greater load can be moved, by an equivalent power, in a wheeled vehicle on a pair of rails than in a similar vehicle on an ordinary road ; (2) that flanged wheels and flat rails are preferable for fast traffic to flat wheels and flanged rails ; and (3) that a railway train should be operated by a locomotive rather than by either animal power or a stationary engine.

It is true that, in regard to the last-mentioned of these three main principles, material changes have been brought about by the resort to electricity as a motive power ; but this, after all, is an improvement in the means of rail transport rather than a complete change in the principle of transport itself; and, though electricity may supersede steam to a considerable extent, especially for suburban traffic, the resort to it is a reversal, in another form, to the earlier idea of motive power distributed from a fixed point, as originally represented by stationary engines, before the locomotive had established its superiority thereto.

In any case, the railway is still the railway, whatever the form of traction employed, and there is, after all, no such fundamental difference between an electric railway and a steam railway as there was between the railway and the canal, or between either railway waggon or canal barge and the carrier's cart travelling on ordinary roads. The question that really arises here is, not whether electricity is likely to supersede steam for long-distance as well as for short-distance rail traffic, but whether the railways themselves are likely to be superseded, sharing the same fate as that which they caused to fall on the stage-coach and, more or less, on the canal barge.

For the physical, economic and other considerations already presented, there is no reasonable ground for expecting much from the projected scheme of canal revival. When the country comes fully to realise (1) the natural unsuitability of England's undulatory surfaces for transport by artificial waterways; (2) the enormous cost which the carrying out of any general scheme of canal revival would involve; (3) the practical impossibility of canal-widening in the Birmingham and Black Country districts; and (4) the comparatively small proportion of traders in the United Kingdom who could hope to benefit from a scheme for which all alike might have to pay;—it is hardly probable that public opinion will sanction the carrying out of a project at once so costly and so unsatisfactory in its prospective results.

Still less than in the case of canals would any attempt to improve the conditions of transport on rivers—serving even more limited districts, and having so many natural drawbacks and disadvantages—be likely to meet any general advantage or to foster any material competition with the railways.

Developments in regard to road transport are much more promising—or, from the point of view of the railways, much more to be feared—than any really practical revival of inland navigation.

Dealing, in this connection, first with personal travel, we find that the main competition with the railways proceeds from (1) omnibuses, motor or otherwise ; (2) electric tramways, and (3) private motor-cars.

An omnibus, whether of the horse or of the motor type, is the equivalent of the carrier's van or of the old stage-coach in so far as it has the complete freedom of the roads. The electric tramway, while having to keep to a certain route, and involved in greater capital expenditure by reason of its need for rails, overhead wires and power stations, may, if owned by a local authority, still be materially aided, directly or indirectly, out of the local rates. Thus the omnibus and the electric tramway may both be able to transport passengers at lower fares than the railways, which, as regards the municipal tramways, may even be called on to pay, through increased taxation, towards the maintenance of their rivals.

In London itself the motor-omnibuses have undoubtedly abstracted a considerable amount of short-distance traffic from the Central London Railway, which, however, still has the advantage in regard to longer distance journeys.

That electric tramways and motor-omnibuses have also diverted a great deal of suburban passenger traffic from the trunk railways is beyond dispute. But here the companies are seeking to meet the position (1) by operating their own suburban lines by electricity, giving their passengers a quicker transport than they would get with tramways or motor-cars stopping frequently, or held up by traffic repeatedly, on the roads or streets ; or (2) by offering to town workers greater facilities for removing from homes in the inner to homes in the outer suburbs, if not in the country proper or even on the coast itself—in other words, to such a distance that they would naturally be dependent on the railway and the business trains that are now run thereon from the places in question to meet their special convenience.[1]

[1] A good example of these tendencies is offered by the Southend district, situate at the mouth of the Thames, a distance of 35 miles from London. Season tickets between London and Southend are issued by the railways at a low rate, and on the London, Tilbury and Southend line there are 6000 holders of these tickets. In the special interests of wives and daughters cheap tickets to London by an express train are issued on Wednesdays to allow of shopping in town, visits to the theatre, etc., and by this train there is an average of from 600 to 700 passengers, consisting almost exclusively of ladies.

Of these two developments the former has not yet been generally adopted, whereas the latter is in full activity, and, in combination with the heavier local taxation which is steadily driving people away from London boroughs, is helping to produce results of much interest and importance.

The population, not only of London, but of great towns in general, is undergoing a considerable redistribution. Land at greater distances from urban centres, and hitherto devoted only to agriculture or market gardens, is being utilised more and more for building purposes ; the increasing values of land within the radius of these outer suburbs improves the position on urban markets of producers in rural centres whose lower rents may more than compensate for their slightly heavier cost of transport as compared with the suburban growers ; the health of town workers taking to what are not merely suburban but country homes should improve. Social and domestic conditions generally are, to a certain extent, in a state of transition ; while the trunk railways are getting back from their long-distance suburban traffic some—though not yet, perhaps, actually the whole—of the revenue they have lost on their short-distance traffic.

On the other hand, results are being brought about in the inner suburbs which are viewed with much uneasiness by the local authorities. The removal from the inner suburbs of considerable numbers of those who can afford to live further away from their business means (1) that population in the inner suburban circle is decreasing, or, alternatively, that a better-class population is giving place to a poorer-class one ; (2) that much of the house property there is either standing empty or is fetching considerably lower rents ; and (3) that the taxable capacity of the areas in question is declining, although the need for raising more by local taxation is to-day greater than ever.

Where the local authorities who are experiencing all these consequences of an interesting social change have themselves helped to bring them about by setting up municipal tramways to compete with the railways, thus, among other consequences, driving the latter to resort to measures of self-defence, they may find that attempts to change, if not to control, the operation of economic forces have their risks and perils ; while the position for the authorities concerned will be even worse if their municipal tramway, in turn, should suffer materially from the competition of the motor-omnibus.

Private motor-cars may appear to have deprived the railways of a good deal of their passenger traffic, and they certainly constitute a most material and much-appreciated increase in the facilities now available for getting about the country. It must, however, be remembered that a very large proportion of the journeys taken in them would probably not be made at all if the motor-car did not exist, and if such journeys had to be made by train instead. The actual diversion of traffic from the railway only occurs when journeys which would otherwise be made by rail are made by motor, in preference. Here the railway certainly does lose.

Against the loss in the one direction in railway revenue, owing to the greater use of motor-cars, there can at least be set the constant growth in the taste for travel which the railway companies (partly, again, to make up for the competition in suburban traffic) have done their best to cultivate by means of abnormally low excursion or week-end fares based, as one leading railway officer put it to me, "not on any idea of distance, but on the amount that the class of people catered for might be assumed to be willing to pay."

The travel habit has thus undergone a greater expansion of late years than has ever before been known, so that a falling-off of railway traffic in some directions ought, sooner or later, to be compensated for by increases in others, if, indeed, that result has not already been attained.

The actual position in regard to passenger travel on the railways of the United Kingdom during the years 1901–10 is shown by the following figures, taken from the Board of Trade Railway Returns :—

YEAR.	PASSENGER JOURNEYS.[1]	RECEIPTS FROM PASSENGERS. £
1901	1,172,395,900	.. 39,096,053
1902	1,188,219,269	.. 39,622,725
1903	1,195,265,195	.. 39,985,003
1904	1,198,773,720	.. 40,065,746
1905	1,199,022,102	.. 40,256,930
1906	1,240,347,132	.. 41,204,982

[1] Exclusive of those by season-ticket holders.

YEAR.	PASSENGER JOURNEYS.	RECEIPTS FROM PASSENGERS. £
1907 . .	1,259,481,315 ..	42,102,007
1908 . .	1,278,115,488 ..	42,615,812
1909 . .	1,265,080,761 ..	41,950,188
1910 . .	1,306,728,583 ..	43,247,345

These figures give evidence of, on the whole, a substantial advance in railway passenger journeys and receipts, notwithstanding all the competition of alternative facilities, and we may assume that although tramways, motor-cars, motor-omnibuses and even the latest new-comer, railless electric traction, may supplement and more or less compete with the railways, there is no suggestion that they are likely entirely to supplant them for passenger travel.

In the matter of goods transport in general, it is the fact that during the last ten or fifteen years, more especially, there has been an increasing tendency for the delivery of domestic supplies to suburban districts or towns within an ever-expanding radius of London and other leading cities to be effected by road, instead of by rail. The same has been the case in the distribution by wholesale houses of goods to suburban shopkeepers, and, also, in the reverse direction, in the sending of market-garden or other produce to central markets.

Where the railway companies have really created new suburban districts through the running of specially cheap workmen's trains, it may seem hard upon them that they should be deprived of the goods transport to which such districts give rise.

The fact must be recognised, however, that when the distances are within, say, a ten-, a fifteen- or even a twenty-mile radius, and when only small or comparatively small parcels or consignments are to be carried, the advantages in economical transport may well be in favour of the road vehicle rather than of the railway. The road vehicle can load up in the streets as it stands opposite the wholesale trader's warehouse ; it pays nothing for the use of the road ; it does not make any special contribution to the police funds in recognition of services rendered in the regulation of the traffic ; nor is it taxed by the local authorities on the basis of the quantity of goods carried and the extent of the presumptive profits made ; whereas the railway company must have a costly goods depôt, acquire land for their track, lay lines of rails, maintain an elaborate organisation to ensure safe working of the traffic, and submit to taxation by every local authority through whose district the goods carried may require to pass. There is, also, the further consideration, of which I have previously spoken, that in the case of short-distance journeys the cost of terminal services makes the rate per ton per mile appear much higher, in proportion, than when, while remaining at the same figure, it is spread over a substantially greater mileage.

While, with the increasing facilities for road transport, the railways must expect to lose more of their short-distance traffic, they should be able to retain their long-distance traffic, and more especially their long-distance traffic in bulk, commercial motors notwithstanding. Where commodities are carried either in considerable quantities or for considerable distances, and more particularly when both of these conditions prevail, transport by a locomotive, operating on rails, and conveying a heavy load with no very material increase in working expenses over the carrying of a light load, must needs be more economical than the distribution of a corresponding tonnage of goods among a collection of commercial motors, for conveyance by road under such conditions that each motor is operated as a separate and distinct unit.

The results, too, already brought about in the case of the suburban passenger traffic may, possibly, be so far repeated that railway companies deprived, also, of suburban goods traffic by the increasing competition of road conveyances, will show further enterprise in encouraging long-distance goods traffic to the same markets, or to the same towns. In this way they might seek to avoid, as far as practicable, any falling-off in their revenue at a time when taxation, wages, cost of materials and other working expenses all show a continuous upward tendency.

Should the policy here in question be adopted, market-gardeners, more especially, may find that, while they have effected a slight saving on their cost of transport by resorting to road conveyance, they will have to face increased competition from produce coming in larger quantities from long-distance growers who, with a lower cost of production, and, also, with increased encouragement from the railways, might have advantages on urban markets fully equal to those of the short-distance grower located in the suburbs.

The whole question of the steadily increasing competition between road and rail has thus become one of special interest, at the present moment, alike for the trading, the motor and the railway interests.

That the use of motor-vehicles is destined to make even greater advance in the immediate future has already here been shown. Yet there are distinct limitations to its possibilities, although this fact is apt to be overlooked by motor enthusiasts, some of whom are, indeed, over-sanguine. One of them proclaims that " the new locomotion " is " designed to be the chief means of transit to be used by humanity at large," and " eventually will probably to a large extent supersede all others." He further writes : " Many of us will live to see railway companies in places pulling up their rails and making their tracks suitable for motor-car traffic, charging a toll for private vehicles and carrying the bulk of the traffic in their own motor-cars."

Granting that motor-vehicles are likely to supersede both tramways and horse-vehicles, what are really the prospects of their superseding railways, as well ? Should railway shareholders at once sell out and put their money, preferably, in motor-omnibus and commercial motor companies ?

In regard to goods we have the fact that the quantities thereof carried by the railways of the United Kingdom in 1910 were :—

Minerals	.	.	405,087,175 tons.
General merchandise		.	109,341,631 ,,
Total	.	.	514,428,806 tons.

Motor transport could obviously not be adapted to the transport of 400,000,000 tons of minerals, and for these, at least, the railways would still be wanted. But the number of motor-vehicles necessary to deal with 109,000,000 tons of general merchandise would still be prodigious, apart from considerations of distance, time taken in transport, wear and tear of roads, and, also, of the question whether a locomotive, doing the work of many motors, would not be the cheaper unit in the conveyance of commodities carried in bulk on long or comparatively long hauls. The suburban delivery of parcels is one thing; the distribution, for example (as mentioned in a footnote on page 399), of 1000 railway waggons of broccoli from Penzance, all over Great Britain, in a single week, is another.

In the matter of passenger traffic, while people of means may prefer to make such journeys as that from London to Scotland in their own motor-car, the railway will continue to form both the cheaper and the quicker means of travel for the great bulk of the population as distinct from private car-owners, whose number must needs be comparatively small.

It is in respect to urban and suburban traffic that motor-vehicles have their best chance of competing with the railways on any extensive scale; yet even here, and notwithstanding all that they are already doing, their limitations are no less evident.

Taking only one of the many railway termini in London, the average number of suburban passengers who arrive at the Liverpool Street station of the Great Eastern Railway Company every week-day (exclusive of 12,000 from places beyond the suburban district) is 81,000, and of these about 66,000 come by trains arriving, in rapid succession, up to 10 a.m. To convey 81,000 suburban dwellers by motor-omnibus instead of by train would necessitate 2382 journeys, assuming that every seat was occupied. On the basis of the average number of persons actually travelling in a motor-bus at one time, it would probably require 4000 motor-bus journeys to bring even the Great Eastern suburban passengers to town each day if they discarded train for bus, and the same number to take them back in the evening. So long, too, as a single locomotive on the Great Eastern suffices for a suburban train accommodating between 800 and 1000 passengers, the company are not likely to pull up their rails and provide tracks in their place for a vast " fleet " of motor-cars or motor-omnibuses.

In some instances tramways and motor-omnibuses have, undoubtedly, deprived the railways of considerable traffic, and certain local stations around London have even been closed in consequence. In other instances tramways and buses have been of advantage to the railways by relieving them of an amount of suburban traffic for which it might have been difficult for them fully to provide. But any *general* supplanting of railways by motor-vehicles is as improbable in the case of passenger travel as it is in that of goods transport. Motor-vehicles are certain to become still more serious rivals of the railways than they are already, but they are not likely to render them obsolete ; and, taking the country as a whole, the " bulk of the traffic " may be expected still to go by rail, motor-vehicles notwithstanding.

Although, at the outset, some of the railway companies were disposed to regard the motor as a rather dangerous rival, the most enterprising have themselves adopted various forms of motor-vehicles, alike for establishing direct communication between country stations and outlying districts unprovided with branch lines, for enabling passengers arriving in London to pass readily from the terminus of one company to that of another, and for the collection and delivery of goods.

In regard, again, to the outlook for the future, important possibilities were foreshadowed by a letter addressed to " The Times " of August 23, 1911, by Lord Montagu of Beaulieu, concerning " Road Transport during Strikes." The hope of the leaders of the then recent railway strike had, of course, been to produce such a paralysis in the transport arrangements of the country that the railway companies would have been forced, owing to the resultant loss, dislocation of traffic, and, possibly, actual famine conditions, to surrender to all the demands made upon them. While the attempt failed on that occasion—thanks to the loyalty of the majority of the workers, the almost complete lack of public sympathy with the strikers, and, also, the employment of troops for the protection of the railways—there will always be the possibility of a renewal of the attempt. Pointing, therefore, to the large number of motorists in the United Kingdom, and mentioning, also, that there are, in addition, at least 10,000 commercial motor-vehicles as well, mostly running in or near the larger industrial centres, Lord Montagu wrote that, if supported by the Royal Automobile Club and the Automobile Association and Motor Union and assisted by his brother motorists in general, he would undertake in the case of a national emergency to carry out the following operations :

(1) The carriage of all mails where railways are now used.

(2) The supply of milk, ice and necessaries to all hospitals and nursing homes.

(3) The supply of milk, fish and perishable produce to London and other large towns.

(4) The supply to country villages of stores not produced in or near their area, such as sugar, tea, etc.

(5) The carriage of troops or police.

(6) The conveyance of passengers if on urgent business in connection with family matters or trade.

Lord Montagu added that "the Government would, of course, have to guarantee open roads and protection for loading and unloading vehicles, and provide for the swearing-in of motorists as special constables, who would be thus engaged in saving the community from starvation and chaos." He further thought that the compilation of a national register of motorists willing to lend their cars should be proceeded with at once.

The existence of such an organisation as this, with the inclusion, also, in the proposed registry, of horsed waggons, waggonettes and other vehicles owned by the country gentry and others, might be of incalculable service both in enabling the railway companies to stand against the coercion of a really general strike, and in saving the transport of the country from any approach to a complete dislocation, pending the time when the full railway services could be resumed.

A further example of the possible usefulness of motor-vehicles was shown by a War Office memorandum, issued on September 26, 1911, giving particulars of a provisional scheme for the subsidising of petrol motor-lorries already manufactured and owned by civilians, complying with certain specified conditions, the War Office thus acquiring the right to purchase such lorries from the owners for military service, in the case of need.

Measures of the kind here in question would, of course, be temporary expedients only, there being, as shown above, no probability that motor transport by road would ever take the place altogether of transport by rail.

Nor is aerial locomotion likely to be a more formidable rival of the railways than either inland navigation or motor transport by road. One may safely anticipate that further great advances are yet to be made in the art of flying ; yet one may, also, assume there is no prospect of aerial locomotion becoming a serious competitor with the railway. It is extremely interesting to know that the journey from London to Scotland has now been made in quicker time by aeroplane than by the fastest express, and that a 1000-mile flight round England has been accomplished with perfect control of the machinery employed. Yet, even allowing for the greatest possible improvements in the construction of the aeroplane, the number of passengers who could be carried is so limited, and the fares charged to cover capital outlay must needs be so high, that there could be no idea of rivalry between the aeroplane and the railway in regard to passenger traffic.

Like considerations should apply in the case of goods traffic.

In theory the idea of an aerial express goods service looks very promising. Yet, as a business proposition, one must needs again consider : (1) the capital cost of the aeroplane ; (2) the comparatively small quantity of goods that could be carried on a single journey ; and (3) the high rates that would necessarily have to be paid for their transport on commercial lines. A " record " in the aerial carriage of a 38-lb. consignment of electric lamps from Shoreham to Hove (Brighton) was established on July 4, 1911, by Mr H. C. Barber, of the Hendon Aviation Grounds ; but this particular exploit was suggestive mainly of an advertisement for the lamps in question. I ventured, therefore, to put the following proposition to Mr Barber :—

" Assume that, owing to a railway strike, no goods trains could pass between London and Liverpool, and that a London merchant had a consignment of goods which it was of the utmost importance should be taken to Liverpool for despatch by a steamer on the point of sailing. Then : (1) What would be the maximum weight, and, also, the maximum bulk, of such consignment as an aeroplane could carry ? (2) In what time, approximately, could the journey from Hendon to Liverpool be made ? (3) What sum would the London trader have to pay for the transport ? "

Mr Barber informs me that the maximum weight of such consignment as could be carried would be about ten stone (1 cwt. 1 qr.) ; that the maximum bulk would be about 30 cubic feet ; that the journey would take about four hours ;

and that the charge for transport would be ten shillings per mile. The distance " as the crow—or the aeroplane—flies " between Hendon and Liverpool being about 200 miles, the charge would come to £100. Mr. Barber adds : " There is no doubt that within the very near future it will be possible to make much smaller charges ; also charges could be very much reduced if there were sufficient business to make it worth while." This is what one would expect to hear. Yet, assuming that the aeroplane rate were reduced even by fifty per cent, it could not, even then, compete with the railway rate under normal conditions ; while to convey through the air the 150 tons of general merchandise which a single locomotive attached to one of the many goods trains passing between London and Liverpool will haul would, on the basis of 1 cwt. 1 qr. per machine, require the use of 2400 aeroplanes. This calculation leaves out of account, too, the much greater weights of grain, timber and other heavy traffic in full truck-loads which pass from Liverpool to various inland places, and could not, of course, be dealt with by aeroplane at all.

After surveying all these possible competitors or alternatives we are left to conclude that, as far as foresight can suggest, the railways are likely still to constitute at least the chief means of carrying on internal transport and communication in this country.

If this be so, then the main proposition as to the outlook for inland transport in general relates to the outlook for the railways in particular.

Here the first consideration which presents itself is that, as regards main lines, our railway system to-day may be regarded as approximately complete.[1] There may still be good scope for the construction of extensions, new links or of short cuts ; but these should count as improvements rather than as fresh lines of communication.

In London there are to be extensions of some of the existing tubes with a view to affording to the public increased facilities both for reaching the termini of the great trunk lines and for

---

[1] In an address delivered by him as president of the Railway Students' Union at the London School of Economics on October 24, 1911, Mr Sam Fay, general manager of the Great Central Railway, said : " There is little prospect of any extensive opening out of new competitive routes in this country, and, but for a few comparatively short lines here and there, the railway system may be considered complete."

a still easier interchange of traffic between the different tube or underground railways themselves.

An exceptionally important scheme of improved transport was announced, on November 18, 1911, by the London and North-Western Railway Company, such scheme comprising (1) the electrification of 40 miles of surburban railway, including a material portion of the North London Railway; (2) the construction by the London Electric Railway Company of a new tube, extending their Bakerloo line from Paddington to the L. & N. W. system at Queens' Park ; and (3) the running, for the first time, and by means of specially-constructed carriages, of through services between a trunk line and a tube.

While the existing tube companies may thus extend their lines, and while the trunk companies may seek to co-operate more with them in providing for suburban traffic, the outlook for any new tube companies in London would not seem to be very promising in view of the fact that the holders of £9,300,000 of ordinary stock in the London Electric Railway (controlling the Bakerloo, Piccadilly and Hampstead lines), out of a total capitalisation of £16,200,000, received in 1911 a dividend equal to only one per cent.

In the country what is most wanted is an increase in transport facilities between existing railways and outlying districts, the traffic from which would not be sufficient to justify the construction of branch lines of ordinary railway. There are fishing villages, agricultural districts, market gardening areas, and innumerable small communities which would gain a material advantage by being provided with better means of communication with the nearest railway.

Whether or not such facilities should be provided by (1) road motors, (2) railless electric traction, or (3) light railways, is a question that must depend on the conditions, circumstances or prospects of the locality concerned ; but if more people are to be sent " back to the land," and if colonies of small holders are to be established thereon with any hope of success, then it is desirable, if not essential : (1) that each colony of such settlers should form an agricultural co-operative society ; (2) that each society should set up its depôt to facilitate the combination of purchases or consignments into grouped lots ; and (3) that between the depôt and a convenient railway station there should be provided some means of collective transport under the most effective and economical conditions.

It is thus mainly in the direction of railway feeders that the need for increased transport facilities exists to-day.

In this absence of any general necessity for additional railways, the policy of the railway companies of late years has been directed more to the consolidation and economical working of the existing system of lines. This policy has especially aimed at the furtherance of those mutual agreements and amalgamations which, as we have seen, have constituted a prominent phase in the development of railways from a very early period in their history. Present-day tendencies in this direction are especially due to the fact that working expenses have greatly increased while the powers of the companies to increase their charges are still subject to the restrictions of the Act of 1894, under which they may be required to justify before the Railway and Canal Commission any increase in a rate since the 31st of December, 1892. Increase of expenditure is found in the higher wages bills, in the ever-expanding items of rates and taxes, in the heavier cost of raw materials, in the greater amount of clerical and other work resulting from the sending of frequent small consignments in place of consignments in bulk, and in the provision of greater conveniences and luxuries in travel.

An increased volume of traffic has, to a certain extent, compensated for these heavier expenses ; but it has not done so sufficiently, and the ideal remedy has appeared to lie in the direction of effecting economies in operation and management, either by individual companies or through arrangements between two or more, to their mutual advantage, and without, as the companies have claimed, any disadvantage to the public.

In some instances companies have had to grant such concessions to local communities as a means of overcoming threatened opposition to their proposed arrangements that the value of the advantages eventually obtained has been represented almost by a negative quantity. In other instances the opposition has been so keen, and the " prices of assent " have been so exacting, that the companies concerned have preferred to abandon their schemes rather than go on with them. In still other instances companies have refrained from attempting to carry out amalgamations requiring Parliamentary sanction, and thus likely to provoke opposition, and have made such arrangements between themselves as were within their powers and were likely to give them some of the advantages they wanted, though not, perhaps, all.

Following on certain developments in these various directions, a Departmental Committee was appointed, in June, 1909, by the Board of Trade to consider and report " what changes, if any, are expedient in the law relating to agreements among railway companies, and what, if any, general provisions ought to be embodied for the purpose of safeguarding the various interests affected in future Acts of Parliament authorising railway amalgamations or working unions." The report of this Committee [Cd. 5631] was issued in May, 1911.

In so far as they deal with the principle that even Parliament itself is powerless to prevent the tendency to co-operation between railway companies originally designed to compete with one another, the Committee do little more than re-echo what was said, not only by the Joint Committee of 1872, but even by Morrison in the speech he made in the House of Commons on May 17, 1836. There is, also, a close resemblance between what I have stated concerning the position in 1836 and at subsequent dates—namely, that there was no allegation that the railway companies *had* abused their powers, only fear that they *might* do so—and the following extract from the report made by the Departmental Committee in 1911 :—

" It is, of course, to the interest of the railway companies not to raise rates or stint accommodation to an extent that will reduce traffic unduly, but, subject to this, a policy of self-interest might frequently lead the companies to charge rates which, judged by any existing standard, would be unreasonable."

So, in 1911, no less than in 1836, and at any time between those dates, the policy of the State towards the railways, as far as it can be summed up in a single word, is represented by this word " might." The attitude of distrust and suspicion originally engendered towards the railways by the canal companies evidently still survives, and is expected to form, even to-day, the approved basis of State action. The principle of railway co-operation is, indeed, frankly and fully accepted by the Departmental Committee, who declare they have come to the unanimous conclusion " that the natural lines of develop-

ment of an improved and more economical railway system
lie in the direction of more perfect understandings and co-
operation between the various railway companies which must
frequently, although not always, be secured by formal agreements of varying scope and completeness, amounting in some
cases to working unions and amalgamations." But, although
they admit that mutual competition between railway companies exists to-day in only a "limited degree," and although
they do not show that the agreements and amalgamations
thus far carried out have been in any way really detrimental
to the public interests they are still influenced, as Parliaments,
Select Committees and Departmental Committees before
them have been for the last three-quarters of a century, by
that one word "might." Railway companies may be allowed
to co-operate—more especially because they cannot be
prevented from doing so ; but fresh restrictions and further
obligations must be imposed lest they *might* abuse the facilities
granted to them, in seeking to cover increased taxation and
other items of heavier working expenses. Thus among the
recommendations of the Departmental Committee are the
following :—

" That it should be provided that when a facility or service
is diminished or withdrawn, it should lie upon the railway
company to show that the reduction or withdrawal is
reasonable.

" That it should lie upon the railway company to justify a
charge made for a service hitherto rendered gratuitously.

" That it should be declared that the law with regard to
increased charges applies to passenger fares and other charges
made for the conveyance of traffic by passenger trains."

These proposals are, no doubt, inspired by a genuine desire
to protect the public interests ; yet the effect of carrying
them out would be effectually to destroy the small amount
of elasticity that is still left in the relations between the
railway companies and the public. If, in addition to having
to " justify " the increase of any rate for goods or minerals,
the companies were required to run the risk of having to
" justify " the taking off of any train they found no longer necessary, or even the slightest increase in any of the now often
extremely low railway fares, the result would be to tie their
hands still further in the making of experimental concessions,

and, in the result, the travelling public, as is the case already with the traders, would stand to lose through a policy nominally designed to protect their interests.

Whatever course may be actually taken in regard to these particular aspects of the question, the trend of events in the railway world will probably be more and more in the direction of continuing the policy of agreements and amalgamations on lines which, while giving the fullest transport facilities to the public, should check wasteful competition and ensure all practicable economy in the matter of working expenses.

That the trade of the country would suffer, in consequence, is hardly to be anticipated. Assuming that three railway companies, who had already agreed as to the rates they would charge, had each been conveying goods between A and B, and that they arranged for the consignments entrusted to all three to be taken in one train by one route, instead of in three trains by separate routes, a clear economy would be effected without any detriment to the traders, since the goods would reach B all the same, while savings in the working expenses should render the companies better able to meet the wishes of traders in other directions.

In regard to the possibility (as already told on page 448) of an increase in railway rates to enable the companies to meet increases of wages or other betterment of the positions of their staffs, any general increase might well occasion uneasiness, and even alarm, to traders who already find it difficult enough to meet foreign competition, and to whom greater cost of transport might be a matter of no little concern. On the other hand there is an undoubted anomaly in the fact that whilst the burdens on railway companies have greatly, if not enormously, increased of late years, and whilst other commercial companies are free to pass on to the consumer increased costs of production or heavier working expenses, including, especially, a much heavier taxation, the statutory standard for railway companies' rates and charges should still be that of the last day of December, 1892.

A further result of the railway strikes in the autumn of 1911 was to revive the agitation in favour of railway nationalisation. In some quarters it was argued that an effective guarantee against the recurrence of railway strikes would be found in State ownership ; but this theory is certainly not confirmed by the actual experiences of Holland, Hungary, Victoria, Italy and France. There is no suggestion that, if the railways were owned by the State, the railwaymen would voluntarily abandon the right to strike ; but State ownership is favoured by the Amalgamated Society of Railway Servants (which passed a resolution approving thereof at the annual conference at Carlisle on October 4, 1911), in the expectation (1) that, under these conditions, the unions would be certain to get " recognition " ; (2) that they would then be able to bring such pressure to bear on the Government that they would be sure to get what they wanted without having to strike ; and (3) that, owing to the economics to which State operation would lead, the Government would be in a position to give the railway workers higher pay and shorter hours. Here, however, the questions arise whether the country would be willing to allow the railway unions practically to control alike the Government and the economic situation ; whether the assumed " economies " under State ownership and operation of the railways would really be effected ; and whether any such changes in railway service conditions as those that were demanded in the National All-Grades Programme could be conceded even under a nationalisation system without imposing on the railway users greater burdens in the way of higher rates and fares than they might be disposed to tolerate.

On the other hand there is the consideration that if the working expenses of the railway companies are to be swollen to still greater proportions by heavier wages bills, abnormal taxation, public demands for greater facilities, and State requirements in equipment or operation ; if, at the same time, the companies are to be subjected to statutory restrictions in regard to the charges they may impose for the services they render ; and if, also, the danger of strikes and of outside control or interference is to be increased, the day may conceivably come when transfer of the railways to the State, under, presumably, fair and equitable conditions, would be the only effectual means of relieving the railways themselves from what might then be an otherwise hopeless position.

While the outlook for the future has various elements of uncertainty, and, in regard to matters of detail, gives rise to some degree of concern, a review of the conditions under which trade, industry and communication have been developed throughout the ages leads to the conclusion that the country may, at least, regard with feelings of profound thankfulness and generous appreciation the efforts of that long succession of individual pioneers, patriots and public-spirited men to whose zeal, foresight and enterprise we are so materially indebted for the advantages we now enjoy.

AUTHORITIES

THE following books, pamphlets, and reports have, among others, been consulted in the preparation of the present work :

" A Cursory View of the Advantages of an Intended Canal from Chesterfield to Gainsborough " (1769).

Adams, William Bridges : " Practical Remarks on Railways " (1854).

"A History of Ten Years of Automobilism, 1896–1906," edited by Lord Montagu (1906).

Aikin, J., M.D. : " A Description of the Country from Thirty to Forty Miles round Manchester " (1795).

Allnutt, Zachariah : " Useful and Correct Accounts of the Navigation of the Rivers and Canals West of London " (2nd ed., 1810).

Anderson, James, LL.D. : " On Cast Iron Rail-ways," in " Recreations in Agriculture," etc., Vol. IV (Nov., 1800).

Ashley, W. J. : " The Beginnings of Town Life in the Middle Ages " (1896) ; " An Introduction to English Economic History and Theory " (1892).

" A View of the Advantages of Inland Navigations, with a Plan of a Navigable Canal intended for a Communication between the Ports of Liverpool and Hull " (1765).

" Avona : or a Transient View of the Benefit of Making Rivers of this Kingdom Navigable." By R. S. (1675).

Badeslade, Thomas : " The History of the Ancient and Present State of the Navigation of the Port of Kings-Lyn and of Cambridge, and the Rest of the Trading Towns in those Parts " (1766).

Bailey, J. : " General View of the Agriculture of the County of Durham " (1810).

Bailey, J., and Culley, G. : " General View of the Agriculture of the County of Northumberland " (1794).

Baines, Thomas : " History of the Commerce and Town of

Liverpool " (1852) ; " Lancashire and Cheshire, Past and Present " (1867).

Bateman, J. : " The General Turnpike Roads Acts " (1854) ; " The General Highways Acts " (2nd ed., 1863).

Blome, Richard : " Britannia : or a Geographical Description of England, Scotland and Ireland " (1673).

Bourn, Daniel : " A Treatise upon Wheel Carriages " (1763).

Boyle and Waghorn : " The Law Relating to Railway and Canal Traffic " (1901).

Bradfield, J. E. : " Notes on Toll Reform and the Turnpike Ticket System " (1856) ; " Observations on the Injustice, Inequalities and Anomalies of the Present System of Taxation of State Carriages " (1854).

Brand, John : " History and Antiquities of Newcastle " (1789).

Brunlees, James, c.e. : Presidential Address, Mechanical Science Section, British Association Meeting, 1883.

Buddle, John : " Description of a Coal Waggon," in the " General Magazine of Arts and Sciences " for June, 1764.

Butterworth, A. Kaye : " The Law Relating to Maximum Rates and Charges on Railways " (1897).

Cheyney, Edward P. : " English Towns and Gilds " (1895).

Clifford, Frederick, of the Inner Temple : " A History of Private Bill Legislation " (2 vols., 1885 and 1887).

Copnall, H. H. : " A Practical Guide to the Administration of Highway Law " (1905).

Cressett, John : " The Grand Concern of England Explained " (1673) ; Harleian Miscellany, Vol. VIII.

Cumming, T. G. : " Illustrations of the Origin and Progress of Rail and Tram Roads " (1824).

Cunningham, W. : " The Growth of English Industry and Commerce " (1890-92).

Curr, John : " Coalviewer and Engine Builder's Practical Companion " (1797).

Defoe, Daniel : " A Tour through the Whole Island of Great Britain " (1724).

Dehany, William Knight, of the Middle Temple : " The General Turnpike Acts " (1823).

Denton, The Rev. W. : " England in the Fifteenth Century " (1888).

De Salis, Henry Rodolph : " A Chronology of Inland

Navigation in Great Britain " (1897) ; " Bradshaw's Canals and Navigable Rivers of England and Wales " (1904).

" Description of a Coal Waggon, Staith, and Waggon-way," in the " Commercial and Agricultural Magazine," October, 1800.

Dowell, Stephen : " A History of Taxation and Taxes in England " (2nd ed., 1888).

Eaton, J. Shirley : "Education for Efficiency in Railroad Service," United States Bureau of Education (1909).

Edgeworth, Richard Lovell : " An Essay on the Construction of Roads and Carriages " (2nd ed., 1817).

Edington, Robert : " A Treatise on the Coal Trade " (1813).

Findlay, Sir George : " The Working and Management of an English Railway " (4th ed., 1891).

Forbes and Ashford : " Our Waterways " (1906).

Fowler, J. Kersley : " Records of Old Times " (1898).

Francis, John : " A History of the English Railway " (1851).

Franks, W. Temple : " History of Traffic Legislation and Parliamentary Action in Connection with Railways " ; London School of Economic Lectures (1907).

Fulton, R. : " A Treatise on the Improvement of Canal Navigation, exhibiting the numerous advantages to be derived from Small Canals and boats of two to five feet wide, containing from two to five tons burthen " (1796).

Galloway, R. L. : " Annals of Coal Mining and the Coal Trade " (1898 and 1904) ; " A History of Coal Mining in Great Britain " (1862) ; " Papers Relating to the History of the Coal Trade " (1906).

Gilbey, Sir Walter : " Early Carriages and Roads " (1903).

Gordon, Alexander : " An Historical and Practical Treatise upon Elemental Locomotion by Means of Steam Carriages on Common Roads " (1832).

Gray, Thomas : " Observations on a General Iron Railway " (2nd ed., 1821 ; 5th, 1825).

Grierson, J. : " Railway Rates, English and Foreign " (1886).

Hackworth, T. : " Jubilee of the World's First Public Railway " (1892).

Hadley, A. T. : " Railway Transportation : Its History and Its Laws " (1906).

Harper, C. G. : " The Holyhead Road " (1902) ; " The Great North Road " (1910).

Harris, Stanley : " Old Coaching Days " (1882) ; " The Coaching Age " (1885).

Herepath, John : " Railway Magazine " (1836–39).

Homer, Henry : " An Inquiry into the Means of Preserving Publick Roads " (1767).

Humpherus, Henry : " History of the Origin and Progress of the Company of Watermen and Lightermen of the River Thames " (1887).

Hunter, The Rev. Joseph : " The History and Topography of the Deanery of Doncaster " (1828).

Hutton, William : " History of Birmingham " (1781).

Jacob, Giles : " Law Dictionary " (4th ed., 1809).

Jeans, J. Stephen : " Waterways and Water Transport " (1890) ; " Jubilee Memorial of the Railway System " (1875).

Jessop, William : " On Inland Navigation and Public Roads," Georgical Essays, Vol. VI (1804).

Jusserand, J. J. : " English Wayfaring Life in the Middle Ages " (1889).

Kinderley, Nathaniel : " The Ancient and Present State of the Navigation of the Towns of Lyn, Wisbech, Spalding and Boston, of the Rivers that pass through those Places and the countries that border thereupon " (2nd ed., 1751).

Law, H., and Clark, D. K. : " The Construction of Roads and Streets " (1887).

Lloyd, John : " Papers Relating to the Rivers Wye and Lug " (1873).

McAdam, John Loudon : " Remarks on the Present System of Road Making " (9th ed., 1827).

Macaulay, Lord : " History of England," chapter III.

McCulloch, J. R. : " Dictionary of Commerce and Commercial Navigation " (1882).

Macdonald, Sir J. H. A. : " The Triumph of Motor Traction," in " Chambers's Journal," August 1, 1911.

Macpherson, David : " Annals of Commerce " (1805).

Maitland, F. W. : " Township and Borough " (1898).

Marriott, H. : " The Fixing of Rates and Fares " (2nd ed., 1910).

Marshall, A. : " Principles of Economics " (4th ed., 1898).

Mathew, Francis : " Of the Opening of Rivers for Navigation : The Benefit exemplified by the two Avons of Salisbury and Bristol, with a Mediterranean Passage by Water for Billanders of Thirty Tun, between Bristol and London " (1655) ; " A Mediterranean Passage by Water from London to Bristol and from Lynne to Yarmouth, and so consequently to the City of York, for the great Advancement of Trade and Traffique " (1670).

Maxwell, William H. : " The Construction of Roads and Streets " (1899).

May, George : " Descriptive History of Evesham " (1845).

Mayo-Smith, Richmond : " Statistics and Economics " (1895–99).

Midleton, Viscount : Article on " Our Highways," in " The Nineteenth Century " for Oct., 1881.

Moore, H. C. : "Omnibuses and Cabs: their Origin and History" (1902).

Morrison, James, M.P. : " Rail Roads : A Speech Delivered in the House of Commons, 17th May, 1836 " ; " Influence of Railway Legislation on Trade and Industry " (1848).

Nash, T. : " The History and Antiquities of Worcestershire " (1781).

Nicholson, J. Shield : " Principles of Political Economy " (1893).

Ogilby, John : " Britannia : A Geographical and Historical Description of the Roads of England and Wales " (1675).

"On the Country Manners of the Present Age." Annual Register (1761).

Palgrave, R. H. I. : " Dictionary of Political Economy " (1900).

Parliamentary Reports and Papers :—

Census of Production (1907). [Cd. 5254.]

Departmental Committee on Railway Agreements and Amalgamations (1911). [Cd. 5631.]

Joint Committee on the Amalgamation of Railway Companies (1872). [364.]

Local Taxation, by H. H. Fowler (Lord Wolverhampton) (1893). [168.]

Railway Returns for 1910 (1911). [Cd. 5796.]

Road Board, First Report of (1911). [292.]

Royal Commission on Canals and Waterways : Fourth and Final Report (1909). [Cd. 4979.]

Royal Commission on the Railway Conciliation Scheme of 1907 (1911). [Cd. 5922.]

Select Committee on the Expediency of Abolishing Turnpike Trusts (1864). [383.]

Select Committee on the Highways of the Kingdom (1819). [509.]

Select Committee on Turnpike Trusts and Tolls (1836). [547.]

Parnell, Sir Henry : " A Treatise on Roads " (1st ed., 1833 ; 2nd, 1838).

Pearson, Charles H. : " Historical Maps of England during the first thirteen centuries, with Explanatory Essays and Indices " (1870).

Penny Cyclopædia : Articles on " Railways," " Rivers " and " Roads " (1841).

Phillips, J. : " A General History of Inland Navigation " (4th ed., 1803).

Plymley, Joseph, Archdeacon of Salop : " General View of the Agriculture of Shropshire " (1803).

Porter, G. R. : " The Progress of the Nation " (1846).

Porter, Robert P. : " The Dangers of Municipal Trading " (1907).

Postlethwayt, Malachy : Article on " Roads " in " Universal Dictionary of Trade " (1751).

Potter, F. : " The Government in Relation to the Railways," a Paper read before the Great Western Railway (London) Lecture and Debating Society (1909).

Pratt and Mackenzie : " Law of Highways " (15th ed.).

Priestley, Joseph : " Historical Account of the Navigable Rivers, Canals and Railways of Great Britain " (1831).

Rees' Cyclopædia : Articles, " Canal " and " Road " (1819).

" Reprints of Rare Tracts : Letters of William Scott " (1847).

Rogers, J. E. Thorold : " History of Agriculture and Prices in England."

Sandars, Joseph : " A Letter on the Subject of the Proposed Rail Road between Liverpool and Manchester, pointing out the necessity for its adoption and the manifest advantages it offers to the Public, with an Exposure of the exorbitant and unjust charges of the Water Carriers " (1824).

Smiles, Samuel : " Lives of the Engineers " (1861).

Smith, Adam : " The Wealth of Nations " (1776).

Stretton, Clement E. : " Early Tramroads and Railways in Leicestershire " ; " History of the Loughborough and Nanpantan Edge-rail-way " : " The Leicester and Swannington Railway," etc.

Stukeley, William, M.D. : " Itinerarium Curiosum " (2nd ed., 1776).

" Survey of London " ; edited by Walter Besant.

Sydney, William Connor : " England and the English in the Eighteenth Century " (1891).

Tatham, William : " The Political Economy of Inland Navigation " (1799).

" The Motor Car in the First Decade of the 20th Century," compiled by W. Eden Hooper (1908).

" The Rating of Railways," Great Western Railway Magazine Booklet (1908).

" The Tourists' Guide to Bridgnorth " (1875).

Thoresby, Ralph, F.R.S. : " Ducatus Leodiensis ; or the Topography of Leedes " (1715).

Thrupp, George A. : " The History of Coaches " (1877).

Tredgold, Thomas : " A Practical Treatise on Rail-roads and Carriages " (1825).

Tristram, W. Outram : " Coaching Days and Coaching Ways " (1888).

Tylor, Alfred : " New Points in the History of Roman Britain," in " Archæologia," Vol. XLVIII.

Vernon-Harcourt, L. F. : " Rivers and Canals " (1896).

Walford, Cornelius : " Fairs Past and Present " (1883).

Walker, Thomas : " Change in Commerce," in " The Original," No. XI (1835).

Wheeler, W. H. : " Tidal Rivers " (1893).

Whitaker, T. D. : " Loidis and Elmete " (1846).

Whitworth, Richard : " The Advantages of Inland Navigation ; or Some Observations offered to the Public to show that an Inland Navigation may be easily effected between the three great ports of Bristol, Liverpool and Hull " (1766).

Whyte, A. G. : " Electricity in Locomotion " (1911).

Williams, F. S. : " Our Iron Roads " (7th ed.,1888) ; " The Midland Railway " (5th ed., 1888).

Wilson, T. : " The Railway System and its Author " (1845).

Wood, Nicholas : " A Practical Treatise on Rail-roads " (1st ed., 1825 ; 3rd, 1838).

Wright and Hobhouse : " An Outline of Local Government and Local Taxation in England and Wales."

Yarranton, Andrew : " England's Improvement by Sea and Land. . . . With the Advantages of making the Great Rivers of England Navigable " (1672).

Young, Arthur : " A Six Weeks' Tour through the Southern Counties " (1769) ; " A Six Months' Tour through the North of England " (1770).

INDEX

WILLIAM BRENDON AND SON, LTD., PRINTERS, PLYMOUTH